HANDBOOK OF RESEARCH ON INNOVATION AND ENTREPRENEURSHIP

Handbook of Research on Innovation and Entrepreneurship

Edited by

David B. Audretsch

Distinguished Professor of Economic Development, Indiana University, Bloomington, USA, Honorary Professor, WHU, Germany and Visiting Professor, King Saud University, Saudi Arabia

Oliver Falck

Senior Researcher, Department of Human Capital and Innovation, Ifo Institute for Economic Research, University of Munich, Germany

Stephan Heblich

Lecturer, Economics Division, School of Management, University of Stirling, UK

Adam Lederer

DIW Berlin, Germany

Edward Elgar
Cheltenham, UK • Northampton, MA, USA

Published by
Edward Elgar Publishing Limited
The Lypiatts
15 Lansdown Road
Cheltenham
Glos GL50 2JA
UK

Edward Elgar Publishing, Inc.
William Pratt House
9 Dewey Court
Northampton
Massachusetts 01060
USA

A catalogue record for this book
is available from the British Library

Library of Congress Control Number: 2010927657

MIX
Paper from
responsible sources
FSC   FSC® C018575
www.fsc.org

ISBN 978 1 84844 087 6 (cased)

Typeset by Servis Filmsetting Ltd, Stockport, Cheshire
Printed and bound by MPG Books Group, UK

Contents

Contributors

Zoltan J. Acs is University Professor at the School of Public Policy and Director of the Center for Entrepreneurship and Public Policy at George Mason University (USA). His research interests are in entrepreneurship and innovation, global and domestic business environment, managerial economics and public policy, new venture creation, technology management, and the global economic environment. He is founding editor of the *Small Business Economics Journal*.

Philippe Aghion is Robert C. Waggoner Professor of Economics at Harvard University, USA. His main research work is on growth and contract theory. With Peter Howitt, he developed the so-called Schumpeterian Paradigm, and extended the paradigm in several directions.

David B. Audretsch is Distinguished Professor, Ameritech Chair of Economic Development, and Director of the Institute for Development Strategies at Indiana University, Bloomington, USA, Honorary Professor at WHU, Germany, and Visiting Professor at King Saud University, Saudi Arabia. His research focuses on the links between entrepreneurship, government policy, innovation, economic development and global competitiveness. He is founding editor of the *Small Business Economics Journal*.

Gil Avnimelech is a faculty member at Ono Academic College, Israel. Previously, he worked with Professor Maryann Feldman as a postdoctoral research associate at the Public Policy Department, UNC-CH. He conducted his PhD at the School of Management, Ben Gurion University. His fields of interest are entrepreneurship venture capital, innovative cluster development and innovation policy. He also lectures at the Business Schools of Tel Aviv University and Ben Gurion University.

William J. Baumol is the Harold Price Professor of Entrepreneurship and Academic Director of the Berkley Center for Entrepreneurship and Innovation in the Stern School of Business at New York University (USA); and Senior Economist and Professor Emeritus at Princeton University, USA. He is the author of more than 45 books, which have been translated into a dozen languages. His honors and awards include 12 honorary degrees and membership in the US National Academy of Sciences, the American Philosophical Society, the Accademia Nazionale Dei Lincei (Italy) and the British Academy.

Werner Bönte is Professor of Industrial Organization of the Schumpeter School of Business and Economics at the University of Wuppertal, Germany. He received a PhD from the University of Hamburg, Germany. His primary research interests are the economics of innovation, industrial organization, entrepreneurship and the economic performance of regions.

Pontus Braunerhjelm is Leif Lundblad's Chair in International Business and Entrepreneurship, The Royal Institute of Technology, Stockholm, Sweden. One strand of his research is on industrial dynamics, cluster analysis, entrepreneurship and the 'knowledge' economy. A second strand of research is on international economics, with an emphasis on economic geography, foreign direct investment (FDI), agglomeration and spatial patterns.

Uwe Cantner is Professor of Economics of the Department of Economics of the Friedrich Schiller University Jena, Germany, and Professor of Economics at the Department of Marketing and Management of the University of Southern Denmark at Odense; he is also Director of the DFG doctoral program 'The Economics of Innovative Change' and Director of the Jena Graduate School 'Human Behavior in Social and Economic Change'. He received a PhD from the Ludwig Maximilians University, Munich, Germany. His research interests are the economics of innovation, evolutionary economics, industrial economics and productivity analysis. He is editor of the *Journal of Evolutionary Economics*.

Bo Carlsson is Professor of Economics at the Weatherhead School of Management, Case Western Reserve University, USA. His research focuses on industrial dynamics, especially the nature and role of innovation systems and entrepreneurship in economic growth; the formation of industry clusters; intellectual property management and technology transfer.

Marcus Dejardin is Assistant Professor at Université Catholique de Louvain and FUNDP-University of Namur (Belgium). He is Invited Assistant Professor at Erasmus School of Economics, Rotterdam, the Netherlands and Université de Caen-Basse Normandie, France. He holds a PhD in economics from FUNDP-University of Namur. He is associate editor of *Small Business Economics*. His research explores the inter-relationships between entrepreneurship and regional economic development. He has developed expertise in entrepreneurship, industrial organization – market structures, macroeconomics, and in spatial and regional economics.

Gilles Duranton holds the Noranda Chair in Economics and International Trade in the Department of Economics at the University of Toronto, Canada. He obtained his PhD in economics jointly from the London School of Economics and the École des hautes études en sciences sociales in Paris. His research interests are both theoretical and empirical, including modelling of urban systems, the scope and micro-foundations of agglomeration economies, traffic congestion and the impacts of local public policies.

Andreas Eisingerich is Assistant Professor in Marketing at Imperial College Business School, London, UK. He holds a PhD from the University of Cambridge, Judge Business School. His research focuses on brand management, consumer behavior and service innovation.

Oliver Falck is Senior Researcher in the Ifo Institute for Economic Research at the University of Munich, Germany. He received a PhD from the Technical University of Freiberg, Germany. His research interests include entrepreneurship, innovation, human capital and urban economics.

Maryann P. Feldman is the S.K. Heninger Distinguished Chair in Public Policy at the University of North Carolina, Chapel Hill, USA. Her work focuses on the ways in which universities transfer technology and the implications for economic development.

She explores the means by which geographic clusters produce economic growth and has special expertise in university-generated technologies and the commercialization of academic research.

Kathy Fogel is Assistant Professor of Finance at the Sam M. Walton College of Business, University of Arkansas, USA. Her research focuses on corporate finance, international corporate governance and entrepreneurial finance.

Michael Fritsch is Professor of Economics and Chair of Business Dynamics, Innovation, and Economic Change at the Friedrich Schiller University Jena, Germany. He is also Research Professor at the German Institute for Economic Research (DIW-Berlin) and at the Max-Planck Institute for Economics, Jena. His main fields of research are entrepreneurship and new business formation, innovation systems and economic development strategies. He received his PhD from the Technical University of Berlin, Germany.

Robert Gold is Graduate Student at the Max Planck Institute of Economics, Germany. He received an MA in political science from the University of Passau. His research interests include regional development and institutional influences on entrepreneurship.

Marco Guerzoni is Assistant Professor at the Department of Economics of the University of Jena, Germany. He received a PhD from the University of Milan, Italy. His research interest are the economics and management of innovation, entrepreneurship, industrial dynamics and competition, and the economics and management of knowledge and information.

Dietmar Harhoff is Professor of Business Administration at the Ludwig-Maximilian University (LMU) Munich, Germany. He is the Director of the Institute of Innovation Research, Technology Management and Entrepreneurship and a co-director of the LMU Entrepreneurship Center. His research focuses on issues in innovation, entrepreneurship, industrial economics and technology management.

Stephan Heblich is Lecturer in the Economics Division in the School of Management, University of Stirling, UK. He received a PhD in economics from the University of Passau, Germany. His fields of specialization are urban economics, entrepreneurship and innovation.

Richard A. Jensen is Professor and Chairperson of the Department of Economics at the University of Notre Dame, USA. He received a PhD from Northwestern University. His fields of specialization are microeconomic theory, industrial organization, and university invention and technology transfer.

Max Keilbach was a Senior Researcher at the Max Planck Institute of Economics in Jena, Germany, from 2004 to 2007. His main research interests were in the area of innovative entrepreneurship and its economic impact using empirical, econometric and simulation-based approaches. Between 1998 and 2002 he worked as a Senior Researcher at the Department of Industrial Economics at the Centre for European Economic Research (ZEW) in Mannheim, Germany. There his research was on the causes and impact of the demography of firms and on the development of corresponding databases.

William R. Kerr is Associate Professor at the Harvard Business School, USA. His research focuses on entrepreneurship and innovation. One research strand considers agglomeration and entrepreneurship, with special interest in how government policies aid or hinder the entry of new firms and cluster formation. A second research strand examines the role of immigrant scientists and entrepreneurs in US technology development and commercialization, as well as the subsequent diffusion of new innovations to the immigrants' home countries. A final interest area is entrepreneurial finance and angel investments.

Israel M. Kirzner is Emeritus Professor of Economics at New York University, USA. He is a leading economist in the tradition of the Austrian School and a leading authority on Ludwig von Mises's thinking and methodology in economics. Kirzner's major work is in the economics of entrepreneurship and ethics and economics.

Alfred Kleinknecht is Professor in the Economics of Innovation at TU Delft, the Netherlands. He obtained a PhD in economics at the Free University of Amsterdam, the Netherlands. He belonged to the team that developed the Community Innovation Survey (CIS) that became part of the standard data collection program in statistical agencies all over the European Union. He also contributed to the OECD Oslo Manual on innovation measurement.

Tobias Kretschmer is Professor of Strategy, Technology and Organization at the University of Munich, Germany. He is also Head of the Department Industrial Organization and New Technologies at the Ifo Institute for Economic Research. He received a PhD from London Business School. His main research interests are empirical industrial organization, organization design and strategy.

Kevin Lee is Assistant Professor of Finance and the Coordinator of the International Business concentration at the Craig School of Business at the California State University, Fresno starting August 2011. His dissertation focuses on formal and informal institutions and their impact on firm performance and economic outcomes.

Albert N. Link is Professor of Economics in the Department of Economics at the University of North Carolina, Greensboro, USA. His areas of expertise include science and innovation policy and the economics of entrepreneurship, and he is the editor of the *Journal of Technology Transfer*. He received a PhD from Tulane.

William McCumber is a PhD student at the Department of Finance at the Sam M. Walton College of Business, University of Arkansas (USA). As a former practitioner of asset management, McCumber has research interests that include financial institutions, corporate finance, asset pricing and the impact of institutions on economic decision-making.

Ramana Nanda is Assistant Professor at the Harvard Business School, USA. His research focuses on the ways in which the financial sector impacts innovation and entrepreneurship in the economy. One strand of research examines the role of financial intermediaries such as banks and VCs (venture capital firms) in shaping the founding and growth of new ventures in a region. A second, related strand, examines how government policy towards the financial sector impacts innovation, entrepreneurship and productivity growth in the economy.

Nicos Nicolaou is Lecturer in Management at the Department of Public and Business Administration at the University of Cyprus and a Visiting Fellow at the Innovation & Entrepreneurship Group, Imperial College Business School, London. His research interests include entrepreneurship, behavioral genetics, innovation management and university spinouts. He received a PhD from Imperial College London.

Bart Nooteboom is Professor of Innovation Policy at Tilburg University, the Netherlands. His current research interests are Schumpeterian and evolutionary economics, institutional economics, industrial/innovation/technology policy, innovation systems, trust within and between organizations, and learning within and between organizations.

Gerben van der Panne defended a PhD on regional knowledge spillovers in 2004. Since then he has been Assistant Professor in Management Economics at TU Delft, the Netherlands.

Simon C. Parker is Associate Professor of Entrepreneurship at the Richard Ivey School of Business, University of Western Ontario, Canada. He received a PhD from the University of Durham. His primary research interests are in the field of the economics of entrepreneurship.

Gabriele Pellegrino is Graduate Student of the Department of Economics and Social Sciences at the Università Cattolica del Sacro Cuore, in Italy. Gabriele's main field of specialization is the economics of innovation.

Mariacristina Piva, PhD in economics, is Associate Professor of Economic Policy at the Università Cattolica del Sacro Cuore, Italy. Her main field of specialization is the economics of innovation.

Mirjam van Praag is Professor of Entrepreneurship and Organization at the Faculty of Economics and Business of the Universiteit van Amsterdam (UvA), the Netherlands. She is also the founding director of the Amsterdam Center for Entrepreneurship (ACE). Mirjam van Praag's research is in the field of entrepreneurship and organization.

Susanne Prantl is a Senior Research Fellow at the Max Planck Institute for Research on Collective Goods in Bonn, Germany. Her main research areas are industrial economics and applied econometrics. In her recent work she has considered the relationship between economic performance and institutions, public policy as well as regulation, focusing on firm entry, product market competition and innovation.

Charles F. Sabel is the Maurice T. Moore Professor of Law and Social Science at Columbia Law School, USA. His research centers on public innovations, European Union governance, labor standards, economic development and ultra-robust networks. His 1984 book, *The Second Industrial Divide: Possibilities for Prosperity* (Basic Books), co-written with Michael J. Piore, has been widely influential among labor scholars.

AnnaLee Saxenian is Professor and Dean of the University of California (USA) Berkeley's School of Information and has a joint faculty appointment with the Department of City and Regional Planning. She has made a career of studying regional economics and the conditions under which people, ideas and geographies combine and connect into hubs of economic activity. She is author of two books about Silicon Valley: *Regional*

Advantage: Culture and Competition in Silicon Valley and Route 128 (Harvard University Press, 1994) and *The New Argonauts: Regional Advantage in a Global Economy* (Harvard University Press, 2006).

Scott Shane is the A. Malachi Mixon III Professor of Entrepreneurial Studies in the Department of Economics at the Weatherhead School of Management at Case Western Reserve University, Cleveland, Ohio, USA. He received a PhD from the University of Pennsylvania.

Donald S. Siegel is Professor and Dean of the School of Business at the University at Albany, SUNY, USA. He received his PhD from Columbia University. He is the incoming co-editor of *Academy of Management Perspectives* and editor of the *Journal of Technology Transfer*. Don has published 92 articles and six books on issues relating to university technology transfer and entrepreneurship, the effects of corporate governance on economic performance, productivity analysis, and corporate social responsibility in leading journals in economics, finance, and management. His most recent books are *Innovation, Entrepreneurship, and Technological Change* (Oxford University Press) and the *Handbook of Corporate Social Responsibility* (Oxford University Press).

Daniel F. Spulber is the Elinor Hobbs Distinguished Professor of International Business and Professor of Management Strategy at the Kellogg School of Management, Northwestern University, USA. He received his PhD from Northwestern University. He is the founding editor of the *Journal of Economics & Management Strategy*.

Erik Stam is Associate Professor of Innovation and Organizational Economics at Utrecht University, the Netherlands. He is also Research Fellow at the University of Cambridge, UK, and Research Fellow at the Scientific Council for Government Policy, the Netherlands. His primary research interests are entrepreneurship, innovation and economic development.

Marco Vivarelli, PhD in economics and PhD in science and technology policy, is Full Professor of Economic Policy at the Università Cattolica del Sacro Cuore, Italy; he is Research Fellow at the Institute for the Study of Labor (IZA, Bonn), and at the Centre for the Study of Globalisation and Regionalisation (CSGR, Warwick University). He is associate editor of *Small Business Economics* and associate editor of *Industrial and Corporate Change*. His main field of specialization is the economics of innovation.

Charles W. Wessner is Director of the Program on Technology, Innovation and Entrepreneurship at the National Academy of Sciences, USA. His fields of specialization are innovation policy, including public–private partnerships, entrepreneurship, early-stage financing for new firms, and the special needs and benefits of high-technology industry. He received a PhD from the Fletcher School of Law and Diplomacy.

Preface

This *Handbook of Research on Innovation and Entrepreneurship* compiles the outstanding expertise of leading researchers in the field of innovation and entrepreneurship. Such a project inevitably goes back to Schumpeter, and we adopt the motivation of his entrepreneur as our starting point. 'The joy of creating, of getting things done' allows us to revisit and connect seminal contributions in the research on innovation and entrepreneurship. Hereby we assume that just as entrepreneurship is needed for the innovative process, without innovation, entrepreneurship would be of little economic interest.

As a first step, we selected a collection of seminal contributions in innovation and entrepreneurship to be included in Edward Elgar's *International Library of Entrepreneurship* (ISBN 978 1 84844 099 9). This volume includes research beginning with the history of economic thinking, continues with the macro-level modern growth theory, the process of innovation, zooms in on the entrepreneur as the individual and, finally, considers institutions as determining framework conditions.

It was during the process of choosing articles for the aforementioned volume that we thought to ask leading scholars in the field of innovation and entrepreneurship research to share their current thoughts on this topic with us. The result is a marvelous collection of contributions that cover many fields within innovation and entrepreneurship research.

This volume starts with analyses of the social desirability of innovation and entrepreneurship, with contributions by William Baumol, Israel Kirzner, Marcus Dejardin and Mirjam van Praag. Contributions by Philippe Aghion, Dietmar Harhoff, Susanne Prantl, William Kerr, Ramana Nanda, AnnaLee Saxenian, Charles Sabel, Kathy Fogel, Kevin Lee and William McCumber then investigate institutions as determining framework conditions for innovation and entrepreneurship. The impact of new knowledge and knowledge spillovers on growth is analyzed in contributions by Gilles Duranton, Maryann Feldman, Gil Avnimelech, Pontus Braunerhjelm, Bo Carlsson, Zoltan Acs, David Audretsch and Max Keilbach. These contributions also reveal the geography of innovation and entrepreneurship. Closely related to the aforementioned topic is the role of technology transfer for innovation and entrepreneurship, which is studied in contributions by Richard Jensen, Albert Link, Charles Wessner, Donald Siegel, Daniel Spulber and Werner Bönte. Contributions by Simon Parker, Michael Fritsch, Uwe Cantner, Marco Guerzoni, Gabriele Pellegrino, Mariacristina Piva, Marco Vivarelli, Erik Stam, Bart Nooteboom, Alfred Kleinknecht, Gerben van der Panne, Andreas Eisingerich and Tobias Kretschmer look inside the firm and analyze in detail the firm's innovation process. Finally, Nicos Nicolaou, Scott Shane, Oliver Falck, Robert Gold and Stephan Heblich study the making of the entrepreneur.

We owe our friends, colleagues and family a great debt for their patience and support with the undertaking of this project. We especially must note the support of Madeleine Schmidt and Kirstin Ziegler at the Max Planck Institute of Economics, and Betty Fiscus at Indiana University, Bloomington. Without their able assistance this book would not be half the book that it is.

David Audretsch
Oliver Falck
Stephan Heblich
Adam Lederer
Bloomington, Jena, and Munich
March 2010

PART I

THE SOCIAL DESIRABILITY OF INNOVATION AND ENTREPRENEURSHIP

1 Invention and social entrepreneurship: social good and social evil
William J. Baumol[1]

The fault, dear Brutus, is not in our stars, but in ourselves . . . (*Julius Caesar*, Act 1, Scene 2)

The words 'inventor' and 'entrepreneur' are often used in a manner implying the unassailable virtues of such an occupational choice. Indeed, inventors and entrepreneurs are hailed as the hope of the future and as indispensable contributors helping to eliminate the world's remaining ills. Many also are regarded as self-sacrificing individuals, surrendering their leisure time and often family in pursuit of their goals. A moment's reflection, however, reveals that these issues are more complex. Indeed, inventors and entrepreneurs pursuing their inventions can damage society, sometimes severely.

I shall argue here, following Douhan and Henrekson (2008), that some of the activities that appear to damage social welfare actually have (second-best) beneficial consequences that mitigate other shortcomings in current economic arrangements. At the same time, there are other apparently beneficial acts of invention and entrepreneurship that are ultimately counterproductive. I shall conclude that, despite these important complications, the work of the inventor and his entrepreneurial partner is, on balance, enormously beneficial to the community. As such, both activities fully merit encouragement.

Readers concerned with policy design will also note that the instances in which invention and entrepreneurship prove damaging underscore the idea that one size does not fit all. In other words, any encouragement of invention and entrepreneurship adopted in accord with our general conclusion should be circumscribed, or at least nuanced, so as not to promote the detrimental along with the beneficial.

ILLUSTRATIONS: SOME POLAR CASES

It is easy to find examples of invention and entrepreneurial activities that are generally accepted as having promoted the general welfare, as well as others whose benefits are surely more questionable or worse. Indeed, it is easy to provide examples of changes in technology and their effects upon our lives that are so radical that our ancestors would be unable to comprehend them: television, commercial aviation and the Internet are only some of the most obvious.

But I shall cite just one simple historic episode in order to offer some sense of the magnitude of the changes and how difficult it is to grasp yesterday's living conditions today. The example shows the challenges faced by a wealthy and powerful individual living before the Industrial Revolution, as compared with today's common manner of existence. It is a description of the 1732 journey of the pregnant Wilhelmina, favorite sister of Frederick the Great. She was returning from Berlin, where she had gone to visit Frederick, to her home in Bayreuth, to whose ruler she was married (Wright, 1965, p. 142):

> Ten strenuous, abnormally frigid days were spent upon roads, bad enough in summer, now deep with snow. On the second day the carriage in which Wilhelmina was riding turned over. She was buried under an avalanche of luggage . . . Everyone expected a miscarriage and wanted Wilhelmina to rest in bed for several days . . . Mountains appeared after Leipzig had been passed . . . Wilhelmina was frightened by the steepness of the roads and preferred to get out and walk to being whacked about as the carriage jolted from boulder to boulder.

As much as we resent airport delays and what used to be airline food service (or, rather, what passed as food), this account surely brings out the degree to which invention and entrepreneurship make us strikingly better off in our travels than eighteenth-century royalty.

On the other side, there are no shortages of technical changes where the contribution to the welfare of humanity is questionable at best. The carbon emissions that poison our atmosphere and threaten our health and quality of life are one such questionable contribution.

But there are consequences of the work of the inventor and the entrepreneur that are even more extreme, either in the benefits provided or in the damage they threaten. Beneficial examples are rather easy to think of, notably in the arena of human health. One very obvious indicator of the state of health that prevails in a community is life expectancy at birth. Longevity data for earlier centuries are, of course, hardly reliable. Nevertheless, the evidence leads specialists to estimate that life expectancy has risen in England from about 35 years (for both nobility and the population as a whole) to its current level in excess of 70 years (Fogel, 1986). There are many other such indicators, notably the rise in productivity that has put an end to the famines, which at intervals of some ten years subjected the inhabitants of continental Europe to widespread starvation that littered the streets with corpses.

Progress is striking, but the need for further advance remains pressing. It is clear when we seek to make sense of the reports of the hundreds of millions of humans who continue barely to subsist on incomes tantamount to less than two dollars a day. I urge readers to take a moment to consider what their lives would be like if they were reduced to such a standard.

But the entrepreneurs of past and present are not all models of absolute virtue. If we define an innovative entrepreneur as someone who ensures the introduction and utilization of some novelty into the workings of the economy, in the hope of garnering wealth, power and prestige in exchange, we must recognize that for most of human history the instruments of successful entrepreneurs were far more straightforward than they are today. Indeed, for many centuries, superstar entrepreneurs accumulated wealth simply by grabbing it from a neighbor in the course of warfare. These evidently enterprising individuals – Caesar, Alexander and Napoleon, to name a notable few – remain the heroes of history, despite the fact that their methods hardly benefited society. Caesar's crippling of captured Gauls, for instance, pales in comparison to the grisly execution procedure favored by Vlad 'the Impaler', who inspired the Dracula legend. Lest these extreme examples be considered outside the range of relevance, one can instead recall the more businesslike activities of the entrepreneur who invented the Ponzi scheme, the questionable activities of the post-Civil War robber barons, and the boldly innovative attempt by Jay Gould and Jim Fisk to corner the USA's gold supply under the Grant Administration.

These individual actions, as deplorable as they may seem to us, are surely nothing in comparison with some of the truly major threats that innovative and entrepreneurial activity have brought to humankind. The damage done to our waterways and the atmosphere, culminating in the prospect of severe global warming, is surely, at least in good part, the result of modern industry. Before the Industrial Revolution, humanity simply did not possess the means to do such extreme damage to our planet.

More recently, humankind, via the agency of its inventors, discovered the means to bring all of human life to an end, and entrepreneurial activity throughout the world is relentlessly promoting the successful search for ways to make these doomsday instruments cheaper and more accessible. Can one really delude oneself into believing that such activity is not being actively encouraged inside the world's rogue regimes that seek to impose what they deem to be 'God's will' upon all of humanity? With newspaper headlines repeatedly reporting random killings in schools and post offices by individuals gone berserk, who can be confident that Adolf Hitler, at the end of his tether in his Berlin bunker, would not have pressed the red button had today's destructive technology been available.

At first, these examples may strike the reader as melodramatic exaggeration. However, a little thought will surely confirm that it seems so only because we do not want to think about these less than cheerful developments – all of which were made possible by the systematic and determined efforts of the world's inventors and their entrepreneurial partners.

ON BENEFICIAL CONTRIBUTIONS OF UNPRODUCTIVE ENTREPRENEURS IN A SECOND-BEST WORLD

The preceding discussion and its focus on extreme cases implies that it is relatively simple to determine whether a particular type of entrepreneurial activity benefits the community or works to its detriment. In reality, matters are more convoluted, and the complications are of considerable importance in a real economy whose workings are unlikely even to approximate optimality. As Douhan and Henrekson (2008) note, in an imperfect world, at least some entrepreneurial activities of questionable virtue can sometimes be distinctly beneficial. A clear example is provided by Adam Smith's smuggler, who provides to the consuming public commodities that irrational legislation sought to deny them. Accordingly, when the smuggler is caught by the authorities, the consequence is apt to be distinctly damaging:

> By the ruin of the smuggler, his capital, which before had been employed in maintaining productive labor, is absorbed either in the revenue of the state or in that of the revenue-officer, and is employed in maintaining unproductive, to the diminution of the general capital of the society, and of the useful industry which it might otherwise have maintained. (Smith [1776], 1937, p. 849)

From my own past, I can recall a related experience, in which my father, a shopkeeper, was solicited by racketeers for the payment of 'protection money'. Absent payment, the racketeers implied that damage to my father's property could confidently be expected. Having little choice, he acquiesced, only to find that it was worth the money because the racketeers provided surveillance, which kept freelance burglars away, and notified him if the doors or windows had not been shut properly. This example is, of course, trivial, but the far-reaching implications for the community surely can be understood.

Aside from the value of the insight this observation provides, it is significant for the design of policy in the arena of entrepreneurship. Sociologists and economic historians, following the work of Max Weber (2001), Douglass North (1981, 1987, 1991, 1994) and David Landes (1999), provide evidence leading to the conclusion that the magnitude and vigor of entrepreneurial activity is heavily influenced – indeed, perhaps primarily determined – by current culture and institutions. Recognition of the role that second-best entrepreneurial activity plays is a caveat pertinent to effective policy design. Smith's smuggler demonstrates how misconceived public policy can impede enterprising activities that might otherwise serve the public interest with reasonable efficiency. In this and other similar instances, the community must instead turn to entrepreneurs who seek out the rewarding second-best opportunities created when the smuggler, for example, can no longer operate. Thus the individual 'would have been, in every respect, an excellent citizen, had not the laws of his country made that a crime which nature never meant to be so' (Smith [1776], 1937, p. 849).

ON THE MORALITY OF ENTREPRENEURS

The enormous range, in terms of public interest, spanned by entrepreneurial careers suggests one critical conclusion: entrepreneurs, as a group, are neither uniformly moral nor immoral. The same is true for those engaged in most economic activities: they span the relevant range – with many falling in that in-between category, led by the prevailing structure of incentives provided by current culture, institutions and economic organizations.

At this point, it is useful to digress in order to clarify three key points. First, my use of the term 'entrepreneur' evidently entails a considerable stretch beyond the usual usage that confines itself to businesspeople. I allow it to include warriors, politicians and Mafia chieftains. Justifying this expansion is surely appropriate. Second, given my focus on *innovative* entrepreneurship, rather than the *imitative* entrepreneurship entailed in the establishment of yet another new firm of a standard pre-existing variety, I have yet to provide evidence suggesting that more heterodox variants of entrepreneurial activity introduce distinct innovations. Finally, I shall comment on the choice of activity by entrepreneurs who can be deemed 'amoral'. What, for example, leads them into activities distinctly damaging to the general welfare? Let me, then, offer some remarks on all three issues, with the aid of a few clear examples.

Heterodox Entrepreneurs

That the careers of political and military leaders or crime bosses can be entrepreneurial should be obvious. An organization dealing in narcotics – acquiring them from the growers, processing them as necessary, transporting them to market, and then delivering them to resellers – differs from conventional business firms in only one respect: its violation of the law. Similarly, a warlord organizing a mercenary private army provides a service and can be expected to carry out his activities on terms as businesslike as those of the CEO of any firm listed on any stock exchange. These unconventional entrepreneurs are even likely to operate in a similar manner; seeking ways to stimulate demand for their products, rather than leaving it to chance. Moreover, for all of these activities, the goals are similar: the pursuit of wealth, power, and perhaps even prestige, albeit in a rather distorted form. Thus, as regards the creators of what are evidently business enterprises in all but name, the appropriate approach for analyzing the activities of these unorthodox entrepreneurs need not differ fundamentally from an investigation into the operations of the most legitimate business firm.

Entrepreneurship that is Heterodox and *Innovative*

What has just been said is equally true for economic organizations working in the public interest at the other end of the spectrum of the general welfare. It is difficult, for instance, to think of anyone more enterprising than Florence Nightingale and her revolutionary reconstitution of the organizations dedicated to caring for the wounded on battlefields and in hospitals at home. As can be true of any effective entrepreneur, the improved procedures Nightingale introduced to the medical profession were not her own invention – at least not exclusively. She was, however, among the first to understand the importance of good sanitation, and her struggle was to ensure that the medical profession put these new insights into practice. In this sense, Nightingale's extraordinary efforts to improve the general welfare were not merely entrepreneurial, but also *innovative*, in the most fundamental sense.

However, one must not confuse innovation with virtue. Some of the most socially damaging acts have been innovative. New weapons, new military tactics and new ways of committing mass murder were innovations actively sought and introduced by warlords throughout history. For instance, Vlad the Impaler was enterprising, using methodical mass execution to preserve his power.

More recently (and in a more businesslike vein), narcotics smugglers have reportedly improved their ability to evade the authorities by using mini-submarines that are difficult to detect or to capture, once spotted. Surely this qualifies as innovation in pursuit of business objectives.

On Determinants of the Choice between Virtue and Vice

As already stated, there is reason to surmise that a considerable number of entrepreneurs, like the members of any profession, are neither outstandingly idealistic nor dedicated to vice as a goal in and of itself. That said, it seems safe to assume that Florence Nightingale would never have turned her abilities to crime or, on the other side, that Vlad the Impaler would have dedicated himself to establishing well-equipped nurseries for abandoned children. For entrepreneurs falling between the extremes that Nightingale and Vlad represent, what determines their course? As noted above, sociologists and economic historians, following the work of Weber, North and Landes, provide evidence leading to the conclusion that the prevailing culture and institutions heavily influence entrepreneurial activity.

ENTREPRENEUR LEADERS: REVISION OF THE RULES BY DESIGN

Among the different types of entrepreneurs discussed so far, one group has been omitted – a group occupying a leadership position in the field. Where the laws or other relevant institutions constitute unreasonable constraints, one cannot expect capable entrepreneurs simply to sit back and accept them as inevitable and immutable – nor will many of them be willing to undergo the inconvenience and risks of outright violation. Instead, one can surely be confident that some vigorous and capable entrepreneurs will act to cut the Gordian knot by attacking the rules directly and undertaking actions designed to modify the offending institutions. Indeed, in this process there emerges a group of entrepreneurs who specialize in modifying the rules of the game. I shall refer to these entrepreneurs who serve the interests of other entrepreneurs as 'mega-entrepreneurs.'

History is full of such enterprising individuals, whose most noted means of operation is the *coup d'état*. Where the currently governing institutions have been inconvenient, the obvious way to improve matters has frequently involved getting rid of those whose role entailed preservation of the status quo. When Augustus took on the role of emperor, following Caesar's failed attempt, he was surely showing enterprise in his pursuit of wealth, power and prestige. More than that, Augustus radically changed the institutions that stood in his way, most notably by ending the Roman republic.

History also provides plentiful examples of a far more abundant type of entrepreneur – one whose activities are rather more routine, but whose immediate goal, the replacement of inconvenient institutions, is similar to that of Augustus. These are the modern mega-entrepreneurs, who are exemplified by lobbyists. Today they occupy a prominent role in the US political process, for example, but this modern entrepreneurial field is hardly a recent invention – evidence indicates that lobbying activity preceded the onset of England's industrial revolution (Colley, 1992, p. 68; italics added):

> The papers of virtually every Member of Parliament and peer from this time (after the Hanoverian succession of 1714) show just how large initiatives to do with trade – petitions for new bridges, new roads, new market places or better street lighting, plans for improvements to ports and lighthouses, or demands for an end to old monopolies – loomed in the political business of the day. Lesser tradesmen would band together to petition for what they wanted. More powerful men lobbied directly, or employed agents to do so for them. In 1739, for example, the prosperous merchants who ran the Convention of the Royal Burgs in Edinburgh *paid a London-based solicitor* called Thomas White the sum of 100 pounds to lobby in support of legislation for Scotland's linen industry. Over the next dozen years, this same body petitioned Parliament on the state of the coinage, on the problem of smuggling, in support of convoy protection for merchantmen in times of war, in favor of standardization of weights and measures, and on behalf of legislation changing the bankruptcy laws.

Today, lobbying itself has been reorganized by its own cadre of entrepreneurs, and is conducted in a most businesslike manner. Lobbyists' services are hired by others, with the commodity sold in this market being activity directed to the modification of legal institutions so as to benefit the purchasers of lobbying services. In this instance, one class of mega-entrepreneurs does well by helping others engaged in different entrepreneurial activities to further their business objectives. Moreover, the organizers of such profitable lobbying firms are themselves mega-entrepreneurs of a higher order, who seek to reorganize the institutions under which other entrepreneurs conduct their activities.[2]

Under US law, lobbyists must register themselves in order to prevent concealed or illicit activities. Information from this registry indicates that, since the Second World War, the population of registered lobbyists in Washington, DC is reported to have exploded, which suggests that lobbying activities have not been unsuccessful. The scale of the lobbying efforts reported also is impressive. Recent figures indicate that there are approximately 35 000 individuals engaged in lobbying the federal government. Moreover, between the years 2000 and 2005, the fees charged by these firms to new clients doubled (Birnbaum, 2005, p. A01).

As such, lobbying is not an activity conducted haphazardly. Rather, it is a well-organized industry with at least one professional association of its own, the American League of Lobbyists. The industry also has at least one public-interest 'watchdog' group, The Center for Responsive Politics, monitoring its activities.

The number of clients to which professional lobbyists devote themselves ranges from one or two clients to as many as 50. Few, if any, of the economy's giant enterprises (including non-profit organizations) eschew lobbying activities, but it is important to note that small enterprises, which can purchase small amounts of a busy lobbyist's time, are not excluded from this arena. In other words, lobbying is a prime example of a well-organized industry founded and maintained by entrepreneurs.

Enterprising lobbyists pursue a wide variety of concrete goals. While many of these objectives are self-serving and may even provide no benefit to the general public, the record in this arena is more mixed than one might expect. For one thing, charitable and non-profit organizations that focus on promoting the general welfare are also driven to engage in lobbying activity. Healthcare institutions, educational institutions, and arts and cultural organizations are among those lobbying for their interests. (Full disclosure: the author of this chapter was once an unpaid member of a lobbying group made up of representatives of the USA's leading institutions of higher education, which worked to promote higher education and expand its funding.)

As expected, however, it is often true that much of the effort of the lobbying industry is directed at eliminating or emasculating requirements that are expensive and onerous to the firms hiring lobbyists. In particular, rules governing modes of manufacture, product quality and safety are institutions of enormous interest to the business firms. Enterprising efforts to modify these regulations very often call for weakening constraints, such as standards of product quality, and reducing enforcement capabilities. Despite their obvious public benefits, such requirements can be very costly to businesses engaged in producing and supplying the products in question.

However, matters are not always so straightforward. In 2007 and 2008, there were a number of instances in which products, particularly imported items, were found to be defective – contaminated by lead paint or other dangerous substances. The resulting threat to health and survival extended from animals kept as pets to human infants, triggering a substantial public outcry. At that point, the suppliers of these items and related products apparently realized that their interests would be promoted by tougher rules and more vigorous enforcement, as a means of restoring customer confidence in their products. As a result, the affected firms reportedly switched their stance toward these rules – at least temporarily – and began pressing for more effective constraints.

Even firms whose products have not yet raised any safety issues can be expected, on occasion, to favor more constraining rules. This exemplifies Akerlof's lemons analysis (1970), which posits that because customers generally have little ability to test such products for dangerous components – and possess little knowledge of what ingredients are dangerous – the unacceptable performance of *some* suppliers must unavoidably raise customer suspicions about products of other suppliers that do satisfy reasonable standards of safety. As such, even firms that already provide acceptable performance can be driven to favor more constraining regulations as certification to potential customers of the quality of their products.

Returning to our main theme, among the influences that account for the appearance of entrepreneurs and their choice of activities, it is important to emphasize the influence exerted by current culture and institutions, which determines the magnitude of the rewards each activity offers. However, entrepreneurs are not prone to leave matters to chance and let happenstance determine the gains that are available to them. Instead, as might have been expected, a group has emerged, whom I have called the 'mega-entrepreneurs' – entrepreneurs who serve other entrepreneurs by working to modify the characteristics of current institutions, making them more favorable to their entrepreneur clients. Lobbyists are the prime prototype of this group, and it has been noted here that this activity and the number of those who carry it out have expanded significantly in recent decades. For society that may be a mixed blessing, but it is not uniformly undesirable.[3] As such, impeding lobbyists' activities completely is not in society's best interest. Instead, constraining these mega-entrepreneurs in ways that benefit the community – as the requirement of reporting by lobbyists already does – may be a wiser policy approach.

CONCLUDING COMMENT

At every level of entrepreneurial activity, the implications for the general welfare are generally mixed. From the promoter of a new invention to the innovative influence peddler within a government agency, entrepreneurs contribute to growth, prosperity and general welfare – in many cases, but not always. This is why it is so important for society to pay attention to the more mutable current institutions that provide incentives for innovative entrepreneurship. That said, government should avoid over-regulating and adhere instead to a self-denying ordinance that keeps regulators from entering arenas in which they have no competence and which are best left to market forces. In those instances where restrictions are required and their logic is understood, regulators must take the utmost care to avoid preclusion or hobbling of the vast benefits that innovative entrepreneurship has provided in the past – and promises to make possible in the future.

NOTES

1. I am deeply indebted to the Ewing Marion Kauffman Foundation for its generous support of this work.
2. This upper echelon of mega-entrepreneurs specializes in intervening in the process that sets the 'rules of the game' – a country's laws and institutions. Those rules determine which activities are most rewarding to other entrepreneurs and, in turn, influence how entrepreneurs of the more usual variety spend their time and effort.

3. For example, hospitals and universities have their lobbyists, whose mission is to facilitate and expand the provision of healthcare and education. Lobbying activity also is sponsored by the arts and by environmentalists, although some of this is carried out by profit-seeking lobbyist firms.

REFERENCES

Akerlof, G.A. (1970), 'The market for "lemons": quality uncertainty and the market mechanism', *Quarterly Journal of Economics*, **84** (3), 488–500.

Birnbaum, J.H. (2005), 'The road to riches is called K Street: lobbying firms hire more, pay more, charge more to influence government', *Washington Post*, p. A01.

Colley, L. (ed) (1992), *Britons: Forging the Nation 1707–1837*, New Haven, CT and London: Yale University Press.

Douhan, R. and M. Henrekson (2008), 'Entrepreneurship and second-best institutions: going beyond Baumol's typology', IFN Working Paper No. 766.

Fogel, R.W. (1986), 'Nutrition and the decline of mortality since 1700: some preliminary findings', in S.L. Engerman and R.L. Gallman (eds), *Long-Term Factors in American Economic Growth*, Chicago, IL: University of Chicago Press, pp. 439–556.

Landes, D.S. (ed.) (1999), *The Wealth and Poverty of Nations: Why Some are so Rich and Some So Poor*, New York: Norton.

North, D.C. (ed.) (1981), *Structure and Change in Economic History*, New York: Norton.

North, D.C. (1987), 'Institutions, transaction costs and economic growth', *Economic Inquiry*, **23** (3), 419–28.

North, D.C. (1991), 'Institutions', *Journal of Economic Perspectives*, **5** (1), 97–112.

North, D.C. (1994), 'Economic performance through time', *American Economic Review*, **84** (3), 359–68.

Smith, A. (ed.) (1776) (1937), *The Wealth of Nations*, New York: Modern Library.

Weber, M. (ed.) (2001), *The Protestant Ethic and the Spirit of Capitalism*, New York and London: Routledge.

Wright, C. (1965), *A Royal Affinity*, London: Frederick Muller.

2 Between useful and useless innovation: the entrepreneurial role
Israel M. Kirzner

For many years I have argued for a theoretical understanding of the entrepreneurial role that differs significantly, in certain respects, from that pioneered by Joseph Schumpeter in his celebrated works (e.g. Schumpeter, 1934). Schumpeter identified the entrepreneurial role with the creative and innovative element in the human make-up. So far, so good. No one need take serious issue with this identification. But Schumpeter went further. For Schumpeter, the entrepreneur's out-of-the-box thinking disrupts the equilibrium that would otherwise tend to emerge in the market economy. The creativity that Schumpeter's entrepreneur displays is a destructive creativity (in the sense that it disturbs pre-existing stable patterns of production and commercial relationships). At this point there is substantial scope for disagreement. Building on the work of Ludwig von Mises, I have, contrary to Schumpeter, seen the entrepreneurial role as benignly responding to perceived imbalances, to the pockets of perceived or anticipated disequilibrium being continuously revealed in markets. The entrepreneur who correctly identifies and exploits such a perceived imbalance is correcting a poorly coordinated set of decisions that would otherwise have been made. As I see it, the sequence of events set in motion by entrepreneurial discovery is a sequence to which we owe whatever equilibrating tendencies markets possess – rather than (as with Schumpeter) an extraneous (albeit possibly creative and ultimately beneficial) disruption jolting the market *away* from any initial equilibrium positions that might otherwise have emerged.[1]

Over the years I have, in response to repeated, valuable (and valued) criticisms, more than once felt compelled to clarify my position. Certainly the importance of Schumpeterian innovation and creativity is not to be denied. Certainly, in the activity of successful real-world-market entrepreneurs such innovation and creativity (and the qualities of imagination and unorthodox brashness that are the basics for such creativity) are the most obvious of observables. My insistence that profitable entrepreneurial activity be seen as a response to existing disequilibrium (rather than disruptive of equilibrium) calls not for denial of the importance of creativity, but for a broader perspective on creativity itself. Creativity is inspired, my position runs, by alertness to opportunities that 'await' exploitation. To the extent that such opportunities are 'waiting' to be exploited, the existing situation must be seen as one that is not in balance: existing decisions are not perfectly coordinated. The profits to be won by creative innovation are the pure profits that characterize markets that have not yet attained equilibrium. It is these prospective profits that inspire entrepreneurial alertness and entrepreneurial creativity. My concession to my critics (that is, my whole-hearted acknowledgment of the primacy of Schumpeterian creativity) turns out to be, at the same time, a challenge calling upon critics to recognize that the 'disruptive', disequilibrating Schumpeterian entrepreneur is, at a deeper level, a 'responding, equilibrating' entrepreneur.[2]

In some of my work, clarifying my position has required me to emphasize the overlap between my view of the entrepreneurial process and that of Schumpeter. At other times it has required me to insist on the differences between these two views. This present chapter, too, emphasizes (one facet of) these differences. Perhaps it is important to underline that this emphasis should not be misinterpreted in any sense, or in any degree, as a denial of the primacy of Schumpeterian creativity in real-world capitalist entrepreneurship, properly understood as an expression of the more fundamental sense in which entrepreneurship is seen as responding to existing imbalances 'waiting' for the entrepreneurial, alert individual who can 'correct' them.

USELESS INNOVATION

The issue discussed here, which draws attention to the difference between Schumpeter's understanding of the entrepreneurial role and my own, has to do with the possibility of useless innovation. It should be intuitively obvious that there is no law of nature ensuring that all innovations are of potential economic benefit to society. The mere fact that a product is new does not guarantee that it will (permanently) rank high on the value scales of consumers (although it can readily be conceded that the mere fact of its novelty *may* inspire some consumer interest – while it is still new). The mere fact that a technologically novel method of production is able to produce a given product in a differently new manner does not in any way guarantee that this new method of production is an economically desirable use of society's resources (permitting society to squeeze out a greater aggregate of consumer satisfaction [however this latter term may be understood] from its available resources).[3]

But once all this is recognized as obviously true, it is equally obvious that our admiration for innovativeness and for creativity cannot be an unqualified admiration. Before endorsing social policies that may be designed to promote and enhance Schumpeterian creativity, one must ask how we can be confident that these policies will not only promote creativity, but will also channel that creativity into socially valuable, rather than socially inefficient, lines of innovation. This is a question that certainly begs for a response with respect to fully socialist societies. To pursue this latter point in a real-world instead of theoretical setting, in the Soviet Union substantial attention was devoted to the deliberate encouragement of innovation in processes of production.[4] But it was by no means clear how, in an economy where resource prices did not freely emerge from the market, it was possible to distinguish between new methods of production that constitute an economic improvement, and new methods of production that do not.[5] In a market economy, one is disposed to argue, this is not a fundamental difficulty. One can argue that the very same competitive-market discipline upon which market economies depend to weed out inefficient methods of production in favor of more efficient methods, and to direct resources away from the productions of less highly valued consumer products toward more highly valued products will steer the creative forces of entrepreneurship away from wastefully new products and techniques toward socially desirable innovations in output mix and in production techniques. This chapter certainly confirms this argument, but also points out that this argument, when articulated within a purely Schumpeterian framework, is not quite the same argument that can be made from the perspective of my understanding of the impact of the entrepreneurial role.

SCHUMPETERIAN CREATIVITY AND USELESS INNOVATIONS

From the purely Schumpeterian theoretical perspective, there does not, in the purely creative role of the entrepreneur, appear to be any built-in guarantee that useless innovation will be avoided. The very same qualities of creativity, imagination and boldness that produced the technological revolutions responsible for the extraordinary rate of growth in Western capitalist countries can also generate new products that consumers do not want, as well as new production techniques that cost far more than they are worth. The pure entrepreneurship responsible for innovation cannot by itself ensure socially valuable innovation. What has steered Western capitalism away from such wasteful innovation, one would have to argue, has been the efficiency-inducing pressure of competitive capitalism. Useless new products would tend to command prices so low as to deter their production; wasteful new technological processes of production would generate prohibitively high costs of production. The price system would, in a freely competitive market, tend to squash entrepreneurial activity that generates wasteful innovation and encourages profitable entrepreneurial innovation. The market ensures that which could not be ensured under central planning: that entrepreneurial innovations tend to be valuably, rather than wastefully, channeled.

However, one must note that from this purely Schumpeterian theoretical perspective, the successful avoidance of wasteful, useless, innovation is to be attributed to a process – the competitive market process – that is distinct from the creative entrepreneurial process responsible for innovation itself. It is only because this latter creative entrepreneurial process is embedded in the larger process of the competitive market that entrepreneurial creativity is channeled to useful rather than to wasteful innovation. There are thus two distinct processes at work in the entrepreneurial market: (1) that which generates entrepreneurial creativity and innovation; and (2) the competitive market process which, by virtue of the price-signaling potential in a competitive market, steers producers away from wasteful innovations toward economically useful innovations. This latter process is, from the purely Schumpeterian theoretical perspective, not an entrepreneurial process at all. For Schumpeter, entrepreneurship is only the disruptive aspect of creativity; he sees the competitive market process, which standard theory sees as tending towards equilibrium (i.e. towards a pattern from which all waste has been eliminated through competitive pressure), as the work, not of entrepreneurs, but rather of 'imitators'.

While it remains true that market capitalism is successful in its tendency to steer entrepreneurial innovation into socially valuable directions, as argued previously, this turns out to be attributable to a fortunate 'accident'. This accident is the circumstance that Schumpeterian entrepreneurship is, in a capitalist world, embedded in the competitive market economy. As we shall see, on the other hand, no such fortunate 'accident' is necessary when (Schumpeterian) entrepreneurial creativity is understood within the wider framework that I have advocated over the years.

THE ENTREPRENEURIAL MARKET PROCESS

This latter perspective recognizes that the equilibrative properties of dynamically competitive markets are themselves driven by entrepreneurial alertness to opportunities for profit from existing market imbalances.[6] What tends to ensure a single price throughout any given market for any given product or input service is the lure (to potential entrepreneurs) of the pure arbitrage profit (created by any initial differences among prices). What tends to ensure that costs of production and product prices tend towards a no-pure-profit equilibrium configuration is the lure (to potential entrepreneurs) of the pure profits to be won by producing at production costs lower than the relevant attainable selling prices. It turns out, from this perspective, that Schumpeterian creativity is simply an example of such more broadly conceived patterns of entrepreneurship. The Schumpeterian innovator, seeing 'around the corner', as it were, glimpses the possibility of acquiring resources at prices that are, when seen from the perspective of his creative imagination, lower than the relevant prices of the output that (in that very same creative imagination) he sees as possibly forthcoming from those resources. Ludwig von Mises presented this perspective with crystalline clarity: 'What makes profit emerge is the fact that the entrepreneur who judges the future prices of the products more correctly than other people do buys some or all of the factors of production at prices which, seen from the point of view of the future state of the market, are too low' (Von Mises, 1962, p. 109). What is added to this Misesian insight, by explicit recognition of Schumpeterian creativity, is that 'the future prices of the products' are now to be understood as those of (possibly novel) products able to be produced (by possibly innovative techniques of production) that other, less creative, less imaginative, producers have not as yet imagined as possible.

In other words, the very same entrepreneurial alertness that drives the equilibrative market process is at work in the decision making of the Schumpeterian innovator. Or, to put it equivalently, the very same entrepreneurial vision that inspires the Schumpeterian innovator is responsible for the competitive-entrepreneurial process that is credited, in the market economy, with weeding out inefficient production: the generation of powerful tendencies in capitalism that operate to (i) replace the production of less-valued products by the production of more-valued products; and to (ii) replace use of more costly production techniques by the use of available (or 'imaginable') less costly techniques.

Thus, from the perspective provided by this broader entrepreneurial–theoretical framework (embracing at once both the pure Schumpeterian creative entrepreneur and the theoretical construct of a purely non-creative arbitrage entrepreneur), what steers innovation and creativity into socially useful channels is a single entrepreneur-driven market process. In this process, entrepreneurs appraise future possibilities, probing the market for its existing imbalance. Such imbalances arise continually as a result of changing consumer tastes, changing patterns of resource availability and, very importantly, of potential changes in technological possibilities. These possible imbalances present themselves to the visionary entrepreneur as pockets of available pure profit. It is these profit opportunities that inspire the entrepreneurial creativity, which manifests itself in the form of innovation. But such innovation, seen from the broader ('Misesian') perspective that I advocate is inspired, not by any abstract creativity detached from market prices, but precisely by prescient awareness of the price imbalances generated by the earlier suboptimal patterns of production.

From this broader perspective, it is no accident that the entrepreneurial creativity responsible for market innovation tends to be channeled in socially beneficial directions. After all, the very same profit-motivated inspiration that drives entrepreneurial creativity drives that creativity towards socially valuable applications, and away from socially wasteful applications.

From my perspective, this latter insight constitutes a significant consideration supporting our long-standing contention that Schumpeterian creativity can best be understood as existentially and essentially embedded within a broader ('Misesian') theoretical understanding of the market as a competitive–entrepreneurial process.

NOTES

1. The original, extensive exposition of this position was presented in Kirzner (1973).
2. For a recent discussion of the place of Schumpeterian creativity in the broader, 'Misesian', framework that I advocate, see Kirzner (2009).
3. Throughout the chapter, we speak loosely about 'socially valuable' or 'socially wasteful' innovation, without attempting to grapple with the well-known subtle theoretical issues (central to welfare economic theory) surrounding such terminology.
4. On this aspect of the Soviet economy see Berliner (1976).
5. On this point see Kirzner (1985), pp. 35f.
6. On this, see Kirzner (1973), chs 1 and 2.

REFERENCES

Berliner, J.S. (ed.) (1976), *The Innovation Decision in Soviet Industry*, Cambridge, MA: MIT Press.
Kirzner, I.M. (ed.) (1973), *Competition and Entrepreneurship*, Chicago, IL: University of Chicago Press.
Kirzner, I.M. (ed.) (1985), *Discovery and the Capitalist Process*, Chicago, IL: University of Chicago Press.
Kirzner, I.M. (2009), 'The alert and creative entrepreneur: a clarification', *Small Business Economics*, **32**, 145–52.
Von Mises, L. (ed.) (1962), *Planning for Freedom and Other Essays*, 2nd edn, South Holland: Libertarian Press.
Schumpeter, J.A. (ed.) (1934), *The Theory of Economic Development*, Cambridge, MA: Harvard University Press.

3 Entrepreneurship and rent-seeking behavior
Marcus Dejardin

Entrepreneurship is now pervasively recognized in economic theory for its contribution in carrying innovation into the economic process and, consequently, in feeding economic growth (Aghion and Howitt, 1992; Carree and Thurik, 2003). *Ceteris paribus*, different entrepreneurial endowments may explain different rhythms of growth between nations. Among the theoretical discussions of the several conditions entering the *ceteris paribus* assumption, one appears tremendously fruitful. It relates to the allocation of entrepreneurial resources between more or less socially productive activities. All activities in a maximizing economy are not equally conducive to production and economic growth. Some can even affect growth negatively. The idea is linked with the concept of rent-seeking behavior. The connections between entrepreneurship and rent-seeking behavior constitute the topic of this chapter.

Having defined the general framework and employed concepts, we shall discuss the allocation of entrepreneurs between different types of economic projects (in other words, between innovative entrepreneurship and rent-seeking), as well as the explicative factors of this allocation. A dynamic set-up follows where interactions between project categories and relations to growth are scanned. We conclude by briefly examining some policy implications.

INTRODUCING ENTREPRENEURSHIP AND RENT-SEEKING BEHAVIOR

Assuming that the individual arbitrage between different remunerative occupations ends up, in all cases, in the development of socially productive activities, the economy is sketched as a strict income economy. Maximizing individuals exploit their skills as best they can. Moreover, in a perfectly competitive economy, private and social benefits coincide.

Now, let us introduce an activity that is remunerated by transfers. We note that, by definition, transfers do not imply a productive counterpart. Transfers result in the possibility that distortions between private and collective interests may occur. This distortion is undoubtedly effective when rent-seeking is involved when compared with the classical competitive benchmark model. That is, the actual net effects of rent-seeking (whether positive or negative) is a matter of concern since optimal allocation and dynamic efficiency of the economy are not taken for granted, as suggested later on.

Although Tullock introduced the basic argument corresponding to rent-seeking behavior to public choice theory in 1967, the term 'rent-seeking' was not coined until Krueger published 'Political economy of the rent-seeking society' in the *American Economic Review* in 1974 (see Tullock, 2003). According to its most common and widespread definition, rent-seeking (behavior) refers to 'the socially costly pursuit of wealth transfers' (Tollison, 1997, p. 506). Rent-seekers' private returns result from redistribution of wealth and not from wealth creation (Murphy et al., 1991).

The rent at stake here is to be distinguished from entrepreneurial creation of rents: rents due to better use of resources, arising from specific assets or technology, securable (by patents, for example) but limited in time from the pressure of competitors and progress (Douhan and Henrekson, 2007; see also Alvarez, 2007; Douhan and Henrekson, 2008a). On the other hand, Tollison's definition of rent-seeking allows for an expression of social opportunity costs in terms of resources diversion to, or following, the rent-seeking activity. Examples of rent-seeking include corruption, stealing, bribery, as well as seeking abusive judicial compensation or protection-seeking with the express purpose of limiting economic competition and promoting a particular interest. Rent-seeking can originate from both the public and private sectors.

For the connection between entrepreneurship and growth, the occurrence of unproductive but remunerated activities means that not only are projects with socially positive or negative impacts in competition, but also that there is a direct potential diversion of entrepreneurial talents. For this diversion to take place, it is assumed that the skills and abilities required by entrepreneurship and by rent-seeking correspond.

Following these introductory considerations, at least two remarks can be formulated that are considered as important additions. The first refers to public action and public services. The economic rationale for public intervention refers generally to market failures, magnificent evidence-jigging from economic reality and questioning the benchmark of the perfectly competitive model.[1] Public services are generally financed by transfers. That being the case, transfers are not a sufficient condition for defining rent-seeking. Public services are not included in rent-seeking given their socially productive contribution. We note further that, while a discussion of the redistribution role of the state is outside the framework of this chapter, things may appear differently if we look at legal institutions that organize productive activities, as they might, for example, create rent-seeking behaviors by limiting competition.

The second remark concerns entrepreneurial initiatives and goes back to the entrepreneurial creation of rents through innovation. Through innovation, the entrepreneur seeks to create a monopoly position, from which he will derive overprofit. In the Schumpeterian model, this position is necessary as it motivates the innovation activity. However, it is temporary, as competition will quickly reduce this position in favor of a new monopoly created by a new innovation. The institutional framework of competition is of primary importance. In this case, a dynamic assessment of the entire process will justify the existence of an abnormal profit, as it will distinguish its positive net contribution to the social benefit.[2]

Rent-seeking behavior thus defined, as well as the general framework of this chapter, we address in the following discussion the allocation of talents between socially productive entrepreneurship and rent-seeking or unproductive activities.

EXPLAINING THE ALLOCATION OF TALENTS

Attempting to explain the allocation of talents implies considering a variety of arguments explaining individual arbitrage between distinct remunerative activities. Together with relative remunerations, institutions or non-pecuniary factors may also play a role. According to Murphy et al. (1991, p. 506), 'talent goes into activities with the highest private returns, which need not have the highest social returns'. These authors assume increasing returns on talent. In other words, the greater the ability of an individual, the greater his private benefits will be. Because the exercise of talent is physically limited (by the period of human activity in a day), talented individuals tend to invest themselves and their abilities in reward-maximizing occupations. It follows that their occupational choice is almost directly determined by the size of the market, the compensation contract (rewards on talent application) and the technology.

Furthermore, the allocation of talent can be linked with both institutional context and non-pecuniary explicative factors. The legal framework and its effective use define a propitious environment for entrepreneurship and, contrarily, for rent-seeking behavior. Property rights, the conditions of their application, and the respect of these rights, joined with governance and fiscal organization, appear to be crucial factors. They contribute particularly and decisively to determine compensation schemes. Information is also important as it determines the efficiency of allocation and how far it is possible to link talent's application with its social and economic results (Baumol, 1990, 1993; Murphy et al., 1991; Acemoglu, 1995; Mohtadi and Roe, 2003; Gradstein, 2004; Corchón, 2008).

Social esteem may play a role. The question therefore becomes how much entrepreneurship is socially valued over other less socially productive occupations (see the seminal Baumol, 1990 and 1993). Finally, entrepreneurs or rent-seekers may influence, by voting or lobbying, political organization and political decisions. The idea is that the political equilibrium, responding to one or another group's interests, will make decisions favoring its maintenance (Acemoglu, 1995). Regarding this last argument, we point out that the innovative entrepreneur would be strongly inclined, when in a (temporary) monopoly position, to adopt rent-seeking behavior.

ENTREPRENEURSHIP AND RENT-SEEKING IN MOTION

The interaction between entrepreneurship and rent-seeking is an interesting question to examine. Formalized models show that multiple equilibria – an equilibrium being defined by an entrepreneur share in the population and a rate of growth – may exist (Murphy et al., 1993; Acemoglu, 1995; Mehlum et al., 2003a, 2003b). Readers interested in model developments may consult the above references. To give a brief overview, we note that results may be derived from the specification of two functions, both with negative slopes, and consequently the potential for multiple intersections. Because it places burdens on entrepreneurial rewards, rent-seeking negatively affects entrepreneurship. Moreover, given competition in the rent-seeking sector itself,[3] rent-seeking rewards will depend negatively on the number of rent-seekers. Baland and François (2000) formalize the effect of entrepreneurial activities on rent-seeking. Their model applies to an economy with import licenses. The production of direct substitutes by local entrepreneurs tends to limit the rents obtained by importers. Results suggest the existence of multiple equilibria. Additionally, these authors discuss the effect of an exogenous resource boom such as an increase in income resulting from an increase in the world price of exports. In their model, the result, more entrepreneurship or more rent-seeking, depends on the importance of the proportion of entrepreneurs and rent-seekers in the population preceding the shock.

Lane and Tornell (1996) initiate an important and often connected literature with the introduction of the 'voracity effect', which is 'a more than proportional increase in aggregate redistribution in response to an increase in the raw rate of return' (p. 226). Recent contributions, also related to the 'natural resource curse', include those by Torvik (2002), Mehlum et al. (2006), Perroni and Proto (2009), and Do and Levchenko (2009). For the sake of illustration, Tornell and Lane (1999) analyze the consequences of windfall gains in a two-sector economy. The first sector can be taxed, the second cannot. Moreover, the first sector uses more efficient technology than the second. Weak legal and political institutions as well as the existence of powerful lobbies characterize the economy. Each tries to support their own interests in an effort to increase their share of the national wealth through additional transfers. This leads to higher tax rates, where they can be applied, i.e. in the first sector. This provokes the reallocation of production factors toward the non-taxed and less productive sector. The result, the so-called voracity effect, is that a positive exogenous shock is followed by a more than proportional increase in transfers and a decline in growth.

Rent-seeking behavior may affect entrepreneurial activities and innovation. Several contributions can be found modeling the relationships. Recent contributions include Acemoglu and Robinson (2006a), and Chaudhry and Garner (2007). A simple, non-formalized but clear-cut discussion of the problem is proposed by Murphy et al. (1993, pp. 412–13). These authors suggest that rent-seeking, whether from private or public origins, can undoubtedly jeopardize the profits of established productive sectors. The innovation sector, however, might be described as the reserved hunting ground of public rent-seeking. In particular, their arguments rely on the nature of innovation. While the project develops, the innovative entrepreneur is confronted with legal and environmental constraints. Innovation may need production permits, licenses, dispensations, as well as amendment to local zoning regulations. This results in demand for government intervention and provides opportunities for corruption. Moreover, the socially unproductive transfers that corruption implies may inhibit some innovative activity, given that innovators may not have equal lobbying power compared to that of established firms, or the same financial resources to pay bribes. To avoid expropriation, important funds are then consumed instead of invested. The *ex post* existence of rent-seeking should increase project risk and effective cost. The authors mention, following these arguments, that the negative effects of rent-seeking could be limited if the rent-seeker became a stakeholder in the innovation project. In the long run, rent-seekers should be interested in such involvement. This idea can be generalized as: rent-seeking, by jeopardizing current entrepreneurial profits, limits its future transfer opportunities. See Mehlum et al. (2003b).

The interaction between entrepreneurship and rent-seeking can generate multiple equilibria that correspond to an allocation of talents and an economic growth rate. Starting from a dynamic extension of his basic model, Acemoglu (1995) discusses the history dependence of an economy.[4] Past and current allocation of talents influences the future structure of rewards. Given historical circumstances (particularly describing successive states of determining factors and allocation), the economy can be locked in low or high steady-state equilibrium. The extremes are high rent-seeking with low growth rate versus highly active and socially productive entrepreneurship with high growth rate.

Under these circumstances, for economies trapped in inferior equilibrium, it seems that only an exogenous shock will have any positive and sustainable effect.

That being the case, if rent-seeking affects innovation and economic growth, the actual net effects of rent-seeking are not always as clear as the above cited literature on rent-seeking suggests. One may expect the effects to be obviously negative. But rent-seeking should also be discussed in comparison with a reference situation that could be far from the benchmark of the perfectly competitive model. In some circumstances – for a reference situation that is not the first best but could be more comparable with the actual situation of a given jurisdiction, the net effects could be positive, as has been suggested by some authors (Samuels and Mercuro, 1984; Douhan and Henrekson, 2007). Distorted allocation may render rent-seeking necessary to attain greater efficiency. For example, accepting the rent-seeking behavior of some official (or even taking it as an opportunity) and bearing the cost of bribery may sometimes be the only way for an entrepreneur to make concrete efficiency-enhancing innovation. Both from a private and a social viewpoint, efficiency gains can be greater than rent-seeking costs – and achieving the new situation would be impossible without accepting rent-seeking.

ENTREPRENEURSHIP, RENT-SEEKING AND PUBLIC POLICY

The allocation of entrepreneurial supply between socially productive and unproductive, or rent-seeking, projects relies on an arbitrage. The result contributes to determining economic growth. In contrast to entrepreneurial supply, which is ultimately explained by the distribution of skills and abilities in the population and on which it is difficult to intervene, the allocation presents some opportunities for public actions (Baumol, 1990, 1993; Naudé, 2008). It could, for example, take the form of (additional) fiscal measures in favor of innovation rewards. Another way could consist in (heavier) penalties on socially unproductive activities. Dutz et al. (2000), referring more particularly to economies that are developing or in transition, and Minniti (2008) stress the primordial role that could be played by governments in creating (or reinforcing) institutions that foster entrepreneurship. An emphasis on better institutions and regulation can be included in a more general framework helping to define entrepreneurial policy guidelines (see Audretsch et al. 2007).

ACKNOWLEDGMENT

The author thanks Jean-Marie Baland, Pierre Perrin, Margaret Main, Michel Mignolet and Adam Lederer for comments on earlier versions.

NOTES

1. Observation of reality would not only lead to point market failures but state failures as well, as public choice theorists would note.
2. On this question, see Buchanan (1980).

3. Acemoglu (1995, p. 29) discusses the case where barriers to entry in rent-seeking activities are established by insiders.
4. Also see some more recent contributions: Acemoglu et al. (2005), Acemoglu and Robinson (2006b) and Douhan and Henrekson (2008b).

REFERENCES

Acemoglu, D. (1995), 'Reward structures and the allocation of talent', *European Economic Review*, **39**, 17–33.
Acemoglu, D. and J.A. Robinson (2006a), 'Economic backwardness in political perspective', *American Political Science Review*, **100** (1), 115–31.
Acemoglu, D. and J.A. Robinson (2006b), 'Persistence of power, elites and institutions', *American Economic Review*, **98** (1), 267–93.
Acemoglu, D., S. Johnson and J.A. Robinson (2005), 'Institutions as the fundamental cause of long-run growth', in P. Aghion and S. Durlauf (eds), *Handbook of Economic Growth*, Amsterdam: North-Holland, pp. 385–472.
Aghion, P. and P. Howitt (1992), 'A model of growth through creative destruction', *Econometrica*, **60** (2), 323–51.
Alvarez, S. A. (2007), 'Entrepreneurial rents and the theory of the firm', *Journal of Business Venturing*, **22** (3), 427–42.
Audretsch, D.B., I. Grilo and A.R. Thurik (2007), 'Explaining entrepreneurship and the role of policy: a framework', in D.B. Audretsch, I. Grilo and A.R. Thurik (eds), *Handbook of Research on Entrepreneurship Policy*, Cheltenham, UK and Northampton, MA, USA: Edward Elgar, pp. 1–17.
Baland, J.-M. and P. François (2000), 'Rent-seeking and resource booms', *Journal of Development Economics*, **61** (2), 527–42.
Baumol, W.J. (1990), 'Entrepreneurship: productive, unproductive, and destructive', *Journal of Political Economy*, **98** (5) part 1, 893–921.
Baumol, W.J. (1993), *Entrepreneurship, Management, and the Structure of Payoffs*, Cambridge, MA: MIT Press.
Buchanan, J.M. (1980), 'Rent seeking and profit seeking', in J.M. Buchanan, R.D. Tollison and G. Tullock (eds), *Toward a Theory of the Rent-seeking Society*, College Station, TX: Texas A&M University Press, pp. 3–15. [Reprinted in *The Economic Analysis of Rent Seeking*, ed. R.D. Congleton and R.D. Tollison, The International Library of Critical Writings in Economics, 49, Aldershot: Edward Elgar, 1995, pp. 46–58.]
Carree, M.A., A.R. Thurik (2003), 'The impact of entrepreneurship on economic growth', in D.B. Audretsch and Z.J. Acs (eds), *Handbook of Entrepreneurship Research*, Dordrecht: Kluwer Academic Publishers, pp. 437–71.
Chaudhry, A. and P. Garner (2007), 'Do governments suppress growth?: institutions, rent-seeking, and innovation blocking in a model of Schumpeterian growth', *Economics and Politics*, **19** (1), 35–52.
Corchón, L.C. (2008), 'Forms of governance and the size of rent-seeking', *Social Choice and Welfare*, **30** (2), 197–210.
Do, Q.-T. and A.A. Levchenko (2009), 'Trade, inequality, and the political economy of institutions', *Journal of Economic Theory*, **144**, 1489–520.
Douhan, R. and M. Henrekson (2007), 'The political economy of entrepreneurship', Working Paper Series 716, Research Institute of Industrial Economics.
Douhan, R. and M. Henrekson (2008a), 'The political economy of entrepreneurship: an introduction', in M. Henrekson and R. Douhan (eds), *The Political Economy of Entrepreneurship Vols I and II*. The International Library of Entrepreneurship 11. Cheltenham, UK and Northampton, MA, USA: Edward Elgar, xi–xxxi.
Douhan, R. and M. Henrekson (2008b), 'Productive and destructive entrepreneurship in a political economy framework', Working Paper Series 761, Research Institute of Industrial Economics.
Dutz, M.A., J.A. Ordover and R.D. Willig (2000), 'Entrepreneurship, access policy and economic development: lessons from industrial organization', *European Economic Review*, **44**, 739–47.
Gradstein, M. (2004), 'Governance and growth', *Journal of Development Economics*, **73** (2), 505–18.
Krueger, A. (1974), 'The political economy of the rent-seeking society', *American Economic Review*, **64** (3), 291–303.
Lane, P.R. and A. Tornell (1996), 'Power, growth, and the voracity effect', *Journal of Economic Growth*, **1**, 213–41.
Mehlum, H., K.O. Moene, and R. Torvik (2003a), 'Predator or prey? Parasitic enterprises in economic development', *European Economic Review*, **47** (2), 275–94.
Mehlum, H., K.O. Moene, and R. Torvik (2003b), 'Destructive creativity', *Nordic Journal of Political Economy*, **29**, 77–84.

Mehlum, H., K.O. Moene and R. Torvik (2006), 'Institutions and the resource curse', *Economic Journal*, **116**, 1–20. [Reprinted in *40 Years of Research on Rent Seeking*, eds R.D. Congleton, A.L. Hillman and K.A. Konrad, Volume 2, Berlin: Springer, pp. 245–64].
Minniti, M. (2008), 'The role of government policy on entrepreneurial activity: productive, unproductive, or destructive?', *Entrepreneurship Theory and Practice*, **32** (5), 779–90.
Mohtadi, H. and T. Roe (2003), 'Democracy, rent-seeking, public spending and growth', *Journal of Public Economics*, **87**, 3–4, 445–66.
Murphy, K.M., A. Shleifer and R.W. Vishny (1991), 'The allocation of talent: implications for growth', *The Quaterly Journal of Economics*, **CVI**, May, 503–30.
Murphy, K.M., A. Shleifer and R.W. Vishny (1993), 'Why is rent-seeking so costly to growth?', *American Economic Review*, Papers and Proceedings, May, pp. 409–14.
Naudé, W. (2008), 'Entrepreneurship in economic development', UNU-WIDER Research Paper No. 2008–20.
Perroni, C. and E. Proto (2009), 'Entrepreneurial drain under moral hazard: a high-yield sector curse?', *Journal of Development Economics*, forthcoming [available online first].
Samuels, W.J. and N. Mercuro (1984), 'A critique of rent-seeking theory', in D.C. Colander (ed.), *Neoclassical Political Economy*, Cambridge, MA: Ballinger, pp. 57–70.
Tollison, R.D. (1997), 'Rent seeking', in D.C. Mueller (ed.), *Perspectives on Public Choice*, Cambridge: Cambridge University Press, pp. 506–25.
Tornell, A. and P.R. Lane (1999), 'The voracity effect', *American Economic Review*, **89** (1), 22–46.
Torvik, R. (2002), 'Natural resources, rent seeking and welfare', *Journal of Development Economics*, **67** (2), 455–70.
Tullock, G. (1967), 'The welfare costs on tariffs, monopolies, and theft', *Western Economic Journal*, **5**, June, 224–32. [Reprinted in R.D. Congleton and R.D. Tollison (eds), *The Economic Analysis of Rent Seeking*, The International Library of Critical Writings in Economics, 49, Aldershot: Edward Elgar, 1995, pp. 3–11.]
Tullock, G. (2003), 'The origin rent-seeking concept', *International Journal of Business and Economics*, **2** (1), 1–8.

4 Who values the status of the entrepreneur?
Mirjam van Praag

INTRODUCTION

Recent research reveals the relevance of (inter)personal factors in occupational choice preference development. For instance, empirical studies by Falck et al. (2008) as well as Nanda and Sørensen (2008) address identity and peer group effects as determinants of the choice for entrepreneurship. Parker and Van Praag (2009) show, based on theory, that the group status of 'entrepreneurship' shapes people's occupational preferences and thus their choice behavior. Moreover, the status of entrepreneurship enters individuals' utility functions, leading to a spillover effect: while people base their occupational decisions on their own relative utility from entrepreneurship versus employment, their decisions may simultaneously affect the composition and status of the profession.

This chapter addresses empirically the following explorative questions: does perceived occupational status affect occupational choice or preferences and, in particular, the choice and preferences for entrepreneurship? What are the determinants of occupational status? Which (job) characteristics affect status? What individual characteristics determine an individual's view on the status of the entrepreneurial profession? Are the individual determinants of their perceived status of the entrepreneurial profession related to the determinants of the choice and preferences for entrepreneurship? These questions are addressed using the results of a survey of 800 university students in the Netherlands.

Answering these questions is instructive: if it is the case that individual choices are affected by perceived status, one can affect choices by changing status. In particular, the study of the occupational or personal determinants of status may reveal where to start changing status and preferences (also given the spillover effects as discussed by Parker and Van Praag, 2009 and the peer group effects discussed by Nanda and Sørensen, 2008) thus encouraging entrepreneurship.

The motivation for the student focus is based on recent studies that collectively demonstrate (1) that the preference for entrepreneurship is not high among more highly educated individuals (Van Der Sluis et al., 2008); whereas (2) the relative private returns to education are higher for entrepreneurs than for employees (Van Der Sluis and Van Praag, 2004, Van Der Sluis et al. 2007, Van Der Sluis and Van Praag, 2007), apparently also in the Netherlands (Parker and Van Praag, 2006); (3) the economic benefits from entrepreneurship are large (Van Praag and Versloot, 2007; Parker, 2004) but a large fraction is derived from a small number of entrepreneurs (Parker, 2009; Henrekson and Johansson, 2008); and finally (4) people who tend to generate high incomes as entrepreneurs are also – on average – the ones likely to grow their firms (Van Der Sluis et al., 2008). Hence, since these performance measures (income and growth) are correlated positively, one can safely assume that higher education levels not only lead to higher incomes but also to higher growth and the creation of economic benefits. Therefore, from a policy perspective, it is important to find instruments motivating this group to become entrepreneurs, and one such instrument might be status. This may be of particular relevance in European countries such as the Netherlands: evidence shows that the desire to become an entrepreneur is lower in Europe than in the USA, especially among people with higher levels of education (CBS, 2007, 2008). This motivates the choice for sampling Dutch students.

This chapter is organized as follows. The next section will introduce the theoretical notion of (group) status. In particular we shall develop this notion in relationship to professions and entrepreneurship. Needless to say, this introduction is partly based on studies outside the field of economics and business. The third section will discuss the data set, variables and empirical methodology. The fourth section discusses the results; the final section concludes.

PROFESSIONAL STATUS: THE DEVELOPMENT OF A CONCEPT

A Little History of the Concept 'Status' and its Determinants

Max Weber (1864–1920) introduced the term 'status' as part of his three-component theory of stratification (social class, social status and religion). He defined status as 'an effective claim for social esteem'. He defined occupations as status groups, i.e. a group of persons who successfully claimed a specific social esteem within a larger group.

Max Weber also had explicit ideas about the determinants of professional status ranking – the determinants of status. He argued that occupational status depends, above all, on the amount of training required and the opportunities for earnings (Weber, 1978 [1922], p. 144). Individual factors, however, would play no role: the status of occupations is uniform and set (Balkwell et al., 1982). Weiss and Fershtman (1998) show that, consistent with early Weber, people ranking occupations according to status do so irrespective of their own individual attributes, such as education, age, income or their country of residence. Furthermore, status rankings of occupations correlate strongly across countries and persist over time (Treiman, 1977). Any variance in the subjective evaluations of occupational status of different occupations is best explained by observable characteristics of the occupations themselves, specifically by the mean income and education in each occupation (Fershtman and Weiss, 1993, p. 948).

Brown (1955) identifies eleven possible occupation-related determinants of occupational status, based on North and Hatt (1947): (i) necessity to the public welfare, (ii) respect, (iii) cleanness of the job, (iv) education or training needed, (v) talent or skills needed, (vi) income, (vii) leisure time/vacations, (viii) personal references ('Do you know people who perform the occupation, and is that a positive association?'), (ix) rich history, (x) hard work needed and (xi) the social or altruistic level of the job. Villemez (1974) adds 'power' as the twelfth occupation-related determinant.

However, other studies show that, in addition to job characteristics, individual characteristics determine the perceived status of occupations (Hendrickx and Ganzeboom, 1998; Katz, 1992). How the relative status of entrepreneurship is affected by professional and individual characteristics is a matter for empirical study – as yet unperformed.

Status of Professions in Economics

Only recently have economists become interested in concepts such as social status. It was recognized that economic theory fails to explain a number of socioeconomic phenomena by ignoring possible interdependencies of preferences across people (Bisin and Verdier, 1998). The social status of a profession is possibly affected by other people's preferences or behavior (Parker and Van Praag, 2009). In turn, status itself may affect people's preferences.

Frank (1984, 1988) was one of the first economists to recognize the importance of status. Frank (1984) claimed that a person's status among his peers is no less important than his absolute income level in determining his sense of well-being.

Since the early 1990s, status is incorporated in models as a determinant of individual utility (and thus of behavior; see, for instance, Fershtman and Weiss, 1993; Weiss and Fershtman, 1998; Ederer and Patacconi, 2007; Clark et al, 2007; Kwon and Milgrom, 2007; Grund and Sliwka, 2007, and Parker and Van Praag, 2009).

How to Measure the Status of a Profession

Traditionally there are two ways of measuring status. The first is based on the occupational prestige study by North and Hatt (1947). Their study, performed at the National Opinion Research Center and known as the NORC study, analyzed public attitudes regarding the prestige of 90 selected occupations. The 1989 NORC general social survey includes an evaluation of the status of occupations (Hodge et al., 1964). Respondents rank occupations according to their social standing. We call this subjective status measurement.

This original NORC study was extended by Duncan (1961), who developed an objective rather than a subjective measure of occupational status, the so-called socioeconomic index (SEI). This was accomplished by linking the prestige scores from the NORC study to the income and education information in the census, thus producing a formula to calculate and predict prestige based solely on education and income for all occupations (Nakao and Treas, 1994; Hodge, 1981), leading to the 1989 Total Based SEI.

Consistent with Weber (and Weiss and Fershtman, 1998), the status of a profession is operationalized, in most economics studies, by the mean income for the profession (Ederer and Patacconi, 2007; Kwon and Milgrom, 2007; Parker and Van Praag, 2009).

Status and Entrepreneurship

Status and entrepreneurship have been little studied so far. Besides the theoretical study by Parker and Van Praag (2009), we know of only one empirical study addressing some of the central questions of this chapter. Malach-Pines et al. (2005) show that the perception of high-tech entrepreneurs as cultural heroes, thus endowed with high social status, among MBA students in a particular country is correlated with the level of entrepreneurial activity in that country as well as with the average risk-taking propensity and willingness to engage in entrepreneurial activity of the sampled MBA students in a country. The sample includes three countries: Hungary, Israel and the USA.

Positioning of this Study

In this study the status of the profession 'entrepreneurship' is empirically evaluated as well as its determinants and the association between an individual's status rank and her willingness and plans to become an entrepreneur. In terms of the determinants of status, both characteristics of the profession and of the individual may determine a person's rank as entrepreneur among other professions. The possible profession-related determinants presented to the respondents are based on Brown (1955) (except iii, viii and xi) and Villemez (1974). The possible individual determinants of status rank analyzed are sourced from the entrepreneurship literature. In terms of the measurement of status, we conform to the method of the original (1989) NORC study. Thus respondents simply state their perceived status of the entrepreneur and of 19 other occupations. Hence we shall test empirically which are determinants of the perceived status of the occupation 'entrepreneur' relative to 19 other professions that are in the choice set of students.

The current study differs from that of Malach-Pines et al. (2005) in several ways: the analysis is not limited to high-tech entrepreneurs;[1] the unit of analysis is the individual student, not the country, as in Malach-Pines et al.; and, unlike Malach-Pines et al., the determinants of entrepreneurial status are analyzed, which might be a relevant instrument for conceiving policy measures to stimulate entrepreneurship if evidence is found that status and entrepreneurial activity are indeed positively related. In the next section, we discuss the data and the methodology used.

DATA AND METHODOLOGY

Sample

Our quantitative analysis is based on a sample of university students, normally between 18 and 23 years old, in the Netherlands taken in 2007. Questionnaires were distributed to students in university libraries, at exams, by email and through websites. We recollected 818 complete questionnaires. Below, we discuss the variables collected through this questionnaire, along with their basic descriptive statistics.

Questionnaire and its Core Questions

A questionnaire was developed including survey questions of a subjective nature.[2] In the key question, number 19, respondents are asked to establish the ranking of the occupation 'entrepreneur' within a selection of 20 occupations, randomly listed (see Table 4.1).[3]

Each respondent graded each occupation on a scale from 1 to 10. Based on this, a ranking was made per individual respondent. The average grade of the entrepreneur is 7.0, whereas the average rank is 8. Twelve percent of the individuals graded the entrepreneur highest, whereas 22 percent put the entrepreneur in the top 3 of the ranking.

The two occupational rankings previously discussed, NORC (1989) and the Total Based SEI (1989), are used as benchmarks. Please note that these measures are from different decades, continents and sub-populations. As shown in Table 4.2, the entrepreneur ranks higher in our study than in the others, although, in general, the patterns in of the

Table 4.1   Questionnaire, question no. 19

19. Please rate the following occupations according to their 'status', in other words which occupations in your opinion have a very low status (1) or a very high status (10)?

Occupation	1	2	3	4	5	6	7	8	9	10
University professor										
Policeman										
Physician										
Mailman										
Actuary										
Management consultant										
Lawyer										
Marketing manager										
Architect										
Teacher (high-school)										
Journalist										
Electrician										
Computer programmer										
Entrepreneur										
Engineer										
Barber										
Real-estate agent										
Accountant										
Mayor										
High-court judge										

rankings are similar. Nevertheless, we conclude from Table 4.2 that the ranking of occupational status is not universal and will probably diverge across countries and/or over time and may therefore depend on individual characteristics as well (see the discussion in the second section).

Question 20 establishes the occupation-related determinants of occupational status:[4]

20. *What is occupational status dependent on, according to you? (multiple answers possible)*

Income	*Required education/training*	*Public importance*
Respect	*Talent*	*Amount of spare time*
Rich history of occupation	*Power*	*Hard work*

. . . .

Dependent Variables

Three variables are considered endogenous and used as dependent variables in the regressions. The first is the perceived status of the entrepreneur, measured in three ways, all relative to the status of other occupations. The first measure of status positions the status rank in the average of the percentile in the sample distribution of the rank and is estimated by means of OLS (ordinary least squares). The second measure of status is a dummy variable that takes on the value one if an individual ranks entrepreneur first

Table 4.2 Occupational status and reference rankings

Rank	Occupation	Status	Std	NORC (1989)	Total 1989 SEI
1	High-court judge	8.7	1.36	Physician	Physician
2	Physician	8.5	1.25	Lawyer	University professor
3	University professor	8.3	1.47	University professor	Lawyer
4	Lawyer	7.9	1.34	Architect	Actuary
5	Mayor	7.7	1.68	Engineer	Engineer
6	Engineer	7.6	1.51	High-court judge	High-court judge
7	Architect	7.4	1.39	Mayor	Architect
8	**Entrepreneur**	**7.0**	**1.55**	High-school teacher	Management consultant
9	Accountant	6.9	1.55	Accountant	High-school teacher
10	Marketing manager	6.7	1.53	Management consultant	Accountant
11	Management consultant	6.7	1.51	Computer programmer	Computer programmer
12	Actuary	6.1	1.64	Journalist	Journalist
13	Journalist	6.1	1.57	Policeman	Marketing manager
14	Real-estate agent	5.9	1.67	Marketing manager	**Entrepreneur**
15	High-school teacher	5.6	1.60	**Entrepreneur**	Real-estate agent
16	Computer programmer	5.5	1.63	Electrician	Policeman
17	Policeman	5.3	1.84	Real-estate agent	Mayor
18	Electrician	4.4	1.70	Mailman	Mailman
19	Barber	3.8	1.66	Actuary	Electrician
20	Mailman	3.7	1.69	Barber	Barber

and zero otherwise. The third measure is a dummy variable taking on the value one for individuals who rank the entrepreneur in the status top 3 and zero otherwise. The latter two measures are estimated in a probit regression. The descriptive statistics for the status measure are shown in Table 4.2.[5]

The second dependent variable measures the willingness of individuals to become an entrepreneur. It is a dummy variable, taking on the value of one if the respondent answers 'entrepreneur' to the question 'If you could choose, would you rather be an entrepreneur or an employee?' and zero if they answer 'employee'. The majority of the respondents, 61 percent, turn out to be willing to become an entrepreneur. The variable's determinants are estimated using a probit equation.

The third dependent variable measures the perceived likelihood of becoming an entrepreneur. It is the answer, on a 10-point scale, to the question: 'What is the likelihood that you will become an entrepreneur within the next ten years?' The distribution of this likelihood variable, estimated by means of OLS, is shown in Table 4.3.

Explanatory Variables

We are particularly interested in the similarity and differences of the determinants of the perceived status of entrepreneurship and the common factors found in the literature that determine (i) the likelihood of entrepreneurship and (ii) the performance of entrepreneurs. Hence the questionnaire includes the most important potential determinants of

Table 4.3   Sample frequencies of the subjective likelihood of becoming an entrepreneur

Stated likelihood of becoming an entrepreneur (scale 1–10), %			
1	12.7	6	11.5
2	11.9	7	12.1
3	14.5	8	9.2
4	10.1	9	3.7
5	9.7	10	4.6

likelihood and performance as derived from the entrepreneurship literature. We further assess to what extent one's willingness and likelihood to become an entrepreneur are associated with these factors as well as with the perceived status of entrepreneurship. Thus entrepreneurial status is used both as a dependent and as an independent variable. Factors are categorized into human capital, social capital and peer group effects, attitudes and background variables. Information on financial capital is lacking.

Human capital
Human capital is measured along various dimensions; see Table 4.4 for sample averages. The first is education. We measure whether students are enrolled in a vocational or academic program. First-year students are distinguished from Bachelor and Master students respectively. An individual's education level is found to be positively associated with entrepreneurship performance, whereas the empirical results on the relationship with the likelihood of becoming an entrepreneur are found to be ambiguous (Van der Sluis et al., 2008). Five education fields are distinguished: economics and business; social sciences; health; science and technical studies; and humanities (including law). Previous studies find that science and technical orientations lead to better performance as an entrepreneur (Van Praag and Cramer, 2001; Hartog et al., 2008).

The second measure of human capital included as a potential explanatory factor is experience. In general, empirical evidence indicates that the success of entrepreneurship is positively related to (the variety of) previous general labor market and, in particular, to entrepreneurship experience (e.g. Davidsson and Honig, 2003; Lazear, 2005; Van Der Sluis et al., 2008). Respondents have indicated whether they are or have been an entrepreneur and how many different previous jobs they have held.

Social capital and the peer group
Social capital is expected to have a positive relationship with entrepreneurship choices and outcomes: it can provide networks that facilitate the discovery of opportunities, as well as the identification and collection of resources (Birley, 1985; Greene and Brown, 1997; Uzzi, 1999; Davidsson and Honig, 2003). We concentrate on the effect of an entrepreneurial environment (see also Gianetti and Simonov, 2004; Nanda and Sørensen, 2008), which is indicated by a dummy variable and a count variable based on the following two questions respectively; see Table 4.4 for statistics:

32.   *Do you know somebody in your surroundings that started as an entrepreneur in the last two years?*

Table 4.4   Sample averages (%) of the human and social capital variables

Education variables	
Education level	
• Professional or vocational Bachelor	83
• University (Bachelor or Master phase)	17
Education stage	
• First year	27
• Bachelor	50
• Master	23
Education field	
• Economics and business	62
• Social sciences	15
• Health	8
• Science and technical studies	7
• Humanities (including law)	8
Experience variables	
Dummy for entrepreneurship experience (1 = 'yes'; 0 = 'no')	6
Number of different jobs ever held:	
• 0–1	9
• 2	17
• 3	23
• 4	17
• 5	12
• 6–7	14
• 8 or more	8
Social capital and peer group variables	
Respondent knows someone who started up a business in the past two years	71
The number of entrepreneurs in one's environment	
• None	4
• Very few	17
• Few	26
• Average	35
• Many	16
• Very many	2

33. How many entrepreneurs are there in your environment *(friends/acquaintances/ family)?*

   None   Very few   Few   Normal   Many   Very many

Attitudes

Various studies show that attitudes, such as risk attitude, locus of control, need for achievement, self-efficacy and self-esteem are intimately related to entrepreneurship choices and outcomes.

   Risk aversion is usually negatively related to the choice for entrepreneurship. We measure risk attitude based on survey questions in two ways: the reservation price for a ticket in a hypothetical lottery (see Cramer et al., 2002)[6] and a measure based on

Table 4.5   Sample averages (%) of background characteristics

Background characteristics	
Percentage female (dummy)	46
Age (in years)	
• 19 or younger	32
• 20–21	28
• 22–23	19
• 24–26	21
Nationalities	
• Respondent not Dutch	7
• Mother not Dutch	15
• Father not Dutch	12
Parental education levels	
• Mother has a (vocational) Bachelor or Master degree	44
• Father has a (vocational) Bachelor or Master degree	57
Parental entrepreneurship experience	
• Mother	16
• Father	37

Dohmen et al. (2005) which is the answer to: 'Are you generally a person who is fully pre-pared to take risks or do you try to avoid taking risks?'[7] Internal locus of control beliefs have been shown to relate positively to the choice for and performance in entrepreneur-ship. The first measure used here is similar to that in Grilo and Thurik (2005), whereas the second is a simplified Rotter (1966) test derived from Pettijohn (1999). The measure we use for need for achievement is based on the validated Ray–Lynn AO scale (Ray, 1979). Self-efficacy and self-esteem measures are based on the self-assessed expectancy of finding a job after graduation (see Oosterbeek and Van den Broek, 2008). Based on Boyd and Vozikis (1994), it is expected that self-efficacy and esteem are positively related to the development of entrepreneurial intentions and behavior.

Background

Control variables, gender, age, nationality (of the respondent and her parents, see Fairlie, 2005), parental education levels and entrepreneurial experience are used in this study. Descriptive statistics are provided in Table 4.5.

We are interested not only in what determines entrepreneurial status, willingness and the perceived likelihood of becoming an entrepreneur, but also in the interrelations between the endogenous variables, i.e. whether the perceived entrepreneurial status is related to one's willingness to become an entrepreneur and the likelihood of becoming an entrepreneur. Based on Malach-Pines et al. (2005), the relationships between perceived status, willingness and likelihood of becoming an entrepreneur are expected to be posi-tive. Table 4.6 shows the correlations of the endogenous variables acknowledged in this study. They are significantly positive. The regression analysis in the next section will show whether and to what extent these correlations hold, conditional upon the inclusion of the independent and control variables.

Table 4.6   Correlations between the endogenous variables

		I	II	III
I	Status ranking of the entrepreneur among other professions	1.00	0.206	0.235
II	Willingness to become an entrepreneur [dummy]		1.00	0.567
III	Perceived likelihood of becoming an entrepreneur [1–10]			1.00

Table 4.7   Occupation-related determinants of the status of occupations*

Determinant	% agreeing that this determines occupational status
Education required	76
Respect	63
Income level	49
Public importance	47
Talent	42
Power	32
Hard work	32
Rich history	15
Leisure time	1
Other	3

Note: * These are the answers to the question:

20.   *What is occupational status dependent on, according to you? (multiple answers possible)*
      Income   Required education/training   Public importance   Respect   Talent   Leisure time
      Rich history of occupation   Power   Hard work   Other . . .

RESULTS

Which Job Characteristics Determine the Status of Occupations?

It turns out that the job characteristic which, according to this sample, is the strongest determinant of the status of professions is the education level required; see Table 4.7. Seventy-six percent of the respondents rate this as the most relevant status criterion. This supports the views of Max Weber, as well as the more recent theoretical study by Parker and Van Praag (2009). The same holds for the income level that has been mentioned as a determinant of occupational status by almost half of the respondents. Respect and public importance are also important determinants of occupations, as suggested by the literature.

Which Perceived Occupational Status Determinants are Important for the Status of Entrepreneurship?

As discussed, the status attached to the profession of the entrepreneur is measured in three ways, corresponding to the columns in Table 4.8. The individual answers (in

Table 4.8   Perceived entrepreneur status and occupation-related determinants of status

Dependent variable: entrepreneur status	(i)	(ii)	(iii)
	Rank (1–20)	Ranked first	Ranked top 3
Regression	OLS[†]	Probit	Probit
Occupational determinants of professional ranking			
Education required	−0.030	−0.078***	−0.107***
	(0.019)	(0.031)	(0.037)
Respect	0.005	0.024	−0.009
	(0.016)	(0.023)	(0.030)
Income level	0.025	0.051**	0.049
	(0.016)	(0.023)	(0.031)
Public importance	0.011	−0.023	0.033
	(0.015)	(0.023)	(0.029)
Talent	0.006	−0.023	−0.020
	(0.015)	(0.025)	(0.029)
Power	−0.034**	−0.0035	−0.062**
	(0.017)	(0.023)	(0.029)
Hard work	0.039**	0.039	0.042
	(0.016)	(0.026)	(0.032)
Rich history	−0.0004	0.042	0.028
	(0.022)	(0.037)	(0.044)
Leisure time	−0.021	0.222*	0.133
	(0.105)	(0.161)	(0.160)
Number of observations	818	818	818
(Pseudo) R^2	0.017	0.035	0.020

Notes:
Probit regressions report marginal effects. The results are based on robust standard errors shown in parentheses. */**/*** indicates that the estimated coefficient is significant at the 10%/5%/1% confidence level.
[†] Equivalent results are obtained when estimated by ordered probit.

dummy form) to question 20 (see Table 4.7) are included as independent variables in these regressions. Table 4.8 shows that the more individuals perceive status to be determined by income levels or hard work, the higher they value the status of the entrepreneur. In addition, the more value one attaches to education or power for the determination of status, the lower the entrepreneur's status is valued. It thus seems that entrepreneurship is associated with hard work, high incomes, but little power and education.

Does the Perceived Status of the Entrepreneur Profession Differ Systematically across Individuals? If so, which Individual Characteristics Determine an Individual's View on the Status of the Entrepreneurial Profession?

In Table 4.9, the status of the entrepreneurial profession – according to the same three measures as in Table 4.8 – is estimated again. The independent variables included in the regressions are individual characteristics this time, rather than profession-related

Table 4.9   Perceived entrepreneur status determined by individual-specific characteristics

Dependent variable: entrepreneur status	(i)	(ii)	(iii)
	Rank (1–20)	Ranked first	Ranked top 3
Regression	OLS[†]	Probit	Probit
Human capital			
Education level			
Education stage (benchmark is first year)			
● Bachelor	−0.012	0.016	−0.058*
	(0.018)	(0.026)	(0.034)
● Master	−0.039	−0.035	−0.093**
	(0.025)	(0.033)	(0.040)
Education field (benchmark is econ. and bus.)			
● Social sciences	0.065***	−0.090***	−0.151***
	(0.020)	(0.021)	(0.028)
● Health	−0.085***	−0.080**	−0.145***
	(0.025)	(0.026)	(0.036)
Dummy for entrepreneurship experience	0.060**	0.022	0.044
	(0.026)	(0.043)	(0.056)
Number of different jobs ever held			
Social capital and peer group variables			
Respondent knows someone who started up a business in the past two years			
The number of entrepreneurs in one's environment	0.028***	0.032***	0.062***
	(0.006)	(0.010)	(0.013)
Attitudes			
Risk aversion[a]			
Internality of locus of control[b]	0.034**	0.035	0.091***
	(0.015)	(0.019)	(0.029)
Need for achievement			
Self-efficacy			
Self-esteem			
Background characteristics			
Female (dummy)	−0.037**	−0.020	−0.076***
	(0.016)	(0.022)	(0.029)
Age (in years)	0.006**	0.004	0.010**
	(0.003)	(0.004)	(0.005)
Nationality			
Parents' nationality			
Parental education levels			
Parental entrepreneurship experience			
Number of observations	818	818	818
(Pseudo) R^2	0.096	0.074	0.116

Table 4.9   (continued)

Notes:
a   Two measures of risk aversion are found to be insignificantly related to the perceived status of the
    entrepreneur: the first based on a lottery (Cramer et al., 2001) and the second based on Dohmen et al.
    (2005).
b   As measured by Grilo and Thurik (2005). The other locus of control measure (measure 2) is insignificantly
    related to the perceived status of the entrepreneur.
    Probit regressions report marginal effects. The results are based on robust standard errors shown in
    parentheses. */**/*** indicates that the estimated coefficient is significant at the 10%/5%/1% confidence
    level.
†   Ordinary least squares.

characteristics. Table 4.9 shows the results when the human capital, social capital, attitude and background characteristics as discussed in the previous section are included as potential determinants. The coefficients that were insignificantly different from zero in all of the three equations have been omitted. The reported results have been obtained while omitting these regressors from the equations.

There are, indeed, individual factors associated with the status of the entrepreneurship profession. We find weak support (significant at the 10 percent level only) for a decline in the perceived occupational status of the entrepreneur when individuals proceed further in their educational trajectories (from first year, to Bachelor to Master). Moreover, there is strong evidence for differences among students across fields. Whereas students in economics and business attach similar status to the entrepreneur as students in the fields of science, technical studies and humanities, students in health and social sciences attach lower value to the status of the entrepreneur. Students who have been entrepreneurs themselves attach a higher value to the status of the entrepreneur (although this effect is only significant in one of the four equations). Previous job variety is no determinant of the perceived status of the entrepreneur.

Variation across individuals in terms of their social capital and peer group is associated with systematic variation across these individuals in terms of the perceived occupational status of the entrepreneur. In particular and very significantly and consistently so, the more entrepreneurs the student has in her direct personal environment, the higher she perceives the status of the entrepreneur. However, causality is unattributable to this strong relationship.

Attitudes that the literature shows determining entrepreneurial spirit or performance are unrelated to the perceived status of the entrepreneurial profession. The only exception is one's locus of control beliefs (as measured in Grilo and Thurik, 2005). The more internal someone's locus of control beliefs, the higher is the perceived status of the entrepreneur.

Finally, individual background characteristics associated with the entrepreneur's perceived status ranking are gender and age. Male students hold entrepreneurs in higher esteem than female students, while older students are more positive about entrepreneurship status than younger students.

We conclude that the human and social capital determinants of the status of the entrepreneur are mainly (positively) related to knowledge of and familiarity with entrepreneurship. Entrepreneurship experience and presence of entrepreneurs in one's environment increase the perceived status (rank) of the entrepreneur. Moreover, students in fields where the probability of becoming an entrepreneur is higher (economics and business; science and technical studies) perceive the status of the entrepreneur as higher.

Is the Perceived Entrepreneur Status Associated with the Willingness and Subjective Likelihood of becoming an Entrepreneur?

Table 4.6 shows that the status ranking of the entrepreneur is positively correlated with the individual's willingness and likelihood of becoming an entrepreneur. The next question is: are the determinants of the perceived status of the entrepreneur also associated with an individual's willingness and subjectively assessed likelihood of becoming an entrepreneur within ten years' time? This question is addressed by including these individual determinants into regressions explaining an individual's measured willingness and likelihood of becoming an entrepreneur by means of a probit and OLS regression respectively. Table 4.10 shows the results.

There are several individual determinants of status determining an individual's stated likelihood of becoming and willingness to become an entrepreneur. Three observations stand out. First, the determinants of the status rank attached to entrepreneurship coincide to a large extent with determinants of the perceived likelihood of becoming an entrepreneur and to a somewhat lesser extent with the determinants of willingness. Second, these determinants explain almost 30 percent of the variance in the stated likelihood of becoming an entrepreneur (see the R^2, first column), which is quite high in such a cross-section. Third, the status ranking of the entrepreneur is significantly and strongly associated with likelihood and willingness, also when controlling for all these other relevant factors. This means that the unexplained variance across individuals in the status rank of the entrepreneurial profession, shown in Table 4.9, is significantly related to an individual's willingness and stated likelihood.

CONCLUSION

'Traditional economics has been based on methodological individualism' (Akerlof, 1997, p. 1005). Since the early 2000s, economists have been demonstrating and acknowledging that individuals' utility depends on the utility or the action of other individuals: social interaction plays a determining role (Akerlof, 1997; Akerlof and Kranton, 2000). The group status of a profession is just one example. Status has only recently begun to play a part in economic models as a determinant of utility (see, e.g., Fershtman and Weiss, 1993; Weiss and Fershtman, 1998; Ederer and Patacconi, 2007). Empirical evidence shows that this avenue of search for the determinants of utility is fruitful (Clark et al., 2007; Kwon and Milgrom, 2007).

Parker and Van Praag (2009) develop a model along these lines where the occupational status of entrepreneurs plays a role in the occupational choice of individuals between wage employment and entrepreneurship. Since each individual's choice for entrepreneurship affects the social status of the group, an individual's choice for entrepreneurship has externalities and affects other people's choices.

The current study focuses on the determinants and consequences of the group status of a profession, entrepreneurship in particular. If the group status of entrepreneurship is

Table 4.10   Are individual factors – determinants of status – associated with an individual's willingness to become and likelihood of becoming an entrepreneur?

Dependent variable	Likelihood (1–10)	Likelihood (1–10)	Willingness	Willingness
Regression	OLS	OLS†	Probit	Probit
Status included as a regressor	No	Yes	No	Yes
Status ranking of the	No	1.127***	No	0.301***
entrepreneur		(0.386)		(0.086)
Human capital				
● Bachelor	−0.315	−0.301	−0.053	−0.052
	(0.196)	(0.195)	(0.046)	(0.046)
● Master	−0.856***	−0.811***	−0.093	−0.082
	(0.259)	(0.257)	(0.062)	(0.062)
Education field (benchmark is econ. and bus.)				
● Social sciences	−0.727***	−0.654***	−0.082	−0.064
	(0.234)	(0.238)	(0.053)	(0.053)
● Health	−0.572	−0.476	−0.069	−0.043
	(0.366)	(0.368)	(0.069)	(0.070)
Dummy for entrepreneurship	2.797***	2.729***	0.291***	0.284***
experience	(0.336)	(0.340)	(0.053)	(0.055)
Social capital and peer group variables				
The number of entrepreneurs in	0.695***	0.663***	0.117***	0.110***
one's environment	(0.074)	(0.075)	(0.016)	(0.016)
Attitudes				
Internality of locus of control	0.428***	0.390**	0.010	0.001
beliefs (Grilo and Thurik,	(0.161)	(0.160)	(0.037)	(0.037)
2005)[a]				
Background characteristics				
Female (dummy)	−0.783***	−0.741***	−0.169***	−0.161***
	(0.173)	(0.172)	(0.037)	(0.037)
Age (in years)	0.022	0.015	−0.005	−0.007
	(0.029)	(029)	(0.007)	(0.007)
Number of observations	818	818	817	817
(Pseudo) R^2	0.291	0.295	0.115	0.126

Notes:
[a]   The other locus of control measure (measure 2, based more directly on the measure proposed by Rotter) is found to be insignificantly related to the perceived status of the entrepreneur.
    Probit regressions report marginal effects. The results are based on robust standard errors shown in parentheses. */**/*** indicates that the estimated coefficient is significant at the 10%/5%/1% confidence level.
†   Ordinary least squares.

related to individual choice behavior, it is policy relevant to better understand this relationship and the determinants of the status of the entrepreneur. For reasons discussed earlier, this study focuses on students in the Netherlands. Our measurement of status and its possible determinants are based on the existing theoretical and empirical literature, both within and outside the field of entrepreneurship and economics. The most important findings can be summarized and interpreted as follows.

First, the status of occupations as perceived by Dutch students is mostly determined by the required level of education, the income level to be expected, and respect. This is consistent with Max Weber (1978 [1922]) as well as with Fershtman and Weiss (1993, p. 948), who pinpoint education and income as the strongest determinants of occupational status. Given the assumed causality implied in this relationship, we can conclude that attracting people with higher levels of education to a profession will improve the status attached to that profession.

Second, the more individuals perceive status to be determined by income levels or hard work, the more they value the status of the entrepreneur. On the contrary, the more value one attaches to education or power for the determination of the status of an occupation, the lower the entrepreneur's status is valued. It thus seems that entrepreneurship is associated with hard work, high incomes, but not with power and education. Since education is one of the main drivers of the perceived status of occupations, it seems useful, if raising the status of entrepreneurs is deemed desirable, to communicate that entrepreneurial success is indeed associated with education. Thus people would realize that successful entrepreneurs have higher levels of education and this would, in turn, according to these results, lead to a higher perceived status of the entrepreneurial profession.

Third, our results indicate, in relation to the discussion in the literature as to whether individual characteristics – such as human capital, social capital, attitudes and background variables – vary systematically with the perceived status of occupations by individuals, that there is indeed such systematic variation. We find weak support for a decline in the perceived occupational status of the entrepreneur when individuals proceed further in their educational trajectories. The strongest human and social capital factors associated with the status of the entrepreneur are (positively) related to the knowledge and familiarity one has with entrepreneurship. Entrepreneurship experience and the presence of entrepreneurs in one's environment increase the perceived status (rank) of the entrepreneur. Moreover, students in fields where the probability of becoming an entrepreneur is higher (economics and business; science and technical studies) perceive the status of the entrepreneur more highly than students in other fields (such as social sciences and health).

Fourth, we find support for a strong association between the perceived status of the entrepreneur by any individual student and her estimated likelihood of becoming and willingness to become an entrepreneur. Both the variation in the systematic determinants of the status of the entrepreneur and the unexplained residual vary systematically with willingness and likelihood.

Given the relatively high private (Van Der Sluis et al., 2004, 2007; Parker and Van Praag, 2006) and presumably social returns to education (Versloot and Van Praag, 2007; Parker, 2004, 2009; Henrekson and Johansson, 2008; Van Der Sluis et al., 2008) for entrepreneurs relative to employees, it is important, from a policy perspective, to find instruments that motivate students to become entrepreneurs, and one such instrument might be status. As the results suggest, although the causality of any of the relationships established is unclear, offering students more entrepreneurial environments, either within or outside their schools, will go together with a higher esteem of the entrepreneurial profession. This, in turn, may then lead to increased willingness to become and a higher likelihood of becoming an entrepreneur for the average student. This, then, would have a positive external effect (as in Parker and Van Praag, 2009): the more highly educated individuals opt for a certain profession, the higher will be its status (also caused indirectly by a higher average income level resulting from the returns to education) and the more desirable it becomes for other (highly educated) individuals. Thus a virtuous circle results. The clear implication of this study is to pay more (positive) attention to entrepreneurship in universities and colleges.[8]

This policy implication is obtained under some untested assumptions, and these form the main limitations of this study (besides the already discussed subjective nature of some of the key survey information). The first untested assumption is that education causes status (and higher income levels and thus even higher status) and not the other way around, albeit consistent with theory. Second, and more far-fetched, we implicitly assume that more entrepreneurs in one's environment (and more own experience as such) cause a higher status attached to the entrepreneur instead of the other way around. Third, and this so far also remains questionable, we assume that the perceived status of a profession causes the willingness to choose, and likelihood of choosing, this profession, instead of the other way around. If it were the other way around, the manipulation of the status of the entrepreneur would have few behavorial consequences (although its underlying determinants that co-determine willingness and likelihood would still be worthwhile to affect). Gaining more insight into the causalities of these relationships should probably be the subject of future studies in this seemingly fruitful area of entrepreneurship and status.

ACKNOWLEDGMENTS

The author is grateful to Thomas Hemels and Taco Slagter for their excellent research assistance, and to Oliver Falck for his valuable comments on an earlier version of this chapter.

NOTES

1. Also, the wording 'high-tech' in the specification by Malach-Pines et al. (2005) might induce individuals to rate the entrepreneur as having higher social status.
2. Bertrand and Mullainathan (2001) discuss some of the problems attached to using subjective survey data. We have set up the questionnaire with extreme caution in order to minimize the problems they address.
3. Other occupations are randomly selected, varying from barber to university professor in accordance with the original NORC questionnaires
4. The descriptive results are presented in Table 4.7.
5. The correlations between the various measures of status range from 0.56 to 0.72. They will therefore not be inserted simultaneously as explanatory variables into regression equations.
6. A drawback of this measure is that it reflects the attitude towards upside risk only.
7. Dohmen et al. (2005) claim that this is the best predictor of risk-taking behavior in different contexts.

8.   Especially in the Master phase, the willingness to become, and likelihood of becoming an entrepreneur as well as the perceived status attached to this profession seem to go stale.

REFERENCES

Akerlof, G.A. (1997), 'Social distance and social decisions', *Econometrica*, **65** (5), 1005–27.
Akerlof, G.A. and R.E. Kranton (2000), 'Economics and identity', *The Quarterly Journal of Economics*, **115** (3), 715–53.
Balkwell, J.W., F.L. Bates and A.P. Garbin (1982), 'Does the degree of consensus on occupational status evaluations differ by socioeconomic stratum? Response by Guppy', *Social Forces*, **60** (4), 1183–9.
Bertrand, M. and S. Mullainathan (2001), 'Do people mean what they say? Implications for subjective survey data', *The American Economic Review*, **91** (2), 67–72.
Birley, S.J. (1985), 'The role of networks in the entrepreneurial process', *Journal of Business Venturing*, **1** (1), 107–17.
Bisin, A. and T. Verdier (1998), 'On the cultural transmission of preferences for social status', *Journal of Public Economics*, **70** (1), 75–97.
Boyd, N.G. and G.S. Vozikis (1994), 'The influence of self-efficacy on the development of entrepreneurial intentions and actions', *Entrepreneurship Theory and Practice*, **18** (4), 63–77.
Brown, M.C. (1955), 'The status of jobs and occupations as evaluated by an urban negro sample', *American Sociological Review*, **20** (5), 564–65.
CBS (2007, 2008), Het Nederlandse ondernemingsklimaat in cijfers Centraal Bureau voor de Statistiek, Voorburg, available at www.cbs.nl.
Clark, E.A., N. Kristensen and N. Westergård-Nielsen (2007), 'Job satisfaction and co-worker wages: status or signal?', IZA Discussion Paper No. 3073, IZA, Bonn.
Cramer, J.S., J. Hartog, N. Jonker and C.M. Van Praag (2002), 'Low risk aversion encourages the choice for entrepreneurship: an empirical test of a truism', *Journal of Economic Behaviour and Organization*, **48** (1), 29–36.
Davidsson, P. and B. Honig (2003), 'The role of social and human capital among nascent entrepreneurs', *Journal of Business Venturing*, **18** (3), 301–31.
Dohmen, T.J., A. Falk, D. Huffman, J. Schupp, U. Sunde and G.G. Wagner (2005), 'Individual risk attitudes: new evidence from a large, representative, experimentally-validated survey', IZA Discussion Paper No. 1730, IZA, Bonn.
Duncan, O.D. (1961), 'A socioeconomic index for all occupations', in A.J. Reiss (ed.), *Occupations and Social Status*, New York: Free Press of Glencoe, pp. 388–98.
Ederer, F. and A. Patacconi (2007), 'Interpersonal comparison, status and ambition in organizations', Economics Series Working Papers No. 222, University of Oxford, Department of Economics.
Fairlie, R.W. (2005), 'Entrepreneurship among disadvantaged groups: an analysis of the dynamics of self-employment by gender, race and education', in S.C. Parker, Z.J. Acs and D.R. Audretsch (eds), *Handbook of Entrepreneurship*, Dordrecht: Kluwer Academic Publishers.
Falck, O., S. Heblich and A. Luedemann (2008), 'Identity and entrepreneurship', CESifo Working Paper No. 2661, CESifo GmbH.
Fershtman, C. and Y. Weiss (1993), 'Social status, culture and economic performance', *Economic Journal*, **103**, 946–59.
Frank, R. H. (1984), 'Are workers paid their marginal products?', *The American Economic Review*, **74** (4), 549–71.
Frank, R.H. (ed.) (1988), *Passions Within Reason*, New York: Norton.
Gianetti, M and A. Simonov (2004), 'Social interactions and entrepreneurial activity', Working Paper, University of Stockholm, School of Economics.
Greene, P.S. and T.E. Brown (1997), 'Resource needs and the dynamic capitalism typology', *Journal of Business Venturing*, **12** (3), 161–73.
Grilo, I. and A.R. Thurik (2005), 'Entrepreneurial engagement levels in the European Union', Papers on entrepreneurship, growth and public policy No. 20-0, Max Planck Institute of Economy, Jena.
Grund, C. and D. Sliwka (2007), 'Reference dependent preferences and the impact of wage increases on job satisfaction: theory and evidence', *Journal of Institutional & Theoretical Economics*, **163** (2), 313–35.
Hartog, J., C.M. Van Praag and J. Van Der Sluis (2008), 'If you are so smart, why aren't you an entrepreneur? Returns to cognitive and social ability entrepreneurs versus employees', Discussion Paper No. 08-073, Tinbergen Institute: 3 – Labour, region and environment, Amsterdam.
Henrekson, M. and D. Johansson (2008), 'Gazelles as job creators – a survey and interpretation of the evidence', IFN Working Paper Series No. 733, Research Institute of Industrial Economics.

Hendrickx, J. and H.B.G. Ganzeboom (1998), 'Occupational status attainment in the Netherlands 1920–1990: a multinomial logistic analysis', *European Sociological Review*, **14** (4), 387–403.

Hodge, R.W. (1981), 'The measurement of occupational status', *Social Science Research*, **10** (4), 396–415.

Hodge, R.W., P.M. Siegel and P.H. Rossi (1964), 'Occupational prestige in the United States 1925–1963', *American Journal of Sociology*, **70** (3), 286–302.

Katz, J.A. (1992), 'A psychological cognitive model of employment status choice', *Entrepreneurship: Theory and Practice*, **17** (1), 29–37.

Kwon, I. and E.M. Meyersson-Milgrom (2007), 'Status, relative pay and wage growth: evidence from M & A', SIEPR Discussion Paper No. 07-26.

Lazear, E.P. (2005), 'Entrepreneurship', *Journal of Labor Economics*, **23** (4), 649–80.

Malach-Pines, A., H. Levy, A. Utasi and T.L. Hill (2005), 'Entrepreneurs as cultural heroes: a cross-cultural, interdisciplinary perspective', *Journal of Managerial Psychology*, **20** (6), 541–55.

Nakao, K. and J. Treas (1994), 'Updating occupational prestige and socioeconomic scores: how the new measures measure up', *Sociological Methodology*, **24** (24), 1–72.

Nanda, R. and J.B. Sørensen (2008), 'Peer effects and entrepreneurship', Harvard Business School Working Paper No. 08-051, Cambridge.

North, C.C. and P.K. Hatt (1947), 'Jobs and occupations: a popular evaluation', *Opinion News*, **9**, 3–13.

Oosterbeek, H. and A. Van Den Broek (2008), 'An empirical analysis of borrowing behaviour of higher education students in the Netherlands', *Economics of Education Review*, **28**, 170–77.

Parker, S.C. (ed.) (2004), *The Economics of Self-Employment and Entrepreneurship*, Cambridge: Cambridge University Press.

Parker, S.C. (ed.) (2009), *The Economics of Self-Employment and Entrepreneurship*, Cambridge: Cambridge University Press.

Parker, S.C. and C.M. van Praag (2006), 'Schooling, capital constraints and entrepreneurial performance: the endogenous triangle', *Journal of Business and Economic Statistics*, **24** (4), 416–31.

Parker, S.C. and C.M. van Praag (2009), 'Group status and entrepreneurship', *Journal of Economics and Management Strategy*, forthcoming 2010.

Pettijohn, T.F. (ed.) (1999) *Psychology: A Connectext*, 4th edn, Guilford, CT: Dushkin/McGraw-Hill.

Ray, J.J. (1979), 'Quick measure of achievement motivation – validated in Australia and reliable in Britain and South Africa', *Australian Psychologist*, **14** (3), 337–44.

Rotter, J.B. (1966), 'Generalized expectancies for internal versus external control of reinforcement', *Psychological Monographs*, **80** (1), 1–28.

Treiman, D.J. (ed.) (1977), *Occupational Prestige in Comparative Perspective,* New York: Academic Press.

Uzzi, B. (1999), 'Embeddedness in the making of financial capital: how social relations and networks benefit firms seeking financing', *American Sociological Review*, **64** (4), 481–505.

Van Der Sluis, J. and C.M. van Praag (2004), 'Economic returns to education for entrepreneurs: the development of a neglected child in the family of economics of education?', *Swedish Economic Policy Review*, **11** (2), 183–226.

Van Der Sluis, J. and C.M. van Praag (2007), 'Returns to education for entrepreneurs and employees: identification by means of changes in compulsory schooling laws', Working Paper, University of Amsterdam, Amsterdam: Netherlands.

Van Der Sluis, J., C.M. van Praag and W. Vijverberg (2008), 'Education and entrepreneurship selection and performance: a review of the empirical literature', *Journal of Economic Surveys*, **22** (5), 795–814.

Van Der Sluis, J., C.M. van Praag and A. Van Witteloostuijn (2007), 'Comparing the returns to education for entrepreneurs and employees', Discussion Paper No. 104/3, Tinbergen Institute.

Van Praag, C.M. and J.S. Cramer (2001), 'The roots of entrepreneurship and labor demand: individual ability and low risk aversion', *Economica*, **68** (269), 45–62.

Van Praag, C.M. and P.H. Versloot (2007), 'What is the value of entrepreneurship? A review of recent research', *Small Business Economics*, **29** (4), 351–82.

Villemez, W.J. (1974), 'Ability versus effort: ideological correlates of occupational grading', *Social Forces*, **53** (1), 45–52.

Weber, M. (ed.) (1922), *Economy and Society*, translated and reprinted, Berkeley, CA: University of California Press, 1978.

Weiss, Y. and C. Fershtman (1998), 'Social status and economic performance: a survey', *European Economic Review*, **42** (3/5), 801–20.

PART II

INSTITUTIONS, INNOVATION AND ENTREPRENEURSHIP

5 Industrial policy, entrepreneurship and growth
Philippe Aghion

INTRODUCTION

New growth theories, particularly the Schumpeterian approach (see Aghion and Howitt, 2009), emphasize the central role of entrepreneurial investments and of institutions and policies that maximize innovation incentives. Of particular importance for innovation-led growth appears to be free entry and product market competition, with the idea that increased competition or entry threat induces firms to invest more in innovation in order to escape the competitive threat. That competition or entry should enhance innovation and growth is supported by a whole set of empirical contributions. Thus Frankel and Romer (1999) and Wacziarg (2001) point to a positive effect of trade liberalization on growth. Wacziarg (2001) showed that increasing trade restrictions by one standard deviation would reduce productivity growth by 0.264 percent annually. Similarly, Keller (2002, 2004) showed that 70 percent of international R&D spillovers are due to cross-country trade flows. More recently Aghion et al. (2008) pointed to large growth-enhancing effects of the trade liberalization and delicensing reforms introduced in India in the early 1990s, particularly in more advanced sectors or in Indian states with more flexible labor market regulations. And several studies summarized in Aghion and Griffith (2006) point to a positive effect of liberalizing product market competition and entry on innovation and productivity growth by incumbent firms, particularly those that are more advanced in their sector. All these studies have lent support to the recent waves of product and trade liberalization worldwide, and have lent support to an argument against any form of government intervention targeted at particular firms or sectors, in other words against any form of industrial policy.

Industrial policies had been implemented after the Second World War in a number a countries, with the purpose of promoting new infant industries and of protecting local traditional activities against competition by products from more advanced foreign countries. Thus several Latin American countries advocated import substitution policies whereby local industries would benefit more fully from domestic demand. East Asian countries like Korea or Japan, rather than advocate import substitution policies, would favor export promotion, which in turn would be achieved partly through tariffs and non-tariff barriers and partly through maintaining undervalued exchange rates. And in Europe, a country like France engaged in a so-called 'Colbertist' policy of targeted subsidies to industries or to 'national champions'.

For at least two or three decades after the Second World War, these policies remained fairly non-controversial as countries implementing them were growing at relatively fast rates. However, the slow-down in Latin America in the 1970s, and then in Japan in the late 1990s, contributed to the growing skepticism about the role of industrial policy in the process of development. Increasingly since the early 1980s, industrial policy has raised serious doubts among academics and policy advisers in international financial institutions. In particular, it was criticized for allowing governments to pick winners and losers in a discretionary fashion, and consequently for increasing the scope for capture of governments by local vested interests. Instead, policy makers and growth/development economists now advocate non-targeted policies aimed at improving the investment climate: the liberalization of product and labor markets, a legal and enforcement framework that protects (private) property rights, and macroeconomic stabilization. This new set of growth recommendations came to be known as the 'Washington consensus', as it was primarily advocated by the IMF, the World Bank and the US Treasury, all based in Washington, DC.

In this chapter we discuss some pros and cons of industrial policy, and in particular we point to new arguments in favor of sectoral intervention even in the context of advanced economies where competition and innovation play a central role. The chapter is organized as follows. The next section summarizes the infant industry argument as traditionally stated, and then discusses recent empirical work that partly refutes this argument. The third section develops a first counter-argument, based on the idea that innovation activities in a pure *laissez-faire* economy may go in the wrong direction. The fourth section develops a second potential counter-argument that, like the initial infant industry argument, emphasizes the existence of cross-sectoral learning spillovers, but proposes a different strategy to test for such spillovers. The final section concludes by suggesting avenues for future research.

INDUSTRIAL POLICY IN CATCHING-UP COUNTRIES: THE TRADITIONAL INFANT INDUSTRY ARGUMENT

The Argument in a Nutshell

The infant industry argument, as formalized by Greenwald and Stiglitz (2006),[1] can be summarized as follows: consider a local economy which comprises a traditional (agricultural) sector and a nascent (industrial) sector. The industrial sector's new activities involve high costs initially: however, production and the resulting learning by doing reduce these costs over time. Moreover, suppose the existence of knowledge externalities between these new industrial activities and the traditional sector. Then two conclusions immediately obtain in this setting.

First, full trade liberalization will make it very costly for domestic industrial sectors to invest in learning by doing: this involves producing but not selling in the short run since domestic costs are initially higher than foreign costs. Second, the social benefits from learning by doing are not fully internalized by industrial sectors, since they do not internalize the knowledge externalities they have on the agricultural sector. It is the combination of these two considerations that justifies domestic policies aimed at (temporarily) protecting nascent industries. Such policies may either take the form of targeted subsidies or import restrictions, or they may involve non-targeted policies, for example maintaining undervalued exchange rates that will benefit the local industry as a whole as long as it does not import too many inputs from abroad themselves.

Criticisms

The main objections to the infant industry argument have been empirical. Thus Krueger and Tuncer (1982) saw no systematic tendency for non-protected firms or industries in Turkey over the 1960s to display higher productivity growth than less protected industries; moreover, they saw no apparent tendency for a new industrial activity to display higher rates of growth than the overall industry to which it belongs.[2]

However, the most compelling case against the traditional infant industry argument was recently made by Nunn and Trefler (in press), henceforth NT. Nunn and Trefler's argument goes as follows: if we were to believe the above infant industry argument, then we should see a positive correlation between growth and the extent to which the domestic tariff structure is skills-biased, the idea being that learning by doing on new activities with knowledge spillovers on the rest of the economy should require more skills than other activities. Thus NT regress average per capita GDP growth, measured by the log of (y_{c1}/y_{c0}), where y_{c1} (resp. coefficient y_{c0}) denotes per capita GDP at the end (resp. the beginning) of the period, on the extent to which the tariff structure is skills-biased (which in turn is measured by the correlation coefficient between skill intensity and the level of tariffs across sectors). A straight cross-country regression with region and cohort fixed effects shows a positive and significant correlation between growth and the skills bias of the tariff structure.

Thus, at first sight, NT's regression results seem to confirm the infant industry argument. However, NT push the analysis further by regressing, for each sector in each country, per capita growth on both the country-level measure of skill bias of tariffs and a new (industry-level) tariff–skill interaction term: this latter term interacts the tariff for that particular industry with the ratio of skilled over unskilled labor in that same industry. The intriguing result is that the coefficient for this industry-level tariff–skill interaction drops significantly. In other words, the positive coefficient on the aggregate measure of skills-biased tariff found in the previous regression reflects something more than simply the growth effect of protecting more skill-biased industries. In fact NT argue that the explanation for the positive coefficient also involves a third variable, namely the quality of local institutions, which is positively correlated with growth and also with the government's propensity to emphasize skill-intensive sectors.

INDUSTRIAL POLICY IN CATCHING-UP COUNTRIES: INDUSTRIAL NICHES

The notion that the existing pattern of specialization may limit the evolution of comparative advantage over time has not received much attention in the growth literature so far. For example in Romer's (1990) product variety model, the current set of inputs displays the same degree of imperfect substitutability with respect to any new input that might be introduced, and therefore does not make one new input more likely than any other: this property stems directly from the fully symmetric nature of the Dixit–Stiglitz model of product differentiation upon which the Romer model is built. However, an important insight that emerges from the work of Young (1991), Lucas (1993), and more recently Hausmann and Klinger (2007) is that successful growth stories involve gradual processes whereby neighboring sectors experiment with new technologies one after the other because experimentation involves learning-by-doing externalities across sectors.

To illustrate the case for targeted intervention based on the existence of cross-sectoral externalities in the simplest possible way, consider the following toy model. Individuals each live for one period. There are four potential sectors in the economy, which we number from 1 to 4, but only one sector, namely sector 1, is active at date zero. Thus the economy at date zero can be represented by the 4-tuple $\Omega_o = (1, 0, 0, 0)$, where the number 1 (resp. 0) in column i refers to the corresponding sector i being currently active (resp. inactive). At date t, a sector that is active produces at the frontier productivity level $\overline{A}_t = (1 + g)^t$. Once activated, a sector automatically remains active forever. Aggregate output at date t is $Y_t = A_t = N_t\overline{A}_t$, where N_t is the number of active sectors at date t.

R&D investments activate new sectors, but there is a cost of learning about distant sectors. Specifically, there is a fixed R&D cost $\gamma(1 + g)^t$ of activating a sector in period t, but this is only possible if (a) the sector is adjacent to an already active sector or (b) the R&D cost $\gamma(1 + g)^{t-1}$ was also incurred in that sector last period.

Consider first the economy under *laissez-faire*. Being populated by one-period-lived individuals, the economy will never invest in a sector that is not adjacent to a sector already active. At best, a local entrepreneur will find it optimal to activate a sector adjacent to an already active sector. This will be the case whenever $\gamma < \theta$, where θ is the fraction of output that can be appropriated by a private innovator. Note however that if $\theta < \gamma$, then private firms will not explore new sectors, even neighboring ones, even though it might be socially optimal to do so.

Coming back to the case where $\gamma < \theta$, in this case the *laissez-faire* sequence of active sectors will be:

$$\Omega_1 = (1, 1, 0, 0)$$
$$\Omega_2 = (1, 1, 1, 0)$$
$$\Omega_t = (1, 1, 1, 1), t \geq 3$$

Now consider a social planner. The social planner will invest in sector 2 in period 1, whenever the cost $\gamma(1 + g)$ of doing so is less than the net present revenue of activating sector 2, namely

$$\sum_{t=1}^{\infty}\frac{\overline{A}_t}{(1 + r)^t} = \frac{1 + g}{r - g}$$

that is, whenever

$$\gamma < \frac{1}{r - g}$$

For g sufficiently close to r or for γ sufficiently small, this inequality is automatically satisfied, in which case it will also be optimal to invest in sector 3 in period 2 because at that date sector 3 will be adjacent to an already active sector (namely sector 2).

But in addition, whenever γ is sufficiently small, it will be optimal to invest in sector 4 in period 1, because that will allow sector 4 to be activated in period 2 whereas otherwise it can be activated only in period 3. Investing in period 1 instead of period 2 in sector 4 will yield an additional $\overline{A}_2/(1 + r)$, and will cost an additional $\gamma(1 + g)$. So, if γ is small enough, namely if

$$\gamma < \frac{1 + g}{1 + r}$$

the optimal sequence of active sectors will be:

$$\Omega_1 = (1, 1, 0, 0)$$
$$\Omega_2 = (1, 1, 1, 1)$$
$$\Omega_t = (1, 1, 1, 1), t \geq 3$$

The *laissez-faire* equilibrium is suboptimal because people do not invest far enough away from already active sectors. In this example output will be lower than optimal in period 2 ($3\overline{A}_2$ versus $4\overline{A}_2$) because individuals were not far-sighted enough to invest in sector 4, which was too far away from already active sectors, in period 1.

Thus this model suggests a role for targeted industrial policy: namely, to overcome the potential underinvestment in new sectors. In particular, if targeted subsidies were to be implemented by a government, we conjecture that such subsidies should be more growth-enhancing (i) if they target sectors that are currently inactive but close 'input-wise' to already active sectors, and (ii) if the country experiences low levels of financial development or low labor mobility or low average levels of education. (i) implies that the targeted sectors are more likely to benefit from learning-by-doing externalities from already active sectors; (ii) makes it less likely that market forces will spontaneously take advantage of these externalities.

The idea that the product space is heterogeneous, with an uneven density of active product lines, and that the current density distribution of active sectors impacts on the evolution of comparative advantage is applied to the data by Hausmann and Klinger (2007), henceforth HK. HK measure the relatedness between two product lines by the probability $\varphi_{i,j}$ that on average countries export enough of the two goods simultaneously.[3] Then, HK define the density around good i in country c as the average relatedness of that product with other products exported by the same country, namely:

$$density_{i,c,t} = \frac{\sum_k \varphi_{i,k,t} x_{c,k,t}}{\sum_k \varphi_{i,k,t}}$$

where $x_{c,k,t}$ is the volume of export of product k by country c at time t.

A main finding in HK is that the probability of a country exporting product i in year $t + 1$, is positively and significantly correlated with the country's density around product i in year t. This in turn provides empirical support to the idea that countries move toward new product lines that are adjacent to existing lines, even though this may be suboptimal, as discussed above.

Two arguments at least can be opposed to targeted interventions of the kind suggested in this section: (a) such policies may serve as a pretext for government favors, particularly if input–output information can be manipulated by politicians or bureaucrats; (b) what guarantees that temporary support to industries will be terminated, especially if the investment turns out to be inefficient? One possible answer to these two objections would be to involve third parties (e.g. private partners) that would access input–output information and would also act as cofinanciers.

INDUSTRIAL POLICY IN DEVELOPED COUNTRIES: REDIRECTING TECHNICAL CHANGE

Previous work based on Acemoglu et al. (2006) argued that the closer a country or sector is to the corresponding world technology frontier, the more growth relies on frontier innovation rather than on imitation. In the above two sections we discussed instances where industrial policy might help in the catching-up process. In this section we argue that even in a developed economy already endowed with a full range of sectors and activities, and where frontier innovations are a main driving force of the growth process, there is a case to be made for industrial policy. Our main idea in this section is that a *laissez-faire* economy may sometimes innovate in the 'wrong direction', i.e. in a direction that may be detrimental to long-run growth. In this case, subsidizing research and production in particular sectors, at least temporarily, can help 'redirect' research efforts so as to enhance long-run growth.

More specifically, Acemoglu et al. (2009), or AABH, develop an endogenous growth model where a consumption good (or final good) can be produced using a clean and/or a dirty input. Only the production of dirty inputs harms the environment. The environment in turn affects consumers' utility. Inputs are produced with labor and machines, and innovation can improve the efficiency of production of either of these. Innovation results from the work of scientists who can try to improve either the quality of dirty machines or the quality of clean machines. An important assumption is what AABH refer to as the 'building on the shoulders of giants' effect, namely that technological advances in one sector make future advances in that sector more effective.

Innovators direct their efforts to the sector where the expected profits from innovation are the highest. Thus, under *laissez-faire*, when the dirty technology enjoys an initial installed-base advantage and given the 'building on the shoulders of giants' effect, the innovation machine will work in favor of the dirty technology. The clean technology may never take off unless the government intervenes. What AABH show is that the *laissez-faire* equilibrium will typically lead to environmental disaster, where environmental quality falls below the level at which it can be regenerated and therefore utility collapses. Where the dirty technology is based on exhaustible resources, this may help to prevent such a disaster, as the dirty technology is eventually priced out of the market. But even in this case, the innovation machine left on its own works suboptimally, favoring the dirty technology for too long.

A critical parameter for the effectiveness of policy intervention is the extent to which the dirty and the clean technologies are substitutable. In particular, when the clean and dirty technologies are sufficiently close substitutes, a temporary policy involving both, a tax on dirty input production (a 'carbon tax') and a subsidy to clean research activities will be sufficient to avoid an environmental disaster and thus to guarantee long-run

Table 5.1 Delaying action is costly

Discount rate (%)	1	1.5
Lost consumption, delay of 10 years (%)	5.99	2.31
Lost consumption, delay of 20 years (%)	8.31	2.36

Source: Calibrations from the AABH (2009) model.

growth sustainability. Indeed, by redirecting technical change towards clean innovation, such a policy will make clean technologies catch up and eventually leap-frog dirty technologies, at which point, by virtue of the 'building on the shoulders of giants' effect (but which now plays in the right direction), private firms will spontaneously choose to innovate in clean machines.

Thus the optimal policy is targeted, i.e. it is directed towards clean production and innovation, but it also relies on a complementarity of roles between the government and the private sector. Delaying such directed intervention not only leads to further deterioration of the environment. In addition, the dirty innovation machine continues to strengthen its lead, making the dirty technologies more productive and widening the productivity gap between dirty and clean technologies even further. This widened gap in turn requires a longer period for clean technologies to catch up and replace the dirty ones. As this catching-up period is characterized by slower growth, the cost of delaying intervention, in terms of foregone growth, will be higher. In other words, delaying action is costly. This is illustrated in Table 5.1.

The AABH (2009) model shows the cost of delaying intervention. This cost is computed as the 'lost' consumption in each period expressed as a percentage of the level of consumption that would result from 'best-time' policy intervention.

Not surprisingly, the shorter the delay and the higher the discount rate (i.e. the lower the value put on the future), the lower the cost will be. This is because the gains from delaying intervention are realized at the start in the form of higher consumption, while the loss occurs in the future through more environmental degradation and lower future consumption. Moreover, because there are basically two problems to deal with, namely the environmental one and the innovation one, using two instruments proves to be better than using one. The optimal policy involves using (i) a carbon price to deal with the environmental externality and, at the same time, (ii) direct subsidies to clean R&D (or a profit tax on dirty technologies) to deal with the knowledge externality.

Of course, one could always argue that a carbon price on its own could deal with both the environmental and the knowledge externalities at the same time (discouraging the use of dirty technologies also discourages innovation in dirty technologies). However, relying on the carbon price alone leads to excessive reduction in consumption in the short run. And because the two-instrument policy reduces the short-run cost in terms of foregone short-run consumption, it reinforces the case for immediate implementation, even for values of the discount rate under which standard models would suggest delaying implementation.

In fact the AABH model allows one to calibrate the cost of using only the carbon price instead of a combination of a carbon price and a subsidy to clean R&D. This cost can be expressed as the amount of 'lost' consumption in each period as a percentage of the level of consumption that would result from optimal policy, which involves using both types of instrument. Using a discount rate of 1 percent, this cost in terms of lost consumption amounts to 1.33 percent.

An alternative way of showing the higher cost when using only one instrument (i.e. the carbon price) rather than a combination of carbon pricing and more industrial-policy-related subsidies is to express how high the optimal carbon price would have to be when used as a singleton relative to its optimal level when used in combination. Simulating this scenario in the AABH model reveals that the carbon price would have to be about 15 times higher during the first five years and 12 times higher over the following five years. The intuition behind the initial high differential is that the early period in particular is the key to inducing the catch-up by clean technologies. By the same token, using only the subsidy instrument, while keeping the carbon-price instrument inactive, would imply that subsidies would have to be on average 115 percent higher in the first ten years compared to their level when used in combination with a carbon price.

The good news is that government intervention to trigger green innovation and growth (through pricing carbon and subsidizing clean technologies) can be reduced over time. As soon as clean technologies have gained sufficient productivity advantage over dirty technologies, the private innovation machine for these clean technologies can be left on its own to generate further improvements resulting in even better and more efficient clean technologies. And with cleaner technologies in place, the environmental damage problem, which the carbon tax needs to address, gradually abates. However, the longer intervention is delayed, the longer intervention will have to be maintained.

In fact, simulations with the AABH model indicate how the carbon price and the clean innovation subsidy should be set optimally over time. The graphs show (i) that subsidies for new clean technologies should be granted immediately but can be quickly reduced as soon as innovation has taken off for these technologies; and (ii) that the carbon price can decrease over time. With the emergence of perfectly clean backstop technologies that have zero emissions, and with the innovation gap between clean and dirty technologies eliminated and the stock of past emissions diminishing, the environmental externality gradually disappears, thus reducing the need for a carbon price over time.

CONCLUSION

In this chapter we have tried to push the debate on the pros and cons of industrial policy somewhat beyond what can be found in the current literature on trade and development. In particular we have identified (extreme) situations where targeted intervention might be called for, even in developed economies where growth relies mainly on frontier innovation. We conclude by making two remarks.

The first is that industrial policy should not be systematically opposed to competition policy. In particular, in current work with Mathias Dewatripont and Patrick Legros, we argue that targeted subsidies could be used to induce several firms to operate in the same sector, instead of escaping competition through excessive horizontal differentiation. This in turn could enhance innovation, both by maintaining a higher equilibrium degree of competition (i.e. by reducing horizontal differentiation) and also because firms operating in the same sector are more likely to benefit from knowledge spillovers or communication among them. Of course, much depends upon the design of industrial policy. Such policy should target sectors, not particular firms (or 'national champions'). And appropriate exit mechanisms should be put in place, for example through cofinancing between public and private sources, so that funding would be eventually withdrawn from sectors where targeted intervention proves unprofitable *ex post*.

An additional case for intervention can be made in relation to the business cycle. More specifically, recent work by Aghion et al. (2009) uses a sample of 45 industries across 17 OECD countries over the period 1980–2005 to show that growth in industrial sectors that are more dependent upon external finance (using Rajan and Zingales's, 1998, methodology) benefit more from more countercyclical fiscal policies, i.e. from policies that involve larger deficits in recessions (compensated by bigger surpluses during booms). Moreover, it is more the expenditures side than the revenues side of governments' budgets whose countercyclicality matters for growth in such sectors. A natural issue, then, is whether government support to such sectors during recessions does or does not amount to some other form of industrial policy.

Whether these latter arguments are in some cases stronger than the powerful political economy counter-argument(s) needs to be assessed depending upon characteristics of the country or the sector, and also with regard to the economy's location in the business cycle. In any case, the general recommendation made by the Spence report with regard to industrial policy strikes us as stemming from common sense: namely, experiment, and then make sure you can stop the intervention if it turns out not to be efficient.

NOTES

1. See also Young (1991).
2. However, Harrison (1994) questions these findings.
3. More specifically, relatedness between products *i* and *j* is measured by:

$$\varphi_{i,j} = \min \{ P(x_i/x_j), P(x_j/x_i) \},$$

where $P(x_i/x_j)$ is the probability that a country exports (enough of) good *i* conditional upon exporting (enough of) good *j*.

REFERENCES

Acemoglu, D. P. Aghion and F. Zilibotti (2006), 'Distance to frontier, selection and economic growth', *Journal of the European Economic Association*, **4**(1), 37–74.

Acemoglu, D. P. Aghion, L. Bursztyn and D. Hemous (2009), 'The environment and directed technical change', NBER Working Paper.

Aghion, P. and R. Griffith (2006), *Competition and Growth*, Cambridge, MA: MIT Press.

Aghion, P. and P. Howitt (2009), *The Economics of Growth*, Cambridge, MA: MIT Press.

Aghion, P. R. Burgess, S. Redding and F. Zilibotti (2008), 'The unequal effects of liberalization: evidence from dismantling the license Raj in India', *American Economic Review*, **98**(4) 1397–412.

Aghion, P., D. Hemous, and E. Kharroubi (2009), 'Cyclical budgetary policy, credit constraints, and industry growth', mimeo, Harvard.

Frankel, J. and D. Romer (1999), 'Does trade cause growth?', *American Economic Review*, **89**, 379–99.

Greenwald, B. and J. Stiglitz (2006), 'Helping infant economies grow: foundations of trade policies for developing countries', *American Economic Review*, Papers and Proceedings, 141–6.

Harrison, Ann E. (1994), 'An empirical test of the infant industry argument: comment', *American Economic Review*, **84**(4), 1090–95.
Hausmann, R. and B. Klinger (2007), 'The structure of the product space and the evolution of comparative advantage', CID Working Paper No. 146.
Keller, W. (2002), 'Technology diffusion and the world distribution of income: the role of geography, language, and trade', University of Texas, unpublished.
Keller, W. (2004), 'International technology diffusion', *Journal of Economic Literature*, **42**, 752–82.
Krueger, A. and B. Tuncer (1982), 'An empirical test of the infant industry argument', *American Economic Review*, **72**, 1142–52.
Lucas, Robert E. Jr (1993), 'Making a miracle', *Econometrica*, **61**(2), 251–72.
Nunn, N. and D. Trefler (in press), 'The political economy of tariffs and long-term growth', *American Economic Journal: Macroeconomics*, forthcoming
Rajan, R. and L. Zingales (1998), 'Financial dependence and growth', *American Economic Review*, **88**, 559–86.
Romer, Paul M. (1990), 'Endogenous technological change', *Journal of Political Economy*, **98**(5), S71–102.
Wacziarg, R. (2001), 'Measuring the dynamic gains from trade', *World Bank Economic Review*, **15**, 393–429.
Young, A. (1991), 'Learning by doing and the dynamic effects of international trade', *Quarterly Journal of Economics*, **106**, 369–405.

6 The role of patents and licenses in securing external finance for innovation
Dietmar Harhoff

INTRODUCTION

Economic literature analyzes a number of problems that stand in the way of an efficient allocation of resources to research and development (R&D) and innovation in a market economy. Among those are the well-known externalities that emanate from knowledge having public goods characteristics. Moreover, it is suggested in theoretical and empirical studies that there are financing constraints for particular types of firms and for specific activities, such as R&D. These constraints limit the extent to which firms engage in R&D and innovation, even if no knowledge externalities are present. Recent literature focuses on a third problem and argues that the market for intermediate outputs of the innovation process (such as ideas, patents, licenses, blueprints, prototypes etc.) is incomplete. The first two problems lead to inefficiently low investment in innovation. The third leads to an inefficiently low extent of division of labor, since transactions have to be internalized, and gains from specialization are lost.

This chapter is concerned with the latter two problems, which are intricately linked. At the root of them lies the idiosyncratic nature of technology, often following firm-specific paths of development, coupled with asymmetric information on alternative uses, substitutes and values. If a market for intermediate results of innovation processes existed, then the financing constraints of innovative firms would presumably be less pronounced. Intermediate results could be licensed, sold, leased or become part of other financial transactions, which would relax the financing constraints problem. The topic of this chapter is the role that patent rights and licenses play in the establishment of such markets for technology and as an instrument to support the financing of innovation.

The following sections develop these thoughts in some detail. First, a brief summary of the classical theoretical arguments pertaining to financing constraints, pecking orders and cost of capital is given. The third section discusses relatively novel uses of patents as instruments for securing external finance that go beyond the classical argument of securing property rights. The fourth section discusses how modern patent systems should be designed to support the financial functions of patents. The final section concludes.

THEORETICAL AND EMPIRICAL EVIDENCE ON FINANCING GAPS

Asymmetric Information, Moral Hazard and Pecking Orders

The impact of asymmetric information on financing has been studied in particular detail for debt finance. Credit markets differ from standard commodity markets in that the lender delivers a loan on the borrower's promise to pay back the loan and interest. The lender's evaluation of the borrower's ability to pay back is crucial for the lending decision. Equilibrium quantity rationing emerges endogenously due to asymmetric information (the lender knows less about the borrower than the borrower himself) and incompleteness of contracts (contractual agreements to control all aspects of borrower behavior are infeasible). In the case of rationing, the lender will decide not to grant a loan to the borrower, even if the borrower offers a higher interest rate than is observed in the market for loans. Thus the supply of loans does not equate the demand at the market interest rate.

The underlying cause for credit-rationing phenomena can be traced back to selection and incentive effects imposed by interest rates. Adverse selection occurs, since the average quality of borrowers will be a decreasing function of the interest rate charged by the lender. Moreover, as the interest rate increases, a borrower will be tempted to undertake riskier projects unless the loan is fully collateralized. Consequently, either some borrowers are not able to obtain loans, or the loan's size will be below that demanded by the borrower (Bester, 1985). If collateral is in short supply for a firm, then the firm may have projects that would be worth financing, but cannot be pursued because of the lack of debt finance. As discussed later, this is particularly likely in innovation projects that largely produce intangible assets as intermediate output.

If debt financing is lacking, firms may want to issue equity. But asymmetric information and moral hazard may prevent managers from doing so, as shown by Myers and Majluf (1984). They analyze the effects of asymmetric information if managers have knowledge of the true value of investment projects and the firm's other assets while investors (or lenders) do not. The model shows that if management acts in the interest of existing shareholders, firms will prefer internal finance over debt financing, and debt financing over the issuance of new shares. In this 'pecking order' model, there is no well-defined optimal capital structure as exists in the static Modigliani–Miller model with taxation, but rather a ranking of capital costs. Once internal resources (free cash flows) are exhausted, the firm must borrow to satisfy its capital needs. The most expensive type of capital is new equity. In some cases, the firm will prefer to forego an investment opportunity rather than issue debt or equity. Exogenous variations in cash flow should therefore have an impact on investment, at least for some firms.

Different Types of Investment: Tangibles versus Intangibles

Are financing constraints particularly important for investment in R&D? There are a number of reasons why investment in physical capital and knowledge capital should be affected differentially by financing constraints, and why obtaining external finance for innovation and R&D projects may be more costly than obtaining such funding for capital investment. At the same time, fundamental technological differences with respect to the adjustment costs of investment in R&D and differences in tax treatment may work against excess sensitivity of R&D spending to transitory shocks in cash flow.

For the purpose of the present discussion, first assume that, contrary to capital investment goods (plant, property and equipment), most R&D results, such as a new prototype, design or patent, cannot be used as collateral. Important exceptions from this rule will be considered in a later section. Most inputs and intermediate outputs of the innovation process are likely to be firm-specific or specific to the new products or processes being developed. Under these conditions there is no market where these assets could be liquidated in the case of insolvency. Thus external financiers cannot expect to recover a significant share of their funds from collateralized intangibles.

Second, for obvious reasons firms may be hesitant to reveal the content and objectives of their R&D efforts, since this knowledge may leak to competitors. Strategic considerations of this kind tend to maintain and reinforce informational asymmetries. But even without secrecy undermining the incentives to provide information about R&D projects, the evaluation of long-term risky projects by external financiers may be more costly than the assessment of more short-term-oriented ones. Thus, if providers of finance face greater uncertainty and longer planning horizons with respect to R&D than capital investment projects, financiers will require a higher 'lemons' premium' for the former type of investment. Hence, even without rationing behavior on the part of banks and other financial institutions, a premium will have to be paid for obtaining external funding for R&D projects. These arguments suggest that R&D-intensive firms will face larger differences between capital costs for internal and for external funds than firms with only a few R&D projects.

The cost of capital for investment and for R&D projects may also be affected differentially due to the tax treatment of R&D and intangibles.[1] Traditionally, R&D is expensed. This is a preferential treatment (full depreciation in the year of investment) when compared to capital investment, but only if the firm has a tax debt which can be reduced by the expensed R&D. Young firms with extended periods in which no positive tax debt occurs usually do not profit from this treatment. Moreover, carrying the tax losses forward does not fully compensate this disadvantage, either because the value of the tax loss declines over time or because some taxation regimes limit the extent to which firms can offset current profits with past losses. While a young firm may not be able to derive much benefit from the classical tax treatment of R&D, dangers come with it. Since the firm does not capitalize its intangibles, it runs an increased risk of ending up over-indebted. New taxation and accounting rules have therefore tried to address this issue. The US General Accounting Principles (GAP) have included a limited right to choose between capitalization and expensing for some time. Such an option is now available in most accounting and taxation systems (e.g. under the International Accounting Standards IAS 38 and IAS 39). To summarize, for most young firms the R&D expensing rule has not historically generated any advantages and the current trend toward explicitly listing some intangible assets (but only the development component) on the asset side of the balance sheet does not create a particular advantage for R&D.

These theoretical arguments suggest that finance for R&D and innovation should be more constrained and thus more susceptible to cash-flow variations than capital investment. However, there are other considerations that run counter to this conclusion. For one, adjustment costs are likely higher for R&D than for physical investment. Indeed, it is likely that the R&D process cannot be delayed or accelerated to the extent that this is possible for capital investment. Scientists cannot be fired and rehired without substantial loss of human capital to the firm (and potential gains to competitors), and resources employed in R&D cannot simply be used in production (or vice versa). This effect actually dampens the long-term response of R&D to cash-flow variation. Moreover, firms that anticipate high adjustment costs and expect to encounter financing constraints with some probability may not enter R&D at all (Bond et al., 2005). Sample selection may therefore work against the detection of cash-flow effects in R&D spending.

The arguments described in the previous sections (and, in some cases, countervailing ones) have been tested in a large number of empirical studies. This evidence will not be reviewed in detail, but attention will be drawn to survey results, in particular to the overviews presented by Hall (2002, 2009). Summarizing a large number of empirical studies, she concludes that the empirical evidence regarding financing constraints or 'funding gaps' is reasonably clear by now. First, innovation is mostly financed out of equity or retained earnings – debt is disfavored as a source of innovation finance. Second, financing differs across countries and governance regimes: the sensitivity of R&D to cash-flow variations is greater in Anglo-Saxon countries than in continental European economies. Finally, there is strong empirical evidence favoring the view that relatively small and young firms (small and medium-sized enterprises – SMEs – and start-ups) attempting to undertake innovation face particularly strong financing contraints. Classical financing institutions such as banks or public equity markets are not well prepared to support the financing of innovation in these firms. Hall (2002) also points out that there is little empirical evidence for the existence of financing constraints in large, established firms. R&D and innovation in these firms may still be subject to important externalities (such as knowledge spillovers), but funding gaps appear to be most pronounced in SMEs and young firms.

Private Equity and the Emergence of the Venture Capitalist

The literature summarized above considers debt and public equity markets, but not private equity. For the purpose of this study, the most interesting form of private equity is venture capital, which explicitly addresses the financing needs of young firms with strong growth prospects but no assets that can be collateralized. Venture capital (VC) is equity or equity-based investment in private companies with high potential for growth (see Gompers and Lerner, 2000; Kaplan and Strömberg, 2003). VC is usually organized as a limited partnership. The limited partners – typically wealthy individuals and institutional investors – enter a partnership with experienced venture capitalists (VCs) who act as general partners. Normally the partnership lasts for about ten years. The funds are invested in young firms in return for preferred stock. VCs also receive important special rights that allow them to influence the management of the start-up even if they hold a minority share. Venture capital emerged first at the end of the Second World War and gained in importance in the USA during the 1980s after the clarification of the Employee Retirement Income Security Act's 'prudent-man' rule allowed pension funds to invest in high-risk assets, including VC. While VC is now important for economic development in the USA, it has not been universally successful, with the UK, Israel, Canada and New

Zealand being major exceptions. The lack of an initial-public-offering (IPO) exit channel is presumably one of the most important impediments to the evolution of a functioning VC market. The emergence of VC can be interpreted as evidence that other financing institutions – in particular banks and public markets – have not been able to address the financing problems of young firms.

The positive role of VC in supporting innovation is now well established (Kortum and Lerner, 2000). But it should be pointed out that VC is restricted in scope – it addresses the financing needs of a very important, yet small segment of start-ups with particularly high growth potential. Even with a working VC market, in most countries a relatively large segment of innovative SMEs would continue to experience financing problems.

Summary

To summarize, there is considerable evidence that funding gaps exist, and that they are particularly problematic for SMEs and young firms. The emergence of VC, a new financing intermediary, in the 1960s and 1970s, and its subsequent success (at least in some countries and regions) can be interpreted as evidence that the financing needs of innovative SMEs and young firms were not met by the classicial institutions. However, VC financing is only a partial solution since it is not applicable to most SMEs and young firms. Meanwhile, a host of relatively new financing arrangements has emerged. These have not yet received detailed attention in the academic discussion, while some investors are already betting considerable sums on the new financing models.

PATENTS AS FINANCING TOOLS

The Market for Technology

Research following the work by Arora et al. (2004) emphasizes the importance of a market for technology. This notion refers to the market exchange of non-embodied technology. Most of economics literature assumes that trading non-embodied technology, for example ideas, know-how, licenses and patents, is considerably more difficult than trading the material forms of knowledge, for example machines and other artifacts. Recent literature seeks to answer the question of whether licensing and patent sales have become more frequent.

The overall incidence of licensing[2] and the monetary volume of licensing transactions are the subject of some research and considerable speculation. It is important to note that licensing (in the sense of granting access to technology) occurs for a number of reasons, some of which have little to do with genuine market exchange. A large share of international trade occurs within multinational enterprises (MNEs) (Maskus, 2000). Licensing may be used by MNEs to shift profits to low-tariff tax jurisdictions. Following the transfer of a patent right to a subsidiary in a low-tax country at a relatively low transfer price, the new patent-holder in the low-tax country may then demand royalty payments from the high-tax location. The use of intangibles for 'tax optimization' purposes is an important aspect in the empirical picture, but its extent is unknown. Furthermore, it is difficult to separate licensing as an exchange from cross-licensing for the mere purpose of avoiding litigation. In the latter case, there is no genuine trade or transaction indicative of a market, but merely avoidance of legal conflicts.

Arora et al. (2004) estimate that the world market for technology was about US$ 35–50 billion in the mid-1990s. The estimate includes licenses and the transfer of know-how as well as transfers based on other forms of collaboration such as production and marketing. Athreye and Cantwell (2007) employ data from the IMF balance of payments statistics and from the World Development Indicators database to compute global licensing revenues. Their time series indicates that worldwide royalty and licensing revenues amounted to about US$ 10 billion in 1980, and about US$ 80 billion in 1998 (Athreye and Cantwell, 2007, Fig. 2). It is unclear what share of this growth is accounted for by within-MNE transactions and to what extent transfer pricing issues are relevant. A 2005 special issue of *The Economist* (2005) includes an estimate for technology licensing revenues of around US$ 100 billion in 2005. Slightly less than half of this figure (US$ 45 billion) is estimated for licensing and royalties within the USA. Survey evidence (as in Zuniga and Guellec, 2009, p. 16) points to increases in the frequency of licensing and of licensing revenues. Their survey data are particularly telling since they restrict the analysis to licensing transactions with unaffiliated firms. Recent data on international US licensing with unaffiliated entities (1997–2007) confirm this view, but the rate of growth is modest at best (Arora and Gambardella, 2010, Fig. 3).

Another component of technology markets might be the outright sale of patent rights. However, the sparse evidence available on patent trade leads to the conclusion that markets for patents are not particularly liquid. Recent studies by Serrano (2008) and Burhop (2009) indicate that there is a moderate degree of patent trade. Burhop (2009) finds that about 8.3 percent of all patents granted by the German Imperial Patent Office between 1884 and 1913 were transferred to other owners. Serrano (2008) reports that the rate of transfers in the USA was 13.5 percent between 1983 and 2002. But in both contexts, the share of patents ever traded during their respective statutory lifetime is small, confirming that there may be a high degree of illiquidity in the market for patents. One reason for the low degree of trade may lie in the idiosyncratic nature of technology. Many patents protect inventions that firms pursue on firm-specific development paths. At the same time, the lack of trade may simply reflect the high degree of asymmetric information, which may lead to a market failure.

Patents may contribute to the growth of markets for technology in manifold ways. They can safeguard the value of assets, lower the costs of transactions, facilitate licensing and technology trade and serve as collateral or provide important signals to investors. As Epstein and Pierantozzi (2009) point out, patents may also help to recover value in the case of distress or bankruptcy – which will again lower the *ex ante* cost of capital.

Growth in the market for technology would allow more firms to trade intermediate inputs and outputs of the innovation process. Specialized firms may emerge that focus and specialize on particular stages of innovation, for example the design stage. Arora et al. (2001) study this phenomenon in the context of the chemical processing industry. They show that the presence of specialized engineering firms supplying chemical plant projects and technologies increases investments in chemical plants by downstream chemical firms. Hall and Ziedonis (2001) study the relevance of patents for the emergence of specialized design firms in the semiconductor industry.

Leaving aside economies of specialization, a liquid and transparent market for technology would also alleviate financing constraints by allowing firms to shorten the time period from first investment to arriving at an output that can be taken to a market. Financing needs for the intermediate steps would be smaller, so that the likelihood of financing these steps internally would increase. Moreover, with a market at hand, loans could possibly be collateralized, opening the path to more debt finance. Finally, the highly illiquid nature of private equity currently translates into a high premium for the investor, and thus into high financing costs for the start-up. With improved markets for technology, the likelihood of obtaining private equity finance may ultimately be enhanced, since start-ups could be liquidated more quickly.

As Gambardella (2002) points out, markets for technology are not a magical cure. Technology markets may introduce new forms of market failures while alleviating others. In particular, they may generate externalities related to the complementarity of intermediate inputs to innovation processes. While much more needs to be learned about markets for technology, for present purposes a focus on the positive properties seems appropriate.

Hybrid Business Models and 'Financial Bootstrapping'

Patents and licenses may facilitate transactions between collaborating firms (Merges, 2005). Growth-oriented firms are subject to highly volatile financial environments. Venture capital supply and demand see wide fluctuations over time. It is not surprising that firms have tried to survive periods of scarce finance by somehow reverting to their own means. One strategy is referred to as 'bootstrapping' – the start-up seeks to survive with the financial means at hand. 'Bootstrapping' can be supported by performing R&D services for other firms. This allows the firm to maintain a functional R&D group that can switch back to working on internal development targets once financial conditions improve.

In this context, even the promise of the future delivery of know-how and patented inventions may serve to support the financing of start-ups. In the 1990s, biotechnology firms developed hybrid business models that allowed them to survive extended periods of underfinancing by engaging in contract R&D for larger firms, mostly from the pharmaceuticals sector. Pharmaceuticals producers have been eager to replenish their product pipelines, which were threatened by expiring patents and low incidence of new clinical entities (NCEs). Rather than internalizing the costly search for NCEs, large firms increasingly sought cooperation with smaller biotechnology firms during the early phases of drug development.

Haagen et al. (2007), in a comparative assessment of UK and German biotechnology firms, evaluate the extent to which firms make use of such approaches. Some firms have adopted a hybrid business model that allows them to offer contract research or services to third parties in order to finance the company's own R&D activities. In essence, the contractual relationship between firms is that of *ex ante* licensing. Sixty-three percent of the German firms as compared to 55 percent of UK firms follow this 'bootstrapping' mode of finance. Focusing on the subgroup of firms that are younger than five years, Haagen et al. find that 66 percent of German firms compared to 60 percent of British firms pursue a hybrid business model. Nearly half of German firms' personnel resources are devoted to conducting contract research or services to finance the company's own research. Somewhat unexpectedly, the proportion of UK firms' personnel committed to contract research or services is also relatively large at about 45 percent.

The bootstrapping approach may conflict with the rapid development of the firms' own products and technologies. After all, firms pursuing a bootstrapping approach choose a form of finance that may delay the growth of the start-up. This may not be optimal, but the approach may help to sustain the start-up. However, there are often considerable rewards for early entry in large but immature markets. The dominance of US firms in emerging technology markets may be due to the fact that they can access additional financial channels, which allows them to grow quickly. This is presumably not the only reason for the (relative) scarcity of fast-growing European high-technology firms, but it may contribute significantly to the phenomenon.

Patents as Signals and Attractors of External Equity Finance

The relevance of patents for companies attempting to obtain financial resources, especially in their early stages, is repeatedly noted in the literature (Hayes, 1999; Lemley, 2000; Graham et al., 2009). The notion that patents facilitate the acquisition of VC is quite intuitive. From an investor's perspective, a start-up with strong patent rights should be preferred since the patent protects the start-up's market position by allowing it to exclude others from using its proprietary technology. Hence patents increase appropriability and provide incentives for innovation. In addition, patents facilitate the licensing of technology (e.g. Gans et al., 2002). They increase the attractiveness of companies as acquisition targets (Cockburn and Wagner, 2007) and enable VCs to recover a salvage value from failing companies. In this regard, patents may serve as valuable assets that enhance the value of the investment both in the case of success and in the case of failure. Patents may also serve as signals that certify to some extent that the start-up has available a novel and inventive technology. In the latter case, the patent's function is mainly to act as a seal of quality, possibly reducing the information problem on the investor's side. This function could even work for industries in which patent protection is not effective, as long as the patent office's assessment contains new information for the venture capitalist.

Several contributions in the empirical literature suggest that patents can indeed work in the two ways just described. Baum and Silverman (2004) examine selection criteria used by VCs and subsequent company performance. They find a positive association between patent applications at the US Patent Office (USPTO) and pre-IPO financing defined as VC financing and private placements. Interestingly, patent grants have a positive but smaller effect than patent applications.

Mann and Sager (2007), building on a qualitative study by Mann (2005), investigate the relationship between patents and VC availability. They show that there is a significant positive correlation between various success measures (number of financing rounds, overall investment, exit status, acquisition of late-stage financing and survival span) and measures of patenting activity. They also demonstrate that in the software industry, only a few start-ups ever patent (hence they are a relatively scarce asset), that patenting behavior varies strongly, and that the size of the patent portfolio does not matter as much as the simple indicator of patenting activity. Mann and Sager (2007) do not have strong evidence in favor of a causal relationship; hence the results could be caused by 'good start-ups' being active in patenting and simultaneously being favored by VC investments without a causal impact of patent rights on the financing decision.

VCs make investment decisions under considerable uncertainty. Technology start-ups are difficult to evaluate, since they lack a track record that outsiders can use to evaluate the potential, are often years away from first revenues, have mostly intangible assets, and are plagued by a high failure rate. These perils force VCs to spend much effort in searching for and assessing signals of ventures' growth potential (Amit et al., 1990; Hall and Hofer, 1993) and have led entrepreneurs to engage in symbolic action in order to gain legitimacy (Zott and Huy, 2007).

While a large strand of literature investigates the traditional view of patents as a means of protecting intellectual property, Long (2002, p. 625) notes that scholars have overlooked the informational function of patents, which 'may be more valuable to the rights holder than the substance of the rights'. Moreover, the information that is relevant to a financier may not just come from the grant event, but from other aspects of the patenting process. The value of information generated during the patenting process is the reduction of information asymmetries between VCs and the new and unproven company seeking capital, thus minimizing information costs for the financiers. Even a pending patent application may constitute such a signal. The preparation of patent applications requires effort and time, since applicants must follow strict guidelines and include technical information in a structured manner. This may allow individuals familiar with the patent application requirements to quickly assess the strengths and weaknesses of an invention and of the technology employed by the start-up.

Hsu and Ziedonis (2008) treat patents as quality signals for entrepreneurial ventures that have to fight the liabilities of smallness and youth. They find that patent filings have a strong association with investor estimates of company value – a doubling of the stock of applications is associated with a 28 percent increase in market valuation. Patents are particularly important in early financing rounds, valued more highly by prominent VCs, and positively correlated with the likelihood of an IPO. Theoretical considerations would predict that founders with more experience should profit less from the signalling effect than less experienced ones, but this expectation cannot be confirmed.

Haeussler et al. (2009) accept the notion that patents might be signals, but point to a weakness in the argument. Usually, the VC investment decision precedes the patent grant considerably. Hence the signal (if there is any) cannot lie in the grant decision of the patent office itself, but must reside in other information generated in the course of patent examination. In the US patent system, patents are usually taken to be patent grants, since the application was previously unknown to the public. Conversely, the European Patent Office (EPO) data used by Haeussler et al. (2009) can be employed to trace unsuccessful applications as well as successful ones. The European patent system thus affords a much more detailed view of the patenting process, since applications, search reports, grants, oppositions and communications between applicant and examiner are observable. This allows the authors to test if VCs react more strongly to patents that become – much later on – highly cited, and to patent oppositions.

Using the timing of events to identify effects, Haeussler et al. (2009) find that in the presence of patent applications, VC financing occurs earlier. The results also show that VCs pay attention to patent quality, financing those ventures faster that later turn out to have high-quality patents. Patent oppositions increase the likelihood of receiving VC, but ultimate grant decisions do not spur VC financing, presumably because they are anticipated. The empirical results and additional interviews with VCs suggest that the process of patenting generates signals that help to overcome the liabilities of newness faced by new ventures. However, it is not the patent application or patent grant *per se* that certifies the start-up's quality. It is a diverse set of events that, taken together, allow VCs sufficiently familiar with the patent system to assess the quality of the firm in their portfolio.

Taken together, these studies suggest that patents have an important but complex function for start-ups in securing external finance from VC channels. Patents may in part reflect enhanced appropriability, but they may also act as signals that would be hard to obtain in the absence of a patent system. Since these functions of patents have been investigated only in recent literature, there is still no quantitative measure of how strongly the institution contributes to the financing of new firms. Clearly, more research is needed to address these important issues.

Patents as Collateral in Debt Finance

Researchers have studied the nexus of finance and innovation for more than 30 years now. The financing-gap problem has already been described. Venture capital provides a solution in some of the cases. However, a large number of firms are subject to financing constraints for R&D and innovation, but unlikely to receive VC. Reasons could be that the growth prospects of the firm's projects – although substantial – are not as high as required from a VC's point of view. Moreover, the entrepreneur or owner may not wish to give up their independence.

In these cases, innovative firms typically tend to lack tangible capital that could be used as collateral to obtain external finance. Why can they not make use of their intangible assets to provide collateral? In the presence of liquid markets for intellectual property such as patent rights, and with some certainty given their scope and value, managers could resort to using patents as collateral in debt financing transactions.[3] The literature states that there are two potential reasons why the use of intangibles as collateral in debt finance has been limited (e.g. Lev, 2001). The first is that it is often exceedingly difficult to come up with an objective valuation of such assets, even from the proprietor's perspective. Even if a valuation existed, asymmetric information could make it hard to communicate the assessment to the financier. The second is that in the case of the loan being defaulted, the bank will find it typically very difficult to sell the asset or commercialize it in some other way. Markets for intellectual property are still not well developed. In other words, the collateral will not provide the intended function as an asset that can compensate the bank for the default.

This classical view may need to be amended, since extending debt finance against intellectual property (IP) collateral is apparently becoming more common. This observation coincides with the argument that technology is increasingly being traded in some form of market transactions. While there is some quantitative evidence of the latter, there are no comprehensive statistical data that would capture the extent to which loans are granted in exchange for IP collateral. As an upper bound, a recent KfW (Kreditanstalt für Wiederaufbau) survey of 4300 German SMEs yielded the result that in 2007, only 2.2 percent of the surveyed firms used intangible assets as collateral (KfW, 2007). Given that these assets may include trademarks, copyright, patents and other IP rights, the share of firms using patents as collateral is likely to be less than 1 percent.

This phenomenon should nonetheless not be ignored. It is true that only few specialist financiers offer such services today, and the use of patents for collateral is still largely experimental and non-standard. But this form of financing innovation has potential and could make a major contribution toward improving overall conditions for innovation, in particular in SMEs. To get a flavor of such transactions, consider the example of ESKA Implants GmbH & Co. KG, a producer of joint replacements reported in Schlemvogt (2009). The company needed capital for expanding its product range and service network to complete a turnaround. The main bank was willing to accept patents as collateral. An external valuation specialist identified 320 relevant patent rights valued at €3.5 to €5.0 million. The bank then accepted the respective portfolio (with a risk adjustment of 30 to 50 percent) as collateral. The company retained ownership of the patents in these transactions.

Several factors discourage the use of patents as collateral at this point. Banks are still highly skeptical, and loan officers typically point to the lack of expertise in dealing with complex IP issues. The inclusion of IP specialists could alleviate this problem, but would increase the costs of such transactions. Moreover, the high risk regarding the liquidation value of the collateralized IP also reduces the extent to which it can be used. It is not uncommon that the collateral value of IP in such debt finance transactions is below 10 percent of its value to the owner. Nonetheless, even such a low valuation may provide the firm with sufficient credit to perform sizable innovation activities. Consequently, an increase in innovation activity would be the result of past inventive activities.

It is too early to assess the relevance of these developments and make predictions about the future potential of IP-collateralized debt finance for innovation. With improvements and standardization in valuation techniques, with greater liquidity in markets for patents and licenses, and with greater openness toward innovative financing instruments on the part of banks, a significant source of financing could emerge. Some banks could evolve into specialists handling such transactions and become lead debt-holders in syndicated transactions. Debt transactions of this type could be handled either by 'house banks' with the support of patent valuation specialists or by specialist, banks that offer one-stop valuation and debt extension. Clearly, the new form of financing would require both relational as well as transactional competencies.

Patent Funds

Patent funds are one of the most interesting types of commercialization vehicles. While IP funds are not a recent invention,[4] the importance of such funds increased during the first decade of the second millennium. Patent funds have been controversial – some US patent funds have gained a reputation for extorting license payments by making intensive use of legal threats or full-fledged litigation (e.g. see *Business Week*, 2006). The European situation is different, presumably because the litigation system does not grant the kind of strategic opportunities available in the US court system. There are other differences as well. In the USA, patent funds are often financed by public equity while European patent funds are typically closed investment vehicles that require investors to hold on to their investments for at least four years. Investors are compensated for the illiquidity of the investment with relatively high returns – most patent funds announce expected returns of between 10 and 20 percent after taxes.

In Europe, two types of funds have emerged: 'blind pools' and 'asset pools'.[5] In blind pools, the patent portfolio to be commercialized is not selected prior to fund establishment – the performance of the pool rides mostly on the fund managers' talent in detecting, acquiring and commercializing patents. In asset pools an intermediary makes an up-front investment in selecting and purchasing the patent portfolio and then invites investors to fund the subsequent commercialization process. Asset pools are considerably less risky for the investor than blind pools, but the intermediary will have to be compensated for the set-up costs and shifting of risk. Thus returns are lower than in the case of blind-pool funds. While the first generation of European patent funds was privately placed, subsequent funds have been marketed as investments to a broader group of investors.

From an analytical perspective, investments in patent funds are largely unknown quantities, and more research is needed to reliably describe their characteristics. Understandably, the information provided by fund managers themselves tends to veer to the optimistic side. The claim made by fund managers that patent fund investments are largely uncorrelated with investments in other asset classes (e.g. Lipfert and Ostler, 2008 (p. 265) and BIT, 2008 (pp. 51 and 71)) has not yet been substantiated in independent research. Moreover, the performance expectations appear to be relatively high at this point, and may be seriously affected by the 2008/09 economic crisis. How patent funds will respond to the decline in IP activity and the trend toward a more restrictive granting of such rights (as is apparent in some patent offices) is unknown. Despite these skeptical remarks, this new form of IP monetization can support the financing of innovative companies. As the collateralization of patents, it should be welcome. The set-up of funds whose commercialization strategy relies heavily on litigation and threat of litigation is likely to receive a more negative response. The discussion of these practices is taken up in the next section.

PATENT SYSTEMS AND THE FINANCING OF INNOVATION

Parameters of Patent System Design

Patent rights may facilitate the financing of innovation activities.[6] How should a patent system be designed that supports the financing function of patents? And do real-world patent systems actually perform this function?

The main issue to be considered here is the extent of uncertainty over the scope and value of patent rights. Patent rights will support the financing of innovative companies if they help to reduce informational asymmetries. But if patent rights themselves are inherently uncertain in terms of the scope of the exclusion right and thus of their value, then the effect of reducing informational asymmetries in financial transactions is likely to be small. With uncertain patent rights it is difficult to establish liquid and transparent markets for patents and licenses. For a patent system to support the supply of innovation financing, it must provide well-delineated patent rights. Moreover, the granting and scope decision should come quickly in order to support firms in the initial stages of innovation, when financial constraints are particularly pronounced.

From the perspective of many stakeholders, the optimal patent system would arrive at precise and reliable decisions almost immediately and at almost no cost to the applicant or society at large. Obviously, this ideal system does not exist due to trade-offs between precision, duration and costs. Consider the issue of precision first. To simplify somewhat, decisions by patent authorities are subject to two types of errors. A Type I error consists in not granting a patent to an applicant with a truly novel and inventive technology, colloquially speaking a 'false negative'. Conversely, a Type II error, the 'false positive', occurs when a patent is granted to an undeserving application, when, for example, the technology already exists or the inventive step is too small to actually qualify for patent protection. Clearly, minimizing the likelihood of either type of error will require resources. Moreover, it may require time – irrespective of resources. Some information is simply generated by time passing by and cannot be replicated easily. Hence an immediate examination would not be recommended, especially in new technical fields. Regibeau and Rockett (2007) present this argument in detail.

A look at the empirical literature yields interesting insights into these trade-offs. There is evidence that (i) longer time lags in patent examination create uncertainty (Gans et al., 2008); (ii) some applicants seek to increase uncertainty for their rivals and therefore delay examination proceedings (Harhoff and Wagner, 2009); (iii) quick decisions are typically less precise than slower ones, particularly in new technical fields (Regibeau and Rockett, 2007); (iv) systems that allow applicants to delay examination (deferred examination) lead to a significant reduction of the examination workload, but also to additional uncertainty (McGinley, 2008); and (v) systems with a large inflow of 'marginal' applications create additional uncertainty for all players because the state of the art is no longer reliably determined (McGinley, 2008; Opperman, 2009).

How do real-world patent systems accommodate the financing function of patents? Consider the situation of the European Patent Office (EPO) and of the national patent offices in Europe as an example. A major backlog of applications exists within the EPO. Moreover, applicants are increasingly resorting to tactics of delay and artificial complexity in their filings (McGinley, 2009). After intially attempting to accommodate the quantity objectives of applicants, the EPO appears to have switched to a quality-oriented approach. It has established practices aimed at 'raising the bar', which should result in lower grant rates and, simultaneously, provide for sanctions (higher fees) when abusive practices are found. This new approach has been broadly supported in the academic literature.[7] But it is not without controversy. Some stakeholders see private value in an ever-expanding patent system. Moreover, patent offices themselves may be 'self-interested'. These are organizations with legal and implicit commitments to their employees who would wish to see secure pension funds, high degrees of job security and comparatively high salaries. Complex issues of fairness, labor market competition and long-term incentives in the patent office must be considered. The political economy of patent systems is quite complex, and it is one of the most neglected aspects in the current academic discussion.

While it is clear that patent office operations should be as efficient as possible, there is no reason to believe that the price of patenting should necessarily be as low as the marginal costs of processing an application at the patent office. The cost of patenting (as perceived from the applicant) functions as a screening device that can deter applicants with low-value, marginal applications. A patent system with excessively low prices is likely to invite a large number of marginal applications, which may clog the system, with subsequent problems for examination quality (Oppermann, 2009). Fees and filing costs are an important determinant of actual applicant behavior – they should therefore be considered appropriate instruments of patent policies (Harhoff et al., 2009).

Finally, the backlogs at major patent offices create uncertainty with respect to the state of the art and the scope of protection. If granting decisions cannot be produced quickly and if backlogs cannot be reduced fast, then the patent system should generate information that allows knowledgeable experts to arrive at reasonably precise predictions of subsequent decisions.[8] Search reports as published by many patent offices can serve a valuable purpose in that regard.

Patent Litigation

Despite the infrequent occurrence of patent litigation (in particular at appellate levels), the patent litigation framework has a particularly important impact on patenting practice, patent office behavior, and on emerging markets for technology. Patent-litigation cases occur in two basic forms: either as revocation proceedings challenging the validity of patents granted by the respective patent authority, or as infringement proceedings seeking to enforce patent rights. The likelihood of a patent being involved in litigation at some point during its term is estimated at between 1 and 3 percent in most patent systems, with some variation across technical domains, industries and countries.[9] Patent litigation is known to occur particularly frequently (i) for valuable patents; (ii) as assessments of case quality become more divergent; and (iii) as the distribution of information becomes increasingly asymmetric. Patent litigation is 'the tail that wags the dog of the patent system' – litigated cases provide legal precedence and important signals to patent-holders, potential infringers, and third parties seeking to steer clear of patent conflicts. A well-designed litigation system is the critical capstone of any patent system. Conversely, a flawed litigation system may effectively counteract any welfare gains from the system or cause welfare losses of its own.

The 'ascendancy of intangibles', as Lev (2001) has termed patent developments, led to the emergence of new types of players and intermediaries. The so-called 'patent troll' is the most notable one. Using the patent litigation system to extort license payments is referred to in the literature as 'trolling', which is not an illegal practice, but seeks to exploit structural and procedural weaknesses of the patent and judicial system to earn rents. See Reitzig et al. (2007) for a detailed analysis of the 'troll' business model. Since these rents may not be compensated by welfare gains, trolling is likely to be welfare-reducing.

Various features of the US patent and litigation system may contribute to the widespread occurrence of trolling in the USA. The following aspects are considered to support patent trolling:

- high costs of legal proceedings;
- cost allocation rules in court (both parties bear their own costs);
- contingency fee payments for lawyers, creating incentives for lawsuits;
- high damage awards and risk of treble damages in the case of 'willful infringement';
- pro-patentee posture of courts and juries;
- low examination quality creating uncertainty about the scope of protection;

- general and broadly defined extension of patentable subject matter to software and business methods; and
- quick and indiscriminate availability of injunctions[10] that can be used to create economic pressure.

The exact extent of 'trolling' in Europe is unknown. Certainly, the practice is not playing as prominent a role as it does in the USA. On the other hand, several patent funds have purchased several thousand patents, and the first court actions by 'trolls' may already be pending in Europe. The weaker presence of 'trolls' is presumably due to the fact that the patent system in Europe deviates from the US system in several crucial respects. In Europe, (i) court proceedings are much less costly; (ii) cost allocation favors the winning party; (iii) damage awards are not excessive; (iv) most courts have sought a careful balance between the rights of the parties and do not follow a systematic pro-patent posture; (v) injunctions are not issued automatically; and (vi) the quality of patent examination is higher than in the USA. However, one should not assume that the European patent and court system is 'troll-proof'.

Efforts seeking to transform the fragmented European patent litigation system into a unified court system must take these and other considerations into account. Currently parties may duplicate their controversies in multiple national courts. New proposals[11] foresee the establishment of a unified patent court covering both European patents and future community patents. These plans have revived the policy discussion and describe a suitable starting point for creating a unified system without creating loopholes exploitable by patent trolls.[12] Most importantly, patent litigation should occur at relatively low cost to litigants.[13]

CONCLUSIONS AND POLICY IMPLICATIONS

There is some agreement among economists that innovation activities are not only impeded by classical knowledge externalities but also by financing constraints. This finding appears to apply in particular to SMEs and young firms. Financial constraints are facilitated by informational asymmetries that are particularly pronounced in the early stages of innovative processes and technology creation. Traditional debt finance and public equity markets cannot close these funding gaps, and relatively new forms of private equity, such as venture capital, reach only the small portion of start-up firms that are likely to generate a particularly high rate of return.

New forms of innovation finance are emerging, however. While these do not play a major role as of 2010, policy-makers and managers should pay attention to the new developments. Supported by changes in valuation techniques and accounting regulation, it seems possible that patent rights will increasingly be used as collateral in debt finance. Moreover, patent funds may become an important source of finance for some innovators. As intermediate outputs of the innovation process become increasingly tradable for financing purposes, a more liquid and transparent market for technology may emerge.

These two developments – enhanced availability of finance and improved markets for technology – are complementary, but both depend to some degree on the design of patent systems. The more uncertain patent rights are, the less likely is it that the new forms of finance will play a major role. Thus current trends toward large quantities of low-quality patents should be discouraged, if not stopped. The pro-quantity stance of some patent offices needs to give way to a strategy in favor of well-delineated and reasonably secure property rights. Paradoxically, this path toward improvements in innovation financing may require cutting down the number of patents granted from currently inflationary numbers to much lower levels.

These suggestions are partly speculative. To advise policy makers and managers more objectively, reliable and objective data as well as sober analysis are needed. In future research, a comprehensive survey of banks could help to measure the extent to which patents are employed as collateral in debt financing. More detailed data on licensing and patent transfers are required to study the development of markets for technology. Moreover, a systematic collection of information on patent funds would be helpful in describing the state of the emerging fund market more reliably.

Summing up, there are some indications that markets for technology have been growing lately. Ultimately, this may lead to improved innovation financing, in particular when measures are taken to make these exchanges more transparent and less prone to opportunistic rent extortion. Such a development would reduce informational asymmetries and quasi-rents, yield lower prices for technology as well as allowing for greater specialization and lower capital costs for innovative firms. This would be welcome news for entrepreneurs, managers and policy makers alike.

ACKNOWLEDGMENTS

I would like to thank Alfonso Gambardella, Bronwyn Hall and Stuart Graham for discussions on the topic of this chapter, and Rosemarie Wilcox for assistance with preparing the manuscript. The chapter builds in part on earlier work with Carolin Häussler and Elisabeth Müller. The usual caveats apply.

NOTES

1. See the discussion in Hall (2009) and Hall and Lerner (2010).
2. As Giuri et al. (2007) show, licensing is indeed relatively rare. See also Gambardella et al. (2007).
3. Firms could also securitize the assets or sell the intellectual property rights and lease them back. The fund activities described in the next subsection can involve securitization. See Jarboe and Furrow (2008) for a discussion of other forms of monetization in the USA. The description given here focuses on the recent European experience.
4. Less recent examples include the British Technology Group (BTG), which was founded in 1995. BTG seeks to commercialize patent rights in the field of pharmaceutical and medical inventions. BTG has been expanding its portfolio by several large-scale acquisitions, e.g. in 2000 when Siemens AG transferred a portfolio of about 1800 patents to BTG.
5. Deutsche Bank has set up three asset-pool funds, starting with Patent Select I in 2006, while Credit Suisse established a blind-pool fund as early as 2004/05. Euram Bank has set up three blind-pool patent funds, starting in 2007. Little is known about fund performance to date; returns from the first fund are supposed to be distributed in 2009/10. Fund volume has been increasing, and minimum investments have been declining from €50000 in 2005 to €10000 in 2008. The total fund volume is currently of the order of €300 million and is expected to grow further. For a practitioner's view on these funds, see Lipfert and Ostler (2008).

6. This is a welfare component of the patent system gaining attention and needing further study. Hall (2007) contains a detailed discussion of the role of patents for start-up firms and for competition.
7. See Harhoff (2006) as well as Guellec and van Pottelsberghe (2007) for a discussion of the issues and the literature.
8. For example, most of the written communication between applicant and examiner is made public in the EPO's file inspection system.
9. See Lanjouw and Schankerman (2001) for the USA. A survey of the literature is included in Harhoff (2009).
10. In May 2006, the US Supreme Court put an end to quasi-automatic injunctions in the US litigation system. These were one of the major instruments used by trolls to exert pressure on presumed infringers. See *eBay Inc v. MercExchange*, L.L.C., 547 U.S. 388(2006).
11. The Czech EU Presidency, in Working Document 5072/09 (Draft Agreement on the European and Community Patents Court and Draft Statute, dated 8 January 2009) proposed a unified patent court to be named the 'European and Community Patents Court'.
12. A more detailed discussion is given in Harhoff (2009).
13. Ellis (2000, p. 22) points out that high litigation costs can significantly distort patent trade and the patent system: 'It is, simply put, that the escalating, indeed skyrocketing litigation costs of the 1970's and 1980's have distorted patent markets and patent economics.' This comment concerns the development in the USA.

REFERENCES

Amit, R., L. Glosten and E. Muller (1990), 'Entrepreneurial ability, venture investments, and risk sharing', *Management Science*, **36**, 1232–45.
Arora, A., A. Fosfuri and A. Gambardella (2001), 'Specialized technology suppliers, international spillovers and investments: evidence from the chemical industry', *Journal of Development Economics*, **65** (1), 31–54.
Arora, A., A. Fosfuri and A. Gambardella (2004), *Markets for Technology: The Economics of Innovation and Corporate Strategy*, Cambridge, MA: MIT Press.
Arora, A. and A. Gambardella (2010), 'Markets for technology', in B. Hall and N. Rosenberg (eds), *Handbook of Economics of Innovation*, Amsterdam: Elsevier, forthcoming.
Athreye, S. and J. Cantwell (2007), 'Creating competition? Globalisation and the emergence of new technology producers', *Research Policy*, **36**, 209–26.
Baum, J.A. and B.S. Silverman (2004), 'Picking winners or building them? Alliance, intellectual, and human capital as selection criteria in venture financing and performance of biotechnology start-ups', *Journal of Business Venturing*, **19**, 411–36.
Bester, H. (1985), 'Screening vs. rationing in credit markets with imperfect information', *American Economic Review*, **75**, 850–55.
BIT (Beteiligungs- & Investitions-Treuhand AG (2008), 'Prospect for Alpha Patent Fund 3', http://basis-plusweb.bit-ag.com/6YXN-NYAD-674Y-PX89/de/beteiligung/downloads/alpha_patentfonds_prospekt.pdf.
Bond, S., D. Harhoff and J. Van Reenen (2005), 'Investment, R&D and financial constraints in Britain and Germany', *Annales d'Économie et de Statistique*, **79/80**, 435–62.
Burhop, C. (2009), 'The transfer of patents in imperial Germany', preprints of the Max Planck Institute for Research on Collective Goods No. 2009/26, Bonn, http://www.coll.mpg.de/pdf_dat/2009_26online.pdf.
Business Week (2006), 'Inside Nathan Myhrvold's mysterious new idea machine', http://www.businessweek.com/print/magazine/content/06_27/b3991401.htm?chan=gl.
Cockburn, I. and S. Wagner (2007), 'Patents and the survival of Internet-related IPOs',. National Bureau of Economic Research, Working Paper No. 13146.
The Economist (2005), 'A market for ideas', Special section, 22 October, pp. 3–6.
Ellis, T.S. (2000), 'Distortion of patent economics by litigation costs: proceedings of the 1999 Summit Conference on intellectual property', University of Washington, Seattle, USA, CASRIP Symposium Publication Series, **5**, pp. 22–26, http://www.law.washington.edu/CASRIP/Symposium/Number5/pub-5atcl3.pdf.
Epstein, R. and M. Pierantozzi (2009), 'Obtaining maximum value from distressed patent assets', *American Bankruptcy Institute Journal*, **28**, 48–51.
Gambardella, A. (2002), 'Successes and failures in the markets for technology', *Oxford Review of Economic Policy*, **18**, 52–62.
Gambardella, A., P. Giuri and A. Luzzi (2007), 'The market for patents in Europe', *Research Policy*, **36**, 1163–83.

Gans, J.S., D.H. Hsu and S. Stern (2002), 'When does start-up innovation spur the gale of creative destruction?', *RAND Journal of Economics*, **33**, 571–86.
Gans, J.S., D.H. Hsu and S. Stern (2008), 'The impact of uncertain intellectual property rights on the market for ideas: evidence from patent grant delays', *Management Science*, **54**, 982–97.
Giuri, P., M. Mariani, S. Brusoni, G. Crespi et al. (2007), 'Inventors and invention processes in Europe: results from the PatVal-EU survey', *Research Policy*, **36**, 1107–27.
Gompers, P. and J. Lerner (2000), *The Venture Capital Cycle*, Cambridge, MA: MIT Press.
Graham, S., R. Merges, P. Samuelson and T. Sichelman (2009), 'High-technology entrepreneurs and the patent system: results of the 2008 Berkeley patent survey', http://ssrn.com/abstract=1429049.
Guellec, D. and B. van Pottelsberghe (2007), *The Economics of the European Patent System: IP Policy for Innovation and Competition*, Oxford: Oxford University Press.
Haagen, F., C. Haeussler, D. Harhoff, G. Murray and B. Rudolph (2007), 'Finding the path to success – the structure and strategies of British and German biotechnology companies', AGBO Report, LMU München.
Haeussler, C., D. Harhoff and E. Mueller (2009), 'To be financed or not . . . – the role of patents for venture capital financing', Centre for Economic Policy Research, London, Discussion Paper No. 7115.
Hall, B.H.H. (2002), 'The financing of research and development', *Oxford Review of Economic Policy*, **18**, 35–51.
Hall, B.H.H. (2009), 'The financing of innovative firms', *EIB Papers*, **14** (2), 9–29.
Hall, B.H.H. (2007), 'Patents and innovation (and competition)', in OECD (ed.), *Competition, Patents and Innovation*, Directorate for financial and enterprise affairs, Competition committee, pp. 243–51.
Hall, B.H.H. and J. Lerner (2010), 'The financing of R&D and innovation', in B. Hall and N. Rosenberg (eds), *Handbook of Economics of Innovation*, Amsterdam: Elsevier, forthcoming.
Hall, B.H.H. and R.H. Ziedonis (2001), 'The patent paradox revisited: an empirical study of patenting in the U.S. semiconductor industry 1979–1995', *RAND Journal of Economics*, **32**, 101–28.
Hall, J. and C. Hofer (1993), 'Venture capitalists' decision criteria in new venture evaluation', *Journal of Business Venturing*, **8**, 25–42.
Harhoff, D. (2006), 'Patent quantity and quality in Europe – trends and policy implications', in B. Kahin and F. Foray (eds), *Advancing Knowledge and the Knowledge Economy*, Cambridge, MA: MIT Press, pp. 331–50.
Harhoff, D. (2009), 'Economic cost–benefit analysis of a unified and integrated European patent litigation system', Final Report to the European Commission, DG Market, No. MARKT/2008/06/D.
Harhoff, D. and S. Wagner (2009), 'The duration of patent examination at the European Patent Office', *Management Science*, **55** (12), 1969–84.
Harhoff, D., K. Hoisl, B. Reichl and B. van Pottelsberghe (2009), 'Patent validation at the country level – the role of fees and translation costs', *Research Policy*, **38**, 1423–37.
Hayes, D.L. (1999), 'What the general intellectual property practitioner should know about patenting business methods', *Computer Lawyer*, **16**, 3–18.
Hsu, D. and R.H. Ziedonis (2008), 'Patents as quality signals for entrepreneurial ventures', *Academy of Management Best Paper Proceedings*.
Jarboe, K.P. and R. Furrow (2008), 'Intangible asset monetization: the promise and the reality', Athena Alliance Working Paper 03, Washington, DC: Athena Alliance, http://www.athenaalliance.org.
Kaplan, S. and P. Strömberg (2003), 'Financial contract theory meets the real world: an empirical analysis of venture capital contracts', *Review of Economic Studies*, **70**, 281–315.
KfW (2007), 'Immaterielle Vermögenswerte und Unternehmensfinanzierung', KfW-Research, Sonderband 'Innovationen im Mittelstand', **37**, 149–65, http://www.kfw.de/DE_Home/Research/Publikatio94/Mittelstan45/Mittelstnd99/Per_39_Periodikum_immat_Sicherheiten_071030_final_online.pdf.
Kortum, S. and J. Lerner (2000), 'Assessing the contribution of venture capital to innovation', *RAND Journal of Economics*, **31**, 674–92.
Lanjouw, J.O. and M. Schankerman (2001), 'Characteristics of patent litigation: a window on competition', *The RAND Journal of Economics*, **32**, 129–51.
Lemley, M.A. (2000), 'Reconceiving patents in the age of venture capital', *Journal of Small and Emerging Business Law*, **4**, 137–48.
Lev, B. (2001), *Intangibles – Management, Measurement, and Reporting*, New York Brookings Institution Press.
Lipfert, S. and J. Ostler (2008), 'Patentverwertungsfonds als effiziente Intermediäre zwischen Kapital- und Patentmarkt', *Mitt. Heft*, **6**, 261–6.
Long, C. (2002), 'Patent signals', *University of Chicago Law Review*, **69**, 625–79.
Mann, R.J. (2005), 'Do patents facilitate financing in the software industry?', *Texas Law Review*, **83**, 961–1030.
Mann, R.J. and T.W. Sager (2007), 'Patents, venture capital, and software start-ups', *Research Policy*, **36**, 193–208.
Maskus, K. (2000), *Intellectual Property Rights in the Global Economy*, Institute for International Economics.
McGinley, C. (2008), 'Taking the heat out of the global patent system', IAM Magazine, July, http://www.iam-magazine.com/issues/Article.ashx?g=6a2efdac-2023-4f35-956b-a9577cd908b9.

Merges, R. (2005), 'A transactional view of property rights', *Berkeley Technology Law Journal*, **20**, 1477–520.

Myers, S.C. and N.S. Majluff (1984), 'Corporate financing and investment decisions when firms have information that investors do not have', *Journal of Financial Economics*, **13**, 187–221.

Opperman, C.P. (2009), 'The elephant in the room', *Intellectual Asset Magazine*, July/August, 53–9.

Regibeau, P. and K. Rockett (2007), 'Are more important patents approved more slowly and should they be?', Centre for Economic Policy Research, London, Discussion Paper No. 6178.

Reitzig, M., J. Henkel and C. Heath (2007), 'On sharks, trolls, and their patent prey – unrealistic damage awards and firms' strategies of "being infringed"', *Research Policy*, **36**, 134–54.

Schlemvogt, T. (2009), 'Wachstumsfinanziening mit Patenten', *IP Manager*, 3 August.

Serrano, C. (2008), 'The dynamics of the transfer and renewal of patents', National Bureau of Economic Research, Working Paper No. 13938.

Zott, C. and Q.N. Huy (2007), 'How entrepreneurs use symbolic management to acquire resources', *Administrative Science Quarterly*, **52**, 70–105.

Zuniga, M. and D. Guellec (2009). 'Who licenses out patents and why? Lessons from a business survey', Organisation for Economic Co-ordination and Development, Paris, STI Working Paper 2009/5.

7 Entry regulation and firm entry: evidence from German reunification

Susanne Prantl

INTRODUCTION

Regulation of firm entry and entry into self-employment is widespread across countries and industries. Many of the relevant rules and laws worldwide have been changed since the beginning of the twenty-first century. Most of the implemented reforms were aimed at increasing entry and competition in order to foster technological progress, economic growth and social welfare (see, e.g., World Bank, 2008, 2009). Concomitantly with these reforms, the empirical literature on the effects of entry regulation has started to grow.

This chapter provides first empirical evidence on the effects of the entry regulation in the German Limited Liability Company Law on firm entry in general and sustained entry, that is the entry of firms that survive for several years after market entry. Identification relies on a substantial natural experiment in entry regulation accompanying German reunification. This empirical investigation is presented along with a survey of recent, methodologically similar studies of the consequences of the entry regulation in the German Trade and Crafts Code on entry into self-employment, sustained entry and the employment that long-living entrants attain several years after market entry.

Germany after reunification is well suited for investigating entry regulation due to the exploitable natural experiment in entry regulation and its strict regulatory setting. The German Limited Liability Company Law implies an expensive and complex incorporation process for limited liability companies; in particular during the 1990s, the observation period of the subsequent empirical analyses, this involved a substantial statutory minimum capital requirement. Sizable statutory minimum capital requirements were then also common in many other European countries, for example in Austria, Denmark and Greece (Becht et al., 2008; World Bank, 2003). Moreover, the German Trade and Crafts Code imposes a costly, mandatory standard, the master craftsman certificate (*Meistertitel*), on entrepreneurs who want to start a legally independent firm in regulated occupations. Similar standards are also applied in some occupations in other European countries, for example in Austria, the Netherlands or Sweden, but the entry regulation in Germany is particularly strict (Monopolkommission, 1998).

After reunification, the same versions of the German Limited Liability Company Law and the German Trade and Crafts Code regulated firm entry and entry into self-employment in both East and West Germany, but entrants faced very different economic conditions in these two regions. In the regulatory context of the East German transition economy with an unexpected, substantial need for industry dynamics and restrictions on the pool of individuals fulfilling the entry requirements imposed in regulated groups (legal forms or occupations), entry regulation should exert stronger effects on entry than in the more stable West German market economy. Building on this conjecture, average effects of the West–East shift in the regulatory context can be estimated by comparing differences between average outcomes in regulated groups and unregulated groups in East Germany after reunification to the corresponding differences in West Germany. In this chapter, I consider regulatory effects on entry in general, sustained entry of firms that survive for several years after market entry and the employment that these long-living entrants attain after their initial years of market activity.

The empirical analyses presented and discussed here relate to the empirical literature on the effects of entry regulation in two respects. First, they extend the literature documenting reductions of firm entry and entry into self-employment in response to entry regulation for different countries, time periods and types of entry regulation. Bruhn (2008), Kaplan et al. (2009) or Mullainathan and Schnabl (2010), for example, provide country-specific micro-data evidence exploiting recent policy reforms to identify such regulatory effects in Mexico and Peru. Ciccone and Papaioannou (2007), Fisman and Sarria-Allende (2004) and Klapper et al. (2006), among others, contribute cross-industry, cross-country evidence by estimating empirical models along the lines of Rajan and Zingales (1998).[1] In this chapter I cover empirical analyses exploiting the substantial natural experiment in entry regulation accompanying German reunification. Entry regulation, based on the German Limited Liability Company Law, is shown to reduce entry after reunification more for incorporated firms in the regulatory context of the East German transition economy than in the more stable West German market economy. The corresponding results of Prantl and Spitz-Oener (2009) are summarized and discussed: post reunification, the entry regulation imposed by the German Trade and Crafts Code lowers entry into self-employment more in regulated occupations in East than in West Germany.

Second, and most importantly, this chapter focuses on the average effects of entry regulation on sustained entry, as opposed to entry in general, and the effects on the employment that long-living entrants attain several years after market entry. Such evidence is relevant in order to explore the specific mechanisms linking entry regulation to technological progress, economic growth and social welfare. It is, however, rarely provided in the literature to date,[2] whereas a larger number of studies offer detailed evidence on the effects of entry regulation on aggregate employment creation and productivity growth in industries and regions, or on the consequences of broader product market deregulation and banking deregulation for industry dynamics.[3] For the entry regulation in the German Limited Liability Company Law, the presented empirical results indicate a negative effect on sustained entry of firms that survive for at least five years after market entry. This finding corresponds to those of Prantl (2010). As shown there, the entry regulation in the German Trade and Crafts Code suppresses not only entrants in general, but also those entrants that have a much higher potential of positively impacting technological progress, economic growth and social welfare. This regulatory effect on the number of long-living entrants is not accompanied by a counteracting effect on the employment attained by these entrants several years after market entry. Altogether, the empirical results presented and discussed in this chapter strengthen the view that the entry regulation under scrutiny here may hinder technological progress as well as economic growth, and may ultimately reduce social welfare.

The next section offers a brief overview of the two types of entry regulation in Germany that are relevant here. In the third section, I summarize and discuss recent evidence on how entry regulation in the German Trade and Crafts Code affects firm entry in general, sustained entry and the employment attained by long-living entrants. The fourth section provides first empirical evidence on the effects of the entry regulation in the German Limited Liability Company Law and the final section concludes.

ENTRY REGULATION IN GERMANY

In Germany, firm entry and entry into self-employment are regulated in many ways. Several geographical entry restrictions are relevant to specific product markets and different laws and regulations imply high administrative entry costs. Djankov et al. (2002) find that starting a domestically owned limited liability firm with standard characteristics in Germany requires the successful completion of ten procedures, taking, on average, 42 business days and costing 15.7 percent of per capita GDP in 1999. In the USA, on the contrary, the respective numbers are substantially lower: four procedures, four business days and 0.5 percent of per capita GDP in 1999. These differences in regulatory entry costs reflect, in part, differences between the German Limited Liability Company Law and US corporate law. Further substantial entry regulation is imposed by the German Trade and Crafts Code. As this chapter centers on these two types of entry regulation, the following paragraphs provide the relevant details.

An entrepreneur who wants to start a new firm in Germany can choose the legal status of the firm, most importantly he can decide whether to incorporate or not. The most common type of corporate firm in Germany, and particularly among small and medium-sized businesses, is the limited liability company (Gesellschaft mit beschränkter Haftung, GmbH). The relevant law is the German Limited Liability Company Law (Gesetz betreffend die Gesellschaften mit beschränkter Haftung, GmbHG).[4] The incorporation process as determined by the GmbHG involves various steps and legal fees. The main requirement during the 1990s, the observation period of the subsequent empirical analyses, is, however, statutory minimum capital of €25 000 (DM 50 000).[5] Altogether, the entry costs imposed on entrants in the group of corporate firms are much higher than those imposed on entrants in the group of non-incorporated firms.

For entrepreneurs of new firms, the core implications of incorporation are limited liability, standardized and facilitated firm (share) transfer in the case of an ownership change and different tax treatment. Firm owners with limited liability are – as regards legal status – liable only up to their firm equity share. Firm owners with full liability in non-incorporated firms risk all their distrainable personal wealth. Accordingly, the main argument usually given for high statutory minimum capital requirements is creditor and customer protection. Opponents argue that other means for protecting creditors or consumers should be preferred as entry costs are expected to suppress firm entry and may consequently reduce innovation, economic growth and social welfare.

The German Trade and Crafts Code (Gesetz zur Ordnung des Handwerks, HwO) imposes a mandatory standard, the master craftsman certificate, on entrants into some, but not all, occupations in Germany. Entrepreneurs wanting to start a legally independent business in one of the regulated occupations are required to have a relevant master craftsman certificate. Regulated occupations are in fields as diverse as metalworking, food, as well as clothing and textiles. In addition, regulated and unregulated occupations can be in similar fields: for example, confectionery and hairdressing are regulated, but ice-cream production and beautician services are not. The master craftsman certificate is an educational degree that an individual can earn after several stages of training, collecting work experience, and taking several exams. Typically, the individual first completes two or three years of apprenticeship (*Lehre* and *Lehrabschluss*). Then he has to work in the occupation for several years and has to earn the related journeyman degree (*Gesellenzeit* and *-brief*). The journeyman degree certifies a high level of vocational training in all occupation-specific tasks and is the prerequisite for admission to the master examination (*Meisterprüfung*). In the master exam, many candidates do not pass (Deregulierungskommission, 1991). Altogether, earning a master craftsman certificate involves not only direct costs, such as fees for preparation courses, but also a substantial investment of time.[6]

Proponents of the entry regulation in the HwO list many benefits; among these are higher average product quality in the regulated markets and surplus vocational training relevant to other sectors of the economy. Opponents stress that individuals with a journeyman degree have a similar occupational qualification to those with a master craftsman certificate. They expect various negative consequences of the entry regulation. For example, the German Monopoly Commission and several other German or EU institutions mention higher product prices, lower production quantities, less entry, lower competition, slower job creation and less innovation (Deregulierungskommission, 1991; Monopolkommission, 1998, 2002).

THE EFFECTS OF THE ENTRY REGULATION IN THE GERMAN TRADE AND CRAFTS CODE

The average effects of the entry regulation in the German Trade and Crafts Code on entry into self-employment, sustained entry and the employment in long-living entrants several years after market entry are investigated by Prantl and Spitz-Oener (2009) and Prantl (2010).

Empirical Approach and Data

A straightforward starting point for estimating these regulatory effects is the comparison of average outcomes in regulated and unregulated occupations. Consider the following estimation equation:

$$Y_{io} = \beta_0 + \beta_1 R_o + X_i' \delta + u_{io} \qquad (7.1)$$

In this equation, the dependent variable is the outcome variable Y, a measure of entry or entrants' employment. Entry regulation is indicated by R. Subscript i indexes individuals, o refers to occupations, and u is the error term. The parameters β_0, β_1 and δ represent the regression coefficients. The vector X includes individual characteristics.

If regulated occupations were randomly selected from the population of occupations, the estimate for the coefficient β_1 would represent the average effect on Y. Systematic, unobserved factors may, however, influence both regulation and the outcome variable of interest. Then, the difference between the average outcomes in regulated and unregulated occupations provides a biased estimate of the average regulatory effect. To account for systematic unobserved factors, Prantl and Spitz-Oener (2009) and Prantl (2010) use the substantial natural experiment in entry regulation accompanying German reunification. The experiment provides data variation across regions and occupations that can be used to control for two types of unobserved effects: (a) additive unobserved effects on the outcome variable Y that differ across the groups of regulated and unregulated occupations while being constant across regions; (b) additive unobserved effects on Y that are common to all occupations, but differ across regions.[7]

The empirical approach builds on the following two main characteristics of German reunification. First, the West German Trade and Crafts Code was extended to East Germany in July 1990 and the elements of the Code regulating firm entry remained essentially unmodified. Since then, the same regulatory rules have applied to the same set of occupations in both German regions. Second, the regions differ fundamentally with respect to the economic context, while falling under the same law. West German market structures were relatively stable after reunification, and opportunities for firm entry opened up on a regular basis due to, for example, random exit of incumbents or incremental technological change. Moreover, the West Germans who held the educational degrees necessary for firm entry in regulated occupations after reunification had chosen their education freely and had access to information on the relevant entry regulation when making that choice. East Germany underwent an unanticipated transition from a planned economy to a market economy after reunification, and new entrepreneurial activities, both firm entry as well as industry restructuring, suddenly dominated. Most East Germans with master craftsman certificates after reunification had earned their degrees under the GDR's planned economy system. At that time, training choices were restricted in various respects and German reunification was unanticipated, including the entrepreneurial opportunities and the regulation of firm entry after reunification.

Entry regulation based on the Trade and Crafts Code is expected to be more binding in East than in West Germany given the unexpected, substantial need for industry dynamics during economic transition and the lower probability that individuals fulfill the entry requirements imposed in regulated occupations in East Germany: stronger effects on firm entry should arise in the regulatory context of the East German transition economy than in the context of the more stable West German market economy.

Comparing the difference between the average outcomes of interest in regulated and unregulated occupations in East Germany after reunification to the corresponding difference in West Germany provides an estimate of the average effect of the West–East shift in the regulatory context in regulated occupations. As outcome variables, Prantl and Spitz-Oener (2009) and Prantl (2010) consider entry indicators and a measure of entrants' employment. The estimation equations are as follows:

$$Y_{ior} = \beta_0 + \beta_1 R_o + \beta_2 E_r + \beta_3 R_o \cdot E_r + X_i'\delta + u_{ior} \tag{7.2}$$

$$Y_{ior} = \beta_0 + \gamma_o + \beta_2 E_r + \beta_3 R_o \cdot E_r + X_i'\delta + u_{ior} \tag{7.3}$$

In these equations, E indicates East Germany, β_2 is the related regression coefficient, and r indexes regions. All other variables and parameters are defined as above. Equation (7.3) represents a more flexible model specification than equation (7.2); it includes occupation fixed effects denoted by γ_o. These occupation effects account for unobserved occupation-specific determinants of the outcome variable Y and, thus, for systematic variation in the occupational composition of the group of regulated occupations across regions, or of the group of unregulated occupations. The set of occupation effects represents a flexible replacement for the level effect of entry regulation (equivalent to β_1 in equation (7.2) which averages across all the regulated occupations).[8]

Most important in equations (7.2) and (7.3) is β_3, the coefficient of the interaction between entry regulation R and East Germany E. From the exposition above, it follows that β_3 reflects the average effect of the West–East shift in the regulatory context on the considered outcome variable in the regulated occupations.

The data come from a large survey that has been carried out repeatedly since 1978 by the German Federal Institute for Vocational Training (Bundesinstitut für Berufsbildung, BIBB) and the Research Institute of the Federal Employment Service (Institut für Arbeitsmarkt- und Berufsforschung, IAB). Approximately every six to seven years, these institutions collect data for the 'Qualification and Career Survey' using representative, unlinked cross-sections of about 30 000 employed individuals. Prantl and Spitz-Oener (2009) use the survey waves launched in 1985/86, 1991/92 and 1998/99. Prantl (2010) uses the survey wave 1998/99 only. This wave includes self-employed individuals in East and West Germany who started self-employment after reunification (up to nine years before the survey was taken), and it provides information on the employment in these firms at the time of the survey.

The main dependent variable in Prantl and Spitz-Oener (2009) is a general entry indicator: it is coded one for individuals who are self-employed at the time of the survey and started that activity after 1989. Prantl (2010) focuses on a more specific indicator of sustained entry: it is coded one for self-employed individuals in 1998/99 with a venture that they started at least five years earlier, but after 1989. The main firm size variable distinguishes six size classes: (a) 1 employed individual (including working entrepreneur), (b) 2, (c) 3 or 4, (d) 5 to 9, (e) 10 to 49 employed individuals, and (f) 50 or more employed individuals. The main explanatory variables are dummy variables for entry regulation, East Germany and the interaction of these variables (R, E and $R*E$). Entry regulation is coded one for individuals in occupations with entry regulation, otherwise zero, using survey data on the occupation individuals currently work in and information from the German Trade and Crafts Code as enforced during the 1990s. The dummy variable for East Germany indicates current residence in East Germany. To capture influences of individual heterogeneity on the dependent variables, demographic and educational variables are used for vector X.

Estimation Results

Implementing the empirical approach described above, Prantl and Spitz-Oener (2009) investigate how the mandatory standard imposed on entrepreneurs influences a general measure of entry into self-employment.[9] They find negative and significant estimates for the coefficient of the interaction between entry regulation and East Germany in equations explaining the probability of being self-employed with a venture started after 1989.[10] The result suggests that entry regulation reduces a general measure of entry into self-employment more in regulated occupations in the regulatory context of the East German transition economy than in the context of the more stable West German economy.

Prantl and Spitz-Oener (2009) provide additional evidence supporting the view that their basic finding depends crucially on entry costs in the form of the mandatory master craftsman certificate. The regulatory effects on entry into self-employment are stronger among individuals who should be more restricted in their entrepreneurial choices than others as a result of these entry costs. Such individuals did not enter their current occupation with their initial training, and thus had, *ceteris paribus*, less time to earn the relevant occupation-specific educational degrees than individuals who never changed their occupation.

Furthermore, the estimated effect on the general entry measure is robust in model specifications that allow for exploring the relevance of additional factors varying across occupations and regions. These are, in particular, occupation-specific demand shocks in West Germany, occupation-specific restructuring requirements in East Germany, occupation- and region-specific levels of incumbent self-employment started before reunification, and skill structures that are heterogeneous across industries and regions.

The findings for the general measure of entry into self-employment raise two important questions. Does more entry in the case of no or less such regulation imply more technological progress, higher economic growth and higher social welfare? What are the specific mechanisms linking entry regulation to technological progress, growth and welfare?

Prantl (2010) takes a first step toward answering these broad questions by investigating the effects of the entry regulation in the German Trade and Crafts Code on a specific entry measure – sustained entry by firms that survive for several years after market entry – and on the employment that these long-living entrants attain. The empirical results indicate that the entry regulation reduces the probability of being self-employed in 1998/99 with a venture that was started after reunification and sustained for at least five years to a stronger extent in regulated occupations in the East German transition context after reunification than in the West German context.[11] This finding suggests that the entry regulation suppresses long-living entrants and, thus, that the finding of Prantl and Spitz-Oener (2009) for entry in general cannot be driven by transient, short-living entrants only. Transient entrants are more likely than other, longer-living entrants to cause welfare losses that a social planner or regulator may try to reduce. Welfare losses can, in particular, arise in the case of repetitive market experimentation of similar entrants. The group of long-living entrants, instead, includes entrants that have grown successfully after entry. These entrants have not only created new jobs; they may innovate successfully, may displace inefficient incumbents or foster efficiency improvements and innovation in incumbents, and should have a much higher potential of positively impacting technological progress, economic growth and social welfare than transient, short-living entrants. In addition, the regulatory effects on the probability of sustained entry into self-employment and, thus, the number of long-living entrants are not found to be accompanied by a counteracting effect on the employment attained by long-living entrants in 1998/99. As the average firm size in the group of long-living entrants remains unaffected, there is no indication of entry regulation causing higher contributions per group member to technological progress, economic growth and social welfare.

Altogether, these empirical results strengthen the view that the entry regulation imposed by the German Trade and Crafts Code may hinder technological progress as well as economic growth, and it may ultimately reduce social welfare.

THE EFFECTS OF THE ENTRY REGULATION IN THE GERMAN LIMITED LIABILITY COMPANY LAW

This section addresses how the entry regulation in the German Limited Liability Company Law impacts entry and sustained entry in regulated firm groups using the substantial natural experiment in entry regulation accompanying German reunification.

The West German version of the Limited Liability Company Law was extended to East Germany in May 1990 (Vertrag über die Schaffung einer Währungs-, Wirtschafts- und Sozialunion, 18 May 1990), and since then, the same rules have applied to both German regions, except for the temporarily lower statutory minimum capital requirement in East Germany (see note 5). As explained earlier, West Germany had relatively stable market structures after reunification and firms entered on a rather regular basis, but East Germany represented a region in economic transition with substantial industry restructuring and unusually high firm entry. Potential East German entrepreneurs were more likely to be financially constrained than potential West German entrepreneurs. Throughout the 1990s, housing and financial wealth in East German households was substantially lower than in West German households (Deutsche Bundesbank, 1999; Fuchs-Schündeln and Schündeln, 2005). In addition, no one anticipated German reunification. East Germans suddenly faced the new entrepreneurial opportunities and the regulation of entry after reunification without having had time to prepare, including accumulating preparatory savings.

Building on these differences between East and West Germany, I conjecture that the incorporation costs reduce entry more in the regulated group of incorporated firms in East German counties than in West German counties. Following a similar empirical approach as described earlier, the effects of the West–East shift in the regulatory context can be identified by comparing differences between regulated and unregulated legal form groups in East German counties to the corresponding differences in West German counties.

For the subsequent empirical analysis, two different measures of firm entry are calculated using a large firm sample with 5788 East and 6652 West German firms entering between May 1990 and December 1993. The underlying raw data consist of two stratified random samples with 10 000 East and 12 000 West German firms that were drawn from two complementary firm databases at the Centre of European Economic Research in Mannheim. Additional firm information was extracted from extensive free-flow text material and collected in a large telephone survey (see Prantl, 2003 for details). Firm records contain, in particular, comprehensive information on firm entry and exit events. Data on the population density at the level of counties (*Stadt-* and *Landkreise*) in 1992 come from the Federal Office for Building and Regional Planning (Bundesamt für Bauwesen und Raumordnung). Entry is measured as the general entry rate per county and legal form group: the number of entrants in a county and legal form group per 1000 inhabitants in that county who are between 18 and 65 years old and are considered as the

Table 7.1   Incorporation law and firm entry after reunification

	1 East Germany	2 West Germany	3 Difference within legal form groups between regions	4 Difference- in-difference
1 Entry rate, incorporated firms	1.642 (0.057)	0.630 (0.023)	1.012 (0.061)	
2 Entry rate, non-incorporated firms	4.346 (0.101)	1.341 (0.038)	3.005 (0.108)	
3 Difference between legal form groups within regions	−2.704 (0.112)	−0.711 (0.039)		−1.993 (0.118)

Notes: The table shows averages of the general entry rates of incorporated and non-incorporated firms that started between May 1990 and December 1993 in 215 East German and 326 West German counties. The general entry rate is defined as the number of entrants between May 1990 and December 1993 per working age population (in thousands) in the county. In addition, the average general entry rate differences within legal form groups between regions, the differences between legal form groups within regions and the difference-in-difference estimate are also shown. Standard errors are reported in parentheses.

Table 7.2   Incorporation law and sustained firm entry after reunification

	1 East Germany	2 West Germany	3 Difference within legal form groups between regions	4 Difference- in-difference
1 Sustained entry rate, incorporated firms	1.259 (0.050)	0.484 (0.020)	0.775 (0.054)	
2 Sustained entry rate, non-incorporated firms	3.465 (0.093)	1.093 (0.034)	2.372 (0.099)	
3 Difference between legal form groups within regions	−2.206 (0.104)	−0.609 (0.036)		−1.597 (0.110)

Notes: The table shows averages of the sustained entry rates of incorporated and non-incorporated firms that started between May 1990 and December 1993 and survived at least five years in 215 East German and 326 West German counties. The sustained entry rate is defined as the number of entrants between May 1990 and December 1993 that survived at least five years per working age population (in thousands) in the county. In addition, the average sustained entry rate differences within legal form groups between regions, the differences between legal form groups within regions and the difference-in-difference estimate are also shown. Standard errors are reported in parentheses.

pool of potential entrepreneurs. The sustained entry rate refers to entrants that survived at least five years.

Tables 7.1 and 7.2 provide empirical evidence on how the entry regulation in the German Limited Liability Company Law influences the general firm entry rate and the sustained entry rate. Regression analyses using similar models as in equations (7.2) and (7.3) are part of a currently ongoing project and the regression results confirm the findings presented here.

The four cells in the first two columns and rows of Table 7.1 provide county-level averages of the general entry rate of incorporated and non-incorporated firms in East and West Germany. At the right and lower margins of Table 7.1, differences and the difference-in-difference are shown. The upper cell in column 3 shows the difference between the average rate of incorporated entrants in East and in West Germany; the bottom cell in column 3 displays the corresponding difference for the firm group of non-incorporated entrants. Row 3 shows the differences between firm groups within regions and in column 4 the difference-in-difference, calculated as the difference between the two differences on the left-hand side of row 3 (or between the two differences in column 3).

The difference results in column 3 illustrate that economic transition in East Germany goes along with unusually high levels of firm entry: in the group of incorporated entrants the difference between East and West Germany is 1, as, on average, 1.6 incorporated firms enter per 1000 working age inhabitants in East German counties between May 1990 and December 1993 and 0.6 such entrants in West German counties. In addition, the average rate of non-incorporated entrants in East German counties is also higher than in West German counties.

The main finding is the negative and statistically significant difference-in-difference result: the entry regulation in the German Limited Liability Company Law reduces the general entry rate in the group of incorporated firms on average by about two firms more in East than in West Germany. In line with expectations, the average effect of the shift in the regulatory context is negative and the entry regulation binds more in East than in West Germany.

For sustained entry, Table 7.2 indicates that the corresponding difference-in-difference is also negative and statistically significant. Accordingly, the entry regulation in the German Limited Liability Company Law not only suppresses the general entry rate more in the group of incorporated firms in East than in West Germany, but also the rate of long-living entrants with the ability to sustain at least five years of market activity.

CONCLUSIONS

This chapter focuses on empirical evidence regarding the effects of entry regulation in Germany on entry in general, sustained entry of firms that survive for several years after market entry, as well as employment attained by long-living entrants. Germany at the dawn of the twenty-first century is well suited for studying entry regulation: the regulatory framework is restrictive and regulatory effects can be identified from the substantial, natural experiment in entry regulation accompanying German reunification. Two distinct types of entry regulation are considered: (1) the German Limited Liability Company Law, which implies an expensive and complex incorporation process for limited liability companies with a substantial statutory minimum capital requirement during the 1990s, the observation period of the empirical analysis; (2) the German Trade and Crafts Code, which imposes a costly, mandatory standard, the master craftsman certificate, on entrepreneurs who want to start a legally independent firm in regulated occupations.

The empirical results presented here indicate that entry regulation based on the

German Limited Liability Company Law reduces the general entry rate after reunification more for incorporated firms in the regulatory context of the East German transition economy than in the context of the more stable West German market economy. This corresponds to the related finding of a stronger reduction of entry into self-employment after reunification in regulated occupations in East than in West Germany in response to the entry regulation imposed by the German Trade and Crafts Code. Both types of entry regulation not only reduce entry in general, but also entry of firms that survive for at least five years after market entry. Not only are transient, short-living entrants suppressed, but also long-living entrants that have a much higher potential of positively impacting technological progress, economic growth and social welfare. In case of the entry regulation in the German Trade and Crafts Code, the regulatory effect on the number of long-living entrants does not go along with a counteracting effect on the employment of long-living entrants several years after market entry. Altogether, the empirical results presented and discussed in this chapter strengthen the view that the entry regulations studied here may hinder technological progress as well as economic growth, and may ultimately reduce social welfare.

ACKNOWLEDGMENTS

I wish to thank Philippe Aghion, Ulrike Böhme, Jan Boone, Richard Blundell, Tomaso Duso, Bernd Fitzenberger, Nicola Fuchs-Schündeln, Michael Fritsch, Adam Lederer, Rachel Griffith, Paul Heidhues, Martin Hellwig, Jennifer Hunt, Markus Nöth and Alexandra Spitz-Oener for helpful comments and discussions. Brian Cooper and Christoph Wigger provided excellent editorial support and research assistance. All remaining errors are my responsibility.

NOTES

1. Djankov (2009) and Schiantarelli (2008) survey further related studies.
2. Related are, however, Ardagna and Lusardi (2010), Bruhn (2010), Capelleras et al. (2008) and Kaplan et al. (2009).
3. Examples are, among others, Aghion et al. (2009), Bertrand and Kramarz (2002), Bertrand et al. (2007), Cetorelli and Strahan (2006), Chari (2008), Kerr and Nanda (2009), Sadun (2008) and Viviano (2008).
4. The limited liability company is a type of a non-public corporate company and, as such, much more important in Germany than in Anglo-Saxon countries (Harhoff et al., 1998). The GmbH is often used in group structures and is a constituting element of the limited commercial partnership that combines corporate and non-corporate entities (GmbH & Compagnie Kommanditgesellschaft, GmbH & Co. KG). Besides the GmbH, other forms of corporate companies are the stock company (Aktiengesellschaft) and the commercial partnership limited by shares (KG auf Aktien), but these legal forms are rarely chosen for new firms. The most common non-incorporated legal form among new firms is the sole proprietorship (Einzelunternehmung, Gewerbebetrieb). In addition, there are the civil law association (Gesellschaft bürgerlichen Rechts) and commercial partnerships (KG, Offene Handelsgesellschaft).
5. The GmbHG allows for allotting (a share of) the required statutory minimum capital in other form than cash, for example in form of adequate firm assets (GmbHG, §5(4) and §9c(1)). In addition, the statutory minimum capital requirement was temporarily, between July 1990 and July 1992, lowered to €10 000 for firms in East Germany.
6. The German Trade and Crafts Code dates back to the end of the nineteenth century, when parts of the historic guild system became institutionalized as a first backlash to the introduction of the freedom of trade in the German Reich. The master craftsman certificate was first imposed only on individuals who

wanted to train apprentices in a regulated occupation, but in 1935 it became relevant to all individuals wanting to start a legally independent business in an occupation covered by the Code. After the Second World War, the West German Trade and Crafts Code of 1953 confirmed the master craftsman certificate as an entry requirement in the Federal Republic of Germany (FRG) in the region of West Germany. The planned economy system of the German Democratic Republic (GDR) in East Germany enforced strict entry regulation for all occupations, also keeping, in a rather *pro forma* manner, an entry regulation that was derived from the German Trade and Crafts Code before the Second World War and the respective educational degrees. Owing to the same historical origins, the set of occupations with Code-based regulation in East Germany was similar to that in West Germany. As the reunification treaty recognized all educational degrees earned in the GDR, East Germans with a GDR master craftsman certificate met the formal requirement relevant for running a business in the respective regulated occupation immediately following reunification. This is important for the empirical analyses discussed below, as the regulatory effects should otherwise be even larger than reported there.

7. The empirical approach is similar to a standard difference-in-difference approach due to the natural experiment in entry regulation that is exploited and the two types of fixed effects that are allowed for (Angrist and Pischke, 2009; Blundell and MaCurdy, 1999; Blundell and Costa Dias, 2009). The average effect of the regulatory change on treated individuals is estimated, and this effect is equivalent to the average effect on the population if individuals' responses to the regulatory change are homogeneous or if individuals with heterogeneous responses are randomly assigned to treatment.

8. As Prantl and Spitz-Oener (2009) use data from two survey waves, they allow for wave-specific occupation effects.

9. Prantl and Spitz-Oener (2009) also study the regulatory effects on occupational mobility among workers. Entry regulation is found to reduce occupational mobility after reunification more in regulated occupations in East than in West Germany, and this result is explained by entry regulation hampering entry and competition more in regulated occupations in the East than in the West.

10. The authors focus on linear probability estimates for a sample of about 27000 employed individuals surveyed in 1991/92 or 1998/99. Linear probability estimates are preferred, in line with Angrist and Pischke (2009) or Wooldridge (2002), and are shown to be similar to average marginal effect estimates as computed from non-linear probit estimates along the lines of Ai and Norton (2003) and Norton et al. (2004).

11. The main result follows from linear probability estimates for a sample of about 15600 employed individuals surveyed in 1998/99.

REFERENCES

Aghion, P., R. Blundell, R. Griffith, P. Howitt and S. Prantl (2009), 'The effects of entry on incumbent innovation and productivity', *Review of Economics and Statistics*, **91** (1), 20–32.

Ai, C. and E.C. Norton (2003), 'Interaction terms in logit and probit models', *Economics Letters*, **80** (1), 123–9.

Angrist, J.D. and J.-St. Pischke (2009), *Mostly Harmless Econometrics: An Empiricist's Companion*, Princeton, NJ: Princeton University Press.

Ardagna, S. and A. Lusardi (2010), 'Explaining international differences in entrepreneurship: the role of individual characteristics and regulatory constraints', in J. Lerner and A. Schoar (eds), *International Differences in Entrepreneurship*, Chicago, IL: University of Chicago Press, pp. 17–62.

Becht, M., C. Mayer and H.F. Wagner (2008), 'Where do firms incorporate? Deregulation and the cost of entry', *Journal of Corporate Finance*, **14** (3), 241–56.

Bertrand, M. and F. Kramarz (2002), 'Does entry regulation hinder job creation? Evidence from the French retail industry', *Quarterly Journal of Economics*, **117** (4), 1369–413.

Bertrand, M., A. Schoar and D. Thesmar (2007), 'Banking deregulation and industry structure: evidence from the French banking reforms of 1985', *Journal of Finance*, **62** (2), 597–628.

Blundell, R. and M. Costa Dias (2009), 'Alternative approaches to evaluation in empirical microeconomics', *Journal of Human Resources*, **44** (3), 565–40.

Blundell, R. and T. MaCurdy (1999), 'Labour supply: a review of alternative approaches', in O. Ashenfelter and D. Card (eds), *Handbook of Labor Economics*, 3, Elsevier, Amsterdam, pp. 1559–695.

Bruhn, M. (2010), 'License to sell: the effect of business registration reform on entrepreneurial activity in Mexico', forthcoming in: *Review of Economics and Statistics*; online at doi: 10.1162/REST_a_00059.

Capelleras, J.-L., K.F. Mole, F.J. Greene and D.J. Storey (2008), 'Do more heavily regulated economies have poorer performing new ventures? Evidence from Britain and Spain', *Journal of International Business Studies*, **39** (4), 688–704.

Cetorelli, N. and P.E. Strahan (2006), 'Finance as a barrier to entry: bank competition and industry structure in local U.S. markets', *Journal of Finance*, **61** (1), 437–61.
Chari, A.V. (2008), 'The aggregate productivity effects of entry and output restrictions: an analysis of license reform in India', mimeo, Ithaca, NY: Cornell University, December.
Ciccone, A. and E. Papaioannou (2007), 'Red tape and delayed entry', *Journal of the European Economic Association*, **5** (2–3), 444–58.
Deregulierungskommission (1991), *Marktöffnung und Wettbewerb*, Gutachten der Unabhängigen Experten-kommission zum Abbau marktwidriger Regulierungen, Stuttgart, Germany: Pöschel Verlag.
Deutsche Bundesbank (1999), 'Zur Entwicklung der privaten Vermögenssituation seit Beginn der neunziger Jahre', *Monatsbericht Januar 1999*, **51** (9), Frankfurt am Main, 33–50.
Djankov, S. (2009), 'The regulation of entry: a survey', *World Bank Research Observer*, **24** (2), 183–203.
Djankov, S., R. La Porta, F. Lopez-De-Silanes and A. Shleifer (2002), 'The regulation of entry', *Quarterly Journal of Economics*, **117** (1), 1–37.
Fisman R. and V. Sarria-Allende (2004), 'Regulation of entry and the distortion of industrial organization', NBER Working Paper No. 10929, Cambridge, MA: National Bureau of Economic Research.
Fuchs-Schündeln, N. and M. Schündeln (2005), 'Precautionary savings and self-selection: evidence from the German reunification "Experiment"', *Quarterly Journal of Economics*, **120** (3), 1085–120.
Gesetz betreffend die Gesellschaften mit beschränkter Haftung, *Bundesgesetzblatt* (III, Gliederungsnummer 4123-1), as changed on 15 May 1986 (*Bundesgesetzblatt*, 1986 (I, 21), 721–9).
Gesetz zu dem Vertrag vom 18. Mai 1990 über die Schaffung einer Währungs-, Wirtschafts- und Sozialunion zwischen der Bundesrepublik Deutschland und der Deutschen Demokratischen Republik (1990), *Bundesgesetzblatt*, 1990 (II, 20), 518–68.
Gesetz zur Ordnung des Handwerks (Handwerksordnung), *Bundesgesetzblatt*, 1966 (I, 1), 1–33, as changed on 24 April 1986 (*Bundesgesetzblatt*, 1986 (I, 17), 560–68) and on 19 March 1989 (*Bundesgesetzblatt*, 1989 (I, 15), 551).
Harhoff, D., K. Stahl and M. Woywode (1998), 'Legal form, growth and exit of West German firms – empirical results for manufacturing, construction, trade and service industries', *The Journal of Industrial Economics*, **46** (4), 453–88.
Kaplan, D.S., E. Piedra and E. Seira (2009), 'Entry regulation and business start-ups: evidence from Mexico', mimeo, Washington, DC: The World Bank, August.
Kerr, W.R. and R. Nanda (2009), 'Democratizing entry: banking deregulations, financing constraints, and entrepreneurship', *Journal of Financial Economics*, **94** (1), 124–49.
Klapper, L., L. Laeven and R. Rajan (2006), 'Entry regulation as a barrier to entrepreneurship', *Journal of Financial Economics*, **82** (3), 591–629.
Monopolkommission (1998), *Marktöffnung umfassend verwirklichen*, 12. Hauptgutachten der Monopolkom-mission 1996/97, Baden-Baden, Germany: Nomos Verlag.
Monopolkommission (2002), *Reform der Handwerksordnung*, 31. Sondergutachten der Monopolkommission, Baden-Baden, Germany: Nomos Verlag.
Mullainathan, S. and P. Schnabl (2010), 'Does less market entry regulation generate more entrepreneurs? Evidence from a regulatory reform in Peru', in J. Lerner and A. Schoar (eds), *International Differences in Entrepreneurship*, Chicago, IL: University of Chicago Press, pp. 159–77.
Norton, E.C., H. Wang and C. Ai (2004), 'Computing interaction effects and standard errors in logit and probit models', *Stata Journal*, **4** (2), 154–67.
Prantl, S. (2003), 'Bankruptcy and voluntary liquidation: evidence for new firms in East and West Germany after unification', ZEW Discussion Paper No. 03-72, Mannheim: Centre for European Economic Studies.
Prantl S. (2010), 'The impact of entry regulation on long-living entrants', forthcoming in *Small Business Economics*; online at doi:10.1007/s11187-010-9293-4.
Prantl, S. and A. Spitz-Oener (2009), 'How does entry regulation influence entry into self-employment and occupational mobility?', *Economics of Transition*, **17** (4), 769–802.
Rajan, R.G. and L. Zingales (1998), 'Financial dependence and growth', *American Economic Review*, **88** (3), 559–86.
Sadun, R. (2008), 'Does planning regulation protect independent retailers?', CEP Discussion Paper No. 888, London: Centre for Economic Performance.
Schiantarelli, F. (2008), 'Product market regulation and macroeconomic performance: a review of cross-country evidence', Boston College Working Papers in Economics 623, first version 2005, Boston, MA: Boston College.
Viviano, E. (2008), 'Entry regulations and labour market outcomes: evidence from the Italian retail trade sector', *Labour Economics*, **15** (6), 1200–22.
Wooldridge, J.M. (2002), *Econometric Analysis of Cross Section and Panel Data*, Cambridge, MA: MIT Press.

World Bank (2003), *Doing Business in 2004 – Understanding Regulations*, Washington, DC: The World Bank.
World Bank (2008), *Doing Business 2009*, Washington, DC: The World Bank.
World Bank (2009), *Doing Business 2010 – Reforming through Difficult Times*, Washington, DC: The World Bank (www.doingbusiness.org).

8 Financing constraints and entrepreneurship
William R. Kerr and Ramana Nanda

INTRODUCTION

Surveys of current and potential entrepreneurs suggest that obtaining adequate access to capital is one of the biggest hurdles to starting and growing a new business. Given the important role that entrepreneurship is believed to play in the process of creative destruction – and hence economic growth – it is not surprising that attempts to alleviate financing constraints for would-be entrepreneurs is an important goal for policy makers across the world. For example, the US Small Business Administration funded or assisted in the funding of about 200 000 loans in fiscal year 2007, at an administrative cost of about $1000 per loan (SBA, 2008). Financial assistance for entrepreneurs is also high on the agenda in the European Union and the OECD, where member states are urged to promote the availability of risk capital financing for entrepreneurs (OECD, 2004).

The underlying premise behind these policies is that there are important frictions in the credit markets precluding high-quality entrepreneurs with good ideas (i.e. positive net present value projects) from entering product markets because they are unable to access adequate capital to start a new business. Much of the academic literature has therefore focused on analyzing the nature of these frictions, the effect they have on access to finance, and the impact of reduced financing constraints on rates of entrepreneurship.

This chapter reviews two major streams of work examining the relevance of financing constraints for entrepreneurship. The first research stream considers the impact of financial market development on entrepreneurship. These papers usually employ variations across regions to examine how differences in observable characteristics of financial sectors (e.g. the level of competition among banks, the depth of credit markets) relate to entrepreneurs' access to finance and realized rates of firm formation. The second stream employs variations across individuals to examine how propensities to start new businesses relate to personal wealth or recent changes therein. The notion behind this second line of research is that an association of individual wealth and the propensity for self-employment or firm creation should be observed only if financial constraints for entrepreneurship exist.

These two streams of research have remained mostly separate literatures within economics, driven in large part by the different levels of analysis. Historically their general results have been mostly complementary. More recently, however, empirical research using individual-level variation has questioned the extent to which financing constraints are important for entrepreneurship in advanced economies. This new work argues that the strong associations between the financial resources of individuals and entrepreneurship observed in previous studies are driven to a large extent by unobserved heterogeneity rather than substantive financing constraints. These contrarian studies have led to renewed interest and debate in how financing environments impact entrepreneurship in product markets.

This chapter begins with an overview of the main findings of these two research streams. We highlight the areas where they seem to pose a puzzle based on potentially contradictory implications. We then develop a framework that can reconcile these contradictory findings and outline a set of implications for ongoing research and policy analysis in the area of financing constraints and entrepreneurship.[1]

FINANCIAL MARKET DEVELOPMENT AND ENTREPRENEURSHIP

Metrics of financial market development quantify the ease with which individuals in need of external finance can access the required capital and the premium they pay for these funds. The role entrepreneurship plays in linking a country's financial market development to its subsequent economic growth is highlighted by King and Levine (1993a, 1993b) and Levine (1997). Their work highlighted the role of finance in Schumpeter's creative destruction, whereby entrepreneurs with new ideas and technologies displace incumbents with old technologies, leading to a continued increase in productivity and economic growth. This contrasts with the view, put forth by Joan Robinson and others, that development of financial sectors and institutions simply follows economic growth.

Central to this idea is the notion that a large fraction of the productivity growth in the economy may take place at the extensive margin (e.g. the birth of new firms, the closure of unproductive firms) rather than at the intensive margin (e.g. firms becoming more productive internally). Since most start-ups need to raise capital in order to implement their new ideas, cross-sectional differences in the ability of capital markets to select and finance the most promising entrepreneurs may lead to important differences in entrepreneurship and productivity growth across economies (Greenwood and Jovanovic, 1990; Jayaratne and Strahan, 1996; Levine, 1997; Beck et al., 2000; Guiso et al., 2004).

Thus a growing line of research has examined the sources of friction in the capital markets that may lead to financing constraints (or the misallocation of capital more broadly) and hence negatively impact productivity growth. In the following subsections, we outline three important mechanisms through which frictions in the capital markets lead to financing constraints for entrepreneurs.

Financial Market Depth

Perhaps the most important factor governing the ability of startups to raise sufficient capital for their projects is the depth of the local capital markets. This depth is therefore a natural starting point for measuring financial market development for funding new capital-intensive projects, through metrics like the ratio of bank deposits to GDP or stock market capitalization to GDP. For example, Rajan and Zingales (1998) show that industrial sectors with a greater need for external finance develop faster in countries with deeper capital markets. Fisman and Love (2003) find that, in particular, startup firms struggle to overcome weaknesses in financial market development, even where established firms are able to use trade credit as a substitute for formal financing. Comin and Nanda (2009) show how the difficulties faced by startups in raising capital might adversely impact the commercialization of new technologies. Using historical data on banking-sector development and technology diffusion, they find that capital-intensive technologies are adopted much faster relative to less capital-intensive technologies in countries that are over a certain threshold in banking-sector development.

Why do some regions have greater financial depth than others? The lack of financial market liquidity has been traced to several related factors. At the most basic level, the willingness of financial intermediaries to lend to entrepreneurs (and the willingness of depositors to save with intermediaries) depends on financial and securities laws in a country. For example, La Porta et al. (1997, 1998) and Beck et al. (2001) trace the relationships between the legal origins of financial market laws across countries and relate them to the degree of investor protection and hence the ability of financial intermediaries to raise and lend capital. Paravisini (2008) shows in the context of Argentina that banks not only face frictions in their access to external financing, but that these frictions prevent them from undertaking profitable investment opportunities in the real economy. Banerjee and Duflo (2008) have similar findings in the context of a directed lending program in India.

While the issues of financial market depth may be particularly acute in emerging markets, startups in advanced economies are not immune to these issues. For example, Berkowitz and White (2004) find that entrepreneurs are less likely to get credit for their startups in US states with stronger bankruptcy protection for individuals. When banks are less certain of recovering their loans in the event that a startup fails, they are less likely to extend credit in the first place. Guiso et al. (2004) examine local variation in the supply of credit across regions in Italy. They find that even in a well-developed and integrated financial market like Italy, regions with deeper capital markets promote the entry and growth of new firms and increase the propensity of individuals to start new businesses.

These findings are important in that they underscore the importance of local capital markets for entrepreneurship. The degree of asymmetric information associated with small, entrepreneurial ventures is very high. As a result, the intermediaries best able to overcome the costs of screening and monitoring these ventures are often local. Deep, national capital markets alone may not be sufficient to alleviate financing constraints for startups.

The importance of access to local finance seems equally relevant for venture capital (VC) financing as it is for bank financing. Sorenson and Stuart (2001) find that VC firms are much more likely to fund entrepreneurs located within a short geographic distance from where they are based (or to provide funding on the condition that entrepreneurs move closer to the VC firms). Similarly, Black and Gilson (1998) relate the lack of a large biotechnology industry in Germany to the local institutional environment for VCs. They argue that the institutional environment in Germany, which is more bank oriented compared to the USA's market orientation, reduces the ability of German startups to achieve liquidity events via stock listings. As a consequence, the VC community in Germany is less developed, and the flow of risk capital to good biotechnology projects in Germany is weaker. Other studies find that VC investors appear particularly effective in funding innovative startups (Kortum and Lerner, 2000) and that the ebbs and flows in the capital markets may have important consequences for rates of innovation in the economy (Nanda and Rhodes-Kropf, 2009).

While capital market depth is a key factor impacting the ability of entrepreneurs to finance their startups, the organization of the financial sector can also have profound effects on financing constraints for potential entrepreneurs. In the next two subsections, we explore two related dimensions in which the organization of the financial sector can impact startup activity – the level of competition between financial intermediaries and the internal structure of the financial intermediaries.

Competition between Financial Intermediaries

The level of competition between financial intermediaries can impact the terms of credit to startups as well as the degree to which capital is allocated to the highest-quality projects (Levine, 1997). This issue is particularly acute in developing countries where the banking system may be subject to political capture (Banerjee et al., 2003; Cole, 2009). However, bank deregulation is shown to have first-order effects on the *ex ante* allocation of capital to large firms in France (Bertrand et al., 2007) and on entrepreneurship in the USA (Black and Strahan, 2002; Kerr and Nanda, 2009a, 2009b). For example, Bertrand et al. (2007) find that banks were less willing to bail out poorly performing firms in the product markets after the French banking reforms of 1985. As a result, French firms in sectors with a greater reliance on bank finance were more likely to restructure.

The US branch banking deregulations provide a particularly useful laboratory to study the effect of bank competition on entrepreneurship. Prior to liberalization, US banks faced multiple restrictions on geographic expansion both within and across states. The most restrictive of these, known as unit banking, limited each bank to a single branch. From the 1970s through the mid-1990s, banks experienced significant liberalization in the ability to establish branches and to expand across state lines, either through new branches or through acquisitions.

Greater bank competition and markets for corporate control due to US deregulations are thought to have improved allocative efficiency by allowing capital to flow more freely towards projects yielding the highest returns. Moreover, although the number of banks fell over this period, the number of bank branches increased considerably, reflecting greater competition and increased consumer choice in local markets. From a theoretical perspective, these reforms would have had a strong positive effect on entrepreneurship if startups faced substantial credit constraints. Moreover, since entrepreneurs typically would have faced fewer non-bank options for financing their projects relative to existing firms (e.g. internal cash flow, bond markets), more efficient allocation of capital within the banking industry should have led to larger increases in startup entry relative to facility expansions by existing firms if startups faced barriers in their ability to raise sufficient external capital to grow.[2]

Black and Strahan (2002), Cetorelli and Strahan (2006) and Kerr and Nanda (2009a) find dramatic increases in startup activity subsequent to interstate branch banking deregulation. Moreover, Kerr and Nanda (2009a) show that these increases continue to be significant when compared to the baseline of facility expansions by existing firms – particularly so for firms entering at a smaller size where financing constraints are likely to be most acute. In addition to these changes at the extensive margin, Kerr and Nanda (2009b) also find that startups were likely to be larger at entry relative to their maximum size in the first four years of operation, suggesting intensive margin effects of the reforms as well.

These results are particularly strong in light of theories suggesting that an increase in bank competition has the potential to impede startup activity. For example, Petersen and Rajan (1995) argue that startups may benefit from concentrated banking markets because monopolist banks can engage in intertemporal cross-subsidization of loans. As a monopolist bank can charge above-market interest rates to mature firms, it can, in turn, charge below-market rates to potential entrepreneurs. By doing so, the bank can maximize the long-term pool of older firms to which it lends. Increased competition weakens the market power of local banks, reducing their ability to charge above-market rates, and thereby weakening the incentives for subsidizing new entrants as well. Despite this possibility, the strong elasticity of entry with respect to the reforms suggests that the overriding impact of the increased competition between banks was to facilitate the provision of cheaper credit and better allocation of capital to new projects.

Structure of Financial Intermediaries and their Relationship with Firms

Financial intermediaries have an important role in deciding which projects to fund and in monitoring these projects after funding them. As the costs of acquiring information about borrowers increase, it becomes harder to fund them profitably. Established firms have several advantages in this respect, such as history of audited financial statements, greater collateral to pledge against loans, and potentially the ability to partially fund expansion through retained earnings. On the other hand, information asymmetry and limited assets are particularly acute for potential entrepreneurs, resulting in good projects going unfunded because intermediaries are unable to evaluate them effectively.

Stiglitz and Weiss (1981) outline why these large costs of screening and monitoring startups cannot be completely overcome by raising interest rates. They observe that raising interest rates may lead to adverse selection, where only entrepreneurs starting the most risky projects would agree to the bank's loan terms. In such an instance, the banks would face greater default probabilities, making the loans unprofitable in expectation. They show theoretically that in such an instance, banks may be forced to ration credit rather than raise interest rates to market-clearing levels. Credit rationing causes entrepreneurs to face financing constraints. Thus innovations within the financial sector that lower information costs can have important effects on reducing financing constraints for entrepreneurs.

A large body of work finds that close ties between financial intermediaries and firms reduce information asymmetries and lower financing constraints. For example, Petersen and Rajan (1994) and Berger and Udell (1995) show that borrowers with longer banking relationships are less likely to pledge collateral, less likely to rely on expensive trade credit, and hence are less constrained in their investment decisions than firms with shorter banking relationships. Related work suggests that small or decentralized banks – where branch managers have greater authority to make adjudication decisions – are much more likely to lend to startups and small businesses. These banks have a comparative advantage for evaluating informationally opaque or 'soft information' businesses (Berger et al., 2001). They also are more likely to have appropriate incentives to act on the information than branch managers in large, hierarchical banks where adjudication decisions are centrally made (Stein, 2002).

Berger et al. (2005) find that differences in bank organizational structures impact the credit constraints of small firms across the USA. Canales and Nanda (2008) demonstrate a similar effect for terms of lending to small businesses in Mexico. In many respects, the recent innovations for microfinance in developing countries, such as the Grameen Bank founded by Muhammad Yunus, can be seen as reducing monitoring cost for informationally opaque micro-businesses. These innovations enable financial intermediaries to lend smaller amounts to entrepreneurs at a profit due to the lower fixed costs of evaluating and monitoring projects.

Although we have outlined these sources of financing constraints as distinct channels impacting entrepreneurship, they are of course interlinked. For example, Canales and Nanda (2008) show the important effects of the interaction between bank structure and the competitive environment when studying the terms of lending to small businesses in Mexico. Bozkaya and Kerr (2007) show that countries with strong employment protection laws – where firing workers is more difficult – are associated with weaker VC and private equity markets. Their findings suggest that institutional environments can have first-order effects on the presence and structure of certain types of financial intermediaries, and hence on the availability of startup capital in certain types of industries.

PERSONAL WEALTH AND ENTREPRENEURSHIP

We now turn to the second broad stream of research on financing constraints and entrepreneurship. While the first stream of research relies on cross-sectional differences in the institutional environment to study the impact of financial development and financial frictions on entrepreneurial activity, the second stream analyzes the propensity of individuals to become entrepreneurs depending upon their financial resources.

Entrepreneurs tend to be significantly wealthier than those who work in paid employment. For example, Gentry and Hubbard (2004) find that entrepreneurs comprise just under 9 percent of households in the USA, but they hold 38 percent of household assets and 39 percent of the total net worth. Not only are entrepreneurs wealthier, but also the wealthy are more likely to become entrepreneurs.

The canonical model to understand this relationship between individual wealth and entrepreneurship was developed by Evans and Jovanovic (1989). In their model, the amount an individual can borrow to fund a new venture is a function of the collateral that he or she can post, which in turn is a function of personal wealth. If the amount the entrepreneur needs to borrow is sufficient to cover the capital required to start the business, then the entrepreneur is said to be unconstrained. On the other hand, if the entrepreneur needs to invest more than he or she can borrow, then a financing constraint leads to suboptimal investment for the project at hand. Since returns to projects are a positive function of the capital invested, some projects that would have been profitable for an unconstrained entrepreneur become unprofitable for a constrained entrepreneur.

Thus a central prediction of this model is that the propensity to become an entrepreneur is a function of personal wealth if potential entrepreneurs are credit constrained. Wealthy individuals are less likely to be constrained for a given project. On the other hand, a null relationship between wealth and entrepreneurship would suggest that borrowing constraints are not binding for potential entrepreneurs. Looking at whether there is a strong association between personal wealth and the propensity to become an entrepreneur may thus shed light on the nature of financing constraints in the economy.

Evans and Jovanovic (1989) estimate their model using data from the National Longitudinal Survey of Youth (NLSY) and find significant support for the presence of financing constraints in their data. They argue that the positive relationship between personal wealth and entry into entrepreneurship can be seen as evidence of market failure, where talented but less wealthy individuals are precluded from entrepreneurship because they lack sufficient wealth to finance their new ventures. This finding has been extremely influential in both academic and policy circles.

While a null relationship between personal wealth and entrepreneurship points to a lack of financing constraints, Evans and Jovanovic (1989) note that unobserved heterogeneity may lead to a spurious correlation between personal wealth and entrepreneurship in empirical studies even if individuals do not face financing constraints. Subsequent work in this second strand of research has built on this canonical model, while attempting to better control for sources of endogeneity in order to understand the causal relationship between personal wealth and the propensity to enter into entrepreneurship. Below, we organize the subsequent work by two major categories of potentially spurious correlation.

Endogenous Wealth Creation

In the Evans and Jovanovic (1989) model, returns to entrepreneurship are greater for high-ability individuals. An important concern with empirical findings that show wealthier individuals become entrepreneurs is that personal wealth accumulation is endogenous. That is, if individuals with high ability are more likely to generate savings (because they earn more in wage employment relative to the mean person) and are also more likely to become entrepreneurs, the observed correlation between personal wealth and entrepreneurship may reflect this unobserved attribute rather than the causal effect of financing constraints (Holtz-Eakin et al., 1994; Blanchflower and Oswald, 1998). A similar concern may apply to results showing that those who are less wealthy start smaller firms (Cabral and Mata, 2003).

In order to address such concerns, researchers have sought to find exogenous shocks to personal wealth and study their effects on selection into entrepreneurship. In addition, dynamic models of occupational choice have aimed to characterize better the intertemporal savings and consumption paths of individuals who eventually become entrepreneurs (Buera, 2009).

An early innovation to overcome the endogeneity of wealth accumulation came from Holtz-Eakin et al. (1994) and Blanchflower and Oswald (1998), who looked at bequests as a way to untangle the endogeneity of wealth creation. Blanchflower and Oswald (1998) find that bequests increase the likelihood of entry into self-employment, especially for younger workers who are less likely to have saved as much. Relatedly, Holtz-Eakin et al. (1994) look at the continuation probabilities of self-employed individuals as a function of bequests. They find that those who received bequests were less likely to shut down their businesses and had better firm performance conditional on continuing operations.

As Blanchflower and Oswald (1998) note, a potential concern with the use of bequests as an instrument for personal wealth is that the bequests may not be truly exogenous.

For example, bequests may be factored into the financial calculations of children. Children of wealthy parents may choose to consume more in the present and invest in the business once they receive the bequest. Consistent with this idea, Hurst and Lusardi (2004) find that future bequests predict entry into self-employment as much as past bequests do. Other novel attempts to overcome this endogeneity concern – for example, Lindh and Ohlsson (1998) – examine self-employment entry among lottery winners, finding a strong positive relationship between shocks to personal wealth and subsequent self-employment entry. It is debated, however, whether these techniques can ultimately account for wealth effects associated with large changes in personal assets that may impact preferences or relative ability, as later discussed.

Wealth Effects, Preferences and Sorting

A second source of spurious correlation arises from the fact that observed and unobserved individual abilities and preferences for entrepreneurship may be systematically correlated with personal wealth. For example, wealthy people may have lower absolute risk aversion, making them more likely to become entrepreneurs (Evans and Jovanovic, 1989; Kihlstrom and Laffont, 1979). People may also have a preference for being their own boss that increases with greater personal wealth (Hurst and Lusardi, 2004). Further, if wealthy individuals are more effectively able to exploit certain networks that help them gain access to scarce resources, the relative ability of an individual as an entrepreneur compared to a wage worker may systematically change as they get wealthier – irrespective of their absolute ability in each sector. This may make wealthier individuals more likely to sort into entrepreneurship even if less wealthy individuals do not face financing constraints.

Hurst and Lusardi (2004) argue in favor of this perspective. They document that the propensity to enter self-employment is relatively flat up to the 80th percentile of the US wealth distribution. Moreover, the strongest association between wealth and entry into self-employment is in the top 5 percent of the wealth distribution. As these very wealthy individuals do not generally start very capital-intensive firms, Hurst and Lusardi (2004) conclude that entrepreneurship may be a luxury good. People may derive non-pecuniary benefits of being their own boss (Hamilton, 2000), in which case the wealthy may be more likely to sort into entrepreneurship due to these unobserved preferences rather than due to substantive financing constraints, and hence may have lower-performing firms (Hvide and Moen, 2008).

In a similar vein, Moskowitz and Vissing-Jorgensen (2002) find that the returns to private equity investments among wealthy business owners are not large enough relative to public markets to account for the undiversified and illiquid stakes that they have in their businesses. These authors also point to the presence of unobserved preferences for self-employment that may drive this 'private equity premium puzzle'.

Using microdata from Denmark, Nanda (2009) finds the same non-linear relationship between personal wealth and entrepreneurship identified for the USA by Hurst and Lusardi (2004). Moreover, he also finds that the wealthiest entrepreneurs are more likely to fail, particularly those founding businesses in less capital-intensive industries. Nanda argues that an important factor explaining this may be the disciplining role of the external capital markets. Wealthy individuals are less likely to have their ideas screened and vetted by potential investors, lowering the threshold level of ability required for wealthy individuals to start businesses. In such an instance, a far greater proportion of wealthy individuals may become entrepreneurs because they do not face the discipline of external finance, even if less wealthy individuals with high ability do not face financing constraints. This view is similar to that of de Meza (2002), who provides a theoretical framework where an individual who is indifferent between becoming an entrepreneur and staying a wage earner is higher ability than the wage earners, but lower ability than the entrepreneurs. When the cost of finance falls, these marginal individuals are most likely to select into entrepreneurship.

   This subsection has highlighted a growing set of studies that have noted either a potentially spurious association between personal wealth and entrepreneurship or provided explanations for the correlations that do not invoke financing constraints. The conclusions of these studies suggest that in advanced economies, financing constraints may not play as important a role in impacting entrepreneurship as was previously believed. They also suggest caution about implementing policies to reduce financing constraints for entrepreneurs under every scenario. Yet regional-level studies discussed in the second section suggest a very consistent pattern of financing constraints faced by firms. How should we reconcile these different views?

AN APPROACH TO RECONCILING THE DIFFERENT EXPLANATIONS

In this section, we propose a simple framework that may help to reconcile these different views. We also highlight some fruitful areas of research that may help to better explain the nature of financing constraints faced by entrepreneurs.

   Figure 8.1 places entering businesses into a two-dimensional space. The vertical axis documents the firm size or capital intensity of the new business. At lower levels, the entrepreneur may be part time and self-employed, without any significant investment or employment of others. At higher levels, the firm is entering with a substantial number of employees in the first year. Most hobby entrepreneurs or sole proprietors will never seek to hire someone else, remaining permanently in the lower bubble. In some cases, the startup will grow much larger, following the path of famous Silicon Valley firms like Hewlett-Packard that began in a garage.

   The horizontal axis considers the technological novelty of the project. This includes both the actual technical challenges required and the difficulty that investors have in assessing the technologies in advance. Most entrepreneurs use off-the-shelf business models with proven technologies, such as restaurants, consulting firms, franchised dealerships and construction firms, among others. Other projects have unproven technologies, where the technology generalizes to include many aspects of the business model, such as design combinations, delivery methods and so on. This definition would cover, for example, the launch of Federal Express as well as pure technology-oriented startups. The right-hand bubble in Figure 8.1 represents these latter cases, which we label as 'Schumpeterian entrepreneurship' for short.

   The first point of this taxonomy is to highlight that the two literature strands identified earlier tend to sample different forms of entrepreneurship. Regional studies, at either the

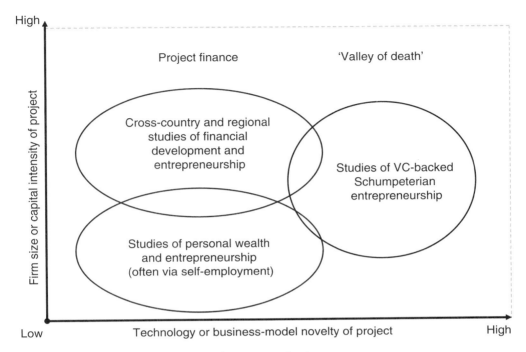

Figure 8.1   Two-dimensional space for entering businesses

country or sub-country level, typically consider financial development and entrepreneurship among firms that are above a certain explicit or implicit size. The top left bubble in Figure 8.1 represents this group. This selection may be due to the legal status of businesses in the sample (e.g. incorporated firms only) or how the data are collected (e.g. payroll tax registers). The data often build from administrative and tax records, and only the firms that have reached a corresponding size or status are included. Moreover, the collection agency may explicitly subsample small firms that are below a certain number of employees, using imputation techniques for other firms. This selection factor from government records can be particularly acute in developing countries where many entrepreneurs operate in informal sectors.

On the other hand, studies looking at personal wealth and entrepreneurship often use self-employment as a proxy for entry into entrepreneurship. Questions regarding self-employment are the most prevalent in household surveys from which these studies draw, and this definition of entrepreneurship is easily linked to the notion of the number of people leading independent enterprises. This metric, however, weighs small-scale, independent operators very heavily *vis-à-vis* high-growth entrepreneurship. This can be seen in self-employment rankings that list West Palm Beach, Florida, as the USA's most entrepreneurial city while San Jose, California, home to a large portion of Silicon Valley, is near the bottom of the rankings. This contrasts with measures of firm startups or VC funding that rank San Jose near the top. This self-employment group is the bottom left bubble in Figure 8.1.[3]

Thus studying different populations may be an important factor in explaining some of the differences in the results. The bottom, left bubble represents the vast majority of entrants. The USA provides a vivid illustration. Of the 26 million firms in the USA, 20 million are self-employed individuals, full or part time, without paid employees. Of the remaining six million businesses, 80 percent have 20 employees or fewer. When looking at new entrants subject to payroll tax, Kerr and Nanda (2009b) find that only 5 percent of startups are formed with more than 20 employees in the first year. This share would be substantially lower if calculated relative to the large majority of entrants that are not paying payroll tax.

A threshold of 20 employees, however, is not an uncommon bar for observing entrepreneurship in many cross-country or cross-regional studies employing official statistics on business startups. These government entry figures capture a very small share of the total entrepreneurial activity that may be reported in individual-level surveys. This observation does not mean that studies based on firm-level administrative data are weaker or less reliable than inquiries employing individual-level data. Indeed, the small share of businesses in the former sample captures most of the job creation and innovation that policy makers typically seek with entrepreneurship initiatives. This trade-off is even more acute in studies employing samples of VC-backed firms. VC-backed samples are not representative for the overall landscape of entrepreneurship even among employer firms, but they do capture well the very high-growth entrepreneurship that some researchers hope to analyze.

Both types of studies are important, but it is essential to position findings regarding financial constraints within the landscape of entry activity and its various metrics. As an example from our own work, Kerr and Nanda (2009a) show that US banking deregulations led to significant increases in churning entry – that is, very small entrants that survive three years or fewer. This extensive margin effect suggests large increases in weaker entrants following relaxed constraints. This churning growth helps reconcile why prior work found that the US interstate reforms resulted in entry increasing by over 10 percent a year (Black and Strahan, 2002), but no measured effects on the firm size distribution and limited productivity gains (Cetorelli and Strahan, 2006; Jayaratne and Strahan, 1996). In a similar vein, Nanda (2009) finds a substantial fall in weak entrants after financing constraints increased in Denmark.

On the other hand, Kerr and Nanda (2009a, 2009b) find that deregulation promoted somewhat larger entry sizes for those startups that survived four years, along the lines of the theoretical predictions by Evans and Jovanovic (1989). Moreover, the overall effects for reducing incumbent market shares were consistent with other regional-level findings. These patterns suggest that the reduced financing constraints brought about by US banking deregulations also facilitated a group of stronger entrants that before the reforms would have not entered or would have entered at suboptimal firm sizes.

The US Census Bureau data that undergird these results are built from payroll tax information. They thus include very small firms with fewer than five employees that are often incompletely measured. This was important for seeing the first effect, which is where the two bubbles overlap. The data also include the larger entrants that lie behind the second result, which is more typical of firm-level data. A consideration of different effects and samples is important in this context.[4]

Additional studies employing microdata can shed further light on how the motivations and needs of these sub-populations differ, along with the ultimate response to changes in local financing environments. Data advances worldwide are helping in this effort. While the Kerr and Nanda (2009a, 2009b) sample lacks many entrants in the bottom, left bubble – the non-employer firms that are missing from payroll records – recent efforts by the US Census Bureau incorporate income tax data about self-employed entrepreneurs. Moreover, the self-employed records are matched to subsequent employer firms where appropriate. These types of data are also emerging in many European countries. Richer data should provide deeper insight into how changes in financial conditions impact different forms of entrepreneurship and transitions across the types.

In addition to more detailed government registers, there is a complementary element of expanding data from additional sources. For example, Braguinsky et al. (2009) study whether scientists who work on startups related to their field of study seem to have similar levels of non-pecuniary benefits from self-employment as those who work in startups unrelated to their field of study (Hamilton, 2000). They find substantial differences between these groups, suggesting that the motivations for starting new businesses can also vary in important ways across sub-populations.

This study also relates to the second dimension of Figure 8.1, which measures the technological novelty of a new project. The vast majority of new firms started in the economy are not undertaking major technological advances or changes to existing methods of production. This is true even among Bhide's (2000) sample of growth-oriented founders in the Inc. 100 list. Moreover, many of the newly founded small businesses require little capital or have a set of hard assets that banks can take as collateral (Fluck et al., 2000). On the other hand, the more novel and unverifiable the technology proposed by the entrepreneur, the more difficult it is for traditional financial institutions to evaluate the creditworthiness of the project at hand. Many such startups are likely to have fewer tangible assets with verifiable valuations that can be pledged for a bank loan. This axis thus highlights why it is the case that projects towards the left of the horizontal axis tend to be bank financed, but why equity and more complex financial contracts (e.g. the convertible preferred stock forms used by VCs) may be necessary to finance projects based on novel technologies.

VC firms attempt to fill at least part of this gap in the USA and other countries. VCs screen entrepreneurial projects, structure financing deals, and monitor the performance of the companies in which they take equity stakes. VCs also provide non-financial resources such as customer and supplier contacts, technical expertise, employee recruitment and so on, which may improve the chances of success for unproven technologies and business models. While institutions such as VC have evolved in some countries to cover these extreme market failures, they have not taken root in all countries, as discussed earlier. The absence of such intermediaries may thus help to explain differences in the kinds of entrepreneurship prevalent across regions – for example, the weaker relative entry of Silicon Valley type startups in Europe – as well as the types of industries that emerge or do not emerge in different regions.

Even in the USA, extremely capital-intensive and novel technologies like wind turbines, refineries for biofuels, and other clean-energy projects, which would lie in the top right-hand corner of Figure 8.1, are said to fall into the 'valley of death' (Nanda and Stuart, 2009). They are too capital intensive for traditional VC and too risky for project finance. While these latter financiers are very comfortable funding highways, dams, coal powered-plants and other well-proven technologies, they are reluctant to fund risky projects with long financing cycles and the potential to become obsolete before the investment pays off. On the other hand, clean technologies may be too capital intensive for traditional VC investors. VC investors typically fund $5–10 million investments, and syndicate out larger investments, but the risk capital and coordination costs involved in funding a $250 million demonstration bio-refinery may be too great for VC investors, even if the projects have positive net present value.

While in theory such types of innovation can be done within the context of large firms (or through financing from strategic investors in such sectors), the interests of strategic investors are not always aligned with the success of these new technologies. Often the new technology has the potential to cannibalize the core business of the incumbents, as is the case of biofuels and oil companies, making incumbents much less likely to focus on commercializing new technologies. In other instances, the bureaucracies associated with larger firms may stifle new innovations. It is for these reasons that the process of creative destruction is said to be so important in leading to continued economic growth, and, hence, it is perhaps in such areas that government subsidies to alleviate credit constraints may have the greatest leverage.

CONCLUSIONS

Financing constraints are one of the biggest concerns impacting potential entrepreneurs around the world. The academic literature has focused on understanding several dimensions of financing constraints. In this chapter, we outlined two major streams of research examining this question. While many of the findings are complementary, some of the results pose a puzzle regarding the extent to which financing constraints may be a problem for entrepreneurs in advanced economies.

Our framework is a starting point for reconciling these seemingly contradictory findings. The slice of entrepreneurship examined is very important for the appropriate positioning of research on financing constraints, but studies too often fail to consider this dimension in the conclusions drawn from empirical results. The choice of where in the space of capital intensity and technological novelty to found a firm may reflect a whole set of unobserved factors that researchers need to be careful about when they look at the question of financing constraints in entrepreneurship. This framework is also useful for thinking about the appropriate role of public policy in stimulating entrepreneurship. Promoting entrepreneurship is an important goal of many governments, and researchers need to define for policy makers a more unified perspective for how studies and samples fit together.

NOTES

1.   There are two important literature strands that we do not review. The first strand studies financing constraints for entrepreneurship in developing economies, with recent innovations using randomized experiments for causal analysis. Representative papers include Morduch (1999), Paulson and Townsend (2004), Paulson et al. (2006), McKenzie and Woodruff (2006, 2008), Banerjee and Duflo (2008), and De Mel et al. (2008). A second literature uses quantitative techniques to evaluate financing constraints, entrepreneurship and economic outcomes. Representative papers include Quadrini (2000), Li (2002), Castaneda et al. (2003), Cagetti and De Nardi (2006), Buera (2008), Meh (2005), and Mondragón-Vélez (2007).

2. Only 12 states had some form of intrastate deregulation prior to 1970, and no state allowed interstate branch banking. Starting in the 1970s, and especially in the 1980s, most states passed both forms of deregulations. Accounts of the political economy of these reforms suggest their passage was mostly exogenous to product markets, driven in part by federal actions and state-level structures of the banking industry. Moreover, Kerr and Nanda (2009a) show that the timing of the reforms is not systematically related to the level of entrepreneurial activity in states prior to the reforms. Exploiting cross-state timing in the passage of the reforms provides a useful way to study the effect of an increase in bank competition on entrepreneurship.
3. Glaeser and Kerr (2009) discuss further measurements of entrepreneurship. The self-employment pattern is also evident in country rankings. For example, Southern European countries (e.g. Portugal, Greece) rank very high on European self-employment scales but tend to have very small VC markets. On the other hand, Scandinavian countries rank low on self-employment indices but have been among the most successful European countries in attracting VC investments (Bozkaya and Kerr, 2007).
4. This sensitivity to entrepreneurship definition and scope is not exclusive to financing constraints. A consistent finding in the labor economics literature is that stricter employment protection increases entrepreneurship defined through self-employment indices (Blanchflower et al., 2001; Addison and Teixeira, 2003). Studies of entrepreneurial finance, however, show that stricter regulations reduce VC investment and high-growth entrepreneurship (Jeng and Wells, 2000, Da Rin et al. 2006, Bozkaya and Kerr, 2007). Autor et al. (2007) also find employment protections reduce entry rates for firms with payroll. A similar mapping of entry distributions and the entrant types considered can reconcile these two findings.

REFERENCES

Addison, J.T. and P. Teixeira (2003), 'The economics of employment protection', *Journal of Labor Research*, **24** (1), 85–129.

Autor, D., W. Kerr and A. Kugler (2007), 'Does employment protection reduce productivity? Evidence from U.S. states', *Economic Journal*, **117** (521), 189–217.

Banerjee, A. and E. Duflo (2008), 'Do firms want to borrow more? Testing credit constraints using a directed lending program', Working paper series No. 02-25, MIT Department of Economics.

Banerjee, A., E. Duflo and K. Munshi (2003), 'The (mis)allocation of capital', *Journal of the European Economic Association*, **1** (2–3), 484–94.

Beck, T., R. Levine and N. Loayza (2000), 'Finance and the sources of growth', *Journal of Financial Economics*, **58** (1–2), 261–300.

Beck, T., A. Demirgüç-Kunt and R. Levine (2001), 'Legal theories of financial development', *Oxford Review of Economic Policy*, **17** (4), 483–501.

Berger, A.N. and G.F. Udell (1995), 'Relationship lending and lines of credit in small firm finance', *Journal of Business*, **68** (3), 351–81.

Berger, A.N., L.F. Klapper and G.F. Udell (2001), 'The ability of banks to lend to informationally opaque small businesses', *Journal of Banking & Finance*, **25** (12), 2127–67.

Berger, A.N., N.H. Miller, M.A. Petersen, R.G. Rajan and J.C. Stein (2005), 'Does function follow organizational form? Evidence from the lending practices of large and small banks', *Journal of Financial Economics*, **76** (2), 237–69.

Berkowitz, J. and M. White (2004), 'Bankruptcy and small firms' access to credit', *RAND Journal of Economics*, **35** (1), 69–84.

Bertrand, M., A. Schoar and D. Thesmar (2007), 'Banking deregulation and industry structure: evidence from the French banking reforms of 1985', *Journal of Finance*, **62** (2), 597–628.

Bhide, A.V. (ed.) (2000), *The Origin and Evolution of New Business*, Oxford: Oxford University Press.

Black, B.S. and R.J. Gilson (1998), 'Venture capital and the structure of capital markets: banks versus stock markets', *Journal of Financial Economics*, **47** (3), 243–77.

Black, S.E. and P.E. Strahan (2002), 'Entrepreneurship and bank credit availability', *Journal of Finance*, **57** (6), 2807–33.

Blanchflower, D.G. and A.J. Oswald (1998), 'What makes an entrepreneur?', *Journal of Labor Economics*, **16** (1), 26–60.

Blanchflower, D.G., A. Oswald and A. Stutzer (2001), 'Latent entrepreneurship across nations', *European Economic Review*, **45** (4–6), 680–91.

Bozkaya, A. and W. Kerr (2007), 'Labor regulations and European private equity', HBS Working Paper No. 08-043.

Braguinsky, S., S. Klepper and A. Ohyama (2009), 'Schumpeterian entrepreneurship: the Schumpeterian entrepreneur is alive and well', Atlanta Competitive Advantage Conference Paper.

Buera, F. (2009), 'A dynamic model of entrepreneurship with borrowing constraints: theory and evidence', *Annals of Finance*, **5** (3), 443–64.

Cabral, L.M.B. and J. Mata (2003), 'On the evolution of the firm size distribution: facts and theory', *The American Economic Review*, **93** (4), 1075–90.

Cagetti, M. and M. De Nardi (2006), 'Entrepreneurship, frictions, and wealth', *Journal of Political Economy*, **114** (5), 835–70.

Canales, R. and R. Nanda (2008), 'Bank structure and the terms of lending to small businesses', HBS Working Paper No. 08-101.

Castaneda, A., J. Diaz-Gimenez and J.-V. Rios-Rull (2003), 'Accounting for the U.S. earnings and wealth inequality', *Journal of Political Economy*, **111** (4), 818–57.

Cetorelli, N. and P.E. Strahan (2006), 'Finance as a barrier to entry: bank competition and industry structure in local U.S. markets', *Journal of Finance*, **61** (1), 437–61.

Cole, S. (2009), 'Fixing market failures or fixing elections? Agricultural credit in India', *American Economic Journals: Applied Economics*, **1** (1), 219–50.

Comin, D. and R. Nanda (2009), 'Finance and the diffusion of new technologies', *mimeo*.

Da Rin, M., G. Nicodano and A. Sembenelli (2006), 'Public policy and the creation of active venture capital markets', *Journal of Public Economics*, **90** (8–9), 1699–723.

de Meza, D. (2002), 'Overlending?', *Economic Journal*, **112** (477), F17–31.

de Mel, S., D. McKenzie and C. Woodruff (2008), 'Returns to capital in microenterprises: evidence from a field experiment', *The Quarterly Journal of Economics*, **123** (4), 1329–72.

Evans, D.S. and B. Jovanovic (1989), 'An estimated model of entrepreneurial choice under liquidity constraints', *Journal of Political Economy*, **97** (4), 808–27.

Fisman, R. and I. Love (2003), 'Trade credit, financial intermediary development and industry growth', *Journal of Finance*, **58** (1), 353–74.

Fluck, Z., D. Holtz-Eakin and H.S. Rosen (2000), 'Where does the money come from? The financing of small entrepreneurial enterprises', Working Paper Series No. 98-038, Leonard N. Stern School Finance Department.

Gentry, W.M. and R.G. Hubbard (2004), 'Entrepreneurship and household saving', *Advances in Economic Analysis & Policy*, Berkeley Electronic Press, **4** (1), Article 8.

Glaeser, E. and W. Kerr (2009), 'Local industrial conditions and entrepreneurship: how much of the spatial distribution can we explain?', *Journal of Economics and Management Strategy*, **18** (3), 623–63.

Greenwood, J. and B. Jovanovic (1990), 'Financial development, growth, and the distribution of income', *Journal of Political Economy*, **98** (5), 1076–107.

Guiso, L., P. Sapienza and L. Zingales (2004), 'Does local financial development matter?', *The Quarterly Journal of Economics*, **119** (3), 929–69.

Hamilton, B.H. (2000), 'Does entrepreneurship pay? An empirical analysis of the returns to self-employment', *Journal of Political Economy*, **108** (3), 604–31.

Holtz-Eakin, D., D. Joulfaian and H.S. Rosen (1994), 'Sticking it out: entrepreneurial survival and liquidity constraints', *Journal of Political Economy*, **102** (1), 53–75.

Hurst, E. and A. Lusardi (2004), 'Liquidity constraints, household wealth, and entrepreneurship', *Journal of Political Economy*, **112** (2), 319–47.

Hvide, H. and J. Moen (2008), 'Lean and hungry or fat and content? Entrepreneurs' wealth and startup performance', *Management Science* (forthcoming), online at doi: 10.1287/mnsc. 1100.1177.

Jayaratne, J. and P.E. Strahan (1996), 'The finance–growth nexus: evidence from bank branch deregulation', *The Quarterly Journal of Economics*, **111** (3), 639–70.

Jeng, L.A. and P.C. Wells (2000), 'The determinants of venture capital funding: evidence across countries', *Journal of Corporate Finance*, **6** (3), 241–89.

Kerr, W. and R. Nanda (2009a), 'Democratizing entry: banking deregulation, financing constraints, and entrepreneurship', *Journal of Financial Economics*, **94** (1), 124–49.

Kerr, W. and R. Nanda (2009b), 'Banking deregulation, financing constraints, and firm entry size', *Journal of European Economic Association*, **8** (2–3), 582–93.

Kihlstrom, R.E. and J.-J. Laffont (1979), 'A general equilibrium entrepreneurial theory of firm formation based on risk aversion', *Journal of Political Economy*, **87** (4), 719–48.

King, R.G. and R. Levine (1993a), 'Finance and growth: Schumpeter might be right', *The Quarterly Journal of Economics*, **108** (3), 717–37.

King, R.G. and R. Levine (1993b), 'Finance, entrepreneurship, and growth: theory and evidence', *Journal of Monetary Economics*, **32** (3), 513–42.

Kortum, S. and J. Lerner (2000), 'Assessing the contribution of venture capital to innovation', *RAND Journal of Economics*, **31** (4), 674–92.

La Porta, R., F. Lopez-de-Silanes, A. Shleifer and R.W. Vishny (1997), 'Legal determinants of external finance', *Journal of Finance*, **52** (3), 1131–50.

La Porta, R., F. Lopez-de-Silanes, A. Shleifer and R.W. Vishny (1998), 'Law and finance', *Journal of Political Economy*, **106** (6), 1113–55.

Levine, R. (1997), 'Financial development and economic growth: views and agenda', *Journal of Economic Literature*, **35** (2), 688–726.

Li, W. (2002), 'Entrepreneurship and government subsidies: a general equilibrium analysis', *Journal of Economic Dynamics and Control*, **26** (11), 1815–44.

Lindh, T. and H. Ohlsson (1998), 'Self-employment and wealth inequality', *Review of Income and Wealth*, **44** (1), 25–42.

McKenzie, D.J. and C. Woodruff (2006), 'Do entry costs provide an empirical basis for poverty traps? Evidence from Mexican microenterprises', *Economic Development and Cultural Change*, **55** (1), 3–42.

McKenzie, D.J. and C. Woodruff (2008), 'Experimental evidence on returns to capital and access to finance in Mexico', *World Bank Economic Review*, **22** (3), 457–82.

Meh, C. (2005), 'Entrepreneurship, wealth inequality and taxation', *Review of Economic Dynamics*, **8** (3), 688–719.

Mondragón-Vélez, C. (2007), 'The transition to entrepreneurship: human capital, wealth and the role of liquidity constraints', International Finance Corporation Working Paper.

Morduch, J. (1999), 'The microfinance promise', *Journal of Economic Literature*, **37** (4), 1569–614.

Moskowitz, T.J. and A. Vissing-Jorgensen (2002), 'The returns to entrepreneurial investment: a private equity premium puzzle?', *The American Economic Review*, **92** (4), 745–78.

Nanda, R. (2009), 'Entrepreneurship and the discipline of external finance', HBS Working Paper No. 08-047.

Nanda, R. and M. Rhodes-Kropf (2009), 'Financing risk and bubbles of innovation', *mimeo*.

Nanda, R. and T. Stuart (2009), 'KiOR: Catalyzing clean energy', Harvard Business School Case 809-092.

OECD (2004), 'Financing innovative SMEs in a global economy', Second OECD Conference of Ministers Responsible for SMEs, Istanbul, Turkey.

Paulson, A.L. and R.M. Townsend (2004), 'Entrepreneurship and financial constraints in Thailand', *Journal of Corporate Finance*, **10** (2), 229–62.

Paulson, A.L., R.M. Townsend and A. K. Karaivanov (2006), 'Distinguishing limited liability from moral hazard in a model of entrepreneurship', *Journal of Political Economy*, **114** (1), 100–44.

Paravisini, D. (2008), 'Local bank financial constraints and firm access to external finance', *Journal of Finance*, **63** (5), 2161–93.

Petersen, M.A. and R.G. Rajan (1994), 'The benefits of lending relationships – evidence from small business data', *Journal of Finance*, **49** (1), 3–37.

Petersen, M.A. and R.G. Rajan (1995), 'The effect of credit market competition on lending relationships', *The Quarterly Journal of Economics*, **110** (2), 407–43.

Rajan, R.G. and L. Zingales (1998), 'Financial dependence and growth', *The American Economic Review*, **88** (3), 559–86.

Quadrini, V. (2000), 'Entrepreneurship, saving, and social mobility', *Review of Economic Dynamics*, **3** (1), 1–40.

SBA (2008), *SBA Fiscal Year 2008 Annual Report*, available at www.sba.gov.

Sorenson, O. and T. Stuart (2001), 'Syndication networks and the spatial distribution of venture capital investments', *American Journal of Sociology*, **106** (6), 1546–88.

Stein, J.C. (2002), 'Information production and capital allocation: decentralized versus hierarchical firms', *Journal of Finance*, **57** (5), 1891–922.

Stiglitz, J.E. and A. Weiss (1981), 'Credit rationing in markets with imperfect information', *The American Economic Review*, **71** (3), 393–410.

9 The new Argonauts and the rise of venture capital in the 'periphery'

AnnaLee Saxenian and Charles F. Sabel

The emergence of technology entrepreneurship and innovation outside, but closely connected to, the advanced core of the world economy is one of the most striking features of contemporary capitalism. Israel and Taiwan, both small, peripheral agricultural economies in the postwar period, became home to dynamic clusters of entrepreneurial experimentation in the 1980s and 1990s. Today Taiwan's specialized producers define the state-of-the-art logistics and flexible manufacturing of low-cost, high-quality electronic systems. Israel, with a population of just over six million, is home to more than a hundred internet security and software-related technology companies listed on NASDAQ, more than any other country outside North America. In both countries venture capital systemically encourages the proliferation of companies that in effect co-design specialized components or subsystems for firms in the core economies.

The emergence of clusters of, for example, software firms in mid-income developing economies like China and India is if anything more striking still. Vital urban hubs like Bangalore and Hangzhou are not only peripheral to the world economy, but also located in large national economies that – (partial) liberalization of trade policy aside – lack most of the institutions economists view as preconditions for growth: the rule of law, secure property rights, good corporate governance, flexible labor markets, transparent capital markets and so forth. If it is surprising that firms in the 'periphery' can co-design crucial components with firms in the core, then it is at least as surprising that institutions good enough to permit and sustain continuing growth can be built locally before such governance institutions are installed nationally, if at all.

This chapter looks at yet another surprising, but less understood, aspect of these cases that grows directly from the connection of the first two: the growing importance of global, or external, search networks that firms and other actors rely upon to locate collaborators who can either solve (part) of a problem they face, or require (part of) a solution they may be able to provide.[1] We focus here on the creation in emerging economies of publicly supported institutions – venture capital in particular – organized to search systematically for, and foster the development of, firms and industries that can in turn collaborate in specialized co-design.

The emergence of venture capital in the periphery sheds light on current discussions in development economics of 'self-discovery' – the search process by which an enterprise or entrepreneur determines what markets it can (come to be able to) serve (Hausmann and Rodrik, 2002). The success of the new high-tech clusters strongly suggests that production is decomposable in ways that allow decentralized co-design of parts and their periodic reintegration into complex wholes. Enterprises in these clusters systematically look for collaborators who are already solving (parts of) the problems they face, rather than trying to elaborate comprehensive solutions on their own.[2] At the same time as production is becoming more collaborative, relying more and more on co-design, so too is the process of self-discovery. Firms and entrepreneurs seeking to enter a new market must demonstrate not just the ability to produce a certain component or product, but also the ability to improve its design or the process by which it is produced in cooperation with the potential customer and their suppliers (Sabel and Zeitlin, 2004).

Producers in less developed economies face distinct challenges when seeking to enter these partnerships, and increasingly require bundles of inputs or services – standards, certification, *de facto* property rights and specific regulations – that only public authorities can provide. This means that self-discovery also typically entails collaborative search with (parts of) government for institutional solutions that will facilitate certain kinds of transactions. Thus understood, self-discovery shades into open-ended industrial policy: a process by which firms and governments collaborate in the identification and pursuit of promising opportunities for development.[3]

This chapter examines the creation of venture capital in emerging economies as an illustration of the way that public and private actors, building on networks they 'find', can construct an institution that systematically creates further networks to foster and monitor the progress of new firms and industries. We focus on the case of Taiwan, where highly skilled first-generation immigrant professionals in US technology industries collaborated with their home-country counterparts to develop the context for entrepreneurial development. The chapter refers to the members of these networks as the new Argonauts, an allusion to Jason and the Argonauts, who centuries ago sailed in search of the Golden Fleece, testing their mythic heroism while seeking earthly riches and glory. While most of the evidence here is drawn from Taiwan, relevant aspects of analogue developments in Israel, India and China are considered as well.

Our central argument is that new Argonauts are ideally positioned (as both insiders and outsiders at home and abroad) to search beyond prevailing routines to identify opportunities for complementary 'peripheral' participation in the global economy, and to work with public officials on the corresponding adaptation and redesign of relevant institutions and firms in their native countries. They are, in other words, exemplary protagonists of the process of self-discovery or open industrial policy – though surely there are in other contexts different institutional arrangements that are as exemplary as well. We argue further that in the cases considered here, the Argonauts' contributions to domestic institution building crystallized most clearly in the development of domestic venture capital, one of the, if not the most important, supports for technology entrepreneurship.

Venture capital is itself a powerful search network: it is an institution for identifying and combining pieces of companies – finance, technical expertise, marketing know-how, business model, standard-setting capacity and so on. Once integrated, these enterprises succeed by becoming nodes in the search networks for designing and building products in their domain. By supporting a diverse portfolio of ventures, and combining hands-on monitoring and mentoring with market selection, investors in developing countries are thus institutionalizing a process of continuous economic restructuring – and learning about how to improve restructuring itself – that transforms the domestic economy by linking it to the most demanding and capable actors in global markets.

The new Argonauts are therefore at once the product of search networks among the professionals and companies for whom they have worked and with which they associate, and – in collaboration with parts of government and other domestic public institutions

– the co-architects of further networks that extend and adapt to home-country conditions the web of relations they already know.

Networks of overseas professionals are central to this story, so we begin with the role of diasporas in development. We review the current debates to claim that the most enduring contributions of skilled professionals to their home countries are not direct transfers of technology or knowledge, but participation in the process of external search and domestic institutional reform. We argue that the focus on the high-skill diaspora as an asset has obscured processes of micro-level reform that, diffusing and cascading, can ultimately produce structural transformations.

The third section illustrates this argument with the example of the creation of the venture capital industry in Taiwan, which provided the context for entrepreneurial growth in high-tech clusters. The following section situates search networks with respect to current debates about the structuring principles of the new, global economy. We show that these networks are based on and transmit knowledge that is more formalized than that circulating in the local networks typical of clusters (where knowledge is, at the limit, purely tacit), but less complete than the knowledge said to flow in modular global production networks (where knowledge is assumed to be fully explicit). The final coda draws early conclusions for our understandings of the process of institutional reform and economic development.

DIASPORAS AND DEVELOPMENT

In spite of the outpouring of research in the past decade, evidence that diaspora networks, taken as various forms of intellectual capital or as 'knowledge networks', have a positive impact on economic development is limited. Diasporas are not new phenomena, nor is the interest of policy makers and scholars in their developmental potential.[4] What is new, or relatively so, is the focus of recent research and policy on the highly educated (e)migrants who have long been viewed as a serious loss to poor economies (the brain drain). Low transportation and communications costs now allow those who go abroad for further training or in search of work to interact and collaborate with their home-country counterparts far more extensively than was feasible in earlier eras of emigration. A small but growing number of migrants have even become fully 'transnational' – with dual citizenship and residences in both their home and their adopted countries.

Early research on diaspora contributions investigated remittances or direct investments, which can provide a stable source of finance and alleviate poverty, but typically have limited long-term impact. The recent literature, by contrast, suggests that skilled migrants can alter the development trajectory of a poor country through the diffusion of knowledge and/or technology transfers – as for example in the shift from a brain drain of talent away from the home country to 'brain circulation' between it and the core economies (Saxenian et al., 2002). Despite this attention to positive development impacts, much of the newer literature (and the public policies with which it is in dialog) continues to treat the diaspora as an asset, valuable insofar as it adds to the home country's stock of capital not through remittances but in intellectual property or reputational capital or related forms of wealth. There is, however, little evidence that diasporas have contributed substantially to development in this way.

The most direct mechanism for transferring intellectual capital to the home country would be for the highly educated migrants to return to work. Yet in spite of the aggressive recruitment efforts of home-country policy makers, and some evidence of rising return rates (from a very low base) in places like India and China, there is no evidence that educated migrants to the USA and other advanced economies are substantially more likely to return permanently to their home economies than they were a decade or two ago. Nor is there evidence that the brain drain has abated, except in small countries that have experienced rapid growth, such as Taiwan.[5]

Some researchers suggest that there is a diaspora effect in scientific collaboration by documenting how knowledge, as measured by patent citations and co-authorship, flows disproportionately among members of the same ethnic community, even over long distances (Kerr, 2008, 2010; Jin et al., 2007; Agrawal et al., 2004). Yet efforts to demonstrate that diaspora scientific collaboration contributes to economic growth in the home country remain unconvincingly incomplete. Above all, they have not identified a causal mechanism by which the findings of collaborative research are usefully transferred to firms and other domestic actors.

Research in related areas has yielded similarly promising but incomplete findings. Studies have found, for instance, that ethnic networks in the USA increase trade with the home country, suggesting that a diaspora can help to reduce reputational and informational and barriers to trade (Kapur, 2001; Rauch and Trindade, 2002; Lucas, 2005). Similarly, case studies suggest that diaspora members can for the same reasons help direct corporate investments or contracts toward their home country. However, the most significant findings from both the quantitative studies and the extensive case study research come from a small number of Asian cases, particularly China and India (Lucas, 2005; Lowell and Gerova, 2004). As critics point out, there are many more cases of failed attempts to mobilize diaspora contributions to development, from Armenia to Argentina, that remain unexplained in current frameworks.

The rise of dynamic clusters in the periphery, and the experience of the new Argonauts generally, suggest that the debate on diasporas and development has been misdirected. The increased salience of diaspora networks to economic development does not lie in the direct contribution of assets, but rather in their role in the design and construction of new institutions in their home countries. While these contributions are often incremental, thus difficult to detect and even more difficult to quantify, over time they have the potential to create a context that supports self-sustaining growth.

In part because of the treatment of diasporas as assets, discussions focus on the macrolevel: the relation of 'the' diaspora to 'its' home country. They overlook the internal heterogeneity of the diaspora, as well as the heterogeneity of the economy and the public sector in developing (as well as the developed) nations. The new Argonauts, for example, are only a subset of the diaspora, normally first-generation emigrants who work with ease in the institutions and environment of their home country, where they continue to have friends, family and colleagues. (Second- or third-generation immigrants, even if they speak the language of their country of origin, have greater difficulty doing business there because they lack both these personal connections and first-hand knowledge of local institutions and culture.)

The spatial differentiation of economic activity typically linked to industrial specialization (another manifestation of heterogeneity) means that a focus on national indicators and institutions can obscure critical transformations occurring at a sub-national level.[6] Likewise the state, in developing as well as in developed counterparts, is not a unified whole, but rather consists of multiple, differently organized units with varying political and economic resources, jurisdictions and interests. Yet it is precisely this heterogeneity that permits innovation and growth within a generally hostile context (Kuznetsov and Sabel, 2006).

The new Argonauts bring to their home countries expertise in specific industries that are located in a small number of urban areas or regions, and they collaborate only with a subset of domestic entrepreneurs and policy makers. This means that economic and institutional change begins in certain locations and/or domains, and advances through partial and incremental (micro-level) reforms that only with time aggregate into larger-scale transformations. Only by disaggregating the diaspora and its interactions with (parts of) the equally differentiated public and private sectors it is possible to see whether and eventually how they are (re)building the institutions of economic development.

A small example from India illustrates how a micro-level reform can facilitate matching of collaborators, and how such reform can diffuse. In the early 1990s Indian products in general were suspect because of their reputation as low quality. Quality problems in software were an important obstacle to collaboration between local suppliers and customers in world markets. In software the problem was not particular to India: almost from the beginning of large software development projects, such as the operating system for the IBM 360 in the 1960s, it has been well known that quality problems can arise from the very partitioning of tasks, which allows different groups to work on separate parts of programs simultaneously. Fixing performance specifications for each 'chunk' or module of the program introduces ambiguities that come to light as defects only when the parts are finally connected to each other (Brooks, 1995). Long-range collaboration could only be expected to exacerbate a problem inherent to software production (and latent, as we shall see in production and design generally).

Anticipating this problem, an Indian engineer from the Software Engineering Institute (SEI) at Carnegie-Mellon University traveled to Bangalore to speak at software firms about the Institute's recently introduced Capability Maturity Model (CMM) for software engineering process improvement. The core of the CMM is a process of periodic peer review of development 'pieces' to insure, by ongoing clarification of specifications, that the rate of error detection is higher than the rate of 'error injection'. Many firms immediately picked up the idea and sponsored conferences and consultations on the topic. By the end of the decade virtually all large Indian software companies had adopted the CMM. Today India is widely recognized for its high-quality software development processes; the country has more SEI-CMM Level V (the top level) certified companies than any other.

The development of a globally competitive software services and technology industry in Bangalore involved a multiplicity of similar micro-level reforms, both within the cluster and externally. In this case the best practice in software engineering processes was transferred to Indian firms as soon as they were being developed. Indeed, the most extensive and practical guide to the use of the quality model today is a study of its application and development at Infosys, one of India's largest and most successful software firms, and published by the SEI (Jalotte, 2000). Such changes occur incrementally, and there is no guarantee that they will continue. But, as we shall see in detail in the next section, when they accumulate, they have the potential to alter the institutional fabric of the economy.

INSTITUTIONALIZING VENTURE CAPITAL: THE TAIWAN CASE

The collaboration of overseas Chinese professionals with government officials in Taiwan to create a venture capital industry exemplifies the contribution of global search to domestic institution building. The institutionalization of venture capital was a critical turning point for Taiwan. It insured that a few, isolated early entrepreneurial successes were followed by growing investment and collective learning in the electronics-related industries. Ultimately it supported the creation of a self-reinforcing cluster, or critical mass, of firms.

The creation of venture capital in Taiwan also shows how such institution building is enabled by, and helps encourage, new political alliances rooted in the incipient forms of cooperation that it fosters. The reform was initiated by an entrepreneurial former finance minister who leveraged both the search capabilities and the political influence of the diaspora to mobilize support for initiatives that were strongly opposed by older-line policy makers and traditional industries.

Last, but perhaps most importantly, the collaborative construction of venture capital in Taiwan shows how search networks can transform and give new meaning to the institutions they connect to and 'import'. Venture capital in Taiwan was as much a means of reorienting the country's emerging high-tech economy from competition to collaborative complementarity with Silicon Valley firms, and of redirecting investment by old-line industry and cautious commercial banks and family networks, as it was a tool for providing finance to startups that otherwise could not find it.

In the 1970s Taiwan was a poor, agricultural nation. Its economy was controlled by a combination of state-owned enterprises (in finance and strategic industrial sectors) and risk-averse family-owned and -run businesses.[7] The 'high-tech' manufacturing sector consisted mainly of low-end, labor-intensive firms manufacturing calculators and electronic components almost exclusively for foreign customers. Intellectual property rights were notoriously disregarded, allowing in the early 1980s for the reverse engineering and production of 'clones' of the IBM PC and Apple's Macintosh. Few would have predicted that entrepreneurs in this peripheral economy would compete in the most technologically advanced sectors of the world economy. Yet by the end of the 1990s Taiwan was a leading center of technology entrepreneurship; today its specialized semiconductor and computer-related firms define the state-of-the-art logistics and manufacturing of low-cost, high-quality electronic systems.

Scholarly accounts of the growth of Taiwan's technology sector typically focus on a farsighted development strategy focused on industrial 'catch-up', and particularly the transfer of leading-edge semiconductor technology through the creation of institutions like the Industrial Technology Research Institute (ITRI), a public–private research agency, and the Hsinchu Science-based Industrial Park (HSIP) (Amsden and Chu, 2003; Mathews and Cho, 1999). Yet they leave a puzzle. How did domestic policy makers manage to identify and supply precisely the institutional pieces required to support entrepreneurial growth in a highly competitive global economy – particularly when many other nations, often far better endowed, tried and failed to develop venture capital and technology industries in the same period?

The answer to this puzzle is that the growth of the sector was only in part a planned or designed process; and the part that *was* designed was aimed less at moving Taiwan to a well-defined technology frontier than at creating institutions for identifying and pursuing appropriate economic opportunities – search networks. A plainly unplanned but crucial part was the decision by tens of thousands of Taiwan's most talented university students to pursue engineering graduate degrees in the USA in the 1960s and 1970s. A majority took jobs in the USA after graduation because the professional and economic opportunities in regions like Silicon Valley far exceeded anything then available in Taiwan. Policy makers complained bitterly about these losses and even sought to control them. None foresaw that the 'brain drain' might prove advantageous.

The initial adjustment of the job seekers to their new environment was also spontaneous. As outsiders in Silicon Valley, the immigrants created technical associations and alumni networks that allowed them to find one another, as well as to stay in touch with their counterparts at home. Some participated in government-sponsored policy discussions or gave talks at universities and technical conferences in Taiwan, but few considered returning home permanently.

The decision not to return home was as self-evident as the decision to go abroad in the first place: Taiwan's personal computer industry in the early 1980s was small and fragile, despite sizable public investments in higher education and technology research, and the efforts of the handful of entrepreneurs who did go back. The Hsinchu Science-based Industrial Park (HSIP) opened in 1980, but was unable to find tenants in spite of aggressive efforts to lure multinationals, including those run by Chinese.

The turning point, and the beginning of a deliberate policy – in the sense of a strategy for building institutions to fix and revise strategies – came in the following years, when Minister without Portfolio Kuo-Ting Li formed an alliance with a group of foreign advisors, including members of the diaspora, to establish a venture capital industry in Taiwan. An engineer who headed both the Ministry of Economic Affairs (1965–69) and then the Ministry of Finance (1969–76), K-T Li is widely regarded as the architect of Taiwan's technology strategy. He had met regularly with Chinese engineers and entrepreneurs in Silicon Valley during the 1960s and 1970s (many were his college classmates) to seek their advice on making Taiwanese industry more globally competitive. Li was especially impressed with the newly emerging USA venture capital industry and the institutional support it created for entrepreneurship.

While serving as the Minister of Finance, Li had hired a team of US-educated engineers to develop a plan for the creation and organization of private industrial investment companies in Taiwan. They concluded that Taiwan should import the venture capital model from the USA; and their conclusions resonated with those of then Minister of Economic Affairs, Li-Te Hsu, as well as Stan Shih, the CEO of Acer, a leading PC maker, both whom had also visited the USA to study its new high-technology industries. During this period an IBM executive based in Silicon Valley, Ta-Lin Hsu, also used his status as a leading figure in the diaspora and an 'outside' expert to promote new policy measures to support technology entrepreneurship by contacting key individuals in various governmental units.

By 1982 Li was able to persuade the Ministry of Finance to introduce legislation to create, develop and regulate venture capital in Taiwan, including comprehensive tax incentives and financial assistance. The concept of venture capital, uncontroversial today, was foreign to the Taiwanese of the day, where family members closely controlled all the financial affairs of a business. Leaders of traditional industries such as chemicals and textiles opposed Li's ideas. So did an influential consultant to the government, Dr Simon Ramo (a pioneer of systems engineering and a co-founder of the company that eventually became TRW), who argued that Taiwan lacked the capabilities to develop a VC industry.

Supporters of the project understood that venture capital would play a different role in Taiwan than in the USA, and that the difference would help redirect the developing economy in a crucial way. They argued that rather than trying to replicate the high-level research and technological innovation of places like Silicon Valley, Taiwan should exploit its own strengths: a supply of relatively low-cost, high-skilled engineers. In this view, Taiwan would position itself to develop commercial applications derived from US innovations, and lower-skill, mass production could be carried out elsewhere. Li envisioned the HSIP as the place for Taiwanese entrepreneurs to undertake this commercialization, collaborating with each other and with foreign companies. The availability of venture capital, and the networking and mentoring that it provides in addition to finance, would be key to this strategy.

Proponents of Li's vision recognized that the conservatism of Taiwan's established financial institutions was a major hindrance to the incubation of high-technology ventures. Most financial institutions at that time were commercial banks, which provided only mortgage or debt financing. The risk aversion of the government officials who managed the public 'Development Fund' and other financial-incentive programs limited the ability of these capital sources to spawn risky new technology enterprises. Only a publicly supported venture-capital industry would provide sufficient capital for such high-risk, high-return ventures.

In addition, Taiwan's businesses were overwhelmingly (95 percent) small- and medium-sized enterprises and most, as we have noted, were family-run. Family-owned and -managed enterprises of this type were typically oriented toward survival, rather than growth, and had little incentive to adopt modern management techniques. Policy makers believed that a venture capital industry could help promote the introduction of modern financial and management skills by institutionalizing the separation of ownership and control. Finally, proponents understood that the introduction of venture capital would entail the development of a public capital market that provided an exit option for investments in startups.

Close scrutiny of the US experience had taught Li's group both that Taiwan could profit from domestic venture capital, but also that the country lacked the relevant institutional know-how to start a venture capital industry and the incentives to draw local actors into the process. Policy makers therefore organized collaborations with large US financial institutions to facilitate the transfer of relevant financial and managerial expertise. For example, young Taiwanese were sent to the USA to be trained in venture capital management. The Ministry of Finance created tax incentives to encourage domestic firms to enter the venture capital industry; 20 percent of the capital invested in strategic (technology-intensive) ventures by individual or corporate investors was tax-deductible for up to five years. The Ministry also offered substantial matching funds through a 'Seed Fund' with NT$800 million from the Executive Yuan Development Fund. In addition, regulation governing security and exchange was modified to support the development of a public capital market.

But even with these incentives, development was hesitant. When Acer founded Taiwan's first venture capital firm in 1984 as a joint venture with the old-line Continental Engineering Group, there were at first no followers. K.T. Li invited the Overseas Chinese community to establish venture capital businesses in Taiwan. In response, Ta-Lin Hsu, a prominent diaspora member and policy advisor, set up Hambrecht & Quist Asia Pacific in 1986. Hsu reports that it was not easy to raise the initial $50 million fund: Li 'twisted lots of arms' to raise $26 million from leading Taiwanese industrial groups such as Far East Textile, President Enterprises and Mitac. The balance (49 percent) came from the government.[8] The first general manager in H&Q Asia Pacific's Taipei office, Ding-Hua Hu, was a classic returnee. After earning a PhD in engineering at Princeton in 1970, Hu had played a lead role in building Taiwan's semiconductor industry as the first general director of the Electronics Research and Service Organization and as a professor of electrical engineering at the elite Chiao Tung University.

In 1987, two other overseas Chinese engineers, Peter Liu and Lip-Bu Tan, responded to Li's invitation as well, establishing Taiwan's second US-style venture fund, the Walden International Investment Group (WIIG) as a branch of the San Francisco-based Walden Group. Both H&Q Asia Pacific and WIIG (along with Peter Liu's spin-off firm, WI Harper) were able to raise capital for Taiwanese funds with relative ease from the networks of overseas Chinese in Silicon Valley who were familiar with venture capital.

It was only after these investments showed returns – after companies like Acer and Microtek (a scanner company started by an engineer who returned to the USA in 1980) were publicly listed on the Taiwan Stock Exchange in the late 1980s – that that the venture capital industry in Taiwan took off. The 'Seed Fund' with matching grants for venture investments was depleted and the Executive Yuan committed a second fund of NT$1.6 billion that was also allocated quickly. Domestic IT firms began to create their own venture funds, including D-Link, Macronix, Mosel, Taiwan Semiconductor Manufacturing Company (TSMC), SiliconWare, UMAX Data Systems, UMC and Winbond. Old-line firms in traditional industries like petrochemicals that had been reluctant earlier to get involved in the 'new economy' also began investing in technology-related venture funds and businesses.

The emergence of Taiwan's venture capital industry and the early successes of venture-backed startups attracted growing numbers of overseas Chinese to return from the USA to start businesses. Miin Wu, a Stanford graduate who worked in Silicon Valley for over a decade before returning in 1988 to start Macronix International, one of Taiwan's first semiconductor companies, in HSIP with funding from H & Q Asia Pacific, is a well-known example. The availability of venture capital finally transformed HSIP into a fertile environment for the growth of indigenous technology firms. By 1996 over 2500 engineers and scientists had returned to work in the Science Park and 40 percent of the 203 companies based in the park were started by returnees. The industry remained highly localized as it grew, with the personal computer industry in greater Taipei region and semiconductor and component firms in Hsinchu, creating a corridor roughly the same size as the Silicon Valley cluster.

The availability of venture capital in the 1980s also distinguished Taiwan from the rest of Asia: outside of Taiwan, capital was then available in the region only to large corporations with ties to governments or to wealthy families. One measure of the success of Taiwan's venture capital industry is the performance of venture-funded firms in public capital markets. Ten of the 32 new ventures started in the HSIP in 1996 received funding from local venture funds. By 1998 over 130 venture-funded companies were listed on the Taiwan Stock Exchange and some 40 were listed on NASDAQ.

The new Argonauts have influenced policy in other developing nations, using best practices and models from Silicon Valley to lever open and animate discussion of institutional reform in their home countries. The experience of the coalition of policy makers and overseas entrepreneurs and engineers that created Israel's venture capital industry from the mid-1980s to the mid-1990s is a striking example: in Israel, as in Taiwan, the introduction of venture capital linked together, in an economically viable way, the capabilities or firm fragments (e.g. research outputs, managerial talent, engineering skill, market knowledge and so on) – created by government's earlier investment in national defense and technological development. In Israel these took the form of policy 'experiments' fostering commercial applications of military high-tech, and R&D cooperation between Israeli and foreign firms.[9] As in Taiwan, early initiatives faced considerable opposition, and success grew from improvements on failures. Thus the first effort to institutionalize venture capital through a government insurance fund, Inbal, failed: under the program the state insured 70 percent of initial investments, but in effect limited the investors' rights to capital appreciation – and so attracted VC firms more interested in minimizing risk than in increasing returns by selection and monitoring of porfolio firms. Inbal's successor – Yozma – was a success: this time the state bought minority stakes in competing, private venture capital firms, structured as limited partnerships between Israeli venture capitalists and their foreign counterparts, thus insuring connections to global as well as local networks (Avnimelech and Teubal, 2004). Indian and Chinese Argonauts have similarly participated in the creation of institutions for venture capital in their home countries (Saxenian, 2006). Each has not only transformed domestic institutions but also altered the development trajectory for those that followed.

Policy makers and entrepreneurs in Taiwan and elsewhere clearly learned from the Silicon Valley model; some even believed that they were replicating that model. But solving problems of domestic economic development by adapting venture capital to domestic contexts, they changed both the model and the contexts themselves. Indeed, as the next section will show, they also helped transform Silicon Valley, in ways that suggest the broad generalizability of these experiences to other industries and settings.

GLOBAL SEARCH NETWORKS AND CROSS-REGIONAL COLLABORATION

In focusing on connections between the new Argonauts and Silicon Valley, the discussion so far invites the objection that the construction of search networks is founded on, and therefore limited to, the prior, 'natural' occurrence of tacit knowledge of technologies and persons associated with industrial clusters or professional and technical 'communities of practice' generally (Brown and Duguid, 2002; Lave and Wenger, 1991). Indeed, one pole in the current discussion of links among firms in the emerging global economy sees that economy as a shift away from coordination by managerial hierarchies in vertically integrated firms toward informal coordination among networks of independent companies. These relations are said to be long term and grounded in 'informal restraints on self-interested behavior' (Lamoreaux et al., 2003, p. 62). This view generalizes to the economy at large the stylized experiences of the industrial districts or clusters, based on local cultures of trust, and the co-design relations among Japanese automobile firms and their subcontractor, based on an ethos of reciprocity, as these were understood in the 1990s. At the limit, this view suggests the information needed to initiate, engage in and judge the performance of collaboration must be so deeply embedded in particular social relations that it is possible to foster collaboration institutionally only when social connections have become so dense and reliable that it is almost superfluous to do so.

However accurate this view may have been of the tacit or 'cultural' coordination of flexible networks of firms in past decades, it ignores the extent to which formalization of key aspects of collaboration is not only possible but necessary to sustain the co-design relations prevailing today. Recall the CMM method of software engineering process improvement and its use of peer review of development 'pieces' to reduce errors. The CMM is just one of a wide array of similar devices for creating information-pooling regimes in which cooperating firms can teach each other to be better collaborators even as they monitor one another's capacities and intentions to do so.[10] Thus it is routine in contracts between, for instance, producers of computers or automobiles and suppliers of key components to specify not only acceptable quality levels but target rates of price reduction, procedures for jointly and regularly reviewing progress towards all these goals, agreeing on joint action when necessary to achieve them, and periodic consultation on emergent features of the next-generation components. Analogous regimes are common between firms co-developing new drugs or innovative computer hard- or software.

These regimes do not of course eliminate the need for personal connections among buyers and sellers. But they do make a firm's capacities and disposition to cooperate much more accessible not only to current but also to potential partners than the informal, tacit view of linkages suggests. Because the regimes make it easier for firms to scan the world, they make it easier for the firm to find partners itself; because in scanning successfully the firm becomes known for its ability to search, the regimes make it more attractive to potential partners (Gilson et al., 2008). Thus the new nature of interfirm networks facilitates rather than obstructs the creation of higher-order search networks and open industrial policy, formalizing the information exchange that give rise to the metrics on which venture capital and like institutions depend in the monitoring performance of firms with which they are engaged.

The prevalence of these collaborative, information-pooling regimes also casts substantial doubt on the modular view of interfirm links at the opposite pole of current discussion of the global economy. In this view, collaborative knowledge is not tacit and informal but rather fully explicit and formalized: new design and production tools allow development of technical standards and design rules that standardize the interfaces between organizationally separate stages of production. This standardization so drastically reduces the volume of information required for interfirm coordination that products can be decomposed into distinct and further decomposable modules, each produced in virtual isolation from the others (Langlois, 2003 and Sturgeon, 2002, p. 374).

Some codification of this kind is obviously necessary to allow specialist producers to focus on their specializations. But too much codification just as obviously becomes a barrier to systematic innovation, locking component manufacturers and those who combine their products into more complex wholes into potentially obsolete product architectures (Sabel and Zeitlin, 2004). Hence the prevalence, among all but the least sophisticated producers, of the information-pooling regimes just noted, whose goal is the continuing elaboration of product and process specification, and the consideration of alternatives – not the clarification of fixed standards. So common are regimes of this type that *their* organization – the way in which quality control information is to be collected and evaluated – has itself been standardized.

A more graphic demonstration of the limits of this view is the rapidly evolving relation between the economic core and periphery in general, and Silicon Valley and Taiwan and Israel in particular. The model of modular networks, with a relatively stable and hierarchical production chain dominated by global flagship producers, suggests that there is no potential for engineering improvements and innovation at any level of the supply chain but the top. In spatial terms, there is no room in a fully modular world for indigenous entrepreneurship and innovation outside the core.

Development in Taiwan demonstrates the opportunities for innovation in the periphery, even at the lowest level of the supply chain. By the early 1990s Taiwan had become a highly efficient and flexible producer of low-cost integrated circuits, components and motherboards – and left new product definition, high-end design and equipment manufacturing to Silicon Valley. Producers in both regions benefited from distinctive capabilities that allowed them to deepen their specialized expertise, in part by recombining it with that of other specialists. A decade later Taiwan's firms had significantly upgraded their design and manufacturing capabilities; they were not only designing and making increasingly sophisticated and complex components such as LCD screens, microprocessors and miniature optical components for cameras, but they were also responsible for the logistics and final integration of advanced products like laptop PCs and mobile devices. During the same decade, they moved virtually all of their high-volume manufacturing to the Chinese mainland, where they could exploit economies of scale and lower cost inputs.

The semiconductor industry, in which Taiwan played an important role, corroborates the importance of venture capital to this process of technological upgrading. In the 1970s, vertically integrated independent device manufacturers (IDM) based in the USA and Japan controlled the design, manufacturing, marketing and distribution of semiconductors. When Morris Chang returned to Hsinchu in the mid-1980s after decades of experience in the US semiconductor industry, he pioneered the 'foundry' model by focusing Taiwan Semiconductor Manufacturing Co. exclusively on chip manufacturing.[11] The availability and rapid growth of Taiwan's contract foundry capacity coincided with the growth of venture capital, triggering a new generation of advanced chip packaging, assembly and materials firms in Taiwan and an unprecedented wave of new chip design startups in Silicon Valley.

Investments over the next two decades by venture capitalists in both regions, sometimes joint, accelerated entrepreneurial experimentation (and learning from failure) and innovation. New semiconductor ventures identified still more highly specialized niches, such as the intellectual property components for chip design, or 'design foundries' with deep expertise in both fabrication technologies and design; and system startups incorporated the more complex, often cheaper and smaller components into new generations of computing products. And as US and Taiwanese producers became increasingly sophisticated, they ceded the lower end of their markets to new generations of entrepreneurs based in locations such as China and India.

In sum, open or external search networks, such as those that helped create venture capital in Taiwan, represent an intermediate form between the tacit networks of industrial districts and the fully explicit networks of modular production systems. Actors in these networks contribute, through intensive information exchange and comparisons, to the construction of shared, domain-specific, understandings and languages (or interpretations) that allow them to search for new models of products and of organizing production, even in distant localities, and to collaborate in incorporating these new possibilities into existing practice. This process blurs the boundaries among firms, industries and regional economies – and, perhaps most fundamentally of all, between linkages and organizations that arise or are 'found', and those that can by reflection and design be made.

CONCLUSION

The experience of the new Argonauts in creating venture capital in peripheral locations such as Taiwan suggests that development today is a process of experimentation and learning in particular contexts. Economic decentralization creates possibilities for entrepreneurs almost anywhere in the world to identify promising market niches and opportunities at many points along supply chains. Diasporas, especially in the form of professional communities like the new Argonauts, can begin to connect suppliers and customers, producers and policy makers.[12] But even in the presence of the social bonds and trust that grow from shared ethnic identities, the challenges of self-discovery – of identifying appropriate partners in a decentralized economy, and of insuring the public inputs needed to work with them – remain substantial. The crucial step in reducing the obstacles to faster, more sustained growth occurs when individuals, firms and policy makers jointly create institutions – or search networks – that extend the connections, not least by creating more nodes and links in the currently existing networks, and by connecting them to others.

We have seen that venture capital can serve as a powerful search network in developing economies when the investors have global as well as local connections. By supporting a diverse portfolio of ventures, and combining hands-on monitoring and mentoring with market selection, they are institutionalizing a process of continuous economic restructuring – and learning about how to improve the institutions of restructuring – that transforms the domestic economy by linking it to the most demanding and capable actors in global markets. In other contexts such search networks have taken the form of publicly supported supply chain development and quality assurance programs. In essence, venture capital is a search network that helps transform the domestic economy by itself creating search networks.

Put another way, search networks can help link partners in micro-level innovations in public institutions and the organization of production. Over time, these changes can cumulate into, or inform programs for, larger-scale transformations that 'endow' the economy with institutions that, on some views of development, it would have needed to grow in the first place. Learning more about how this contemporary form of economic development was possible in places where – improbable at first – it has already occurred can teach how it might be done in settings where it today seems unimaginable.

NOTES

1. See Sabel (2005), which argues that search routines offer an alternative to the hierarchical decomposition of tasks as a solution to the problem of bounded rationality in organizations.
2. If this were not the case it would be impossible for high-tech clusters to emerge in developing economies by specializing in complex components or special-purpose software, and to grow by collaborating more and more closely with their customers in the elaboration of successive, more sophisticated generations and generalizations of the original specialties.
3. See Hausmann et al. (2008) and generally Rodrik (2007).
4. See, e.g., Brinkerhoff (2006), Kapur and McHale (2005), Kuznetsov (2006), Lowell and Gerova (2004), Lucas (2005), Saxenian (2006).
5. Ironically there is now concern in policy circles in Taiwan that they have lost the 'bridge' to Silicon Valley as a result – at least implicitly recognizing the importance of the diaspora as a search network.
6. The literature on national institutions and development overlooks the evidence from India, China and many other cases suggesting that parts of economies grow rapidly and reliably even if the wholes to which they are connected do not have the institutions thought to be necessary for growth. The evidence suggests that the institutions of governance sufficiently 'good' to permit and encourage sustained growth can be built piecemeal, in particular sectors of the economy, and the regions in which they are located, in advance of comprehensive, national reform. No one looking only, say, at national legislation (or its absence) regarding property rights in China would have been able to predict that country's growth.
7. Taiwan's per capita GNP in 1962 was US$170, on par with Zaire (not the Democratic Republic of the Congo).
8. Interview with Ta-Lin Hsu, San Francisco, CA, 1 June 1997.
9. Avnimelech and Teubal (2004 p. 88) speak explicity of 'business experiments' and 'policy experimenta-tion' in this period.
10. On such 'pragmatist' mechanisms such as benchmarking, simultaneous engineering, and 'root cause' error detection and correction, see Helper et al. (2000). All of these generate information for collaborative improvement or design innovation by triggering 'routine questioning of routines'.
11. This organizational innovation, which transformed the global semiconductor industry, is at direct odds with claims that Taiwan is not innovative.
12. The new Argonauts have contributed actively to policy reform in India and China in the areas of telecom-munications regulation, science and technology policy, and reform of educational institutions as well as capital markets (Saxenian, 2006).

REFERENCES

Agrawal, Ajay, Devesh Kapur and John McHale (2004), 'Defying distance: examining the influence of the diaspora on scientific knowledge flows', mimeo.

Amsden, Alice and Wan-wen Chu (2003), *Beyond Late Development: Taiwan's Upgrading Policies*, Cambridge, MA: MIT Press.

Avnimelech, Gil and Morris Teubal (2004), 'Targeting venture capital: lessons from Israel's Yozma program', in Anthony Bartzokas and Sunil Mani (eds), *Financial Systems, Corporate Investment in Innovation, and Venture Capital*, Cheltenham, UK and Northampton, MA, USA: Edward Elgar, pp. 85–116.

Brinkerhoff, Jennifer M (2006), 'Diasporas, skills transfer, and remittances: evolving perceptions and potential', in C. Wescott and J. Brinkerhoff (eds), *Converting Migration Drains into Gains. Harnessing the Resources of Professionals*, Manila: Asian Development Bank.

Brooks Jr, Frederick P. (1995), *The Mythical Man-Month: Essays on Software Engineering*, Reading, MA: Addison-Wesley.

Brown, John Seeley and Paul Duguid (2002), *The Social Life of Information*, Cambridge, MA: Harvard Business School Press.
Gilson, Ronald, Victor Goldberg, Charles Sabel and Robert Scott (2008), 'Contracting for innovation', draft, Columbia Law School.
Hausmann, Ricardo and Dani Rodrik (2002), 'Economic development as self-discovery', NBER Working Paper No. 8952.
Hausmann, Ricardo, Dani Rodrik and Charles Sabel (2008), 'Reconfiguring industrial policy: a framework with an application to South Africa', HKS Working Paper No. RWP08-031.
Helper, Susan, John Paul MacDuffie and Charles Sabel (2000), 'Pragmatic collaborations: advancing knowledge while controlling opportunism', *Industrial and Corporate Change*, 9 (3), 443–88.
Jalotte, Pankaj (2000), *CMM in Practice: Processes for Executing Software Projects at Infosys*, Reading, MA: Addison-Wesley/Software Engineering Institute.
Jin, Bihui, Ronald Rousseau, Richard P. Suttmeier and Cong Cao (2007), 'The role of ethnic ties in international collaboration: the Overseas Chinese phenomenon', *Proceedings of the ISSI 2007*, CISC, Madrid, pp. 427–36.
Kapur, Devesh (2001), 'Diasporas and technology transfer', *Journal of Human Development*, 2 (2), 265–86.
Kapur, Devesh and John McHale (2005), 'The global migration of talent: what does it mean for developing countries?', CGD brief, Washington, DC: Center for Global Development, October.
Kerr, William (2008), 'Ethnic scientific communities and international technology diffusion', *The Review of Economics and Statistics*, 90 (3), 518–37.
Kerr, William (2010), 'The agglomeration of U.S. ethnic inventors', in Edward Glaeser (ed.), *Agglomeration Economics*, Chicago, IL: University of Chicago Press, pp. 237–76.
Kuznetsov, Yevgeny (ed.) (2006), *Diaspora Networks and the International Migration of Skills*, Washington, DC: World Bank Institute.
Kuznetsov, Yevgeny and Charles Sabel (2006), 'Towards a new open economy industrial policy: sustaining growth without picking winners', presentation at World Bank Institute, Asian Policy Forum, Seoul, Korea, 30 November.
Lamoreaux, Naomi R., Daniel M.G. Raff and Peter Temin (2003), 'Beyond markets and hierarchies: toward a new synthesis of American business history', *The American Historical Review*, 108 (2), 404–33.
Langlois, Richard N. (2003), 'The vanishing hand: the changing dynamics of industrial capitalism', *Industrial and Corporate Change*, 12 (2), 351–85.
Lave, Jean and Etienne Wenger (1991), *Situated Learning: Legitimate Peripheral Participation*, Cambridge UK: Cambridge University Press.
Lowell, B. Lindsay and Stefka G. Gerova (2004), 'Diasporas and economic development: state of knowledge', prepared for the World Bank.
Lucas, Robert B (2005), *International Migration Regimes and Economic Development*, Cheltenham, UK and Northampton, MA, USA: Edward Elgar.
Mathews, John A. and Dong-Sung Cho (1999), *Tiger Technology: The Creation of a Semiconductor Industry in East Asia*, Cambridge: Cambridge University Press.
Rauch, James E. and Vitor Trindade (2002), 'Ethnic Chinese networks in international trade', *The Review of Economics and Statistics*, 84 (1), 116–30.
Rodrik, Dani (2007), *One Economics, Many Recipes*, Princeton, NJ: Princeton University Press.
Sabel, Charles F (2005), 'A real-time revolution in routines', in Charles Heckscher and Paul Adler (eds.), *The Corporation as a Collaborative Community*, Oxford: Oxford University Press, pp. 105–56.
Sabel, Charles. F. and Jonathan Zeitlin (2004), 'Neither modularity nor relational contracting: inter-firm collaboration in the new economy', *Enterprise & Society*, 5 (3), 388–403.
Saxenian, AnnaLee (2006), *The New Argonauts: Regional Advantage in a Global Economy*, Cambridge, MA: Harvard University Press.
Sturgeon, Timothy J. (2002), 'Modular production networks: a new American model of industrial organization', *Industrial and Corporate Change*, 11, 451–96.

10 Institutional impact on the outreach and profitability of microfinance organizations
Kathy Fogel, Kevin Lee and William McCumber

INTRODUCTION

In 2006, Dr Muhammad Yunus shared the Nobel Peace Prize with the institution he founded, Grameen Bank, a microfinance organization and community development bank in Bangladesh. More than three decades after its founding, formalized microfinance (as opposed to traditional, often predatory, money-lending) has expanded to hundreds of countries by way of thousands of institutions, all extending financial services to the traditionally underserved, whom we call the 'non-banked', especially the rural poor and micro-entrepreneurs.

As microfinance organizations continue to grow and expand their services, various forms of organizational structure emerge. Some remain purely philanthropic, relying on governments and NGOs for funds. These organizations focus on reaching the poor; loan performance is a lesser concern. Others introduce funds from the private sector and gradually move away from the micro-loan models and shift resources toward larger loans. Yet many others aspire to strike a subtle balance between profitability and outreach, aiming at financial self-sustainability while providing needed social services to the poor. The organizational structure chosen by a microfinance institution largely depends on the community it serves, which has its unique social characteristics, including cultural heritage and popular values, commonly referred to as 'informal institutions', and legal rules, government effectiveness, and regulatory environment, known as 'formal institutions'.

This chapter attempts a first-pass analysis to understand the impact of formal and informal institutions on the success of microfinance institutions. We are interested to see how a microfinance organization's external environment affects its profitability and outreach goals. This study will provide policy makers and investors with some guidance as to what changes are necessary to accompany the improved access to capital in an effort to reduce and ultimately eradicate poverty.

The rest of this chapter is organized as follows. The next section introduces microfinance business models around the world. The third section explores the definitions of formal and informal institutions and explains why they matter in the context of microfinance. The fourth section introduces the data used in this chapter. Then two sections discuss what constitutes success by exploring profitability and outreach metrics and their relation to the external institutions of a society. The final section concludes.

MICROFINANCE AND MICROFINANCE INSTITUTIONS

While microfinance service has expanded in some areas to include savings accounts, deposit taking and insurance services, most microfinance service is microcredit, that of granting small (or 'micro') loans to the poor, usually without pledges of traditional collateral. There are a number of reasons why traditional banks cannot or choose not to provide services to the poor. The poor often have little or no net worth and therefore cannot pledge collateral as a personal guarantee of loan repayment. They often need very small loans but the costs to service loans do not depend upon loan size; that is, the costs incurred by the bank in servicing a small loan are comparable to those of servicing a large loan. It is therefore much more cost efficient for a bank to lend larger amounts and have minimum loan amounts that exclude small borrowers. And in the absence of collateral, financial statements and credit histories, the risk that micro-borrowers may default is difficult for traditional banks to gauge accurately. Physical distance may also be an issue for both the borrower and the traditional bank, as it is difficult for borrowers to travel any distance to repay their loans and costly for bank representatives to visit rural borrowers and monitor loans.

Microfinance institutions (MFIs) charge higher interest rates to their borrowers to cover the higher costs of servicing microloans. Reported interest rates vary considerably, and are reported as high as 20 percent per day, or 18 percent–200 percent annually on declining loan balance (Robinson, 2001). How, one may ask, would 20 percent per day be satisfactory to the borrower? One must take into consideration the explosive gains in efficiency that credit affords the rural, poor, entrepreneur. For example, consider a small grocer in a rural village in a developing country. With relatively poor infrastructure, transportation, and limited financial resources, the grocer must close her shop every other day as she travels a great distance to buy inventory for her shelves, which she pays for with the profits from the previous day's sales. If, however, she has a small loan for a week, she is able to buy a week's worth of inventory and close the shop only on the one day needed to travel for supplies. Her store is better stocked with a larger and broader inventory, is open for business more frequently, and the efficiencies gained mean more opening hours, more product sold, and more attention paid to other business needs (other than inventory procurement). More efficiency ultimately means more revenues at lower cost and part of these 'efficiency improvement profits' are used to repay the loan and interest. And much like business in the developed world that relies upon short-term credit and liquidity, the grocer then gets another week-long loan for another week of inventory.

If MFIs can charge higher fees to cover their higher administrative costs, one large impediment to providing financial services to the underserved is overcome. As important, however, are the combined effects of several innovations in microfinance that allow MFIs to be successful where traditional banks are not.

A profound innovation in microfinance is the practice of joint liability through group lending. The MFI harnesses the power of group dynamics, the intimate communal knowledge shared by locals, and collective advancement or consequences to outsource a significant portion of information gathering and loan monitoring. Groups, as opposed to individuals, apply for a loan. Members of the group are then jointly responsible for loan repayment. If the loan is repaid, the group is in good standing to receive another loan. If one member defaults, the entire group is responsible and is less likely to get a loan in the future (Khandker, 1998). Progressive lending practices allow for future loans to be larger than the initial loans, adding incentive for groups to repay their loans. Importantly, where traditional banks would increase interest rates to offset increased repayment risk, MFIs use group monitoring – as members monitor each other and have to rescue defaulting members on their own – to reduce repayment risk and/or offset default costs (Armendariz de Aghion and Morduch, 2005). Furthermore, there is a smaller probability of strategic default[1] since members jointly suffer even if only one member defaults.

Frequent and public loan payments also serve to increase the likelihood of repayment. Frequent repayments reduce the likelihood that excess funds – from a profitable business, for example – are used by extended family members in need, a common practice in rural and developing communities, instead of meeting loan obligations. Of course, most of us share the common temptation to spend more as funds increase and are otherwise idle. The rural poor are no different. Public repayment increases the social stigma of non-repayment and potentially increases the village or group's trust in those who make payments. Frequent and public repayment also reduces the possibility that MFI officials or loan representatives are corrupted as the public knows who paid, how much, and how often. It also keeps MFI administrative costs in check if representatives are able to meet with many clients locally at one time.

MFIs may also accept pledges of non-traditional collateral as a guarantee of repayment. Non-traditional collateral may be anything that the owner values, regardless of how the market would price the collateral. Often items with family history or sentimental value attached are 'worth' more to their owners than to the market.

As a condition of granting loans, MFIs may make savings requirements. Savings serve as collateral, as a means of providing other loans as savings are mobilized among the community, and/or simply serve as an additional applicant screening mechanism.

Many MFIs work disproportionally with women clients as, regardless of local or regional gender equity norms, women have higher repayment rates than men. Women often have less access to traditional banking services than men. Women may also be more attuned to group dynamics, social advancement and repercussions, making them less risky in group lending environments.

MFIs started simply by offering small loans to rural poor entrepreneurs; in the ensuing decades microfinance became a dynamic subset of global finance offering diverse financial services to the traditionally underserved (see Table 10.1). MFIs differ in size, scope, services offered, organizational structure, regulatory environment, profitability, dependence upon government or non-governmental subsidies and grants, outreach, as well as client mix, among other measures.

Many MFIs, particularly those financed by non-philanthropic funds, find themselves serving two – although not necessarily mutually exclusive – masters: social outreach and profitability. MFIs strive to be an agent of development in the greater community as well as self-sustaining – not relying upon the vagaries of external grants and donations. However, outreach and profitability are often at odds and MFIs face trade-offs between social outreach metrics, which are more difficult to quantify and traditional profitability measures.

The business model and organizational structure chosen by an MFI depends to a large degree upon the community it serves, taking into account such things as cultural norms, values, infrastructure, the regulatory environment, size of the community, existence of competition and many other factors. Flexibility, the ability of an MFI to adapt to

Table 10.1   Key differences between traditional banking and microfinance

	Traditional banking	Microfinance
Lending	Competitive interest rates; borrowers sensitive to rates	Access to credit more important than rate charged, high rates prevalent
Client relationship	Contractually formal, arm's length	Ongoing intimate knowledge of client/business/needs, actively collaborative relationships
Loan security	Primarily collateral	Collective monitoring, trust, reputation, nontraditional collateral
Client base	Small	Large
Loan size	Large; minima apply	Very small on average
Administrative costs	Proportional	Very high

Source: Compiled by authors; source material Koveos and Randhawa (2004).

changing circumstances, is important for survival. Some of the more common permutations of the MFI model are presented in Table 10.2.

An MFI is born of both social needs and entrepreneurial activity. The practices and organizational structure of each institution evolve over time within the structure and norms of local formal and informal institutions. The rest of this chapter explores the definitions of formal and informal institutions and explains why they matter in the context of microfinance. We then examine what constitutes success by exploring profitability measures and outreach metrics. We provide a snapshot of microfinance around the world, and conclude with closing comments and suggest areas requiring future research and development.

INSTITUTIONAL ATTRIBUTES AND MFI SUCCESS

The financial success and self-sustainability of microfinance institutions depend upon the social, political, economic and cultural environments of the host country, aggregated as the institutional attributes of a society. As all other players in society, MFIs are subject to the constraints required by the formal 'rules of the game', including the nature of its host country's legal system, the strength of property right protection, the regulatory stance and efficiency of its government, as well as the breadth and strength of industry-specific regulations. The success of MFIs also hinges on the set of societal factors that affect the behavioral norms of citizens, commonly termed informal institutions, which include culture, religious beliefs, social hierarchy and trust among strangers. The following subsection describes how each institutional feature affects the financial and social performance of microfinance institutions in different countries.

Formal Institutions

Formal institutions include governance, regulation, legal origin and the rule of law, property rights, as well as the level of bureaucratic corruption. Governmental structure

Table 10.2   Common MFI models

Model	Grameen Bank	Bangladesh Rural Advancement Community (BRAC)	Co-operative	Village Bank
Institutional form	Licensed bank	Non-governmental organization (NGO)	Owner-managed firm	Limited bank
Clientele	Poor women, no net worth	Poor households	Non-banked households	Rural groups, micro-enterprises
Loan type	Short-duration small loans	Short-duration small loans	Members' savings mobilization	Rural savings mobilization
Regulation of services	Mutual assistance and monitoring by small groups, access to legal system	Group monitoring and delivery	Members are owners of entity, have interest in performance	Legal enforcement
Funding	Financial institutions	NGOs	Savings mobilization	Financial institutions and rural savings
Allocation of funds	Group procedures for screening, monitoring	Socially oriented to the needy, *a priori*	Allocated to members, mutual responsibility	As per traditional banking, though mobile and closer to rural clients

Sources: Koveos and Randhawa (2004), World Bank Publications, online sources.

and the degree to which the citizenry can lend their voice to governmental action are important. The relative freedom of individuals to change their status and move freely within the system encourages or discourages entrepreneurial activity, and thus microfinance lending. In contrast to London and Hart (2004), we find that formal institutions, such as property rights protection and formal contract enforcement, are still relevant in determining MFI success.

As the legal system of many countries is in large part a function of prior colonial rule, legal origin lends itself to governance, legal and regulatory norms. Civil law holds legislation as the primary source of law, and precedent is not binding for courts. An example of a civil law system is the Napoleonic Code. Common law, on the other hand, is the compilation of court rulings that forms legal precedent. New issues and cases are decided keeping in mind how similar preceding cases were decided. The UK and the USA have common law systems. The common – but contested – wisdom in academic literature is that common law systems tend to foster more developed financial markets, wherein market mechanisms steer the rise and fall of business developments. Economic resources are more likely to be prioritized and/or directed by the state in civil law countries.

Regulatory environment, especially with regard to the financial system, is an important issue for microfinance. Regulation of financial institutions adds a layer of bureaucratic requirements, filings and oversight that increases institutional costs. However, regulation should come with benefits as regulated firms also have access to lines of credit or insured deposits that they would not enjoy without regulation. Many MFIs can choose, at least at the beginning, whether or not to be regulated, with all of the opportunities and costs associated with such status. Once an MFI grows to a certain size, the state may require it to be regulated. Efficient regulation can help an MFI grow; burdensome regulation with high compliance costs could drive smaller, weaker MFIs to fail. One would expect regulated MFIs, with their higher costs, to have stronger profitability metrics and weaker outreach metrics, while unregulated organizations would be freer to pursue social outreach but at the expense of profitability.

Corruption, as related to government, bureaucracy and regulation, is an added cost to MFIs, in terms of both social cost and actual cost. Significant corruption increases the cost of doing business and erodes the level of trust between bureaucrats and MFIs as well as between MFIs and their clients, to the extent that the clientele view the MFI as part of the establishment.

Informal Institutions

The financial sustainability of microfinance institutions also depends upon the implicit rules of the game, or informal institutions. Dimensions of informal institutions include culture, religion, hierarchical structure and the perception of trustworthiness among strangers. The lending and borrowing relationships between a microfinance institution and its borrowers reflect not only a formal contract that specifies the terms of the loans and repayments, but also an implicit agreement involving trust and a mutual understanding of the consequences of a particular outcome. These consequences may include culturally embedded rewards and punishments such as increases in status or loss of reputation. The strength of informal institutions will have a direct impact on the severity of punishment, such as social stigma, when an agreement is violated.

Cultural differences also manifest in a society's ability to create new enterprises. Research shows that some cultures value entrepreneurial spirit more than others (see, e.g., Casson, 1993). A culture valuing strict hierarchy in organizations and demanding docile respect from subordinates tends to discourage entrepreneurial activity, as it is unlikely the entrepreneur would be 'allowed' an increase in status. This reduces the demand for microloans, thus adversely affecting the outreach and financial performance of microfinance institutions in these circumstances.

In order to make meaningful comparisons, we employ Geert Hofstede's four cultural dimensions: power distance, individualism, masculinity and uncertainty avoidance. Each dimension is presented as an index.

A higher value on the power distance index (PDI) indicates that members of the lower strata of society more willingly accept hierarchical structure and the unequal distribution of wealth and power. For example, the PDI values for the UK and the USA are 35 and 40, respectively, as citizens in these countries value their ability to question authority and pursue their dreams. In contrast, the PDI index for both China and the Arab countries is 80. In these societies, people have significantly less upward mobility, obey authority, and tolerate both unequal power and wealth distributions.

A higher value on the individualism index indicates a societal preference for maximizing personal as opposed to collective well-being. The USA, the UK and Australia have the greatest individualism. China, Guatemala and Colombia are at the other end of the scale. An individualist culture may encourage independent thinking and stimulate entrepreneurial ventures, thus increasing the demand for microloans and the success of microfinance institutions.

Hofstede's third cultural dimension, masculinity, reflects the distribution of gender roles. A higher index value implies that the culture's men are more aggressive, assertive and competitive, and that their societal role is distinctly separate from that of women than in societies with lower values. Although these 'masculine' tendencies – assertiveness, competitiveness and so on – are also more prevalent in women in cultures with high masculinity values, the gap between male and female behavior is still wider in these countries than in those with lower values.

The last dimension, uncertainty avoidance, measures societal tolerance for uncertainty and risk. Higher levels of uncertainty avoidance – preference for certainty – indicate a lower societal preference for 'taking a chance'. Entrepreneurs, by definition, take greater risk and explore new ideas. Countries that value certainty over risk taking are therefore expected to have less entrepreneurial activity and, therefore, less demand for microcredit.

DATA

The Microfinance Information Exchange (or MIX market) provides detailed data on the financial and social performance of microfinance institutions in our study. The data include observations from 1997 to 2008, approximately 6000 firm–year observations. Table 10.3 provides a yearly summary of different types of MFIs in our sample.

An international comparison of microfinance lenders must take into account the level of regulation to which each entity is subject. We hand collect this information on each

Table 10.3   Sample by organizational forms

Year	Non-profit (NGO)	Bank	Co-op or credit union	Non-bank financial institution	Rural bank	Other	Total
1997	21	8	2	12	1	0	44
1998	36	11	5	27	0	1	80
1999	48	14	9	38	0	1	110
2000	73	17	17	50	4	3	164
2001	103	21	49	69	4	8	254
2002	196	33	77	106	10	11	433
2003	269	40	110	147	43	16	625
2004	356	49	129	192	51	16	793
2005	395	56	160	218	58	16	903
2006	376	57	151	229	65	14	892
2007	332	59	154	218	61	20	844
2008	271	54	134	198	61	18	736

Table 10.4 Selected performance and outreach measures

Variables	Obs.	Mean	Std dev.	Min.	Max.
Total assets	6595	3.04e+07	1.92e+08	0	6.45e+09
Active borrowers	6535	51756	326421.2	0	6792978
Depositors	5692	85453	1093258	0	3.23e+07
% of women borrowers	5702	66%	28%	0	100%
Avg. loan to GNI per capita	6488	1.466	52.672	0	4236
Borrowers per staff	6505	137	252	0	13709
Operating expense to assets	5249	0.197	0.170	0	2.215
Loan write-off percentage	4743	1.7%	5.5%	0	100%
Return on assets	5250	0.75%	13.95%	−214%	101%

entity in MIX market, creating a binary variable equal to one if the entity is regulated, zero if not. Banking literature (Flannery et al., 2004 and Stiroh and Rumble, 2006) generally suggests that regulation increases the cost of doing business, thus reducing financial performance. This cost is often called regulatory burden. A simple t-test[2] comparing regulated and unregulated MFIs shows that regulated MFIs tend to be older, have greater assets, and are more likely to be for-profit rather than non-profit entities. Regulated MFIs issue larger, traditionally safer loans. Regulated MFIs tend to show higher performance but lower outreach measures, and the clientele of regulated MFIs tend to be wealthier.

Our MFI financial and social performance indicators build upon United Nations Capital Development Fund (UNCDF) publications. Financial performance indicators include profitability, as measured by return on assets (ROA), efficiency, as measured by operating expense as a percentage of total outstanding loans and cost per client, and loan performance, measured by the ratio of loan write-offs to outstanding loans. Social performance, or outreach, measures include the number of accounts, the percentage of women borrowers to total active borrowers, and client poverty level, measured by the average outstanding loan size as a percentage of per capita gross national income (see Table 10.4).

PROFITABILITY

Our primary interest is a cross-country comparison of the effect of national characteristics on MFI profitability and outreach. We adopt a random effect panel approach to model the institutional differences among countries. Because our sample includes multiple microfinance organizations coupled with country-level institutions, we cannot treat each organization as separate, independently identically distributed observations. Statistically, those locally correlated factors produce biased estimates of standard errors. We therefore use random effects panel regressions with the Moulton correction (Moulton, 1986) to cluster the standard errors at country level to account for unobserved, locally correlated factors.[3]

In this section we investigate the effects of selected formal and informal institution measures on profitability (ROA), collection performance (impaired loans to assets) and efficient cost control (operating expense to assets). Table 10.5 shows the results from random effects panel regressions using robust clustered standard errors at the country level. Columns 1, 2 and 3 investigate select formal institution measures on profitability, collection performance and cost control, respectively. We control for year and country to take into account economic development measures and firm-specific measures. We use 11 economic development variables divided into two distinct types: infrastructure and economic development. Infrastructure variables include, for example, the number of miles of roads, road density, and whether or not the roads are paved. Economic variables include gross domestic product the percentage of agriculture to total economic activity. As representatives of these two types, we chose roads and gross domestic product at purchasing power parity per capita (GDPpercapita-PPP) for our regressions. Our results are robust using alternative measures. For firm-specific controls, we control for the age, size, capital structure and non-profit status. Age and size must be controlled because MFIs can suffer 'mission drift' as they grow in size, scope or age. Also an MFI's capital structure may affect the extent to which they may lend and under what conditions. For-profit and non-profit MFIs will also differ in business modeling.

For formal institution measures we use the control of corruption index (Kaufmann et al., 2003) and a dummy variable for common law legal origin. Although other measures can be substituted, such as the regulation, rule and voice indices, they are highly correlated. In one way or another each variable measures the quality of government and the power of the citizenry. Legal origin, however, is specifically correlated with the quality of laws. Variables such as investment protection, director liability and disclosure indices specifically address commercial law. All are found to be highly related to legal origin and greater in common law countries than in civil law countries. Legal origin is therefore our independent variable. Column 1 shows a negative relationship between performance (ROA) and the strength of formal institutions. The coefficient for control of corruption is −0.0164 but statistically insignificant while the coefficient for common law origin is −0.1006 and statistically significant at the 1 percent level. This indicates that MFIs operating in a less corrupt environment have lower performance. This may seem puzzling, but our results indicate that these same firms tend to offer smaller loans at lower interest rates than MFIs in civil law countries, and therefore receive lower returns (see Table 10.6). Columns 2 and 3 show mixed results for impaired loans and operating expenses. Overall, better corruption control is associated with lower levels of loan impairment and a lower operating expense to asset ratio. On the other hand, common law legal origin is positively associated with levels of impairment and operating expense.

The control variables for economic development are all significant in the first three columns. The road variable coefficient is 0.1002, −0.0237 and −0.3037 for ROA, impairment and operating expense respectively. The better the infrastructure, the more efficient and profitable the MFIs. This is probably due to the fact that it is easier for MFIs to monitor their loans and meet with their clientele in sparsely populated rural areas with better roads. GDP per capita shows the opposite signs of infrastructure development. MFIs tend to perform more poorly in richer nations. For example, attempts to provide microcredit to the rural poor in the USA have proved unsuccessful. For firm-specific control variables, age and for-profit measures are significant and show similar relationships with performance and efficiency. As expected, older MFIs tend to be more profitable. This may be due in part to 'mission drift' as these institutions move to serve wealthier

Table 10.5   *Effects of formal and informal institutions on performance and efficiency measures*

	ROA (1)	Impaired loans to assets (2)	Operating expense to assets (3)	ROA (4)	Impaired loans to assets (5)	Operating expense to assets (6)
Formal institutions						
Control of corruption	−0.0164 *(0.23)*	−0.0045** *(0.02)*	−0.0280 *(0.19)*			
Common law legal origin	−0.1006*** *(0.00)*	0.0078** *(0.03)*	0.1378*** *(0.00)*			
Informal institutions:						
Individualism				−0.0036* *(0.06)*	0.0004*** *(0.00)*	0.0061*** *(0.00)*
Masculinity				0.0013 *(0.36)*	0.0002** *(0.00)*	9.87E−05 *(0.95)*
Power distance				0.0011 *(0.34)*	−5.7E−05 *(0.58)*	0.0010 *(0.28)*
Uncertainty avoidance				0.0012 *(0.31)*	0.0002 *(0.21)*	0.0008 *(0.55)*
Economic development						
Roads	0.1002*** *(0.00)*	−0.0236*** *(0.00)*	−0.3056*** *(0.00)*	0.2525*** *(0.01)*	−0.0565*** *(0.00)*	−0.5941*** *(0.00)*
GDP per capita (PPP)	−1.1E−05*** *(0.01)*	1.35E−06*** *(0.00)*	2.09E−05*** *(0.00)*	−7.15E−06 *(0.45)*	−3.00E−07 *(0.67)*	1.81E−05** *(0.04)*
Firm-specific controls						
Age	0.0011** *(0.02)*	−0.0002** *(0.02)*	−0.0030*** *(0.00)*	5.60E−04 *(0.30)*	−0.0003 *(0.01)*	−0.0026*** *(0.00)*
Debt to equity	9.95E−07 *(0.26)*	−8.20E−07*** *(0.00)*	−3.60E−06*** *(0.01)*	6.71E−07 *(0.24)*	−7.51E−07 *(0.00)*	−2.89E−06*** *(0.00)*
Total assets	−3.08E−14 *(1.00)*	4.17E−12 *(0.17)*	−5.42E−11* *(0.10)*	1.86E−11 *(0.51)*	5.23E−12 *(0.22)*	−8.76E−11 *(0.20)*
For-profit	0.0140** *(0.05)*	−0.0034** *(0.05)*	−0.0556*** *(0.00)*	2.15E−02* *(0.08)*	−0.0019 *(0.49)*	−0.0627*** *(0.00)*
Constant	0.0322 *(0.25)*	0.0201*** *(0.00)*	0.2410*** *(0.00)*	−0.1871 *(0.27)*	0.0039 *(0.68)*	0.0030 *(0.98)*

Table 10.5   (continued)

	ROA (1)	Impaired loans to assets (2)	Operating expense to assets (3)	ROA (4)	Impaired loans to assets (5)	Operating expense to assets (6)
Number of observations	4408	4389	4407	1806	1801	1808
R^2	0.3730	0.2541	0.4412	0.5355	0.5910	0.7551

Note: *, **, and *** represent statistical significance at the 10, 5 and 1 percent levels, respectively.

clients. Debt to equity does not seem to affect profitability of the MFIs measured by ROA, but shows significantly negative coefficients for efficiency.

Columns 4 through 6 re-examine performance and efficiency using informal institution measures. The economic development and firm-specific control variables are largely consistent with the first three models. Using Hofstede's cultural dimensions as defined above, we find that individualism leads to lower profits, higher loan impairment and higher expenses. The last two are both significant at the 1 percent level. Individualism appears to be the most important determinant in performance and efficiency among all cultural measures. Although group lending reduces monitoring costs, MFIs in high-individualism areas may not benefit if less importance is placed upon group dynamics and collective well-being. Power distance and uncertainty avoidance seem to have little explanatory power in MFI performance or efficiency. Masculinity is also insignificant in models 4 and 6. However, it is positively and significantly related to impairment of loans, indicating poorer loan performance in male-dominated societies and societies intolerant of new ideas.

OUTREACH

In this section we investigate the effects of select formal and informal institution measures on outreach (number of active borrowers) and target clientele (percentage of women borrowers and average loan size). Table 10.6 shows the results from random effects panel regressions using robust clustered standard errors at the country level. Columns 1, 2 and 3 investigate select formal institution measures on outreach and target clientele. Columns 4 through 6 re-examine these models using informal institution measures. With controls for year and country, we take into account economic development measures and firm-specific measures as in prior regressions.

Starting with the economic development variables, we see roads contributing to better outreach overall although the coefficient in the first model is insignificant. Increasing roads also show a negative impact on the proportion of female borrowers as well as an increase in loan size. This is similar to what we would expect for larger, older MFIs. The roads variable is an infrastructure development variable. It is conceivable that there is a correlation between infrastructure development and microfinancing development. If

Table 10.6   Effects of formal and informal institutions on outreach measures

	Borrowers (1)	% women borrowers (2)	Loan size (3)	Borrowers (4)	% women borrowers (5)	Loan size (6)
Formal Institutions						
Government corruption	10807.95	0.0114	−435.55			
	(0.30)	*(0.64)*	*(0.19)*			
Common law legal origin	57505.53*	0.1662***	−765.96***			
	(0.09)	*(0.00)*	*(0.00)*			
Informal institutions						
Individualism				1944.20***	0.0051*	−46.63***
				(0.00)	*(0.08)*	*(0.00)*
Masculinity				790.27	−0.0020	−16.97
				(0.13)	*(0.42)*	*(0.25)*
Power distance				−223.35	0.0036*	−31.89***
				(0.48)	*(0.09)*	*(0.00)*
Uncertainty avoidance				713.17*	−0.0026	−8.56
				(0.06)	*(0.23)*	*(0.31)*
Economic development						
Roads	43563.44	−0.2350***	1522.78	54274.75	−0.2994*	3554.79***
	(0.25)	*(0.00)*	*(0.17)*	*(0.49)*	*(0.10)*	*(0.00)*
GDP per capita (PPP)	−9.26*	1.86E−06	0.1742**	−8.17**	−2.03E−06	0.1531**
	(0.06)	*(0.74)*	*(0.02)*	*(0.05)*	*(0.90)*	*(0.04)*
Firm-specific controls						
Age	2600.0	−0.0022**	23.10***	815.02*	−0.0011	22.57***
	(0.27)	*(0.02)*	*(0.00)*	*(0.08)*	*(0.34)*	*(0.00)*
Debt to equity	−5.23***	−6.14E−06***	0.0194*	−4.85***	−6.77E−06***	0.0083**
	(0.00)	*(0.00)*	*(0.08)*	*(0.00)*	*(0.00)*	*(0.02)*
Total assets	0.0014**	−5.10E−11	2.60E−06*	0.0005***	−1.34E−11	2.07E−06
	(0.03)	*(0.10)*	*(0.08)*	*(0.01)*	*(0.65)*	*(0.13)*
For-profit	−15999.3	−0.1186***	244.68**	10554.88	−0.1409***	120.29
	(0.22)	*(0.00)*	*(0.03)*	*(0.27)*	*(0.00)*	*(0.37)*
Constant	13715.21	0.7408***	−305.28	−76500	7.01E−01***	4172.05**
	(0.62)	*(0.00)*	*(0.59)*	*(0.31)*	*(0.01)*	*(0.00)*
Number of observations	5273	4634	5251	1957	1791	2123
R^2	0.3497	0.3587	0.2358	0.4256	0.4486	0.5692

Note: *, **, and *** represent statistical significance at the 10, 5 and 1 percent levels, respectively.

this is the case, then we expect MFIs to have grown in these countries and have more clientele. At the same time we expect them to shift away from the poor and toward profit-generating lines of business by issuing larger, more secure loans. GDP per capita is associated with fewer borrowers and larger loan sizes. As the citizenry is better off, they may take their businesses to more traditional banks rather than MFIs since the citizens are in a better position to provide credit histories, financial statements, traditional collateral, and thereby pay lower interest rates on their loans. Therefore there is probably more competition between MFIs and traditional banks in richer countries. Loan size should also be expected to be larger with greater client wealth.

Firm-specific control variables indicate the importance of age, size, capital structure and non-profit status to outreach and target clientele. As MFIs get older and/or larger, they tend to increase the number of borrowers but issue larger loans to relatively fewer women. The coefficients for size are all significant for the first three models while those for age are significant in two of the first three models. For-profit MFIs shift away from female borrowers and the poor and toward a more traditional clientele. However, location will affect the number of clients that profit institutions have. MFIs with high debt ratios reach fewer total borrowers, shift away from female borrowers and offer larger loans. High debt ratios may hamper MFIs from being able to offer riskier loans to women and the poor. The results for debt to equity ratio are consistent and highly significant across all six models.

The corruption variable in columns 1 through 3 is not significant in any of the models but the signs of the coefficients are consistent with expectations. Better protection against corruption increases participation in MFIs and allows smaller average loan size. The common law legal origin variable shows signs consistent with those of the corruption protection variable. In this case, however, all coefficients are significant at the 10 percent level or better. MFIs in countries with common law have significantly more borrowers, a higher percentage of female borrowers, and offer smaller loans on average. This means these MFIs have greater market penetration and reach a greater percentage of the traditionally underserved, namely women and the rural poor.

In columns 4 through 6 we re-examine the relationships between outreach and target clientele measures with informal institution measures. The economic development and firm-specific control variables are consistent with the first three models with the notable exception of for-profit in models 1 and 4. Using Hofstede's cultural dimensions, we find that individualism shows a positive and significant impact on number of borrowers. Individualism likely increases the number of borrowers as individuals, as opposed to groups or villages, that apply for loans. This is consistent with the result that individualism is negatively associated with the size of the loan (see column 6) as individual loans are usually smaller than village or group loans. Masculinity shows a similar pattern (although statistically insignificant), as individuals may be more assertive and aggressive in pursuing goals by acquiring loans. Power distance has an insignificantly negative impact on the number of borrowers but a negative significant impact on the size of the loan. It may be that the poor in high power distance countries have realistic expectations as to social mobility, or lack thereof, and do not bother seeking credit. Those who do may require smaller loans. High power distance may suffocate entrepreneurial spirit in the lower-income populace. We also see that individualism and power distance have a positive statistical impact on the proportion of female borrowers. The only unexpected result again involves uncertainty avoidance. Contrary to expectations, it appears that societies with a greater preference for certainty also have more borrowers. The findings are significant at the 10 percent level. It is also robust to a different specification that controls for the size of total population in the country.

SUMMARY AND CONCLUSIONS

As commercial, governmental and philanthropic organizations continue to channel resources to providing microfinance services to the poor, it is essential to understand what makes such efforts successful. In this chapter, we conduct a first-pass analysis attempting to understand the impact of formal and informal institutions, the legal, political, economic and cultural aspects of society, on the financial performance and outreach of microfinance services.

We show that societies with strong formal institutions, as represented by common law legal origin, foster more efficient MFIs in terms of social outreach. These MFIs often must endure lower profitability, relatively, to provide greater outreach and communal economic development. Lower corruption assists by lowering loan impairment, which in turn should lower overall costs to MFIs.

The effects of cultural dimensions on MFI performance are more complex, as one might expect. Individualism increases the number of borrowers and reduces the size of the loans but at the expense of increasing the cost and risk of lending. In addition, a society more comfortable with certainty, rather than entrepreneurial spirit, has better outreach performance as measured by number of borrowers, but seems to shift away from female and poor borrowers.

Microfinance is in many ways still in its infancy as a subset of global finance. More work needs to be done to help tailor the availability of microcredit and other financial services to those unable to access the traditional banking system. Just like the clients they serve, MFIs can benefit greatly if they have access to better tools, which in turn aids the continued development and well-being, of the groups, villages, women and entrepreneurs served by microfinance institutions. MFIs, on the other hand, must also be profitable and sustainable in order to continue to serve the rural poor and break the cycle of poverty.

NOTES

1. Strategic default refers to the decision of a borrower to default because the perceived cost of default to the borrower is less than the cost of keeping the loan current. For example, a homeowner may choose to strategically default on her mortgage (walk away from her home and let the property fall into foreclosure) if home prices have plummeted, making her loan balance much greater than the market value of her home.
2. Results are not reported but are available from the authors.
3. We thank Oliver Falck for pointing out the appropriateness of using this methodology.

REFERENCES

Armendariz de Aghion, Beatriz and Jonathan Morduch (2005), *The Economics of Microfinance*, Cambridge, MA and London: MIT Press.
Casson, Mark (1993), 'Entrepreneurship', in David R. Henderson (ed.), *Fortune Encyclopaedia of Economics*, New York: Warner Books, pp. 631–4.
Flannery, Mark, Simon H. Kim and M. Nimalendran (2004), 'Market evidence on the opaqueness of banking firms' assets', *Journal of Financial Economics*, **71**, 419–60.
Hofstede, Geert (1980), *Culture's Consequences: International Differences in Work-related Values*, Beverly Hills: Sage Publications.

Kaufmann, Daniel, Aart Kraay and Massimo Mastruzzi (2003), 'Governance matters III: governance indicators for 1996–2002', World Bank Working Paper.

Khandker, S.R. (1998), *Fighting Poverty With Microcredit: Experience in Bangladesh*, Oxford: Oxford University Press.

Koveos, P. and D. Randhawa (2004), 'Financial services for the poor: assessing microfinance institutions', *Managerial Finance*, **30** (9), 70–95.

London, T. and Hart, S.L (2004), 'Reinventing strategies for emerging markets: beyond the transitional model', *Journal of International Business Studies*, **35**, 350–70.

Moulton, B.R. (1986), 'Random group effects and the precision of regression estimates', *Journal of Econometrics*, **32**, 385–97.

Robinson, Marguerite S. (2001), *The Microfinance Revolution, Volume 1: Sustainable Finance for the Poor*, Washington, DC: World Bank.

Stiroh, Kevin and Adrienne Rumble (2006), 'The dark side of diversification: the case of US financial holding companies', *Journal of Banking & Finance*, **30**, 2131–61.

PART III

KNOWLEDGE, KNOWLEDGE SPILLOVERS, THE GEOGRAPHY OF INNOVATION AND ENTREPRENEURSHIP, AND GROWTH

11 Innovation in cities: classical and random urban growth models
Gilles Duranton

It was an honour to have my paper 'Nursery cities' (Duranton and Puga, 2001), republished in a recent Edward Elgar Reference Collection, edited by the editors of this volume. That paper attempts to make a connection between the literature on growth and innovation and urban economics. More precisely, it uses a model of process innovation through experimentation to derive a number of implications about the urban landscape. The insights delivered by this model shed light on a variety of stylized facts about cities and how they link with economic growth. However, the approach taken in nursery cities and much of the 'classical' urban growth literature does not square well with a well-known regularity about the size distribution of cities. Namely, the size of cities appears to be well approximated by a Pareto distribution with exponent minus one. Recently, another literature developed to generate this type of distribution from well-articulated economic models. This literature proposes a radically different modelling approach to urban growth. It highlights randomness and granularity in the urban growth process whereas the classical literature views urban growth as smooth and deterministic. The object of this chapter is first to clarify the tension between the classical urban growth literature *vis-à-vis* random growth models and, second, to explore to what extent these approaches are compatible.

NURSERY CITIES AND CLASSICAL URBAN GROWTH MODELS

The model of Duranton and Puga (2001) can be summarized as follows. Entrepreneurs can introduce new products by paying a fixed cost of entry. At first, entrepreneurs do not fully master the production process for their products and can only produce 'prototypes' (to use the jargon of the model). Mass production of a product requires process innovation. Mass production is desirable because it allows entrepreneurs to produce with greater productivity.

Process innovation, which in the real world is enormously complex, is modelled in a simple way and tailored to deal with urban issues. There is a finite set of inputs in the economy. Among them, one is the 'ideal' set of inputs that each entrepreneur needs for mass production. That is, process innovation is synonymous with discovering one's own ideal set of inputs for a new product. To do this, each entrepreneur needs to engage in sampling. In each period, an entrepreneur can sample at most only one new set of inputs and use them for prototype production. As soon as an entrepreneur samples her ideal set of inputs, she knows this is it and can start mass production.

The use of a particular set of inputs, either for prototype production or mass production (if it is the ideal one), requires physical proximity with its producers. One possibility is for input producers to be dispersed and for entrepreneurs to change location every time they want to sample a new set of inputs. There is a problem with this learning strategy: moving is costly. As a result, entrepreneurs would like to be able to sample different sets of inputs at the same location.

Besides, input producers benefit from agglomeration economies. Having more input producers of the same kind, in the same location, increases their efficiency. This assumption reflects a fundamental fact about cities: the increased concentration of firms and particularly firms from the same sector increases firm efficiency. This fact was noted first by Alfred Marshall back in 1890. Modern econometric studies have confirmed it over and over again (see Rosenthal and Strange, 2004, for a review). In practice, as well as in the model, this tendency for producers to concentrate is limited by the existence of urban costs.

That moving is costly and that input producers want to be together to increase productivity creates an interesting tension. Learning entrepreneurs who try to discover their ideal set of inputs would like to sample everything at the same place. That is, entrepreneurs who have not yet discovered their ideal set of inputs want to locate in a very diversified local economy. However, producers of a particular type of inputs would like to locate together with producers of the same type of inputs. This pushes towards the existence of specialized cities.

Provided moving costs are neither too high nor too low, an interesting equilibrium emerges. It reconciles the needs for specialization and diversity along the life cycle of firms. Entrepreneurs develop new products in cities with a diversified production structure. It allows them to sample easily and discover their ideal set of inputs. After discovering this ideal set of inputs, entrepreneurs are no longer interested in urban diversity. Because input producers in different sectors do not benefit from each other directly, industrial diversity makes cities bigger and thus more costly. As a result, entrepreneurs who know what their ideal inputs are would like to be in a city that is specialized only in the production of those inputs.[1] Put differently, provided moving is not prohibitively costly, entrepreneurs who have discovered their ideal set of inputs will want to move away from a diversified city to a specialized city in order to benefit from agglomeration effects in their sector. In this sense, we can think of diversified cities as 'nursery cities' where learning takes place and specialized cities as the places where the production of mature goods occurs.

To summarize, the model of Duranton and Puga (2001) proposes a set of predictions of how the process of growth and innovation takes place spatially. Beyond this, it rationalizes a number of stylized facts about cities. First, there is a key new prediction originating from the model. Firms that relocate will predominantly relocate away from diversified cities to specialized cities in their sector of activity. The evidence presented in the introduction of Duranton and Puga (2001) supportes this prediction. This model also predicts the coexistence in equilibrium of specialized and diversified cities, a prominent feature of the urban landscape of advanced countries (Duranton and Puga, 2000). Consistent with the growth in cities literature initiated by Glaeser et al. (1992) and more particularly with the work of Henderson et al. (1995), specialized cities seem to bring benefits to firms in mature industries whereas firms in high-tech industries appear to benefit more from diversified cities. The patterns of entry and exit predicted by the nursery city model are consistent with empirical results from firm-level studies (e.g. Dumais et al., 2002; Bernard and Jensen, 2007).

Although it is not strictly speaking a model of endogenous growth, the model of Duranton and Puga (2001) fits well within the literature that extends urban models to consider economic growth. Let us call this class of models the classical urban growth models. While this is not the place to discuss this literature in depth, a number of papers are worth mentioning.[2] Eaton and Eckstein (1997) consider a model where there are agglomeration effects in the accumulation of human capital. They formalize the suggestion of Lucas (1988) that human capital accumulation takes place primarily in cities. Interestingly, the dynamic human capital externality at the core of Eaton and Eckstein's model is at the root of both economic growth and of the existence of cities. Glaeser (1999) proposes a different form of dynamic externality through direct interactions. His argument is that learning can only occur through the teaching of 'young unskilled' workers by 'old skilled' workers. Cities favour learning by providing more opportunities for young workers to meet old workers. While obviously very stylized, this model captures the idea that the greater possibilities for direct interactions between workers in cities may be at the origin of the accumulation and diffusion of knowledge. Black and Henderson (1999) propose a model with a static human capital externality in cities. Larger cities make workers more productive. In turn, workers spend part of their time accumulating human capital. This accumulation of human capital reinforces the human externality that takes place within cities. In turn, that makes cities more attractive. As cities grow in population, the human capital externality is reinforced. A particularly nice feature of Black and Henderson (1999) is that human capital accumulation, output growth and population growth in cities all go hand in hand.

Despite differing emphases on aspects of how the growth process and urban development interact, these models share a number of elements. First, they follow primarily Lucas's (1988) pioneering work on human capital externalities and growth. The framework of Romer (1990) in which growth occurs through new innovations that are patented and increase the general stock of knowledge has arguably less relevance when one is interested in the spatial aspects of growth.[3] The Schumpeterian insights for growth as modelled in Aghion and Howitt (1992) is discussed below.

Second, cities are viewed as an equilibrium outcome between agglomeration forces that make larger cities more productive and urban costs such as increased land scarcity and congestion. Both sets of forces are usually modelled in a detailed fashion with a particular focus on the microeconomic foundations of agglomeration. A fundamental property of this class of models is the existence of a bell-shaped curve for earnings net of urban costs as a function of population size. As a city grows, both agglomeration economies and urban costs increase. The increase in agglomeration economies initially dominates for small cities while higher urban costs eventually take over to limit the growth of large cities.

Third, these models are 'smooth' in the sense that growth proceeds smoothly through atomistic agents. At each period, a fraction of prototype producers learn about their ideal production process (Duranton and Puga, 2001), a fraction of workers become skilled after being taught by others (Glaeser, 1999), or existing residents increase their human capital by some fraction (Eaton and Eckstein, 1997; Black and Henderson, 1999).

Fourth, and related to the previous point, these models are deterministic. Structural characteristics of cities predict its growth. For instance, in Duranton and Puga (2001), the sectoral composition of activities in cities predicts how much learning by firms will take place.[4] In Glaeser (1999), learning by workers is predicted by the composition of cities in terms of both skills and demographics. In Eaton and Eckstein (1997) and Black and Henderson (1999), it is the initial level of human capital of cities, its initial size and its sectoral activity that predict how much growth will take place. Introducing a stochastic element in the model would obviously attenuate this determinism at the city level.[5] For instance, random city effects at each period could influence human capital accumulation. However, what these models tell us is that some urban characteristics like the average level of human capital positively relate with urban growth (Black and Henderson, 1999). In Black and Henderson (1999), a higher level of human capital leads to faster population growth in cities and this is of first-order importance in the sense that what is left unexplained is a residual. While this point may seem obvious (most models in applied theory are about deriving some comparative statics that can be brought into a regression), random urban growth models work very differently.

Before investigating that point more deeply, let me highlight the main limitation of this class of models. It lies in its inability to generate a plausible distribution of city sizes. In Duranton and Puga (2001), the model in its simplest form predicts that in equilibrium all cities are of the same size. We can easily relax this prediction by considering that agglomeration effects in cities have different intensities for different sectors. This is a well-established empirical fact (Henderson, 2003; Rosenthal and Strange, 2004). It implies that specialized cities each achieve a particular size depending on their sector of specialization. This is because the balance between agglomeration economies and urban costs differs across sectors of specialization. It is also possible to assume that agglomeration effects weaken at the margin as a sector grows locally. This immediately implies that diversified cities are much larger than specialized cities, a well-established stylized fact in urban literature (Duranton and Puga, 2000).[6] However, it remains the case that city size is determined by its 'type', and this naturally maps into the observed distribution of city sizes. This feature is not specific to Duranton and Puga (2001), but common to this entire class of models (with one exception to be discussed below) since Henderson (1974). Eaton and Eckstein (1997) and Black and Henderson (1999) also have several types of cities growing in parallel and thus do not have much to say about the size distribution of cities.

To summarize, the literature steming from Henderson (1974) and to which Duranton and Puga (2001) belongs, offers a theory of why there are cities (an equilibrium between agglomeration and dispersion forces), a theory (or a set of related theories) of what those cities do and their production structure, and a theory of their population size and growth, which depends on type. The evidence of tension between agglomeration and dispersion forces seems incontrovertible. The insights delivered by this literature about what cities do and the production structure are also convincing and backed by a large body of evidence. As a set of theories about city size(s), this literature seems much weaker, a point to which we now turn.

ZIPF'S LAW AND RANDOM GROWTH MODELS

Academic interest in the size distribution of cities pre-dates the approach just described. Since Auerbach (1913), many have approximated the distribution of city sizes with a Pareto distribution. In a nutshell, the idea is to rank cities in a country from the largest to the smallest and then to correlate this ranking against their population in the following manner:

$$\text{logRank} = \text{Constant} - \xi\,\text{logSize} \tag{11.1}$$

The estimated coefficient ξ is the exponent of the Pareto distribution. Zipf's law (Zipf, 1949) corresponds to the statement that $\xi = 1$. This implies that the expected size of the second-largest city is half the size of that of the largest, that of the third-largest is a third of that of the largest etc.[7]

The empirical validity of Zipf's law is hotly debated. The classic cross-country assessment of Rosen and Resnick (1980) is ambiguous because their average Pareto exponent of 1.14 for 44 countries is simultaneously interpreted as evidence both for and against Zipf's law. Follow-up work by Soo (2005) broadly confirms these results, albeit with a more negative tone and a claim that Zipf's law is rejected for a majority of countries. This evidence should, however, be interpreted with care because countries differ in the definition of what is a city and quality of data.[8]

The fact that the Zipf coefficient in a large majority of countries is between 0.8 and 1.2 suggests that there is 'something' in the data and it would be hard to argue against any regularity in the size distribution of cities altogether. Zipf's law is both an important stylized fact and a useful benchmark. But it should not be viewed as something miraculous. Whether Zipf's law should take primacy over other stylized facts about cities is also debatable.

Let us now explore the statistical processes leading to Zipf's law. There are two (related) avenues: multiplicative and additive processes. These processes do not tell us much about the underlying economic forces behind urban growth. An important goal of literature is to embed them in well-articulated economic models. For expositional reasons, let us follow the same path and start with the mechanics of Zipf's law.

Following Gabaix (1999a, 1999b), multiplicative processes have attracted a lot of attention. These processes are referred to as Kesten processes (Kesten, 1973). Some formal modelling is now needed. We borrow from Gabaix and Ioannides (2004) and consider an economy with fixed population size. Between t and $t + 1$, city i grows according to $S_{it+1} = (1 + \tilde{\gamma}_{it+1})S_{it}$. We impose Gibrat's law. The $\tilde{\gamma}$s are independently and identically distributed with density $f(\gamma)$.

After T periods, the size of city i is:

$$\begin{aligned}\log S_{iT} &= \log S_{i0} + \sum_{t=1}^{t=T}\log(1 + \gamma_{it}) \\ &\approx \log S_{i0} + \sum_{t=1}^{t=T}\gamma_{it}\end{aligned} \tag{11.2}$$

We note that the approximation in this equation holds only when the shocks are small enough. By the central limit theorem, $\log S_{iT}$ is normally distributed and the distribution of S_{iT} is thus log normal. This distribution of city sizes does not admit a steady state and its variance keeps increasing.

To obtain a steady state, one must impose a lower bound for city sizes (Gabaix, 1999a). Without this, the distribution is single-peaked with thin tails at both ends, as made clear above. This is because very few cities consistently get positive or negative shocks. With a lower bound on city size, things change dramatically because the thin lower tail disappears and there is instead a maximum of the density function at the lower bound. Preventing cities from becoming too small also allows the upper tail to be fed by more cities. As a result, it is fatter. This lower bound also allows for the existence of a steady state instead of an ever-widening distribution. Interestingly, this steady state implies a Pareto distribution.[9]

The main alternative to the multiplicative process described above was originally proposed by Simon (1955). In essence, Simon's model assumes that aggregate population grows over time by discrete increments. With some probability, a new lump goes to form a new city. Otherwise it is added to an existing city. The probability that any particular city gets it is proportional to its population. This mechanism generates a Pareto distribution for city sizes. The Pareto exponent falls to one at the limit as the probability of new cities being created goes to zero.

Despite important differences, both multiplicative and additive processes have some version of Gibrat's law at their core, either directly through multiplicative shocks or through increases of fixed size that occur proportionately to population.

Among existing models of random growth with an economic content, that proposed by Eeckhout (2004) is the simplest. There is a continuum of cities. City i at period t offers productivity A_{it} for labour, the only factor of production. Agglomeration economies increase the productivity of labour by a factor S_{it}^{θ} and congestion costs reduce it by a factor $S_{it}^{-\sigma}$, where S_{it} is the population of city i at time t. Hence output per worker in this city is $A_{it}S_{it}^{\theta-\sigma}$. To avoid complete concentration into a single city, we need $\theta < \sigma$. Free mobility across cities then implies the equalization of output per worker across all cities.

Even though each city faces shocks, the law of large numbers applies in aggregate so that output per worker is deterministic. After normalizing it to unity, the equilibrium size of city i is given by:

$$S_{it} = A_{it}^{\frac{1}{\sigma-\theta}} \qquad (11.3)$$

With small i.i.d. shocks productivity evolves according to $A_{it+1} = (1 + \gamma_{it+1})A_{it}$. It is easy to see that after T periods, we have

$$\log S_{iT} \approx \log S_{i0} + \frac{1}{\sigma - \theta}\sum_{t=1}^{t=T}\gamma_{it} \qquad (11.4)$$

Equation (11.4) is derived in the same way as (11.2). The main difference is that instead of imposing 'arbitrary' population shocks, the model assumes cumulative productivity shocks. In a setting where free mobility implies that population is a power function of productivity (equation 11.3), the log normal distribution of city productivity maps into a log normal distribution of city population. As argued above, adding a lower bound for city size would imply Zipf's law instead.[10]

The model of Rossi-Hansberg and Wright (2007) also relies on cumulative productivity shocks.[11] The main difference between this model and that of Eeckhout (2004) is that it treats cities, as in classical urban growth literature, as an equilibrium between agglomeration and dispersion forces. It is important to show that random growth models can accommodate a standard modelling of cities. The main difference between random and classical urban growth models is not in the static modelling of cities but in what drives the dynamics.

Gabaix (1999a) considers a model where workers are mobile only at the beginning of their life when they need to pick a city. Workers derive (multiplicatively) separable utility from consumption and local amenities. The level of amenity in a city is i.i.d. and drawn every period. With such shocks, the location problem of young workers boils down to the static maximization of the product of the local amenities and the local wage. At the steady-state equilibrium, this product for young workers is equalized across cities.

The production function is homogeneous of degree one between young workers and incumbent residents (a fraction of survivors from previous-period population). An interesting part of Gabaix's model is to show how temporary shocks have permanent effects. This arises through workers becoming immobile after their original choice and the production function which is homogeneous of degree one so that the wage of young workers depends only on the ratio of young mobile workers to immobile incumbents. In this context, amenity shocks that multiply the wage lead to Gibrat's law. Following the argument developed above, adding a lower bound leads to Zipf's law in steady state. There are two differences with the previous two models. First, the shocks apply to amenities and not to technology. Second, the shocks are temporary.

The models of Gabaix (1999a), Eeckhout (2004), and Rossi-Hansberg and Wright (2007) are the three main multiplicative random growth models. Duranton (2006, 2007) proposes two related economic mechanisms that lead to additive random growth.

Duranton (2006) builds on Romer's (1990) endogenous growth model. Research is tied to production through local spillovers. As a result, research activity in one location is proportional to the number of local products. With mobile workers and no cost or benefits from cities, city population is proportional to the number of local products. In equilibrium, small discrete innovations occur in cities proportionately to its population size. Innovations need to be discrete to avoid the law of large numbers from applying and leading to parallel growth for all cities. Newly invented products are either produced where they were developed or, alternatively, where some natural resource forces them to be produced at a new location. The latter leads to the creation of a new city. After each innovation in a city, there is an increase in labour demand to produce the new product. In turn, this implies population growth. In essence, this model puts a geographical structure on a discrete version of Romer (1990). As shown by Duranton (2006), this maps directly into Simon (1955) and generates Zipf's law as a limit case when the probability of a new city tends to zero.[12]

Duranton (2007) uses a related model that builds instead on the Schumpeterian growth model of Grossman and Helpman (1991). In this framework, profit-driven research tries to develop the next generation of a product up a quality ladder. A success gives it a monopoly, which lapses when the next innovation on the same product occurs. Products are discrete to ensure the necessary granularity for shocks to affect cities. Again, local spillovers tie research on a given product to the location of its production. The core of the model is that research might succeed in improving the products it seeks to improve (same-product innovation) or, sometimes, because of serendipity in the research process, it might succeed in improving another product (cross-product innovation).

With same-product innovation, the location of activity is unchanged by innovation and successful new innovators only replace incumbent producers in the same city. With cross-product innovation, the old version of the improved product stops being produced where it used to be and starts being produced in the city where the innovation took place. This typically leads to a relocation of production with a population gain for the innovating city and a loss for the city of the incumbent producer. An example of cross-product innovation is xerography.

In the late 1950s a Rochester (NY) firm, Haloid Company, attempted to improve on Eastman Kodak's technology in the photographic industry. Its innovation was instead an improvement in the reprographic industry. As a result, the reprographic industry moved from New York, where it was originally located, to Rochester, where Haloid and the photographic industry were located.

To prevent cities from disappearing for ever, the model also assumes that there is a core product in each city that cannot move. Symmetry and the absence of other costs and benefits from cities also ensure that city population is proportional to the number of products manufactured locally.

In steady state, this model does not quite lead to Zipf's law because new innovations are not exactly proportional to city size. Because they already have more products, large cities have fewer of them to capture from elsewhere. On the other hand, the smallest cities with just one fixed product can only grow. Hence growth is less than proportional to city size and this leads to a distribution of city sizes that is less skewed than Zipf's law. This distribution does well at replicating the US city size distribution. Unlike other models of random growth, it does not focus exclusively on the size distribution of cities. It also replicates the fast churning of industries across cities, a well-documented fact (Simon, 2004; Duranton, 2007; Findeisen and Südekum, 2008).

TWO MUTUALLY EXCLUSIVE APPROACHES TO URBAN GROWTH?

Classical urban growth models and random urban growth models both appear to contain a grain of truth. They address different aspects of the urban growth process and are able to replicate different stylized facts. At first glance the models seem to complement each other. The key question is whether they are compatible. There are two main differences between these two classes of models. First, in classical urban growth models growth is smooth whereas in random growth models it is granular as growth proceeds through discrete shocks.[13] With infinitesimal shocks, the law of large numbers would apply within each city and the interesting results of random growth models would disappear. Even though random growth models cannot be smoothed, the smoothness of classical urban growth models can easily be roughened. In fact, classical urban growth models are smooth for tractability and aesthetic reasons. Adding shocks or some other form of granularity would be conceptually easy but would make solving these models much more complicated. This suggests that granularity is not an issue from the theoretical perspective and that there is no real opposition here between the two classes of model.

The second main difference between classical and random growth models of cities regards the role of shocks. Classical urban growth models follow the traditional approach where growth is driven by city characteristics and what is left unexplained is treated as a residual. In random growth models, the 'residual' is everything.

To understand this point better, consider a simple urban growth regression:

$$\log S_{it+1} - \log S_{it} = a_1 \log S_{it} + a_2 \log X_{it} + \varepsilon_{it+1} \tag{11.5}$$

where the growth of city i between t and $t + 1$ depends on its population size in t, a set of characteristics X, and a random term, ε. As starting point, it is useful to consider that classical urban growth models focus on S and X whereas random growth models focus on ε. The issue is whether Zipf's law is compatible with $a_1 \neq 0$ or $a_2 \neq 0$.

While there is some disagreement in the literature about the importance of mean reversion in city population data (e.g. Black and Henderson, 2003 versus Eeckhout, 2004), past city population is more often than not a significant determinant of city growth and its coefficient appears with a negative sign in urban growth regressions. However, mean reversion is not sufficient to invalidate random growth models. As made clear by Gabaix and Ioannides (2004), what matters is not mean reversion in itself but the existence of a unit root in the urban growth process. That is, random growth models rely on a 'weak' version of Gibrat's law, not on its strong version. To understand this point more precisely, let us follow Gabaix and Ioannides (2004) and assume the following error structure $\varepsilon_{it} = \gamma_{it} + \mu_{it} - \mu_{it-1}$ where γ_{it} is i.i.d. and μ_{it} is stationary. In that case, there is mean reversion since growth between t and $t + 1$ is negatively correlated with size in t. On the other hand, absent other determinants of urban growth, one can easily show that this error structure implies:

$$\log S_{iT} = \log S_{i0} + \sum_{t=1}^{t=T} \gamma_{it} + \mu_{iT} + \mu_{i0} \tag{11.6}$$

This equation has much in common with (11.2), where the summation of the γ shocks combined with a lower bound for city size leads to Zipf's law. The main difference is the contemporaneous error term μ_T. The heuristic developed by Gabaix and Ioannides (2004) argues that if the tail of the summation in γ is fatter than that of μ, Zipf's law should still occur in steady state. Intuitively, mean reversion does not matter provided it is 'dominated' by the cumulated 'Gibrat's shocks'. While insightful, this example remains very particular. Much remains to be done in this area. We need to know what is the weakest version of Gibrat's law compatible with Zipf's law.

Turning to the other determinants of urban growth, let us return to equation (11.5), assume $a_1 = 0$, allow for a_2 to be time varying, and consider that $\varepsilon_{it} = \gamma_{it}$ which is i.i.d. After simplification, we obtain:

$$\log S_{iT} = \log S_{i0} + \sum_{t=1}^{t=T} \gamma_{it} + \sum_{t=1}^{t=T} a_{2t} X_{it} \tag{11.7}$$

It is now easy to understand that any term $a_2 X$ that is constant over time and differs across cities would lead to a distribution that differs from Zipf's law. Simply put, when cities experience city-specific trends, there is divergence in the long run and no steady-state distribution.

This basic incompatibility between classical and random urban growth models should not be exaggerated. First, the upper tail of the city size distribution may remain Pareto despite different growth trends. To understand this point, consider two groups of cities, fast- and slow-growing cities (corresponding to the case where X is an indicator variable in equation 11.5). Provided the lower bound city size for each group of cities grows with its trend, there is a Pareto distribution emerging for each group of cities and divergence between the two groups.[14] If this divergence is slow, at any point in time the overall distribution will be a mixture of two Pareto distributions with coefficent minus one but different lower bounds. Above the largest of the two lower bounds, this distribution will be Pareto. Over one century, a difference of 1 percent per year in the trend implies a factor of only 2.7 for city size differences. With a lower bound for slow growing cities of, say, 10 000 people, the corresponding lower bound for fast growing cities will be 27 000 after one century. Above 27 000 the size distribution of cities is Pareto. Thus slow divergence is difficult to observe in the data.

If divergence between groups is fast, the slow-growth group will quickly become vanishingly small. For instance, it may be that contemporaneous distributions of city sizes that are typically truncated at some threshold between 10 000 and 100 000 may only contain 'good sites'. 'Bad sites' have not developed into large cities and led only to small settlements. The evidence of a Pareto distribution in the lower tail of the distribution is much weaker than in the upper tail (Eeckhout, 2004; Michaels et al., 2008; Rozenfeldet al., 2009). This is consistent with this argument. Put differently, fast divergence is also difficult to observe in the data. Only 'intermediate' divergence will be easily observed.

Second, classical and random urban growth models are also compatible when the effects of $a_{2t}X_{it}$ are short-lived, that is when there is mean reversion in a_2 or in X. Mean reversion in a_2 corresponds to the situation where a permanent characteristic has a positive effect over a period of time and negative effect over another. In the USA, for instance, it is possible that hot summers were conducive to population growth after the development of air-conditioning but not before. Proximity to coal and iron was arguably a factor of growth during the late nineteenth and early twentieth century. It became irrelevant after.

Mean reversion in X corresponds instead to the situation where the determinants of growth are temporary in cities. For instance, it could be that receiving roads is a factor of urban growth, as suggested by Duranton and Turner (2008), and that the growth of roads is proportional to population.[15] In that case, what growth regressions and classical urban models treat as explanatory variables need to be thought of as the shocks in random growth models. This observation suggests that shocks in the context of random growth models need not be equated with residuals in urban growth regressions. It also highlights the need for more microfoundations for the shocks in random growth models.

These remarks suggest that different time horizons between classical and random growth models may go a long way towards making them compatible with each other. Classical urban growth models, which constitute the theoretical underpinning of standard urban growth regressions, may be looking at the growth of cities around a particular period whereas random growth models may have a much longer time horizon. In that case, classical urban growth models help us uncover short-run proximate factors of urban growth whereas random growth models help us understand the fundamental mechanics that drive urban growth in the long run.

CONCLUSION

'Nursery cities' (Duranton and Puga, 2001), the paper reproduced in this book's companion reference volume, belongs to a broader class of classical urban growth models. These models deliver important insights about the growth cities and illuminate a number of other issues such as the respective roles of diversity and specialization in urban development. These models also make some suggestions about the relative sizes of cities. However, they do not naturally generate a key stylized fact, Zipf's law.

Random urban growth models propose a number of explanations for this stylized fact. This presents a challenge for classical urban growth models working under radically different principles. In a nutshell, classical growth models are all about trends whereas random growth models are all about shocks. As shown above, these frameworks can coexist, but only under fairly restrictive conditions. An exact statement of these conditions is still needed. A more systematic empirical exploration of random growth models is also needed. Urban economists will need to use techniques that are outside their normal toolbox.

NOTES

1. A proportion of firms die every period to ensure that new firms keep entering and learning is never exhausted.
2. See Berliant and Wang (2005) for a review of this literature.
3. There is an interesting literature on the spatial dimension of patents, as represented for instance by Jaffe et al. (1993) or, more recently, Agrawal et al. (2006). As shown below, Romer (1990) nevertheless serves as the basis for a couple of urban growth models.
4. All the learning takes place in diversified cities. However, process innovations are implemented in specialized cities. This is where TFP (total factor productivity) growth is then recorded. In this model, more innovation implies employment growth in diversified cities and more TFP growth in specialized cities. This prediction is consistent with the empirical findings of Cingano and Schivardi (2004).
5. Proper modelling of microeconomic foundations for these shocks would be needed. We return to this issue below.
6. Under some conditions, equilibrium city size is such that marginal agglomeration economies are equal to marginal urban costs. If marginal agglomeration economies are constant, the sectoral composition of cities does not matter in determining their size and all cities regardless of what they do reach the same size. With marginal agglomeration economies decreasing with size, a city with only one sector has lower marginal agglomeration economies than another city of the same size whose activity is split across many sectors. As a result, we expect diversified cities to be larger than specialized cities.
7. The deterministic reformulation of Zipf's law is usually referred to as the 'rank size rule'.
8. For more about these issues, see the excellent survey by Gabaix and Ioannides (2004).
9. See Gabaix (1999a) for a complete proof.
10. Zipf's law is not desired by Eeckhout (2004). The empirical part of his paper makes the case for a log normal distribution for city sizes.
11. Zipf's law is obtained in two cases by Rossi-Hansberg and Wright (2007). The first is the case described here with permanent shocks. The second is a situation with temporary shocks that affect factor accumulation. For alternative ways to generate Zipf's law with cumulative shocks, see also Córdoba (2008).
12. It also avoids some pitfalls of Simon (1955), which converges slowly towards Zipf's law. The cumulative and exponential nature of the growth process in Romer (1990) ensures that shocks, although additive, occur more frequently as time passes, which leads to much faster convergence.
13. Although random growth models can be specified in continuous time, as in Gabaix (1999a), some form of granularity is needed.
14. The lower bound needs to increase with the trend, otherwise cities of smaller relative size would occur over time, which would weaken the reflection leading to a Pareto distribution. In the extreme case of a fast-receding lower bound, it is easy to see that one would return to a log normal distribution.

15. Duranton and Turner (2008) reject this second condition for the last quarter of the twentieth century but not for the 25 years prior to this, which saw a major expansion in the US road system.

REFERENCES

Aghion, Philippe and Peter Howitt (1992), 'A model of growth through creative destruction', *Econometrica*, **60** (2), 323–51.

Agrawal, Ajay, Iain Cockburn and John McHale (2006), 'Gone but not forgotten: knowledge flows, labor mobility, and enduring social relationships', *Journal of Economic Geography*, **6** (5), 571–91.

Auerbach, F. (1913), 'Das Gesetz der Bevölkerungskonzentration', *Petermanns Geographische Mitteilungen*, **59**, 73–6.

Berliant, Marcus and Ping Wang (2005), 'Dynamic urban models: agglomeration and growth', in Roberta Capello and Peter Nijkamp (eds), *Advances in Urban Economics*, Amsterdam: Elsevier, pp. 533–81.

Bernard, Andrew B. and J. Bradford Jensen (2007), 'Firm structure, multinationals, and manufacturing plant death', *Review of Economics and Statistics*, **89** (2), 193–204.

Black, Duncan and J. Vernon Henderson (1999), 'A theory of urban growth', *Journal of Political Economy*, **107** (2), 252–84.

Black, Duncan and J. Vernon Henderson (2003), 'Urban evolution in the US', *Journal of Economic Geography*, **3** (4), 343–72.

Cingano, Federico and Fabiano Schivardi (2004), 'Identifying the sources of local productivity growth', *Journal of the European Economic Association*, **2** (4), 720–42.

Córdoba, Juan-Carlos (2008), 'On the distribution of city sizes', *Journal of Urban Economics*, **63** (1), 177–97.

Dumais, Guy, Glenn Ellison and Edward L. Glaeser (2002), 'Geographic concentration as a dynamic process', *Review of Economics and Statistics*, **84** (2), 193–204.

Duranton, Gilles (2006), 'Some foundations for Zipf's law: product proliferation and local spillovers', *Regional Science and Urban Economics*, **36** (4), 542–63.

Duranton, Gilles (2007), 'Urban evolutions: the fast, the slow, and the still', *American Economic Review*, **97** (1), 197–221.

Duranton, Gilles and Diego Puga (2000), 'Diversity and specialisation in cities: why, where and when does it matter?', *Urban Studies*, **37** (3), 533–55.

Duranton, Gilles and Diego Puga (2001), 'Nursery cities: urban diversity, process innovation, and the life cycle of products', *American Economic Review*, **91** (5), 1454–77.

Duranton, Gilles and Matthew A. Turner (2008), 'Urban growth and transportation', processed, University of Toronto.

Eaton, Jonathan and Zvi Eckstein (1997), 'Cities and growth: theory and evidence from France and Japan', *Regional Science and Urban Economics*, **27** (4–5), 443–74.

Eeckhout, Jan (2004), 'Zipf's law for (all) cities', *American Economic Review*, **94** (5), 1429–451.

Findeisen, Sebastian and Jens Südekum (2008), 'Industry churning and the evolution of cities: evidence for Germany', *Journal of Urban Economics*, **64** (2), 326–39.

Gabaix, Xavier (1999a), 'Zipf's law for cities: an explanation', *Quarterly Journal of Economics*, **114** (3), 739–67.

Gabaix, Xavier (1999b), 'Zipf's law and the growth of cities', *American Economic Review* (Papers and Proceedings), **89** (2), 129–32.

Gabaix, Xavier and Yannis M. Ioannides (2004), 'The evolution of city size distributions', in Vernon Henderson and Jacques-François Thisse (eds) *Handbook of Regional and Urban Economics*, vol. 4, Amsterdam: North-Holland, pp. 2341–78.

Glaeser, Edward L. (1999), 'Learning in cities', *Journal of Urban Economics*, **46** (2), 254–77.

Glaeser, Edward L., Heidi Kallal, José A. Scheinkman and Andrei Schleifer (1992), 'Growth in cities', *Journal of Political Economy*, **100** (6), 1126–52.

Grossman, Gene M. and Elhanan Helpman (1991), 'Quality ladders in the theory of growth', *Review of Economic Studies*, **58** (1), 43–61.

Henderson, J. Vernon (1974), 'The sizes and types of cities', *American Economic Review*, **64** (4), 640–56.

Henderson, J. Vernon (2003), 'Marshall's economies', *Journal of Urban Economics*, **53** (1), 1–28.

Henderson, J. Vernon, Ari Kuncoro and Matt Turner (1995), 'Industrial development in cities', *Journal of Political Economy*, **103** (5), 1067–90.

Jaffe, Adam B., Manuel Trajtenberg and Rebecca Henderson (1993), 'Geographic localization of knowledge spillovers as evidenced by patent citations', *Quarterly Journal of Economics*, **108** (3), 577–98.

Kesten, Harry (1973), 'Random difference equations and renewal theory for products of random matrices', *Acta Mathematica*, **131** (1), 207–48.

Lucas, Robert E. Jr (1988), 'On the mechanics of economic development', *Journal of Monetary Economics*, **22** (1), 3–42.

Marshall, Alfred (1890), *Principles of Economics*, London: Macmillan.

Michaels, Guy, Ferdinand Rauch and Stephen J. Redding (2008), 'Urbanization and structural transformation', processed, London School of Economics.

Romer, Paul M. (1990), 'Endogenous technical change', *Journal of Political Economy*, **98** (5(2)), S71–S102.

Rosen, Kenneth and Mitchell Resnick (1980), 'The size distribution of cities: an examination of the Pareto law and primacy', *Journal of Urban Economics*, **8** (2), 165–86.

Rosenthal, Stuart S. and William C. Strange (2004), 'Evidence on the nature and sources of agglomeration economies', in Vernon Henderson and Jacques-François Thisse (eds), *Handbook of Regional and Urban Economics*, vol. 4, Amsterdam: North-Holland, pp. 2119–71.

Rossi-Hansberg, Esteban and Mark L.J. Wright (2007), 'Urban structure and growth', *Review of Economic Studies*, **74** (2), 597–624.

Rozenfeld, Hernán D., Diego Rybski, Xavier Gabaix and Hernán A. Maske (2009), 'Zipf's law for the bulk of the distribution of city sizes', processed, New York University.

Simon, Curtis J (2004), 'Industrial reallocation across US cities, 1977–1997', *Journal of Urban Economics*, **56**(1), 119–43.

Simon, Herbert (1955), 'On a class of skew distribution functions', *Biometrika*, **42** (2), 425–40.

Soo, Kwok Tong (2005), 'Zipf's law for cities: a cross country investigation', *Regional Science and Urban Economics*, **35** (3), 239–63.

Zipf, George K. (1949), *Human Behavior and the Principle of Least Effort: An Introduction to Human Ecology*, Cambridge, MA.: Addison-Wesley.

12 Knowledge spillovers and the geography of innovation – revisited: a 20 years' perspective on the field on geography of innovation
Maryann P. Feldman and Gil Avnimelech

INTRODUCTION

Economic growth is one of the major goals of national and regional economic policy. Thus an important economic inquiry is: why do some regions grow more than others? The neoclassical answer to this question is that economic growth is determined by the stocks of capital and labor (Solow, 1956). The endogenous growth theory (Romer, 1986; Lucas, 1988) claims that another important element in determining economic growth is the stock of economic knowledge of an economy. Accordingly, knowledge impacts growth by enhancing the rate of innovation and technical change. Moreover, not only is knowledge an important factor generating growth, but, because it spills over for use by third-party agents, it is actually a prevailing powerful factor. Romer (1990) also argues that knowledge is the only factor that can be the source of long-term growth of per capita GDP, e.g. the rate of per capita GDP growth equals the rate of technological change on the steady-state growth path.

Krugman (1991) argues that the most striking feature of the geography of economic activity is the concentration of production in space. Feldman (1994) and Audretsch and Feldman (1996) provide evidence that the concentration of innovation activity in space is even more dominant. This concentration of innovation activity has significant implications for regional economic growth. While, since the 1980s, many regions implemented regional development strategies based on enhancement of innovation capabilities, one major element that still differentiates the pace of innovation of different geographical regions is the level of their knowledge stocks (Lucas, 1993).

Eliminating these differences is difficult because the sources of knowledge are often embedded in local institutions, social structures and human capital (Sweeney, 1987). Moreover, Dosi (1988) notes that innovation may have a strong geographical stickiness due to the path-dependent and cumulative nature of knowledge and learning processes. This cumulative nature of knowledge development is related to the notion of knowledge spillovers. Knowledge is said to spill over when the economic agent utilizing that knowledge is distinct from the one that produced the knowledge.

THE FOUNDATIONS OF GEOGRAPHY OF INNOVATION

The Knowledge Production Function

The starting point in most theories of innovation is the firm. In such theories, firms are exogenous and their ability to generate new economic knowledge is endogenous (Scherer, 1984; Cohen and Klepper, 1992). In these theories, the greatest source generating new economic knowledge is generally considered to be the level of investment in R&D (Cohen and Klepper, 1992). For example, in the model of the knowledge production function, introduced by Griliches (1979), firms engage in R&D activity as an input into the process of generating innovations. Other inputs in the knowledge production function include measures of human capital, skilled labor and educational levels (Audretsch and Feldman, 2004).

However, empirical estimation of this simplistic model of the knowledge production function is found to be stronger at broader levels of aggregation. For example, when the unit of observation is sectors at the state level, the empirical evidence obviously supports the existence of the knowledge production function, while at the enterprise or local establishment levels this relationship is less robust (Audretsch and Feldman, 2004).

As it became apparent that the firm is not a completely adequate unit of analysis for estimating the knowledge production function model, scholars began looking for empirical evidence of local knowledge externalities. More specifically, the finding on one hand that the knowledge production function model holds only at aggregated levels of economic activity such as states or regions and, on the other hand, that there are clear differences in innovation levels between different regions, suggests that both the presence of an externality from new knowledge generation and these externalities are probably geographically bounded.

Knowledge Externalities and Spillovers

Nelson (1959) and Arrow (1962) argue that there are externalities associated with knowledge production due to its non-exclusive and non-rival characteristics. However, what is challenging both theoretically and empirically is to identify the mechanisms through which knowledge spillovers occur (Breschi and Lissoni, 2001). More specifically, in refocusing the model of the knowledge production function on the spatial unit, scholars confronted three challenges. The first was theoretical: what is the theoretical basis for knowledge spillovers that are geographically bounded? The second challenge involved measurement: how could knowledge spillovers be identified and measured? The third was empirical: how can we determine the causality in the spatial knowledge production function?

During the 1980s, a new theoretical understanding about the role of knowledge spillovers and the way in which they are localized emerged. These theories claim that knowledge spillovers do not spread without cost with respect to geographic distance. While the costs of transmitting codified information may be invariant to distance, it appears that the cost of transmitting tacit knowledge (Polanyi, 1966) rises along with distance (Audretsch and Feldman, 1996). Based on this new understanding, scholars began estimating the knowledge production function incorporating a spatial dimension.

Industrial Clusters

The concept of regional cluster is also related to the notion of spatially bounded knowledge spillovers. The phenomenon of regional clusters[1] has been an integral part of economic geography theories since the works of Marshall (1890). The traditional explanation for the existence of regional clusters focuses on cost saving through agglomeration economics. Marshall (1890) proposed three main advantages of industrial clustering: (1) the development of a local pool of specialized labor; (2) the availability of specialized input factors and specialized business services; and (3) efficient information flows.

Jaffe et al. (1993) point out that one explanation why innovative activity in some industries tends to cluster geographically is the fact that the location of production in these industries is also concentrated spatially. However, in practice the role of clusters in knowledge-intensive industries seems to be even more significant than in traditional industrial clusters (Maskell, 2001). Many explanations are given for this phenomenon. Dahlman (1979) emphasizes the role of the reduction of transaction costs involving search costs, bargaining costs and enforcement costs in knowledge-intensive clusters. Griliches (1992) argues that as knowledge has incomplete property rights, geographic concentrations of innovative activity generate knowledge spillovers as one firm's activities aid the advancement of other firms. Ellison and Glaeser (1999) argue that the knowledge-intensive activities are more dependent on frequent face-to-face contacts due to the complexity of the knowledge and its tacit nature.

LOCALIZED KNOWLEDGE SPILLOVERS

The literature tends to use the term 'localized knowledge spillovers', which could be seen as geographically bounded knowledge externalities (Breschi and Lissoni, 2001). Localized knowledge spillovers are the focus of significant econometric studies in the field of economic geography.

Krugman (1991, p. 53) argues that it is impracticable to directly measure innovative activity because 'knowledge flows are invisible; they leave no paper trail by which they may be measured and tracked, and there is nothing to prevent the theorist from assuming anything about them that she likes'. However, Jaffe et al. (1993) point out that 'knowledge flows do sometimes leave a paper trail – in the form of patent citations'. Jaffe et al. (1993) used such patent citation in their research on localized knowledge spillovers. Other scholars find various ways to measure directly or indirectly innovation activity. For example, Jaffe (1989) links the patent activity related to a specific technological sector located within a specific state to R&D activity related to the same technological sector located within the same state.

Considerable evidence suggests that location and proximity clearly matter in exploiting knowledge spillovers. Jaffe (1986) finds that firm patents are a function of both the firm's own R&D expenditure and state-level R&D expenditure. Jaffe (1989) finds empirical evidence that supports the notion of localized knowledge spillovers from university and industrial research laboratories. He found that firm-level patents are related to internal R&D level, and the level of industrial and university research in the firm's sector within the relevant state. Jaffe et al. (1993) analyze patent citations, comparing the probabilities of patents citing prior patents awarded to inventors from the same city against a randomly drawn control sample of cited patents. Their results suggest that citations are significantly more localized than in the control group. Almeida and Kogut (1997) use the same methodology on patenting in the semiconductor industry, and find that patent citations are highly localized.

However, none of these studies explicitly examines the propensity for innovative activity to cluster spatially (Feldman, 1994, 1999). Acs et al. (1992, 1994), Feldman (1994), as well as Audretsch and Feldman (1996) explicitly measure geographical knowledge spillovers in innovation using a database of commercial innovation collected by the Small Business Administration (SBA) in 1982. This database gathered information on announcements of new innovation in over 100 scientific and trade journals. This empirical work also supports the notion of localized knowledge spillovers. Acs et al. (1992) confirm that the knowledge production function held at a spatial unit of observation using a direct measure of innovative activity, new product introductions in the market. Feldman (1994) extends the model to consider other knowledge inputs to the commercialization of new products such as related industries and business services. Audretsch and Feldman (1996) calculate Gini coefficients for the geographic concentration of innovative activity. They find that the propensity of innovative activity to cluster geographically tends to be greater in industries where new economic knowledge plays a more important role. This effect is found to hold even after holding the degree of production at that location constant. Their results suggest a greater propensity for innovative activity to cluster spatially in industries in which industry R&D, university research and skilled labor are important inputs.

Localized Knowledge Spillovers from Academic Institutions

Of particular importance in providing new economic knowledge are research scientists at universities. Jaffe (1989) finds that corporate patents at the state level are a function both state-level industrial R&D expenditure and state-level university research expenditure. Acs et al. (1992) find that the knowledge created in university laboratories contributes to the generation of commercial innovations in the private sector. Acs et al. (1994) and Feldman (1994) find evidence that spillovers from university research contribute substantially to the innovative activity of private corporations.

The empirical evidence suggests that knowledge spillovers from universities are not homogeneous across different types of firms. In estimating knowledge absorption by large and small enterprises separately, Acs et al. (1994) find that expenditures on research by universities serve as a key input for generating innovation activities in small enterprises. Apparently large firms are more adept at exploiting knowledge created by their own laboratories, while smaller counterparts have a comparative advantage at exploiting spillovers from both university laboratories and from knowledge created by large corporations.

Powell et al. (1996), Florida and Cohen (1999) and Feldman et al. (2002) also demonstrate the ways in which research universities provide a link that facilitates knowledge spillovers by recruiting talent into the region, transferring technology through local linkages, placing students in industry, and by providing a platform for firms, individuals and government agencies to interact.

Mechanisms of Knowledge Spillovers

The aforementioned empirical evidence suggests that location and proximity clearly matter in exploiting knowledge spillovers. However, although previous research has produced a certain degree of empirical evidence on the existence of local knowledge spillovers, there is still limited understanding of how spillovers actually take place. It is difficult to distinguish between different channels of knowledge spillovers (Fritsch and Slatchev, 2007). Understanding the mechanisms underlying knowledge spillovers is obviously essential for a comprehensive theory of geography of innovation and for designing effective innovation policies (Breschi and Lissoni, 2001).

Audretsch et al. (2006) argue that the spillover processes that the endogenous growth theory assumes to be automatic are not actually automatic; rather they are actively driven by economic agents and specific mechanisms. Examples of such spillover mechanisms are when a skilled employee changes his job – labor mobility (Almeida and Kogut, 1999) establishes a new firm or spin-offs (Klepper, 2009), or exchanges knowledge informally with employees in other companies – informal networks (Dahl and Pederson, 2005). These spillover mechanisms are known to be spatially bounded (Breschi and Lissoni, 2001).

Knowledge spillovers and entrepreneurship

Evolutionary economics focuses on two central principles – diversity and selection (Nelson and Winter, 1982). Evolution takes place via a process of selection among diverse entities, which propels an economy in a new direction. Nelson and Winter (1982) argue that diversity often originates from investments in R&D. However, R&D does not directly lead to innovation. Arrow (1962) suggested that knowledge is characterized by radical uncertainty, considerable asymmetries and high transaction costs. This means that knowledge is not the equivalent of economic knowledge, but rather a gap exists between knowledge and economically commercialized knowledge. This implies that firm investment in R&D does not automatically result in the generation of diversity and enhanced growth.

Audretsch et al. (2006, 2008) argue that, contrary to the assumption of the endogenous growth theory (Lucas, 1988; Romer, 1986, 1990), growth resulting from knowledge is not equally spread across individuals, firms and regions. Rather, a filter between investments in new knowledge and its commercialization exists (Acs et al., 2009). Various mechanisms are required to facilitate spillovers from the agents creating that knowledge to its commercialization (Acs et al., 2009). The ability to transform new knowledge into economic opportunities involves a set of skills, attitudes, insights and circumstances that is not widely distributed in the population. Audretsch (1995) argues that this unique ability is what characterizes entrepreneurs. Acs and Audretsch (1990) argue that entrepreneurs play an important role in the economy, serving as agents of change, acting as a considerable source of innovation activity, and stimulating industry evolution. Entrepreneurs play a special role in the cluster formation (Avnimelech and Teubal, 2006; Saxenian, 1994; Feldman, 2001). They start new firms and new economic activities that exploit new technological opportunities and create new markets (Feldman and Francis, 2004; Feldman et al., 2005).

Audretsch and Keilbach (2004) suggest that entrepreneurship is an important mechanism for creating diversity of knowledge, which in turn serves as a mechanism facilitating innovation and economic growth. More specifically, entrepreneurs are the economic agents bridging the gap between knowledge and economic knowledge. What enables entrepreneurs to create this diversity of knowledge is the fact that they are often the carriers of knowledge spillovers within an economy. Entrepreneurs' role as carriers of knowledge spillovers includes two main elements: selection of economically valuable knowledge and commercialization of this knowledge. Thus entrepreneurship is an important source of diversity by transforming knowledge into economic knowledge. This suggests that those regions with a greater amount of entrepreneurial activity also have a greater degree of diversity, which should result in higher rates of growth (Audretsch and Keilbach, 2004). Michelacci (2003) contend that the low rates of social return to R&D in specific regions may be due to lack of entrepreneurial skills.

The willingness and potential of individuals to serve as a conduit of knowledge spillovers via entrepreneurship is not homogeneous across geographic space. Rather, it is a function not only of personal preferences but also of regional characteristics, such as social acceptance of entrepreneurial behavior and other cultural parameters, the availability of venture capital finance, and the institutional setting of the region. A region in which these and other factors are conducive to entrepreneurship can be characterized as having a high level of 'entrepreneurship capital' (Audretsch and Keilbach, 2004). Since startups can serve as a conduit for knowledge spillovers, those regions with a high level of entrepreneurship capital would be expected to exhibit high levels of economic growth (Audretsch and Keilbach, 2004).

Knowledge spillovers and labor mobility
Building on Arrow's (1962) seminal work on the link between labor mobility and knowledge spillovers, economists also consider labor mobility as an important spillover conduit. Skilled engineers often hold knowledge tacitly. Labor mobility is quite likely to be bounded in space, due to sunk costs for relocation and aversion to the risk of unemployment. Thus the observations that tacit knowledge is embedded within individuals and that there is a spatially bounded labor market are critical components in explaining why the localization of knowledge and innovation activity may vary significantly by region (Almeida and Kogut, 1999).

In the literature on localized knowledge spillovers, employee mobility is often mentioned as one of the mechanisms through which spillovers occur (Dahl, 2002). In Audretsch and Feldman (1996), skilled labor is included as a mechanism through which knowledge spillovers may be realized as workers move between jobs within an industry taking their accumulated skills and know-how with them. For example, Almeida and Kogut (1999), tracking the movements of over 400 engineers, show that their patterns of mobility influenced the interregional and intraregional patterns of knowledge flow. They argue that interregional labor mobility may be a cause of knowledge localization. Their findings suggest regions such as Silicon Valley, which experience higher than average levels of interfirm labor mobility, tend to experience a greater degree of localized knowledge spillovers. This finding is also supported by Breschi and Lissoni (2006, 2009). Dosi (1988) suggests that hiring people away from a rival firm is a way of transferring knowledge that is otherwise immobile. Song et al. (2003) argue that learning-by-hiring is mostly useful for innovation beyond the firm's current technological and geographic boundaries.

Knowledge spillovers and networks
Another potential mechanism for knowledge spillovers is social networks. Diffusion of knowledge tends to be local, particularly for technologies characterized by relatively high degrees of tacitness and complexity, and thus cannot be completely codified into blueprints, contracts and journal articles (Audretsch and Feldman, 1996). When tacitness and complexity are relatively high, repeated face-to-face contact and personal interaction are increasingly valuable for effective knowledge transfer (Sorenson et al., 2004). Repeated interactions promote development of informal networks that serve as conduits for information exchange about important technological developments and emerging market opportunities (Saxenian, 1994; Stuart and Sorenson, 2003).

Many social networks dedicated to the production of knowledge are geographically bounded, since spatial proximity helps network members to communicate more effectively and monitor each other's behavior. The literature emphasizes the impact of networks and social capital within a geographic region on knowledge spillovers. For example, Saxenian (1990, 1994) emphasizes that it is the communication between individuals that facilitates the knowledge spillovers across agents, firms and industries. Florida and Kenney (1988) provide evidence on the local dimension of venture capital activity and examine the connections and access to talent and resources that venture capital firms provide their local portfolio companies.

The literature suggests that social relationships facilitate knowledge spillovers. Spatial proximity is important for mediating social relationships between individuals from different fields. As Agrawal et al. (2006) argue, geography is likely to be less important in mediating social relationships between individuals in the same field since they have various alternative mechanisms through which to establish relationships. Agrawal et al. (2006) posit that geographic proximity works to overcome social distance and, once relationships are established, that individuals can remain socially close even if they become geographically separated.

Criticism of the Concept of Localized Knowledge Spillovers

The concept of localized knowledge spillovers is strongly criticized by Breschi and Lissoni (2001), who argue that it is no more than a 'black box' with ambiguous contents. Furthermore, they argue that this literature neglects to explore how spillovers occur and how knowledge actually is transferred between individuals and firms located in the same geographical area.

Breschi and Lissioni (2001) argue that there is usually no unambiguous empirical evidence that the local externalities observed are actually knowledge spillovers rather than other types of urbanization or agglomeration economics such as economics of specialization (the existence of a variety of specialized suppliers and other business services), supply and demand markets economies of scale, and labor market economies of scale (the existence of a pool of specialized employees).

In addition, even when the observed externalities are related to knowledge transfer, it is not clear whether it is a public good (i.e. pure knowledge spillovers) or market-intended knowledge transfer such as cooperative networks or acquiring skilled employees previously employed by other companies. Breschi and Lissioni (2001) argue that market-intended knowledge transfer should not be considered as knowledge externalities or seen as a local advantage, as the absorbing agent often pays the full economic value of this production input.

This criticism is based on the observation that the units of analysis in most studies examining spillovers are often too broad to explain knowledge spillovers in both the geographical and in the technological sense (Breschi and Lissioni, 2001). Moreover, the variables usually used to measure innovation (patents and counts of innovations) are not similar to innovation and, therefore, result in methodological problems (Breschi and Lissioni, 2001). In addition, one cannot be sure that there are no unobserved variables (such as culture) that affect both the dependent and independent variables in the models (Breschi and Lissioni, 2001). The pre-existing pattern of technology-related activities makes it difficult to separate spillovers from the correlation (rather than causality) of variables at the geographic level. Economic activity may be co-located, but the pattern of causality is difficult to decipher.

Breschi and Lissoni (2006) argue that spatial proximity is used by most localized knowledge spillover studies as a proxy for social proximity. To the extent that many social networks are concentrated in space, spatial proximity would appear as a significant determinant of access to knowledge spillovers. If this is true, by replacing spatial proximity with direct measurers of social proximity we would diminish the importance of geography as an explanatory variable of spillovers. Breschi and Lissoni (2009) also find that after controlling for inventors' mobility and for the resulting co-invention network, the residual effect of spatial proximity on knowledge diffusion is greatly reduced.

SUMMARY, POLICY IMPLICATIONS AND FUTURE CHALLENGES

Innovation is widely seen as the key to regional economic development. Many countries and regions seek to develop economic development strategies that encourage increased regional innovation levels. The theory and findings on the issue of geography of innovation are extremely influential in shaping the approach for these policies. For example, the suggestion that localized knowledge flows create positive knowledge spillovers has prompted the intervention of local policy makers in enhancing knowledge production through support of R&D activities at local universities and public research centers. Moreover, regional policy makers shift their focus toward policies that enable and facilitate knowledge diffusion and absorption by local economic agents such as network development and entrepreneurship enhancement policies.

Yet the economic benefits of innovation can be captured only if new knowledge leads to commercial innovations. Thus additional effort should be channeled toward better understanding the barriers to and channels for regional innovation commercialization. The entrepreneurial capital theory is a significant step in this direction. However, other aspects should also be explored such as regional innovation systems, regional institutions and regional culture. Regional entrepreneurial capital may be the result of other unexplored omitted regional factors.

Much has been written about the 'death of distance'. Modern information and communications technologies (ICTs) are thought to have diminished the obstacles to economic interaction created by geographic separation. Yet the tendency for high-technology industries to be geographically clustered suggests that proximity to sources of knowledge flows as inputs to R&D is still critically important. However, one cannot ignore the fact that rapid advances in ICTs and the wide social impact that they may have in the near future will significantly impact the geography of innovation. One example is the possibility that tacit knowledge may be transferred through different types of communication platforms. Another example may be that social proximity will become less related to spatial proximity and more related to online social network association. On the other hand, new technological revolutions may be more dependent on spatial proximity than the ICT revolution. For example, personal medicine may be much more strongly associated with specific geographical areas.

In addition, there is evidence that globalization has had two conflicting impacts. On one hand, due to the ICT revolution people around the world are becoming more aware of different cultures and life, thus creating a greater possibility for common culture. On the other hand, the economics of scope and flexible technologies enable much greater personalization of products, processes and services, which may actually lead to a world with increasing cultural difference.

NOTE

1. Marshall (1890) defined clusters as geographic areas containing a number of firms producing similar products, including firms operating at different stages of a production process that gain advantages through co-location. Porter (1998) defined clusters as geographical concentrations of interconnected firms and institutions in a particular field, linked by commonalities and complementarities.

REFERENCES

Acs, Z.J. and D.B. Audretsch (1990), *Innovation and Small Firms*, Cambridge, MA: MIT Press.
Acs, Z.J., D.B. Audretsch and M.P. Feldman (1992), 'Real effects of academic research', *American Economic Review*, **82** (1), 363–7.
Acs, Z.J., D.B. Audretsch and M.P. Feldman (1994), 'R&D spillovers and recipient firm size', *Review of Economics and Statistics*, **100** (2), 336–67.
Acs, Z.J., P. Braunerhjelm, D.B. Audretsch and B. Carlsson (2009), 'The knowledge spillover theory of entrepreneurship', *Small Business Economics*, **32**, 15–30.
Agrawal A., I. Cockburn and J. McHale (2006), 'Gone but not forgotten: labor flows, knowledge spillovers, and enduring social capital', *Journal of Economic Geography*, **6** (5), 571–92.
Almeida, P. and B. Kogut (1997), 'The exploration of technological diversity and the geographic localization of innovation', *Small Business Economics*, **9** (1), 21–31.
Almeida, P. and B. Kogut (1999), 'Localisation of knowledge and the mobility of engineers in regional networks', *Management Science*, **45**, 905–17.
Arrow, K.J. (1962), 'Economic welfare and the allocation of resources for invention', in R.R. Nelson (ed.), *The Rate and Direction of Inventive Activity*, Princeton, NJ: Princeton University Press, pp. 609–25.
Audretsch, D.B. (1995), *Innovation and Industry Evolution*, Cambridge, MA: MIT Press.
Audretsch, D.B. and M.P. Feldman (1996), 'Knowledge spillovers and the geography of innovation and production', *American Economic Review*, **86**, 630–40.
Audretsch, D.B. and M.P. Feldman (2004), 'Knowledge spillovers and the geography of innovation', in V. Henderson and J.F. Thisse (eds), *Handbook of Regional and Urban Economics, volume 4: Cities and Geography*, Amsterdam: Elsevier, pp. 2713–39.
Audretsch, D.B. and M. Keilbach (2004), 'Entrepreneurship capital and economic performance', *Regional Studies*, **38** (8), 949–59.

Audretsch, D.B., Bonte, W. and M. Keilbach (2008), 'Entrepreneurship capital and its impact on knowledge diffusion and economic performance', *Journal of Business Venturing*, **23** (6), 687–98.

Audretsch, D.B., Keilbach, M. and E. Lehmann (2006), *Entrepreneurship and Economic Growth*, New York: Oxford University Press.

Avnimelech, G. and M. Teubal (2006), 'Creating VC industries which co-evolve with high tech: insights from an extended industry life cycle (ILC) perspective to the Israeli experience', *Research Policy*, **35** (10), 1477–98.

Breschi, S. and F. Lissoni (2001), 'Knowledge spillovers and local innovation systems: a critical survey', *Industrial and Corporate Change*, **10**, 975–1005.

Breschi, S. and F. Lissoni (2006), 'Cross-firm inventors and social networks: localised knowledge spillovers revisited', *Annales d'Economie et de Statistique*, **79–80**, special issue, part II.

Breschi, S. and F. Lissoni (2009), 'Mobility of skilled workers and co-invention networks: an anatomy of localized knowledge flows', *Journal of Economic Geography*, **9** (4), 1–30.

Cohen, W.M. and S. Klepper (1992), 'The anatomy of industry R&D intensity distributions', *The American Economic Review*, **82** (4), 773–99.

Dahl, M. (2002), 'Embedded knowledge flows through labor mobility in regional clusters in Denmark', DRUID's New Economy Conference, Copenhagen.

Dahl, M.S. and C.R. Pederson (2005), 'Social networks in the R&D process: the case of the wireless communication industry around Aalborg, Denmark', *Journal of Engineering and Technology Management*, **22** (1–2), 75–92.

Dahlman, C.J. (1979), 'The problem of externality', *The Journal of Law and Economics*, **22** (1), 141–62.

Dosi, G. (1988), 'Sources, procedures, and microeconomic effects of innovation', *Journal of Economic Literature*, **26** (3), 1120–71.

Ellison, G. and E.L. Glaeser (1999), 'The geographic concentration of industry: does natural advantage explain agglomeration?', *American Economic Review*, **89** (2), 311–16.

Feldman, M.P. (1994), *The Geography of Innovation*, Boston, MA: Kluwer Academic Publishers.

Feldman, M.P. (1999), 'The new economics of innovation, spillovers and agglomeration: a review of empirical studies', *Economics of Innovation and New Technology*, **8** (1–2), 5–25.

Feldman, M.P. (2001), 'The entrepreneurial event revisited: an examination of new firm formation in the regional context', *Industrial and Corporate Change*, **10**, 861–91.

Feldman, M.P. and J.L. Francis (2004), 'Homegrown solutions: fostering cluster formation', *Economic Development Quarterly*, **18** (2), 127–37.

Feldman, M.P., I. Feller, J.E.L. Bercovitz and R.M. Burton (2002), 'University–technology transfer and the system of innovation', in M.P. Feldman and N. Massard (eds), *Institutions and Systems in the Geography of Innovation*, Boston, MA: Kluwer Academic Publishers, pp. 55–78.

Feldman, M.P., J.L. Francis and J. Bercovitz (2005), 'Creating a cluster while building a firm: entrepreneurs and the formation of industrial clusters', *Regional Studies*, **39** (1), 129–41.

Florida, R. and M. Kenney (1988), 'Venture capital-financing innovation and technological change in the U.S.', *Research Policy*, **17**, 119–37.

Florida, R.L. and W.M. Cohen (1999), 'Engine or infrastructure? The university role in economic development', in L.M. Branscomb, F. Kodama and R. Florida (eds), *Industrializing Knowledge: University–Industry Linkages in Japan and the United States*, Cambridge, MA: MIT Press; pp. 589–610.

Fritsch, M. and V. Slatchev (2007), 'Universities and innovation in space', *Industry and Innovation*, **14**, 201–18.

Griliches, Z. (1979), 'Issues in assessing the contribution of research and development to productivity growth', *The Bell Journal of Economics*, **10** (1), 92–116.

Griliches, Z. (1992), 'The search for R&D spillovers', *Scandinavian Journal of Economics*, **94**, 29–47.

Jaffe, A.B. (1986), 'Technological opportunity and spillovers of R&D: evidence from firms, patents, profits and market value', *American Economic Review*, **76** (5), 984–1001.

Jaffe, A.B. (1989), 'Real effects of academic research', *American Economic Review*, **79** (5): 957–70.

Jaffe, A.B., M. Trajtenberg and R. Henderson (1993), 'Geographic localization of knowledge spillovers as evidenced by patent citations', *Quarterly Journal of Economics*, **63** (3), 577–98.

Klepper, S. (2009), 'Spinoffs: a review and synthesis', *European Management Review*, **6** (3), 159–71.

Krugman, P. (1991), 'Increasing returns and economic geography', *Journal of Political Economy*, **99** (3), 483–99.

Lucas, R.E. (1988), 'On the mechanics of economic development', *Journal of Monetary Economics*, **22** (1), 3–42.

Lucas, R.E. (1993), 'Making a miracle', *Econometrica*, **61**, 251–72.

Marshall, A. (1890), *Principles of Economics*, 8th edn, New York: Macmillan, 1948.

Maskell, P. (2001), 'Toward a knowledge-based theory of the geographical cluster', *Industrial and Corporate Change*, **10** (4), 921–43.

Michelacci, C. (2003), 'Low returns in R&D due to the lack of entrepreneurial skills', *The Economic Journal*, **113**, 207–25.

Nelson, R.R. (1959), 'The simple economics of basic scientific research', *Journal of Political Economy*, **67**, 297–306.
Nelson, R. and S. Winter (1982), *An Evolutionary Theory of Economic Change*, Cambridge, MA and London: Harvard University Press (Belknap Press).
Polanyi, M. (1966), *The Tacit Dimension*, New York: Doubleday.
Porter, M.E. (1998), *On Competition*, Boston, MA: Harvard Business School Press.
Powell, W., K.W. Koput and L. Smith-Doerr (1996), 'Interorganizational collaboration and the locus of innovation: networks of learning in biotechnology', *Administrative Science Quarterly*, **42** (1), 116–45.
Romer, P.M. (1986), 'Increasing returns and long-run growth', *Journal of Political Economy*, **94** (5), 1002–37.
Romer, P.M. (1990), 'Endogenous technological change', *Journal of Political Economy*, **98** (5), 71–8.
Romer, P.M. (1994), 'The origins of endogenous growth', *The Journal of Economic Perspectives*, **8** (1), 3–22.
Saxenian, A. (1990), 'Regional networks and the resurgence of Silicon Valley', *California Management Review*, 33, 89–111.
Saxenian, A. (1994), *Regional Development: Silicon Valley and Route 128*, Boston, MA: Harvard University Press.
Scherer, F. (1984), 'Using linked patent and R&D data to measure interindustry technology flows', in *R&D, Patents, and Productivity*, Cambridge, MA: National Bureau of Economic Research.
Solow, R.M. (1956), 'A contribution to the theory of economic growth', *The Quarterly Journal of Economics*, **70** (10), 65–94.
Song, J., P. Almeida and G. Wu (2003), 'Learning-by-hiring: when is mobility more likely to facilitate interfirm knowledge transfer?', *Management Science*, **49** (4), 351–65.
Sorenson, O., J.W. Rivkin and L. Fleming (2004), 'Complexity, networks and knowledge flow', mimeo, University of California, Los Angeles, CA.
Stuart, T. and O. Sorenson (2003), 'The geography of opportunity: spatial heterogeneity in founding rates and the performance of biotechnology firms', *Research Policy*, **32**, 229–53.
Sweeney, G.P. (1987), *Innovation, Entrepreneurs and regional Development*, New York: St Martin's Press.
Zucker, L.G., M.R. Darby and J. Armstrong (1998), 'Geographically localized knowledge: spillovers or markets?', *Economic Inquiry*, **36**, 65–86.

13 Entrepreneurship, innovation and economic growth: interdependencies, irregularities and regularities[1]
Pontus Braunerhjelm

The greatest danger for most of us is not that our aim is too high and we miss it but that it is too low and we reach it. (Michelangelo)

INTRODUCTION

Considerable advances, even breakthroughs, have undoubtedly been made during the last decades in our understanding of the relationship between knowledge and growth on the one hand, and entrepreneurship and growth on the other. Similarly, more profound insights have also been gained as to how entrepreneurship, innovation and knowledge are interrelated. Yet a comprehensive understanding is still lacking concerning the interface of all of those variables: knowledge, innovation, entrepreneurship and growth. The knowledge–innovation–entrepreneurship–growth nexus is intricate and influenced by forces that are likely to simultaneously affect all variables, at least partially, while others can be expected to have a unidirectional impact or affect only a few of these variables. The link between the microeconomic origin of growth and the macroeconomic outcome is still too rudimentarily modeled to grasp the full width of these complex and intersecting forces.

Growth can basically be attributed the following fundamental forces: an increase in factors of production; improvements in the efficiency of allocation across economic activities; knowledge; and the rate of innovation. Given full employment and efficient allocation, growth is thus driven by knowledge accumulation and innovation. The process of innovation is typically modeled as a function of the incentive structure, i.e. institutions, assumed access to existing knowledge, and a more systemic part. Innovation also implies that the stock of (economically) useful knowledge increases. In other words, innovation is one vehicle that diffuses and upgrades already existing knowledge, thereby serving as a conduit for realizing knowledge spillovers. The process of innovation is consequently considered to be one of the critical issues in comprehending growth.

Irrespective of the advances made in this vein of economics, a number of basic questions related to the dynamics of the growth process, and the ensuing normative conclusions, are only fragmentally understood and just partially explored. Even quite basic issues as the definition of the concept of innovation are clearly not settled, not to mention how they come about and by whom, i.e. the connection to entrepreneurial activities. Moreover, in precisely what way does innovation contribute to new knowledge (through scientific/technical discoveries or through a much broader view on innovation) and which knowledge bases and cognitive abilities are critically important for innovation to take place? Exactly how does innovation substantiate into growth and how are the effects spatially diffused? And which policy measures should be taken in order to boost the probability of sustained knowledge-based growth? Those are the questions that will be focused on in this chapter through a selected survey of the literature.

The lack of detailed insight into these issues implies that our knowledge concerning the microeconomic foundations of growth is at best partial, but could potentially also be quite flawed. Without accurate microeconomic specification of the growth model there is also an obvious risk that the derived policy implications are incorrect. The recipes for growth are likely to be inconsistent over time and also to vary over different stages of economic development. Today's developing countries may learn from policies previously pursued by the developed countries, while developed countries themselves confront a more difficult task in carving out growth policies for the future. Hence the relationship between the level of development, entrepreneurship, innovation and growth will also be considered.

Background

Despite the enhanced understanding of the building blocks of dynamic processes, economics-based theories and models largely fall short of addressing the influence of the independent innovator or entrepreneur on important economic outcomes. The accumulation of factors of production, i.e. knowledge, human and/or physical capital, cannot alone explain economic development. Innovation and entrepreneurship are needed to transform these inputs in profitable ways, an insight already expressed by Adam Smith (Andersson and Tollison, 1982).

At the same time there seem to be preconceived perceptions at the policy level concerning the effects of activities by entrepreneurs and entrepreneurial firms. For instance, it is more or less taken for granted that setting up a new company, or the performance of new ventures, automatically translate into societal benefits. However, this is an oversimplification; entrepreneurship may under certain conditions reduce rather than enhance economic progress. This would be the case for illegal enterprising, but also when entrepreneurial talent is spent on rent-seeking activities such as litigation, or whenever the Coasian transaction costs arguments for internalizing economic activities are violated through policy-induced incentives. In other words, it is fully conceivable for successful new enterprise at the micro level to translate into economic regress at the societal level and for a failed entrepreneurship at the micro level to contribute to economic development. The societal implications of the actions of individual entrepreneurs, i.e. how that translates into growth and prosperity, is thus not fully considered.

In connecting knowledge, innovation and entrepreneurship, it is essential to emphasize the non-routine processes that are conspicuous phenomena of the dynamics of economic development. Knowledge-driving innovation is frequently thought of as a linear process, being an outcome of activities labeled R&D. Obviously a set of other processes, such as learning-by-doing, cognitive abilities, networking, combinatorial insights and so on, also fuse societal knowledge. Uncertainty, search and experiments are crucial parts of the innovative process. The knowledge-generating activities of entrepreneurs and small firms have been shown to be spread across a number of different functional areas. Disregarding these aspects means that several studies neglect a substantial share of the knowledge creation relevant to innovation and economic growth.

Consequently, despite making small investments in R&D and other formal knowledge-generating activities, entrepreneurs and small firms may still substantially contribute to aggregate innovation, thanks to their entrepreneurial abilities. Still, there is no guarantee that new knowledge with commercial potential is immediately transformed into entrepreneurial initiatives; these effects could fail to show up at all, or appear with a time lag.

Because entrepreneurship entails the actions and activities of individuals working within firms or for themselves, incentives that encourage the risky endeavor of entrepreneurial activity seem essential, as is the infrastructure allowing the transfer of knowledge from knowledge-generating actors to knowledge-exploiting entrepreneurs. In addition, firms and entrepreneurs have to develop strategies to balance slow knowledge development processes with fleeting windows of opportunity and find ways of speeding up knowledge generation and exploitation. Here the financial system, by evaluating prospective entrepreneurs, mobilizing and channeling savings to finance the most productivity-enhancing activities, diversifying risks and so on, plays a vital role. Thus the design of financial systems influences growth by increasing the probabilities of successful innovation (King and Levine, 1993). The question is how that is accounted for in standard knowledge-driven growth models.

The view that entrepreneurship could play an important role in a knowledge-based economy seems to contradict much of the conventional wisdom. For instance, according to Galbraith (1967), Williamson (1968) and Chandler (1977), it seemed inevitable that exploitation of economies of scale by large corporations would become the main engine of innovation and technical change. But also the 'late' Joseph Schumpeter (1942) shared these views, albeit he was considerably more skeptical about the beneficial outcome than his colleagues. Rather, Schumpeter feared that the replacement of small and medium-sized enterprise by large firms would negatively influence entrepreneurial values, innovation and technological change. Despite these early prophecies of prominent scholar, there is ample empirical evidence that the development has actually reversed since the early 1970s for most industrialized countries. The tide has turned: the risk-prone entrepreneur has experienced a virtual renaissance and is increasingly seen as indispensable to economic development.

Theoretical advances and empirical research seem to support the view that knowledge generation, innovation and entrepreneurship are localized processes. Irrespective of knowledge flows largely being bounded in space, it is however also possible to observe how knowledge, innovations and entrepreneurial initiatives flow between functional urban regions and even countries. Thus, even though regions are characterized by their varying internal economic and infrastructure networks, they are also connected by a multitude of such networks. It is obvious that there is an important interplay between localized processes of knowledge generation, innovation and entrepreneurship, but current insights are basically lacking concerning the relative importance of interregional and international networks. An increasingly global knowledge base serves to enhance and diversify the local knowledge base, i.e. what has been coined 'local buzz and global pipelines'.

In terms of policy, it is a well-established result that market economies normally do not generate a socially optimal volume of knowledge creation, innovation and entrepreneurship. However, there is no consensus concerning what institutional frameworks and policy measures might generate such a social optimum given the imperfections in both the economic and the political markets. This has not stopped policy makers from launching a large number of institutional changes and policy measures to stimulate knowledge creation, innovation and entrepreneurship. Nevertheless, the number of carefully carried through policy evaluations is rather limited, which implies that there is a huge knowledge gap concerning which policies actually work and whether they are worth their costs.

The main objective of this chapter is hence to shed light on recent advances in our understanding of the forces that underpin the creation of knowledge, its diffusion and commercialization through innovation, and the role of the entrepreneur in the growth process. The following section discusses the definition, origin and measurement of entrepreneurship, and how it relates to knowledge production, while the third section is devoted to innovation and the innovation process. The fourth section presents how these components have been integrated into a growth context, and discusses the weak links in current models of growth. In the subsequent section the regional aspects of entrepreneurship, knowledge extraction and growth are highlighted. The chapter is concluded by a policy discussion and a summary of the main findings, together with suggestions for future research.

ENTREPRENEURSHIP – DEFINITION, MEASURE AND ORIGIN

Why do individuals engage in entrepreneurial ventures with uncertain and risky outcomes?

The earlier entrepreneurship literature suggests a plethora of reasons as to why individuals become entrepreneurs, albeit institutions are always at the heart of the matter when the extent of entrepreneurial activities is explained. The alleged explanations of entrepreneurship comprise a mix of clear-cut economic explanations, specific attributes that are claimed to characterize entrepreneurs, as well as forces related to culture and path-dependency. Sometimes they are classified according to the level of aggregation, starting at the macro-level and working their way down to industry-related factors, microeconomic incentive structures and cognitive abilities of individuals. Alternatively, similar forces triggering entrepreneurship are presented in a supply and demand taxonomy. In this section I shall briefly survey the most frequent explanations for entrepreneurial activities, focusing on the empirical findings concerning the role of institutions and access to knowledge. The idiosyncrasies pertaining to the definition and production of knowledge are likewise addressed.[2]

The Austrian Heritage

Within the last decades we have witnessed an Austrian renaissance in economics – putting the entrepreneur, structural change and creative destruction in the forefront – both from an academic point of view as well in policy making. Most contemporary theories of entrepreneurship, and the implications of entrepreneurship, thus build on the seminal contributions by, in particular, Schumpeter (1911/1934). He stressed the importance of innovative entrepreneurs as the main vehicle to move an economy forward from static equilibrium, based on the combinatorial capabilities of entrepreneurial individuals.[3] In his own words:

> Whatever the type, everyone is an entrepreneur only when he actually carries out new combinations and loses that character as soon as he has built up his business, when he settles down to running it as other people run their business. (Schumpeter, 1911/1934, p. 78)

> And what have they done: they have not accumulated any kind of goods, they have created no original means of production, but have employed means of production differently, more advantageously. They have carried out new combinations! They are the entrepreneurs. And their profit, the surplus to which no liability corresponds, is the entrepreneurial profit. (Ibid., p. 132)

Schumpeter viewed the creation of technological opportunity as basically outside the domain of the entrepreneur. Rather, the identification and exploitation of such opportunities are what distinguish entrepreneurs, i.e. innovation. Also in this respect Schumpeter's original thoughts on entrepreneurial opportunity have had a considerable influence on the succeeding generation of entrepreneurship researchers. Nor did Schumpeter view entrepreneurs as risk takers, even though he did not completely dismiss the idea, and was aware that innovation contains elements of risk also for the entrepreneur. But basically that task was attributed to the capitalists who financed entrepreneurial ventures.

A decade later, Knight (1921) proposed the role of the entrepreneur as someone who transforms uncertainty into a calculable risk. Schumpeter's model was thereby complemented by the explicit introduction of cognitive abilities as an explanation of entrepreneurial activity. Somewhat later, the definition of the entrepreneur as someone who moved the economy toward equilibrium (partly contrasting Schumpeter) by taking advantage of arbitrage possibilities was forwarded by Kirzner (1973, 1996, 1997). The Austrian heritage can be traced even further back. Menger (1871) stressed the uncertainties and subjectivities that he claimed must be inherent phenomena in economies characterized by extensively distributed and fragmented economic activities.[4] These ideas were further elaborated by von Hayek (1945). Thus there seems to be a rather clear connection between Menger's view on the subjective economy, von Hayek's ideas about the distribution of knowledge, and Kirzner's arbitraging entrepreneur, which in turn basically links well with Schumpeter's definition of the entrepreneur's innovative capacity, including the detection of new markets.[5]

More recently, the research field of entrepreneurship has been defined as analyses of 'how, by whom and with what consequences opportunities to produce future goods and services are discovered, evaluated and exploited' (Shane and Venkataraman, 2000, p. 220). As regards by 'whom', an eclectic definition of the entrepreneur that has become increasingly accepted is suggested by Wennekers and Thurik (1999). The entrepreneur: (i) is innovative, i.e. perceives and creates new opportunities; (ii) operates under uncertainty and introduces products to the market, decides on location, and the form and use of resources; and (iii) manages his business and competes with others for a share of the market. Apparently, this definition can be linked to all three contributions referred to above. Note that invention is not explicitly mentioned (albeit creation of opportunity is) in this definition, nor excluded from the interpretation of entrepreneurship. A summary of different definitions of entrepreneurs over time is presented in Table 13.1.

Table 13.1   Some definitions and characteristics of entrepreneurship, 1755–2001

R. Cantillon (1755)	• Entrepreneurs are defined as self-employed
	• Self-employment deals with additional uncertainty
	• Entrepreneurs should balance their activities with market demand
J.-B. Say (1803)	• Entrepreneurs shift economic resources from low- to high-productivity areas with higher yield
	• Entrepreneurship implies many obstacles and uncertainties
A. Marshall (1890)	• Entrepreneurs and managers have different but complementary characteristics
J. Schumpeter (1911)	• Entrepreneurship is the main vehicle by which to move an economy forward from static equilibrium, based on the combinatorial capabilities of entrepreneurial individuals
	• Combinatorial capabilities result in recognition of a new good/quality, a new method/process, a new market, a new source of supply or a new way of organizing the firm/production
	• Entrepreneurs' role is distinct from the role of inventors
F. Knight (1921)	• Entrepreneurs are a special social class who direct economic activity
	• Uncertainty is the primary aspect of entrepreneurship
E. Penrose (1950)	• Entrepreneurial and managerial abilities should be distinguished
	• Detecting and exploiting opportunities for smaller firms is the basic aspect of entrepreneurship
H. Leibenstein (1968)	• Entrepreneurial activity mainly implies reducing organizational inefficiencies and reversing organizational entropy
	• There are two types of entrepreneurs: a managerial type, who allocates inputs into the production process in an effective manner, and a Schumpeterian type, who fills observed market gaps by introducing new products or processes
I. Kirzner (1973, 1997)	• Entrepreneurial activity moves the market towards equilibrium as entrepreneurs discover profitable arbitrage possibilities
M. Casson (1982)	• Entrepreneurs specialize in taking judgmental decisions about the coordination of scarce resources
W. Gartner (1985), H. Aldrich and C. Zimmer (1986)	• Entrepreneurship is the outcome of actions of individuals who act in and are influenced by the organizational and regional environment in which they live and work
W. Baumol (1990)	• Entrepreneurial activity is crucial for (radical) innovation and growth
	• Institutions decide the allocation of entrepreneurial activity between productive (innovation) and unproductive activities (rent-seeking, organized crime etc.)
R. Holcombe (1998)	• Entrepreneurs promote a more productive economy due to more efficient and innovative ways of production; this is the foundation for economic growth
OECD (1998)	• Entrepreneurs represent the ability to marshall resources to seize new business opportunities; defined broadly, they are central to economic growth
S. Wennekers and R. Thurik (1999)	• Entrepreneurs have multi-tasking abilities.
	• Entrepreneurs perceive and create new opportunities, operate under uncertainty and introduce products to the market, decide on location and the form and use of resources and, finally, manage their business and compete with others for a share of the market

Table 13.1   (continued)

H. Aldrich and M. Martinez (2001)	• Entrepreneurial activity is not necessarily synonymous with innovation since entrepreneurial activities also involve imitation • The distinction between innovation and reproduction in entrepreneurial activities should be supported.

Source: Own compilation based on Salgado-Banda (2005).

Many Explanations but Few Theories

The above brief and, of course, incomplete presentation theorizes and describes the perceived characteristics the entrepreneur is believed to possess. Even though explanations as to why entrepreneurial activities are embarked upon can be inferred from those entrepreneurial characteristics, this is far from presenting a rigorous theoretical model of entrepreneurship. There are few, if any, compelling theoretical models of entrepreneurial behavior, which stems from the heterogeneity and stochastic elements that seem to be an indisputable part of entrepreneurship. The closest contemporary attempt to model entrepreneurship is probably the occupational-choice models (Evans and Leighton, 1989; Banerjee and Newman, 1993; van Praag and Cramer, 2001). Still, the distinction between these and other models of profit-maximizing agents based on perfect information is fine. Instead, entrepreneurship models are based on processes driven by stochastically distributed abilities and learning capacities.[6]

For instance, in Jovanovic's (1982) model, new firms, or entrepreneurs, face costs that are not only random but also differ across heterogeneous firms. A central feature of the model is that new firms do not know their cost functions, that is, their relative efficiency, which is discovered through the process of learning from its actual post-entry performance once the business is established. Hence, entry *per se* is not important and dynamics is characterized by a noisy selection process where performance is partly exogenous. Jovanovic and Lach (1989) present a modified version of the 1982 model that also builds on learning by doing, and generates a S-shaped diffusion pattern of innovation (and entry) over time.

Neither of these approaches is particularly satisfactory, and whether they can offer insights more valuable than an eclectic approach based on empirical observations is questionable. We therefore restrict the remaining presentation to an overview of the most common empirical explanations as to why entrepreneurship occurs.

Empirical Explanations of Entrepreneurship

According to the literature, the fundamental source of economic development, dynamism and changes can be ascribed to the institutional setting in which agents operate. Even though needs may drive individual actions, the way those needs are fulfilled, and the efficiency in accomplishing them, depends on institutions. Hence, at an overarching level, the extent and type of entrepreneurship can always be attributed to institutions, formal and informal (de Soto, 1989, 2000; Baumol, 1990; North, 1990, 1994; Henrekson,

2005).[7] Institutions also appear at all levels of economic activities: the macroeconomic framework, industrial policies, knowledge creation, attitudes and individual incentives.

In the following we shall classify the empirical explanations of entrepreneurship by the different factors and levels of aggregations that have been presented in the literature. These will also be briefly related to other contextual concepts, such as push and pull factors, and the demand and supply of entrepreneurs. The section concludes with some observations on the definition, role and production of knowledge. However, before plunging into the observed empirical regularities in explaining entrepreneurship, the measurement problems related to entrepreneurship will be considered.

Measuring entrepreneurship

Rather than being synonymous with starting a new venture, entrepreneurship refers to a set of abilities embodied within an individual. Adequately capturing such abilities in data that are comparable over individuals, not to mention comparisons across regions or nations, are simply not possible. Thus the measures of entrepreneurship will always be partly erroneous and subject to criticism since empirical studies have to rely on proxies which (it is hoped) are correlated with entrepreneurship.

A considerable share of studies on entrepreneurship relies on self-employment data. One obvious reason is that these were simply available for a large number of regions and countries (Evans and Leighton, 1989; Blanchflower and Oswald, 1998; Georgellis et al., 2000; OECD, 2000; Audretsch and Thurik, 2001; Blanchflower et al., 2001; Bruce and Holtz-Eakin, 2001; Fonseca et al., 2001). Yet, as noted by Blanchlower (2000) and Earle and Sakova (2000), self-employment consists of a very heterogeneous group more or less involved in productive entrepreneurial activities, it could just as well represent employment push factors.

Alternative but related measures of entrepreneurship are the number of establishments (Beck and Levine, 2001), density of firms (Klapper et al., 2010) or business ownership (Carree, et al., 2002). As pointed out above, self-employment is less likely to capture productive entrepreneurship. Net birth rate (entries minus exits) has also been suggested as an indicator of entrepreneurship, in addition to tracing structural industrial changes (Dejardin, 2009). Firm demography is, however, quite different between industries, implying that sectorally adjusted indicators are needed to capture structural changes using net birth rates (Geroski, 1995; Caves, 1998). But also turbulence (entries plus exits) has been advocated as an approximation of entrepreneurship (Fritsch, 1996).

A relatively new set of data has been compiled by the Global Entrepreneurship Monitor (GEM). These data are based on questionnaires designed to capture both potential entrepreneurs and other respondents. The data also contain additional information, for example, motives for embarking on entrepreneurial activity. Comparison with other data sets, for instance those collected by Eurostat (Flash Eurobarometer) and the World Bank, reveals a high degree of correlation (Reynolds et al., 2005). That they catch roughly the same phenomena does not however mean that they are good indicators of entrepreneurial activity.

Entrepreneurship is often categorized as opportunity- or necessity-based ventures. The former represents a profitable opportunity as perceived by an individual, while the latter is associated with entrepreneurship as a last resort, i.e. due to impossibility of finding other sources of income. The distinction between opportunity- and necessity-based entrepreneurs could also be interpreted as the separation between self-employment and high-growth entrepreneurship (Glaeser and Kerr, 2009).[8]

Macro-level explanations of entrepreneurship
The most commonly defined determinants of entrepreneurship at the macro level in the literature are the level and growth of GDP, together with (un)employment, investments, cost levels, inflation and the interest rate level (Highfield and Smiley, 1987; Bosma et al., 2005; Wang, 2006). Factors such as government spending on education, infrastructure and health seems to be positively correlated with startups (Reynolds and Storey, 1993).

Some of these factors relate to the business cycle – i.e. there may be a cyclical component in entrepreneurship activity – while other, albeit less explained, can be associated with long waves influencing economic activity, innovation and entrepreneurship (Schumpeter, 1939).[9] See also Fritsch (1996), who shows that entry and exit varies during the product cycle, i.e. it is particularly high in the earlier stages.

Regions, industry and firm-level factors
One strand of entrepreneurial economics looks at how differences in regional characteristics and preconditions influence entrepreneurship. Low transportation costs, concentration of human capital and extensive R&D activities together with availability of financial capital, seems to be the most critical factors.[10] Also population (demand), employment and income growth turn out to be important determinants of entrepreneurship (Acs and Armington 2002). We shall further elaborate on the regional dimension of entrepreneurship in a later section.

On the industry level the most prominent factors that have been identified to impact entrepreneurship are the level of profits, entry barriers, level of demand, and the extent of agglomerated or urbanized production structures (Reynolds, 1992; Reynolds and Storey, 1993).[11] The determinants of entrepreneurship thus relate to variables derived from industrial organization, economic geography and standard microeconomic theories of economics. There are mixed results for different variables in different countries, but basically profits, industry growth and industry size are positively related to startups while increasing capital requirements and need for product differentiation seem to negatively impact entry.

Disaggregating to the firm level, human capital (education) shows up as one of the fundamental variables explaining entrepreneurship (Evans and Leighton, 1990; Kim et al., 2006). Overall, the likelihood of becoming an entrepreneur is strongest for skilled individuals, particularly for entrepreneurs seeking to exploit an opportunity. Human capital signals quality, works as a sorting mechanism, helps to overcome barriers in obtaining credit/equity, as well as improving network forming.[12] Social networks can in turn be expected to reduce transaction costs (Williamson, 1971), which also has gained empirical support, particularly for opportunity-based entrepreneurship.[13]

Regulation as such has been shown to influence entrepreneurship and size of startups (Ciccone and Papaioannou, 2006; Ardagna and Lusardi, 2009).[14] Particularly detrimental effects are attributed high startup costs (Fonseca et al., 2001, 2007). Glaeser and Kerr (2009) present (regional) evidence that cost levels are one of the major impediments to entrepreneurship, while Gordon (1998) and Cullen and Gordon (2007) conclude that higher taxes have a distinct and significant negative impact on entrepreneurship. Moreover, indirect effects have been reported through the effects of taxes on wealth formation (Evans and Jovanovic, 1989; Banerjee and Newman, 1993). Individual wealth has been shown to be a robust predictor of the probability of starting a firm.

At the individual level, progressive marginal tax rates seem to negatively impact entry, even though the magnitude depends on the difference between taxes on wages and taxes on profits (Gentry and Hubbard, 2000; Hansson, 2010). It is also noteworthy that individuals in either the highest or the lowest income brackets are most likely to start a firm, which probably mirrors the fact that individual abilities govern whether opportunity- or necessity-based entrepreneurial ventures are embarked upon.

Norms and culture

A number of studies find that social norms, or entrepreneurial culture, influence entrepreneurship.[15] An obvious indicator of this is the parent effect; that is, the likelihood of becoming a firm-owner or starting a new firm increases if the parents had their own firms (Dunn and Holtz-Eakin, 2000; Davidsson and Honig, 2003; Gianetti and Simonov, 2004). It also seems to be the case that an environment dominated by smaller and independent firms is more conducive to entrepreneurship than environments hosting larger firms (Glaeser et al., 2009, Glaeser and Kerr, 2009). Holding an industry's establishment size constant, entrepreneurs increase when the surrounding city has a greater number of small establishments. In addition, there is a remarkably strong correlation between average establishment size and subsequent employment growth through startups, particularly in manufacturing (see also Rosenthal and Strange, 2010). Growth of new startups is thus correlated with the number of existing establishments in the area. The direction of causality is however not clear.

Glaeser and Kerr (2009) also find that higher amenities (defined as exogenous regional differences in climate factors) tend to drive up the price of land, which attracts low fixed cost industries correlated with a higher share of entrepreneurship. Hence high-amenity places attract people and firms, and labor-intensive industries, thereby inducing a positive impact on entrepreneurship.[16] A related observation is that the fraction of entrepreneurs that are active in the region where they were born is significantly higher than the corresponding fraction of workers. This local preference seems to be strongest in developed regions with well-developed financial sectors. In addition, Michelacci and Silva (2007) show that firms created by locals are more valuable, bigger, more capital-intensive and obtain more financing per unit of capital invested.

Individual and cognitive factors

A considerable part of the literature is preoccupied with the cognitive processes by which individuals discover opportunities and take the decision to start a new firm (Braunerhjelm, 2008). These studies find that a number of individual abilities and cognitive capabilities are characteristic for entrepreneurs. For instance, risk acceptance (Knighterian uncertainty) is claimed to distinguished entrepreneurs from other individuals, as is their tolerance for ambiguity. They are also claimed to have a stronger need to achieve, for reasons of self-efficacy as well as preferences for autonomy.[17] In some studies such individual characteristics are broken down at the regional level in order to capture how variations in social capital, creativity and tolerance may influence entrepreneurship

(Coleman, 1988, 1990; Putnam, 1993; Lee et al., 2004; Florida, 2002, Florida et al., 2008).[18]

In a recent empirical analysis, Sutter (2009) sets out to test the impact of a composite factor defined as 'psychological capital'. Compared to previous studies, Sutter's embraces a more varied set of individually defined characteristics, such as those related to enjoying other people and one's own life, ability to control emotions, capability to enthuse other people and so on, which are all incorporated in a 'psychological capital' index. Controlling for other individual factors related to access to opportunities, education, social capital, creativity and trust, the empirical analysis concludes that the psychological index is an important determinant of entrepreneurial endeavor.

Demand- and supply-side explanations of entrepreneurship
In the previous literature there are frequent references to demand- and supply-side determinants of entrepreneurship.[19] I am not convinced that this is the path forward to a better understanding of entrepreneurship and its effects. Empirically it also seems hard to pin down whether entrepreneurial activities descend from the demand or supply factors; some places just seem to have a greater supply of entrepreneurs (see Chinitz, 1961; Sassens, 2006; Glaeser and Kerr, 2009). Such regional differences are likely to be a consequence of local norms, traditions, serendipitous events, i.e. a residual of 'unmeasurables'. Moreover, in some cases the distribution between supply-side and demand-side forces seems somewhat ambiguous. For instance, is unemployment a variable that can be derived from the demand or the supply side of the economy?

Framing the sources of entrepreneurship in terms of demand and supply implicitly also suggests that equilibrium could be attained, i.e. a stationary point exists where either entries equal exits or that dynamics cease. That is of course quite contradictory when one is discussing phenomena characterized by extensive dynamics, non-linear behavior and experimentally organized processes.

Notwithstanding that the distinction between demand- and supply-side factors may be imprecise, previous research seem to allot most explanatory power to the latter. Among the most important are knowledge, broadly defined, and how it ties in with human capital and knowledge resources for production.[20]

Knowledge, its Organization and Entrepreneurship

Knowledge
Knowledge is sometimes defined as a process. Preceding that discussion is the question of how information and knowledge are related. Information normally refers to data that can be easily codified, transmitted, received, transferred and stored. Knowledge, on the other hand, is seen as consisting of structured information that is difficult to codify and interpret due to its intrinsic indivisibility; it is embodied in individuals and organizations. Even though the ability to use knowledge relates to the human cognitive abilities to absorb and select among available information, individual competence may have little or no value in isolation, but combined with other competencies in an organization it may constitute an important part of the organization's knowledge capital. Part of knowledge is likely always to remain 'tacit' and thus non-codifiable (Polanyi, 1966).

In contrast to information that may be interpreted as factual, knowledge may be considered as establishing generalizations and correlations between variables. Generally, knowledge can be described as somewhere between the completely tacit and the completely codified. Tacit, sticky or complex knowledge, i.e. highly contextual and uncertain knowledge, seems best transferred via face-to-face interactions (von Hippel, 1988). Proximity thus matters since knowledge developed for any particular application can easily spill over and find additional applications.

There will always be limitations in accessing knowledge. Measures concerning access and level of knowledge tend likewise to be partial. Indeed, even if the total stock of knowledge were freely available, knowledge about its existence would not necessarily be. The knowledge space is in itself unbounded, implying that decisions are made under 'bounded rationality' (Simon, 1955). Hence, partiality and subjectivity tend to influence decisions. Building on these insights, Hayek (1945) concluded that a key feature of a market economy is the distribution of knowledge across a large number of individuals. Consequently, divergence in the valuation of new ideas across economic agents, or between economic agents and decision-making hierarchies of incumbent enterprises, can also be expected. That constitutes one fundamental source of entrepreneurial opportunity and also implies a market structure dominated by imperfect information and imperfect competition.

Another typical characteristic of knowledge is its non-excludability, implying that only part can be appropriated by the 'owner' while part may diffuse to an indefinite number of users. Low costs in transmitting codified knowledge, together with considerable fixed costs in acquiring and compiling knowledge, points to the difficulties in knowledge-producing activities.

Organization of knowledge production and entrepreneurship
The way knowledge production is organized has shifted over the years and distinct differences can also be observed between Europe and the USA.[21] Furthermore, its organization is shown to have influenced the rate of entry of new firms. In the nineteenth century an interdependence emerged between the needs of the growing US economy and the contemporary rise of university education – what Rosenberg (1985) has called 'endogenous institutions'. In Europe the role of the universities was more oriented towards independent and basic research, as manifested by the Humboldt University in 1809. The difference in knowledge production seems to have given the USA a technological lead in the twentieth century, even though basic science was weak in the USA until the 1930s/40s. The research university in the USA was a post-Second World War institution, basically designed as a modified version of the Humboldt system, where competition and pluralism were retained.

To develop and improve the findings/inventions that were the base of the second Industrial Revolution in the late nineteenth century, the beginning of the twentieth century saw the development of corporate labs, where basic research was conducted (the first corporate lab was set up in Germany in the 1870s). The close links between industry and science, characterized by collaborative research and two-way knowledge flows, were thus reinforced. Within-firm research was much greater in the USA than in Europe; employment of scientists and engineers grew ten-fold in the USA between 1921 and 1940.

During the 1940s there was a huge increase in R&D spending driven by the war, while the following decades saw a decrease in R&D relative to GDP. Basic and government-funded research diminished, but also firms cut down on their R&D spending. As a result, firms seemed to lose touch with their knowledge base, spin-offs declined and there was also less growth in large firms.

At the beginning of the 1980s the situation changed again, propelled by a number of institutional reforms directed towards intellectual property rights, pension capital and taxes. That was coupled with a partly new set-up of organizations, such as SBIR, where 2.5 percent of federal agencies' research funding had to go to the SMEs, and deregulations of a large part of the US economy gave rise to new entrepreneurial opportunities. Thus, entrepreneurial opportunities were created through scientific and technical discoveries that were paralleled by governmental policies which inserted a new dynamism in the US economy. A shift followed from large incumbent firms to small, innovative, skilled-labor-intensive and entrepreneurial entities (Carlsson et al., 2009).

Even though entrepreneurship is shown to be important for opportunity recognition, discovery and creation (Shane and Venkatamaran, 2000), little is said about the origin of opportunities in the entrepreneurship literature. This thread was taken up by Acs et al. (2004b, 2009), suggesting that knowledge endowments, and the way knowledge spillovers are materialized, constitutes perhaps the most important source of entry and entrepreneurship. Obviously, new insights – knowledge – should be instrumental in the dynamics and has been described by Schumpeter in the following way: '[I]ncessantly revolutionizing the economic structure from within, incessantly destroying the old one, incessantly creating a new one' (Schumpeter, 1942, p. 83). How higher rates of entrepreneurship increase the possibilities of turning knowledge into innovations and set forces of creative destruction in motion will be further considered in the next section.

ENTREPRENEURSHIP, OPPORTUNITIES AND INNOVATION

As discussed in the previous section, the idea that opportunities are objective but their perception subjective has long persisted in economic theory. The realm of opportunities is always present; it is the ability to identify such opportunities that determines whether they are revealed and exploited. Thus there is virtual consensus in the contemporary literature on entrepreneurship that it revolves around the recognition of opportunities and the pursuit of those opportunities (Venkataraman, 1997).[22] Identification of innovation opportunities is thus argued to constitute the specific tool of entrepreneurs (Drucker, 1985).

For this tool to be efficiently used, a proper institutional setting is required that allows exploitation of entrepreneurial opportunities. Intellectual property rights have been shown to be critical in making entrepreneurship attractive (Murphy et al., 1991), but a broader perspective on institutions is required, including incentive structures, market structures, openness and so on. Obviously, these are factors that fall largely under the control of a society and thus impact the opportunity space for entrepreneurs. Thus the predominant view that the opportunity space is assumed exogenous in relation to entrepreneurship, whereas individual abilities determine how entrepreneurs can exploit the given opportunities, seems too agnostic. From a policy point of view, such a deterministic attitude towards the possibilities of influencing entrepreneurial activity within an economy is far too passive. We shall return to the policy implications in a later section.

The previous section emphasized the role of innovation but said little about the prime source of entrepreneurial opportunities. The rest of this section will focus on the role of knowledge in creating opportunities that can be exploited through innovation, examine how different types of entrepreneurs accomplish different tasks, and also give a brief account of the empirical evidence in this strand of research. Initially we shall discuss the differences between innovation and imitation, and the measurement problems related to innovation.

How to Define and Measure Innovation?

Perhaps more than any other economist, Schumpeter (1911/34) is explicit about the economic function of the entrepreneur. According to Schumpeter, the process of economic development can be divided into three separate stages. The first stage implies technical discovery of new things or new ways of doing things, which Schumpeter refers to as invention. In the subsequent stage innovation occurs, i.e. the successful commercialization of a new good or service stemming from technical discoveries or, more generally, a new combination of knowledge (new and old). The final step in this three-stage process – imitation – concerns a more general adoption and diffusion of new products or processes to markets.[23]

Schumpeter was also clear about the difference between roles played by the inventor as compared to the innovator. Even though he foresaw situations when the roles could coincide, that was, according to Schumpeter, an exception to the rule.

Obviously there are numerous pitfalls in the measurement of inventions and innovations. No matter what scale is applied, measurement difficulties and subjective evaluation criteria may to a various extent distort data on knowledge and can always be subject to criticism.[24] Some frequently implemented knowledge variables are likely to miss essential parts, while others tend to exaggerate the knowledge content. The most commonly applied measure of knowledge exploitation and innovative activities is R&D expenditures and patents.[25]

R&D expenditures suffer from the apparent drawback of applying input measures in order to approximate innovative output. Patent is a better performance variable but also suffers from serious limitations. Patents can be expected to reflect conditions (red tape, financial sector quality and so on) that affect the decision to innovate.[26] They are also likely to be more closely related to the type of innovative and productive entrepreneurship that has been emphasized by Schumpeter and Baumol (Earle and Sakova, 2000). Patent authorities, however, rarely know whether patents have been commercialized, nor whether commercialization was successful, or the size of the inventing firm. Still, patents are widely used and are claimed to be a fairly reasonable measure of innovativeness (Acs et al., 2002).

An interesting and more relevant measure to separate invention and innovation using patent data is to implement quality-adjusted patents (Lanjouw and Schankerman, 1999; Hall et al., 2000). As shown, for instance, by Ejermo and Gråsjö (2008) and Ejermo (2009), regional innovation is better explained by quality-adjusted patent data and is shown to be highly correlated with regional R&D, whereas interregional R&D fails to reveal any significant impact on regional innovation.[27]

Turbulence, i.e. entry and exit of firms, is yet another indicator proposed to capture innovative activity. However, firms' death and birth seem correlated with many factors, some of which are internal to firms (mismanagement, inexperience, retirement and so on), while others are associated with innovation by incumbents and threat of entry (Baumol et al., 1982). In addition, some sectors with many entries and exits (e.g. consumer services) can hardly be identified as innovative; rather entry takes place due to imitation. Net entry, supposed to capture expansion of new and innovative industries, has therefore been suggested as a better proxy for innovative entry.[28]

A Symbiotic Relationship between Large and Small Firms?

The Schumpeterian separation between the inventor and the entrepreneur has repeatedly been challenged (see, e.g., Schmookler, 1966). At the same time good reasons for integrating the inventive and innovative stages have been presented in the industrial organization literature. Grossman and Hart's (1986) seminal article refers to the contractual problems when information is asymmetric, which could be overcome through vertical integration. On a more aggregate level, the merging of the inventive and innovative stages is present in the earlier neo-Schumpeterian growth models.[29] Baumol (2002) emphasizes the symbiosis between small and large firms in his David and Goliath innovation framework.

In the management literature, Teece (1986, 2006) presents a 'nascent neo-Schumpeterian theory', where he outlines the strategic implications of commercializing an invention in an independent firm set up by inventors, as compared to licensing it to an incumbent firm. He identifies three key factors that determine whether it would be the inventor, the following firms, or firms with related capacity – or complementary assets – that extract the profits from an invention: (i) the institutions tied to IPRs, (ii) the extent to which complementary assets were needed for commercialization; and (iii) the emergence of a dominant design. Teece was thus not primarily preoccupied with the organizational regime between the inventor and the innovator; rather he stressed the prerequisites governing the entry mode irrespective of whether it was the inventor or the innovator/ entrepreneur that was about to launch a new product. Furthermore, the presence of large incumbents could be essential for the emergence of a market for 'ideas', i.e. large firms could procure and develop small firms' inventions (Norbäck and Persson, 2010).

Thus there seem to be a number of important reasons why small and large firms complement each other, and these are likely to influence the innovation processes. The gains of specialization are at the root of this argument, where entrepreneurs/small firms simply perform better than large firms with respect to certain activities. And vice versa. Related to this is the issue of agglomeration and knowledge spillovers, to which we return in a later section.

Leads, Laggards and Technological Regime

In a series of papers, Aghion et al. (2001, 2004, 2005, 2006) have examined the innovative activities in technologically leading industries as compared to other industries (laggards). A number of interesting results emerge from those studies.[30] In particular, the induced effects of entry on incumbents' innovation and productivity are shown to differ across heterogeneous industries. How does firm entry influence innovation incentives and productivity growth in incumbent firms? In the earlier contributions it was shown that incumbents in more advanced industries increase their innovative activities, hoping to circumvent the negative effects of competition based on innovative entry. The authors refer to this mechanism as the 'escape entry effect through innovation'. However, laggards have little or no hope of winning against entrants, thus they tend rather to reduce innovation due to entry, which is referred to as the Schumpeterian appropriability effect of product market competition.

In Aghion et al. (2006) the analysis is extended to account for entry by foreign firms, i.e. foreign direct investments. A similar dynamics is shown to induce incumbents in technologically advanced industries to increase their innovative efforts due to foreign entry (or threat thereof), whereas the opposite prevails in laggard industries. Successful innovation prevents entry. In laggard industries it discourages innovation since entry reduces the expected return from innovating, which is called the discouragement effect.

Thus entry of new firms – domestic or foreign – initiates an improved allocation of inputs, and outputs that tend to trigger knowledge spillovers and affect innovation incentives among incumbents. But the dynamics will differ between industries, and in order to reap the potential welfare effects of a structural adjustment within and between industries, different policies are required for different industries.

In the evolutionary framework developed by Nelson and Winter (1982), the questions of the origin of variation (innovation), how selection of innovations take place, and the way in which such selected variation is transmitted between periods, are addressed. According to Nelson and Winter, the answer refers to routines that are claimed to have gene-like stability (inheritance) properties, combined with an ability to mutate, i.e. induce variation. Thus routines drive evolution and different modes of innovation are suggested to occur through the exploitation of opportunities due to specific knowledge regimes associated with the particular industry context. Hence large incumbent firms are modeled as investors of R&D and other knowledge-creating efforts, which are referred to as a routinized technological regime. These are then exploited by the same firms, where the selection of winners (innovation and higher productivity) is influenced by exogenous, stochastic factors.[31] Alternatively, other regimes based on imitations or where entrepreneurs or small firms are considered to have the capacity of exploiting commercial opportunities without relying on R&D, may also exist. Winter (1964, 1984) refers to those as entrepreneurial technological regimes.[32]

Endogenous Entrepreneurship

Summarizing the above discussion and drawing on the discussion in the previous section, knowledge, broadly defined, and the institutions governing its diffusion and ownership, seems to constitute the most important aspect of innovative entrepreneurship. Individuals with a certain mix of abilities and characters, described in the previous section, tend to engage in entrepreneurial processes characterized by search, uncertainty and randomness. A conspicuous feature of entrepreneurs seems to be that they constantly get involved in experiments, where many different varieties and models may be tried out before the right one is found (Rosenberg and Birdzell, 1986). In order to function, such an experimentally organized economy requires a proper institutional setting. Property rights, intellectual as well as those relating to entrepreneurial rent, and non-stigmatizing failure mechanisms seem to be some of the cornerstones of an institutional setting that is conducive to entrepreneurial activities.[33]

Taking that as their point of departure, Acs et al. (2004b, 2009) argue that the exploitation of knowledge depends on the broad spectrum of institutions, rules and regulations, or, in their terminology, an economy's knowledge filter. The knowledge filter is the gap between new knowledge and economic knowledge. The thicker the knowledge filter, the more pronounced the gap between new knowledge and new economic – i.e. commercialized – knowledge. This relates to Arrow's (1962) perception of knowledge, stressing that knowledge differs from other factors of production. The expected value of any new idea is highly uncertain, and as Arrow pointed out, has a much greater variance than would be associated with the deployment of traditional factors of production. Arrow emphasized that when it comes to innovation, there is uncertainty about whether the new product can be produced, how it can be produced, and whether sufficient demand for that visualized new product might actually materialize.

Thus both the individuals and the contexts in which agents operate have to be integrated in the model. In other words, the individual–opportunity nexus has to be operationalized. The key issue – often disregarded – is that even though new knowledge leads to opportunities that can be exploited commercially, it has to be converted into commercial applications. Such opportunities rarely present themselves in neat packages; rather they have to be discovered and applied commercially (Shane and Eckhardt, 2003). In particular, the uncertainty, asymmetries and high transaction costs inherent in knowledge generate a divergence in the assessment and evaluation of the expected value of new ideas. This means that ability to commercialize knowledge – to become entrepreneurs – also varies across individuals.

Building on these insights, Acs et al. (2004b, 2009) model the supply of entrepreneurs as a function of (i) the societal investments in knowledge, i.e. the existing knowledge stock at a given point in time, (ii) how efficient the economy works (the knowledge filter, i.e. the design of the institutional setup), and (iii) the given individual entrepreneurial ability. In addition, culture and traditions and institutions, i.e. country- or region-specific factors, influence entrepreneurship. Those are the building blocks of the knowledge spillover theory of entrepreneurship, presented by Acs et al. (2004b, 2009). More precisely, production of new products/qualities can either occur due to an invention of incumbent firms investing in R&D, or by entrepreneurial startups where existing knowledge is combined in innovative ways that do not require any investment in R&D.[34] Instead, individuals combine their given entrepreneurial ability (where higher ability increases the probability of success) with the overall knowledge stock within an economy to discover commercial opportunities. The societal knowledge stock is a composite of previous knowledge stemming from activities by incumbents and startups, i.e. knowledge refers not only to scientific discoveries but also to knowledge associated with novel ways of producing and distributing in traditional businesses, changing business models, new marketing strategies and so on.

Concluding, endogenous entrepreneurs seem to be one crucial vehicle in transforming knowledge into useful goods and services. In other words, spillovers are actually generated through entrepreneurs, simultaneously as commercial opportunities are increasing in a larger stock of knowledge. By serving as a conduit for the spillover of knowledge that might not otherwise be commercialized, entrepreneurship is one mechanism that links knowledge to commercialization and economic growth (see the next section). A mobile working force may be another mechanism. From that perspective there are undoubtedly many mechanisms that may also impede the commercialization of knowledge – and growth – which opens up a new field of economic policies as compared to the traditional growth instruments of taxes and subsidies (see final section).

Innovation, Entrepreneurs and Small Firms: The Empirical Evidence

Audretsch et al. (2006) note that there is an interesting contrast between most predominant theories of the firm and the entrepreneurial literature's assumption about opportunity. According to the former, innovative opportunities are the result of systematic and purposeful efforts to create knowledge and new ideas by investing in R&D, which are subsequently appropriated through commercialization of such investments (Griliches, 1979; Chandler, 1990; Cohen and Levinthal, 1989; Warsh, 2006), which stands in sharp contrast to the entrepreneurial tradition of a given, exogenous opportunity space.

As regards the empirical evidence, several studies reach the conclusion that irrespective of modest R&D investments, small and entrepreneurial firms contribute substantially to aggregate innovation (Audretsch, 1995; Feldman and Audretsch, 1999). Micro studies also suggest that entrepreneurs/small firms have their knowledge-producing activities spread across a number of different functional areas apart from formal R&D activities (Freel, 2003) and that these firms draw on many knowledge sources other than R&D in their innovation (Shane, 2000).

In a couple of papers, Acs and Audretsch (1988, 1990) provide interesting results for the USA. Notwithstanding that the large corporations account for most of the country's private R&D investments, there are substantial differences across industries and large firms did not account for the greatest amount of innovative activity in all industries. For example, in the pharmaceutical and aircraft industries, the large firms were much more innovative, while in computers and process control instruments small firms contributed the bulk of innovations. More precisely, their results indicate a small-firm innovation rate in manufacturing of 0.309, compared to a large-firm innovation rate of 0.202. Their findings link to the suggested restraints on innovation capacities in large firms discussed below. Similar results are obtained by Baldwin and Johnson (1999), who confer a particular important role on small-firm innovations in the electronics, instruments, medical equipment and biotechnology industry. Baldwin (1995) suggests that more successful firms adopt more innovative strategies.

Based on a detailed Swedish data set, Andersson and Lööf (2009) show that one-third of patent applications in the manufacturing sector emanate from firms with fewer than 25 employees. Moreover, compared to non-patenting firms, firms engaged in patenting have more skilled labor, larger profit margin and better access to bank loans, and also belong to the high-technology segment of industry. In addition, a substantial share of patenting small firms has links to a Swedish multinational enterprise (MNE). Persistence is also shown to be high: 99 percent of those not applying for patents in one year did not do so in the subsequent year, while 50 percent firms with more than 25 employees applied in the subsequent year and 17 percent of those with fewer than 25 employees. Access to skill, internationalization (export share) and links to an MNE are most strongly correlated with small-firm patenting.

Patent data have also been used to examine differences in commercialization perform-ance between new firms and existing firms. Braunerhjelm and Svensson (2009), also using a Swedish data set, show that commercialization performance is superior when a patent is sold or licensed, or when the inventor is employed in an already existing firm, as compared to the alternative when the inventor commercializes in his own existing or new firm. This supports Schumpeter's view that entrepreneurs have superior skills in com-mercializing new knowledge (innovating). On the other hand, the analysis also shows that inventor participation during the commercialization is important. One interpreta-tion is that the inventor is crucial for further adaptation (custom-specific, etc.) of the innovation, but also in order to reduce uncertainty about the firm's capacity.

Thus entrepreneurs and small firms exploit existing knowledge – through their network and links to other knowledge producers – to satisfy their specific needs in the production of goods and services. Thereby they also produce new knowledge, even if it does not show up in the R&D statistics. Sometimes they do so independently, sometimes in conjunction with other firms, e.g. inventors or MNEs. But the process differs radically as compared to large, R&D-investing, firms.

Another difference relates to the intertemporal dynamics within large enterprises. As they set out to attain established growth targets, this tends to make incumbents less adaptable to changing a system that may affect the usefulness or value of an existing production structure (Christensen, 1997). Similarly, Aldrich and Auster (1986) make the simpler argument that the larger and older the firm, the less receptive to change the organization becomes. As a result, incumbents have an inherent tendency to develop and introduce less risky, incremental innovations into the market.

Contrast that with new ventures. These are more prone to develop, use and introduce radical, market-making products that give the firm a competitive edge over incum-bents (Casson, 2002a, 2002b; Baumol, 2007). Thus new firms are not constrained by path dependencies and partial lock-in effects; rather they compete through innovation and Schumpeterian means of creative destruction.[35] That also suggests that radical innovations will more likely stem from new ventures (Scherer, 1980; Baumol, 2004), in particular if new firms have access to knowledge spillovers from the available stock of knowledge. Therefore they are likely to play a distinct and decisive role in the transfor-mation of knowledge-based economies. Moreover, an impressive share of radical break-through innovations stems from entrepreneurs and small firms. Almeida and Kogut (1997) and Almeida (1999) show that small firms innovate in relatively unexplored fields of technology.[36]

Also Block et al. (2009) emphasize the role of entrepreneurs and small firms in their empirical test of the knowledge spillover theory. As a starting point they conclude that knowledge (in terms of R&D outlays) has been shown to positively influence growth, but that there remain large and unexplained differences across countries. They attribute those differences to varying thickness of the respective country's knowledge filter. The empirical analysis covers 21 European countries for the period 1998–2006, and innova-tion is defined as either the share of turnover accounted for by new products in firms, or the share of turnover from new or improved goods that are new to the market. A country's level of knowledge is defined as the share of firms that have applied for at least one patent. In the empirical analysis, where community innovation data are pooled with country-level data, they find statistical support for entrepreneurship as an important vehicle for turning knowledge into innovative product, contrasting imitating firms/products where no such effect could be detected. They also show that innovative activities have increased compared to imitative activities in the investigated period. Their interpretation is that this reflects a switch to a more entrepreneurial regime, replacing the traditional managerial regime.

Thus empirical evidence stresses the new and growing firms' role in introducing new products and processes, making business-model innovations, and developing new markets as well as changing the rules of the game in their industries (Bhide, 2000). Apart from those changes, they also generate employment. Apparently those processes are in turn likely to deliver substantial knowledge spillovers. The implication is that only a subset of innovations is normally taken into account in the most commonly applied measures, such as patents and outlays on R&D.

So far we have explored how entrepreneurial activity impacts innovation, the measurement difficulties in identifying innovative activities, and the role of institutions. In particular, we have emphasized the role of institutions that governs ownership, knowledge production and knowledge diffusion and its interface with entrepreneurship. In the next section the objective is to show how these processes integrate into the growth process, and the extent to which this is captured in contemporary growth models.

ENTREPRENEURSHIP AND GROWTH

Contemporary models of economic growth are based on investment and exploitation of knowledge as the prime source of economic development. Growth performance may however differ across countries, even though countries may have similar, albeit not identical, knowledge endowments and institutional design. Simultaneously, a frequent empirical regularity seems to suggest that economic growth is highly correlated with abundance of small, entrepreneurial firms. In fact, an emerging empirical literature concludes that entrepreneurial startups are important links between knowledge creation and the commercialization of such knowledge, particularly at the early stage when knowledge is still fluid. About two-thirds of all empirical studies on entrepreneurship/small firms and growth reach the conclusion that there is a positive, and generally quite strong, correlation between these variables (Karlsson and Nyström, 2008).[37] Hence knowledge by itself may only constitute a necessary – but far from sufficient – condition for growth.

In this section we shall review the theoretical growth models and present the empirical evidence concerning the relationship between knowledge, entrepreneurship and economic growth.

Knowledge-based Growth

The seminal contribution of the knowledge-based (endogenous) growth models that appeared in the mid-1980s was to show that investments in knowledge and human capital were undertaken by profit-maximizing firms in a general equilibrium setting.[38] Whereas firms invested in R&D to get a competitive edge over their competitors, part of that knowledge spilled over to a societal knowledge stock that influenced the production function of all other firms, augmenting their productivity. Hence growth was disentangled from investments in capital and increases in labor supply: even if those remained constant, increases in knowledge meant that growth would increase.

The first wave of endogenous growth models (Romer, 1986; Lucas, 1988; Rebelo, 1991; and others) emphasized the influence of knowledge spillovers on growth without specifying how knowledge spills over.[39] Yet the critical issue in modeling knowledge-based growth rests on the spillover of knowledge. That is, even though an economy invests heavily in R&D, the mechanisms by which this knowledge spills over and is converted into goods and services is basically unknown.

This was to some extent remedied in the second generation of endogenous growth models (Schmitz, 1989; Segerstrom et al., 1990; Segerstrom, 1991; Aghion and Howitt, 1992; Cheng and Dinopoulos, 1992; Segerstrom, 1995). Predominantly the neo-Schumpeterian models designed entry as an R&D race where a fraction of R&D turns into successful innovations. While this implies a step forward, the essence of the Schumpeterian entrepreneur is missed. The innovation process stretches far beyond R&D races that predominantly involve large incumbents and concern quality improvements of existing goods.

In the most recent vein of knowledge-based growth models the focus is narrowed and better defined. Most prominent among those are the effects of technology-based entry on the innovativeness and productivity of incumbents, and the implications of firm heterogeneity for creative destruction and growth (Aghion and Griffith, 2005). As regards the first issue, the analysis follows an industrial organization tradition that examines the effects of preemption, entry regulation and strategic interaction (Gilbert and Newbery, 1982; Tirole, 1988; Laffont and Tirole, 1993; Nickell, 1996; Blundell et al., 1999; Berry and Pakes, 2007; Aghion et al., 2006). The new element is that these models take into account the effects of competition and innovation of both incumbents and new firms. For instance, Aghion et al. (2006) have shown that entry – or entry threats – has positive effects on the innovative behavior by incumbents close to the technological frontier, while no such effects could be found for technological laggards (see the discussion in the previous section).

Concerning the analysis of firm heterogeneity, entry and productivity, the basic reasoning is that elevated firm specificity in performance (stock evaluation, profits etc.) is associated with a growing number of smaller and new firms (Pastor and Veronesi, 2005; Fink et al., 2005). Moreover, firm specificity is seen as reflecting creative destruction, enhanced efficiency and higher productivity and growth (Durnev et al., 2004; Aghion et al., 2004, 2005; Acemoglu et al., 2006; Chun et al., 2007). An increased influence of small firms and startups is associated with deregulation and increased competition but is also due to the fact that new and young firms are more prone to exploit new technologies and knowledge (Jovanovic and Rousseau, 2005).

Klette and Kortum (2004), building on Penrose's (1959) resource-based theory of the firm, present a multi-firm, multi-variety model where the innovation production function combines codified (or known) knowledge with current ongoing R&D to produce new or improved goods. Entry occurs when startups produce higher-quality products as compared to those varieties produced by the incumbents. Based on a standard endogenous growth model, Acs et al. (2004a) and Braunerhjelm et al. (2009) present a theoretical model that includes the Schumpeterian entrepreneurs that innovate but are not involved in R&D activities (see the appendix).

Thus, notwithstanding that knowledge-based growth models imply a huge step forward in understanding growth, the precise microeconomic mechanisms need to be further pinned down. A number of empirical studies find ambiguous support for knowledge variables as explanations of aggregate growth (Jones, 1995a, 1995b, 2006). Based on these empirical irregularities, and the previous discussion concerning knowledge dissemination and innovation, the key issue in growth still revolves around the exact implementation and transformation of knowledge into commercial value, i.e. knowledge spillovers. A conceivable missing link in much of the contemporary growth literature relates to the incorporation of the 'true' Schumpeterian entrepreneur. The latter, as shown in previous sections, constitutes a bridge between opportunity and economic outcome, thereby influencing how knowledge is more or less smoothly filtered into and substantiated in business activity. Coming to grips with the microeconomic foundations of growth also has an important bearing on the effectiveness of policy recommendations.

The microeconomic foundation of contemporary growth models
Scrutinizing the knowledge-based growth models reveals that they rest on three cornerstones: knowledge externalities, increasing returns in the production of goods, and decreasing returns in the production of knowledge. These are considered to provide a microeconomic foundation for explaining the mechanisms that promote growth at the macro level. Here we narrow down the discussion to how representative some of the properties of these building blocks are for real-world behavior.

First, the ability of incumbents to absorb knowledge spillovers can be questioned. As shown above, the potential advantages in knowledge sourcing are often impeded by the firm's inherent incentive structures. If we take the view proposed by Cohen and Levinthal (1990) that at any given point in time absorption capacity depends on the knowledge accumulated in prior periods, i.e. the need to remain within a well-defined product space when innovating, it is not surprising that absorption and transformation of knowledge become path-dependent. Empirical evidence quite persuasively also reveals that a large number of radical breakthrough innovations originate in small, less R&D-intensive, but entrepreneurially geared firms. Some of the current examples are Microsoft and Google, which exploit, develop and use existing technologies but had none – or modest – R&D facilities initially. In fact, the entrepreneurs behind these firms share several of the typical characteristics of the Austrian prototype entrepreneur. Other likely examples of growth-enhancing entrepreneurial firms are Ikea and HM of Sweden, and Walmart and Starbucks of the USA. These firms have no research departments (but do undertake activities that could be labeled development), but have certainly contributed to knowledge by introducing new business models and developing new markets.[40]

Whereas the production of knowledge shifted from being exogenous in neoclassical growth models to becoming endogenous in the knowledge-based models, the critical issue for growth – diffusion of knowledge – is by and large still exogenous. Knowledge is thus a necessary but far from sufficient condition of attaining growth (Nelson and Pack, 1999; Acs et al., 2004a; Braunerhjelm et al., 2010). In a sense, the Solowian technical residual can be argued to have been transformed into an entrepreneurial residual.

A second strand of criticism concerns the intertemporal and indirect effects of entrepreneurship on aggregate growth. These are largely unaccounted for. Assuming an influx of firms that intensifies forces of creative destruction and raises the 'adjustment pressure', knowledge regarding 'when and how' is still quite rudimentary.[41] The indirect effects – such as increasing competition, the replacement of older and less productive firms – may be more important than the direct effects (Robinson et al., 2006). These dynamic effects have largely been ignored. Similarly, exits, being the other critical component of creative destruction and dynamics, not least because they release the resources needed to expand other parts of the economy, are much less researched than entry.[42]

The Empirical Evidence

Entrepreneurship, knowledge and national growth
The link between knowledge production and productivity at the micro level is well established.[43] At a higher level of aggregation, empirical analyses become more intricate as endogenity and causality issues make the interpretation of the results considerably harder. Still, a number of recent empirical studies suggest that entrepreneurship – measured as startup rates, the relative share of SMEs or self-employment rates – is instrumental in converting knowledge into products and thereby propelling growth.

For example, Thurik (1999) provided empirical evidence from a 1984–94 cross-sectional study of the 23 countries that are part of the OECD that increased entrepreneurship, as measured by business ownership rates, was associated with higher rates of employment growth at the country level. Similarly, Audretsch et al. (2002) and Carree and Thurik (1999) find that OECD countries exhibiting higher increases in entrepreneurship have also experienced higher rates of growth and lower levels of unemployment. See also Wennekers and Thurik (1999).

In a study for the OECD, Audretsch and Thurik (2002) undertook two separate empirical analyses to identify the impact of changes in entrepreneurship on growth. Each one used a different measure of entrepreneurship, sample of countries and specification. This provides some sense of robustness across different measures of entrepreneurship, data sets, time periods and specifications. The first analysis measures entrepreneurship in terms of the relative share of economic activity accounted for by small firms. It links changes in entrepreneurship to growth rates for a panel of 18 OECD countries over five years to test the hypothesis that higher rates of entrepreneurship lead to higher subsequent growth rates. The second analysis uses a measure of self-employment as an index of entrepreneurship and links changes in entrepreneurship to unemployment at the country level between 1974 and 1998. The different samples including OECD countries over different time periods reach consistent results – increases in entrepreneurial activity tend to result in higher subsequent growth rates and a reduction of unemployment.

Acs et al. (2004a) and Braunerhjelm et al. (2009) find a positive relationship between entrepreneurship and growth at the country level examining 20 OECD countries for the period 1981–2002. The impact is considerably stronger in the 1990s than in the 1980s, while the importance of R&D seems to diminish in the latter time period. Salgado-Banda (2005) implements a measure of innovative entrepreneurship based on quality-adjusted patent data for 22 OECD countries, which is reported to positively influence growth, while no such effect could be established for self-employment.

Acs and Armington (2002) examined the relative contribution of new firms in terms of new jobs. They concluded that new firm startups play a far more important role in the economy than has previously been recognized. For the US economy as a whole they show that for the first half of the 1990s new establishments accounted for a considerably larger share of job creation than already existing establishments. As discussed in a previous section, at more disaggregated spatial units – i.e. a city, region or state – the empirical evidence corroborates the results at the national level. The authors also find that new firms are more important than the stock of firms in a region, but the manufacturing sector appears to be an exception. This is consistent with prior research on manufacturing.

Similar results are found in studies by van Stel and Storey (2004), Baptista et al. (2008) and van Stel and Suddle (2008). In addition, Fritsch and Mueller (2004) argue that these effects are strongest in the earliest stage of the firm's life cycle. In a recent paper by Glaeser and Kerr (2009), it is shown how a 10 percent increase in the number of firms per worker increases employment growth by 9 percent, while a 10 percent increase in average size of firms is claimed to result in a 7 percent decrease in employment growth due to new startups.[44]

At the firm level, startups are more likely to grow and create new jobs (Johnson et al., 2000; Lingelbach et al., 2006, Haltiwanger et al., 2010). The pattern seem however to differ between the USA and Europe. The probable reason for these differences is the institutional set-up (Storey, 1994; Davies and Henrekson, 1997). While in Europe the main effect is attributed to firms employing one or two new persons (Wiklund, 1998; Davidsson and Delmar, 2000), growth in the USA is claimed to be dominated by a small number of new entrepreneurial firms exhibiting extraordinary growth ('gazelles'). Of course, gazelle effects also exist in other countries (Wiklund and Shepherd, 2004). They can also be found in all types of industries, even though they seem to emerge more frequently from exploiting new knowledge (at least in the USA). As shown by Henrekson and Johansson (2009), the importance of gazelles seems to have increased over the years.

At the regional level, numerous studies – which have the advantage of being exposed to basically the same institutional setup – appear where regional entrepreneurship but also knowledge seems significantly related to regional prosperity.[45] Different variables have been used to capture entrepreneurial activities. Using an industry turbulence variable, Fritsch (1996) concluded that entry and exits impact growth. Dejardin (2009), implementing a net entry variable to capture entrepreneurship, found positive lagged effects for entry in the service sector on growth in 1982–96.

A recent study by Sutter (2009) on US data attributes 90 percent of regional variation in growth (total factor productivity) to the regional knowledge stock (patent) and regional new firm formation. Entrepreneurship is however claimed to have an effect on growth that is five times larger than knowledge.[46] Thus the empirical evidence hints that knowledge is important for economic growth at the same time as its commercial introduction through new ventures/firms has a dramatically larger impact.

Countries at different levels of economic development

Do the effects of entrepreneurship on growth and productivity differ with respect to countries' level of development? We take Rostow (1960) as our point of departure. He suggested that countries go through five different stages of economic growth as they develop, ending in a stage labeled the age of high mass consumption. Following that thread, Porter et al. (2002) presented a growth cycle consisting of three stages: the factor-driven, the efficiency-driven and the innovation-driven. Hence countries at different levels of development can be expected to display diverging production structures, but so also can the presence of smaller firms and entrepreneurs (Acs and Szerb, 2009).

In a neo-Schumpeterian growth model context, innovative entrepreneurship is claimed to be the specific mechanism through which productivity growth is introduced in advanced economies, contrasting less developed countries where diffusion of previous innovations and previously developed technology spur productivity growth (Acemouglu et al., 2006). Hence technological innovation is brought about through the creation of new knowledge made manifest in production by entrepreneurs in developed economies, while diffusion to a larger extent is driven by capital investment channeled through established firms (Ertur and Koch, 2008). The presence of technological interdependence between countries is claimed to facilitate the diffusion of technologies from leading to lagging economies, thereby speeding up productivity among laggards.

The causes of structural change thus differ between economies at different levels of development (Nelson and Pack, 1999; Gries and Naudé, 2008, 2010). In developing countries with advantageous cost structures, entrepreneurship based on imitation, together with inflows of foreign firms and investments by large incumbents, serves to achieve this end (Rodrik, 2007). In more advanced economies innovation and structural change are more likely to take place through the combined efforts by entrepreneurial small ventures and large innovative firms (organized R&D) complementing each other (Nooteboom, 1994; Baumol, 2002).

Some empirical support for the different kinds of technology diffusion and dynamics is provided by Stam and van Stel (2009). They pool microeconomics data (GEM) with more aggregate data and find that entrepreneurship has no growth effect in low-income countries.[47] In high-income and transition countries the opposite prevails, particularly with regard to opportunity-based entrepreneurship. The positive effects are most pronounced in the transition economies, which is attributed to ample entrepreneurial opportunities, a highly educated population and qualified entrepreneurs that are well connected to local networks. In addition, opportunity costs are low for potential entrants since alternative occupations are sparse.

To summarize this section, theoretical advances, supported by empirical findings, clearly point to an increasing role for entrepreneurs in the growth process. Simultaneously, there are considerable gaps in our understanding of the structure and working of the microeconomic mechanisms in the growth process.

THE GEOGRAPHY OF ENTREPRENEURSHIP, INNOVATION AND GROWTH

This section is devoted to a brief exploration of some of the dominant explanations as regards the spatial distribution or, more precisely, the lumpiness of entrepreneurship and knowledge, which seems to be a distinct feature of the economic landscape. We shall also touch upon the expected, and actual, consequences of geographically concentrated structures of economic activities. An investigation of the mechanisms that have been identified as tending to generate geographically concentrated production structures more generally is, however, beyond the scope of the current chapter. Rather, the ambition is to highlight some aspects of particular interest when it comes to the inter-locus of entrepreneurs and knowledge on one hand, and geographic proximity and growth, on the other.[48]

Why is Geographical Proximity Important?

The modeling pillars of the geographical distribution of economic activities are transport and trade costs, together with pecuniary and non-pecuniary externalities. The former type of externality refers to demand and supply linkages, while the latter has to do with knowledge spillovers. If trade and transport costs are high, economic production structures will be dispersed with no or little trade. On the other hand, if they are very low or even zero, then location of economic activity is arbitrary.[49] The largest consequences for the spatial distribution of production can be expected to be somewhere in between. Changing trade costs could thus induce an endogenous change in the location of production.[50] Once a critical mass has been established, self-reinforcing and centripetal forces are set in motion. The counter-effects, i.e. those that prevent all economic activities from being located in one place, are associated with congestion costs and rising costs of locally fixed production factors.

Serendipity is also involved when it comes to explaining spatial differences, particularly in the initial stages of the emergence of a cluster or agglomerated production milieu (Chinitz, 1961; Kenney and Patton, 2006; Scott, 2006; Glaeser and Kerr, 2009). One frequently cited example is the move by William Schockley's semiconductor business from the east coast to San Francisco. It was not the abnormal – if any – difference in returns that made Schockley relocate, but the fact that his sick mother lived close to San Francisco.

Entrepreneurship
When it comes to entrepreneurship and firm location, there is a large literature pointing to a positive effect of geographically concentrated environment on the location of firms and entrepreneurs. For instance, access to finance and services, higher flow of ideas, larger markets and fewer swings in demand, together with lower entry costs, are among the most commonly cited advantages of agglomerated economic milieux.[51] A theoretical model of regional differences in startups has been presented by Gries and Naudé (2008), in which, amongst other dynamic features, entrepreneurs can identify and exploit region-specific opportunities, through either imitation or innovation. They supply intermediates to final goods producers, which link entrepreneurs to qualitative and structural change, and increased numbers of startups imply more diversity and higher regional growth.

It is also claimed that environments characterized by small firms cause more entrepreneurship by lowering the effective cost of entry through the development of independent suppliers, together with a larger and a more diversified supply of venture capital where risk capital investors more easily can spread risks.[52] Grek et al. (2009) argue that the impact of regional size (local and external accessibility to gross regional product) is found to positively influence entrepreneurship in the service sector, whereas a negative influence of entrepreneurship seems to prevail in manufacturing and primary sectors. Verheul et al. (2001) present an overview of how decisions at the individual level are influenced by regional characteristics, including culture but also other region-specific institutions as well as demand and supply factors, generating differences in regional entrepreneurship.

The regional economic milieu, as manifested in culture, knowledge base and business attitude, is also reported to be important for regional success and entrepreneurship (Camagni, 1991). Nijkamp (2003) claims that access to knowledge, skill density, opportunities and networks offers more favorable conditions for innovative entrepreneurship. In addition, new firms are frequently built around product knowledge that is geographically bounded (Wong et al., 2005; Koster, 2006). Van Oort and Stam (2006) argue that agglomeration effects have a stronger impact on entrepreneurship than on growth of incumbents (examining the information and communication industry). The reasons are, allegedly, spatially more distributed organizations of large incumbents and a propensity to internalize their knowledge base.

An interesting empirical observation is that once entrepreneurs have established themselves in a region, they rarely move (Stam, 2007), which seems to be particularly prevalent in high-tech firms (Cooper and Folta, 2000). Entrepreneurs are also more likely to be from their region of birth than workers, and they operate stronger businesses than moved in entrepreneurs (Klepper, 2001; Figueiredo et al., 2002; Michelacci and Silva, 2007). These findings suggest that at least semi-permanent differences and path-dependence exist in the spatial distribution of entrepreneurs.

The dynamics due to entry may differ over time.[53] In the short run, entry may yield price competition, which in turn tends to increase purchasing power and over time also boost profits and diversity. It could also attract purchasing power from outside the region and overall make the region more attractive.[54] The region may than gain from both a pull on outside customers, leading to an increase in total regional expenditure, at the same time as there is modest leakage of demand to other regions due to more varied and qualitative supply. In the longer run, or if there are credible innovations-based entry (see previous sections) threats in the short run, innovative activities can be expected to follow suit. Thus entry and expansion of new industries can be expected to strengthen regional attractiveness.

Knowledge
With regard to knowledge production, too, a number of advantages of geographically concentrated structures have been observed. Proximity advantages present themselves in facilitating knowledge diffusion and creating proximity-based communications externalities. The importance of proximity to specific knowledge nodes, such as universities, has also been investigated. It is shown that innovativeness is substantial and increasing in the presence of universities.[55] The effect is attributed to knowledge spillovers.

There is a virtual consensus that spillovers are locally bounded. The distance decay effect has also been established in a large number of studies.[56] Knowledge spillovers tend to be stronger for more technologically sophisticated production, and in more fluid and early stages of production of new knowledge. Innovative processes assessed by either patents or quality-adjusted measures of patents indicate that innovation is more concentrated than inventive or production activities (Paci and Usai, 1999; Ejermo, 2009).

Consequently, innovation processes and entrepreneurial activity are to a high extent localized processes, one reason being that innovation frequently involves the exchange of complex knowledge, which takes place mainly within the borders of a region. Innovation processes are thus governed by interdependencies, complementarities and networking between the different actors. Hence innovation capabilities seem to stem from the interplay between generic knowledge and learning processes that are highly 'localized' and embedded in the knowledge and market environment of each region.[57]

Regional growth
Apparently there is ample empirical evidence of the importance of geographical proximity for knowledge spillovers and innovativeness. But to what extent is that reflected in differences in regional productivity? As shown in Braunerhjelm (2008), a large number of empirical studies, covering different geographical units and industries, reach the conclusion that geographical concentration of entrepreneurship and knowledge is associated with higher productivity.

One of the first studies on regional productivity was undertaken by Ciccone and Hall (1996). They performed a cross-sectional study, based on US data from 1988, on labor productivity and concentration at the county level. Controlling for knowledge (as measured by education levels) and capital intensity, they found that the major explanatory power could be attributed to regional employment density. According to their estimations, doubling the employment density at the county level increased labor productivity by 6 percent. Still, the issues addressed focused on density and knowledge while the impact of entrepreneurs was not included in the analysis. In a subsequent analysis (Ciccone, 2002) on European regions similar results were obtained.

Within the last decade there have been several attempts to pin down the relationship between entrepreneurship and regional growth. Reynolds's (1999) study indicated a positive relationship for the USA, as did Holtz-Eakin and Kao's (2003) analysis of the impact of entrepreneurship on productivity change over time. It is shown that variations in the birth rate and the death rate for firms are related to positive changes in productivity. Corresponding analyses on European data covering roughly the same time period report more ambiguous results. For instance, Audretsch and Fritsch (1996) and Fritsch (1997) using data on Germany from the 1980s and beginning of the 1990s, failed to detect any signs of entrepreneurship augmenting growth. However, rerunning their estimations for a later time period, Audretsch and Fritsch (2002) found that regions with a higher startup rate exhibited higher growth rates. Their interpretation was that Germany had changed over time, implying that the engine of growth was shifting towards entrepreneurship.

Callejon and Segarra (1999) used a data set of Spanish manufacturing industries between 1980 and 1992 to link new-firm birth rates and death rates, which taken together constitute a measure of turbulence, to total factor productivity growth in industries and regions. They adopt a model based on a vintage capital framework in which new entrants embody the edge technologies available and exiting businesses represent marginal obsolete plants. They find that both new-firm startup rates and exit rates contribute positively to the growth of total factor productivity in regions as well as industries. Similar results are reported by Bosma and Nieuwenhuijsen (2002), looking at 40 regions in the Netherlands from 1988 to 1996 and distinguishing between the service and the manufacturing sector. Positive total factor productivity effects were observed for the service sector. The analysis is extended to 2002 in Bosma et al. (2008).

The positive relationship between entrepreneurship and growth at the regional level has also been concluded to prevail in Sweden. For example, Fölster (2002) and Braunerhjelm and Borgman (2004) find similar effects using Swedish data. Fölster (2000) examines not just the employment impact within new and small firms, but the overall link between increases in self-employment and total employment in Sweden between 1976 and 1995. Using a Layard–Nickell framework, he provides a link between micro behavior and macroeconomic performance, and shows that increased self-employment shares have had a positive impact on regional employment rates in Sweden. Braunerhjelm and Borgman (2004) established a positive impact of entrepreneurs on regional growth measured as labor productivity. They also found that the effect was most pronounced for knowledge-intensive industries.

Regional performance may also be affected by the composition of industries (Klepper, 2002; Rosenthal and Strange, 2003). Even though a considerable number of studies have shown how innovative activities and growth seem to be higher in more diversified regions (Glaeser et al., 1992; Feldman and Audretsch, 1999; Henderson and Thisse, 2004), the issue of diversity versus specialization in regional composition of industries has been examined by pooling regional data with information on innovative activities. The empirical evidence as to whether knowledge externalities occur between industries (Jacobian externalities) or within industries (Marshall–Arrow–Romer externalities) is inconclusive (Braunerhjelm, 2008).

Romanelli and Feldman (2006), looking at biotechnology clusters in the USA, conclude that three ingredients are particularly decisive for regional development. First, their study reveals that about two-thirds of the clusters were founded by local entrepreneurs and investors. Second, regions that exhibited sustained growth revealed a higher degree of spin-offs from local, i.e. first-generation, firms. Third, a quite sizable share (one-third) of the entrepreneurs relocated from one metropolitan region to another to found new firms. The conclusion is that entrepreneurs are scanning attractive locations to which they relocate. These results corroborate the findings of Klepper (1996, 2002).

More recently LeSage and Fischer (2008) and LeSage and Pace (2009) assessed the impact of regional knowledge stocks on regional total factor productivity, and reached the conclusion that spatial factors must be taken into account. Both spatial and technological proximity are found to be important when examining the extent of regional spillovers. They implement an extended version of regional knowledge stocks to fully grasp available regional technical knowledge.

Sutter (2009) shows that entrepreneurship is clustered in space, and that there are latent unobservable and region-specific sources of variation in entrepreneurial activities that have an important influence on entrepreneurial activity. Growth in high-tech output as a share of regional output, per capita income and total private employment were the most important structural economic variables in determining regional entrepreneurship, suggesting path-dependence in high technology. Sutter, implementing recent improvements in spatial econometric techniques, also concludes that knowledge and entrepreneurship positively influence regional total factor productivity. In addition, distance to the technological frontiers seems to have no or a modest impact on the contribution by entrepreneurs to total factor productivity. Discovery and exploitation of opportunities seem allied to both individuals and place (Schoonhoven and Romanelli, 2005).

To conclude, a larger number of studies confirm that entrepreneurship, agglomerated knowledge structures and regional growth are interconnected in a complex way, but that the dominant share of spillovers seems to have a local origin.

IMPLICATIONS FOR ECONOMIC POLICIES

The previous sections generated some general observations. First, to achieve sustainable growth, policies must embrace different but complementary parts of an economy. Apparently, economic performance cannot be disentangled from the legal and institutional context of an economy (North and Thomas, 1973; Rosenberg and Birdzell, 1986).[58] In addition, a discrepancy between economic policies at the macro and the micro level may lead to lower growth. A suboptimal policy mix as regards the conditions for diffusion of knowledge, as compared to accumulating knowledge, could impede countries and regions from reaching their potential growth trajectories (Michelacci, 2004).

Thus, irrespective of fact that the macroeconomic setting has improved over the last decade (disregarding the present – 2009 – macroeconomic turmoil), coupled with the ambition to augment countries' knowledge base, the leverage on those changes may turn out to be quite disappointing if too little attention is directed towards the microeconomic conditions for knowledge based growth.

Second, despite technological advances in terms of facilitating information flows and communication channels, proximity still seems to matter. Costs of communication thus remain important, as do institutional and cultural barriers between countries (Hofstede, 2001). That also holds at a finer geographical level, judging from the more ample spillovers within regions.

Third, an emerging empirical literature where micro-level data are pooled with country data provides statistical support for a negative relationship between regulation and aggregate income, while an opposite effect is attributed as regards ownership rights and entry of new firms (Bergoeing et al., 2004). A couple of studies also suggest that high-tech firms and knowledge-intensive startups seems to play a major role in influencing growth (Audretsch and Keilbach, 2004; Mueller, 2007).

Altogether, these observations carry interesting implications for the design of policies. Particularly important components in the microeconomic setting refer to the design of regulation affecting knowledge production, ownership, entry barriers, labor mobility and inefficient financial markets. These all refer to the diffusion of knowledge through entry. Knowledge creation has to be matched by incentives to exploit knowledge.[59]

Policy Implications

Knowledge production, ownership and entry
The US university research system seems to be more pluralistic and decentralized as compared to Europe's (Carlsson et al., 2009). It has been argued that Europe's universities achieved organizational rationality and bureaucratic efficiency at the expense of competition and innovation. The degree to which universities should be autonomous, governed in an alternative way and more exposed to competition, is widely debated (Braunerhjelm, 2009). The US system seems however to have better links to the commercial sector and a more rapid pace of commercialization of new knowledge. That is likely to entail lessons for the European university system.

It would however be a mistake to conclude that these differences can be predominantly attributed to the changes in the intellectual property rights (IPRs) that resulted due to the

Bayh–Dole Act (1980), i.e. where IPRs were transferred to universities. Without policies that promote entrepreneurial activity, commercialization of new knowledge is less likely to be achieved. If we believe that growth and economic development are driven by innovation and creative destruction processes, leading to temporary monopolies, a balanced design of IPRs can be expected to yield such an outcome. This view has also, however, been debated. Still, without legal rights to appropriate the returns from innovations, the incentives to engage in such high-risk activities are likely to decline.

In addition, legal protection of investors has been shown to enhance access to credit for potential entrepreneurs and facilitate entry (Ardagna and Lusardi, 2010). In general, contract enforcement regulation, which affects the efficiency of the legal system, tends to improve the possibilities for entry and enhance innovation (Djankov et al., 2008; La Porta, 2008; Aidis et al., 2009). Djankov et al. (2008) shows that the differences in entry between countries with little regulation, as compared to the most heavily regulated, influences entry rate by 5 percent annually. Thus well-defined and credible ownership institutions should have a positive impact on the rate of innovation and entry.

Regulation of entry
In general terms, regulation is shown to deter growth, but exactly how is less clear, albeit the negative effect on entrepreneurship is one suggested mechanism, together with taxes and liquidity constraints.[60] Ciccone and Papaioannou (2006) provide evidence that entry regulation can delay introduction of new varieties/goods in industries that experience expansionary global demand and/or technology shocks.

The extent of regulation has interesting indirect effects that influence entry. As shown by Ardagna and Lusardi (2009), the positive effect associated with skills (education) diminishes considerably in more regulated countries, particularly for opportunity-based entrepreneurship. In addition, it significantly reduces the propensity for marginalized groups to start firms. Similarly, the positive effects of knowing people who are entrepreneurs, run their own firms, i.e. network and belong to an entrepreneurial culture, is curbed.[61] The results comply with earlier findings of Klapper et al. (2006) and also of Ciccone and Papaioannou (2006), referred to above.

The results reported in Aghion et al. (2006) of entry on innovation imply that entry barriers may reduce innovation rate, productivity and growth. Put differently, more employees in foreign firms may spur productivity growth in incumbents. Openness to encourage an influx of firms, workers and potential entrepreneurs is consequently important. Internationalized firms are also observed to be most innovative (Hessels and Suddle, 2007).

Regulation of labor markets and entry
The impact of regulated labor markets is somewhat more mixed. However, Micco and Pagés (2006), Author et al. (2007) and Kugler and Pica (2008) all report a significant negative impact on entry of higher regulated labor markets, as well as a slower restructuring of the economy. Similarly, studies on the determinants of foreign direct investments find a negative effect of regulated labor markets (Jarvorcik et al., 2006; Gross and Ryan, 2008). In addition, productivity seems to decrease as labor market regulations become more severe (Bassanini and Venn, 2007; Martins, 2009), and the number of fast-growing firms – gazelles – seems to be negatively impacted.

Ciccone and Papaioannou (2006) report several interesting results by interacting different variables, for example, that regulated labor markets negatively influence entry by lowering the social network factor discussed above, particularly for opportunity-based entrepreneurship. In addition, more regulated labor markets imply that individuals' risk-taking attitudes become more important. Hence the perceived threshold to climb before taking the step to become an entrepreneur increases. Ardagna and Lusardi (2010) conclude that labor market regulation has its strongest impact on opportunity-based entrepreneurship, while Caballero and Hammour (2000) stress that 'constrained contractual capabilities' in labor markets (and in the financial system) may hamper the process of creative destruction.[62]

Taxes and entry
There is an extensive literature on the effect of taxes on entrepreneurship, embracing the structure of taxes, the overall tax pressure and marginal tax rates. Most of the empirical studies are based on US, or Anglo-Saxon, data. The results are somewhat inconclusive, but the overall conclusion of these studies seems to be that the level of individual taxes is ambiguous (and even positive), while increased marginal rates have clearly negative effects on the propensity to become an entrepreneur. The impact on entrepreneurship is however sensitive to the possibilities of arbitraging between tax bases (Gentry and Hubbard, 2000; Parker and Robson, 2003; Cullen and Gordon, 2007). Taxes that lower the possibilities for individual wealth, thereby adding to financial constraints, are also reported to have a negative effect on entrepreneurship (Hansson, 2010). Note also that the administrative burden associated with taxes primarily affects entrepreneurs negatively (Djankov et al., 2008).[63]

In a recent study by Djankov et al. (2008), looking at effective corporate taxes in 85 countries for a standardized firm in 2004, a large negative impact is found on investments (by incumbents and foreign direct investments) and on entrepreneurial activity. A 10 percent increase in corporate tax is shown to reduce aggregate investment in relation to GDP by 2 percent and reduce entry by between 2 and 5 percent. A tax rise is also negatively correlated with growth but positively associated with growth of the informal sector.[64] Another statistically significant result is that the corporate debt of firms is much higher (lower solidity) in countries with higher corporate taxes, i.e. debt financing is more common than equity financing.

Sectors and the stage of firms' life cycle
Depending on the stage of the firm's life cycle, different sets of policies are conceivable. In the very early phases of an entrepreneurial venture, individuals' economic status may be hard to disentangle from that of their firms (Autio and Wennberg, 2009). In general, there is little policy attention to the joint implication of public policies at different stages of new firm evolution such as entry, growth and exit. In addition, firms grow at different paces and the requirements of slow-growing firms and gazelles may be quite different. The importance of gazelles for job creation seems to have increased over time. All in all, it is likely that policy variables influencing growth differ over firms' evolutionary stages.

In addition, there are also sectoral differences. For instance, removing entry barriers may not increase productivity and growth in all industries. Hence, doing so should be complemented with means that facilitate the reallocation of resources towards sectors that react positively to entry, thereby releasing resources to be employed in expanding sectors. Exits are often neglected, but constitute a policy area (bankruptcy institutions etc.) as important as policies geared towards entry.

Level of economic development
The design of policies may also vary with countries' level of economic development. As discussed above, the mechanism for structural changes and implementation of a new technology looks very different in developing and developed countries. Building institutions that foster private sector development and provide credible enforcement to protect private ownership, encourage education and attract foreign direct investments and imitative entrepreneurship, should be high-priority issues in developing countries (van Stel, 2005; Saxenian, 2006; Rodrik, 2007). In more developed economies, attention should to a larger extent be directed to production and diffusion of knowledge, together with well-functioning and experimentally organized innovation processes.

The point emphasized in this section is that a supplementary set of policies focusing on strengthening the conduits of knowledge spillover plays a central role in promoting economic growth. Without the appropriate incentive structure for labor, entrepreneurs and investors, the potential beneficial effect of knowledge accumulation policies will not be achieved. Therefore policies that aim to set economies on their potentially long-run sustainable growth trajectory must implement coherent strategies that embrace several levels (micro and macro) and areas (knowledge accumulation and diffusion). The different policy areas must be coordinated and addressed simultaneously. If entry barriers are reduced but exit possibilities are inferior and property rights weak, the result in term of startups, knowledge diffusion and productivity may be modest.

CONCLUSION

A society's ability to increase its wealth and welfare over time critically hinges on its potential to develop, exploit and diffuse knowledge, thereby influencing growth. The more pronounced step in the evolution of mankind has been preceded by discontinuous, or lumpy, augmentations of knowledge and technical progress. As knowledge has advanced and reached new levels, periods of economic development followed, characterized by uncertainty, market experiments, redistribution of wealth, and the generation of new structures and industries. This pattern mirrors the evolution during the first and second Industrial Revolutions in the eighteenth and nineteenth centuries, and is also a conspicuous feature of the 'third', and still ongoing, digital revolution.

Despite the fact that there is a general presumption within the economics discipline that micro-level processes play a vital role in the diffusion of knowledge, and thus the growth process, there is a lack of a stringent theoretical framework but also of empirical analyses to support this allegation. The economic variables knowledge, entrepreneurship and, innovation hang together in a complex manner but are treated as different and separate entities, or reduced to a constant or a stochastic process. It is not until the last 10–15 years that a literature has emerged that aims to integrate these economic concepts into a coherent framework.

Thus knowledge concerning the microeconomic processes that lead to growth is still incomplete. In the neoclassical growth models, production of knowledge was exogenous – the technical residual – whereas in the endogenous growth literature the diffusion of knowledge is either exogenous, stochastic or allotted to large firms, for example pharmaceutical companies where research departments try to come up with the next combination of molecules that will be turned into the next 'magic bullet'. But knowledge is developed, applied and diffused in many other ways, often through smaller innovative firms and by entrepreneurs. The uncertainty, asymmetries and high transaction costs inherent in knowledge also generate a divergence in the assessment and evaluation of the expected value of new ideas. This divergence in valuation of knowledge across economic agents and within the decision-making process of incumbent firms can induce agents to start new firms as a mechanism to appropriate the (expected) value of their knowledge. This would suggest that entrepreneurship facilitates the spillover of knowledge in the form of starting a new firm.

How do we account for that kind of dynamics in the present growth models? To what extent are lagged effects and interaction effects included in an appropriate way? And what is actually endogenized through knowledge accumulation? Should knowledge be seen as the engine of growth, or should we see it as fuel that feeds into the mechanism that converts knowledge into growth, e.g. entrepreneurs, innovation, labor mobility etc.? Has, indeed, the Solowian technical residual been transformed into an entrepreneurial residual?

This chapter has tried to illustrate the relationship between knowledge, entrepreneurship and innovation on the one hand, and how that relates to growth on the other. Based on a (partial) survey of recent and previous theoretical and empirical contributions in this vein of research, the ambition has been to pinpoint some of the weak spots in our current understanding of growth, and to provide some recent insight into the growth process. In addition, policy areas of importance for the microeconomic foundations for growth have also been discussed, stressing the importance of a holistic approach implying that a multitude of measures and instruments must be considered in order to achieve sustainable economic development.

To paraphrase Voltaire: 'Doubt is not a pleasant condition but certainty is absurd', and we can be assured that we do not yet fully comprehend the microeconomic mechanisms of growth. Thus the challenges are still there – let us deal with them!

NOTES

1. This chapter draws partly on the survey in Braunerhjelm (2008).
2. The following section includes a brief and partial presentation of some of the most influential thoughts as regards entrepreneurs. For a more thorough survey, see Sexton and Landström (2000), Acs and Audrestch (2003) and Braunerhjelm (2008).
3. Olsson (2000) and Olsson and Frey (2002) present a theoretical model of entrepreneurs as undertakers of new combinations of ideas.
4. Menger did not, however, define or include the entrepreneur in his work. Von Mises (1949) much later defined entrepreneurs in terms of unevenly distributed talent.
5. Schumpeter defined five different types of innovation: the recognition of a new good/quality; a new method/process; a new market; a new source of supply; or a new way of organizing the firm/production.
6. See Shane (2003).
7. Baumol (1990) emphasizes the role of institutions for the allocation between productive (innovation) and unproductive activities (rent-seeking, organized crime etc.).

8. We shall not consider explanations related to the sociological disciplines (teams, networks etc.), nor those related to nascent entrepreneurship, 'combinators' etc.

9. For alternative approaches in the long-wave literature; see, e.g., Kitchin (1923, long waves appear due to investments cycles), Juglar (1862, investments in machinery), Kuznets (1971, investments in real estate) and Kondratieff (1925/35), who simply concludes that long waves of economic activity seems to be a fact.

10. See Bartik (1989), Evans and Jovanovic (1989), Reynolds et al. (1994), Dunn and Holtz-Eakin (1995, 2000), Quadrini (2000) and Acs et al. (2007).

11. The demand variable goes back to Adam Smith's argument about the size of the market and the scope for specialization.

12. Though, as argued by Leff (1979), capital market imperfections should not be enough to explain entrepreneurial differences, since it could be argued that overcoming such difficulties constitutes a part of entrepreneurial abilities.

13. See Ardagna and Lusardi (2008), where it is shown that knowing someone with entrepreneurial experience increases the likelihood of becoming an entrepreneur by 3 percent. See also Djankov et al. (2006), Guiso et al. (2004), and Nanda and Sorenson (2007).

14. Gordon (2004) and Bosma and Harding (2007) claim that institutional differences explain the growth differences between Europe and the USA.

15. An exception, based on US data, is Kim et al. (2006).

16. Compare the studies by Black et al. (1996), Hurst and Lusardi (2004) and Nanda (2009), where it is shown that higher real-estate processes ease liquidity constraints and positively influence entrepreneurship.

17. See McClelland (1961), Williamson (1971), Timmons (1976), Kihlstrom and Laffont (1979), Brockhaus (1980), Budner (1982), Schere (1982), Chell (1986), Begley and Boyd (1987), Chen et al (1998), Zucker et al (1998), van Praag and Cramer (2001), Markman et al (2002), Agrawal et al (2006), Sorenson and Singh (2007), Benz and Frey (2008).

18. Note the analogy with successful organizations, where psychological capital has been defined as an important explanatory factor (Luthans et al., 2007; Luthans and Youssef, 2007).

19. See, e.g., Fritsch and Mueller (2007), Koster and Karlsson (2009).

20. Globalization is claimed to influence both the demand- (lower transport costs, expansion of markets etc.) and supply-side factors (migration, FDI, spin-offs etc.) of entrepreneurship (Karlsson et al., 2009).

21. See Carlsson et al. (2009), and the references therein, for a more thorough review of the production and organization of knowledge within the modern society.

22. Shane (2003) presents a discussion concerning the differences between Schumpeterian and Kirznerian sources of opportunity where it is claimed that only the Schumpeterian type of opportunity requires 'creation' by the entrepreneur.

23. Baumol (1990) also separates the innovator and the firm-creator (imitator).

24. Obviously the same measurement weaknesses appear with regard to countries' knowledge capital.

25. Patents, and patents citations, are also frequently used as a proxy for knowledge spillovers (Jaffe et al., 1993, 2000; Acs et al., 2002; Furman et al., 2002).

26. See Braunerhjelm and Svensson (2009) and the references therein.

27. Mairesse and Mohnen (2001) suggest using an alternative measure based on the composite of the share in sales attributed to innovative products, R&D, proximity to basic research and market structure (competitiveness).

28. Gort and Klepper (1982), Klepper and Graddy (1990), Jovanovic and McDonald (1994), Klepper (1996) and Agarwal and Gort (1996).

29. See Braunerhjelm (2008) and Aghion and Griffith (2005) for surveys.

30. For references to related papers in the industrial organization vein, see those papers. See also Aghion and Griffith (2005).

31. This implies that the difference for this sector as compared to the neoclassical innovation production function (Dasgupta and Stiglitz, 1981; Pakes and Griliches, 1984; Mairesse and Sassenon, 1991; Mairesse and Kremp, 1993; Mairesse and Mohnen, 2004) is perhaps not that large.

32. See Witt (2002) for a criticism of the evolutionary dynamics in the Nelson and Winter model. Winter (1984) introduces entry and exit where firm-level productivity is stochastically determined. The entering firm decides *ex post* whether it should belong to the routinized regime, which yields lower but safer returns, or the entrepreneurial regime, where potential profits are higher but also uncertain.

33. See Baumol (1990), Eliasson (2007), Johnson et al. (2000), Boetke and Coyne (2003), Acemouglu et al. (2004) and Powell (2008).

34. Compare the resource-based views (Penrose, 1959; Barney, 1991), which stressed heterogeneous internal resources and capabilities. The early evolutionary neo-Schumpeter also acknowledged the role of internal factors but focused on sector characteristics and technological regimes (Malerba and Orsenigo, 1993).

35. However, creative destruction is not solely a function of entry and small, but also relates to innova-

tion within large firms as well as mergers and acquisitions (Jovanovic and Rosseau, 2002; Eliasson and Eliasson, 1996).

36.   Rothwell and Zegveld (1982), Baumol (2004), Ortega-Argilés et al. (2009).
37.   See Braunerhjelm (2008) and van Praag and Versloot (2007) for surveys.
38.   For a survey of neoclassical growth models, see Braunerhjelm (2008).
39.   See also Prescott and Boyd (1987), who modeled production externalities as a function of coalition con-tracts between senior, experienced and younger, less experienced workers. Diminishing returns set as in the number of younger workers increased. Compare Lucas's (1978) work on the role of talented manage-ment and the allocation of resources.
40.   Kim et al. (2006) conclude that startups promote new and more flexible organizations.
41.   This was noted long ago by, e.g., Kirzner (1973), Geroski (1995) and Nickell (1996), and the previous ref-erences to Aghion et al. Johnson and Parker (1996), Dejardin (2009) and Thurik and Carree (2008) show that net entry has a positive lagged effect on regional growth, while Dejardin (1998) failed to find such a relationship. As argued, the entry/exit process is characterized by a considerable degree of heterogeneity and will not necessarily generate creative destruction and economic progress (Manjón-Antolin, 2004, Vivarelli, 2007). Cabral (1997) even claims that most entrepreneurial ventures are entry mistakes.
42.   Bartelsman et al. (2004) show that the faster pace of exits in the USA as compared to Europe has had positive structural effects.
43.   See Adams (1990), Lichtenberg (1993), Caballero and Jaffe (1993), Coe and Helpman (1995), Baumol (2007), LeSage and Fischer (2008) and Naudé (2008).
44.   The results are corroborated by McMillan and Woodruff (2002) and Audretsch et al. (2006).
45.   See Ashcroft and Love (1996), Fritsch (1997), Audretsch and Fritsch (2002), Acs and Armington (2002), van Stel and Storey (2002), Carree et al. (2002) and Klapper et al. (2006). A number of studies report a positive correlation between knowledge and regional prosperity. However, as stressed by several scholars, these studies suffer from numerous problems, e.g. the complex dynamics between R&D and its com-mercial applications (Disney et al., 2003; Scarpetta et al., 2002; Erken et al., 2008), and fail to account for physical and human capital factors/stocks (Holtz-Eakin and Kao, 2003, Heden, 2005; Foster et al., 2006). Thus, much of the variation in productivities may have little to do with differences in knowledge or technology.
46.   See also Glaeser et al. (1992), Miracky (1993), Reynolds et al. (1994), Acs and Armington (2006), Stam (2006) Glaeser (2007) and Naudé et al. (2008) for analyses of the relationship between entrepreneurship and growth, the product cycle, technological progress and competition.
47.   At the same time, the average entrepreneurship rate is shown to be much higher in low- and middle-income countries than in high-income countries (Ardagna and Lusardi, 2010). In addition, in the former two categories of countries, necessity entrepreneurship accounts for about two-thirds of startups, while that drops to 22 percent in high-income countries. The EU has the lowest rate of entrepreneurial activ-ity. This complements Wennekers's (2005) U-shaped model, where higher entrepreneurial activities are expected in low- and high-income countries, by stressing the type of entrepreneurship.
48.   For more general surveys of economic geography models, see Fujita et al. (1999), Fujita and Thisse (2002), Thisse and Henderson (2004) and Braunerhjelm and Feldman (2006).
49.   For electronically transmitted products, trade and transports costs approach zero.
50.   Note that the European economy has a considerably more geographically dispersed production than the USA, which is explained by higher transport and trade costs (Braunerhjelm et al., 2000). As those costs become lower due to European integration, a reshuffling of production and stronger geographic concen-tration can be expected. That will have implications at the regional level.
51.   See for instance Chinitz (1961), Jacobs (1969), Mills and Hamilton (1984), Hansen (1987), Saxenian (1994), Guimarães et al. (2000, 2002) and Braunerhjelm and Feldman (2006).
52.   See Thornton and Flynne (2003), Backman (2009) and Glaeser and Kerr (2009).
53.   Another dynamic feature is the expected correlation between regional entry and exit (Keeble and Walker, 1994; Reynolds et al., 1994). A more dense environment tends to lower survival rates but also implies higher growth prospects for survivors (Fritsch et al., 2006, Weyh, 2006).
54.   The effect is known as Reilly's Law (1931).
55.   The reader is referred to Braunerhjelm (2008) for a more detailed description of the studies regarding proximity to universities, spillovers and growth.
56.   This literature goes way back. For more contemporary contributions, see, e.g., Hoover and Vernon (1959), Vernon (1962), Pred (1977), Leone and Struyck (1976), Acs et al. (1994), Acs (1996), Audretsch and Vivarelli (1996), Anselin et al. (1997), Glaeser (1999), Feldman and Audretsch (1999), Anselin et al. (2000), Keller (2002), Fischer and Varga (2003), Bottazi and Peri (2003), and the refences in those articles.
57.   However, Breschi and Lissoni (2001) argue in a critical article that careful scrutiny reveals that spillovers are more of a pecuniary, market-based nature rather than related to knowledge spillovers.
58.   The remarkable growth in Sweden between 1870 and 1950 was preceded by a number of important insti-

tutional changes: compulsory schooling was initiated in 1842, local monopolies (guilds) were abolished in 1846, whereas a new law for firms with limited liabilities was passed in 1847, followed in 1862 by freedom of trade. Hence the Swedish case illustrates the significance of the institutional set-up (Braunerhjelm, 2005).

59. Theoretically different views on regulation can be found in the public choice (Buchanan and Tullock, 1962) and public-interest (Pigou, 1938) theories. The former claims that public intervention hinders dynamics and economic development, while the latter argues that interventions are necessary to protect the public interest.

60. See Evans and Jovanovic (1989), Hurst and Lusardi (2004), Alesina et al. (2005), Djankov et al. (2007), Fiori et al. (2007), Gentry and Hubbard (2000), Nicoletti and Scarpetta (2003), Djankov et al. (2008) and Arnold et al. (2008). Delmar and Wennberg (2010) discuss the need for a multi-level (individual, firm, industry) policy approach. La Porta (2008) claims that a French legal origin (civil law) tends to weaken the effect of innovation on growth as compared to Anglo-Saxon origin (common law).

61. These effects are quantified by Ardagna and Lusardi (2010). For example, the positive network effects are reduced by more than two-thirds.

62. See also Djankov et al. (2002), Desai et al. (2003) and La Porta et al. (1997, 2008).

63. See Hansson (2010) for a survey. La Porta (2008) reach the conclusion that the tax burden is substantially higher in civil-law countries and the tax rate higher.

64. The empirical analysis controls for other taxes (VAT, personal, etc.).

REFERENCES

Acemoglu, D., Aghion, P. and Zilibotti, F. (2006), 'Distance to frontier, selection and economic growth', *Journal of the European Economic Association*, **4** (1), 37–74.

Acemouglu, D., Johnson, S. and Robinson, J. (2004), 'Institutions as the fundamental cause of long-run growth', NBER WP 10481, Cambridge, MA.

Acs, Z. (1996), 'Small firms and economic growth', in Z. Acs, B. Carlsson and R. Thurik (eds), *Small Business in the Modern Economy*, Oxford: Blackwell Publishers, pp. 1–62.

Acs, Z. and Armington, C. (2002), 'Economic growth and entrepreneurial activity', Center for Economic Studies, US Bureau of the Census, Washington, DC.

Acs, Z. and Armington, C. (2006), *Entrepreneurship, Geography and Economic Growth*, New York: Cambridge University Press.

Acs, Z. and Audretsch, D. (1988), 'Innovation in large and small firms: an empirical analysis', *American Economic Review*, **78**, 678–90.

Acs, Z. and Audretsch, D. (1990), *Innovation and Small Firms*, Cambridge, MA: MIT Press.

Acs, Z. and Audretsch, D. (2003), *Handbook of Entrepreneurship Research: An Interdisciplinary Survey and Introduction*, Boston, MA, Dordrecht and London: Kluwer.

Acs, Z. and Szerb, L. (2009), 'The Global Entrepreneurship Index', *Foundations and Trends in Entrepreneurship*, **5**, 341–435.

Acs, Z., Audretsch, D. and Feldman, M. (1994), 'R&D spillovers and recepient firm size', *The Review of Economics and Statistics*, **76**, 336–40.

Acs, Z., FitzRoy, F. and Smith, I. (2002), 'High technology employment, and R&D in cities: heterogeneity vs. specialization', *Annals of Regional Science*, **36**, 269–371.

Acs, Z., Audretsch, D., Braunerhjelm, P. and Carlsson, B. (2004a), 'The missing link. The knowledge filter and entrepreneurship in endogenous growth', CEPR DP 4783, CEPR, London.

Acs, Z., Audretsch, D., Braunerhjelm, P. and Carlsson, B. (2004b), 'The knowledge spillover theory of entrepreneurship', Cesis WP 77, Royal Institute of Technology, Stockholm.

Acs, Z., Brooksbank, D., O'Gorman, C., Pickernell, D. and Terjesen, S. (2007), 'The knowledge spillover theory of entrepreneurship and foreign direct investment', Jena Economic Research Paper, 07-059, Max Planck Institute of Economics, Jena.

Acs, Z., Braunerhjelm, P., Audretsch, D. and Carlsson, B. (2009), 'The knowledge spill-over theory of entrepreneurship', *Small Business Economics*, **32**, 15–30.

Adams, J. (1990), 'Fundamental stocks of knowledge and productivity growth', *Journal of Political Economy*, **98**, 673–703.

Agarwal, R. and Gort, M. (1996), 'The evolution of markets and entry, exit and survival of firms', *Review of Economics and Statistics*, **78**, 489–98.

Aghion, P. and Griffith, R. (2005), *Competition and Growth: Reconciling Theory and Evidence*, Cambridge, MA: MIT Press.

Aghion, P. and Howitt, P. (1992), 'A model of growth through creative destruction'. *Econometrica*, **60**, 323–51.
Aghion, P. and Howitt, P. (1998), *Endogenous Growth Theory*, Cambridge, MA: MIT Press.
Aghion, P., Harris, C., Howitt, P. and Vickers, J. (2001), 'Competition, imitation and growth with step-by-step innovation', *Review of Economic Studies*, **68**, 467–92.
Aghion, P., Burgess, R., Redding, S. and Zilibotti, F. (2004), 'Entry and productivity growth: evidence from microlevel panel data', *Journal of the European Economic Association*, **2**, 265–76.
Aghion, P., Bloom, N., Blundell, R., Griffith, R. and Howitt, P. (2005), 'Competition and innovation: an inverted U relationship', *Quarterly Journal of Economics*, **120**, 701–28.
Aghion, P., Blundell, R., Griffith, R., Howitt, P. and Prantl, S. (2006), 'The effects of entry on incumbent innovation and productivity', NBER WP 12027, Cambridge, MA.
Agrawal, A. Cockburn, I. and McHale, J. (2006), 'Gone but not forgotten: knowledge flows, labor mobility, and enduring social relationships', *Journal of Economic Geography*, **6**, 571–91.
Aidis, R, Estrin, S. and Mickiwics, T. (2009), 'Entrepreneurial entry: which institutions matter?', CEPR DP 7278, CEPR, London.
Aldrich, H. and Auster, E. (1986), 'Even dwarfs started small: liabilities of age and size and their strategic implications', *Research in Organizational Behavior*, **8**, 165–98.
Aldrich, H. and Martinez, M. (2001), 'Many are called, but few are chosen: an evolutionary perspective for the study of entrepreneurship', *Entrepreneurship: Theory and Practice*, **25**, 41–57.
Aldrich, H. and Zimmer, C. (1986), 'Entrepreneurship through social networks', in D. Sexton and R. Smilor (eds), *The Art and Science of Entrepreneurship*, Cambridge, MA: Ballinger Publishing, pp. 3–23.
Alesina, A., Ardagna, S, Nicoletti, G. and Schiantarelli, F. (2005), 'Regulation and investment', *Journal of European Economic Association*, **3**, 791–825.
Almeida, P. (1999), 'Semiconductor startups and the exploration of new technology territory', in Z. Acs (ed.), *Are Small Firms Important? Their Role and Impact*, Berlin: Springer Verlag, pp. 39–51.
Almeida, P. and Kogut, B. (1997), 'The exploration of technological diversity and the geographic localization of innovation', *Small Business Economics*, **9**, 21–31.
Anderson, G. and Tollison, R. (1980), 'Adam Smith's analysis of joint-stock companies', *Journal of Political Economy*, **90**, 1237–57.
Andersson, M. and Lööf, H. (2009), 'Key characteristics of the small innovative firm', Cesis WP 175, The Royal Institute of Technology, Stockholm.
Anselin, L., Varga, A. and Acs, Z. (1997), 'Local geographic spillovers between university research and high technology innovations', *Journal of Urban Economics*, **42**, 422–48.
Anselin, L., Varga, A. and Acs, Z. (2000), 'Geographic and sectoral characteristics of academic knowledge externalities', *Papers in Regional Science*, **79**, 435–43.
Ardagna, S. and Lusardi, A. (2009), 'Heterogeneity in the effect of regulation on entrepreneurship and entry size', NBER WP 15510, NBER, Cambridge, MA.
Ardagna, S. and Lusardi, A. (2010), 'Explaining international differences in entrepreneurship: the role of individual characteristics and regulatory constraints', in J. Lerner and A. Schoar (eds), *International Differences in Entrepreneurship*, Chicago, IL: University of Chicago Press, pp. 17–62.
Arnold, J., Nicoletti, G. and Scarpetta, S. (2008), 'Regulation, allocative efficiency and productivity in OECD countries: industry and firm-level evidence', OECD Economics Department, OECD, Paris.
Arrow, K. (1962), 'Economic welfare and the allocation of resources for invention', in R. Nelson (ed.), *The Rate and Direction of Inventive Activity*, Princeton, NJ: Princeton University Press, pp. 609–26.
Ashcroft, B. and Love, J. (1996), 'Firm births and employment change in the British counties: 1981–1989', *Papers in Regional Science*, **75**, 483–500.
Audretsch, D. (1995), *Innovation and Industry Evolution*, Cambridge, MA: MIT Press.
Audretsch, D. and Fritsch, M. (1996), 'Creative destruction: turbulence and economic growth', in E. Helmstädter and M. Perlman (eds), *Behavioral Norms, Technological Progress, and Economic Dynamics: Studies in Schumpeterian Economics*, Ann Arbor, MI: University of Michigan Press, pp. 137–50.
Audretsch, D. and Fritsch, F. (2002), 'Growth regimes over time and space', *Regional Studies*, **36**, 113–24.
Audretsch, D. and Thurik, R. (2002), 'Linking entrepreneurship to growth', OECD STI Working Paper, 2081/2, OECD, Paris.
Audretsch, D. and Vivarelli, M. (1996), 'Firm size and R&D spillover: evidence from Italy', *Small Business Economics*, **8**, 249–58.
Audretsch, D., Keilbach, M. and Lehmann, E. (2006), *Entrepreneurship and Economic Growth*, New York: Oxford University Press.
Autio, E. and Wennberg, K. (2009), 'Social peer influences and the transition to entrepreneurship, innovation and entrepreneurship', Group Working Paper, London.
Backman, M. (2009), 'New firm formation and regional accessibility to capital', Ciseg WP, Jönköping International Business School, Jönköping.

Baldwin, R. (1995), *The Dynamics of Industrial Competition*, Cambridge, MA: Cambridge University Press.

Baldwin, J. and Johnson, J. (1999), 'Entry, innovation and firm growth', in Z. Acs (ed.), *Are Small Firms Important? Their Role and Impact*, Dordrecht, Boston, MA and London: Kluwer Academic Publishers, pp. 51–79.

Banerjee, A. and Newman, A. (1993), 'Occupational choice and the process of development', *Journal of Political Economy*, **101**, 274–98.

Baptista, R., Escária, V. and Madruga, P. (2008), 'Entrepreneurship, regional development and job creation: the case of Portugal', *Small Business Economics*, **28**, 49–58.

Barney, J. (1991), 'Firm resources and sustained competitive advantage', *Journal of Management*, **17**, 99–120.

Bartelsman, E., Haltiwanger, J. and Scarpetta, S. (2004), *Microeconomic Evidence of Creative Destruction in Industrial and Developing Countries*, Washington, DC: World Bank.

Bartik, T. (1989), 'Small business start-ups in the United States: estimates of the effects of characteristics of states', *Southern Economic Journal*, **55**, 1004–18.

Baumol, W. (1990), 'Entrepreneurship: productive, unproductive and destructive', *Journal of Political Economy*, **98**, 893–921.

Baumol, W. (2002), *The Free-market Innovation Machine*: *Analysing the Growth Miracle of Capitalism*, Princeton, NJ: Princeton University Press.

Baumol, W. (2004), 'Entrepreneurial enterprises, large established firms and other components of the free-market growth machine', *Small Business Economics*, **23**, 9–21.

Baumol, W. (2007a), 'Small firms: why market-driven innovation can't get along without them', paper presented at the IFN conference in Waxholm.

Baumol, W. (2007b), *Good Capitalism, Bad Capitalism, and the Economics of Growth and Prosperity*, New Haven, CT: Yale University Press.

Baumol, W., Panzar, J. and Willig, R. (1982), *Contestable Markets and the Theory of Industrial Structure*, New York: Harcourt Brace Jovanovich.

Beck, T. and Levine, R. (2001), 'Stock markets, banks, and growth: correlation or causality?', Policy Research Working Paper Series 2670.

Begley, T. and Boyd, D. (1987), 'Psychological characteristics associated with performance in entrepreneurial firms and smaller business', *Journal of Business Venturing*, **2**, 79–93.

Benz, M. and Frey, B. (2008), 'Being independent is a great thing: subjective evaluations of self-employment and hierarchy', *Economica*, **75**, 362–83.

Bergoeing, R., Loayza, N. and Repetto, A. (2004), 'Slow recoveries', *Journal of Development Economics*, **75** (2), 473–506.

Berry, S. and Reiss, P. (2007), 'Empirical models of entry and market structure', in M. Armstrong and R. Porter (eds), *Handbook of Industrial Organization*, Vol. 3, Amsterdam: North Holland, pp. 1845–86.

Bhide, A. (2000), *The Origin and Evolution of New Businesses*, New York: Oxford University Press.

Black, J., de Meza, D. and Jeffrey, D. (1996), 'House prices, the supply of collateral, and the enterprise economy', *Economic Journal*, **106**, 60–75.

Blanchflower, D. (2000), 'Self-employment in OECD countries', *Labor Economics*, **7**, 471–505.

Blanchflower, D. and Oswald, A. (1998), 'What makes an entrepreneur?', *Journal of Labor Economics*, **16**, 26–60.

Blanchflower, D., David, G., Oswald, A. and Stutzer, A. (2001), 'Latent entrepreneurship across nations', *European Economic Review*, **45**, 669–80.

Block, J., Thurik, R. and Zhou, H. (2009), 'What turns knowledge into growth? The role of entrepreneurship and knowledge spillovers', Research Paper ERS -2009-049, ERIM.

Blundell, R., Griffith, R. and van Reenen, J. (1999), 'Market share, market value and innovation in a panel of British manufacturing firms', *Review of Economic Studies*, **66**, 529–44.

Boetke, P. and Coyne, C. (2003), 'Entrepreneurship and development: cause or consequence?', in R. Koppl, J. Birner and P. Kurrild-Klitgaard (eds), *Austrian Economics and Entrepreneurial Studies*, Bingley: Emerald Publishing, pp. 67–87.

Bosma, N. and Harding, R. (2007), *Global Entrepreneurship Monitoring 2006. Summary Results*, Boston, MA and London: Babson College and London Business School.

Bosma, N. and Nieuwenhuijsen, H. (2002), 'Turbulence and productivity: an analysis of 40 Dutch regions in the period 1988–1996', EIM SCALES-paper N200205, Zoetermer.

Bosma, N., de Wit, G. and Carree, M. (2005), 'Modelling entrepreneurship: unifying the equilibrium and the entry/exit approach', *Small Business Economics*, **25**, 35–48.

Bottazi, L. and Peri, G. (2003), 'Innovations and spillovers in regions: evidence from European patent data', *European Economic Review*, **47**, 687–710.

Braunerhjelm, P. (2005), 'Knowledge capital and economic growth: Sweden as an emblematic example', in A. Curzio and M. Fortis (eds), *Research and Technological Innovation*, Heidelberg and New York: Physica-Verlag, pp. 235–65.

Braunerhjelm, P. (2008), 'Entrepreneurship, knowledge and growth', *Foundations and Trends in Entrepreneurship*, **4**, 451–533.
Braunerhjelm, P. (2009), 'Universities and regional development: the old versus the new', *Industry and Innovation*, **15**, 253–75.
Braunerhjelm, P. and Borgman, B. (2004), 'Geographical concentration, entrepreneurship and regional growth: evidence from regional data in Sweden, 1975–99', *Regional Studies*, **38**, 929–48.
Braunerhjelm, P. and Feldman, M. (2006), *Cluster Genesis: The Development of High-Technology Industrial Locations*, Oxford: Oxford University Press.
Braunerhjelm, P. and Svensson, R. (2009), 'The inventor role. Was Schumpeter right?', *Journal of Evolutionary Economics*, on-line version.
Braunerhjelm, P., Acs, Z., Audretsch, D. and Carlsson, B. (2010), 'The missing link. Knowledge diffusion and entrepreneurship in endogenous growth', *Small Business Economics*, **34**, 105–25.
Breschi, S. and Lissoni, F. (2001), 'Knowledge spillovers and the local innovation system: a critical survey', *Industrial and Corporate Change*, **10**, 975–1005.
Brockhaus, R. (1980), 'Risk taking propensity of entrepreneurs', *The Academy of Management Journal*, **23**, 509–20.
Bruce, D. and Holtz-Eakin, D. (2001), 'Who are the entrepreneurs? Evidence from taxpayer data', *Journal of Entrepreneurial Finance and Business*, **1**, 1–10.
Buchanan, G. and Tullock, J. (1962), *The Calculus of Consent: Logical Foundations of Constitutional Democracy*, Ann Arbor, MI: University of Michigan Press.
Budner, S. (1982), 'Intolerance of ambiguity as a personality variable', *Journal of Personality*, **30**, 29–50.
Caballero, R. and Hammour, M. (2000), 'Creative destruction and development: institutions, crises and restructuring', NBER WP 7849, NBER, Boston, MA.
Caballero, R. and Jaffe, A. (1993), 'How high are the giant's shoulders? An empirical assessment of knowledge spillovers and creative destruction in a model of economic growth', *NBER Macroeconomics Annual*, **8**, 15–74.
Cabral, L. (1997), 'Entry mistakes', CEPR DP 1729, CEPR, London.
Callejon, M. and Segarra, A. (1999), 'Business dynamics and efficiency in industries and regions: the case of Spain', *Small Business Economics*, **13**, 253–71.
Cantillon, R., (1755), *Essai Sur la Nature du Commerce en General*, London.
Carlsson, B., Acs, Z., Audretsch, D. and Braunerhjelm, P. (2009), 'Knowledge creation, entrepreneurship, and economic growth: a historical review', *Industrial and Corporate Change*, **18**, 1193–229.
Carree, M. and Thurik, R. (1999), 'Industrial structure and economic growth', in D. Audretsch and R. Thurik (eds), *Innovation, Industry Evolution, and Employment*, Cambridge: Cambridge University Press, pp. 86–111.
Carree, M., van Stel, A., Thurik, R. and Wennekers, S. (2002), 'Economic development and business ownership: an analysis using data of 23 OECD countries in the period 1976–1996', *Small Business Economics*, **19**, 271–90.
Casson, M., (1982), *The Entrepreneur*, Totowa, NJ: Barnes & Noble.
Casson, M. (2002a), 'Entrepreneurship, business culture and the theory of the firm', in Z. Acs and D. Audretsch (eds), *The International Handbook of Entrepreneurship Research*, Berlin and New York: Springer Verlag, pp. 223–47.
Casson, M. (2002b), *The Entrepreneur: An Economic Theory*, Cheltenham, UK and Northampton, MA, USA: Edward Elgar.
Caves, R. (1998), 'Industrial organization and new findings on the turnover and mobility of firms', *Journal of Economic Literature*, **36**, 1947–82.
Chandler, A. (1977), *The Visible Hand*, Cambridge, MA and London: The Belknap Press.
Chandler, A. (1990), *Scale and Scope: The Dynamics of Industrial Capitalism*, Cambridge, MA: Harvard University Press.
Chell, E. (1986), 'The entrepreneurial personality: a review of and some theoretical developments', in J. Curran, J. Stanworth and D. Watkins (eds), *The Survival of the Small Firm: The Economics of Survival and Entrepreneurship*, Aldershot: Gower Publishing, pp. 102–19.
Chen, C., Greene, P. and Crick, A. (1998), 'Does entrepreneurial self-efficiency distinguish entrepreneurs from managers?', *Journal of Business Venturing*, **13**, 295–316.
Cheng, L. and Dinopoulos, E. (1992), 'Schumpeterian growth and international business cycles', *American Economic Review*, **82**, 409–14.
Chinitz, B. (1961), 'Contrasts in agglomeration: New York and Pittsburgh', *American Economic Review*, **51**, 279–89.
Christensen, C. (1997), *The Innovator's Dilemma*, Boston, MA: Harvard Business School Press.
Chun, H., Kim, J.-W. Morck, R. and Yeung, B. (2007), 'Creative destruction and firm-specific performance heterogeneity', NBER WP 13011, Cambridge, MA.
Ciccone, C., (2002), 'Agglomeration effects in Europe', *European Economic Review*, **46**, 213–27.

Ciccone, C. and Hall, R.E. (1996), 'Productivity and the density of economic activity', *American Economic Review*, **86**, 54–70.

Ciccone, A. and Papaioannou, E. (2006), 'Red tape and delayed entry', CEPR DP 5996, CEPR, London.

Coe, D. and Helpman, E. (1995), 'International R&D spillovers', *European Economic Review*, **39**, 859–87.

Cohen, W. and Levinthal, D. (1989), 'Innovation and learning: the two faces of R&D', *Economic Journal*, **99**, 569–96.

Cohen, W. and Levinthal, D. (1990), 'Absorptive capacity: a new perspective on learning and innovation', *Administrative Science Quarterly*, **35**, 128–52.

Coleman, J.S (1988), 'Social capital in the creation of human capital', *American Journal of Sociology*, **94** (suppl.), S95–S120.

Coleman, J.S. (1990), *Foundations of Social Theory*, Cambridge, MA: Harvard University Press.

Cooper, A. and Folta, T. (2000), 'Entrepreneurship and high-technology clusters', in D. Sexton and H. Landström (eds), *Handbook of Entrepreneurship*, Oxford: Blackwell, pp. 348–67.

Cullen, J. and Gordon, R. (2007), 'Taxes and entrepreneurial risk-taking: theory and evidence in the U.S.', *Journal of Public Economics*, **91**, 1479–505.

Dasgupta, P. and Stiglitz, J.E. (1988), 'Learning-by-doing, market structure and industrial and trade policies', *Oxford Economic Papers*, **40** (2), 246–68.

Davidsson, P and Delmer, F. (2000), 'The characteristics of high-growth firms and their job contribution', in B. Green et al. (eds), *Risk Behaviour and Risk Management in Business Life*, Dordrecht: Kluwer, pp. 204–13.

Davidsson, P. and Honig, B. (2003), 'The role of social and human capital among nascent entrepreneurs', *Journal of Business Venturing*, **18**, 301–31.

Davis, S. and Henrekson, M. (1997), 'Industrial policy, employer size and economic performance in Sweden', in R. Freeman, R. Topel and B. Swedenborg (eds), *The Welfare State in Transition*, Chicago, IL: University of Chicago Press, pp. 352–98.

Dejardin, M. (2009), 'Linking net entry to regional growth', *Small Business Economics*, online version.

Delmar, F. and Wennberg, K. (2010), *The Birth, Growth, and Demise of Entrepreneurial Firms in the Knowledge Intensive Economy*, Cheltenham, UK and Northampton, MA, USA: Edward Elgar.

Desai, M., Gompers, P. and Lerner, J. (2003), 'Institutions, capital constraints and entrepreneurial firm dynamics: evidence from Europe', NBER WP 10165, NBER, Cambridge, MA.

Disney, R., Haskel, J. and Heden, Y. (2003), 'Restructuring and productivity growth in UK manufacturing', *Economic Journal*, **113**, 666–94.

Djankov, S., La Porta, R., Lopes de Silanes, F. and Shleifer, A. (2002), 'The regulation of entry', *Quarterly Journal of Economics*, **117**, 1–37.

Djankov, S., Qian, Y., Roland, G. and Zhuravskaya, E. (2006), 'Entrepreneurs in China and Russia compared', *Journal of the European Economic Association*, **4**, 352–65.

Djankov, S., McLiesh, C. and Shleifer, A. (2007), 'Private credit in 129 countries', *Journal of Financial Economics*, **84**, 299–329.

Djankov, S., Glanser, T., McLiesh, C., Ramalho, R. and Shleifer, A. (2008), 'The effect of corporate taxes on investment and entrepreneurship', NBER WP 13765, NBER, Cambridge, MA.

Drucker, P. (1985), *Innovation and Entrepreneurship*, Oxford: Butterworth-Heineman Elsevier.

Dunn, T. and Holtz-Eakin, D. (1995), 'Capital market constraints, parental wealth and the transition to self-employment among men and women', NLS DP Series NLS 96-29, Bureau of Labor Statistics, Washington, DC.

Dunn, T. and Holtz-Eakin, D. (2000), 'Financial capital, human capital and the transition to self-employment: evidence from intergenerational links', *Journal of Labor Economics*, **18**, 282–305.

Durnev, A., Morck, R. and Yeung, B. (2004), 'Value-enhancing capital budgeting and firm-specific stock return variation', *Journal of Finance*, **59**, 65–105.

Earle, J. and Sakova, Z. (2000), 'Business start-ups or disguised unemployment? Evidence on the character of self-employment from transitional economies', *Labor Economics*, **7**, 575–601.

Ejermo, O. (2009), 'Regional innovation measured by patent data – does quality matter?', *Industry and Innovation*, **16**, 141–65.

Ejermo, O. and Gråsjö, U. (2008), 'The effects of research and development on regional invention and innovation', mimeo, Lund University, Lund.

Eliasson, G. (2007), *Entreprenörens roll i tillväxtteorin*, Stockholm: ITPS.

Eliasson, G. and Eliasson, Å. (1996), 'The biotechnical competence bloc', *Revue d'Economie Industrielle*, **78**, 7–26.

Erken, H., Donselaar, P. and Thurik, R. (2008), 'Total factor productivity and the role of entrepreneurship', Jena Economic Research Paper 2008-019, Max Planck Institute of Economics, Jena.

Ertur, C. and Koch, W. (2008), 'International R&D spillovers in the multi-country Schumpeterian growth model', presented at Southern Regional Science Association Meeting.

Evans, D. and Jovanovic, B. (1989), 'An estimated model of entrepreneurial choice under liquidity constraints', *Journal of Political Economy*, **97**, 808–27.
Evans, D. and Leighton, S. (1989), 'Some empirical aspects of entrepreneurship', *American Economic Review*, **79**, 519–35.
Feldman, M. and Audretsch, D. (1999), 'Innovation in cities: science-based diversity, specialization and localized competition', *European Economic Review*, **43**, 409–29.
Figueiredo, O., Guimaraes, P. and Woodward, D. (2002), 'Home-field advantage: location decisions of Portuguese entrepreneurs', *Journal of Urban Economics*, **97**, 808–27.
Fink, J., Fink, K., Grullon, G. and Weston, J. (2005), 'IPO vintage and the rise of idiosyncratic risk', paper presented at the Seventh Annual Texas Finance Festival (http://papers.ssrn.com/sol3/papers.cfm?abstract_id=661321).
Fiori, G., Nicoletti, G., Scarpetta, S. and Schiantarelli, F. (2007), 'Employment outcomes and the interactions between product and labor market deregulation: are they substitutes or complements?', WP 663, Boston College, Boston, MA.
Fischer, M. and Varga, A. (2003), 'Spatial knowledge spillovers and university research: evidence from Austria', *The Annals of Regional Science*, **37**, 303–22.
Florida, R. (2002), *The Rise of the Creative Class*, New York: Basic Books.
Florida, R., Mellander, C. and Stolarich, K. (2008), 'Inside the black box of regional development – human capital, the creative class and tolerance', *Journal of Economic Geography*, **8**, 615–49.
Fölster, S., (2002), 'Do lower taxes stimulate self-employment?', *Small Business Economics*, **19**, 135–45.
Fonseca, R., Lopez-Garcia, P. and Pissarides, C. (2001), 'Entrepreneurship, start-up costs and employment', *European Economic Review*, **45**, 692–705.
Fonseca, R., Michaud, P. and Sopraseuth, T. (2007), 'Enterpreneurship, wealth, liquidity constraints and start-up costs', DP 2874, Institute for the Study of Labor, Bonn.
Foster, L., Haltiwanger, J. and Krizan, C. (2006), 'Market selection, reallocation, and restructuring in the U.S. retail trade sector in the 1990s', *Review of Economics and Statistics*, **88**, 748–58.
Freel, M. (2003), 'Sectoral patterns of small firm innovation, networking and proximity', *Research Policy*, **32**, 751–70.
Fritsch, M., (1996), 'Turbulence and growth in West Germany: a comparison of evidence by regions and industries', *Review of Industrial Organization*, **11**, 231–51.
Fritsch, M. (1997), 'New firms and regional employment change', *Small Business Economics*, **9**, 437–47.
Fritsch, M. and Mueller, P. (2007), 'The persistence of regional new business formation-activity over time – assessing the potential of policy promotion program', *Journal of Evolutionary Economics*, **17**, 299–315.
Fritsch, M., Brixy, U. and Falck, O. (2006), 'The effect of industry, region and time on new business survival – a multi-dimensional analysis', *Review of Industrial Organization*, **28**, 285–306.
Fujita, M. and Thisse, J.-F. (2002), *Economics of Agglomeration*, Cambridge, MA: MIT Press.
Fujita, M., Krugman, P. and Venables, A. (1999), *The Spatial Economy: Cities, Regions and International Trade*, Cambridge, MA: MIT Press.
Furman, J.L., Porter, M.E. and Stern, S. (2002), 'The determinants of national innovative capacity', *Research Policy*, **31**, 899–933.
Galbraith, J.K. (1967), *The New Industrial State*, London: Routledge.
Gartner, W. (1985), 'A conceptual framework for describing the phenomenon of new venture creation', *Academy of Management Review*, **10**, 696–706.
Gentry, W. and Hubbard, G. (2000), 'Tax policy and entrepreneurial entry', *American Economic Review*, **90**, 283–7.
Georgellis, Y, Joyce, P. and Woods, A. (2000), 'Entrepreneurial action, innovation and business performance: the small independent business', *Journal of Small Business and Enterprise Development*, **7**, 7–17.
Geroski, P. (1995), 'What do we know about entry?', *International Journal of Industrial Organization*, **13**, 421–40.
Gianetti, M. and Simonov, A. (2004), 'On the determinants of entrepreneurial activity: social norms, economic environment and individual characteristics', *Swedish Economic Policy Review*, **11**, 269–313.
Gilbert, R. and Newbery, D. (1982), 'Preemptive patenting and the persistence of monopoly', *American Economic Review*, **72**, 514–26.
Glaeser, E. (1999), 'Learning in cities', *Journal of Urban Economics*, **46**, 254–77.
Glaeser, E. (2007), 'Entrepreneurship and the city', Discussion Paper no. 2140, Harvard Institute on Economic Research, Cambridge, MA.
Glaeser, E. and Kerr, W. (2009), 'Local industrial conditions and entrepreneurship: how much of the spatial distribution can we explain?', *Journal of Economics and Management Strategy*, **18**, 623–33.
Glaeser, E., Kerr, W. and Ponzetto, G. (2009), 'Clusters of entrepreneurship', NBER 1WP 5377, NBER, Cambridge, MA.

Glaeser, E., Kallal, H., Scheinkman, J. and Shleifer, A. (1992), 'Growth of cities', *Journal of Political Economy*, **100**, 1126–52.

Gordon, R. (1998), 'Can high personal taxes encourage entrepreneurial activity?', *IMF Staff Papers*, **45**, 49–80.

Gordon, R. (2004), 'Why was Europe left at the station when America's productivity locomotive departed?', NBER WP 19651, NBER, Cambridge, MA.

Gort, M. and Klepper, S. (1982), 'Time path in the diffusion of product innovation', *Economic Journal*, **92**, 630–53.

Grek, J., Karlsson, C. and Klaesson, J. (2009), 'Market potential and new firm formation', Cesis WP 202, Royal Institute of Technology, Stockholm.

Gries, T. and Naudé, W. (2008), 'Enterpreneurship and regional economic growth', UNU-Wider Research Paper 2008/70, UNU-Wider, Helsinki.

Gries, T. and Naudé, W. (2010), 'Entrepreneurship and structural economic transformation', *Small Business Economics*, **34**, 13–29.

Griliches, Z. (1979), 'Issues in assessing the contribution of R&D to productivity growth', *Bell Journal of Economics*, **10**, 92–16.

Gross, D. and Ryan, M. (2008), 'FDI location and size: does employment protection legislation matter?', *Regional Science and Urban Economics*, **38**, 590–605.

Grossman, S. and Hart, O. (1986), 'The costs and benefits of ownership: a theory of vertical and lateral integration', *The Journal of Political Economy*, **94**, 691–719.

Guimarães, P., Figueiredo, O. and Woodward, D. (2000), 'Agglomeration and the location of foreign direct investment in Portugal', *Journal of Urban Economics*, **47**, 115–35.

Guimarães, P., Figueiredo, O. and Woodward, D. (2002), 'Home-field advantage: location decisions of Portuguese entrepreneurs', *Journal of Urban Economics*, **52**, 341–61.

Guiso, L., Sapienza, P. and Zingales, L. (2004), 'Does local financial development matter?', *Quarterly Journal of Economics*, **119** (3), 929–69.

Hall, B., Jaffe, A. and Trajtenberg, M. (2000), 'Market value and patent citation: a first look', NBER WP 7741, NBER, Cambridge, MA.

Haltiwanger, J., Jarmin, R. and Miranda, J. (2010), 'Who creates jobs? Small vs. large vs. small', Working Paper CES 10-17, August.

Hansen, W. (1987), 'How accessability shapes land-use', *Journal of American Institute of Planners*, **25**, 73–6.

Hansson, Å. (2010), 'Tax policy and entrepreneurship: empirical evidence from Sweden', *Small Business Economics*, online version.

von Hayek, F. (1945), 'The use of knowledge in society', *American Economic Review*, **35**, 519–30.

Heden, Y. (2005), 'Productivity, upskilling, restructuring, entry and exit: evidence from the UK and Swedish micro data', University of London, London.

Henderson, V. and Thisse, J.-F. (eds) (2004), *Handbook of Regional and Urban Economics*, Amsterdam: Elsevier.

Henrekson, M. (2005), 'Entrepreneurship – a weak link in the mature welfare state', *Industrial and Corporate Change*, **13**, 1–31.

Henrekson, M. and Johansson, D. (2009), 'Gazelles as job creators: a survey and interpretation of the evidence', *Small Business Economics*, online version.

Hessels, J. and Suddle, K. (2007), *Ambitious Nascent Entrepreneurs and National Innovativeness*, Scales Research Reports H200702, EIM Business and Policy Research.

Highfield, R. and Smiley, R. (1987), 'New business start-ups and economic activity: an empirical investigation', *International Journal of Industrial Organization*, **5**, 51–66.

von Hippel, E. (1988), *The Sources of Innovation*, Oxford: Oxford University Press.

Hofstede, G. (2001), *Culture's Consequences: Comparing Values, Behaviors, Institutions and Organizations Across Nations*, Thousand Oaks, CA: Sage.

Holcombe, R. (1998), 'Entrepreneurship and economic growth', *The Quarterly Journal of Austrian Economics*, **1**, 45–62.

Holtz-Eakin, D. and Kao, C. (2003), *Entrepreneurship and Economic Growth: The Proof is in the Productivity*, Syracuse, NY: Syracuse University.

Hoover, E. and Vernon, R. (1959), *Anatomy of a Metropolis*, Cambridge, MA: Harvard University Press.

Hurst, E. and Lusardi, A. (2004), 'Liquidity constraints, household wealth and entrepreneurship', *Journal of Political Economy*, **112**, 319–47.

Jacobs, J. (1969), *The Economy of Cities*, New York: Vintage.

Jaffe, A., Trajtenberg, M. and Fogarty, M. (2000), 'Knowledge spillovers and patent citations: evidence from a survey of inventors', *American Economic Review*, **90** (2), 215–18.

Jaffe, A., Trajtenberg, M. and Henderson, R. (1993), 'Geographic localization of knowledge spillovers as evidenced by patent citations', *Quarterly Journal of Economics*, **63**, 577–98.

Javorcik, B., Ozden, C. Spatareanu, M. and Neagu, C. (2006), 'Migrant networks and foreign direct investment', World Bank Policy Research Working Paper No. 4654, World Bank, Washington, DC.

Johnson, P. and Parker, S. (1996), 'Spatial variations in the determinants and effects of firm births and deaths', *Regional Studies*, **30**, 679–88.

Johnson, S., McMillan J. and Woodruff, C. (2000), 'Entrepreneurs and the ordering of institutional reform: Poland, Slovakia, Romania, Russia and Ukraine compared', *Economics of Transition*, **81**, 1–36.

Jones, C. (1995a), 'R&D-based models of economic growth', *Journal of Political Economy*, **103**, 759–84.

Jones, C. (1995b), 'Time series test of endogenous growth models', *Quarterly Journal of Economics*, **110**, 495–525.

Jones, C. (2006), 'Knowledge and the theory of economic development', mimeo, Department of Economics, Berkeley, CA.

Jovanovic, B. (1982), 'Selection and evolution of an industry', *Econometrica*, **50**, 649–70.

Jovanovic, B. and Lach, S. (1989), 'Entry, exit and diffusion with learning by doing', *American Economic Review*, **79**, 690–99.

Jovanovic, B. and McDonald, G. (1994), 'The life cycle of competitive industry', *Journal of Political Economy*, **102**, 322–47.

Jovanovic, B. and Rousseau, P.L. (2005), 'General purposes technologies', in P. Aghion and S. Durlauf (eds), *Handbook of Economic Growth*, Amsterdam: Elsevier, pp. 1181–2240.

Juglar, C. (1862), *Des crises commerciales et leur retour périodique en France, en Angleterre et aux États-Unis*, Paris: Librairie Guillaumin et Cie.

Karlsson, C. and Nyström, K. (2008), *Nyföretagande, näringslivsdynamik och tillväxt i den nya världsekonomin*, Report to the Swedish Government's Globalization Council, Ministry of Education, Stockholm.

Karlsson, C., Johansson, B. and Stough, R. (2009), 'Entrepreneurship and development – local processes and global patterns', Cesis WP 160, The Royal Institute of Technology, Stockholm.

Keeble, D. and Walker, S. (1994), 'New firms, small firms and dead firms: spatial patterns and determinants in the United Kingdom', *Regional Studies*, **28**, 411–27.

Keller, W. (2002) 'Geographic localization of international technology diffusion', *American Economic Review*, **92**, 120–42.

Kenney, M. and Patton, D. (2006), 'Coevolution of technologies and policies: Silicon Valley as the iconic high-technology cluster', in P. Braunerhjelm and M. Feldman (eds), *Cluster Genisis: The Development of High-Technology Industrial Locations*, Oxford: Oxford University Press, pp. 38–64.

Kihlstrom, R.E. and Laffont, J.-F. (1979), 'A general equilibrium entrepreneurial theory of firm formation based on risk aversion', *Journal of Political Economy*, **87**, 719–48.

Kim, P., Aldrich, H. and Keister, L. (2006), 'Access (not) denied: the impact of financial, human and cultural capital on entrepreneurship entry in the United States', *Small Business Economics*, **27**, 5–22.

King, R. and Levine, R. (1993), 'Finance and growth: Schumpeter might be right', *Quarterly Journal of Economics*, **108**, 717–38.

Kirzner, I. (1973), *Competition and Entrepreneurship*, Chicago, IL: University of Chicago Press.

Kirzner, I. (1996), *The Meaning of the Market Process*, London: Routledge.

Kirzner, I. (1997), 'Entrepreneurial discovery and the competitive market process: an Austrian approach', *Journal of Economic Literature*, **35**, 60–85.

Kitchin, J. (1923), 'Cycles and trends in economic factors', *Review of Economic Statistics*, **5**, 10–16.

Klapper, L., Laeven, L. and Rajan, R. (2006), 'Entry regulation as a barrier to entrepreneurship', *Journal of Financial Economics*, **82**, 591–629.

Klapper, L., Amit, R. and Guillén, M. (2010), 'Entrepreneurship and firm formation across countries', in J. Lerner and A. Schoar (eds), *International Differences in Entrepreneurship*, Chicago, IL: University of Chicago Press, pp. 129–58.

Klepper, S. (1996), 'Entry, exit, growth, and innovation over the product life cycle', *American Economic Review*, **86**, 562–83.

Klepper, S. (2001), 'Employee start-ups in high-tech industries', *Industrial and Corporate Change*, **10**, 639–74.

Klepper, S. (2002), 'The capabilities of new firms and the evolution of the U.S. automobile industry', *Industrial and Corporate Change*, **11**, 645–66.

Klepper, S. and Graddy, E. (1990), 'The evolution of new industries and the determinants of market structure', *RAND Journal of Economics*, **21**, 27–44.

Klette, J. and Kortum, S. (2004), 'Innovating firms and aggregate innovation', *Journal of Political Economy*, **112**, 986–1018.

Knight, F. (1921), *Risk, Uncertainty and Profit*, Boston, MA: Houghton Mifflin.

Kondratieff, N.D. (1935), 'The long waves in economic life', *Review of Economic Statistics*, **17**, 105–15.

Koster, S. (2006), *Whose Child? How Existing Firms Foster New Firm Formation: Individual Start-ups, Spin-Outs and Spin-Offs*, PhD Dissertation, Groeningen University, Groeningen.

Koster, S. and Karlsson, C. (2009), 'New firm formation and economic development in a globalizing economy', Cesis WP 167, The Royal Institute of Technology, Stockholm.

Kugler, A. and Pica, G. (2008), 'Effects of employment protection on worker and job flows: evidence from the 1990 Italian reform', *Labour Economics*, **15** (1), 78–95.

Kutznets, S. (1971), *Economic Growth of Nations: Total Output and Production Structure*, Cambridge, MA: Harvard University Press.

La Porta, R., Lopes-de-Silanes, F., Schleifer, A. and Vishny, R. (1997), 'Legal determinants of external finance', *Journal of Finance*, **52**, 1131–50.

La Porta, R., Lopes-de-Silanes, F. and Schleifer, A. (2008), 'Economic consequences of legal origins', *Journal of Economic Literature*, **46**, 285–332.

Laffont, J.-J. and Tirole, J. (1993), *A Theory of Incentives and Regulation*, Cambridge, MA: MIT Press.

Lanjouw, J. and Schankerman, M. (1999), 'Patent quality and research productivity: measuring innovation with multiple indicators', *Economic Journal*, **114**, 441–65.

Lee, S., Florida, R. and Acs, Z. (2004), 'Creativity and entrepreneurship: a regional analysis of new firm formation', *Regional Studies*, **38**, 879–91.

Leff, N. (1979), 'Entrepreneurship and economic development: the problem revisited', *Journal of Economic Literature*, **17**, 46–64.

Leibenstein, H. (1968), 'Entrepreneurship and development', *American Economic Review*, **58**, 72–83.

Leone, R.A. and R. Struyck (1976), 'The incubator hypothesis: evidence from five SMSAs', *Urban Studies*, **13**, 325–31.

LeSage, J. and Fischer, M. (2008), 'The impact of knowledge capital on regional total factor productivity', available at http://ssrn.com/abstract=1088301.

LeSage, J. and Pace, R. (2009), *Introduction to Spatial Econometrics*, Boca Raton, FL: Taylor and Francis.

Lichtenberg, F. (1993), 'R&D investments and international productivity differences', NBER WP 4161, NBER, Cambridge, MA.

Lingelbach, D., de la Vina, L. and Asel, P. (2006), 'What's distinctive about growth-oriented entrepreneurship in developing countries?', Center for Global Entrepreneurship, WP 1, College of Business, San Antonio.

Lucas, R.E. (1978), 'On the size distribution of business firms', *Bell Journal of Economics*, **9**, 508–23.

Lucas, R.E. (1988), 'On the mechanisms of economic development', *Journal of Monetary Economics*, **22**, 3–42.

Luthans, F. and Youssef, C. (2007), 'Emerging positive organizational behavior', *Journal of Management*, **33**, 321–49.

Luthans, F., Youssef, C. and Avolio, B. (2007), *Psychological Capital*, New York and Oxford: Oxford University Press.

Mairesse, J. and Kremp, A. (1993), 'A look at the firm level in eight French service industries', *Journal of Productivity Analysis*, **4**, 211–34.

Mairesse, J. and Mohnen, P. (2001), 'To be or not be innovative: an exercise in measurement', NBER WP 8644, NBER, Cambridge, MA.

Mairesse, J. and Mohnen, P. (2004), 'The importance of R&D for innovation: a reassessment using French survey data', NBER WP 10897, NBER, Cambridge, MA.

Mairesse, J. and Sassenou, M. (1991), 'R&D and productivity: a survey of econometric studies at the firm level', *OECD Science – Technology Industry Review*, Paris: OECD, pp. 9–43.

Malerba, F. and Orsenigo, L. (1993), 'Technological regimes and firm behavior', *Industry and Corporate Change*, **2**, 45–71.

Manjón-Antolín, M. (2004), 'Firm size and short-term dynamics in aggregate entry and exit', mimeo, Tilburg University, Tilburg.

Markman, G., Balkin, D. and Baron, R. (2002), 'Inventors and new venture formation: the effects of general self-efficacy and regretful thinking', *Entrepreneurship Theory and Practice*, **27**, 149–65.

Marshall, A. (1890), *Principles of Economics*, reprinted 1997 by Prometheus Books, London.

Martins. P. (2009), 'Dismissal for the cause: the difference that just eight paragraphs can make', *Journal of Labor Economics*, **27**, 257–79.

McClelland, D. (1961), *The Achieving Society*, New York: Free Press.

McMillan, J. and Woodruff, C. (2002), 'The central role of entrepreneurs in transition economies', *Journal of Economic Perspectives*, **16**, 153–70.

Menger, C. (1871), *Grundsätze der Volkverschaftslehre*, Wein: Wilhelm Braumüller.

Micco, A. and Pagés, C. (2006), 'The economic effects of employment protection: evidence from international industry-level data', Discussion paper 2633, IZA, Bonn.

Michelacci, C. (2003), 'Low returns in R&D due to the lack of entrepreneurial skills', *Economic Journal*, **113**, 207–25.

Michelacci, C. and Silva, O. (2007), 'Why so many local entrepreneurs?', *Review of Economics and Statistics*, **89**, 615–33.

Mills, E. and Hamilton, B. (1984), *Urban Economics*, Glenview, IL: Scott, Foresman, and Co.
Miracky, W. (1993), *Economic Growth and Business Cycles in Cities: The Role of Local Externalities*, MIT thesis.
von Mises, F. (1949), *Human Action*, Chicago, IL: Contemporary Books.
Mueller, P. (2007), 'Exploiting entrepreneurial opportunity: the impact of entrepreneurship on growth', *Small Business Economics*, **28**, 355–62.
Murphy, K., Schleifer, A. and Vishny, R. (1991), 'The allocation of talent: the implications for growth', *Quarterly Journal of Economics*, **56**, 503–30.
Nanda, R. (2009), Entrepreneurship and the discipline of external finance', HBS WP 08-047, Harvard, Boston, MA.
Nanda, R. and Sorenson, J. (2007), 'Peer effects and entrepreneurship', Harvard Business School WP 08-051, Harvard, Boston, MA.
Naudé, W. (2008), 'Entrepreneurship in economic development', Research Paper 2008/20, UNU-Wider, Helsinki.
Naudé, W., Gries, T., Wood, E. and Meintjes, A. (2008), 'Regional determinants of entrepreneurial start-ups in a developing country', *Entrepreneurship and Regional Development*, **20**, 111–24.
Nelson, R. and Pack, H. (1999), 'The Asian miracle and modern growth theory', *Economic Journal*, **109**, 416–36.
Nelson, R. and Winter, S. (1982), *An Evolutionary Theory of Economic Change*, Cambridge: Cambridge University Press.
Nickell, S.J. (1996), 'Competition and corporate performance', *Journal of Political Economy*, **104**, 724–46.
Nicoletti, G. and Scarpetta, S. (2003), 'Regulation, productivity and growth: OECD evidence', *Economic Policy*, **18**, 11–72.
Nijkamp, P. (2003), 'Entrepreneurship in a modern network economy', *Regional Studies*, **37** (4), 395–405.
Nooteboom, B. (1994), 'Innovation and diffusion in small firms: theory and evidence', *Small Business Economics*, **6**, 327–47.
Norbäck, P.J. and Persson, L. (2010), 'The organization of the innovation industry: entrepreneurs, venture capitalists, and oligopolists', *Journal of the European Economic Association*, **7**, 1261–90.
North, D. (1990), *Institutions, Institutional Change and Economic Performance*, Cambridge: Cambridge University Press.
North, D. (1994), 'Economic performance through time', *American Economic Review*, **84**, 359–68.
North, D. and Thomas, R.T. (1973), *The Rise of the Western World: A New Economic History*, Cambridge: Cambridge University Press.
OECD (1998), *Fostering Entrepreneurship*, Paris: OECD.
OECD (2000), *Employment Outlook*, Paris: OECD.
Olsson, O. (2000), 'Knowledge as a set in idea space: an epistemological view on growth', *Journal of Economic Growth*, **5**, 253–76.
Olsson, O. and Frey, B. (2002), 'Entrepreneurship as recombinant growth', *Small Business Economics'*, **19**, 69–80.
van Oort, F. and Stam, E. (2006), 'Agglomeration economies and entrepreneurship in the ICT industries', ERIM Report Series, 016-ORG, Erasmus University, Rotterdam.
Ortega-Argilés, R., Vivarelli, M. and Voight, P. (2009), 'R&D in SMEs: a paradox', *Small Business Economics*, **33**, 3–11.
Paci, R. and Usai, S. (1999), 'Externalities, knowledge spillovers and the spatial distribution of innovation', *GeoJournal*, **49**, 381–90.
Pakes, A. and Griliches, Z. (1980), 'Patents and R&D at the firm level: a first report', *Economics Letters*, **5**, 377–81.
Parker, S. and Robson, M. (2003), 'Explaining international variations in entrepreneurship: evidence from a panel of OECD countries', mimeo, University of Durham, Durham, UK.
Pastor, L. and Veronesi, P. (2005), 'Technological revolutions and stock prices', mimeo, University of Chicago, IL.
Penrose, E.T. (1950), 'The patent controversy in the nineteenth century', *Journal of Economic History*, **10**, 1–29.
Penrose, E. (1959), *The Theory of the Growth of the Firm*, Oxford: Oxford University Press.
Phan, P.H. and Siegel, D.S. (2006), 'The effectiveness of university technology transfer', *Foundations and Trends in Entrepreneurship*, **2**, 77–44.
Pigou, A. (1938), *The Economics of Welfare*, London: Macmillan and Co.
Plummer, L., Haynie, L.A. and Godesiabois, J. (2007), 'An essay on the origins of entrepreneurial opportunity', *Small Business Economics*, **28**, 363–79.
Polanyi, M., (1966), *The Tacit Dimension*, New York: Doubleday.
Porter, M., Sachs, J. and McArthur, J. (2002), 'Executive summary: competitiveness and stages of economic development', in M. Porter, J. Sachs, P. Cornelius, J. McArthur and K. Schwab (eds), *The Global Competitiveness Report 2001–2002*, New York: Oxford University Press, pp. 16–27.

Powell, B. (2008), *Making Poor Nations Rich. Entrepreneurship and the Process of Economic Development*, Stanford, CA: Stanford University Press.

van Praag, M. and Cramer, J. (2001), 'The roots of entrepreneurship and labor demand: individual ability and low risk aversion', *Economica*, **68**, 45–62.

van Praag, M. and Versloot, P. (2007), 'What is the value of entrepreneurship? A review of recent research', *Small Business Economics*, **29**, 351–82.

Pred, A. (1977), *City-systems in Advanced Economies: Past Growth, Present Processes and Future Development Options*, London: Hutchinson.

Prescott, E. and Boyd, J. (1987), 'Dynamic coalitions: engines of growth', *American Economic Review*, **77**, 63–7.

Putnam, R. (1993), *Making Democracy Work: Civic Traditions in Modern Italy*, Princeton, NJ: Princeton University Press.

Quadrini, V. (2000), 'Entrepreneurship, saving and social mobility', *Review of Economic Dynamics*, **3**, 1–40.

Rebelo, S. (1991), 'Long-run policy analysis and long-run growth', *Journal of Political Economy*, **99**, 500–21.

Reilly, W. (1931), *The Law of Retail Gravitation*, New York: The Knickerbocker Press.

Reynolds, P. (1992), 'Predicting new-firm births: interactions of organizational and human populations', in D. Sexton and J. Kasarda (eds), *The State of the Art of Entrepreneurship*, Boston, MA: PWS-Kent Publishing, pp. 268–97.

Reynolds, P. (1999), 'Creative destruction', in Z. Acs, B. Carlsson and C. Karlsson (eds), *Entrepreneurship, Small & Medium-sized Enterprises and the Macroeconomy*, Cambridge: Cambridge University Press, pp. 97–135.

Reynolds, P. and Storey, D. (1993), *Local and Regional Characteristics Affecting Small Business Formation: A Cross-National Comparison*, Paris: OECD.

Reynolds, P., Storey, D. and Westhead, P. (1994), 'Cross-national comparisons of the variation in new firm formation rates', *Regional Studies*, **28**, 443–56.

Reynolds, P., Bosma, N., Autio, E., Hunt, S., De Bono, N., Servais, I., Lopez-Garcia, P. and Chin, N. (2005), 'Global entrepreneurship monitoring: data collection, design and implementation 1998–2003', *Small Business Economics*, **24**, 205–31.

Robinson, C., Leary, B. and Rincon, A. (2006), 'Business start-ups, closures and economic churn: a review of the literature', Enterprise Directorate, BERR, UK.

Rodrik, D. (2007), *One Economics, Many Recipes: Globalisation, Institutions and Economic Growth*, Princeton, NJ: Princeton University Press.

Romanelli, E. and Feldman, M. (2006), 'Anatomy of cluster development: emergence and convergence in the US human biotherapeutics, 1976–2003', in P. Braunerhjelm and M. Feldman (eds), *Cluster Genisis: The Development of High-Technology Industrial Locations*, Oxford: Oxford University Press, pp. 87–113.

Romer, P. (1986), 'Increasing returns and long run growth', *Journal of Political Economy*, **94**, 1002–37.

Rosenberg, N. (1985), 'The commercial exploitation of science by American industry', in K. Clark, R. Hayes and C. Lorenz (eds), *The Uneasy Alliance: Managaing the Productivity–Technology Dilemma*, Boston, MA: Harvard Business School Press, pp. 19–51.

Rosenberg, N. and Birdzell, L. (1986), *How the West Grew Rich*, New York: Basic Books.

Rosenthal, S. and Strange, W.C. (2003), 'Geography, industrial organization and agglomeration', *The Review of Economics and Statistics*, **85**, 377–93.

Rosenthal, S. and Strange, W. (2010), 'Small establishment/big effects: agglomeration, industrial organization and entrepreneurship', in E. Glaeser (ed.), *Economics of Agglomeration*, Chicago, IL: University of Chicago Press, pp. 277–302.

Rostow, W. (1960), *The Stages of Economic Growth*, Cambridge: Cambridge University Press.

Rothwell, R. and Zegveld, W. (1982), *Innovation and the Small and Medium Sized Firm*, London: Pinter Publishers.

Salgado-Banda, H. (2005), 'Entrepreneurship and economic growth: an empirical analysis', Direction de Estudios Económicos, Banco de México.

Sassens, S. (2006), *Cities in a World Economy*, Thousand Oaks, CA: Pine Forge Press.

Saxenian, A. (1994), *Regional Advantage: Culture and Competition in Silicon Valley and Route 128*, Cambridge, MA: Harvard University Press.

Saxenian, A. (2006), *The New Argonauts. Regional Advantage in a Global Economy*, Cambridge, MA: Harvard University Press.

Say, J.-B. (1803), *A Treatise on Political Economy*, reprinted 2001, Edison, NJ: Transaction Publishers.

Scarpetta, S., Hemmings, P., Tressel, T. and Woo, J. (2002), 'The role of policy and institutions for productivity and firm dynamics: evidence from micro and industry data', OECD Economics Department WP no. 329, OECD, Paris.

Schere, J. (1982), *Tolerance of Ambuigity as a Discriminating Variable Between Entrepreneurs and Managers*, New York: Proceedings of the Academy of Management.

Scherer, F. (1980), *Industrial Market Performance and Economic Performance*, Chicago, IL: Rand McNally.

Schmitz, J. (1989), 'Imitation, entrepreneurship, and long-run growth', *Journal of Political Economy*, **97**, 721–39.

Schoonhoven, C. and Romanelli, E. (2005), *The Entrepreneurship Dynamic: Origins of Entrepreneurship and the Evolution of Industries*, Stanford, CA: Stanford University Press.

Schmookler, J. (1966), *Invention and Economic Growth*, Cambridge, MA: Harvard University Press.

Schumpeter, J. (1911/34), *The Theory of Economic Development*, Cambridge, MA: Harvard University Press.

Schumpeter, J. (1939), *Business Cycles: A Theoretical, Historical and Statistical Analysis of capitalist Process*, New York: McGraw-Hill.

Schumpeter, J. (1942), *Capitalism, Socialism and Democracy*, New York: Harper & Row.

Scott, A. (2006), 'Origins and growth of the Hollywood motion picture industry. The first three decades', in P. Braunerhjelm and M. Feldman (eds), *Cluster Genisis: The Development of High-Technology Industrial Locations*, Oxford: Oxford University Press, pp. 17–38.

Segerstrom, P. (1991), 'Innovation, imitation and economic growth', *Journal of Political Economy*, **99**, 190–207.

Segerstrom, P. (1995), 'A quality ladders growth model with decreasing returns to R&D', mimeo, Michigan State University.

Segerstrom, P., Anant, T.C. and Dinopoulos, E. (1990), 'A Schumpeterian model of the product life cycle', *American Economic Review*, **80**, 1077–91.

Sexton, D.L. and Landström, H. (2000), *The Blackwell Handbook of Entrepreneurship*, Oxford: Blackwell.

Shane, S. (2000), 'Prior knowledge and the discovery of entrepreneurial opportunities', *Organization Science*, **11**, 448–69.

Shane, S. (2003), *A General Theory of Entrepreneurship*, Cheltenham, UK and Northampton, MA, USA: Edward Elgar.

Shane, S. and Eckhardt, J. (2003), 'The individual-opportunity nexus', in Z. Acs and D. Audretsch (eds), *Handbook of Entrepreneurship Research*, New York: Springer Publishers, pp. 161–91.

Shane, S. and Venkataraman, S. (2000), 'The promise of entrepreneurship as a field of research', *Academy of Management Review*, **25**, 217–21.

Simon, H. (1955), 'A behavioral model of rational choice', *Quarterly Journal of Economics*, **69**, 99–118.

Sorenson, O. and Singh, J. (2007), 'Science, social networks and spillovers', *Industry and Innovation*, **14**, 219–38.

de Soto, H. (1989), *The Other Path: The Invincible Revolution in the Third World*, New York: Harper & Row.

de Soto, H. (2000), *The Mystery of Capital: Why Capitalism Triumphs in the West and Fails Everywhere Else*, New York: Basic Books.

Stam, E. (2007), 'Why butterflies don't leave: locational behaviour of entrepreneurial firms', *Economic Geography*, **83**, 27–50.

Stam, E. and van Stel, A. (2009), 'Types of entrepreneurship and economic growth', Research Paper 2009/47, UNU-Wider, Helsinki.

van Stel, A. and Storey, D. (2002), 'The relationship between firm births and job creation', Tinbergen Institute DP 02-052/3, Tinbergen.

van Stel, A. and Storey, D. (2004), 'The link between firm birth and job creation: is there an upas tree effect?', *Regional Studies*, **38**, 893–909.

van Stel, A. and Suddle, K. (2008), 'The impact of new firm formation on regional development in the Netherlands', *Small Business Economics*, **30**, 31–47.

Storey, D. (1994), *Understanding the Small Business Sector*, London: Routledge.

Sutter, R., (2009), *The Psychology of Entrepreneurship and the Technological Frontier: A Spatial Econometric Analysis of Regional Entrepreneurship in the United States*, PhD Dissertation manuscript, George Mason University, Washington, DC.

Teece, D. (1986), 'Profiting from technological innovation: implications for integration, collaboration, licensing and public policy', *Research Policy*, **15**, 285–305.

Teece, D. (2006), 'Reflections on profiting from innovations', *Research Policy*, **35**, 1131–46.

Thisse, J.-F. and Henderson, V. (2004), *Handbook of Regional and Urban Economics*, Amsterdam: North-Holland.

Thornton, P.H. and Flynn, K.H. (2003), 'Entrepreneurship, networks and geographies', in Z. Acs and D. Audretsch (eds), *Handbook of Entrepreneurship Research*, Dordrecht: Kluwer, pp. 401–33.

Thurik, R. (1999), 'Entrepreneurship, industrial transformation and growth', in G. Libecap (ed.), *The Sources of Entrepreneurial Activity*, Greenwich, CT: JAI Press, pp. 29–66.

Timmons, J. (1976), 'Characteristics and role demands of entrepreneurship', *American Journal of Small Business*, **3**, 5–17.

Tirole, J. (1988), *The Theory of Industrial Organization*, Cambridge, MA: MIT Press.

Venkataraman, S. (1997), 'The distinctive domain of entrepreneurship research: an editor's perspective', in J. Katz and R. Brockhaus (eds), *Advances in Entrepreneurship, Firm Emergence, and Growth*, Greenwich, CT: JAI Press, pp. 199–238.

Verheul, I., Wennekers, D., Audretsch, D. and Thurik, R. (2001), 'An eclectic theory of entrepreneurship', Tinbergen DP 2001-03/3, Tinbergen Institute, Rotterdam.

Vernon, R. (1962), *Metropolis 1985*, Cambridge, MA: Harvard University Press.

Vivarelli, M. (2007), *Entry and Post-entry Performance of Newborn Firms*, London: Routledge.

Vivarelli, M. and Voigt, P. (2009), 'R&D in SMEs: a paradox?', *Small Business Economics*, **33**, 3–11.

Wang, S. (2006), 'Determinants of new firm formation in Taiwan', *Small Business Economics*, **27**, 313–23.

Warsh, D. (2006). *Knowledge and the Wealth of Nations*, New York: W.W. Norton.

Wennekers, S. (2005), 'Entrepreneurship at country level: economic and non-economic determinants', Scales Research Reports 200602, EIM Business and Policy Research.

Wennekers, S. and Thurik, R. (1999), 'Linking entrepreneurship and economic growth', *Small Business Economics*, **13**, 27–55.

Weyh, A. (2006), 'What characterizes successful start-up cohorts?', in M. Fritsch and J. Schmude (eds), *Entrepreneurship in the Region*, Berlin and New York: Springer Verlag, pp. 61–74.

Wiklund, J. (1998), *Small Firm Growth and Performance: Entrepreneurship and Beyond*, Jönköping International Business School, Jönköping.

Wiklund, J. and Shepherd, D. (2004), 'Entrepreneurial orientation and small firm performance: a configurational approach', *Journal of Business Venturing*, **20**, 71–91.

Williamson, O. (1968), 'Economies as an antitrust defense: the welfare tradeoffs', *American Economic Review*, **58**, 18–42.

Williamson, O. (1971), 'The vertical integration of production: market failure considerations', *American Economic Review*, **61**, 112–23.

Winter, S. (1964), 'Economic "natural selection" and the theory of the firm', *Yale Economic Essays*, **4**, 225–72.

Winter, S. (1984), 'Schumpeterian competition in alternative technological regimes', *Journal of Economic Behavior and Organization*, **5**, 287–320.

Witt, U. (2002), 'How evolutionary is Schumpeter's theory of economic development?', *Industry and Innovation*, **9**, 7–22.

Wong, P., Ho, Y. and Autio, E. (2005), 'Entrepreneurship, innovation and economic growth: evidence from GEM data', *Small Business Economics*, **24**, 335–50.

Zucker, L., Darby, M. and Brewer, M. (1998), 'Geographically localized knowledge. Spillovers or markets?', *Economic Inquiry*, **36**, 65–86.

APPENDIX: ENDOGENOUS GROWTH WITH KNOWLEDGE EXPLOITING ENTREPRENEURS[1]

Research departments within incumbent firms employ labor (L_R) as the only production factor, and research activities are influenced by the available stock of knowledge (A) and an efficiency parameter (σ_R) related to research activities. The production function can be written as

$$Z_R(L_R) = \sigma_R L_R A \tag{13A.1}$$

where research production is positively influenced by a larger knowledge stock and higher efficiency.

In order to include the Schumpeterian entrepreneur, we first assume that entrepreneurial ability is embodied in labor but in contrast to raw labor it is distributed unevenly across the population. Thus entrepreneurial activities are assumed to be characterized by decreasing returns to scale ($\gamma < 1$). The production function for entrepreneurial activities takes the following form:

$$Z_E(L_E) = \sigma_E L_E^\gamma A, \ \gamma < 1 \tag{13A.2}$$

Hence, similar to R&D workers, the representative entrepreneur takes advantage of existing knowledge. On the other hand, the production technology differs (decreasing returns to scale) and they do not engage in research. Rather, they combine their entrepreneurial ability with the existing stock of knowledge to introduce new products and business models. The different varieties of capital goods (x_i) produced by entrepreneurs and researchers is employed in the final goods (Y) sector together with labor:

$$Y = (L - L_E - L_R)^\alpha \int_0^A x(i)^{1-\alpha} di \tag{13A.3}$$

where α ($0 < \alpha < 1$) represents the scale parameter. Given that the demand for all varieties in equilibrium is symmetric, i.e. $x_i = \bar{x}$ for all $i \leq A$, we rewrite equation (13A.3) as

$$Y = (L - L_E - L_R)^\alpha A \bar{x}^{(1-\alpha)} \tag{13A.4}$$

Assume that capital goods (K) are produced with the same technology as final goods and that it takes κ units of capital goods to produce one unit of capital. Then it can be shown that

$$K = \kappa A \bar{x} \tag{13A.5}$$

Substituting equation (13A.5) into (13A.4) gives

$$Y = (L - L_R - L_E)^\alpha A^\alpha K^{1-\alpha} \kappa^{\alpha-1} \tag{13A.6}$$

Thus the economy employs three factors of production, i.e. raw labor (producing final goods), together with researchers and entrepreneurs who produce varieties of capital goods. Labor market equilibrium is attained when employment in R&D, entrepreneurship and final production equals total supply:

$$L = L_F + L_E + L_R \tag{13A.7}$$

As a side effect of their efforts, researchers and entrepreneurs produce new knowledge that will be publicly available for use in future capital-goods development, positively influencing coming generations of research and entrepreneurial activities. Equation (13A.8) describes the production of new knowledge, i.e. the evolution of the stock of knowledge, in relation to the amount of labor channelled into R&D (L_R) and entrepreneurial activity (L_E),

$$\dot{A} = Z_R(L_R) + Z_E(L_E) \tag{13A.8}$$

Substituting from equation (13A.1) and (13A.2)

$$\dot{A}/A = \sigma_R L_R + \sigma_E L_E^{\gamma} \tag{13A.9}$$

where, again, the σs represent the knowledge efficiency in invention activities (R&D) and innovation (entrepreneurship), whereas A is the stock of available knowledge at a given point in time. The rate of technological progress is thus an increasing function in R&D, entrepreneurship and the efficiency of these two activities.

Assuming that demand is governed by consumer preferences characterized by constant intertemporal elasticity of substitution ($1/\theta$), the maximization problem can be expressed in the following way:

$$\max_{C, L_E, L_R} \int_0^{\infty} \frac{C^{1-\theta}}{1-\theta} e^{-\rho t} dt \tag{13A.10}$$

subject to the law of motion for knowledge and capital.

$$\dot{A} = \sigma_R L_R A + \sigma_E L_E^{\gamma} A \tag{13A.11}$$

$$\dot{K} = Y - C = (L - L_E - L_R)^{\alpha} A^{\alpha} K^{1-\alpha} \kappa^{\alpha-1} - C \tag{13A.12}$$

The current-value Hamiltonian for the representative consumer is then

$$H_C = \frac{C^{1-\theta}}{1-\theta} + \lambda_A(\sigma_R L_R A + \sigma_E L_E^{\gamma} A) + \lambda_K(\kappa^{\alpha-1} A^{\alpha} K^{1-\alpha}(L - L_R - L_E) - C) \tag{13A.13}$$

The first-order conditions for maximum, letting $\Delta \equiv (L - L_E - L_R)^{\alpha} A^{\alpha} K^{1-\alpha} \kappa^{\alpha-1}$, are as follows:

$$\frac{\partial H_C}{\partial C} = C^{-\theta} - \lambda_K = 0$$

$$\lambda_K = C^{-\theta} \rightarrow \frac{\dot{\lambda}_K}{\lambda_K} = -\theta\frac{\dot{C}}{C} \qquad (13A.14)$$

$$\frac{\partial H_C}{\partial L_E} = \lambda_A\gamma\sigma_E L_E^{\gamma-1}A - \lambda_K\alpha(L - L_E - L_R)^{-1}\Delta = 0 \qquad (13A.15)$$

$$\frac{\partial H_C}{\partial L_R} = \lambda_A\sigma_R A - \lambda_K\alpha(L - L_E - L_R)^{-1}\Delta = 0 \qquad (13A.16)$$

Combining equations (13A.15) and (13A.16) gives

$$L_E = \left(\frac{\sigma_R}{\gamma\sigma_E}\right)^{\frac{1}{\gamma-1}} \qquad (13A.17)$$

Thus, on a balanced growth path, where both R&D and entrepreneurship are profitable, the amount of resources engaged in entrepreneurial activities is independent of consumer preferences (ρ). As γ is less than 1, entry into entrepreneurship is increasing in σ_E and decreasing in σ_R.

The maximization of equation (13A.13) also gives the equations of motion for the shadow prices of capital (K) and knowledge (A) as

$$\frac{\partial H_C}{\partial A} = \lambda_A(\sigma_R L_R + \sigma_E L_E^{\gamma}) + \lambda_K\alpha A^{-1}\Delta = \rho\lambda_A - \dot{\lambda}_A,$$

$$\frac{\dot{\lambda}_K}{\lambda_K} = \rho - (1 - \alpha)K^{-1}\Delta \qquad (13A.18)$$

$$\frac{\partial H_C}{\partial K} = \lambda_K(1 - \alpha)K^{-1}\Delta = \rho\lambda_K - \dot{\lambda}_K$$

$$\frac{\dot{\lambda}_A}{\lambda_A} = \rho + \sigma_R L_E - \sigma_R L - \sigma_E L_E^{\gamma} \qquad (13A.19)$$

$$\frac{\partial H_C}{\partial\lambda_A} = \dot{A} \qquad (13A.20)$$

$$\frac{\partial H_C}{\partial\lambda_K} = \dot{K} \qquad (13A.21)$$

A balanced growth path, i.e. where

$$\frac{\dot{Y}}{Y} = \frac{\dot{C}}{C} = \frac{\dot{K}}{K} = \frac{\dot{A}}{A}$$

requires that $\frac{\dot{\lambda}_K}{\lambda_K} = \frac{\dot{\lambda}_A}{\lambda_A}$. From (13A.14) and the law of motion for knowledge (13A.11),

$$\frac{\dot{\lambda}_K}{\lambda_K} = -\theta\frac{\dot{C}}{C} = -\theta\frac{\dot{A}}{A} = -\theta(\sigma_R L_R + \sigma_E L_E^{\gamma}) \qquad (13A.22)$$

Equalizing equations (13A.18) and (13A.19), using equation (13A.22), yields the following expression:

$$-\theta(\sigma_R L_R + \sigma_E L_E^\gamma) = \rho + \sigma_R L_E - \sigma_R L - \sigma_E L_E^\gamma \qquad (13A.23)$$

Solving for employment in the research sector gives

$$L_R = \frac{1}{\theta \sigma_R}(\sigma_R(L - L_E) + (1 - \theta)\sigma_E L_E^\gamma - \rho) \qquad (13A.24)$$

Inserting the expressions for equilibrium employment in the entrepreneurial (13A.17) and research sectors (13A.24) into the law of motion for knowledge, the steady state growth rate (g) can be derived as

$$g = \frac{\dot{A}}{A} = \sigma_R L_R + \sigma_E L_E^\gamma$$

$$g = \sigma_R\left(\frac{1}{\theta \sigma_R}(\sigma_R(L - L_E) + (1 - \theta)\sigma_E L_E^\gamma - \rho)\right) + \sigma_E L_E^\gamma$$

$$g = \sigma_R\left(\frac{1}{\theta \sigma_R}\left(\sigma_R\left(L - \left(\frac{\sigma_R}{\gamma \sigma_E}\right)^{1/(\gamma-1)}\right) + (1 - \theta)\sigma_E\left(\frac{\sigma_R}{\gamma \sigma_E}\right)^{\gamma/(\gamma-1)} - \rho\right)\right) + \sigma_E\left(\frac{\sigma_R}{\gamma \sigma_E}\right)^{\gamma/(\gamma-1)}$$

$$g = \frac{1}{\theta}\left(\sigma_R L - \rho + (1 - \gamma)\gamma^{\gamma/(1-\gamma)}\left(\frac{\sigma_E}{\sigma_R^\gamma}\right)^{1/(1-\gamma)}\right) \qquad (13A.25)$$

Note that some entrepreneurial activity (equation 13A.17) will always be profitable – i.e. $L_E > 0$ – as long as the stock of knowledge exceeds zero $(A > 0)$, which does not however always apply to R&D activities (equation 13A.24).[2] The model shares a number of characteristics with previous models, e.g. growth is decreasing in the discount factor (ρ) and increasing in a larger labor force.

Notes

1. See also Braunerhjelm et al. (2009).
2. This depends in a non-trivial way on a range of parameters. The degree of entrepreneurial activity is, for instance, decreasing in the productivity of R&D as long as R&D is profitable. Thus R&D and entrepreneurship are to some extent substitutes. If R&D is not sufficiently profitable, then we cannot combine equations (13A.14), (13A.15), (13A.18) and (13A.19) to derive the reduced-form growth. The resulting expression provides little insight and is not shown here.

14 New knowledge: the driving force of innovation, entrepreneurship and economic development
Bo Carlsson

INTRODUCTION

In the 1950s, Abramovitz (1956) and Solow (1956) observed that increased inputs of labor and capital account for only a small portion of economic growth, leaving most of the explanation to a residual factor. Solow referred to this residual as the 'technology factor', while Abramovitz called it 'a measure of our ignorance'. Subsequently, endogenous growth theory (Romer, 1986, 1990; Lucas, 1988, 1993 and others) provides a way to incorporate technology (particularly in the form of technological spillovers) into the macro-production function.

But what are the spillover mechanisms that convert technological change into economic growth? In a series of papers (Acs et al., 2009; Carlsson et al., 2009; Braunerhjelm et al., 2010) my co-authors and I develop a model that distinguishes between knowledge and economically useful knowledge (following Arrow, 1962) and that introduces the notion of entrepreneurship as one of the mechanisms (in addition to incumbent firms) that translates economic knowledge into economic growth. This raises the question of where and how economically useful knowledge is created.

The claim of this chapter is that new knowledge – specifically, the creation of economically useful knowledge – is the main driver of innovation; that innovation is what generates economic development (in Schumpeter's sense, i.e. distinct from 'economic growth' that is associated with the 'circular flow'); and that the institutional arrangements (referred to as innovation systems) that support innovation and entrepreneurial activity vary across time and space.

Innovation creates opportunities for both incumbent firms and startups. It is innovation (the application and diffusion of knowledge) and not invention that stimulates economic growth. Innovation systems at various levels – national, regional, sectoral and technology-focused – generate technological change. They also internalize externalities such as technological spillovers. A historical review of the formation of the US national innovation system shows that the intensity and locus of knowledge creation shift over time. The Second World War represents a watershed by shaping a new set of technology-based innovation systems that may be referred to collectively as the 'national innovation system'. This eventually led to the transformation of the US economy from being large-scale and mass-production-oriented to one based on knowledge while being much more flexible. Similar innovation systems formed in other countries, taking different shapes depending on local circumstances. The main functions of innovation systems are to create, absorb and diffuse new knowledge. Put differently, the functions are to generate/capture ideas (inventions), translate them into innovations and then to diffuse/commercialize them. Sometimes inventions are generated within the system; sometimes they come from outside. Whether innovations are diffused via incumbent firms or new entities depends on the nature of the technology and on the institutional circumstances; there are strong spillover mechanisms in which path dependence plays an important role.

The chapter is organized as follows. In the first section I show how the nature and locus of knowledge creation in the USA have shifted over time and evolved into the present 'national innovation system'. Next I discuss the role of innovation systems in a few other countries. This is followed by a conclusion summarizing the argument.

THE NATURE AND LOCUS OF KNOWLEDGE CREATION: THE EVOLUTION OF THE U.S. NATIONAL INNOVATION SYSTEM

1750–1900

The Industrial Revolution in Britain in the late eighteenth and early nineteenth centuries was based on new technologies causing major changes in agriculture, manufacturing and transportation. Inventions such as the spinning jenny (James Hargreaves, 1764), the power loom (Richard Arkwright, 1769) and the steam engine (Isaac Watt, 1775) signaled a shift from a manual labor-based economy toward machine-based manufacturing. After the invention of the puddling process for producing pig iron through the use of coke rather than charcoal, iron became cheap enough to use for industrial machinery; previous machines were usually made of wood. All these new technologies were invented through trial and error by individual tinkerers and entrepreneurs. The inventions soon spread from Britain to other European countries and to North America.

In connection with the American War of Independence, Great Britain imposed an embargo on exports of machinery and skilled mechanics to the USA. Faced with short-ages of labor (skilled mechanics in particular) and high-quality iron, the Americans had to devise new ways of producing industrial machinery. This led to the so-called 'American system of manufactures' (standardization and interchangeability of parts making possible a high degree of mechanization), applied first to the manufacture of guns and later to sewing machines, farm implements and tools, bicycles, locomotives and automobiles. This was the result of a series of minor adaptations and improvements of existing machine tools in response to the needs of new industries and the diffusion of modern methods of production to older sectors. As a result, the USA surpassed Britain in machine-tool technology in the latter half of the nineteenth century (Carlsson, 1984).

In his *Scale and Scope*, Chandler (1990) describes the rise of the modern industrial enterprise and the emergence of the USA as the world's economic leader. He attributes these developments to new technologies in transportation (railroads and steam ships) and communication (telegraph) that provided unique opportunities for American entre-preneurs as they took advantage of rapid population growth and the creation of a new economy spanning an entire continent:

> As a result of the regularity, increased volume and greater speed of the flows of goods and mate-rials made possible by the new transportation and communication systems, new and improved processes of production developed that for the first time in history enjoyed substantial econo-mies of scale and scope. Large manufacturing works applying the new technologies could produce at lower unit costs than could the smaller works. (Chandler, 1990, p. 8)

The new technologies transformed capital-intensive industries such as the processing of tobacco, grains, sugar, vegetable oil and other foods and they revolutionized oil refining and the making of metals and other materials. The new knowledge created in these industries was practical, shop-floor-oriented, built on experience and largely experimental. Henry Ford's moving assembly line in 1913 is an example. Through such people as Nikola Tesla, Thomas Edison, George Westinghouse and Alexander Graham Bell in the USA, Ernst Werner von Siemens in Germany, Lord Kelvin in the UK and Ottó Bláthy in Hungary, electricity was turned from a scientific curiosity into an essential tool for modern life.

But even though the new industries that emerged based on these innovations depended more on individual ingenuity than on science and higher education, they drew their skilled labor from a growing pool of technically trained personnel, especially engineers, coming out of universities and engineering schools. As the need for standards, testing, measuring and quality control increased, firms began to establish industrial laboratories to carry out such tasks. Many of these laboratories had strong collaboration with universities. American universities and engineering schools were quick to respond as new technical breakthroughs were made. Academia and industry co-evolved.

Until the late nineteenth century, the main focus of universities was on preservation and codification of existing knowledge rather than on new knowledge creation. Certainly the creation of new economically useful knowledge was not seen as the mission of universities. This was true even in the engineering schools that had sprung up in France and Germany in the late eighteenth century and subsequently in the USA. But this began to change with the creation of land-grant universities in the USA by the 1862 Morrill Act, leading to the establishment of universities in every state. Unlike most private universities, these state universities and colleges were created not only to keep up with the educational needs of a rapidly growing population, but also to create a knowledge base needed to support the expansion of the still largely agricultural economy. The land-grant universities were charged with public service obligations in agricultural experimentation and extension services, industrial training, teacher education, home economics, public health and veterinary medicine. One of the main features of the land-grant universities was a strong practical/vocational orientation in both education and research. While the emphasis was on teaching branches of learning related to agriculture and the mechanical arts in addition to the liberal arts, there was also research. The agricultural experiment stations at the land-grant universities played a particularly important role not only in advancing knowledge in fields of practical and economic relevance, but also in making the practical application of research acceptable if not required in US academic institutions (Carlsson et al., 2009).

As the US population grew, partly through immigration and as the country expanded westward, new institutions of higher education, both private and public, were established. The expansion of the US system of higher education allowed it to cater not only to a rapidly growing population but also to increasing percentages of each cohort demanding higher education. This set the USA apart from its European competitors. As a result, by 1910 about 330 000 students were enrolled at almost one thousand colleges and universities in the USA (whose population was 92 million), while at the same time there were only about 14 000 students in 16 universities in France (with a population of 39 million). This represented about 4 percent of the college-age population in the USA versus about 0.5 percent in France (Graham and Diamond, 1997, p. 24). This expansion of higher education contributed importantly to the creation of a relatively highly educated industrial labor force, i.e. a relatively high capacity to absorb new technology. This made it possible for large industrial firms to recruit the skilled labor they needed.

The Morrill Act also stimulated engineering education, and the number of engineering schools grew rapidly. But in contrast to Europe, engineering subjects were taught not only at separate institutions but also in the older elite institutions. For example, Yale introduced courses in mechanical engineering in 1863 and Columbia University opened its School of Mines in 1864 (Rosenberg and Nelson, 1994, p. 327). Soon new engineering disciplines were created.

After the breakthroughs in electricity research around 1880, US universities responded almost instantly to the need for electrical engineers. In the same year (1882) in which Edison's first power station in New York City went into operation, the Massachusetts Institute of Technology (MIT) (founded in 1865) introduced its first course in electrical engineering. Cornell followed in 1883 and awarded the first doctorate in the subject in 1885. By the 1890s schools like MIT had become the chief suppliers of electrical engineers (ibid., pp. 327–8).

The story is similar in chemical engineering. Even though Britain was the 'workshop of the world' and had the largest chemical industry in 1850, this industry was based on its role as supplier to the textile manufacturers, not on professional engineering competence. In fact, there were no departments of chemical engineering in Britain or anywhere else outside the USA until the 1930s. By contrast, MIT offered the first course in chemical engineering in 1888 and established the School of Chemical Engineering Practice in 1915 (Rosenberg, 2000, p. 88). Several other US universities established chemical engineering departments in the first decade of the twentieth century (Rosenberg, 1998, pp. 193–200).

Even though the new industries that emerged in the late nineteenth century – those relying on chemical engineering, electricity and the internal combustion engine – were based on earlier scientific breakthroughs, relatively little of their performance during this era was based directly on science, nor even on advanced technical education. American technology was practical and experimental, built on experience. The new industries needed new knowledge, but the universities did not possess the required specialized knowledge, equipment and organization. Instead, a new mechanism of collaboration between universities and industry emerged in the form of industrial laboratories.

During the latter half of the nineteenth century a number of industrial labs were established in the USA. There were at least 139 by the turn of the century (Mowery, 1981, cited in Rosenberg, 1985, p. 51). The earliest industrial labs did not perform activities that could be regarded as research; they were set up to apply existing knowledge, not to make new discoveries. They were organized to engage in a variety of routine and elementary tasks such as testing and measuring in the production process, assuring quality control, standardizing both product and process and meeting the precise specifications of customers (Chandler, 1985, p. 53). This development was linked to the expansion of higher education in the USA.

Industrialization in the USA in the late nineteenth century was built on mass production and labor-saving technology. But around 1900, industrial growth became science-based: companies such as DuPont, General Electric and Westinghouse, as well as the auto industry, were based on new technologies in chemical, electrical and mechanical engineering. Most of this new knowledge was created in industry, not in academia. While the US universities were creating new engineering and applied science disciplines, they were still lagging behind their European counterparts in basic sciences such as chemistry and physics, and their research capabilities were too small to support the needs of the growing industrial giants. There was little external funding of academic research and none from the federal government. Most R&D was carried out in corporate labs.

US universities played an important role in the creation of corporate R&D laboratories, especially in chemical engineering, via collaborative research and consulting and in developing expanded research capabilities over time, in addition to serving as the launching pad for the careers of individuals who found employment in private firm laboratories. There is also evidence of influence in the opposite direction, from firms to universities.

1900–1945

The new industries contributed to building a new industrial base in the USA during the first two decades of the twentieth century. Several of them were producer-goods-oriented: light machinery, electrical equipment, industrial chemicals and metals. All involved mass production. There were also mass-produced consumer goods in the form of branded packaged products (Chandler, 1990, pp. 63–71). As electrification proceeded, first in industry and later in households, new industries for household appliances such as refrigerators, vacuum cleaners, washing machines and dishwashers emerged. Advances in the organization of automobile production (such as standardization and the moving assembly line) led to mass production of automobiles.

With the stock market crash and the onset of the Great Depression, the demand for new consumer products suddenly diminished. However, innovation continued. After the end of the First World War there was actually a boom in research – little noticed because of the overwhelmingly negative impact of the Great Depression on all sorts of economic activity. Nevertheless:

> Between 1921 and 1938 industrial research personnel rose by 300%. In 1927 approximately 25% of its employees reportedly worked on a part-time basis; by 1938 this proportion had fallen to 3%. Laboratories rose from fewer than 300 in 1920 to over 1,600 in 1931 and more than 2,200 in 1938; the personnel employed increased from about 6,000 in 1920 to over 30,000 in 1931 and over 40,000 in 1938. The annual expenditure [rose] from about $25,000,000 in 1920 to over 120,000,000 in 1931 to about 175,000,000 in 1938. In 1937, industrial research on an organized basis in the United States ranked among the 45 manufacturing industries which provided the largest number of jobs. (Fano, 1987, p. 262)

In connection with the Great Depression during the 1930s, innovation became focused more on cost reduction, particularly labor saving via mechanization. In the metalworking industries there were two major new manufacturing technologies: cemented carbide (first adapted for use in machine tools by the Krupp Steel Works in Germany in 1928 and a few months later by Carboloy in the USA) used for machine tools that could handle high speeds and temperature, and the automatic transfer machine consisting of a large number of work stations arranged so that work pieces can be transferred automatically from one work station to the next. The diffusion of both of these technologies was slowed down by the Depression, but their availability proved crucial in the buildup of new production capacity to support the war effort (Carlsson, 1984). For example, the scaling up of aircraft production from fewer than 1000 a year to more than 10 000 that took place within two years would have been impossible without the application of production and organizational know-how from the auto industry. The buildup of new production capacity for other kinds of military gear (warships, tanks, trucks, jeeps, ammunition etc.) also required similar investments, resulting in an essentially new industrial base that was converted to civilian products after the war.

Other industries were also characterized by increasing utilization of large-scale equipment during the 1930s. The applications ranged from industrial locomotives and power shovels to cement kilns, roller mills in flour milling and milling equipment for mining industries. Along with the extended use of large equipment units came growing importance of industrial measuring, recording and controlling devices (Fano, 1987, p. 257). Also, electricity was used increasingly in industry as well as in agriculture. The innovations during the 1920s and 1930s seem to have been mainly productivity-enhancing (cost-reducing, process-oriented) rather than market-expanding.

Thus, in spite of the Depression, advances in large-scale equipment and mass production technology laid the foundation for wartime production and for economic growth in the postwar period. During the 1920s and 1930s, US universities were still lagging behind Germany and Britain in basic science, but clearly leading in engineering and applied science. External funding of academic research was quite limited. During the interwar period, academic research in the USA was funded primarily by philanthropic foundations and large corporations. The federal government was not involved in funding academic research at this time. The total value of foundation grants to academic institutions was only on the order of $50 million in 1931 and then fell dramatically as the Depression deepened. It rose again in the late 1930s but attained only $40 million (about $450 million in 2006 dollars) in 1940 (Graham and Diamond, 1997, p. 28). The externally funded academic research was also concentrated in just a handful of institutions.

Thus the foundations of the postwar expansion in high-tech industries in the USA were laid over several decades. The buildup of a highly educated labor force began in the late nineteenth century as the university system expanded and the percentage of each cohort of the population receiving post-secondary education became four or five times higher than in the leading countries in Europe. The USA was still catching up with Europe in basic science until the Second World War, but it had developed strong academic programs in chemical and electrical engineering in the late nineteenth and early twentieth centuries, long before Europe. The practical and application-oriented education nature of US higher education, in combination with close collaboration between academic and corporate R&D, created a strong foundation upon which to build the postwar high-tech expansion.

The innovations that provided the foundation for the military buildup during the Second World War were diffused primarily through existing firms. They involved essentially a scaling up of previous activity through the application of technical and organizational know-how that had been developed in the decades preceding the war.

1945–1980

The entry of the USA into the Second World War required mobilization of all kinds of resources. President Roosevelt summoned Vannevar Bush, former dean of engineering at MIT, to lead the mobilization of scientific manpower. For this purpose, Bush organized the Office of Scientific Research and Development (OSRD). Instead of drafting scientists to work in government labs, as had been done in the First World War, the OSRD developed intense collaboration between Washington and the leading universities. Total federal R&D expenditures increased from $83 million in 1940 to $1314 million in 1945 in 1930 dollars (Mowery and Rosenberg, 1998, p. 28). During the war, the Army Corps of Engineers spent $2 billion developing the atomic bomb and the Radiation Laboratory at MIT spent $1.5 billion for radar systems (Geiger, 1993, p. 9). The increased research was guided by military needs and involved both basic research and its immediate application to military goods and services. In addition to the atomic bomb and radar, these efforts led to the development of the computer, jet engines, penicillin, DDT, numerically controlled machine tools, and scientific instrumentation.

Huge investments were also made in production facilities to support the war effort. Tanks, trucks, jeeps, airplanes, warships and ammunition were needed in quantities never seen before. Civilian facilities were converted to military production, but new facilities were also needed that incorporated the new mass production techniques, especially transfer machines, that had been developed during the interwar period. As a result, at the end of the war the USA had massive and modern production capacity unmatched anywhere in the world, a position it maintained for the first two decades after the war.

It is noteworthy that several of the major technologies developed during the war originated in Britain and Germany and came to the USA via Britain; the war effort became a powerful focusing device in building domestic innovation systems and production capacity in each of these areas. For example, the Radiation Lab at MIT was initially set up in 1940 as a joint Anglo-American project to further develop British radar technology and produce radar equipment. Penicillin was mass produced in the USA during the war, organized by the War Production Board on the basis of discoveries made in the UK and Australia. The first American jet engine was built by General Electric in 1943 after a British prototype. The civilian commercialization of these technologies that followed later was carried out primarily by existing companies.

While the conversion from military to civilian production was based in part on imported technology and largely benefited existing companies, the development of the computer industry took place in the USA and US universities played a prominent role.

> The first digital electronic computer, the ENIAC, was brought to the full stage of a working prototype at the Moore School of Electrical Engineering at the University of Pennsylvania, in the fall of 1945 . . . In the case of the computer, moreover, American universities not only designed and assembled the initial hardware of the computer industry; they created an entirely new discipline, of huge economic importance, along with the research infrastructure that had to be built in order to exploit the vast potential of the new hardware (Rosenberg, 2000, p. 49)

The first computer company was Eckert-Mauchly Computer Corporation, formed in 1946. The company was sold in 1950 to Remington Rand (later Sperry Rand), which was an established maker of office equipment and electric shavers. Many other companies entered the emerging computer business during the early postwar years. Some companies were founded *de novo* to pursue computer development opportunities, but most start-ups sold out to become the nucleus of computer operations of established companies (Scherer, 1996, p. 240).

Although one can argue, based on the analysis in the preceding section, that there were innovation systems at work in the USA prior to the Second World War, the war certainly had a fundamental impact on shaping a new innovation system (or actually a whole set of partially overlapping technology-focused innovation systems). In this new system, the universities played a much more prominent role than before both in research (both basic and applied) and in education of a larger segment of the labor force. The research university as we know it today is one of the results; it became an important part of the newly emerging national innovation system. The federal government also played a much more important role than before both in funding and in performing research. Most of the federal funding came via the Department of Defense and was conducted largely in government labs and by defense contractors. But the war-related research was organized in such a way that it also involved universities. For the first time, and quite suddenly, the federal government became the major source of funding for academic research, which now included 'big science' projects (systematic, programmatic research) on a scale never seen before. Basic research started to shift toward the universities. Fortunately, the US universities were ready to respond to the challenges. Several academic institutions, led by MIT, had policies (such as arrangements for consulting) and organizations (such as separate laboratories) in place to allow faculty to engage in classified military research without interfering with their role as educators and academic researchers (Carlsson et al., 2009). Also, as the war ended, the GI bill generated a large increase in college enrollment at all types of universities, not just elite ones.

The war-related products (such as computers, jet engines and radar) that resulted from the R&D were commercialized almost immediately through the military, and soon after the war were converted to civilian products. The commercialization took place mainly through incumbent firms. Even though leading research universities such as MIT began spinning off new companies based on the military technologies they had developed during the war, these new startups were too few to affect the total number of firms materially. Overall, there were few new firms created; entrepreneurial activity declined or stagnated between 1950 and 1965.

The federal funding of defense-related R&D continued to grow until total R&D expenditures reached a peak in the mid-1960s. The total R&D spending then fell as the federal expenditures declined. At the same time, the federal funding of academic research became less focused, dispersed to a much larger number of institutions of higher education and used for building research infrastructure. As a result, much less of the knowledge created was economically useful. Fewer new products emerged and the civilian spin-offs from military products began to decline. The economic growth rate fell.

Even though most R&D was still performed by industrial firms, the enhanced role of universities meant that more basic research was being conducted. There had been little of that before the war, even at universities. The increase in basic research was closely linked to research in the life sciences, conducted primarily at universities. But as their external funding grew, the universities also played an increasingly important role in applied research in chemical and electrical engineering. However, in microelectronics the university role seems to have been largely that of supplying highly trained personnel; many of the important discoveries were made in industry. For example, William Shockley and colleagues at Bell Labs developed the transistor, subsequently sharing it with academic researchers (Rosenberg, 1992, p. 34).

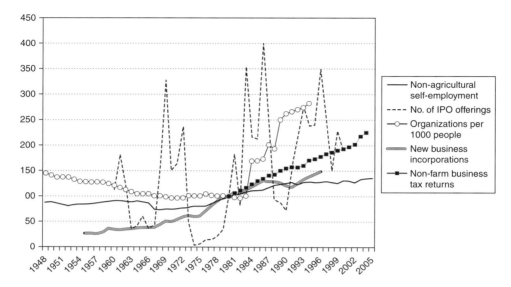

Sources: Number of IPOs: Ibbotson et al. (2001); Ritter (2006). New business incorporations, non-farm
business tax returns and non-agricultural self-employment: *Statistical Abstract of the United States*, various
issues. Organizations per 1000 people: Gartner and Shane (1995), p. 295.

Figure 14.1   Indicators of entrepreneurial activity, 1948–2005 (Index, 1980 = 100)

Thus the economic growth in the early postwar years was largely concentrated in large existing companies, not in startups. The total number of concerns in business increased initially as the return to a civilian economy began from about 2.1 million in 1946 (about the same as in 1930) and rose to 2.7 million by 1949, but then stayed at that level until the end of the 1950s. Few new companies were formed; the number of new business incorporations was around 100000 per year in the latter half of the 1940s, rose gradually in the 1950s and 1960s but did not really take off until the late 1970s. Non-agricultural self-employment remained constant from the late 1940s until the mid-1960s, even though the labor force grew (i.e. the self-employment rate declined). There were few initial public offerings (IPOs), and those that did occur were quite modest in size (in terms of proceeds per IPO) and often involved companies that had been started many years earlier (Ibbotson et al., 2001). The number of organizations per person declined continuously from 1948 to about 1970 and then leveled off (see Figure 14.1).

If there had not been sufficient absorptive capacity in US industry during the Second World War, if the universities had not been at or near the frontier in applied fields of science and engineering, and if they had not been organized appropriately, the transition to a knowledge-based economy would have taken much longer than it did.

> The creation of an institutional infrastructure during this century that, by the 1940s, was capable of training large numbers of electrical engineers, physicists, metallurgists, mathematicians and other experts capable of advancing these new technologies, meant that the postwar American endowment of specialized human capital was initially more abundant than that of other industrial nations. (Mowery and Rosenberg, 1998, p. 165)

The reasons that the USA took the lead after the war even in technologies originally developed elsewhere were: (1) the destruction in Europe, particularly in Germany and the UK; (2) the high absorptive capacity in the USA as a result of both substantial funding of R&D; and (3) the formation of a new set of technology-focused innovation systems that together may be referred to as a 'national innovation system'.

1980–2006

The year 1980 represents something of a turning point. A number of institutional reforms (including strengthening of intellectual property rights, the enactment of the Bayh–Dole Act, changes in tax laws and deregulation of financial institutions that created not only new financial instruments but also a whole new market for venture capital – see Mowery et al., 2004, and Shane, 2004 for details) mark a transition to a new technological regime in which new business formation plays an increasing role in converting new knowledge into economic growth. These institutional changes stimulated not only innovation but also entrepreneurial activity. The breakthrough in DNA research and the microprocessor revolution contributed to this development. Funding for life sciences research increased dramatically both in absolute amounts and as a share of overall R&D funding, which gave rise to numerous university spin-offs. These were dedicated biotechnology firms focused on translating scientific inventions into commercial innovations, sometimes producing and marketing their own products but more often in various collaborative arrangements (ranging from licensing to being acquired by large pharmaceutical firms) with other firms. While this development has created many new firms, the economic results are still pending in many cases. Meanwhile, the microelectronic revolution has spawned many new firms, some of which have grown to be industrial giants, such as Microsoft, Intel and Apple.

These developments have brought a significant shift in the size distribution of firms. The share of large firms in the economy began to decline for the first time, reversing the trend over the previous 100 years (Carlsson, 1992). Entrepreneurial activity (as measured by non-farm business tax returns, new business incorporations, the number of organizations per capita, the number of IPO offerings and non-agricultural self-employment) began to pick up as the dynamism of the economy increased (see Figure 14.1).

The 'big picture' that emerges shows the economy becoming increasingly dependent on economically useful knowledge and on the effectiveness with which that knowledge is converted into economic activity. In the late nineteenth century, knowledge creation was linked to a rise in the share of college-educated people in the population, and codification and standardization of economically useful knowledge in industrial labs. At the turn of the nineteenth century, economic growth was driven primarily by science- and engineering-based industries such as chemicals, electrical equipment and telecommunications. The leading companies in these industries built their own corporate R&D labs. These, as well as several federal laboratories, working closely with academic scientists, were the main producers of economically useful knowledge and they were quick to reap the economic benefits.

The Second World War led to a massive scaling up of R&D in the USA. While most of the funding went to federal and corporate laboratories, the federal government now also began to fund academic research. At first the defense-related R&D was immediately converted into economic activity via incumbent firms producing such products as jet engines, radar and computers. In the mid-1960s, the total R&D expenditures started falling in relation to GDP and the economic impact of the war-related products was diminishing. The decline in R&D spending was reversed in the early 1980s, carried largely by biotechnology and the microprocessor.

THE NATURE AND ROLE OF INNOVATION SYSTEMS IN OTHER COUNTRIES

As indicated above, not only the volume but also the organization of R&D influences the outcome as reflected in economic growth. This is one reason why there is little or no correlation between R&D spending and economic growth (see Acs et al., 2005). But there are many other reasons having to do with history (path dependence) and institutional arrangements. As shown above, institutions evolve, along with technologies. The institutions and the way they evolve involve both private and public actors.

The US national innovation system is unique in that most inventions, particularly science-based ones, are generated within the system. In most other national innovation systems, most of the inventions come from outside and are converted into innovations within the system.

For example, in a study of the technological development in Swedish industry in the 1970s (Carlsson, 1979), it was found that even though Sweden was at or close to the technological frontier in many areas, the genuinely Swedish technological contributions were quite modest. Most technologies had been imported from abroad and then adapted and improved. This had been done largely through the R&D efforts of individual companies. In fact, one of the major findings of the study was that global monitoring of research, both academic and non-academic, was the most important function of corporate R&D even in the most research-intensive firms. Thus many of the large industrial firms could be said to have designed their own innovation systems for their own needs, often with extensive networks both internally and externally – the latter in the form of both formal arrangements such as joint ventures and alliances, and informal participation in conferences, seminars, research consortia and so on. Links with academic researchers were often seen as important but certainly not confined to domestic universities. MIT and Stanford were as likely to be mentioned as the Royal Institute of Technology and Chalmers University of Technology.

After the concept of national innovation system was developed in the late 1980s (Freeman, 1987, 1988; Lundvall, 1988; Nelson, 1988; Pelikan, 1988), a substantial literature has emerged on the structure and evolution of innovation systems in various countries and time periods. See, for example, Lundvall (1992), Nelson (1992, 1993) and Edquist (1997); see Carlsson (2006, 2007) for surveys of the literature. What emerges from this literature is that there are many different ways in which national innovation systems have evolved; the evolutionary processes as well as their outcomes are clearly path-dependent.

Although there is extensive evidence of internationalization of economic activity (including R&D) at the corporate level, involving cross-licensing, joint ventures, acquisitions, licensing agreements, technology alliances and the like, there is not much evidence of internationalization of the institutions that support national innovation systems. But there are numerous studies of internationalization of corporate R&D that point to the continued importance of national institutions to support innovative activity, even though that activity is becoming increasingly internationalized. Such institutions, whether they take the form of business groups such as Japanese *keiretsu*, Korean *chaebol*, Chinese government policy in combination with direct foreign investment or other configurations, can function as mechanisms to facilitate spillovers of technology from outside the national systems. Helping to overcome the spatial boundedness characteristic of knowledge spillovers by importing/absorbing ideas from abroad and then combining, selecting and implementing them is one of the most important functions of innovation systems. In this sense, the innovative activities of firms are significantly influenced by their home country's national system of innovation (Carlsson, 2006).

Strangely missing from most of the innovation systems literature is the notion of entrepreneurial activity; the focus has been mainly on the creation of ideas rather than on innovation and commercialization. As explained in Bergek et al. (2008), there are six basic functions that have to be fulfilled in a well-functioning innovation system: a mechanism is needed to focus the search for solutions; sufficient knowledge needs to be acquired or developed; resources need to be mobilized; given all the uncertainties surrounding new technologies, numerous entrepreneurial experiments are often required; a market (or markets) needs to be formed; and social and political legitimation is needed. Sometimes, but not always, policy intervention is needed in one or more of these functions. It may well be the case that barriers to entrepreneurial activity in the form of entrenched incumbents and interest groups, as well as lack of institutions supporting entrepreneurship, are the most important impediments to economic development.

Given the complexity of both the economic development process and the innovation systems that support it, it is not surprising that there are not many studies of the contributions of innovation systems to economic development. But such studies are now beginning to emerge. For example, Fagerberg and Srholec (2008) tried to find indicators of 'capabilities' representing the main features of national innovation systems as well as indicators of the quality of governance, the character of the political system and the degree of openness of the economy for 115 countries. They found that innovation systems and the quality of governance are particularly important, much more so than the character of the political system and the degree of openness of the economy, in explaining differences among countries in economic development as reflected in GDP per capita. Thus there is now at least some empirical evidence that innovation systems do make a difference, but clearly much more needs to be done.

CONCLUSION

In this chapter I have tried to show that new knowledge is the main driver of innovation in advanced economies and that innovation is translated into economic development via both incumbent firms and new entities. The analysis of the experience in the USA shows that in the late nineteenth and early twentieth centuries, firms in new industries that took advantage of economies of scale and scope were able to grow large and dominate their industries. New ideas came mainly from individual inventors or from corporate R&D

labs rather than from academia. As new industries developed that were based on scientific discoveries, they became dependent on universities for recruiting highly trained, specialized personnel and for research collaboration. The expansion of the US system of higher education, the number and diversity of institutions, the students they educated and the practical orientation of the curriculum created a relatively highly educated labor force, providing the economy with a high absorptive capacity. The early development of new academic disciplines in chemical and electrical engineering gave US firms an advantage over their foreign competitors.

The vast expansion of R&D in conjunction with the Second World War led to the emergence of a new national innovation system in which knowledge creation shifted much more toward the universities while also shifting toward basic sciences, particularly life sciences. Initially, large existing firms were the main vehicles to commercialize the products that resulted from the wartime research. But as new opportunities emerged in microelectronics and biotechnology, and as institutional changes involving intellectual property and venture finance were made, entrepreneurial activity began to flourish.

The analysis shows that technologies and institutions co-evolve and that innovation systems are dynamic and path-dependent phenomena. It also shows that the function of innovation systems is not only to create or absorb ideas, but also to turn ideas into innovations and commercialize them.

REFERENCES

Abramovitz, Moses (1956), 'Resource and output trends in the United States since 1870', *American Economic Review*, **45**, 5–23.

Abramovitz, Moses (1993), 'The search for the sources of growth: areas of ignorance, old and new', *Journal of Economic History*, **53** (2), 217–43.

Acs, Z.J., D.B. Audretsch, P. Braunerhjelm and B. Carlsson (2005), 'Growth and entrepreneurship – an empirical assessment', Working Paper, April.

Acs, Z.J., D.B. Audretsch, P. Braunerhjelm and B. Carlsson (2009), 'The knowledge spillover theory of entrepreneurship', *Small Business Economics*, **32** (1), 15–30.

Arrow, Kenneth (1962), 'The economic implication of learning by doing', *Review of Economics and Statistics*, **80**, 155–73.

Bergek, A., S. Jacobsson, B. Carlsson, S. Lindmark and A. Rickne (2008), 'Analyzing the functional dynamics of technological innovation systems: a scheme of analysis', *Research Policy*, **37** (4), 407–29.

Braunerhjelm, P., Acs, Z.J., D.B. Audretsch and B. Carlsson (2010), 'The missing link: the knowledge filter and entrepreneurship in economic growth', *Small Business Economics*, **34** (2), 105–25.

Carlsson, Bo (1979), *Teknik och industristruktur: 70-talets ekonomiska kris i historisk belysning* (Technology and industrial structure: the economic crisis of the 70s in historical perspective), Stockholm: IUI and IVA, ch. 6, pp. 138–54.

Carlsson, Bo (1984), 'The development and use of machine tools in historical perspective', *Journal of Economic Behavior and Organization*, **5** (1), 91–114.

Carlsson, Bo (1992), 'The rise of small business: causes and consequences', in W.J. Adams (ed.), *Singular Europe: Economy and Polity of the European Community after 1992*, Ann Arbor, MI: University of Michigan Press, pp. 145–69.

Carlsson, Bo (2006), 'Internationalization of innovation systems: a survey of the literature', *Research Policy*, **35** (1), 56–67.

Carlsson, Bo (2007), 'Innovation systems: a survey of the literature from a Schumpeterian perspective', in Horst Hanusch and Andreas Pyka (eds), *Elgar Companion to Neo-Schumpeterian Economics*, Cheltenham, UK and Northampton, MA, USA: Edward Elgar, pp. 257–71.

Carlsson, B., Z.J. Acs, D.B. Audretsch and P. Braunerhjelm (2009), 'Knowledge creation, entrepreneurship and economic growth: a historical review', *Industrial and Corporate Change*, **18** (6), 1193–1229.

Chandler, Alfred D., Jr (1985), 'From industrial laboratories to departments of research and development', in

K.B. Clark, R.H. Hayes and C. Lorenz (eds), *The Uneasy Alliance: Managing the Productivity–Technology Dilemma*, Boston, MA: Harvard Business School Press, pp. 53–61.

Chandler, Alfred D., Jr (1990), *Scale and Scope: The Dynamics of Industrial Capitalism*, Cambridge, MA: Harvard University Press.

Edquist, Charles (1997), *Systems of Innovation: Technologies, Institutions and Organizations*, London: Pinter.

Fagerberg, J. and M. Srholec (2008), 'National innovation systems, capabilities and economic development', *Research Policy*, **37**, 1417–35.

Fano, Ester (1987), 'Technical progress as a destabilizing factor and as an agent of recovery in the United States between the two world wars', *History and Technology*, **3**, 249–74.

Freeman, Christopher (1987), *Technology Policy and Economic Performance: Lessons from Japan*, London: Pinter.

Freeman, Christopher (1988), 'Japan: a new national system of innovation', in G. Dosi et al. (eds), *Technical Change and Economic Theory*, London: Pinter, pp. 330–48.

Gartner, W.B. and S.A. Shane (1995), 'Measuring entrepreneurship over time', *Journal of Business Venturing*, **10**, 283–301.

Geiger, Roger L. (1993), *Research and Relevant Knowledge: American Research Universities since World War II*, Oxford: Oxford University Press.

Graham, H.D. and N. Diamond (1997), *The Rise of American Research Universities: Elites and Challenges in the Postwar Era*, Baltimore, MD: The Johns Hopkins University Press.

Ibbotson, R.G., J.L. Sindelar and J.R. Ritter (2001), 'The market's problems with the pricing of initial public offerings', *Journal of Applied Corporate Finance*, Spring, 66–74. Available at http://bear.cba.ufl.edu/ritter.

Lucas, Robert (1988), 'On the mechanics of economic development', *Journal of Monetary Economics*, **22**, 3–39.

Lucas, Robert (1993), 'Making a miracle', *Econometrica*, **61**, 251–72.

Lundvall, Bengt-Åke (1988), 'Innovation as an interactive process: from user–producer interaction to the national system of innovation', in G. Dosi et al. (eds), *Technical Change and Economic Theory*, London: Pinter Publishers, pp. 349–69.

Lundvall, Bengt-Åke (1992), *National Systems of Innovation: Towards a Theory of Innovation and Interactive Learning*, London: Pinter Publishers.

Mowery, David C. (1981), 'The emergence and growth of industrial research in American manufacturing, 1899–1945', PhD dissertation, Stanford University, CA.

Mowery, D.C. and N. Rosenberg (1998), *Paths of Innovation: Technological Change in 20th-century America*, Cambridge: Cambridge University Press.

Mowery, D.C., R.R. Nelson, B.N. Sampat and A.A. Ziedonis (2004), *Ivory Tower and Industrial Innovation: University–Industry Technology Transfer before and after the Bayh–Dole Act in the United States*, Stanford, CA: Stanford University Press.

Nelson, Richard R. (1988), 'Institutions supporting technical change in the United States', in G. Dosi et al. (eds), *Technical Change and Economic Theory*, London, Pinter Publishers, pp. 312–29.

Nelson, Richard R. (1992), 'National innovation systems: a retrospective on a study', *Industrial and Corporate Change*, **1** (2), 347–74.

Nelson, Richard R. (1993), *National Innovation Systems: A Comparative Analysis*, Oxford: Oxford University Press.

Pelikan, Pavel (1988), 'Can the innovation system of capitalism be outperformed?' in G. Dosi et al. (eds), *Technical Change and Economic Theory*, London: Pinter Publishers, pp. 370–98.

Ritter, Jay R. (2006), 'Some factoids about the 2005 IPO market', http://bear.cba.ufl.edu/ritter.

Romer, Paul (1986), 'Increasing returns and economic growth', *American Economic Review*, **94**, 1002–37.

Romer, Paul (1990), 'Endogenous technical change', *Journal of Political Economy*, **98**, 71–102.

Rosenberg, Nathan (1985), 'The commercial exploitation of science by American industry', in K.B. Clark, R.H. Hayes and C. Lorenz (eds), *The Uneasy Alliance: Managing the Productivity–Technology Dilemma*, Boston, MA: Harvard Business School Press, pp. 19–51.

Rosenberg, Nathan (1992), 'Scientific instrumentation and university research', *Research Policy*, **21** (3), 381–90.

Rosenberg, Nathan (1998), 'Technological change in chemicals: the role of university–industry relations', in A. Arora, R. Landau and N. Rosenberg (eds), *Chemicals and Long-term Economic Growth: Insights from the Chemical Industry*, New York: Wiley, pp. 193–230.

Rosenberg, Nathan (2000), *Schumpeter and the Endogeneity of Technology. Some American Perspectives*, New York: Routledge.

Rosenberg, N. and R.R. Nelson (1994), 'American universities and technical advance in industry', *Research Policy*, **23** (3), 323–48.

Scherer, Frederic M. (1996), *Industry Structure, Strategy and Public Policy*, New York: HarperCollins College Publishers.

Shane, Scott (2004), *Academic Entrepreneurship: University Spinoffs and Wealth Creation*, Cheltenham, UK and Northampton, MA, USA: Edward Elgar.
Solow, Robert (1956), 'A contribution to theory of economic growth', *Quarterly Journal of Economics*, **70**, 65–94.

15 Innovation, entrepreneurship and the search for knowledge spillovers
Zoltan J. Acs

INTRODUCTION

David B. Audretsch and Zoltan J. Acs were attracted to the economics of technological change by the innovative prowls of new-technology-based firms in the 1980s. While the conventional wisdom held that large firms had an innovative advantage over small firms, in a 1988 article in the *American Economic Review* they discovered an anomaly instead of solving a problem:

> A perhaps somewhat surprising result is that not only is the coefficient of the large-firm employment share positive and significant for small-firm innovations, but it is actually greater in magnitude than for large firms. This suggests that, *ceteris paribus*, the greater extent to which an industry is composed of large firms, the greater will be the innovative activity, but that increased innovative activity will tend to emanate more from the small firms than from the large firms. (Acs and Audretsch, 1988, p. 686)

The anomaly of where new technology-based startups acquire knowledge was unresolved.

Building on the work of Griliches (1979), Adam Jaffe (1989) was the first to identify the extent to which university research spills over into the generation of commercial activity. Building on Jaffe's work, Maryann Feldman (1994) at Carnegie Mellon University expanded the knowledge production function to innovative activity and incorporated aspects of the regional knowledge infrastructure. Attila Varga (1998) at West Virginia University extends the Jaffe–Feldman approach by focusing on a more precise measure of local geographic spillovers. Varga approaches the issue of knowledge spillovers from an explicit spatial econometric perspective. The Jaffe–Feldman–Varga spillovers (from here on JFV) go a long way toward explaining the role of knowledge spillovers in technological change. Building on this foundation, the model was recently extended to identify entrepreneurship as a conduit through which knowledge spillovers take place (Acs et al., 2009). Finally, the role of agglomerations in knowledge spillovers represents the frontier in this scientific revolution (Clark et al., 2003). The purpose of this chapter is to catalogue the contribution of JFV – two of them my students – that simultaneously and independently sparked a search for the mechanism of knowledge spillovers.

The second section outlines the main contributions of Jaffe, Feldman and Varga. The third section examines extensions of the model by Jaffe, Trajtenberg and Henderson, as well as recent criticisms of the model by Thomson and Fox-Kean. The fourth section examines spatialized explanations of economic growth by Acs and Varga; Fujita et al.; and Romer. The fifth section presents work on the knowledge spillover theory of entrepreneurship. The sixth section discusses agglomerations, with policy discussed in the seventh section. Conclusions are in the final section.

JAFFE–FELDMAN–VARGA

In his 1989 paper in the *American Economic Review*, Adam Jaffe extended his path-breaking 1986 study measuring the total R&D pool available for spillovers to identify the contribution of spillovers from university research to commercial innovation. Jaffe's findings were the first to identify the extent to which university research spills over into the generation of inventions and innovations by private firms. In order to relate the response of this measure to R&D spillovers from universities, Jaffe modifies the 'knowledge production function' introduced by Zvi Griliches (1979) for two inputs: private corporate expenditures on R&D, and research expenditures undertaken at universities.

Essentially, this is a two-factor Cobb–Douglas production function that relates an output measure for 'knowledge' to two input measures: research and development performed by industry; and research performed by universities. Formally, this is expressed as:

$$\log(K) = \beta_{K1} \log(R) + \beta_{K2} \log(U) + \varepsilon_K \qquad (15.1)$$

where K is a proxy for knowledge measured by patent counts, R is industry R&D and U is university research, with ε_K as a stochastic error term. The analysis is carried out for US states for several points in time and disaggregated by sector. The potential interaction between university and industry research is captured by extending the model with two additional equations that allow for simultaneity between these two variables:

$$\log(R) = \beta_{R1} \log(U) + \beta_{R2} Z_2 + \varepsilon_R \qquad (15.2)$$

and

$$\log(U) = \beta_{U1} \log(R) + \beta_{U2} Z_1 + \varepsilon_U \qquad (15.3)$$

where U and R are as before, Z_1 and Z_2 are sets of exogenous local characteristics, and ε_R and ε_U are stochastic error terms.

Jaffe's statistical results provide evidence that corporate patent activity responds positively to commercial spillovers from university research. The lack of evidence that geographic proximity within the state matters clouds results concerning the role of geographic proximity in spillovers from university research. According to Jaffe (1989, p. 968), 'there is only weak evidence that spillovers are facilitated by geographic coincidence of universities and research labs within the state'. In other words, we know very little where knowledge spillovers go.

Maryann Feldman expands on the work of Jaffe in two ways (Feldman, 1994; Feldman and Florida, 1994; Acs et al., 1992, 1994). First, she uses a new data source – a literature-based innovation output indicator developed by the US Small Business Administration that directly measures innovative activity (Acs and Audretsch, 1988) and extends the knowledge production function (Jaffe, 1989) to account for tacit knowledge and commercialization linkages.

Griliches (1979) introduced a model of technological innovation that views innovative output as the product of knowledge-generating inputs. Jaffe (1989) modified this production function approach to consider spatial and technical area dimensions. However, Jaffe's model considers only what were previously defined as the elements of the formal knowledge base. Such a formulation does not consider other types of knowledge inputs, which contribute to the realization of innovative output. This is important since innovation requires both technical and business knowledge if profitability is to be the guide for making investments in R&D. Following the innovation knowledge base conceptual model, a more complete specification of innovative inputs would include

$$\log(K) = \beta_{K1} \log(R) + \beta_{K2} \log(U) + \beta_{K3} \log(BSERV) + \beta_{K4} \log(VA) + \varepsilon_K \quad (15.4)$$

where K is measured by counts of innovations, and R and U are as before. VA is the tacit knowledge embodied by the industry's presence in an area, and $BSERV$ stands for the presence of business services that represents a link to commercialization.

The last input in the knowledge base model is the most evasive. Various producer services provide knowledge to the market and the commercialization process. For example, the services of patent attorneys are a critical input to the innovation process. Similarly, marketing information plays an important role in the commercialization process.

Substitution of the direct measure of innovative activity for the patent measure in the knowledge production function generally strengthens Jaffe's (1989) arguments and reinforces his findings. Most importantly, use of the innovation data provides even greater support than was found by Jaffe: as he predicted, spillovers are facilitated by the geographic coincidence of universities and research labs within the state. In addition, there is at least some evidence that, because the patent and innovation measures capture different aspects of the process of technological change, results for specific sectors may be, at least to some extent, influenced by the technological regime. Thus it is found that the importance of university spillovers relative to private company R&D spending is considerably greater in the electronics sector when the direct measure of innovative activity is substituted for the patent measure.

However, the relative importance of industry R&D and university research as inputs in generating innovative output clearly varies between large and small firms (Acs et al., 1994). That is, for large firms, not only is the elasticity of innovative activity with respect to industry R&D expenditures more than two times greater than the elasticity with respect to expenditures on research by universities, but it is nearly twice as large as the elasticity of small-firm innovative activity with respect to industry R&D. By contrast, for small firms the elasticity of innovative output with respect to expenditures on research by universities is about one-fifth greater than the elasticity with respect to industry R&D. Moreover, the elasticity of innovative activity with respect to university research is about 50 percent greater for small enterprises than for large corporations.

These results support the hypothesis that private company R&D plays a relatively more important role in generating innovative activity in large corporations than in small firms. By contrast, spillovers from the research activities of universities play a more decisive role in the innovative activity of small firms. Geographic proximity between university and corporate laboratories within a state clearly serves as a catalyst to innovative activity for firms of all sizes. However, the impact is apparently greater on small firms than on large firms.

There were two limitations of the Jaffe–Feldman research. First, the unit of analysis at the state level was too aggregate, requiring a geographical coincidence index to control for co-location. Second, the research did not take into consideration the potential influence of spatial dependence that may invalidate the interpretation of econometric analyses based on contiguous cross-sectional data.

Attila Varga mitigates these limitations, examining both the state and the metropolitan statistical area (MSA) levels and using spatial econometric techniques[1] (Varga, 1998, 2000; Anselin et al., 1997, 2000a, 2000b; Acs et al., 2002). These extensions yielded a more precise insight into the range of spatial externalities between innovation and R&D in the MSA and university research both within the MSA and in surrounding counties. He was able to shed some initial light on this issue for high-tech innovations measured as an aggregate across five two-digit SIC industries and also at a more detailed industrial sector level. He found a positive and highly significant relationship between MSA innovations and university research, indicating the presence of localized university research spillovers in innovation. In comparison with the effect of industrial knowledge spillovers (i.e. knowledge flows among industrial research laboratories), the size of the university effect is considerably smaller, as it is one-third of the size of the industrial research coefficient. University knowledge spillovers follow a definite distance decay pattern, as shown by the statistically significant albeit smaller size university research coefficient for adjoining counties within a 50-mile distance range from the MSA center.

There are notable differences among sectors with respect to the localized university effect as studied at the MSA level. Specifically for the four high-tech sectors such as machinery, chemicals, electronics and instruments, significant localized university spillover impact was found only for electronics and instruments, while for the other two industries the university research coefficient remains consistently insignificant.

Acs et al. (2002) test whether the patent data developed by the US Patent and Trademark Office is, in fact, a reliable proxy measure of innovative activity at the regional level as compared to the literature-based innovation output indicator developed by the US Small Business Administration. This is important, since the patent data are readily available over time and can be used to study the dynamics of localized knowledge flows within regional innovation systems. Before this study, there was some evidence that patents provide a reliable measure of innovative activity at the industry level (Acs and Audretsch, 1989), and some evidence that patents and innovations behave similarly at the state level (Acs et al., 1992). However, this had not been tested at the sub-state level.

The correlation between the PTO patent and SBA innovation counts at the MSA level is reasonably high (0.79), and this could be taken as a first indication that patents might be a reliable measure of innovation at the regional level. However, this correlation coefficient value is not high enough to guarantee that the role of different regional actors in knowledge creation would turn out similar with both measures if applied in the same empirical model. Varga proceeded by replacing innovation counts with the patent measure in the same model as in Anselin et al. (1997) in order to directly compare the results of the two measures of new technological knowledge and assess the extent to which patents may be used as a reliable proxy.

Sizes of all the parameters in the estimated knowledge production function are smaller for innovation than for patents, suggesting that firms in the product development stage rely on localized interactions (with universities as well as with other actors) less intensively than in earlier stages of the innovation process. The other important finding of this comparative study is that the importance of university knowledge spillovers (measured by the size of the university research parameter) compared with that of R&D spillovers among private firms is substantially less pronounced for patents than for innovations. Since patenting reflects more the earlier stages of innovation whereas the direct innovation measure accounts for the concluding stage of the innovation process, the relatively higher weight of local universities in innovation than in patenting appears to reflect the different spatial patterns of basic and applied research collaboration. To collaborate with universities in applied research, firms tend to choose local academic institutions, whereas basic research collaboration can be carried out over larger distances.

EXTENSIONS OF THE JFV MODEL

Jaffe, Trajtenberg and Henderson (1993, 2005) expand on the above work to answer the question if knowledge externalities are localized. This is important since growth theory assumed that knowledge spills over to agents within the country, but not to other countries. This implicit assumption begs the question as to what extent knowledge externalities are localized. Jaffe et al. extend the search for knowledge spillovers by using a matching method that found that knowledge spillovers are strongly localized. Their method matches each citing patent to a non-citing patent intended to control for the pre-existing geographic concentration of production. Using patent data, they came to two conclusions: that spillovers are particularly significant at the local level, and that localization fades slowly over time. These results and the large research issue are reproduced in Jaffe and Trajtenberg (2002).

Audretsch and Feldman (1996) explore the question of the geography of innovation and production. They provide evidence concerning the spatial dimension of knowledge spillovers. Their findings suggest that knowledge spillovers are geographically bounded and localized within spatial proximity to the knowledge source. Feldman and Audretsch (1999) further examine the question of knowledge spillovers by looking into the question of specialization versus industrial diversity in cities. Their research supports the ideas that diversity leads to more innovation.

Recently, Thompson and Fox-Kean (2005a, 2005b) challenged the findings of Jaffe et al. They suggest that the Jaffe et al. method matched case control methodology included a serious spurious component. Controlling for unobservables using matching methods is invariably a dangerous exercise because one can rarely be confident that the controls are doing their job. In some cases, imperfect matching may simply introduce noise and a corresponding loss of efficiency. They suggest at least two reasons why the matching method may not adequately control for existing patent activity. First, the level of aggregation might not be fine enough. Second, patents typically contain many distinct claims, each of which is assigned a technological classification. These two features of the control selection process mean that there is no guarantee that the control patent has any industrial similarity with either the citing or the originating patent. Of course, their conclusion that spillovers stop at the country level also needs explaining.

Empirical research done within the JFV framework and the extensions introduced so far were established and originally carried out in the USA with the use of state, MSA and county-level data sets. However, the issue of the geographic extent of knowledge spillovers has definite international validity. The JFV model has been replicated and continually refined in the search for the geographical boundaries of knowledge flows in Europe, South America and Asia. Varga (2006) provides an assessment of the international literature.

THE 'SPATIALIZED' EXPLANATION OF ECONOMIC GROWTH

Building on the JFV model of knowledge spillovers, Acs and Varga (2002) suggest that a 'spatialized' theoretical framework of technology-led economic growth needs to reflect three fundamental issues. First, it should explain why knowledge-related economic activities concentrate in certain regions, leaving others relatively underdeveloped. Second, it needs to answer the questions of how technological advances occur and what are the key processes and institutions involved, with a particular focus on the geographic dimension. Third, it must present an analytical framework where the role of technological change in regional and national economic growth is clearly explained. In order to answer these three questions, Acs and Varga examine three separate and distinct literatures: the new economic geography, the new growth theory, and the new economics of innovation.

Although the three approaches focus on different aspects, the three are at the same time complements. The 'new' theories of growth endogenize technological change and as such interlink technological change with macroeconomic growth. However, the way technological change is described is strongly simplistic and the economy investigated is formulated in an a-spatial model. On the other hand, systems of innovation frameworks are very detailed with respect to the innovation process but say nothing about macroeconomic growth. However, the spatial dimension has been introduced into the framework in the recently developed 'regional innovation systems' studies (Braczyk et al., 1998).

The idea behind the innovation systems approach is quite simple but extremely appealing. According to this, in most cases, innovation is a result of a collective process and this process is shaped in a systematic manner. The elements of the system are innovating firms and firms in related and connected industries (suppliers, buyers), private and public research laboratories, universities, supporting business services (such as legal or technical services), financial institutions (especially venture capital) and the government. These elements are interconnected by innovation-related linkages where these linkages represent knowledge flows among them. Linkages can be informal in nature (occasional meetings in conferences, social events etc.) or they can also be definitely formal (contracted research, collaborative product development etc.). The effectiveness (i.e. productivity in terms of number of innovations) of the system is determined by both the knowledge already accumulated by the actors and the level of their interconnectedness (i.e. the intensity of knowledge flows). Ability and motivations for interactions are shaped largely by traditions, social norms, values and the countries' legal systems.

New economic geography models investigate general equilibrium in a spatial setting (Krugman, 1991). This means that they provide explanations not just for the determination of equilibrium prices, incomes and quantities in each market, but also for the development of the particular geographical structure of the economy. In other words, new economic geography derives economic and spatial equilibrium simultaneously (Fujita et al., 1999; Fujita and Thisse, 2002). Spatial equilibrium arises as an outcome of the balance between centripetal forces working towards agglomeration (such as increasing returns to scale, industrial demand, localized knowledge spillovers) and centrifugal forces promoting dispersion (such as transportation costs). Until the latest developments, new economic geography models did not consider the spatial aspects of economic growth. However, models of technological change follows the same pattern as endogenous growth models, and fail to reach the complexity inherent in innovation systems studies.

As emphasized by Acs and Varga (2002), although each of the above three approaches has its strengths and weaknesses, each could serve to create the building blocks of an explanatory framework of technology-led economic growth. The three approaches suggest that a specific combination of the Krugmanian theory of initial conditions for spatial concentration of economic activities with the Romerian theory of endogenous economic growth, complemented with a systematic representation of interactions among the actors of Nelson's innovation system, could be a way of developing an appropriate model of technology-led regional economic development.

Following Acs and Varga (2002), Varga (2006) develops an empirical modeling framework of geographical growth explanation. This framework is the spatial extension of the endogenous growth model in Romer (1990) and it integrates elements of the innovation systems and the new economic geography literature. For a more formal treatment, Varga (2006) applies the generalized version of the Romer (1990) equation of macroeconomic level knowledge production developed in Jones (1995):[2]

$$dA = \delta\, H_{\mathrm{A}}{}^{\lambda}\, A^{\varphi} \qquad (15.5)$$

where H_A stands for human capital in the research sector working on knowledge production (operationalized by the number of researchers), A is the total stock of technological knowledge available at a certain point in time, whereas dA is the change in technological knowledge resulted from private efforts to invest in R&D. δ, λ and φ are parameters.

Technological change is generated by research, and its extent depends on the number of researchers involved in knowledge creation (H_A). However, their efficiency is directly related to the total stock of already available knowledge (A). Knowledge spillovers are central to the growth process: the higher A is, the larger the change in technology produced by the same number of researchers. Thus macroeconomic growth is strongly related to knowledge spillovers.

Parameters in the Romer knowledge production function play a decisive role in the effectiveness of macro-level knowledge production. The same number of researchers with a similar value of A can raise the level of already existing technological knowledge with significant differences depending on the size of the parameters. First, consider δ ($0 < \delta < 1$), which is the research productivity parameter. The larger δ, the more efficient H_A is in producing economically useful new knowledge.

The size of φ reflects the extent to which the total stock of previously established knowledge impacts knowledge production. Given that A stands for the level of codified knowledge (available in books, scientific papers or patent documentations), φ is the parameter of codified knowledge spillovers. The size of φ reflects the portion of A that spills over and, as such, its value largely influences the effectiveness of research in generating new technologies.

λ is the research spillover parameter. A larger λ indicates a stronger impact on technological change with the same number of researchers. In contrast to φ and δ, which are determined primarily in the research sector and as such their values are exogenous to the economy, λ is endogenous. Its value reflects the diffusion of (codified and tacit) knowledge accumulated by researchers. Technological diffusion depends on three interactions: first, on the intensity of interactions among researchers (H_A); second, on the quality of public research, and the extent to which the private research sector is connected to it (especially to universities) by formal and informal linkages; and third, on the development level of supporting/connected industries and business services, and the integration of innovating firms into the system. The extensive innovation systems literature evidences that the same number of researchers contribute to different efficiencies depending on the development of the system. In the Romer equation, this is reflected in the size of λ.

Within the JFV framework, a series of papers demonstrates that a significant fraction of knowledge spillovers is bounded spatially. These findings imply that the geographic structure of R&D is a determinant of technological change and ultimately economic growth. *Ceteris paribus*, in an economy where R&D institutions are highly concentrated, intensive knowledge spillovers will result in a higher level of innovation than in a system where research is more evenly distributed over space. Thus λ is also sensitive to the spatial structure of H_A. Even with the same number of researchers, λ can have different values depending on the extent that R&D is spatially concentrated.

Finally, λ depends on the interaction of researchers and entrepreneurs. The distribution of entrepreneurs is also not even over space. The more entrepreneurs are concentrated regionally, where knowledge is produced, the greater the impact of knowledge spillovers on economic growth.

A KNOWLEDGE SPILLOVER THEORY OF ENTREPRENEURSHIP

In this section, the JFV model of knowledge spillovers is extended by Acs and Audretsch, who develop the knowledge spillover theory of entrepreneurship in order to answer the question, 'What is the conduit by which knowledge spillovers occur?' As a first step in this direction, the theory incorporates two of the above contributions to the literature: new growth theory (Romer, 1990) and the new economics of innovation (Nelson, 1993) to explain how entrepreneurship facilitates the spillover of knowledge.

A modern synthesis of the entrepreneur is someone who specializes in making judgmental decisions about the coordination of scarce resources (Lazear, 2005). In this definition, the term 'someone' emphasizes that the entrepreneur is an individual. Judgmental decisions are decisions for which no obvious correct procedure exists – a judgmental decision cannot be made simply by plugging available numbers into a scientific formula and acting based on the resulting number. In this framework, entrepreneurial activity depends upon the interaction between the characteristics of opportunity and the characteristics of the people who exploit them. Since discovery is a cognitive process, it can take place only at the individual level. Individuals, whether working in an existing organization or unemployed, are the entities discovering opportunities. The organizations employing people are inanimate and cannot engage in discovery. Therefore any explanation for the mode of opportunity discovery must be based on choices made by individuals about how they would like to exploit the opportunity that they have discovered (Hayek, 1937).

So where do opportunities come from? Today we know that the technology opportunity set is endogenously created by investments in new knowledge. The new growth theory, formalized by Romer (1986), assumes that firms exist exogenously and then engage in the pursuit of new economic knowledge as input into the process of generating endogenous growth. Technological change plays a central role in the explanation of economic growth, since on the steady state growth path the rate of per capita GDP growth equals the rate of technological change.

However, not only does new knowledge contribute to technological change; it also creates opportunities for use by third-party firms, often entrepreneurial startups (Shane, 2001). The creation of new knowledge gives rise to new opportunities through knowledge spillovers; therefore entrepreneurial activity does not involve simply the arbitrage of opportunities (Kirzner, 1973) but also the exploitation of new opportunities created but not appropriated by incumbent organizations (Hellmann, 2007). Thus, while the entrepreneurship literature considers opportunity to exist exogenously, in the new economic growth literature, opportunities are endogenously created through the purposeful investment in new knowledge. The theory as suggested by Audretsch (1995, p. 48) 'proposes shifting the unit of observation away from exogenously assumed firms to individuals – agents confronted with new knowledge and the decision whether and how to act upon that new knowledge'.

The theory relaxes two central (and unrealistic) assumptions of the endogenous growth model to develop a theory that improves the microeconomic foundations of endogenous growth theory (Acs et al., 2009). The first is that knowledge is automatically equated with economic knowledge. In fact, as Arrow (1962) emphasized, knowledge is inherently different from the traditional factors of production, resulting in a gap between knowledge (K) and what he called economic knowledge (K^c). The second involves the assumed spillover of knowledge. The existence of the factor of knowledge is equated with its automatic spillover, yielding endogenous growth. In the knowledge spillover theory of entrepreneurship, institutions impose a filter between new knowledge and economic knowledge ($0 < K^c / K < 1$) that results in a lower level of knowledge spillovers.

The model is one where new product innovations can come either from incumbent organizations or from entrepreneurial startups (Schumpeter, 1934). According to Baumol (2004, p. 9),

> the bulk of private R&D spending is shown to come from a tiny number of very large firms. Yet, the revolutionary breakthroughs continue to come predominantly from small entrepreneurial enterprises, with large industry providing streams of incremental improvements that also add up to major contributions.

We can think of incumbent firms that rely on the flow of knowledge to innovate as focusing on incremental innovation, i.e. product improvements (Acs and Audretsch, 1988). Entrepreneurial startups that have access to knowledge spillovers from the stock of knowledge and entrepreneurial talent are more likely to be engaged in radical innovation that leads to new industries or completely replace existing products (Acs et al., 1994). Startups play a major role in radical innovations such as software, semiconductors, biotechnology (Zucker et al., 1998) and the information and communications technologies (Jorgenson, 2001). The presence of these activities is especially important at the early stages of the life cycle when technology is still fluid.

Equation (15.6) suggests that entrepreneurial startups (E) will be a function of the difference between expected profits (π^*) minus wages (w). Expected profits are conditioned by the knowledge stock (K) that positively affects startups and is negatively conditioned by knowledge commercialized by incumbent firms. Yet a rich literature suggests that there is a compelling array of financial, institutional and individual barriers to entrepreneurship, which results in a modification of the entrepreneurial choice equation:

$$E = \gamma\ (\pi^*\ (K^\xi) - w)/\beta \tag{15.6}$$

where β represents those institutional and individual barriers to entrepreneurship, spanning factors such as risk aversion, financial constraints, and legal and regulatory restrictions (Acemoglu et al., 2004). The existence of such barriers explains why economic agents might choose not to enter into entrepreneurship, even when confronted with knowledge that would otherwise generate a potentially profitable opportunity. Thus this mode shows how local differences in knowledge stocks, the presence of large firms as deterrents to knowledge exploitation, and an entrepreneurial culture might explain regional variations in the rates of entrepreneurial activity. The primary theoretical predictions of the model are:

- an increase in the stock of knowledge positively affects the level of entrepreneurship;
- the more efficient incumbents are at exploiting knowledge flows, the smaller the effect of new knowledge on entrepreneurship; and
- entrepreneurial activities decrease in the face of higher regulations, administrative barriers and governmental market intervention.

Thus entrepreneurship becomes central to generating economic growth by serving as a conduit, albeit not the sole conduit, by which knowledge created by incumbent organizations spills over to agents who endogenously create new firms. The theory is actually a theory of endogenous entrepreneurship, where entrepreneurship is a response to opportunities created by investments in new knowledge that was not commercialized by incumbent firms. The theory suggests that, *ceteris paribus*, entrepreneurial activity will tend to be greater in contexts where investments in new knowledge are relatively high, since the startups will benefit from knowledge that spills over from the source actually producing that new knowledge. In a low-knowledge context, the lack of new ideas will not generate entrepreneurial opportunities based on potential knowledge spillovers. A series of studies links entrepreneurship and economic growth at the regional level (Acs and Armington, 2006; Audretsch et al., 2006) and at the national level (Acs et al., 2009), finding that entrepreneurship does in fact offer an explanation for how knowledge spillovers occur.

Acs and Varga (2005) empirically test the theory within the JFV framework. They build their modeling approach on the interpretation of the Romerian equation (equation 15.5) presented earlier. They start with the assumption that the value of λ bears the influence of the level of entrepreneurship because the value of new economic knowledge is uncertain. While most R&D is carried out in large firms and universities, this does not mean that the individuals who discover the opportunity will carry out the subsequent exploitation. An implication of the theory of firm selection is that new firms may enter an industry in large numbers to exploit knowledge spillovers. The higher the rate of start-ups, the greater should be the value of λ because of knowledge spillovers.

The empirical model in which the parameter λ in equation (15.5) is endogenized has the following form:

$$\log(NK) = \delta + \lambda\log(H) + \varphi\log(A) + \varepsilon \tag{15.7}$$

$$\lambda = (\beta_1 + \beta_2\log(ENTR) + \beta_3\log(AGGL) \tag{15.8}$$

where *NK* stands for new knowledge (i.e. the change in *A*), *ENTR* is entrepreneurship, *AGGL* is agglomeration, *A* is the set of publicly available scientific–technological knowledge and ε is stochastic error term. Insertion of (15.7) into (15.8) results in the following estimated equation:

$$\log(NK) = \delta + \beta_1\log(H) + \beta_2\log(ENTR)\log(H) + \beta_3\log(AGGL)\log(H)$$
$$+ \varphi\log(A) + \varepsilon \tag{15.9}$$

In equation (15.9), the estimated value of the parameter β_2 measures the extent to which research interacted with entrepreneurship contributes to knowledge spillovers. Applied to European data, Acs and Varga (2005) find a statistically significant value of β_2 that is taken as evidence supporting the knowledge spillover theory of entrepreneurship.

AGGLOMERATION: THE FINAL FRONTIER

The JFV model is extendable for empirically testing agglomeration effects in knowledge spillovers. Agglomeration forces are crucial in technological change, and as such in economic growth explanation. Varga (2006) points out that in equation (15.5) the size of λ is also influenced by agglomeration. Insights from the new economic geography can help explain the dynamic effects of the spatial structure of R&D on macroeconomic growth (Baldwin and Forslid, 2000; Fujita and Thisse, 2002; Baldwin et al., 2003). If spatial proximity to other research labs, universities, firms and business services matters in innovation, firms are motivated to locate R&D laboratories in those regions where actors of the system of innovation are already agglomerated in order to reduce innovation costs.

Thus spatial concentration of the system of innovation is a source of positive externalities and, as such, these externalities (as centrifugal forces in R&D location) determine the strength of the cumulative process that leads to a particular spatial economic structure. However, agglomeration effects can be negative as well. Increasing housing costs and travel time make innovation more expensive and might motivate labs to move out of the region. The actual balance between centrifugal and centripetal forces determines the geographical structure of the system of innovation. Through determining the size of λ in equation (15.5), this also influences the rate of technological progress (dA/A) and, eventually, the macroeconomic growth rate (dy/y).

Within the JFV framework Varga (2000, 2001) estimates the magnitude of agglomeration effects. Based on a data set of 125 US metropolitan areas, he finds that spatial concentration of high-tech production and business services has a definite positive relationship with the intensity of local academic knowledge transfers. Increasing returns resulting from the spatial concentration of economic activities is clearly demonstrated in the study. It is shown that the same amount of local expenditures on university research yields dramatically different levels of innovation output depending on the concentration of economic activities in the metropolitan area. A critical mass of agglomeration is found necessary for regions to experience substantial local economic effects of academic research spending. This critical mass is characterized by a city population of around 3 million, employment in high-tech production facilities and business service firms about 160 000 and 4000, respectively. In Varga (2001), agglomeration effects in university knowledge spillovers for two 'high-tech' sectors (electronics and instruments) are also demonstrated.

How can the JFV framework contribute to study empirically the dynamism of agglomeration (i.e. the dynamism of λ) described in detail by the new economic geography? To model empirically the effects of centripetal and centrifugal forces on spatial structure, researchers develop spatial computable general equilibrium (SCGE) models. These models are empirical counterparts of the new economic geography and are extremely powerful tools for explaining spatial distribution of economic activities under different starting assumptions.

Now it is technically possible to integrate the JFV approach into SCGE modeling in order to study the dynamic effects of knowledge spillovers on geography, technological change and growth. With this step the JFV model becomes a crucial bridge between academic research on the geography of innovation and policy analysis for studying different scenarios of economic development. Varga (2008) demonstrates that incorporating the lessons of the JFV framework into development policy analysis opens up the possibility of building 'new-generation models' with such simulations where regional, interregional and macro effects of different policy scenarios can be studied and compared with each other. The GMR-Hungary model (Varga, 2007) is the first one in this field.

PUBLIC POLICY

Policy-makers are interested in promoting economic growth at the national and the regional level. Politicians look to academia to help them understand the process of economic development and inform their decisions. Academics long ago identified technical change through innovation as a key process for generating long-term stable economic growth. However, that begs the question, 'What causes innovation in a region or economy?' (Acs and Sanders, 2007).

In accordance with the evidence, the entrepreneur is the agent with whom the buck stops. The creation of the knowledge he commercializes is not (necessarily) motivated by the rents that the entrepreneur receives for commercialization. Rents reward the act of commercialization, and as such should not be destroyed, to enhance static efficiency. However, the claim to these rents should also not be transferred to the generators of knowledge that may have had no intent of commercializing and/or require no incentive to create such knowledge in the first place.[3] It is not the generation of new knowledge that is valuable to society at large, but rather its utilization and subsequent economic growth. Knowledge creation, of course, is a necessary but insufficient condition for innovation and growth, and creation without implementation is clearly a waste of resources. We argue, therefore, that policy-makers should stop and think about the bottlenecks in the innovative process before committing large amounts of public money and/or entitlements to profits and rents to the (formal) knowledge generation process.

These results also carry over to the regional level if considering the impact of limited geographical labor mobility, transport costs and communication costs. As the knowledge spillovers that drive economic growth are likely to be regionalized, regional policies should aim to facilitate spillovers. A first requirement is that sufficient resources are available for both knowledge creation and knowledge commercialization. And as entrepreneurial talent is a key resource in the innovation chain, regional policies should try to develop it. Moreover, the impediments to knowledge spillovers from creators to commercializers deserve attention. Legal impediments such as non-competition clauses in labor contracts should be abandoned. By investing in physical and communication infrastructures, and by stimulating or enabling the exchange of knowledge, local and regional governments can support the entire innovation chain. Direct support to new entrants or R&D should be given only as long as that does not reduce the incentives to create or commercialize new knowledge.

The model outlined in this chapter has important policy implications at the aggregate and regional level, but also raises important questions. The presence of knowledge spillovers is well documented in the literature. But the exact channels through which such spillovers arise is a challenging arena for further research. The three propositions predicting regional clustering are empirically indistinguishable in most studies due to data availability issues. The detailed case studies by Klepper (2008) provide support for the first channel that was identified with evidence on importance of physical support infrastructure. Florida (2003) presents evidence in support of the third channel we have discussed, but, to our knowledge, studies that try to distinguish between them have not yet been done. In addition, at the aggregate level, the theory and its underlying assumptions require further empirical scrutiny. The available evidence supports the claim that knowledge spillovers are important for (regional) economic growth but much more can be done to test the model predictions. This empirical research agenda will, it is hoped, inspire other researchers.

CONCLUSIONS

In this review, the Jaffe–Feldman–Varga model is introduced and an assessment as to its relevance for economics research is made. It is highlighted that this approach has become a widely applied tool for testing the spatial extent of knowledge spillovers in different countries, different sectors and at different spatial scales. In addition, this model became a workhorse of empirical studies of entrepreneurship, agglomeration and growth. The JFV approach has also proven to become a crucial element in 'new generation development policy modeling'. Thus the JFV model of knowledge spillovers and its extensions offer an avenue to re-explain the mechanism by which knowledge spillovers operate and open the door for a new understanding of regional and macroeconomic development. If this indeed happens, we would have experienced a paradigm shift in economic science.

NOTES

1. When models are estimated for cross-sectional data on neighboring spatial units, the lack of independence across these units (or the presence of spatial autocorrelation) can cause serious problems of model misspecification when ignored (Anselin, 1988). The methodology of spatial econometrics consists of testing for the potential presence of these misspecifications and of using the proper estimators for models that incorporate the spatial dependence explicitly (for a recent review, see Anselin, 2001).
2. The functional form corresponds to the Jones (1995) version; however, the interpretation of λ and φ is different in Varga (2006).
3. This may well be the effect of stronger patent and IPR protection.

REFERENCES

Acemoglu, D., S. Johnson and J. Robinson (2004), 'Institutions as the fundamental cause of long-run growth', in Philippe Aghion and Steven Durlauf (eds), *Handbook of Economic Growth*, New York: Elsevier North Holland, Vol. 1, pp. 405–72.
Acs, Z.J. and C. Armington (eds) (2006), *Entrepreneurship, Geography and American Economic Growth*, Cambridge, UK: Cambridge University Press.
Acs, Z.J. and D.B. Audretsch (1988), 'Innovation in large and small firms: an empirical analysis', *The American Economic Review*, **78** (4), 678–90.
Acs, Z.J. and D.B. Audretsch (1989), 'Patents as a measure of innovative activity', *Kyklos*, **42** (2), 171–80.
Acs, Z.J and M. Sanders (2008), 'Intellectual property and the knowledge spillover theory of entrepreneurship', Jena Economic Research Papers No. 2008-069, Max Planck Institute of Economics, Jena.
Acs, Z.J. and A. Varga (2002), 'Geography, endogenous growth and innovation', *International Regional Science Review*, **25** (1), 132–48.
Acs, Z.J. and A. Varga (2005), 'Entrepreneurship, agglomeration and technological change', *Small Business Economics*, **24** (3), 323–34.
Acs, Z.J., L. Anselin and A. Varga (2002), 'Patents and innovation counts as measures of regional production of new knowledge', *Research Policy*, **31** (7), 1069–85.
Acs, Z.J., D.B. Audretsch and M.P. Feldman (1992), 'Real effects of academic research: comment', *American Economic Review*, **82** (1), 363–7.
Acs, Z.J., D.B. Audretsch and M. P. Feldman (1994), 'R&D spillovers and recipient firm size', *Review of Economic Statistics*, **76** (2), 336–40.
Acs, Z.J., P. Braunerhjelm, D.B. Audretsch and B. Carlsson (2009), 'The knowledge spillover theory of entrepreneurship', *Small Business Economics*, **32** (1), 15–30.
Anselin, L. (ed.) (1988), *Spatial Econometrics: Methods and Models*, Dordrecht: Kluwer Academic Publishers.
Anselin, L. (2001), 'Spatial econometrics', in B.H. Baltagi (ed.), *A Companion to Theoretical Econometrics*, Oxford: Basil Blackwell, pp. 310–30.
Anselin, L., A. Varga and Z.J. Acs (1997), 'Local geographic spillovers between university research and high technology innovation', *Journal of Urban Economics*, **42** (1), 422–48.
Anselin, L., A. Varga and Z.J. Acs (2000a), 'Geographic and sectoral characteristics of academic knowledge externalities', *Papers in Regional Science*, **79** (4), 435–43.
Anselin, L., A. Varga and Z.J. Acs (2000b), 'Geographic spillovers and university research: a spatial econometric perspective', *Growth and Change*, **31** (4), 501–15.
Arrow, K.J. (1962), 'Economic welfare and the allocation of resources for invention', in R. Nelson (ed.), *The Rate and Direction of Inventive Activity: Economic and Social Factors*, Princeton, NJ: Princeton University Press, pp. 609–25.
Audretsch, D.B. (ed.) (1995), *Innovation and Industry Evolution*, Cambridge, MA: MIT Press.
Audretsch, D.B. and M.P. Feldman (1996), 'R&D spillovers and the geography of innovation and production', *American Economic Review*, **86** (3), 630–40.
Audretsch, D.B., M.C. Keilbach and E.E. Lehmann (eds) (2006), *Entrepreneurship and Economic Growth*, Oxford: Oxford University Press.

Baldwin, R.E. and R. Forslid (2000), 'The core–periphery model and endogenous growth: stabilizing and destabilizing integration', *Economica*, **67**, 307–24.

Baldwin, R., R. Forslid, P. Martin, G. Ottaviano and F. Robert-Nicoud (eds) (2003), *Economic Geography and Public Policy*, Princeton, NJ: Princeton University Press.

Baumol, W.J. (2004), 'Entrepreneurial enterprises, large established firms and other components of the free-market growth machine', *Small Business Economics*, **23** (1), 9–21.

Braczyk, H.J., P. Cooke and M. Heidenreich (eds) (1998), *Regional Innovation Systems: The Role of Governances in a Globalized World*, London: UCL Press.

Clark, G.L., M.P. Feldman and M.S. Gertler (eds) (2003), *The Oxford Handbook of Economic Geography*, Oxford: Oxford University Press.

Feldman, M.P. (ed.) (1994), *The Geography of Innovation*, Dordrecht: Kluwer Academic Publishers.

Feldman, M.P. and R. Florida (1994), 'The geographic sources of innovation: technological infrastructure and product innovation in the United States', *Annals of the Association of American Geographers*, **84** (2), 210–29.

Feldman, M.P. and D.B. Audretsch (1999), 'Innovation in cities: science-based diversity, specialization and localized competition', *European Economic Review*, **43** (2), 409–29.

Florida, R. (2003), *The Rise of the Creative Class*, New York: Basic Books.

Fujita, M., P. Krugman and A.J. Venables (eds) (1999), *The Spatial Economy*, Cambridge, MA: MIT Press.

Fujita, M and J.F. Thisse (eds) (2002), *Economics of Agglomeration. Cities, Industrial Location, and Regional Growth*, Cambridge, MA and London: Cambridge University Press.

Griliches, Z. (1979), 'Issues in assessing the contribution of research and development to productivity growth', *The Bell Journal of Economics*, **10** (1), 92–116.

Hayek, Frederick A. von (1937), 'Economics and knowledge: presidential address to the London Economic Club', *Economica* (New Series), **4**, 33–54.

Hellmann, T. (2007), 'When do employees become entrepreneurs?', *Management Science*, **53** (6), 919–33.

Jaffe, A.B. (1989), 'The real effects of academic research', *American Economic Review*, **79** (5), 957–70.

Jaffe, A.B., M. Trajtenberg and R. Henderson (1993), 'Geography, location of knowledge spillovers as evidence of patent citations', *Quarterly Journal of Economics*, **108** (3), 577–98.

Jaffe, A.B. and M. Trajtenberg (eds) (2002), *Patents, Citations and Innovations: A Window on the Knowledge Economy*, Cambridge, MA: MIT Press.

Jaffe, A.B., M. Trajtenberg and R. Henderson (2005), 'Patent citations and the geography of knowledge spillovers: a reassessment: comment', *American Economic Review*, **95** (1), 461–4.

Jones, C.I. (1995), 'R&D based models of economic growth', *Journal of Political Economy*, **103** (4), 759–84.

Jorgenson, D.W. (2001), 'Information technology and the U.S. economy', *American Economic Review*, **91** (1), 1–32.

Kirzner, Israel M. (ed.) (1973), *Competition and Entrepreneurship*, Chicago, IL: University of Chicago Press.

Klepper, S. (2008), 'Silicon Valley, a chip off the old Detroit bloc', in Z.J. Acs, D.B. Audretsch and R.J. Strom (eds), *Entrepreneurship, Growth, and Public Policy*, Cambridge: Cambridge University Press, pp. 79–118.

Krugman, P. (1991), 'Increasing returns and economic geography', *Journal of Political Economy*, **99** (3), 483–99.

Lazear, E.P. (2005), 'Entrepreneurship', *Journal of Labor Economics*, **23** (4), 649–80.

Nelson, R.R. (ed.) (1993), *National Innovation Systems: A Comparative Analysis*, New York: Oxford University Press.

Romer, P. (1986), 'Increasing returns and long-run growth', *Journal of Political Economy*, **94** (5), 1002–37.

Romer, P. (1990), 'Endogenous technological change', *Journal of Political Economy*, **98** (5), 71–102.

Schumpeter, J.A. (ed.) (1911) [1934], *The Theory of Economic Development: An Inquiry into Profits, Capital, Credit, Interest and the Business Cycle*, Cambridge, MA: Harvard University Press.

Shane, S. (2001), 'Technological opportunities and new firm creation', *Management Science*, **47** (2), 205–20.

Thompson, P. and M. Fox-Kean (2005a), 'Patent citations and the geography of knowledge spillovers: a reassessment', *American Economic Review*, **95** (1), 450–60.

Thompson, P and M. Fox-Kean (2005b), 'Patent citations and the geography of knowledge spillovers: a reassessment: reply', *American Economic Review*, **95** (1), 465–6.

Varga, A. (ed.) (1998), *University Research and Regional Innovation: A Spatial Econometric Analysis of Academic Technology Transfers*, Boston, MA: Kluwer Academic Publishers.

Varga, A. (2000), 'Local academic knowledge transfers and the concentration of economic activity', *Journal of Regional Science*, **40** (2), 289–309.

Varga, A. (2001), 'Universities and regional economic development: does agglomeration matter?', in B. Johansson, C. Karlsson and R. Stough (eds), *Theories of Endogenous Regional Growth: Lessons for Regional Policies*, Berlin: Springer, pp. 345–67.

Varga, A. (2006), 'The spatial dimension of innovation and growth: empirical research methodology and policy analysis', *European Planning Studies*, **14** (9), 1171–86.

Varga, A. (2007), 'GMR-HUNGARY: a complex macro-regional model for the analysis of development policy impacts on the Hungarian economy', Final Report, Project No. NFH 370/2005.

Varga, A. (2008), 'From the geography of innovation to development policy analysis: the GMR-approach', *Annals of Economics and Statistics*, **87** (12), 83–101.

Zucker, L.G., M.R. Darby and M.B. Brewer (1998), 'Intellectual human capital and the birth of U.S. biotechnology enterprises', *American Economic Review*, **88** (1), 290–306.

16 Knowledge spillover entrepreneurship, innovation and economic growth
David B. Audretsch and Max Keilbach

INTRODUCTION

Where do new opportunities come from and what is the response of decision-makers when confronted by such new opportunities? The disparate approaches pursued to answer these questions distinguish the literature on entrepreneurship from that on firm innovation. The model of the knowledge production function of the firm has assumed the firm to be exogenous, while opportunities are endogenously created through purposeful investments in the creation of new knowledge, such as expenditures on R&D and augmentation of human capital.

By contrast, in the entrepreneurship literature the opportunities are generally viewed as exogenous but the startup of the new firm is endogenous to characteristics specific to the individual. The focus of the entrepreneurship literature in general, and entrepreneurship theory in particular, has been on the cognitive process by which individuals recognize entrepreneurial opportunities and then decide to attempt to actualize them through the process of starting a new business or organization. This approach has typically taken the opportunities as given, and focused instead on differences across individual-specific characteristics, traits and conditions to explain variations in entrepreneurial behavior.

The purpose of this chapter is to reconcile these two disparate literatures on entrepreneurship and firm strategy. We do this by considering entrepreneurship to be endogenous – not just to differences in individual characteristics, but rather to differences in the context in which a given individual, with an endowment of personal characteristics, propensities and capabilities, finds herself.

We do not contest the validity of the pervasive entrepreneurship literature identifying individual specific characteristics as shaping the decision to become an entrepreneur. What we do propose, however, is that such differences in the contexts in which any given individual finds herself might also influence the entrepreneurial decision.

Rather than taking entrepreneurial opportunity as exogenous, this chapter places it at the center of attention by making it endogenous. Entrepreneurial opportunity is posited to be greater in contexts that are rich in knowledge but limited in those contexts with impoverished knowledge. According to the 'endogenous entrepreneurship hypothesis', entrepreneurship is an endogenous response to investments in knowledge made by firms and non-private organizations that do not fully commercialize those new ideas, thus generating opportunities for entrepreneurs. Thus, while most of the literature typically takes entrepreneurial opportunities to be exogenous, this chapter suggests that they are, in fact, endogenous, and systematically created by investments in knowledge.

A summary and conclusions are provided in the last section. In contrast to the prevalent approach in entrepreneurship theory, this chapter concludes that entrepreneurial opportunities are not exogenous but rather systematically generated by investments in ideas and knowledge that cannot be fully appropriated and commercialized by those incumbent firms and organizations creating the new knowledge.

WHERE DOES OPPORTUNITY COME FROM?

The Entrepreneurial Firm

Why do (some) people start firms? This question has been at the heart of considerable research, not just in economics, but throughout the social sciences. Hebert and Link (1989) have identified three distinct intellectual traditions in the development of the entrepreneurship literature. These three traditions can be characterized as the German tradition, based on von Thuenen and Schumpeter, the Chicago tradition, based on Knight and Schultz, and the Austrian tradition, based on von Mises, Kirzner and Shackle.

Stevenson and Jarillo-Mossi (1990) assume that entrepreneurship is an orientation towards opportunity recognition. Central to this research agenda are the questions, 'How do entrepreneurs perceive opportunities and how do these opportunities manifest themselves as being credible versus being an illusion?' Krueger (2003) examines the nature of entrepreneurial thinking, and the cognitive process associated with opportunity identification and the decision to undertake entrepreneurial action. The focal point of this research is on the cognitive process identifying the entrepreneurial opportunity along with the decision to start a new firm. Thus a perceived opportunity and intent to pursue that opportunity are the necessary and sufficient conditions for entrepreneurial activity to take place. The perception of an opportunity is shaped by a sense of the anticipated rewards accruing from and costs of becoming an entrepreneur. Some of the research focuses on the role of personal attitudes and characteristics, such as self-efficacy (the individual's sense of competence), collective efficacy, and social norms. Shane (2000) has identified how prior experience and the ability to apply specific skills influence the perception of future opportunities. The concept of the entrepreneurial decision resulting from the cognitive processes of opportunity recognition and ensuing action is introduced by Shane and Eckhardt (2003) and Shane and Venkataraman (2001). They suggest that an equilibrium view of entrepreneurship stems from the assumption of perfect information. By contrast, imperfect information generates divergences in perceived opportunities across different people. The sources of heterogeneity across individuals include different access to information, as well cognitive abilities, psychological differences, and access to financial and social capital.

It is a virtual consensus that entrepreneurship revolves around the recognition of opportunities and the pursuit of those opportunities (Venkataraman, 1997). Much of the more contemporary thinking about entrepreneurship has focused on the cognitive process by which individuals reach the decision to start a new firm. According to Sarasvathy et al. (2003, p. 142), 'An entrepreurial opportunity consists of a set of ideas, beliefs and actions that enable the creation of future goods and services in the absence of current markets for them.' These authors provide a typology of entrepreneurial opportunities as consisting of opportunity recognition, opportunity discovery and opportunity creation.

In asking why some do it, while others don't, scholars have focused on differences across individuals (Stevenson and Jarillo-Mossi, 1990). As Krueger (2003, p. 105) observes, 'The heart of entrepreneurship is an orientation toward seeing opportunities', which frames the research questions, 'What is the nature of entrepreneurial thinking?', and 'What cognitive phenomena are associated with seeing and acting on opportunities?' The traditional approach to entrepreneurship essentially holds the context constant and then asks how the cognitive process inherent in the entrepreneurial decision varies across different individual characteristics and attributes (Shaver, 2003; McClelland, 1961). As Shane and Eckhardt (2003, p. 187) summarize this literature in introducing the individual-opportunity nexus, 'We discussed the process of opportunity discovery and explained why some actors are more likely to discover a given opportunity than others.' Some of these differences involve the willingness to incur risk, others involve the preference for autonomy and self-direction, while still others involve differential access to scarce and expensive resources, such as financial, human, social and experiential capital. This approach, focusing on individual cognition in the entrepreneurial process, has generated a number of important and valuable insights, such as the contribution made by social networks, education and training, and familial influence. The literature certainly leaves the impression that entrepreneurship is a personal matter largely determined by DNA, familial status and access to crucial resources.

Opportunities Created by the Incumbent Firm

In contrast to the prevalent thinking concerning entrepreneurial startups, the most predominant theory of firm innovation does not assume that opportunities are exogenous to the firm. Rather, innovative opportunities are the result of systematic effort by firms and the result of purposeful efforts to create knowledge and new ideas, and subsequently to appropriate the returns to those investments through commercialization of such investments. Thus, while the entrepreneurship literature has taken entrepreneurial opportunities to be exogenous, the literature on firm innovation and technological change has taken the creation of such innovative opportunities to be endogenous.

The traditional starting point in the literature on innovation and technological change for most theories of innovation has been the firm (Chandler, 1990; Cohen and Levin, 1989; and Griliches, 1979). In such theories firms are exogenous and their performance in generating technological change is endogenous (Cohen and Klepper, 1991, 1992).

The most prevalent model of technological change is the model of the knowledge production function, formalized by Zvi Griliches in 1979. According to this model, incumbent firms engage in the pursuit of new economic knowledge as an input into the process of generating the output of innovative activity. The most important input in this model is new economic knowledge. As Cohen and Klepper (1991, 1992) point out, the greatest source generating new economic knowledge is generally considered to be R&D. Other inputs in the knowledge production function have included measures of human capital, skilled labor and educational levels. Thus the model of the knowledge production function from the literature on innovation and technological change can be represented as

$$I_i = \alpha RD_i^\beta HK_i^\gamma \varepsilon_i \qquad (16.1)$$

where *I* stands for the degree of innovative activity, *RD* represents R&D inputs, and *HK* represents human capital inputs. The unit of observation for estimating the model of the knowledge production function, reflected by the subscript *i*, has been at the level of countries, industries and enterprises.

Thus, in this view of firm innovation, the firm exists exogenously. It undertakes purposeful investments to create knowledge endogenously, which results in the output of innovative activity. Opportunities are not exogenous, but rather the result of purposeful and dedicated investments and efforts by firms to create new (knowledge) opportunities and then to appropriate them through commercializing their innovations.

THE INNOVATION PARADOX

When it came to empirical validation of the model of the knowledge production function, it became clear that measurement issues played a major role. The state of knowledge regarding innovation and technological change has generally been shaped by the nature of the data that were available to scholars for analyses. Such data have always been incomplete and, at best, represented only a proxy measure reflecting some aspect of the process of technological change. Simon Kuznets observed in 1962 that the greatest obstacle to understanding the economic role of technological change was a clear inability of scholars to measure it. More recently, Cohen and Levin (1989, p. 146) warned, 'A fundamental problem in the study of innovation and technical change in industry is the absence of satisfactory measures of new knowledge and its contribution to technological progress. There exists no measure of innovation that permits readily interpretable cross-industry comparisons.'

Measures of technological change have typically involved one of the three major aspects of the innovative process: (1) a measure of the inputs into the innovative process, such as R&D expenditures, or else the share of the labor force accounted for by employees involved in R&D activities; (2) an intermediate output, such as the number of inventions which have been patented; or (3) a direct measure of innovative output.

These three levels of measuring technological change have not been developed and analyzed simultaneously, but have evolved over time, roughly in the order of their presentation. That is, the first attempts to quantify technological change at all generally involved measuring some aspects of inputs into the innovative process (Scherer, 1965b, 1965c, 1967; Grabowski, 1968; Mueller, 1967; and Mansfield, 1968). Measures of R&D inputs – first in terms of employment and later in terms of expenditures – were only introduced on a meaningful basis enabling inter-industry and inter-firm comparisons in the late 1950s and early 1960s.

A clear limitation in using R&D activity as a proxy measure for technological change is that R&D reflects only the resources devoted to producing innovative output, but not the amount of innovative activity actually realized. That is, R&D is an input and not an output in the innovation process. In addition, Kleinknecht (1987, 1989) and Kleinknecht and Verspagen (1989) have systematically shown that R&D measures incorporate only efforts made to generate innovative activity that are undertaken within formal R&D budgets and within formal R&D laboratories. They find that the extent of informal R&D is considerable, particularly in smaller enterprises. And, as Mansfield (1984) points out, not all efforts within a formal R&D laboratory are directed towards generating innovative output in any case. Rather, other types of output, such as imitation and technology transfer, are also common goals in R&D laboratories.

As systematic data measuring the number of inventions patented were made publicly available in the mid-1960s, many scholars interpreted this new measure not only as superior to R&D but also as reflecting innovative output. In fact, the use of patented inventions is not a measure of innovative output, but is rather a type of intermediate output measure. A patent reflects new technical knowledge, but it does not indicate whether this knowledge has a positive economic value. Only those inventions that have been successfully introduced in the market can claim that they are innovations as well.

Empirical estimation of the model of the knowledge production function, represented by equation (16.1), was found to be stronger at broader levels of aggregation such as countries or industries. For example, at the unit of observation of countries, the empirical evidence (Griliches, 1984) clearly supported the existence of the knowledge production function. This is intuitively understandable, because the most innovative countries are those with the greatest investments in R&D. Less innovative output is associated with developing countries, which are characterized by a paucity of new economic knowledge.

Similarly, the model of the knowledge production function was found to be empirically corroborated at the level of the industry (Scherer, 1982b; Griliches, 1984). Again, this seems obvious, as the most innovative industries also tend to be characterized by considerable investments in R&D and new economic knowledge. Not only are industries such as computers, pharmaceuticals and instruments high in R&D inputs that generate new economic knowledge, but also in terms of innovative outputs (Scherer, 1983; Acs and Audretsch, 1990). By contrast, industries with little R&D, such as wood products, textiles and paper, also tend to produce only a negligible amount of innovative output.

Where the relationship became less robust was at the disaggregated microeconomic level of the enterprise, establishment, or even line of business: there is no direct deterministic relationship between knowledge inputs and innovative output. While innovations and inventions are related, they are not identical. The distinction is that an innovation is a new product, process, service or organizational form that is introduced into the market. By contrast, an invention may or may not be introduced into the market.

Besides the fact that many, if not most, patented inventions do not result in an innovation, a second important limitation of patent measures as an indicator of innovative activity is that they do not capture all of the innovations actually made. In fact, many inventions that result in innovations are not patented. The tendency of patented inventions to result in innovations and of innovations to be the result of inventions that were patented combine into what F.M. Scherer (1983) has termed the propensity to patent. It is the uncertainty about the stability of the propensity to patent across enterprises and across industries that casts doubt upon the reliability of patent measures According to Scherer (1983, pp. 107–8),

> The quantity and quality of industry patenting may depend upon chance, how readily a technology lends itself to patent protection, and business decision-makers' varying perceptions of how much advantage they will derive from patent rights. Not much of a systematic nature is known about these phenomena, which can be characterized as differences in the propensity to patent.

Mansfield (1984, p. 462) has explained why the propensity to patent may vary so much across markets:

> The value and cost of individual patents vary enormously within and across industries . . . Many inventions are not patented. And in some industries, like electronics, there is considerable speculation that the patent system is being bypassed to a greater extent than in the past. Some types of technologies are more likely to be patented than others.

The implications are that comparisons between enterprises and across industries may be misleading. According to Cohen and Levin (1989, p. 1063), 'There are significant problems with patent counts as a measure of innovation, some of which affect both within-industry and between-industry comparisons.'

Thus, even as superior sources of patent data were introduced, such as the new measure of patented inventions from the computerization by the US Patent Office, the reliability of these data as measures of innovative activity has been severely challenged. For example, Griliches and Pakes (1980, p. 378) warn that 'patents are a flawed measure (of innovative output); particularly since not all new innovations are patented and since patents differ greatly in their economic impact'. And in addressing the question, 'Patents as indicators of what?', Griliches (1990, p. 1669) concludes:

> Ideally, we might hope patent statistics would provide a measure of the (innovative) output . . . The reality, however, is very far from it. The dream of getting hold of an output indicator of inventive activity is one of the strong motivating forces for economic research in this area.

It was not before well into the 1970s that systematic attempts were made to provide a direct measure of the innovative output. Thus it should be emphasized that the conventional wisdom regarding innovation and technological change was based primarily on the evidence derived from analyzing R&D data, which essentially measure inputs into the process of technological change, and patented inventions, which are a measure of intermediate output at best.

The most ambitious database providing a direct measure of innovative activity is the US Small Business Administration's Innovation Data Base (SBIDB). The database consists of 8074 innovations commercially introduced in the USA in 1982. These data are analyzed by Acs and Audretsch (1987, 1988 and 1990) to determine the relationships between firm size and technological change and market structure and technological change, where a direct rather than indirect measure of innovative activity is used.

The knowledge production function has been found to hold most strongly at broader levels of aggregation. The most innovative countries are those with the greatest investments in R&D. Little innovative output is associated with less developed countries, which are characterized by a paucity of production of new economic knowledge. Similarly, the most innovative industries also tend to be characterized by considerable investments in R&D and new economic knowledge. Industries such as computers, pharmaceuticals and instruments are high in R&D inputs that generate new economic knowledge, but also excel in terms of innovative outputs (Audretsch, 1995). By contrast, industries with little R&D, such as wood products, textiles and paper, also tend to produce only a negligible amount of innovative output. Thus the knowledge production model linking knowledge-generating inputs to outputs certainly holds at the more aggregated levels of economic activity.

Where the relationship becomes less compelling is at the disaggregated microeconomic level of the enterprise, establishment, or even line of business. For example, while Acs and Audretsch (1990) found that the simple correlation between R&D inputs and innovative output was 0.84 for four-digit standard industrial classification (SIC) manufacturing industries in the USA, it was only about half, 0.4, among the largest US corporations.

At the heart of the conventional wisdom has been the widely accepted hypothesis that large enterprises able to exploit at least some market power are the engine of technological change. This view dates back at least to Schumpeter, who in *Capitalism, Socialism and Democracy* (1942, p. 101) argued that, 'The monopolist firm will generate a larger supply of innovations because there are advantages which, though not strictly unattainable on the competitive level of enterprise, are as a matter of fact secured only on the monopoly level.' The Schumpeterian thesis, then, is that large enterprises are uniquely endowed to exploit innovative opportunities. That is, market dominance is a prerequisite to undertaking the risks and uncertainties associated with innovation. It is the possibility of acquiring quasi-rents that serves as the catalyst for large-firm innovation.

In one of the most important studies, Scherer (1982c) used the US Federal Trade Commission's Line of Business Data to estimate the elasticity of R&D spending with respect to firm sales for 196 industries. He found evidence of increasing returns to scale (an elasticity exceeding unity) for about 20 percent of the industries, constant returns to scale for a little less than three-quarters of the industries, and diminishing returns (an elasticity less than unity) in less than 10 percent of the industries.

While the Scherer (1982c) and Soete (1979) studies were restricted to relatively large enterprises, Bound et al. (1984) included a much wider spectrum of firm sizes in their sample of 1492 firms from the 1976 COMPUSTAT data. They found that R&D increases more than proportionately along with firm size for the smaller firms, but that a fairly linear relationship exists for larger firms. Despite the somewhat more ambiguous findings in still other studies (Mansfield, 1981, 1983; Mansfield et al., 1982), the empirical evidence seems to generally support the Schumpeterian hypothesis that research effort is positively associated with firm size.

The studies relating patents to firm size are considerably less ambiguous. Here the findings unequivocally suggest that 'the evidence leans weakly against the Schumpeterian conjecture that the largest sellers are especially fecund sources of patented inventions' (Scherer, 1982d, p. 235). In one of the most important studies, Scherer (1965a) used the *Fortune* annual survey of the 500 largest US industrial corporations. He related the 1955 firm sales to the number of patents in 1959 for 448 firms. Scherer found that the number of patented inventions increases less than proportionately along with firm size. Scherer's results were later confirmed by Bound et al. (1984) in the study mentioned above. Basing their study on 2852 companies and 4553 patenting entities, they determined that the small firms (with less than $10 million in sales) accounted for 4.3 percent of the sales from the entire sample, but 5.7 percent of the patents.

Thus, just as there are persuasive theories defending the original Schumpeterian hypothesis that large corporations are a prerequisite for technological change, there are also substantial theories predicting that small enterprises should have the innovative advantage, at least in certain industries. As described above, the empirical evidence based on the input measure of technological change, R&D, tilts decidedly in favor of the

Schumpeterian hypothesis. However, as also described above, the empirical results are somewhat more ambiguous for the measure of intermediate output – the number of patented inventions. It was not until direct measures of innovative output became available that the full picture of the process of technological change could be obtained.

Using the measure of innovative output from the US Small Business Administration's Innovation Data Base, Acs and Audretsch (1990) show that, in fact, the most innovative US firms are large corporations. Further, the most innovative US corporations also tended to have large R&D laboratories and be R&D-intensive. At first glance, these findings based on direct measures of innovative activity seems to confirm the conventional wisdom. However, in the most innovative four-digit standard industrial classification (SIC) industries, large firms, defined as enterprises with at least 500 employees, contributed more innovations in some instances, while in other industries small firms produced more innovations. For example, in computers and process control instruments small firms contributed the bulk of the innovations. By contrast, in the pharmaceutical preparation and aircraft industries the large firms were much more innovative.

Probably their best measure of innovative activity is the total innovation rate, which is defined as the total number of innovations per thousand employees in each industry. The large-firm innovation rate is defined as the number of innovations made by firms with at least 500 employees, divided by the number of employees (thousands) in large firms. The small-firm innovation rate is analogously defined as the number of innovations contributed by firms with fewer than 500 employees, divided by the number of employees (thousands) in small firms.

The innovation rates, or the number of innovations per thousand employees, have the advantage in that they measure large- and small-firm innovative activity relative to the presence of large and small firms in any given industry. That is, in making a direct comparison between large- and small-firm innovative activity, the absolute number of innovations contributed by large firms and small enterprises is somewhat misleading, since these measures are not standardized by the relative presence of large and small firms in each industry. When a direct comparison is made between the innovative activity of large and small firms, the innovation rates are presumably a more reliable measure of innovative intensity because they are weighted by the relative presence of small and large enterprises in any given industry. Thus, while large firms in manufacturing introduced 2445 innovations in 1982, and small firms contributed slightly fewer, 1954, small-firm employment was only half as great as large-firm employment, yielding an average small-firm innovation rate in manufacturing of 0.309, compared to a large-firm innovation rate of 0.202 (Acs and Audretsch, 1988, 1990).

Thus there is considerable evidence suggesting that, in contrast to the findings for R&D inputs and patented inventions, small enterprises apparently play an important generating innovative activity, at least in certain industries. By relating the innovative output of each firm to its size, it is also possible to shed new light on the Schumpeterian hypothesis. In their 1991 study, Acs and Audretsch find that there is no evidence that increasing returns to R&D expenditures exist in producing innovative output. In fact, with just several exceptions, diminishing returns to R&D are the rule. This study made it possible to resolve the apparent paradox in the literature that R&D inputs increase at more than a proportional rate along with firm size, while the generation of patented inventions does not. That is, while larger firms are observed to undertake a greater effort towards R&D, each additional dollar of R&D is found to yield less in terms of innovative output.

The model of the knowledge production function therefore became less compelling in view of a wave of studies that found that small enterprises were an engine of innovative activity in certain industries. The apparent contradiction between the organizational context of knowledge inputs, principally R&D, and the organizational context of small-firm innovative output resulted in the emergence of what has become known as the 'innovation paradox': either the model of the knowledge production did not hold, at least at the level of the enterprise (for a broad spectrum across the firm-size distribution), or else the appropriate unit of observation had to be reconsidered. In searching for a solution, scholars chose the second interpretation, leading them to look beyond the boundaries of the firm for sources of innovative inputs.

THE KNOWLEDGE SPILLOVER THEORY OF ENTREPRENEURSHIP

The Endogenous Entrepreneurship Hypothesis

Resolution of the 'innovation paradox' came after rethinking not the validity of the model of the knowledge production function, but rather the implicit assumptions of independence and separability underlying the decision-making analytical units of observation – the established incumbent firm and the new entrepreneurial firm. Just as the prevailing theories of entrepreneurship have generally focused on the cognitive process of individuals in making the decision to start a new firm, so that the decision-making criteria are essentially internal to the decision-making unit – in this case the individual – the model of the knowledge production function generally limited the impact of the firm's investments in creating new knowledge to that decision-making unit – in this case the firm.

That these decision-making units – the firm and the individual – might actually not be totally separable and independent, particularly with respect to assessing the outcome of knowledge investments, was first considered by Audretsch (1995), who introduced 'the knowledge spillover theory of entrepreneurship'.

The reason for challenging the assumptions of independence and separability between (potential) entrepreneurs and firms emanates from a fundamental characteristic of knowledge that differentiates it from the more traditional firm resources of physical capital and (unskilled) labor. Arrow (1962) pointed out that knowledge differs from these traditional firm resources due to the greater degree of uncertainty, higher extent of asymmetries, and greater cost of transacting new ideas.

The expected value of any new idea is highly uncertain, and as Arrow pointed out, has a much greater variance than would be associated with the deployment of traditional factors of production. After all, there is relative certainty about what a standard piece of capital equipment can do, or what an (unskilled) worker can contribute to a mass-production assembly line. By contrast, Arrow emphasized that when it comes to innovation, there is uncertainty about whether the new product can be produced, how it can be produced, and whether sufficient demand for that visualized new product might actually materialize.

In addition, new ideas are typically associated with considerable asymmetries. In order to evaluate a proposed new idea concerning a new biotechnology product, the decision-maker might not only need to have a PhD in biotechnology, but also a specialization in the exact scientific area. Such divergences in education, background and experience can result in a divergence in the expected value of a new project or the variance in outcomes antici-pated from pursuing that new idea, both of which can lead to divergences in the recognition and evaluation of opportunities across economic agents and decision-making hierarchies. Such divergences in the valuation of new ideas will become greater if the new idea is not consistent with the core competence and technological trajectory of the incumbent firm.

Thus, because of the conditions inherent in knowledge – high uncertainty, asym-metries and transactions costs – decision-making hierarchies can reach the decision not to pursue and try to commercialize new ideas that individual economic agents, or groups or teams of economic agents, think are potentially valuable and should be pursued. The basic conditions characterizing new knowledge, combined with a broad spectrum of institutions, rules and regulations impose what could be termed 'the knowledge filter'. The knowledge filter is the gap between new knowledge and what Arrow (1962) referred to as economic knowledge or commercialized knowledge. The greater the knowledge filter, the more pronounced the gap between new knowledge and new economic, or commercialized, knowledge.

The knowledge filter is a consequence of the basic conditions inherent in new knowl-edge. Similarly, it is the knowledge filter that creates the opportunity for entrepreneur-ship in the knowledge spillover theory of entrepreneurship. According to this theory, opportunities for entrepreneurship are the duality of the knowledge filter. The higher the knowledge filter, the greater are the divergences in the valuation of new ideas across eco-nomic agents and the decision-making hierarchies of incumbent firms. Entrepreneurial opportunities are generated not just by investments in new knowledge and ideas, but by the propensity for only a distinct subset of those opportunities to be fully pursued by incumbent firms.

Thus, as Audretsch pointed out in 1995, the knowledge theory of entrepreneurship shifts the fundamental decision-making unit of observation in the model of the knowl-edge production function away from exogenously assumed firms to individuals, such as scientists, engineers or other knowledge workers – agents with endowments of new economic knowledge. When the lens is shifted away from the firm to the individual as the relevant unit of observation, the appropriability issue remains, but the question becomes, 'How can economic agents with a given endowment of new knowledge best appropriate the returns from that knowledge?' If the scientist or engineer can pursue the new idea within the organizational structure of the firm developing the knowledge and appropriate roughly the expected value of that knowledge, she has no reason to leave the firm. On the other hand, if he places a greater value on his ideas than does the decision-making bureaucracy of the incumbent firm, he may choose to start a new firm to appropriate the value of his knowledge.

In the knowledge spillover theory of entrepreneurship the knowledge production function is actually reversed. The knowledge is exogenous and embodied in a worker. The firm is created endogenously in the worker's effort to appropriate the value of his knowledge through innovative activity. Typically an employee from an established large corporation, often a scientist or engineer working in a research laboratory, will have an idea for an invention and ultimately for an innovation. Accompanying this potential innovation is an expected net return from the new product. The knowledge worker would expect to be compensated for her potential innovation accordingly. If the company has a different, presumably lower, valuation of the potential innovation, it may decide either not to pursue its development, or that it merits a lower level of compensation than that expected by the employee.

In either case, the knowledge worker will weigh the alternative of starting her own firm. If the gap in the expected return accruing from the potential innovation between the inventor and the corporate decision-maker is sufficiently large, and if the cost of starting a new firm is sufficiently low, the employee may decide to leave the large corporation and establish a new enterprise. Since the knowledge was generated in the established corporation, the new startup is considered to be a spin-off from the existing firm. Such startups typically do not have direct access to a large R&D laboratory. Rather, the entrepreneurial opportunity emanates from the knowledge and experience accrued in the R&D laboratories with their previous employers. Thus the knowledge spillover view of entrepreneurship is actually a theory of endogenous entrepreneurship, where entrepreneurship is an endogenous response to opportunities created by investments in new knowledge in a given context that are not commercialized because of the knowledge filter.

The 'Endogenous Entrepreneurship Hypothesis' posits that entrepreneurship is a response to investments in knowledge and ideas by incumbent organizations that are not fully commercialized by those organizations. Thus those contexts that are richer in knowledge will offer more entreperneurial opportunities and therefore should also endogenously induce more entrepreneurial activity, *ceteris paribus*. By contrast, those contexts that are impoverished in knowledge will offer only meager entrepreneurial opportunities generated by knowledge spillovers, and therefore would endogenously induce less entrepreneurial activity.

But what is the appropriate unit of observation to be used to frame the context and observe the entrepreneurial response to knowledge investments made by incumbent organizations? In his 1995 book, Audretsch proposed using the industry as the context in which knowledge is created, developed, organized and commercialized. The context of an industry was used to resolve the paradox concerning the high innovative output of small enterprises given their low level of knowledge inputs that seemingly contradicted the Griliches model of the firm knowledge production:

> The findings in this book challenge an assumption implicit to the knowledge production function – that firms exist exogenously and then endogenously seek out and apply knowledge inputs to generate innovative output . . . It is the knowledge in the possession of economic agents that is exogenous, and in an effort to appropriate the returns from that knowledge, the spillover of knowledge from its producing entity involves endogenously creating a new firm. (Audretsch, 1995, pp. 179–80)

What is the source of this entrepreneurial knowledge that endogenously generated the startup of new firms? The answer seemed to be through the spillover of knowledge from the source creating it to commercialization via the startup of a new firm:

> How are these small and frequently new firms able to generate innovative output when undertaken a generally negligible amount of investment into knowledge-generating inputs, such as

R&D? One answer is apparently through exploiting knowledge created by expenditures on research in universities and on R&D in large corporations. (Ibid., p. 179)

The empirical evidence supporting the knowledge spillover theory of entrepreneurship was provided by analyzing variations in startup rates across different industries reflecting different underlying knowledge contexts (Audretsch, 1995). In particular, those industries with a greater investment in new knowledge also exhibited higher startup rates, while those industries with less investment in new knowledge exhibited lower startup rates which was interpreted as the mechanism by which knowledge spillovers are transmitted.

In subsequent research, Klepper and Sleeper (2000) showed how spin-offs in the automobile industry exhibited a superior performance when the founder came from a high-performing incumbent firm, as compared to a low-performing incumbent firm, or even from outside of the industry. Klepper interpreted this result as indicating that the experience and ability to absorb human capital within the context of the incumbent firm influenced the subsequent entrepreneurial performance. Similar results were found for Agarwal et al. (forthcoming).

Thus compelling evidence was provided suggesting that entrepreneurship is an endogenous response to the potential for commercializing knowledge that has not been adequately commercialized by the incumbent firms. This involved an organizational dimension involving the mechanism transmitting knowledge spillovers – the startup of new firms.

The Localization Hypothesis

The 'endogeneous entrepreneurship hypothesis' involves the organizational interdependency between entrepreneurial startups and incumbent organizations investing in the creation of new knowledge (Audretsch et al., 2006; Audretsch, 2005). A second hypothesis emerging from the knowledge spillover theory of entrepreneurship, 'The localizational hypothesis', has to do with the location of the entrepreneurial activity.

An important theoretical development is that geography may provide a relevant unit of observation within which knowledge spillovers occur. The theory of localization suggests that because geographic proximity is needed to transmit knowledge, and especially tacit knowledge, knowledge spillovers tend to be localized within a geographic region. The importance of geographic proximity for knowledge spillovers has been supported in a wave of recent empirical studies by Jaffe (1989), Jaffe et al. (1993), Acs, Audretsch and Feldman (1992, 1994), Audretsch and Feldman (1996) and Audretsch and Stephan (1996).

As it became apparent that the firm was not adequate as a unit of analysis for estimating the model of the knowledge production function, scholars began to look for externalities. In refocusing the model of the knowledge production to a spatial unit of observation, scholars confronted two challenges. The first one was theoretical. What was the theoretical basis for knowledge to spill over yet, at the same time, be spatially within some geographic unit of observation? The second challenge involved measurement. How could knowledge spillovers be measured and identified? More than a few scholars heeded Krugman's warning (1991b, p. 53) that empirical measurement of knowledge spillovers would prove to be impossible because 'knowledge flows are invisible, they leave no paper trail by which they may be measured and tracked.'[1]

In confronting the first challenge, which involved developing a theoretical basis for geographically bounded knowledge spillovers, scholars turned to the emerging literature of the new growth theory. In explaining the increased divergence in the distribution of economic activity between countries and regions, Krugman (1991a, 1991b) and Romer (1986) relied on models based on increasing returns to scale in production. By increasing returns, however, Krugman and Romer did not necessarily mean at the level of observation most familiar in the industrial organization literature – the plant, or at least the firm – but rather at the level of a spatially distinguishable unit. In fact, it was assumed that the externalities across firms and even industries yield convexities in production. In particular, Krugman (1991a, 1991b), invoking Marshall (1920), focused on convexities arising from spillovers from (1) a pooled labor market; (2) pecuniary externalities enabling the provision of nontraded inputs to an industry in a greater variety and at lower cost; and (3) information or technological spillovers.

That knowledge spills over was barely disputed. Some 30 years earlier, Arrow (1962) identified externalities associated with knowledge due to its non-exclusive and non-rival use. However, what has been contested is the geographic range of knowledge spillovers: knowledge externalities are so important and forceful that there is no reason that knowledge should stop spilling over just because of borders, such as a city limit, state line, or national boundary. Krugman (1991a, 1991b), and others, did not question the existence or importance of such knowledge spillovers. In fact, they argue that knowledge externalities are so important and forceful that there is no reason for a political boundary to limit the spatial extent of the spillover.

In applying the model of the knowledge production function to spatial units of observation, theories of why knowledge externalities are spatially bounded were needed. Thus it took the development of localization theories explaining not only that knowledge spills over but also why those spillovers decay as they move across geographic space.

Studies identifying the extent of knowledge spillovers are based on the model of the knowledge production function applied at spatial units of observation. In what is generally to be considered the first important study refocusing on the knowledge production function, Jaffe (1989) modified the traditional approach to estimate a model specified for both spatial and product dimensions. Empirical estimation essentially shifted the knowledge production function from the unit of observation of a firm to that of a geographic unit. Implicitly contained within the knowledge production function model is the assumption that innovative activity should take place in those regions where the direct knowledge-generating inputs are the greatest, and where knowledge spillovers are the most prevalent. Jaffe (1989) dealt with the measurement problem raised by Krugman (1991a, 1991b) by linking the patent activity within technologies located within states to knowledge inputs located within the same spatial jurisdiction.

Jaffe (1989) found empirical evidence supporting the notion knowledge spills over for third-party use from university research laboratories as well as industry R&D laboratories. Acs et al. (1992) confirmed that the knowledge production function held at a spatial unit of observation using a direct measure of innovative activity, new product introductions in the market. Feldman (1994) extended the model to consider other knowledge inputs to the commercialization of new products. The results confirmed that the knowledge production function was robust at the geographic level of analysis: the output of innovation is a function of the innovative inputs in that location.

While this literature has identified the important role that knowledge spillovers play, it provides little insight into the questions of why knowledge spills over and how it does so. What happens within the black box of knowledge production is vague and ambiguous at best. The exact links between knowledge sources and the resulting innovative output remain invisible and unknown. None of the above studies suggesting that knowledge spillovers are geographically bounded and localized within spatial proximity to the knowledge source actually identified the actual mechanisms that transmit the knowledge spillover; rather, the spillovers were implicitly assumed to automatically exist, or fall like 'manna from heaven', but only within a geographically bounded spatial area.

One explanation was provided by the knowledge spillover theory of entrepreneurship, which suggests that the startup of a new firm is a response to investments in knowledge and ideas by incumbent organizations that are not fully commercialized by those organizations. Thus those contexts that are richer in knowledge will offer more entrepreneurial opportunities and therefore should also endogenously induce more entrepreneurial activity, *ceteris paribus*. By contrast, those contexts that are impoverished in knowledge will offer only meager entrepreneurial opportunities generated by knowledge spillovers, and therefore would endogenously induce less entrepreneurial activity.

Access to knowledge spillovers requires spatial proximity. While Jaffe (1989) and Audretsch and Feldman (1996) made it clear that spatial proximity is a prerequisite for accessing knowledge spillovers, they provided no insight into the actual mechanism transmitting them. As for the Romer and Lucas models, investment in new knowledge automatically generates knowledge spillovers. Their only additional insight involves the spatial dimension – knowledge spills over but the spillovers are spatially bounded. Since we have just identified one such mechanism by which knowledge spillovers are transmitted – the startup of a new firm – it follows that knowledge spillover entrepreneurship is also spatially bounded in that local access is required to access the knowledge facilitating the entrepreneurial startup:

Localization hypothesis Knowledge spillover entrepreneurship will tend to be spatially located within close geographic proximity to the source of knowledge actually producing that knowledge. Thus, in order to access spillovers, new firm startups will tend to locate close to knowledge sources, such as universities.

Systematic empirical support for both the localization hypothesis as well as the endogeneous entrepreneurship hypothesis is provided by Audretsch et al. (2006), who show that the startup of new knowledge-based and technology firms is geographically constrained within close geographic proximity to knowledge sources. Based on data from Germany in the 1990s, their evidence shows that startup activity tends to cluster geographically around sources of new knowledge, such as R&D investments by firms and research undertaken at universities. Their findings provide compelling support for the Knowledge Spillover Theory of Entrepreneurship in that entrepreneurial activity is systematically greater in locations with a greater investment in knowledge and new ideas.

Similarly, the research laboratories of universities provide a source of innovation-generating knowledge that is available to private enterprises for commercial exploitation.

Jaffe (1989) and Acs et al. (1992), for example, found that the knowledge created in university laboratories 'spills over' to contribute to the generation of commercial innovations by private enterprises. Acs et al. (1994) found persuasive evidence that spillovers from university research contribute more to the innovative activity of small firms than to the innovative activity of large corporations. Similarly, Link and Rees (1990) surveyed 209 innovating firms to examine the relationship between firm size and university research. They found that, in fact, large firms are more active in university-based research. However, small- and medium-sized enterprises apparently are better able to exploit their university-based associations and generate innovations. Link and Rees (1990) conclude that, contrary to the conventional wisdom, diseconomies of scale in producing innovations exist in large firms. They attribute these diseconomies of scale to the 'inherent bureaucratization process which inhibits both innovative activity and the speed with which new inventions move through the corporate system towards the market' (Link and Rees, 1990, p. 25).

A Model

The starting point for models of economic growth in the Solow (1956) tradition is that the rate of technical change, the rate with which new technological knowledge is created, is exogenous. This view has been challenged by the endogenous growth theory (Romer, 1986, 1990; Lucas, 1988). Consider the Romer (1990) growth model. The production function is expressed as

$$Y = K^{\alpha}(AL_Y)^{(1-\alpha)} \tag{16.2}$$

where Y represents economic output, K is the stock of capital, L_Y is the labor force in the production of Y, and A is the stock of knowledge capital. The capital accumulation function is standard from the Solow (1956) model:

$$\dot{K} = s_K Y - \Delta K, \tag{16.3}$$

where s_K is the saving rate and Δ is the depreciation rate of capital. The R&D sector is modeled as

$$\dot{A} = \bar{\delta} L_A \tag{16.4}$$

where $\bar{\delta}$ is the 'discovery rate' of new innovations with

$$\bar{\delta} = \delta L_A^{1-\lambda} A^{\phi} \tag{16.5}$$

L_A denotes the amount of labor active in the generation of new knowledge (such as R&D personnel), λ denotes returns to scale in R&D, and ϕ is a parameter that expresses the intensity of knowledge spillovers. Inserting (16.5) into (16.4), we obtain the rate of creation of new knowledge (the rate of endogenous technical change):

$$\dot{A} = \delta L_A^{\lambda} A^{\phi} \tag{16.6}$$

In the Romer, Lucas and Jones (1995) models, knowledge automatically spills over and is commercialized, reflecting the Arrow observation about the nonexcludability and nonexhaustive properties of new knowledge. Thus investment in R&D and human capital automatically affects output in a multiplicative manner because of their external properties, suggesting that new knowledge, A, is tantamount to commercialized economic knowledge A_c, that is, $A = A_c$.

As we discussed earlier, the emphasis on, or rather assumption about, the nonexcludability property is better suited for information than for knowledge. Information has, by its definition, a very low level of uncertainty, and its value is not greatly influenced or shaped by asymmetries across economic agents possessing that information. Thus information can be characterized as being nonexcludable and nonexhaustive. In contrast, as Arrow points out, there is a gap between new knowledge and what actually becomes commercialized, or new economic knowledge, $A - A_c > 0$. In fact, the knowledge filter is defined as the gap existing between investments in knowledge and the commercialization of knowledge, or economic knowledge. We denote the knowledge filter as θ; hence

$$\theta = A_c/A, \quad \text{with} \quad 0 \leq A_c \leq A \quad \text{hence} \quad \theta \in [0, 1] \tag{16.7}$$

Thus θ denotes the 'permeability' of the knowledge filter. It is the existence of the knowledge filter, or knowledge not commercialized by incumbent enterprises, that generates the entrepreneurial opportunities for commercializing knowledge spillovers. As long as the incumbent enterprises cannot exhaust all of the commercialization opportunities arising from their investments in new knowledge, opportunities will be generated for potential entrepreneurs to commercialize that knowledge by starting a new firm. Thus the actual level of new technological knowledge used by incumbent firms is

$$\dot{A}_c = \theta \cdot \delta L_A^\lambda A^\phi \tag{16.8}$$

Correspondingly, the remaining 'untapped' part $(1 - \theta)$ is opportunities *opp* that can be taken on by new firms. We denote this part entrepreneurial opportunities'. Thus we have

$$\dot{A}_{opp} = (1 - \theta)\dot{A} = (1 - \theta) \cdot \delta L_A^\lambda A^\phi \tag{16.9}$$

The observation that knowledge conditions dictate the relative advantages in benefiting from opportunities arising from investments in knowledge of incumbents versus small and large enterprises is not new. Nelson and Winter (1982) distinguished between two knowledge regimes. What they call the routinized technological regime reflects knowledge conditions where the large incumbent firms have the innovative advantage. In contrast, in the entrepreneurial technological regime, the knowledge conditions bestow an innovative advantage on small enterprises (Winter, 1984).

However, there are two important distinctions to emphasize. The first is the view that, in the entrepreneurial regime, the small firms exist and will commercialize the new knowledge or innovate. In the lens provided by the spillover theory of entrepreneurship, the new firm is endogenously created via entrepreneurship, or the recognition of an opportunity and pursuit by an economic agent (or team of economic agents) to appropriate the value of that knowledge. These knowledge-bearing economic agents use the organizational context of new firm creation to attempt to appropriate their endowments of knowledge.

The second distinction is that the knowledge will be commercialized, either by large or small firms. In the lens provided by the knowledge spillover theory of entrepreneurship, the knowledge filter impedes and preempts at least some of the knowledge spillover and commercialization of knowledge. Only select spillover mechanisms, such as entrepreneurship, can permeate the knowledge filter. But this is not a forgone conclusion; rather, the situation will vary across specific contexts and depends on a broad range of factors, spanning individual characteristics, institutions, culture and laws, and is characterized by what we might call 'entrepreneurship capital'. Thus, to merely explain entrepreneurship as the residual from $\dot{A}_{opp} = \dot{A} - \dot{A}_c$ assumes that all opportunities left uncommercialized will automatically result in the commercialized spillover of knowledge via entrepreneurship.

This was clearly not the case in the former Soviet Union and its Eastern European allies, just as, according to AnnaLee Saxenian, in *Regional Advantage* (1994), it was not the case for Silicon Valley or Route 128. That is, the capacity of each context, or *Standort*, to commercialize the residual investments in knowledge created by the knowledge filter through entrepreneurship is not identical. Rather, it depends on the capacity of that *Standort* to generate an entrepreneurial response that permeates the knowledge filter and creates a conduit for transmitting knowledge spillovers.

Both the West and the former Soviet Union invested in the creation of new knowledge. And both innovated in what Nelson and Winter characterized as the routinized regime. The divergence in growth and economic performance emanated from differences in the knowledge filter and the ability to overcome that knowledge filter. Just as the West proved to have the institutional context to generate entrepreneurial spillovers and commercialize a far greater level of knowledge investment, so, too, as Saxenian documents, the organizational structure and social capital of Silicon Valley provided a more fertile context than Route 128 did for knowledge spillovers through entrepreneurship. Both Silicon Valley and Route 128 had the requisite knowledge inputs to generate innovative output. Saxenian's main conclusion is that the differences between the two *Standorts* that resulted in a greater degree of knowledge spillovers and commercialization in Silicon Valley than in Route 128 were institutional. Thus, just as the knowledge filter should also not be assumed to be automatic, entrepreneurship, whether it emanates from opportunities from knowledge spillovers or from other sources, is the result of a cognitive process made by an individual within the institutional context of a particular *Standort*.

This cognitive process of recognizing and acting on perceived opportunities, emanating from knowledge spillovers as well as other sources, E, is characterized by the model of occupational (or entrepreneurial) choice, where E reflects the decision to become an entrepreneur, π^* is the profit expected from starting a new firm, and w is the anticipated wage that would be earned from employment in an incumbent enterprise:

$$E = f(\pi^* - w) \tag{16.10}$$

But what exactly are the sources of these entrepreneurial opportunities based on expected profits accruing from entrepreneurship? As we said, most of the theoretical and empirical focus has been on characteristics of the individual, such as attitudes towards risk and access to financial capital and social capital. Thus the entrepreneurial opportunities are created by variation in individual characteristics within a context held constant. Entrepreneurial opportunities are generated because individuals are heterogeneous, leading to variation in the ability of individuals to recognize opportunities and their willingness to act upon those opportunities. Thus the focus on entrepreneurship, and why it varies across contexts, or *Standorts*, seemingly leads to the conclusion that individuals must differ across different contexts.

In the view presented here, we invert this analysis. Instead of holding the context constant and asking how individuals endowed with different characteristics will behave differently, we take all of the characteristics of the individual, all of his or her various propensities, proclivities and peculiarities, as given. We let the context, or *Standort*, in which he or she finds herself vary and then ask: holding the (characteristics of the) individual constant, how will behavior change as the context changes?

Of course, guided by the knowledge spillover theory of entrepreneurship, we know that the contextual variation of interest is knowledge. We want to know whether and how, in principle, the same individual(s) with the same attributes, characteristics and proclivities will be influenced in terms of the cognitive process of making the entrepreneurial choice, as the knowledge context differs. In particular, some contexts are rich in knowledge, while others are impoverished. Does the knowledge context alter the cognitive process weighing the entrepreneurial choice?

According to the knowledge spillover theory of entrepreneurship, it does. We certainly do not claim that knowledge spillovers account for all entrepreneurial opportunities, or that any of the existing explanations of entrepreneurship are any less valid. The major contextual variable that has been previously considered is growth, especially unanticipated growth. Hence, we can rewrite equation (16.10) as

$$E = f(\pi^*[g_Y, \dot{A}_{opp}, \theta] - w) \qquad (16.11)$$

which states that the expected profits are based on opportunities that accrue from general economic growth, g_Y, on one hand and from potential knowledge spillovers, $\dot{A}_{opp}$, on the other. Therefore the total amount of entrepreneurship can be decomposed into knowledge spillover entrepreneurship, which is denoted as E^*, and entrepreneurship from rather traditional sources, that is nonknowledge sources, such as growth $\overline{E}$, that is,

$$E = \overline{E} + E^*. \qquad (16.12)$$

Economic growth that is anticipated by incumbent firms will be met by those firms as they invest to expand their capacity to meet expected growth opportunities. If, however, there is any type of constraint in expanding the capacity of incumbent enterprises to meet (unexpected) demand, then growth of GDP, g_Y, will generate entrepreneurial opportunities that have nothing to do with new knowledge, or

$$\overline{E} = f(\pi^*[g_Y] - w) \qquad (16.13)$$

Let us distinguish this type of traditional entrepreneurship from the one based on opportunities from knowledge spillovers. As we claimed, investments in new knowledge in a given context will generate entrepreneurial opportunities. The extent of such entrepreneurial opportunities is shaped by two sources. The first is the amount of new knowledge being produced. The second is the permeability of the knowledge filter, which limits the commercialization of that new knowledge by the incumbent firms. If neither new knowledge nor ideas were being generated, then there would be no spillover opportunities for potential entrepreneurs to consider. There might be entrepreneurship triggered by other factors, but not by knowledge opportunities. Similarly, in the absence of a knowledge filter, all opportunities for appropriating the value of that knowledge would be pursued and commercialized by incumbent firms. In this case, knowledge spillovers would be considerable, just not from entrepreneurship.

Thus two factors shape the relative importance of knowledge spillover entrepreneurship: the amount of investment in creating new knowledge, $\dot{A}$, and the magnitude of the knowledge filter, θ. Thus, knowledge spillover entrepreneurship, E^*, is the attempt to appropriate profit opportunities accruing from the commercialization of knowledge not commercialized by the incumbent firms, or $1 - \theta$:

$$E^* = f(\pi^*[\dot{A}_{opp}, \theta] - w). \tag{16.14}$$

Equation (16.14) implicitly suggests that the only contextual influence on entrepreneurship emanating from knowledge spillovers is the extent of knowledge investments and permeability of the knowledge filter. Such a simple assumption neglects the basic conclusion from Saxenian (1994) that some contexts, such as Boston's Route 128, have institutional and social barriers to entrepreneurship, while other contexts, such as Silicon Valley, have institutions and social networks that promote entrepreneurship. The exact nature of such impediments to entrepreneurship spans a broad spectrum of financial, institutional, and individual characteristics (Acs and Audretsch, 2003). Incorporating such impediments or barriers to entrepreneurship, β, yields

$$E^* = \frac{1}{\beta} f(\pi^*[\dot{A}_{opp}, \theta] - w), \tag{16.15}$$

where β represents those institutional and individual barriers to entrepreneurship, spanning factors such as financing constraints, risk aversion, legal restrictions, bureaucratic and red-tape constraints, labor market rigidities, lack of social acceptance, and so on (Lundström and Stevenson, 2005). Although we do not explicitly specify these individual entrepreneurial barriers, we duly note that they reflect a wide range of institutional and individual characteristics, which, taken together, constitute barriers to entrepreneurship. The existence of such barriers, or a greater value of β, explains why economic agents choose not to become entrepreneurs, even when endowed with knowledge that would otherwise generate a potentially profitable opportunity through entrepreneurship.

Since $E > E^*$, the total amount of entrepreneurial activity exceeds that generated by knowledge spillovers. Thus we also restate equation (16.11):

$$E = \frac{1}{\beta} f(\pi^*[g_Y, \dot{A}_{opp}, \theta] - w) \tag{16.16}$$

Equation (16.16) and the corresponding discussion lead to the following propositions:

Entrepreneurial opportunities: Entrepreneurship will be greater in regions with a greater amount of nonknowledge entrepreneurial opportunities, such as growth.

Barriers to entrepreneurship: Entrepreneurship will be lower in regions burdened with barriers to entrepreneurship.

The Hypotheses

On the basis of the arguments presented in the previous sections, we can derive a number of hypotheses concerning the determinants of entrepreneurship and their impact on economic performance. The first hypothesis to emerge from the knowledge spillover theory of entrepreneurship is the following:

Endogenous entrepreneurship hypothesis: Entrepreneurship will be greater in the presence of higher investments in new knowledge, *ceteris paribus*. Entrepreneurial activity is an endogenous response to higher investments in new knowledge, reflecting greater entrepreneurial opportunities generated by knowledge investments.

This hypothesis is consistent with the growth model. Equation (16.9) describes the generation of new opportunities. Investments in new knowledge are denoted L_A within the model. Deriving (16.9) with respect to L_A, we obtain

$$\frac{d\dot{A}_{opp}}{dL_A} = (1 - \theta) \cdot \delta\lambda L_A^{\lambda-1}A^\phi \tag{16.17}$$

which is positive for all L_A and A^ϕ. Hence opportunities increase with investment in new knowledge. Again, these hypotheses are consistent with the formal model given. Deriving (16.8) with respect to A^ϕ, we obtain

$$\frac{d\dot{A}_{opp}}{dA^\phi} = (1 - \theta) \cdot \delta L_A^\lambda \tag{16.18}$$

which is positive for all L_A. Hence opportunities increase with spillovers and therefore firms will locate near the source of spillovers, *ceteris paribus*, which suggests this hypothesis:

Economic performance hypothesis: Entrepreneurial activity will increase the level of economic output since entrepreneurship serves as a mechanism facilitating the spillover and commercialization of knowledge.

On the basis of the arguments given, we state production function (16.2) as

$$Y = K^\alpha(\theta_r A)^{(1-\alpha)}L_Y^{(1-\alpha)} \tag{16.19}$$

where θ_r denotes the 'realized permeability' of the knowledge filter, that is, that level that includes the part of $(1 - \theta)$ that has been taken on by startup firms. Thus we have

$\theta_r \in [0, 1 - \theta]$ or $\theta \le \theta_r \le 1$. An increase in entrepreneurial activity increases θ_r and therefore the distance between θ and θ_r. Deriving

$$\frac{dY}{d\theta_r} = (1 - \alpha)\theta_r^{-\alpha}K^\alpha A^{(1-\alpha)}L_Y^{(1-\alpha)} = \frac{1 - \alpha}{\theta_r}Y \tag{16.20}$$

which is greater than 0 for all Y; thus economic output, or GDP, increases with entrepreneurial activity.

The third hypothesis emerging from the knowledge spillover theory of entrepreneurship concerns the location of the entrepreneurial activity. Access to knowledge spillovers requires spatial proximity. Though Jaffe (1989) and Audretsch and Feldman (1996) showed that spatial proximity is a prerequisite for accessing such knowledge spillovers, they provided no insight about the actual mechanism transmitting such knowledge spillovers. As for the Romer, Lucas and Jones models, the Jaffe (1989) and Audretsch and Feldman (1999) studies assume that investment in new knowledge automatically generates knowledge spillovers. The only additional insight involves the spatial dimension: knowledge spills over but these spillovers are spatially bounded. Since we have identified just one such mechanism by which knowledge spillovers are transmitted – the startup of a new firm – it follows that knowledge spillover entrepreneurship is also spatially bounded in that local access is required to access the knowledge facilitating the entrepreneurial startup:

Localization hypothesis: Knowledge spillover entrepreneurship will tend to be spatially located within close geographic proximity to the source of knowledge actually producing that knowledge.

One of the important findings of Glaeser et al. (1992) and Audretsch and Feldman (1996) is that economic performance is improved by knowledge spillovers. However, their findings, as well as corroborative results from a plethora of studies, focused on a spatial unit of observation, such as cities, regions and states. For example, Glaeser et al. (1992) found compelling empirical evidence suggesting that a greater degree of knowledge spillover leads to greater economic growth rates of cities. If higher knowledge spillovers imply higher growth rates for cities, this relationship should also hold for the unit of observation of the knowledge firm. The performance of entrepreneurial firms accessing knowledge spillovers should exhibit a superior performance:

Entrepreneurial performance hypothesis: Opportunities for knowledge-based entrepreneurship, and therefore performance of knowledge-based startups, is superior when they are able to access knowledge spillovers through geographic proximity to knowledge sources, such as universities, when compared to their counterparts without a close geographic proximity to a knowledge source.

CONCLUSIONS

Something of a dichotomy has emerged between the literatures on entrepreneurial opportunities and firm innovation and technology management. On the one hand, in the entrepreneurship literature, opportunities are taken as being exogenous to the fundamental decision-making unit – the individual confronted with an entrepreneurial decision. On the other hand, in the model of the knowledge production function, opportunities are decidedly endogenous and the result of purposeful investments into the creation of new knowledge and ideas through expenditures on R&D and augmentation of human capital. This dichotomy reflects implicit assumptions about the independence and separability of the two essential decision-making units – the incumbent organization and the (potential) entrepreneur.

This chapter has drawn on emerging theories of entrepreneurship that challenge the assumption that opportunities are exogenous. The knowledge spillover theory of entrepreneurship inverts the assumptions inherent in the model of the knowledge production function for the firm. Rather than assuming that the firm is exogenous and then endogenously creates new knowledge and innovative output through purposeful investments in R&D and human capital, this view instead starts with an individual exogenously endowed with a stock of knowledge and ideas. The new firm is then endogenously created in an effort to commercialize and appropriate the value of that knowledge.

The prevalent and traditional theories of entrepreneurship have typically held the context constant and then examined how characteristics specific to the individual impact the cognitive process inherent in the model of entrepreneurial choice. This often leads to the view that is remarkably analogous to that concerning technical change in the Solow (1956) model – given a distribution of personality characteristics, proclivities, preferences and tastes, entrepreneurship is exogenous. One of the great conventional wisdoms in entrepreneurship is 'Entrepreneurs are born, not made'. Either you have it or you don't. This leaves virtually no room for policy or for altering what nature has created.

This chapter has presented an alternative view. We hold the individual attributes constant and instead focus on variations in the context. In particular, we consider how the knowledge context will impact the cognitive process underlying the entrepreneurial choice model. The result is a theory of endogenous entrepreneurship, where (knowledge) workers respond to opportunities generated by new knowledge by starting a new firm. In this view, entrepreneurship is a rationale choice made by economic agents to appropriate the expected value of their endowment of knowledge. Thus the creation of a new firm is the endogenous response to investments in knowledge that have not been entirely or exhaustively appropriated by the incumbent firm.

In the endogenous theory of entrepreneurship, the spillover of knowledge and the creation of a new, knowledge-based firm are virtually synonymous. Of course, there are many other important mechanisms facilitating the spillover of knowledge that have nothing to do with entrepreneurship, such as the mobility of scientists and workers, and informal networks, linkages and interactions. Similarly, new firms have certainly started that have nothing to do with the spillover of knowledge. Still, the spillover theory of entrepreneurship suggests that there will be additional entrepreneurial activity as a rationale and cognitive response to the creation of new knowledge. Those contexts with greater investment in knowledge should also experience a higher degree of entrepreneurship, *ceteris paribus*. Perhaps it is true that entrepreneurs are made. But more of them will discover what they are made of in a high-knowledge context than in an impoverished-knowledge context. Thus we are disinclined to restate the conventional wisdom and instead propose that entrepreneurs are not necessarily made, but are rather a response

– and in particular a response to high-knowledge contexts that are especially fertile in spawning entrepreneurial opportunities.

NOTE

1. Lucas (2001), and Lucas and Rossi-Hansberg (2002) impose a spatial structure on production externalities in order to model the spatial structure of cities. The logic is that spatial gradients capture some of the externalities associated with localized human capital accumulation.

REFERENCES

Acs, Z.J. and D.B. Audretsch (1987), 'Innovation market structure and firm size', *Review of Economics and Statistics*, **64** (4), 567–75.
Acs, Zoltan J. and David B. Audretsch (1988), 'Innovation in large and small firms: an empirical analysis', *American Economic Review*, **78** (4), 678–90.
Acs, Z.J. and D.B. Audretsch (1990), *Innovation and Small Firms*, Cambridge, MA: MIT Press.
Acs, Z.J. D.B. Audretsch (1991), 'Innovation and size at the firm level', *Southern Economic Journal*, **57** (3), 739–44.
Acs, Z.J. and D.B. Audretsch (2003), *Handbook of Entrepreneurship Research*, Boston, MA: Springer.
Acs, Zoltan J., David B. Audretsch and Maryann P. Feldman (1992), 'Real effects of academic research', *American Economic Review*, **82** (1), 363–7.
Acs, Zoltan J., David B. Audretsch and Maryann P. Feldman (1994), 'R&D spillovers and recipient firm size', *Review of Economics and Statistics*, **100** (2), 336–67.
Agarwal, Rajshree, Raj Echambadi, April Franco and M.B. Sarker (forthcoming), 'Knowledge transfer through inheritance: spin-out generation, development and performance', forthcoming, *Academy of Management Journal*.
Arrow, Kenneth J. (1962), 'Economic welfare and the allocation of resources for invention', in R.R. Nelson (ed.), *The Rate and Direction of Inventive Activity*, Princeton, NJ: Princeton University Press, pp. 609–26.
Audretsch, David B. (1995), *Innovation and Industry Evolution*, Cambridge, MA: MIT Press.
Audretsch, David B. and Maryann P. Feldman (1996), 'R&D spillovers and the geography of innovation and production', *American Economic Review*, **86** (3), 630–40.
Audretsch, David B. and Paula E. Stephan (1996), 'Company–scientist locational links: the case of biotechnology', *American Economic Review*, **86** (3), 641–52.
Audretsch, David B., Max Keilbach and Erik Lehmann (2006), *Entrepreneurship and Economic Growth*, New York: Oxford University Press.
Bound, John, Clint Cummins, Zvi Griliches, Bronwyn H. Hall and Adam Jaffe (1984), 'Who does R&D and who patents?', in Z. Griliches (ed.), *R&D, Patents, and Productivity*, Chicago, IL: University of Chicago Press, pp. 21–54.
Chandler, A. (1990), *Scale and Scope: The Dynamics of Industrial Capitalism*, Cambridge, MA: Belknap Press of Harvard University Press.
Cohen, Wesley M. and Richard C. Levin (1989), 'Empirical studies of innovation and market structure', in Richard Schmalensee and Robert Willig (eds), *Handbook of Industrial Organization*, Volume II, Amsterdam: North-Holland, pp. 1059–107.
Cohen, Wesley M. and Steven Klepper (1991), 'Firm size versus diversity in the achievement of technological advance', in Z.J. Acs and D.B. Audretsch (eds), *Innovation and Technological Change: An International Comparison*, Ann Arbor, MI: University of Michigan Press, pp. 183–203.
Cohen, Wesley M. and Steven Klepper (1992), 'The tradeoff between firm size and diversity in the pursuit of technological progress', *Small Business Economics*, **4** (1), 1–14.
Feldman, M.P. (1994), 'Knowledge complementarity and innovation', *Small Business Economics*, **6**, 363–72.
Glaeser, E., Kallal, H., Scheinkman, J. and Shleifer, A. (1992), 'Growth of cities', *Journal of Political Economy*, **100**, 1126–52.
Grabowski, Henry G. (1968), 'The determinants of industrial research and development: a study of the chemical, drug, and petroleum industries', *Journal of Political Economy*, **76** (4), 292–306.
Griliches, Zvi (1979), 'Issues in assessing the contribution of R&D to productivity growth', *Bell Journal of Economics*, **10** (Spring), 92–116.

Griliches, Zvi (1984), 'Introduction to R & D, patents, and productivity', in National Bureau of Economic Research (ed.), *R & D, Patents, and Productivity*, New York: NBER, pp. 1–20.

Griliches, Zvi (1990), 'Patent statistics as economic indicators: a survey', *Journal of Economic Literature*, **28** (4), 1661–707.

Griliches, Zvi and A. Pakes (1980), 'Patents and R and D at the firm level: a first look', NBER Working Papers 0561.

Hebert, R.F. and Albert N. Link (1989), 'In search of the meaning of entrepreneurship', *Small Business Economics*, **1** (1), 39–49.

Jaffe, Adam B. (1989), 'Real effects of academic research', *American Economic Review*, **79** (5), 957–70.

Jaffe, A., Trajtenberg, M. and Henderson, R. (1993), 'Geographic localization of knowledge spillovers as evidenced by patent citations', *Quarterly Journal of Economics*, **63**, 577–98.

Jones, Charles, I. (1995), 'R & D-based models of economic growth', *Journal of Political Economy*, **103** (4), 759–84.

Kleinknecht, Alfred (1987), *Innovation Patterns in Crisis and Prosperity. Schumpeter's Long Cycle Reconsidered*, London: Macmillan and New York: St Martin's Press.

Kleinknecht, Alfred and Bart Verspagen (1989), 'R&D and market structure: the impact of measurement and aggregation problems', Open Access publications from Maastricht University urn: nbn: NL: ui: 27-18073, Maastricht University.

Klepper, Steven and S. Sleeper (2000), 'Entry by spinoffs', unpublished manuscript, Carnegie Mellon University.

Krueger, Norris F. Jr (2003), 'The cognitive psychology of entrepreneurship', in Zoltan J. Acs and David B. Audretsch (eds), *Handbook of Entrepreneurship Research*, New York: Springer Publishers, pp. 105–40.

Krugman, P. (1991a), 'Increasing returns and economic geography', *Journal of Political Economy*, **99**, 483–99.

Krugman, Paul (1991b), *Geography and Trade*, Cambridge: MIT Press.

Kuznets, Simon (1962), 'Inventive activity: problems of definition and measurement', in R.R. Nelson (ed.), *The Rate and Direction of Inventive Activity*, National Bureau of Economic Research Conference Report, Princeton, NJ, pp. 19–43.

Link, Albert N. and John Rees (1990), 'Firm size, university based research, and the returns to R&D', *Small Business Economics*, **2** (1), 25–32.

Lucas, Robert E., Jr (1988), 'On the mechanics of economic development', *Journal of Monetary Economics*, **22** (1), 3–42.

Lucas, Robert E., Jr (2001), 'Externalities and cities', *Review of Economic Dynamics*, **4** (2), 245–74.

Lucas, Robert E., Jr and Esteban Rossi-Hansberg (2002), 'On the internal structure of cities', *Econometrics*, **70** (4), 1445–76.

Lundstrom, Anders and Lois A. Stevenson (2005), *Entrepreneurship Policy: Theory and Practice*, Dordrecht: Kluwer.

Mansfield, Edwin (1968), *Industrial Research and Technological Change*, New York: W.W. Norton, for the Cowles Foundation for Research Economics at Yale University.

Mansfield, Edwin (1981), 'Composition of R&D expenditures: relationship to size of firm, concentration, and innovative output', *Review of Economics and Statistics*, **63**, 610–15.

Mansfield, Edwin (1983), 'Industrial organization and technological change: recent empirical findings', in John V. Craven (ed.), *Industrial Organization, Antitrust, and Public Policy*, The Hague: Kluwer–Nijhoff, pp. 129–43.

Mansfield, Edwin (1984), 'Comment on using linked patent and R&D data to measure interindustry technology flows', in Z. Griliches (ed.), *R&D, Patents, and Productivity*, Chicago, IL: University of Chicago Press, pp. 462–64.

Mansfield, Edwin, A. Romeo, M. Schwartz, D. Teece, S. Wagner and P. Brach (1982), *Technology Transfer, Productivity, and Economic Policy*, New York: W.W. Norton.

Marshall, Alfred (1920), *Principles of Economics*, London: Macmillan.

McClelland, David (1961), *The Achieving Society*, New York: Free Press.

Mueller, Dennis C. (1967), 'The firm decision process: an econometric investigation', *Journal of Political Economy*, **81** (1), 58–87.

Nelson, Richard R. and Sidney G. Winter (1982), *An Evolutionary Theory of Economic Change*, Cambridge, MA: Harvard University Press.

Romer, Paul M. (1986), 'Increasing returns and long-run growth', *Journal of Political Economy*, **94** (5), 1002–37.

Romer, Paul M. (1990), 'Endogenous technological change', *Journal of Political Economy*, **98** (5), S71–102.

Sarasvathy, Saras D., Nicholas Dew, S. Ramakrishna Velamuri and Sankaran Venkataraman (2003), 'Three views of entrepreneurial opportunity', in Zoltan J. Acs and David B. Audretsch (eds), *Handbook of Entrepreneurship Research*, New York: Springer Publishers, pp. 141–60.

Saxenian, AnnaLee (1994), *Regional Advantage*, Cambridge, MA: Harvard University Press.

Scherer, Frederic M. (1965a), 'Corporate inventive output, profits, and growth', *Journal of Political Economy*, **73**, 290–97.

Scherer, Frederic M. (1965b), 'Firm size, market structure, opportunity, and the output of patented inventions', *American Economic Review*, **55**, 1097–125.

Scherer, Frederic M. (1965c), 'Invention and innovation in the Watt-Boulton steam engine venture', *Technology and Culture*, **6**, 165–87.

Scherer, Frederic M. (1967), 'Market structure and the employment of scientists and engineers', *American Economic Review*, **57**, 524–30.

Scherer, Frederic M. (1982a), 'Demand-pull and technological innovation: Schmookler revisited', *Journal of Industrial Economics*, **30**, 225–38.

Scherer, Frederic M. (1982b), 'Industrial technology flows in the United States', *Research Policy*, **11** (4), 227–45.

Scherer, Frederic M. (1982c), 'Inter-industry technology flows and productivity growth', *Review of Economics and Statistics*, **64** (4), 627–34.

Scherer, Frederic M. (1982d), 'The lag structure of returns to R&D', *Applied Economics*, **14**, 603–20.

Scherer, Frederic M. (1983), 'The propensity to patent', *International Journal of Industrial Organization*, **1**, 107–28.

Schumpeter, Joseph A. (1942), *Capitalism, Socialism and Democracy*, New York: Harper & Row.

Shane, S. (2000), 'Prior knowledge, and the discovery of entrepreneurial opportunities', *Organization Science*, **11** (4), 448–69.

Shane, Scott and Jonathan Eckhardt (2003), 'The individual–opportunity nexus', in Zoltan J. Acs and David B. Audretsch (eds), *Handbook of Entrepreneurship Research*, New York: Springer Publishers, pp. 161–94.

Shane, S. and S. Venkataraman (2001), 'Response to dialogue about the promise of entrepreneurship as a field of research', *Academy of Management Review*, **26** (1), 14–16.

Shaver, Kelly G. (2003), 'The social psychology of entrepreneurial behviour', in Zoltan J. Acs and David B. Audretsch (eds), *Handbook of Entrepreneurship Research*, New York: Springer Publishers, pp. 331–58.

Soete, Luc (1979), 'Firm size and inventive activity: the evidence reconsidered', *European Economic Review*, **12** (4), 319–40.

Solow, Robert (1956), 'A contribution to the theory of economic growth', *Quarterly Journal of Economics*, **70**, 65–94.

Stevenson, H.H. and J.C. Jarillo-Mossi (1990), 'A paradigm of entrepreneurship: entrepreneurial management', *Strategic Management Journal*, **11**, 17–27.

Venkataraman, S. (1997), 'The distinctive domain of entrepreneurship research', in Jerome A. Katz (ed.), *Advances in Entrepreneurship, Firm Emergence and Growth*, Vol. 3, Greenwich, CT: JAI Press, pp. 119–38.

Winter, Sidney G. (1984), 'Schumpeterian competition in alternative technological regimes', *Journal of Economic Behavior & Organization*, **5** (3–4), 287–320.

PART IV

TECHNOLOGY TRANSFER, INNOVATION AND ENTREPRENEURSHIP

17 Startup firms from research in US universities
Richard A. Jensen

INTRODUCTION

As is well known by now, the Bayh–Dole Act led to an explosion in technology transfer efforts by universities, as well as a substantial increase in the commercialization of university inventions. Technology transfer offices (TTOs) at US universities are responsible for making good-faith efforts to commercialize university inventions. This process begins when a faculty member discloses a potential invention to the TTO, which then tries to find a partner for commercialization. The partner may be either an established firm or a new business venture (startup) funded independently by venture capitalists, angel investors or the faculty inventor. Although initially most of this activity took the form of license agreements with established firms, there has been an increase in commercialization via new firms, or startups, with the passage of time.

This chapter empirically examines university entrepreneurship in the form of the commercialization of faculty inventions through startup firms for the period 1994 through 2004. According to data collected by the Association of University Technology Managers (AUTM), for fiscal years 1993–2004, the number of startups emerging from US universities increased by nearly 80 percent, and the average number of startups per university increased by about 45 percent. Several models are estimated of both the annual number of startups initiated per university and the annual cumulative number of operational startups per university. Generally speaking, annual startups initiated measures the number of new firms created in that year, while annual cumulative operational startups measures the number of all startups initiated at any time in the past that remain operational. Therefore, both can reasonably be considered as measures of the success of university research and technology transfer, but the former is perhaps best thought of as a necessary condition for this success, while the latter is a sufficient condition.

In this study the annual number of startups initiated and cumulative operational startups per university are modeled as a function of characteristics of the university itself, its faculty, and general financial conditions. I employ annual university-level data from the surveys by AUTM on the number of startups initiated and operational, the presence of a medical school, land-grant and private status, the size and age of the TTO, the number of invention disclosures, and the levels of federal and industrial funding, as well as data on the size and quality of the life science and engineering faculties from the 1994 Survey by the National Research Council (NRC). The quality measure is a weighted average of the NRC ranks of the individual department in each university, and varies from one to five. I also use annual state-level data on venture capital funding from the *National Venture Capital Association Yearbook*, and the annual NASDAQ composite index.

I test four different specifications of the model, involving four different samples: all US universities in the AUTM surveys; all universities except the University of California (UC) system, omitted because all ten of its campuses report as one, so these observations are substantial outliers; all universities that created their TTOs before passage of the Bayh–Dole Act in 1980;[1] and all universities that created their TTOs after passage of Bayh–Dole.[2]

The results are interesting from several perspectives. First, the main result for the annual number of startups initiated per university is that it is positively related to the quality of the engineering faculty, the levels of federal and industrial funding, the number of invention disclosures of the university, and the level of venture capital funding in the state where the university is located, while negatively related to whether the university is private and whether it has land-grant status.[3] The number of startups initiated is also negatively related to the NASDAQ index in the sample that omits the UC system and the sample of universities with newer TTOs. However, as discussed in detail in a later section, the magnitude of the effect for most of these variables is small, in that the increase in the variable required to induce one additional startup per year is large compared to the sample mean. Conversely, one exception is private status, which generally implies one fewer startup every two years in the full sample, and roughly four fewer startups per year in the sample omitting the UC system and three fewer startups per year in the sample of universities with newer TTOs. The effects of land-grant status are the same in magnitude.

Next, in general, the number of cumulative operational startups per university is positively related to the quality of the engineering faculty, the age of the TTO, the level of industrial funding, and the number of invention disclosures in the university, but negatively related to the land-grant and private status of the university. Again, the magnitude of the effect for many of these variables is small, but there are notable exceptions. As detailed in a later section, the increase in the NRC ranking of a university's engineering faculty required for one additional operational startup is very small in the sample omitting the UC system. Similarly, a very small increase in the ranking of a university's life science faculty is needed for one additional operational startup in the sample of universities with newer TTOs. Private status implies six fewer operational startups in the sample that omits the UC system, and five fewer operational startups in the sample of universities with newer TTOs. Land-grant status implies four and three fewer operational startups in these two samples, respectively.

These results have implications for university administrators or policy-makers interested in generating more startups. First, as the relative sample sizes indicate, in any given year the number of all startups that remain operational is generally less than half of the startups initiated in that year. Thus, although startups must be initiated to become operational, it seems apparent that the cumulative number of startups that remain operational deserves more attention as a metric of success. The results for this measure largely indicate that those universities with older TTOs, and more experience in technology transfer, should simply continue what they are currently doing.

By contrast, those universities with newer TTOs, and less experience in technology transfer, can increase their startup activity with relatively small increases in the quality of their life science and engineering faculties (as measured by the NRC rankings), the level of industrial funding, and the number of annual invention disclosures. The results also show that startup activity for these universities increases with small increases in the age of their TTO, and is higher for those that are not private. The former result suggests substantial learning-by-doing in university startup activity. Although this learning process can be speeded up with the hiring of more experienced staff for the TTO, this may have limited effects because university faculty and administration also need to learn about the process of technology transfer. Similarly, a private university cannot, in general, simply choose to become public. Many private universities need to overcome a culture that has not been conducive to technology transfer via startup firms involving their faculty.

Perhaps the most important contribution of this analysis is the recognition that the UC system is an outlier whose inclusion in the data causes substantial differences in results, and that the universities with newer TTOs are dramatically different from those with older TTOs (including the UC system). Increases in the size and quality of the engineering faculty, the size of the life science faculty, the number of invention disclosures, the level of industrial funding, the age of the TTO and decreases in the NASDAQ index are all more likely to have beneficial effects on startup activity when the UC system is omitted from the analysis. These beneficial effects are even more pronounced for those universities with TTOs created after the passage of the Bayh–Dole Act. The results that emerge from this partitioning of the data indicate that startup activity depends crucially on a university's past success, or perhaps more accurately, lack of past success in technology transfer.

LITERATURE REVIEW

These results contribute to a small but growing literature on university entrepreneurship and startups. Rothaermel et al. (2007) provide a very thorough review of the literature. For the purposes of this chapter the focus is on the most closely related work.

First, there is a small theoretical literature that has predominantly focused on the behavior of faculty in the research, disclosure and commercial development of university inventions, and the behavior of technology transfer officers in licensing those inventions: Jensen and Thursby (2001), Lach and Shankerman (2003), Jensen et al. (2003), Decheneaux et al. (2009), Hoppe and Ozdenoren (2004), and Macho-Stadler et al. (2004).

The empirical literature on university invention is more extensive (Henderson et al., 1998; Mowery et al., 2001; Shane, 2002; Thursby and Thursby, 2002, 2004), but often focuses on case studies of startups in specific universities that have provided exceptionally detailed data sets. For example, Shane studies startups based on inventions by MIT faculty. He shows that startups are more likely when inventors recognize business opportunities (Shane, 2000) or technological opportunities (Shane, 2001), and that licensing to inventor startups is more likely when patents are ineffective at preventing information problems such as moral hazard and adverse selection. However, he also finds that licenses to startups perform poorly compared to licenses to established firms. Similarly, Lowe and Ziedonis (2004) use data from the University of California to show that royalties from startups are higher on average, but successful commercialization tends to occur only after acquisition by an established firm.

There are three more general studies of startups using AUTM data. Di Gregorio and Shane (2003) study startups from US universities using AUTM data for 1994 to 1998, finding a positive relationship between startup formation and faculty quality, as measured by the Gourman Report. O'Shea et al. (2005) also study startups from US universities using AUTM and NRC data for 1995 to 2001, finding positive relationships between startups and faculty quality (measured by NRC rankings), faculty size, federal funding for science and engineering, past success in startups, a high fraction of industry funding and TTO size. The following study extends these analyses by using data through 2004, including measures of university faculty size in the life sciences and engineering, adding financial variables, using time (annual) fixed effects, analyzing the annual number of cumulative operational startups as well as startups initiated, and partitioning the data in new ways. This study often finds different results, as noted below.

Another related work is the unpublished manuscript by Chukumba and Jensen (2005), which develops a theoretical model to explain when university technology is licensed to startup firms versus established firms. This is accompanied by reduced-form estimates of the number of startups initiated and licenses to established firms. The estimation of startups in that working paper uses licensing revenue as a proxy for past success, thus introducing serious endogeneity concerns. Again, this study finds results that are often different, as noted later.

DATA

Generally, the commercialization of university inventions is a process that begins with the faculty conducting research, given funding from various sources, that results in disclosures to the university's technology transfer office (TTO) or office of technology licensing. A disclosure is a relatively short form that describes the invention and suggests possible commercial applications. The TTO then attempts to find a firm to partner with in attempting to develop the invention for commercial application. Generally the university and firm enter a license (or option) agreement for use of the invention. The licensee generally pays the costs of patenting, often provides additional funding for the inventor's research, pays the costs of the further development typically required for commercial application, and commits to pay a stream of royalties if the invention is a commercial success. In this event, the university shares this stream of license revenue with the faculty inventor(s). As shown in Jensen and Thursby (2001), this feature of the Bayh–Dole Act provides a substantial incentive for inventors to engage in the development process, thereby increasing the likelihood of discovering a successful commercial application. Indeed, often the licensing agreement involves a startup firm in which the faculty inventor is a principal.

For each university, the annual measures of entrepreneurship are startups initiated and cumulative operational startups. These outcomes are discrete (integer-valued), of course. The data are provided by AUTM, which has published surveys including startup data for the years 1994 through 2004. This is an unbalanced panel ranging from 145 US universities and 31 US hospitals and research institutes in 1994 to 164 US universities and 33 US hospitals and research institutes in 2004.

We consider explanatory variables that include characteristics of the TTO, the faculty and the university. The literature generally argues and finds support for the hypothesis that the effectiveness of a TTO depends on its experience and expertise both at eliciting disclosures from faculty and at locating potential partners for the inventions (see, e.g., Thursby et al., 2001; Jensen et al., 2003). For each university, AUTM provides data on TTO size (*ttosize*), measured as the number of full-time equivalents (FTEs) devoted to licensing activities, and TTO age (*ttoage*), measured by the number of years since the university first devoted at least one half of an FTE to its licensing activities. The rationale for using the size of a TTO is that larger TTOs not only have greater resources, but also may have more experience among their personnel. The rationale for using the age of a TTO is that older TTOs have more experience and expertise.

Next, the size and quality of the faculty must impact the startups arising from university intentions. Previous studies have used the National Research Council's survey (1995) to construct a quality measure for each university's faculty as a whole, or for its faculty in the life sciences and engineering. These measures are obviously flawed in that they measure quality at a single point in time, and they can be constructed only for those universities with doctoral programs. However, they are reasonable to the extent that the faculty sizes and program rankings do not change too much over time, and these measures have typically had explanatory power in previous studies. Specifically, for each university in the AUTM survey data, we determine the total number of faculty in all engineering doctoral programs (*engsize*), then compute the size-weighted average of the NRC faculty quality score (Q93A) for those programs, which we use as a measure of engineering faculty quality (*engqual*). We do the same for each university's life science doctoral programs to obtain the size (*scisize*) and quality (*sciqual*) of its science faculty.

General university characteristics also may influence success in technology transfer. For example, nearly all prior studies have tested the hypothesis that the presence of a medical school or status as a land-grant institution should matter to technology transfer because faculty inventions from these universities should be generally closer to commercial application. Another university characteristic that should matter is whether it is private or public. Whether they have land-grant status or not, public universities are expected to contribute to local and regional economic development. Therefore faculty inventions in public universities also may be closer to commercial application than those in private universities. Moreover, private universities may not have a culture conducive to commercialization of their research, as suggested by the fact that roughly three-fourths of private universities in the AUTM data did not create a TTO until after passage of the Bayh–Dole Act. However, some private universities, notably MIT and Stanford, are known for having a culture that encourages faculty startups (Shane, 2000; O'Shea et al., 2005), so the net effect of private status on startups is not obvious, *a priori*. I represent these characteristics by the dummy variables *medschool*, *landgrant* and *private*, each equal to 1 if the university has a medical school, is land-grant, or is private.

Because a university's research output, and the resulting technology transfer, depend upon its level of funding, I also include the current (annual) level of research funding for each university provided by the federal government (ln*fedfnd*) and by industry (ln*indfnd*). I use logged values due to the highly skewed nature of these variables. Disclosures are a key input to the technology transfer process, because research success cannot translate into technology transfer unless inventions are disclosed to the TTO. Because it takes time to move from a disclosure to a license (whether to an established firm or a startup), the lagged number of annual invention disclosures for each university is included (*lagdisclose*).

Finally, because university startups are usually funded by venture capitalists or angel investors (Lerner, 1999), it is important to add some financial variables to indicate the availability of funding. I use both the annual level of venture capital spending in the state where the university is located (ln*ventcap*), logged because its distribution is very skewed,

Table 17.1   Summary statistics for full sample

Variable	Observations	Means	Standard deviation	Minimum	Maximum
medschool	2747	0.49	0.50	0	1
landgrant	2004	0.32	0.46	0	1
private	2221	0.29	0.45	0	1
scisize	1858	247.71	326.84	9	3225
sciquality	1858	2.92	0.78	1.04	4.75
engsize	1308	101.75	87.00	7	423
engquality	1308	2.77	0.82	1.01	4.63
ttosize	2337	3.57	5.13	0	73
ttoage	2393	12.25	10.90	0	79
disclose	2473	64.47	86.94	0	973
fedfund (US$ millions)	2418	95.3	144	0	2170
indfund (US$ millions)	2379	13.1	20.4	0	318
ventcap (US$ millions)	2459	1710	4590	0	43,200
nasdaq	2749	17.87	33.80	−41	84.30
startup	2054	1.96	3.06	0	31
cumstartup	983	13.64	21.58	0	206

and the annual change in the composite NASDAQ index (*nasdaq*). Intuitively, greater availability of venture capital funding should imply more startups, whereas increases in the NASDAQ index indicate better alternative opportunities for investors and so fewer startups.

Table 17.1 displays summary statistics. Roughly half of the universities in the AUTM data have medical schools, while about 30 percent are land-grant and another 30 percent are private. These characteristics are not mutually exclusive, of course, because medical schools are present at both private and land-grant universities, and some private universities have land-grant status. The NRC quality rankings use a scale from one to five (low to high), and the weighted averages span nearly the entire range. The data for the sizes of the life sciences faculty are substantially skewed because the UC system submits one report for all ten of its campuses. The means of science and engineering faculty size are 248 and 102, and the medians are 151 and 76. Similarly, the sizes and ages of the TTOs vary substantially, although the typical TTO is still small. Mean TTO size is 3.57 FTE, and the median is two. TTO age is also very skewed. The mean age is about 12 years, but there were 27 TTOs in existence when the Bayh–Dole Act was passed in 1980 (24 of which are included in the data). In fact, five universities have TTOs that were founded more than 50 years ago (Iowa State, Kansas State, MIT, Wisconsin and the UC system). Annual federal and industrial funding per university are both extremely skewed, with values ranging from zero to US$2 billion and US$318 million (respectively). Annual venture capital spending in each state is even more skewed, ranging from zero to 43 billion.

Finally, both the annual number of startups initiated and cumulative operational startups are also skewed, though not as severely as the funding variables. However, it is most important to note that the annual number of startups is frequently zero. In particular, 809, or about 39 percent, of the 2054 observations are zero. The annual number of operational startups is less skewed, but this variable also takes the value zero about 15 percent of the time, or 148 of the 983 observations. The small number of observations (compared to startups initiated) is a clear indication of the high failure rate for university startups.

EMPIRICAL MODEL AND ANALYSIS

For each startup outcome and sample, the specification of the econometric model involves equations of the form

$$Y_{it} = \alpha + \beta_1 \mathbf{X}_{1it} + \beta_2 \mathbf{X}_{2i} + \varepsilon_{it}$$

where i indexes universities, t indexes time, Y_{it} is a measurable outcome of university startup activity, $\mathbf{X}_{1it}$ is a vector of time-varying explanatory variables, $\mathbf{X}_{2i}$ is a vector of time-invariant explanatory variables, and ε_{it} is an error term.

For each of the explanatory variables in this model, causation arguably goes in the correct direction. However, concerns about endogeneity would remain if other variables were omitted from the model that are correlated with both startups and some explanatory variable. I test four specifications for each startup outcome, each corresponding to a different sample. The first is a test on the full sample of all US universities. The second is a test on the sample of all universities except the UC system. There are two reasons to omit the UC system. As noted, many of its observations are outliers because it submits one report for all ten campuses. Moreover, it also has both land-grant status and a medical school, although not all of its campuses fulfill either of these functions. The remaining specifications involve a partition of the data: the third test is for universities that created their TTOs before the passage of the Bayh–Dole Act in 1980, and the fourth test is for those universities that created their TTOs after the passage of the Act. I use a negative binomial specification for all of these regressions because, as previously noted, the number of annual startups initiated and cumulative operational startups are count data that are both skewed and contain a non-trivial fraction of zeros.

Table 17.2 reports the results for the number of annual startups initiated per university. The first column reports the results for the full sample, and this is the benchmark case. The second column reports the results when the UC system is omitted from the data; the third reports the results for those universities with older TTOs (created before the passage of the Bayh–Dole Act in 1980); and the fourth reports results for those universities with newer TTOs (created after the passage of the Bayh–Dole Act in 1980). All specifications include time (annual) fixed effects.

First, the previous studies noted, which use fewer data, generally show no significant effect of a medical school, land-grant status, or private status on startup activity. This study tends to confirm these results for the presence of a medical school. Precisely, the number of annual startups initiated per university is negatively and significantly correlated with the presence of a medical school, but only for the sample of universities with newer TTOs, and only at the 10 percent significance level. However, this study finds that the annual number of startups initiated is negatively and significantly correlated with whether a university has land-grant status in all samples, and is negatively and significantly correlated with whether a university is private in all samples except

Table 17.2   Negative binomial regressions for startups initiated

	Full sample	Without UC	Older TTOs	Newer TTOs
medschool	−0.001	−0.047	−0.191	−0.240**
	(0.077)	(0.079)	(0.146)	(0.102)
landgrant	−0.182***	−0.191***	−0.631***	−0.213***
	(0.067)	(0.068)	(0.150)	(0.085)
private	−0.271***	−0.274***	−0.013	−0.340***
	(0.083)	(0.085)	(0.159)	(0.107)
scisize	−3.04E−04**	−6.97E−05	−1.43E−04	−2.48E−05
	(1.33E−04)	(1.92E−04)	(1.76E−04)	(2.62E−04)
sciquality	−0.049	−0.382	−0.382	0.041
	(0.091)	(0.274)	(0.274)	(0.118)
engsize	0.000	0.000	0.004***	0.000
	(0.001)	(0.001)	(0.001)	(0.001)
engquality	0.440***	0.402***	0.532**	0.242**
	(0.090)	(0.094)	(0.220)	(0.114)
ttosize	0.004	0.019*	−0.009	0.022
	(0.008)	(0.011)	(0.007)	(0.016)
ttoage	0.005*	0.003	0.007	0.012
	(0.003)	(0.003)	(0.005)	(0.008)
lagdisclose	0.003***	0.003***	0.002***	0.005***
	(0.000)	(0.001)	(0.001)	(0.001)
lnfedfnd	0.163**	0.162**	0.025	0.154**
	(0.065)	(0.063)	(0.113)	(0.075)
lnindfnd	0.133***	0.125***	0.126***	0.151***
	(0.046)	(0.046)	(0.086)	(0.058)
lnventcap	0.057***	0.061***	0.130***	−0.010
	(0.021)	(0.021)	(0.031)	(0.025)
nasdaq	−9.21E−04	−1.87E−03**	−1.28E−03	−4.05E−03**
	(9.24E−04)	(7.4E−04)	(9.51E−04)	(1.63E−03)
N	778	769	181	597
Pseudo R^2	0.182	0.166	0.234	0.144

Note: Standard errors in parentheses: *$p < 0.10$, **$p < 0.05$; ***$p < 0.01$.

universities with older TTOs. In terms of initiating startups, private universities that became involved in the technology transfer process before the passage of the Bayh–Dole Act do not differ significantly from their public counterparts, but those who became involved after the passage of the Act do. Private universities that did not create TTOs until after 1980 apparently do not have a culture encouraging technology transfer. And, because universities with land-grant status are generally considered to produce inventions that are, on average, closer to commercial application, it may be that these universities are also more likely to find established firms as partners in technology transfer, and so have relatively less need for startups.

The number of startups is positively and significantly correlated with the quality of the engineering faculty, though, interestingly, this is generally the only faculty characteristic that matters. An exception is that startups are positively and significantly correlated with the size of the engineering faculty for the sample of universities with older TTOs, and again, this is not a surprise because these universities demonstrated a culture of encouraging technology transfer well before the passage of the Bayh–Dole Act. The other exception is that the number of startups is negatively correlated with the size of the life science faculty for the full sample, though only at the 5 percent level. Because this result is not robust to the other specifications, it is not clear how much emphasis should be placed on it. These results confirm those in Chukumba and Jensen (2005), but differ from O'Shea et al. (2005), who find a significant and positive relationship with science faculty quality (for fewer years of data).

Next, the size, experience and expertise of the university TTOs do not seem to have any significant effect on the number of startups initiated. TTO size and age are each significant only for the sample without the UC system. Although both have the antici-pated positive signs in these cases, they are significant only at the 10 percent level. This again stands in contrast to the results of O'Shea et al. (2005), but tends to support the other studies which have found that TTOs are either less effective or less interested in finding partners for startups (e.g. Shane, 2001; Lowe and Ziedonis, 2004; Chukumba and Jensen, 2005).

The number of startups is also positively and significantly correlated with the lagged number of disclosures and levels of federal and industrial funding. This is as expected, of course, because each of these is a measure of inputs that are important to the process of technology transfer. The results for funding confirm those of Chukumba and Jensen (2005) and O'Shea et al. (2005), but they are not robust to the sample of universities with older TTOs. These universities are older, well-established ones whose funding levels did not vary that much over the time period, and have had a culture that encouraged the technology transfer process for many decades.

The results for the financial variables are rather interesting. The number of startups is positively and significantly correlated with the level of venture capital funding in the state where the university is located, except in the sample of universities with newer TTOs (created after passage of the Bayh–Dole Act). This is also as expected, because greater availability of venture capital funding locally should increase the likelihood that university startups can find the necessary funding (Chukumba and Jensen, 2005 also find this for the full sample). However, because there is no significant effect for the sample of universities with newer TTOs, it appears that venture capitalists are reticent to deal with universities that are relatively new to the technology transfer process.

More interesting is the result that the number of startups is negatively and significantly correlated (at the 5 percent level) with the annual change in the composite NASDAQ index both for the sample of all universities except the UC system and the sample of universities with new TTOs. In these cases, more startups are associated with a falling NASDAQ, which is consistent with the view that investors are more drawn to university startups when their alterative investment opportunities are poor.

The annual number of startups initiated, of course, is perhaps best viewed as a measure of university research results that have just enough promise to attract funding from venture capitalists or angel investors. Alternatively, the annual number of cumulative operational startups is perhaps a better measure of the quality, or commercial success, of these research results because it is the number of all startup firms initiated by the

Table 17.3   Negative binomial regressions for operational startups

	Full sample	Without UC	Older TTOs	Newer TTOs
medschool	0.067	0.041	−0.070	−0.232**
	(0.100)	(0.095)	(0.199)	(0.112)
landgrant	−0.296***	−0.297***	−0.995***	−0.297***
	(0.087)	(0.082)	(0.161)	(0.098)
private	−0.470***	−0.2461***	−0.073	−0.564***
	(0.104)	(0.098)	(0.180)	(0.117)
scisize	−7.03E−05	1.81E−04	−1.68E-03***	1.73E−04
	(2.55E−04)	(2.51E−04)	(2.55E−04)	(3.27E−04)
sciquality	0.235**	0.167	−0.274	0.418***
	(0.121)	(0.116)	(0.213)	(0.138)
engsize	−3.02E−04	−5.77E−04	8.60E−03***	−1.37E−03*
	(7.65E−04)	(7.28E−04)	(1.62E−03)	(8.38E−04)
engquality	0.311***	0.293***	0.414*	0.121
	(0.118)	(0.111)	(0.245)	(0.126)
ttosize	0.001	0.022	0.002	0.030
	(0.017)	(0.017)	(0.027)	(0.022)
ttoage	0.015***	0.013***	0.003	0.031
	(0.004)	(0.003)	(0.009)	(0.010)
lagdisclose	0.003***	0.003***	0.001	0.006***
	(0.001)	(0.001)	(0.001)	(0.001)
lnfedfnd	0.066	0.058	0.522***	0.025
	(0.071)	(0.068)	(0.186)	(0.075)
lnindfnd	0.172***	0.162***	−0.241***	0.147***
	(0.058)	(0.055)	(0.118)	(0.062)
lnventcap	0.0523**	0.0494**	−0.013	0.008
	(0.023)	(0.022)	(0.043)	(0.028)
nasdaq	1.89E−03	1.62E−03	−8.51E−04	9.20E−04
	(1.38E−03)	(1.31E−03)	(2.01E−03)	(1.50E−03)
N	383	382	88	295
Pseudo R^2	0.131	0.142	0.162	0.140

Note: Standard errors in parentheses: *$p < 0.10$, **$p < 0.05$; ***$p < 0.01$.

university at any time in the past that are still active in business. Table 17.3 reports the results for the number of cumulative startups that remain operational per university per year. Again, the first column reports the results for the benchmark case of the full sample, the second reports the results omitting the UC system, the third reports the results for universities with older TTOs, and the fourth reports results for those with newer TTOs.

As with startups initiated, the number of cumulative operational startups is negatively and significantly correlated with the presence of a medical school, but only at the 10 percent level for the sample of universities with newer TTOs. And again, the number of operational startups is negatively and significantly correlated with whether a university is land-grant or is private, but private status has no effect in the sample of universities with older TTOs.

The results for size and quality of the engineering faculty are also similar to those for startups initiated. The number of cumulative operational startups is positively and significantly correlated with the quality of the engineering faculty both in the full sample and the sample where the UC system is omitted. It is positively correlated with the quality of the engineering faculty, but with weak significance (at the 10 percent level) for the sample of universities with older TTOs. The lack of significance when the data are partitioned into universities by the age of the TTOs may simply be a function of the small sample sizes in these cases. And again, cumulative operational startups are positively and significantly correlated with the size of the engineering faculty when the sample is restricted to universities with older TTOs (and a history of embracing technology transfer).

One difference from the results for startups initiated, however, is that the size and quality of the life sciences faculty now matter. For the sample of universities with older TTOs, the number of cumulative operational startups is negatively and significantly correlated with the size of the life science faculty. This is a small sample, but among these universities with older TTOs, those with large life science faculties, *ceteris paribus*, have fewer operational startups. Moreover, the number of cumulative operational startups is positively and significantly correlated with the quality of the life science faculty both for the full sample and for those universities with newer TTOs. This suggests that, for these universities, high-quality life science faculty do not initiate as many startups as engineers, but a higher fraction of their startups survive over time.

As with startups initiated, the size of university TTOs does not seem to have any significant effect on the number of cumulative operational startups. TTO size is significant in none of the specifications. However, in stark contrast to the results for startups initiated, the age of the TTO is positive and significant in every specification except the sample of universities with older TTOs. This suggests that learning-by-doing by universities, their faculties, and their TTOs is important to the creation of startups that continue to operate successfully.

Again, the number of cumulative operational startups is, in general, positively and significantly correlated with the lagged number of disclosures and with the level of industrial funding. This is as expected, of course, because each of these is a measure of inputs that are important to the process of technology transfer. But the universities with older TTOs are again exceptions, as in their case lagged disclosures have no significant effect, and cumulative startups are negatively correlated with industrial funding (significant at the 5 percent level). Among this small group with very old and experienced TTOs, those universities with greater funding from industrial sources generate fewer operational startups. This may simply indicate that the sources of industrial funding are likely to be technology transfer partners (i.e. the funding may be tied to an option to license), so startups are less likely.

In contrast to the results for startups initiated, the number of operational startups is positively and significantly correlated to the level of federal funding only for universities with older TTOs. This suggests that, except for those universities with very old and experienced TTOs, greater federal funding may help to initiate more startups, *ceteris paribus*, but not ones that successfully survive.

The results for the financial variables also differ in this case. The number of cumulative operational startups is positively and significantly correlated with the level of venture capital funding in the state where the university is located for only the full sample and when the UC system is omitted. There is no effect when the sample is partitioned by the age of the TTOs. Thus greater availability of venture capital locally, as expected, generally results in a larger number of startups that remain operational. The lack of effect in the case of universities with older TTOs may simply be a function of the small sample size.

Finally, changes in the composite NASDAQ index had no significant effect whatsoever on the cumulative number of operational startups. This is surprising because the number of startups initiated is negatively correlated with the annual change in the NASDAQ index, but this might also simply indicate that although poor alterative investment opportunities are helpful in providing funds to initiate university startups, they do not seem to be essential to the continuing success of those startups.

INTERPRETATIONS

To provide additional context, marginal effects for changes in those explanatory variables that are significant in the estimations are computed. For each specification, marginal effects are computed at the means of the sample. For dummy variables, these effects show the change in the number of startups per university that would occur if that dummy variable changed from 0 to 1. In the case of those explanatory variables that are continuously valued, for the sake of concreteness, the question is: how large a change in this variable would be required to induce one additional startup per university?

For ease of exposition, the results are stated with the presumption that changes in the explanatory variables have an effect on university startups. As noted above, this seems correct for my choice of explanatory variables, although the possibility of an omitted variables bias cannot be ignored. There may be other factors that influence university startup activity that are not included in the study. Indeed, it is likely that there is unobserved heterogeneity among the universities, but this study goes beyond most previous studies in its use of university-specific explanatory variables in the estimation.

For the full sample, land-grant status, *ceteris paribus*, generally implies 0.39 fewer startups initiated, and 0.30 fewer operational startups per university per year. Similarly, private status generally implies 0.55 fewer startups initiated, and 0.47 fewer operational startups, per university per year. When the UC system is omitted, however, land-grant status implies 3.92 fewer annual operational startups per university, and private status implies 5.7 fewer annual operational startups per university. Similarly, for the sample of universities with newer TTOs, land-grant status implies 3.01 fewer annual operational startups, and private status implies 5.12 fewer annual operational startups. As previously noted, land-grant institutions seem to generate research that is closer to commercial application (and so easier to license to existing firms), whereas private universities often lack a culture encouraging startups. Moreover, these effects seem most pronounced among universities that are relatively new to the technology transfer process.

The results for faculty size indicate that the required increase in a university's life science faculty for one additional annual startup is 167 faculty members in the full sample, or 67 percent of the sample mean. An increase in life science faculty has a significant effect on operational startups only for the sample of universities with older TTOs, and in this case the increase required for one more operational startup is 500, roughly doubling the sample mean. The results are somewhat less daunting for engineering faculty, at least for universities with older TTOs, in which case the required increase in faculty size is 71 for one more startup and 166 for one more operational startup, or 55 and 127 percent of the sample mean.

An increase in the quality of the science faculty has essentially no significant effect on the number of startups initiated, and one more operational startup per university in the full sample requires an increase in the NRC ranking of 4.25 (recall the scale runs only from one to five). That is, an increase of one in the life science faculty quality ranking of a university results in one more operational startup every four years. However, for those universities with newer TTOs, the required increase in the NRC ranking of the life science faculty to induce one more operational startup per university per year is only 0.23.

Increases in the quality of the engineering faculty generally have a significant effect on the number of startups initiated and operational. An increase in the NRC ranking of about 1.0 is required for an additional annual startup initiated per university in both the full sample and that without the UC system. However, the required increase in NRC ranking needed for the sample of universities with older TTOs is only 0.48, while that for those universities with newer TTOs is 4.0. The results for cumulative operational startups per year are remarkable. Although the increase in NRC ranking required for one more operation startup for each university in the full sample is 3.2, it is only 0.25 in the sample when the UC system is omitted. This shows dramatically how the size of the UC system influences the results of this analysis.

The size of the TTO has no effect on startups initiated or operational, but the age of the TTO has some effect. Most noteworthy is the result that the increase in TTO age required for one more operational startup per university is only 5.6 years when the UC system is omitted, and only 3.1 years for those universities with newer TTOs. Mean TTO age is 12 and 9 years in these two samples.

The effects of changes in the annual number of invention disclosures are similar to those for TTO age. Additional disclosures do increase the number of startups initiated, but the number required to induce an additional startup initiated per university is generally quite large, ranging from 143 in the sample of universities with older TTOs, or 95 percent of the sample mean, to 208 in those universities with newer TTOs, or a four-fold increase of the sample mean. And the additional disclosures needed for one more operational startup per university per year for the full sample is 333, a five-fold increase of the sample mean. However, the increase in disclosures required for one more operational startup is only 23 when the UC system is omitted, and 15.6 for those universities with newer TTOs, or 38 and 31 percent of the relevant sample means.

Increases in external funding in the university and venture capital funding levels in the state have significant effects on startups, but these effects are not overwhelming. For example, in the full sample, an increase of one startup per university per year requires increases in federal funding of $273 million, industrial funding of $46 million, and venture capital funding of $14 billion. These amounts correspond to roughly a tripling of annual federal and industrial funding per university (the sample means are $95 million and $13 million), and a seven-fold increase in local venture capital funding (the sample mean is $1.7 billion). Similarly, in the full sample, an increase of one operational startup per university per year requires even larger increases in industrial funding of $76 million and venture capital funding of $32 billion.

Nevertheless, once again results differ dramatically for some subsamples of universities.

Specifically, an increase of one operational startup per university per year requires an increase in industrial funding of only $5.6 million per university (46 percent of the sample mean) when the UC system is omitted, and only $7.2 million per university (59 percent of the sample mean) for those universities with newer TTOs. Moreover, an increase of one operational startup per university per year requires an increase in venture capital funding in the state of only $2.5 billion (roughly a 50 percent increase over the sample mean) when the UC system is omitted.

Finally, although changes in the NASDAQ index have no noticeable effect on the number of operational startups, as noted above, declines in the NASDAQ do indicate less attractive alternative investments, and therefore more startups initiated in some sub-samples. Specifically, the annual decrease in the index required for an additional startup initiated per university is 250 points in the sample without the UC system, and 500 points in the sample of universities with newer TTOs. Both of these changes are, of course, large compared to the sample mean of about 18.

CONCLUSIONS

This study examines factors influencing entrepreneurship resulting from university research. The measures of entrepreneurship used were the annual number of startups initiated per university and the annual cumulative number of startups that remain operational per university. The primary results for startups initiated are that they are positively related to the quality of the engineering faculty, the levels of federal and industrial funding, the number of invention disclosures in the university, and the level of venture capital funding in the state, but negatively related to the land-grant and private status of the university. Interestingly, startups initiated are also negatively related to the change in the NASDAQ index both in the sample that omits the UC system and in the sample of universities with newer TTOs. An increase of one in the NRC ranking of a university's engineering faculty implies one more startup initiated each year. The increase in invention disclosures required for an additional startup is quite large, ranging from about 200 in the full sample to 150 in the sample without the UC system. Although the changes in the levels of funding required to induce an additional startup are generally very large for the full sample, they are substantially smaller, and well within the realm of possibility, in the sample that omits the UC system and the sample of universities with newer TTOs. Finally, land-grant or private status generally implies one fewer startup every two years in the full sample. However, land-grant or private status implies roughly four fewer startups in the sample that omits the UC system and three fewer startups in the sample of universities with newer TTOs.

The number of cumulative operational (surviving) startups per university, on the other hand, is a better measure of the success of startups. The general results for operational startups are that they are positively related to the quality of the engineering faculty, the age of the TTO, the level of industrial funding, and the number of invention disclosures in the university, but negatively related to the land-grant and private status of the university. An unlikely increase of 3.2 in the NRC ranking of a university's engineering faculty is needed for one more operational startup per year in the full sample, but an increase of only 0.25 in the NRC ranking is needed for one more operational startup in sample when the UC system is omitted. Although the quality of the life science faculty does not seem to matter for startups initiated, and matters with limited significance for operational startups in the full sample, it is very important for operational startups in the sample of universities with newer TTOs. Specifically, an increase of only 0.23 in the NRC ranking of a university's life science faculty is needed for one more operational startup in this sample. The increase in invention disclosures required for one more operational startup is over 300 for the full sample, but only 23 in the sample without the UC system and about 16 in the sample of universities with newer TTOs. Again, the change in the level of industrial funding required for one more operational startup is very large for the full sample, though less large (roughly half of the sample mean) in the sample that omits the UC system and the sample of universities with newer TTOs. The results for a land-grant status and private status are essentially the same as those for startups initiated: about one fewer operational startup every two years in the full sample, but private (land-grant) status implies six (four) fewer operational startups in the sample that omits the UC system and five (three) fewer operational startups in the sample of universities with newer TTOs.

I examined a variety of alternative specifications of the general model to check the robustness of these results. I estimated these specifications with university fixed effects, but the number of observations was too small to allow meaningful results using both time and university fixed effects. I conducted all the tests using the current number of disclosures instead of the lagged value, and using lagged values of federal and industrial funding. I also estimated these specifications using nominal (instead of logged) values of the funding variables, so as not to omit those few observations with zero funding levels. The results were essentially the same in sign and significance.

Finally, perhaps the most important unanswered question about university startups involves the relationship between licenses made with startups and licenses made with established firms. There is evidence (Shane, 2001; Lowe and Ziedonis, 2004) that universities prefer to license to established firms, and then turn to startups as an inferior alternative. This study also provides evidence in support of this in the result that the presence of a medical school or land-grant status has a negative effect on startup activity. It is frequently argued that universities with medical schools or land-grant status tend to produce inventions that are closer to commercial application. If so, then these universities may be more likely to find established firms as licensees, and less likely to need startups. The unpublished working paper by Chukumba and Jensen (2005) makes an attempt to analyze this interrelationship, but this effort is limited in that the theory relies solely on differences in the costs of licensing to established firms versus startups, and the empirical analysis simply conducts separate reduced-form estimations of licenses with established firms and licenses with startup firms. An analysis of the interaction between these two modes of licensing is essential to understanding university entrepreneurship.

NOTES

1. Those universities with TTOs created before the passage of the Bayh–Dole Act are: Boston, Colorado State, Cornell, Harvard, Iowa State, Johns Hopkins, Kansas State, Montana State, Oregon State, Stanford, Tufts and Washington State universities, the California and Massachusetts Institutes of

Technology, the State University of New York system, the University of California system, and the universities of Georgia, Iowa, Minnesota, Rochester, Southern California, Utah, Virginia and Wisconsin.

2. I thank Bruno Cassiman for suggesting that I stratify the data by the ages of the TTOs in a different context. There are insufficient data to allow for finer partitions by TTO age, but using the Bayh–Dole Act to partition the data seems the most reasonable and intuitive approach.

3. Land-grant institutions are colleges or universities in the USA designated by their state to receive the benefits of the Morrill Acts of 1862 and 1890. Under the acts, each state received a grant of federal land to be used to develop educational institutions to focus on teaching agriculture, science and engineering. The first act was the outcome of a political movement emphasizing both the need for more agricultural and mechanical education, and the need for greater access to higher education (Nemec, 2006). Some institutions that received land-grant status already existed in 1862, such as MIT and Rutgers, while others were created afterwards. See the web site of the Association of Public and Land-grant Universities (www.aplu. org) for a list of the 76 land-grant institutions.

REFERENCES

Association of Public and Land-grant Universities (2009), *Membership Listing*, www.aplu.org, accessed 25 June 2009.

Association of University Technology Managers (1995, 1996, 1997, 1998, 1999, 2000, 2001, 2002, 2003, 2004), *AUTM Licensing Surveys*, Chicago, IL: Association of University Technology Managers.

Chukumba, C. and R.A. Jensen (2005), 'University invention, entrepreneurship, and start-ups', NBER Working Paper No. 11475.

Dechaneaux, E., M.C. Thursby and J.G. Thursby (2009), 'Shirking, sharing risk, and shelving: the role of university license contracts', *International Journal of Industrial Organization*, **27** (1), 80–91.

Di Gregorio, D. and S. Shane (2003), 'Why do some universities generate more start-ups than others?', *Research Policy*, **32** (2), 209–27.

Henderson, R., A.B. Jaffe and M. Trajtenberg (1998), 'Universities as a source of commercial technology: a detailed analysis of university patenting, 1965–1988', *The Review of Economics and Statistics*, **80** (1), 119–27.

Hoppe, H.C. and E. Ozdenoren (2004), 'Intermediation in innovation', *International Journal of Industrial Organization*, **23** (5–6), 483–503.

Jensen, R. and M.C. Thursby (2001), 'Proofs and prototypes for sale: the licensing of university inventions', *The American Economic Review*, **91** (1), 240–59.

Jensen, R., J.G. Thursby and M.C. Thursby (2003), 'The disclosure and licensing of university inventions: the best we can do with the s**t we get to work with', *International Journal of Industrial Organization*, **21** (9), 1271–300.

Lach, S. and M. Shankerman (2003), 'Incentives and invention in universities', *RAND Journal of Economics*, **39** (2), 403–33.

Lerner, J. (1999), 'The government as a venture capitalist: the long run impact of the SBIR Program', *Journal of Business*, **72** (3), 285–318.

Lowe, R. and A.A. Ziedonis (2004), 'Start-ups, established firms, and the commercialization of university inventions', mimeo, paper presented at conference on academic spin-offs, UQAM, 27 February.

Macho-Stadler, I., D. Perez-Castrillo and R. Veugelers (2004), 'Licensing of university innovations: the role of a technology transfer office', *International Journal of Industrial Organization*, **25** (3), 483–510.

Mowery, D.C., R.R. Nelson, B.N. Sampat and A.A. Ziedonis (2001), 'The growth of patenting and licensing by U.S. universities: an assessment of the effects of the Bayh–Dole Act of 1980', *Research Policy*, **30** (1), 99–119.

National Research Council (1995), *Research-Doctorate Programs in the United States: Continuity and Change*, Washington, DC: National Academy of Sciences.

National Venture Capital Association (2004), *National Venture Capital Association Yearbook*, Arlington, VA: National Venture Capital Association.

Nemec, M.R. (2006), *Ivory Towers and Nationalist Minds: Universities, Leadership, and the Development of the American State*, Ann Arbor, MI: The University of Michigan Press.

O'Shea, R.P., T.J. Allen, A. Chevalier and F. Roche (2005), 'Entrepreneurial orientation, technology transfer and spinoff performance of U.S. universities', *Research Policy*, **34** (7), 994–1009.

Rothaermel, F.T., S.D. Agung and L. Jiang (2007), 'University entrepreneurship: a taxonomy of the literature', *Industrial and Corporate Change*, **16** (4), 691–791.

Shane, S. (2000), 'Prior knowledge and the discovery of entrepreneurial opportunities', *Organization Science*, **11** (4), 448–69.

Shane, S. (2001), 'Technological opportunities and new firm creation', *Management Science*, **47** (2), 205–20.

Shane, S. (2002), 'Selling University Technology. Patterns from MIT', *Management Science*, **48** (1), 122–37.

Thursby, J.G. and M.C. Thursby (2002), 'Who is selling the ivory tower? Sources of growth in university licensing', *Management Science*, **48** (1), 90–104.

Thursby, J.G. and M.C. Thursby (2004), 'Are faculty critical? Their role in university–industry licensing', *Contemporary Economic Policy*, **22** (2), 162–78.

Thursby, J.G., R. Jensen and M.C. Thursby (2001), 'Objectives, characteristics and outcomes of university licensing: a survey of major U.S. universities', *Journal of Technology Transfer*, **26** (1), 59–72.

18 Universities as research partners: entrepreneurial explorations and exploitations
Albert N. Link and Charles W. Wessner

INTRODUCTION

According to Schumpeter (1934), innovation can be described in several ways. He initially spelt out a number of new combinations of resources and structures, including: the creation of a new good or new quality of good; the creation of a new method of production; the opening of a new market; the capture of a new source of supply; and/or the new organization of industry. Over time, the forces of these new combinations dissipate as new becomes part of old. This is the dynamic character of innovation, but as such it does not change the essence of the entrepreneurial function. 'Everyone is an entrepreneur only when he actually "carries out new combinations"' (Schumpeter, 1934, p. 78), and he loses that character when his actions become old, or revert to the status quo.

Schumpeter also defined innovation by means of the production function. The production function 'describes the way in which quantity of product varies if quantities of factors vary. If instead of quantities of factors, we vary the form of the function, we have an innovation' (1939, p. 62).

Schumpeter recognized that the knowledge supporting the innovation need not be new, although the combination of resources must. It may be that existing knowledge is used that was previously unused. He wrote (1928, p. 378):

> [T]here has never been any time when the store of scientific knowledge has yielded all it could in the way of industrial improvement, and, on the other hand, it is not the knowledge that matters, but the successful solution of the task *sui generis* of putting an untried method into practice – there may be, and often is, no scientific novelty involved at all, and even if it be involved, this does not make any difference to the nature of the process.

Successful innovation requires an act of will, not intellect, he argued; successful innovation depends on leadership, not intelligence.

When firms initiate a research partnership with a university, or when a university initiates a research partnership with a firm, each is acting entrepreneurially as it systematically and purposely attempts to identify (i.e. explore) and capture a new source of supply – knowledge. Each then uses (i.e. exploits) systematically and purposely this new source of supply to create, among other things, a new method of production, be it a good or service or intellectual output. That new method of production can lead to a new market or organization of industry.[1]

The goal of this chapter is to broaden the scope of interpretation about universities as research partners. As our overview of selected, yet representative, elements of the extant literature on universities as research partners shows, most scholars who have approached this important topic have done so in what we call a structure–conduct–performance paradigm, later defined (and we emphasize that we are loosely borrowing that term from Mason, 1939, and Bain, 1949). We argue that the literature should alternatively, and more broadly, be viewed within the intellectual thought of entrepreneurial activity as related to the creation and use of knowledge, or to innovation. As such, this literature has public policy implications, as discussed later.

A PARADIGMATIC OVERVIEW OF THE LITERATURE

Industry–university relationships have been strengthening in industrialized nations for decades. The Council on Competitiveness (1996, pp. 3–4) notes and emphasized this trend in the USA:

> [P]articipants in the U.S. R&D enterprise will have to continue experimenting with different types of partnerships to respond to the economic constraints, competitive pressures and technological demands that are forcing adjustments across the board . . . [and in response] industry is increasingly relying on partnerships with universities . . .

A number of studies support this trend. For example, Link (1996) shows that university participation in formal research joint ventures (RJVs) has increased steadily since the mid-1980s, Cohen et al. (1997) document that the number of industry–university R&D centers increased by more than 60 percent during the 1980s, and a survey of US science faculty by Morgan (1998) reveals that many desire even more partnership relationships with industry. Mowery and Teece (1996, p. 111) contend that such growth in strategic alliances in R&D is indicative of a 'broad restructuring of the U.S. national R&D system'.

According to Hall et al. (2000, 2003), little is known about the types of roles that universities play in such research partnerships or about the economic consequences associated with those roles.[2] What research there is on the topic of universities as research partners falls broadly into either examinations of industry motivations or of university motivations for engaging in an industry–university research relationship.

As Hall et al. (2000, 2003) note, the literature identifies two broad industry motivations for engaging in an industry–university research relationship. The first is access to complementary research activity and research results.[3] Rosenberg and Nelson (1994, p. 340) emphasize that 'What university research most often does today is to stimulate and enhance the power of R&D done in industry, as contrasted with providing a substitute for it.' Pavitt (1998), based on his review of this literature, was more specific in this regard. He concludes that academic research augments the capacity of businesses to solve complex problems. The second industry motivation is access to key university personnel.[4]

University motivations for partnering with industry seem to be financially based. Administration-based financial pressures for faculty to engage in applied commercial research with industry are growing.[5] Zeckhauser (1996, p. 12746), for example, was subtle when he referred to the supposed importance of industry-supported research to universities as he describes how such relationships might develop: 'Information gifts [to industry] may be a part of [a university's] commercial courtship ritual.' Along those same lines, Cohen et al. (1997, p. 177) argue that:[6] 'University administrators appear to be

Table 18.1   Selected literature on universities as research partners: structure → conduct

Author(s) (alphabetically)	Observations	Findings
Bercovitz and Feldman (2007)	Canadian R&D firms	Firms more likely to establish university research relationships when internal R&D is exploratory
Boardman and Corley (2008)	US university faculty survey data	Likelihood of industry–university research collaboration greater when university scientists are affiliated with an industry-liked university research center
Fontana et al. (2006)	KNOW survey of EU firms	Larger firms more likely to collaborate with public research organizations (i.e. universities)
Hall (2004)	Literature review	IP mechanisms affect the extent and scope of industry–university research relationships
Hall et al. (2001)	Research projects funded by US Advanced Technology Program (ATP)	When research results are expected to be less appropriable, IP issues prevent the industry–university partnership from taking place
Link et al. (2007)	US university faculty survey data	Male-tenured faculty are more likely to engage in informal research relationships with industry
Stuart et al. (2007)	US biotechnology firms	Biotechnology firms' upstream alliances with universities increase as firms mature

Source: Compiled by the authors.

interested chiefly in the revenue generated by relationships with industry.' They are also of the opinion that faculty, who are fundamental to making such relationships work, 'desire support, *per se*, because it contributes to their personal incomes [and] eminence . . . primarily through foundation research that provides the building blocks for other research and therefore tends to be widely cited'.

However, several drawbacks to university involvement with industry have been identified, such as the diversion of faculty time and effort from teaching, the conflict between industrial trade secrecy and traditional academic openness, and the distorting effect of industry funding on the university budget allocation process (in particular, the tension induced when the distribution of resources is vastly unequal across departments and schools).

Table 18.1 summarizes selected, yet representative, early twenty-first-century empirical research related to universities as research partners. Defining 'conduct' as partnering with a university and 'structure' as those firm or university or environmental characteristics that bring about partnering, the structure → conduct literature is summarized.

To generalize, observing universities partnering with firms – conduct – is more likely in the following independent situations – structure:

- the firm is engaged in exploratory internal R&D (Bercovitz and Feldman, 2007);
- the firm is mature and large (Stuart et al., 2007; Fontana et al., 2006);

Table 18.2   Selected literature on universities as research partners: conduct ➤ performance

Author(s) (alphabetically)	Observations	Findings
Bozeman et al. (2008)	North Carolina nanotechnology firms	Lack of access to university faculty is a significant barrier to the growth of nanotechnology firms
Cohen et al. (2002)	Carnegie Mellon survey of industry R&D firms	Key channels through which university research impacts industry R&D are indirect, including publications, conferences and information relationships
Hall et al. (2000, 2003)	Research projects funded by US Advanced Technology Program (ATP)	Projects with universities as research partners are in areas involving 'new' science and thus experience more difficultly and delay; universities contribute to basic research awareness and thus help to ensure the project's successful completion
Hertzfeld et al. (2006)	US firms involved in research joint ventures	Industry learns through prior partnership experiences with universities how to overcome IP problems
Kodama (2008)	Research firms in TAMA cluster region of Japan	No relationship between university research collaboration and firm size of firm profitability
Link (2005)	US research joint ventures	Upward trend in the percent of RJVs with US university as a research member
Link and Rees (1990)	Interview data from US research firms	Productivity of R&D increases with a university is involved, especially in smaller firms
Link and Ruhm (2008)	US Small Business Innovation Research (SBIR) program projects funded by National Institutes of Health (NIH)	Probability of commercialization greater in those projects with university involvement in the research
Link and Scott (2005)	US research joint ventures	Larger RJVs more likely to include university as research partner
Link and Scott (2007)	Literature review on university research parks	Growth of university research parks, which is one indicator of intent of universities to partner with industry in research, is a post-Second World War phenomenon and it continued into the 1980s and then became sporadic but positive

Source: Compiled by the authors.

- there is a lack of intellectual property issues between the firm and the university (Hall, 2004; Hall et al. 2001);
- university faculty are male, with tenure, and are part of a university research center (Boardman and Corley, 2008; Link et al., 2007).

Table 18.2 focuses on conduct–performance where 'performance' is defined in terms of the economic consequences of partnering with a university, so that the conduct → performance literature is summarized.

Given a university–industry research partnership – structure – it is likely that the following attributes – performance – will be observed:

- there will be two-way flows of knowledge through publication and conferences, and through the formation of research joint ventures (Cohen et al., 2002; Link, 2005; Link and Scott, 2005; Hertzfeld et al., 2006);
- firm R&D will be more successful (Link and Rees, 1990; Hall et al., 2000, 2003, Kodama, 2008);
- university research parks will grow, as will attendant industries (Link and Scott, 2007; Bozeman et al., 2008).

DISCUSSION

As stated in the introduction to this chapter, it is our position that the literature on universities as research partners should be viewed within the intellectual thought of entrepreneurial activity as related to the creation and use of knowledge, or to innovation. And, we contend, that it is this nexus between entrepreneurial activity and innovation that implies that this subject has public policy implications.[7] We discuss these implications specifically in light of one important US program, the Small Business Innovation Research (SBIR) program.

The SBIR program is a public–private partnership that funds private R&D with grants both as a means of meeting government mission and of complementing the results of federal research.[8] A prototype of the SBIR program began at the National Science Foundation in 1977 (Tibbetts, 1999). At that time, the goal was to encourage small businesses, increasingly recognized as a source of innovation and employment in the US economy, to participate in NSF-sponsored research, especially research with commercial potential. Because of the early success of the program at NSF, Congress passed the Small Business Innovation Development Act of 1982 (P.L. 97-219; hereafter the 1982 Act).[9]

The 1982 Act required all government departments and agencies with external research programs of greater than $100 billion to establish an SBIR program and to set aside funds equal to 0.20 percent of the external research budget.[10] In 1983, this amount totaled $45 million for all governmental departments and agencies.

The 1982 Act states that the objectives of the program are:

1. to stimulate technological innovation;
2. to use small business to meet federal research and development needs;
3. to foster and encourage participation by minority and disadvantaged persons in technological innovation; and
4. to increase private sector commercialization of innovations derived from federal R&D.

As part of the 1982 Act, SBIR's awards are structured into three phases.[11] Phase I awards are small, generally less than $100 000 for the six-month award period. The purpose of Phase I awards is to assist firms as they assess the feasibility of an idea's scientific and commercial potential in response to the agency's objectives. Phase II awards typically range up to $750 000 over two years. These awards are for the firm to develop further

Table 18.3   *University involvement in Small Business Innovation Research (SBIR)*
             projects

2%	of projects had a university faculty member as the principal investigator
3%	of projects had an adjunct faculty member as the principal investigator
22%	of projects had a faculty or adjunct faculty member as a consultant
15%	of the projects involved graduate students
13%	of the projects relied on university facilities or equipment
3%	of the projects relied on technology licensed from a university
5%	of the projects relied on technology developed at a university by one of the participants in the project
17%	of the projects had a university as a subcontractor

Source: Wessner (2008, p. 167).

its proposed research, ideally leading to a commercializable product, process, or service. The Phase II awards of public funds for development are sometimes augmented by private funding from outside the firm. Further work on the projects launched as SBIR projects occurs in what is called Phase III, and Phase III does not involve SBIR funds. It is the stage when the firm, if it needs additional outside finance, should obtain outside it from sources other than the SBIR program to ensure that the product, process or service can move into the marketplace.

In 1992, the SBIR program was re-authorized until 2000 through the Small Business Research and Development Enactment Act (P.L. 102-564). Under the 1982 Act, the set-aside incrementally increased to 1.25 percent; the re-authorization increased that amount over time to 2.50 percent and re-emphasized the commercialization intent of SBIR-funded technologies (see point (4) of the 1982 Act above).[12] The Small Business Reauthorization Act of 2000 (P.L. 106-554) extended the SBIR program until 2008 and maintained the 2.50 percent set-aside.[13]

Eleven departments and agencies currently participate in the SBIR program: the Environmental Protection Agency (EPA); the National Aeronautics and Space Administration (NASA); the National Science Foundation (NSF); and the Departments of Agriculture (USDA), Commerce (DoC), Defense (DoD), Education (ED), Energy (DoE), Health and Human Services (HHS), Transportation (DoT), and, most recently, Homeland Security (DHS). DoD maintains the largest program: DoD, HHS, NASA, DoE, and NSF have accounted over time for nearly 97 percent of the program expenditures.

According to Wessner (2008), universities are prominently involved in linking SBIR recipient firms to the marketplace. In a recent balanced survey of Phase II award recipients, conducted by the National Research Council, about one-third of all survey respondents indicated that university faculty, graduate students and/or a university itself are involved in the development of technologies from SBIR-funded research. And in addition, more than two-thirds of funded Phase II projects are in firms with at least one academic founder, in nearly one-third of funded Phase II projects a university faculty is the principal investigator or consultant, and in nearly one-fifth of the projects universities serve as subcontractors. See Table 18.3. Relying on the same data, Link and Ruhm (2008) demonstrate that, among NIH-funded Phase II projects, those projects with university involvement enjoyed a greater probability of commercialization of the technology from the project.[14]

Regarding the policy implications flowing from this paradigmatic overview of the literature, albeit selective yet representative, publicly funded research projects could be selected at the margin, holding the quality of the proposed research constant, on the basis of whether or not the funded firm will include university talent as a research resource. Building on the arguments proffered by Leyden and Link (1999), as well as Link and Scott (2005), the university could act as an honest broker providing insights into the research while at the same time preserving appropriability.

Hall et al. (2003) argue, on the basis of publicly funded research through the Advanced Technology Program (ATP) within the National Institute of Standards and Technology (NIST), that universities create research awareness, thus facilitating sooner-than-expected completion of research projects. The inclusion of universities as research partners may be most effective when the research involves 'new' science (Hall et al., 2003, p. 491):

> Industrial research participants perceive that the university could provide research insight that is anticipatory of future research problems and could be an ombudsman anticipating and communicating to all parties the complexity of the research being undertaken.

Thus, well known as an engine of economic growth, incentives for firms to include universities as an industrial research partner could be an important policy innovation and one based on the view that the collaborative search for such knowledge is in itself an entrepreneurial endeavor.

NOTES

1. Bercovitz and Feldman (2007), building on the conceptual advances of Pisano (1991) and Chesbrough (2003), talk about exploration and exploitation in the context of upstream university research alliances.
2. Hall's (2004) subsequent emphasis on industry–university research partnerships in the USA relates to intellectual property. See also the role of intellectual property protection mechanisms (Hertzfeld et al., 2006).
3. Cohen et al. (1997) provide a selective review of this literature, emphasizing the studies that have documented that university research enhances firms' sales, R&D productivity and patenting activity. See Blumenthal et al. (1986); Jaffe (1989); Adams (1990); Berman (1990); Feller (1990); Mansfield (1991, 1992); Van de Ven (1993); Bonaccorsi and Piccaluga (1994); Klevorick et al. (1995); Zucker et al. (1994); Henderson et al. (1995); Mansfield and Lee (1996); Zeckhauser (1996); Campbell (1997); and Baldwin and Link (1998). Cockburn and Henderson (1997) show that it was important for innovative pharmaceutical firms to maintain ties to universities. Hall et al. (2000, 2003) suggest that perhaps such research ties with universities increase the 'absorptive capacity', in the sense of Cohen and Levinthal (1990), of the innovative firms.
4. See Leyden and Link (1992) and Burnham (1997). Link (1995) documents that one reason for the growth of Research Triangle Park (North Carolina) was the desire of industrial research firms to locate near the triangle universities (University of North Carolina in Chapel Hill, North Carolina State University in Raleigh and Duke University in Durham).
5. See Berman (1990), Feller (1990), Henderson et al. (1995) and Siegel et al. Link (1999).
6. Siegel et al. (1999) document that university administrators consider licensing and royalty revenues from industry as an important output from university technology transfer offices.
7. Link and Link (2009) emphasize this point and illustrate its importance using several examples of US public–private partnerships. They argue that viewing government as entrepreneur is a unique lens through which a specific subset of government policy actions can be characterized. This perspective

8. This section draws on Audretsch et al. (2002) and Wessner (2008). For a taxonomy of public–private partnerships, see Link (1999, 2006).

9. Total factor productivity growth, a measure of technological advancement, slowed in the USA, and in most industrial nations, in the early 1970s and then again in the late 1970s. The latter slowdown extended to the early 1980s. In response, a number of technology-based policies were initiated, including the 1980 R&E Tax Credit and the National Cooperative Research Act of 1984. The 1982 Act is one such initiative, although public support for enhancing innovation in small firms can be traced to as early as the 1960s (Turner and Brown, 1999).

10. SBIR is a set-aside program; it redirects existing R&D funds for competitive awards to small business rather than appropriating new monies for R&D for small firms.

11. As stated in the 1982 Act, to be eligible for an SBIR award, the small businesses must be: independently owned and operated; other than the dominant firms in the field in which they are proposing to carry out SBIR projects; organized and operated for profit; the employer of 500 or fewer employees, including employees of subsidiaries and affiliates; the primary source of employment for the project's principal investigator at the time of award and during the period when the research is conducted; and at least 51 percent owned by US citizens or lawfully admitted permanent resident aliens.

12. The percentage increased to 1.5 in 1993 and 1994; then to 2.0 in 1995 and 1996; and finally to 2.5 in 1997.

13. At the time of writing this chapter, re-authorization is still being debated in the US Congress.

14. This finding is not inconsistent with Link and Rees (1990); see Table 18.2.

REFERENCES

Adams, J.D. (1990), 'Fundamental stocks of knowledge and productivity growth', *Journal of Political Economy*, **98** (4), 673–702.

Audretsch, D.B., A.N. Link and J.T. Scott (2002), 'Public private U.S. technology partnerships: evaluating SBIR-supported research', *Research Policy*, **31** (1), 145–58.

Bain, Joe S. (1949), 'Price and production policies of large scale enterprises', in H.S. Ellis (ed.), *A Survey of Contemporary Economics*, Philadelphia, PA: The Blakiston Company, pp. 129–73.

Baldwin, W. and A.N. Link (1998), 'Universities as research joint venture partners: does size of venture matter?', *International Journal of Technology Management*, **15** (8), 895–913.

Bercovitz, J.E.L. and M.P. Feldman (2007), 'Fishing upstream: firm innovation strategy and university research alliances', *Research Policy*, **36** (7), 930–48.

Berman, E.M. (1990), 'The economic impact of industry-funded university R&D', *Research Policy*, **19** (4), 349–55.

Blumenthal, D., M.E. Gluck, K.S. Lewis, M.A. Stoto and D. Wise (1986), 'University industry research relationships in biotechnology: implications for the university', *Science*, **232**, 1361–6.

Boardman, P.C. and E.A. Corley (2008), 'University research centers and the composition of research collaborations', *Research Policy*, **37** (5), 900–913.

Bonaccorsi, A. and A. Piccaluga (1994), 'A theoretical framework for the evaluation of university–industry relationships', *R&D Management*, **24** (3), 229–47.

Bozeman, B., J. Hardin and A.N. Link (2008), 'Barriers to the diffusion of nanotechnology', *Economics of Innovation and New Technology*, **17** (7/8), 749–61.

Burnham, J.B. (1997), 'Evaluating industry/university research linkages', *Research-Technology Management*, **40** (1), 52–5.

Campbell, T.I.D. (1997), 'Public policy for the 21st century: addressing potential conflicts in university–industry collaboration', *The Review of Higher Education*, **20** (4), 357–79.

Chesbrough, H. (ed.) (2003), *Open Innovation: The New Imperative for Creating and Profiting from Technology*, Boston, MA: Harvard Business School Publishing.

Cockburn, I. and R. Henderson (1997), 'Public private interaction and the productivity of pharmaceutical research', NBER Working Paper No. 6018, Cambridge, MA.

Cohen, W.M., R. Florida, L. Randazzese and J. Walsh (1997), 'Industry and the academy: uneasy partners in the cause of technological advance', in R. Noll (ed.), *Challenges to Research University*, Washington, DC: Brookings Institution Press, pp. 171–200.

Cohen, W.M. and D.A. Levinthal (1990), 'The implications of spillovers for R&D and technology advance', in V.K. Smith and A.N. Link (eds), *Advances in Applied Micro-Economics*, Greenwich, CT; JAI Press, pp. 29–46.

Cohen, W.M., R.R. Nelson, and J.P. Walsh (2002), 'Links and impacts: the influence of public research on industrial R&D', *Management Science*, **48** (1), 1–23.

Council on Competitiveness (ed.) (1996), *Endless Frontiers, Limited Resources: U.S. R&D Policy for Competitiveness*, Washington, DC: Council on Competitiveness.

Feller, I. (1990), 'Universities as engines of R&D-based economic growth: they think they can', *Research Policy*, **19** (4), 335–48.

Fontana, R., A. Geuna and M. Matt (2006), 'Factors affecting university–industry R&D projects: the importance of searching, screening and signalling', *Research Policy*, **35** (2), 309–23.

Hall, B.H. (2004), 'University–industry research partnerships and intellectual property', in Jean-Pierre Contzen, David Gibson and Manuel V. Heitor (eds), *Rethinking Science Systems and Innovation Policies*, West Lafayette, IN: Purdue University Press, ch. 17.

Hall, B.H., A.N. Link and J.T. Scott (2000), 'Universities as research partners', NBER Working Paper No. 7643, Cambridge, MA.

Hall, B.H., A.N. Link and J.T. Scott (2001), 'Barriers inhibiting industry from partnering with universities: evidence from the advanced technology program', Working Paper, University of California, Berkeley.

Hall, B.H., A.N. Link and J.T. Scott (2003), 'Universities as research partners', *Review of Economics and Statistics*, **85** (2), 485–91.

Henderson, R., A.B. Jaffe and M. Trajtenberg (1995), 'Universities as a source of commercial technology: a detailed analysis of university patenting 1965–1988', *Review of Economics and Statistics*, **80** (1), 119–27.

Hertzfeld, H.R., A.N. Link and N.S. Vonortas (2006), 'Intellectual property protection mechanisms in research partnerships', *Research Policy*, **35** (6), 825–38.

Jaffe, A.B. (1989), 'Real effects of academic research', *The American Economic Review*, **79** (5), 957–78.

Klevorick, A.K., R.C. Levin, R.R. Nelson and S.G. Winter (1995), 'On the sources and significance of inter-industry differences in technological opportunities', *Research Policy*, **24** (2), 185–205.

Kodama, T. (2008), 'The role of intermediation and absorptive capacity in facilitating university–industry linkages: an empirical study of TAMA in Japan', *Research Policy*, **37** (8), 1224–40.

Leyden, D.P. and A.N. Link (eds) (1992), *Government's Role in Innovation*, Dordrecht: Kluwer Academic Publishers.

Leyden, D.P. and A.N. Link (1999), 'Federal laboratories as research partners', *International Journal of Industrial Organization*, **17** (4), 575–92.

Link, A.N. (ed.) (1995), *A Generosity of Spirit: The Early History of Research Triangle Park*, Chapel Hill, NC: University of North Carolina Press, the Research Triangle Park Foundation.

Link, A.N. (1996), 'Research joint ventures: patterns from federal register filings', *Review of Industrial Organization*, **11** (5), 617–28.

Link, A.N. (1999), 'Public/private partnerships in the United States', *Industry and Innovation*, **6** (2), 191–217.

Link, A.N. (2005), 'Research joint ventures in the United States: a descriptive analysis', in A.N. Link and F.M. Scherer (eds), *Essays in Honor of Edwin Mansfield: The Economics of R&D, Innovation, and Technological Change*, Norwell, MA: Springer, pp. 187–94.

Link, A.N. (ed.) (2006), *Public/Private Partnerships: Innovation Strategies and Policy Alternatives*, New York: Springer.

Link, A.N. and J.R. Link (eds) (2009), *Government as Entrepreneur*, New York: Oxford University Press.

Link, A.N. and J. Rees (1990), 'Firm size, university based research, and the returns to R&D', *Small Business Economics*, **2** (1), 25–31.

Link, A.N. and Ch.J. Ruhm (2008), 'Bringing science to market: commercializing from NIH SBIR awards', NBER Working Paper No. 14057, Cambridge, MA.

Link, A.N. and J.T. Scott (2005), 'Universities as partners in U.S. research joint ventures', *Research Policy*, **34** (3), 385–93.

Link, A.N. and J.T. Scott (2007), 'The economics of university research parks', *Oxford Review of Economic Policy*, **23** (4), 661–74.

Link, A.N., D.S. Siegel and B. Bozeman (2007), 'An empirical analysis of the propensity of academics to engage in informal technology transfer', *Industrial and Corporate Change*, **16** (4), 641–55.

Mansfield, E. (1991), 'Academic research and industrial innovation', *Research Policy*, **20** (1), 1–12.

Mansfield, E. (1992), 'Academic research and industrial innovation: a further note', *Research Policy*, **21** (3), 295–6.

Mansfield, E. and J.-Y. Lee (1996), 'The modern university: contributor to industrial innovation and recipient of industrial R&D support', *research policy*, **25** (7), 1047–58.

Mason, E.S. (1939), 'Price and production policies of large scale enterprises', *The American Economic Review*, **29** (1), 61–74.

Morgan, R.P. (1998), 'University research contributions to industry: the faculty view', in Peter D. Blair and Robert A. Frosch (eds), *Trends in Industrial Innovation: Industry Perspectives & Policy Implications*, Research Triangle Park: Sigma Xi, The Scientific Research Society.

Mowery, D.C. and D.J. Teece (1996), 'Strategic alliances and industrial research', in R.S. Rosenbloom and W.J. Spencer (eds), *Engines of Innovation: U.S. Industrial Research at the End of an Era*, Boston, MA: Harvard Business School Publishing, pp. 111–32.

Pavitt, K. (1998), 'The social shaping of the national science base', *Research Policy*, **27** (8), 793–805.

Pisano, G. (1991), 'The governance of innovation: vertical integration and collaborative arrangements in the biotechnology industry', *Research Policy*, **20**, 237–49.

Rosenberg, N. and R.R. Nelson (1994), 'American universities and technical advance in industry', *Research Policy*, **23** (3), 323–48.

Schumpeter, J.A. (1928), 'The instability of capitalism', *Economic Journal*, **38** (151), 361–86.

Schumpeter, J.A. (ed.) (1934), *The Theory of Economic Development*, Cambridge, MA: Harvard University Press.

Schumpeter, J.A. (ed.) (1939), *Business Cycles*, New York: McGraw-Hill.

Siegel, D., D. Waldman and A.N. Link (1999), 'Assessing the impact of organizational practices on the productivity of university technology transfer offices: An exploratory study', NBER Working Paper No. 7256, Cambridge, MA.

Stuart, T.E., S.Z. Ozdemir and W.W. Ding (2007), 'Vertical alliance networks: the case of university–biotechnology–pharmaceutical alliance chains', *Research Policy*, **36** (4), 477–98.

Tibbetts, R. (1999), 'The small business innovation research program and NSF SBIR commercialization results', mimeograph.

Turner, J. and G.J. Brown (1999), 'Reworking the federal role in small business research', *ISSUES in Science and Technology*, **15** (4), 51–8.

Van de Ven, A.H. (1993), 'A community perspective on the emergence of innovations', *Journal of Engineering Technology Management*, **10**, 23–51.

Wessner, C.W. (ed.) (2008), *An Assessment of the SBIR Program*, Washington, DC: National Academy Press.

Zeckhauser, R. (1996), 'The challenge of contracting for technological information', *Proceedings of the National Academy of Science*, **93** (23), 12743–8.

Zucker, L.G., M.R. Darby and J. Armstrong (1994), 'Intellectual capital and the firm: the technology of geographically localized knowledge spillovers', NBER Working Paper No. 4946, Cambridge, MA.

19 The rise of university technology transfer and academic entrepreneurship: managerial and policy implications
Donald S. Siegel

INTRODUCTION

A salient trend is the establishment and growth of technology transfer offices (henceforth TTOs) at research universities around the globe. These offices attempt to commercialize the university's intellectual property, via patenting, licensing, and startup creation. The US-based Association of University Technology Managers (AUTM, 2008) reports that the annual number of patents granted to US universities rose from fewer than 300 in 1980 to 3662 in 2007, while licensing of new technologies increased almost five-fold between 1991 and 2007. Annual licensing revenue generated by US universities rose from about $160 million in 1991 to $1.8 billion in 2007. In 2007 a total of 555 university-based startup companies were launched, while 6321 new firms based on university-owned intellectual property were created between 1980 and 2007.

This pattern in the USA is part of an international phenomenon, with substantial increases in patenting, licensing, and startup creation reported in Europe, Australia, Canada and elsewhere (Wright et al., 2007). Examples of key technologies transferred from universities to firms include the famous Boyer–Cohen 'gene-splicing' technique that launched the biotechnology industry, diagnostic tests for breast cancer and osteoporosis, Internet search engines (e.g. Google), music synthesizers, computer-aided design (CAD) and green technologies.

TTOs constitute an 'intermediary' between suppliers of innovations (academic scientists) and those who can potentially commercialize these innovations: firms, entrepreneurs and venture capitalists. TTOs facilitate commercial knowledge transfers of intellectual property resulting from university research through licensing to existing firms or the establishment of startup companies launched to commercialize inventions. The activities of these intermediaries have key policy implications, since licensing agreements and university-based startups can yield additional revenue for the university, employment opportunities for university-based researchers (especially post-docs) and graduate students, as well as local economic and technological spillovers through the stimulation of additional R&D investment and job creation.

As noted in Siegel et al. (2003), the traditional emphasis of the TTO is on licensing and patenting. Increased attention is devoted, however, to the creation of spin-off firms by university scientists. Scholars examine university technology commercialization and entrepreneurship, typically focusing on the 'performance' of TTOs, while also analyzing agents engaging in commercialization, such as academic scientists. Several authors evaluate the antecedents and consequences of faculty involvement in technology commercialization, such as the propensity of academics to patent, disclose inventions, co-author with industry scientists, and form university-based startups.

In this chapter, I review the burgeoning academic literature and attempt to synthesize these findings. The remainder of the chapter is organized as follows: in the second section, I provide a review of the literature on the productivity of TTOs. In the following section, I summarize studies of academic entrepreneurship – university-based startups. In the final section, I attempt to synthesize these findings and identify some key recommendations for policy-makers.

REVIEW OF SELECTED PAPERS ON UNIVERSITY TTOS

Table 19.1 summarizes some of the key theoretical and empirical papers on university TTOs. Following Siegel et al. (2003), most of the papers start with the concept of a production function, leading to the construction of measures of 'productivity', based on indicators of 'outputs' and 'inputs' of university technology transfer (e.g. Siegel et al., 2003; Thursby and Thursby, 2002; Friedman and Silberman, 2003; and Chapple et al., 2005). Several papers in this realm utilize non-parametric methods of productivity measurement, such as data envelopment analysis (henceforth DEA), a linear programming method. Others employ parametric estimation procedures, such as stochastic frontier estimation.

Siegel et al. (2003) conducted the first systematic econometric analysis of the relative productivity of university TTOs. In their econometric analysis, the (single) output is licensing activity and the inputs are invention disclosures, full-time equivalent (FTE) employees in the TTO, and legal expenditures. The authors report that the production function model yields a good fit. Based on estimates of their 'marginal product', it appears that technology licensing officers add significant value to the commercialization process. The findings also imply that spending more on lawyers reduces the number of licensing agreements but increases licensing revenue. Licensing revenue is subject to increasing returns, while licensing agreements are characterized by constant returns to scale. An implication of increasing returns for licensing revenue is that a university wishing to maximize revenue should spend more on lawyers. Perhaps this would enable technology licensing officers to devote more time to eliciting additional invention disclosures and less time to negotiating with firms.

The authors supplement their econometric analysis with qualitative evidence, derived from 55 structured in-person interviews of 100 university technology transfer stakeholders (i.e. academic and industry scientists, university technology managers, as well as corporate managers and entrepreneurs) at five research universities in Arizona and North Carolina. The field research allowed them to identify intellectual property policies and organizational practices that can potentially enhance technology transfer performance.

The qualitative analysis identified three key impediments to effective university technology transfer. The first was informational and cultural barriers between universities and firms, especially for small firms. Another impediment was insufficient rewards for faculty involvement in university technology transfer. This includes both pecuniary and non-pecuniary rewards, such as credit towards tenure and promotion. Some respondents even suggested that involvement in technology transfer might be detrimental to their

Table 19.1   Selected papers on the performance of university technology transfer offices

Author(s)	Data sets	Methodology	Key results
Siegel et al. (2003a)	AUTM, NSF, and US Census data, interviews	Total factor productivity (TFP) of university licensing – stochastic frontier analysis and field interviews	TTOs exhibit constant returns to scale with respect to the no. of licenses; increasing returns to scale with respect to licensing revenue; organizational and environmental factors have considerable explanatory power
Link and Siegel (2005)	AUTM, NSF, and US Census data, interviews	TFP of university licensing – stochastic frontier analysis	Land-grant universities are more efficient in technology transfer; higher royalty shares for faculty members are associated with greater licensing income
Friedman and Silberman (2003)	AUTM, NSF, NRC, Milken Institute 'Tech-Pole' data	Regression analysis – systems equations estimation	Higher royalty shares for faculty members are associated with greater licensing income
Lach and Schankerman (2004)	AUTM, NSF, NRC	Regression analysis	Higher royalty shares for faculty members are associated with greater licensing income
Rogers et al. (2000)	AUTM, NSF, NRC	Correlation analysis of composite technology transfer score	Positive correlation between faculty quality, age of TTO, and no. of TTO staff and higher levels of performance in technology transfer
Thursby et al. (2001)	AUTM, authors' survey	Descriptive analysis of authors' survey/ regression analysis	Inventions tend to disclose at an early stage of development; elasticities of licenses and royalties with respect to invention disclosures are both less than one; faculty members are increasingly likely to disclose inventions
Bercovitz et al. (2001)	AUTM and case studies, interviews	Qualitative and quantitative analysis	Analysis of different organization structures for technology transfer at Duke, Johns Hopkins and Penn State; differences in structure may be related to technology transfer performance
Thursby and Kemp (2002)	AUTM	Data envelopment analysis and logit regressions on efficiency scores	Faculty quality and no. of TTO staff have a positive impact on various technology transfer outputs; private universities appear to be more efficient than public universities; universities with medical schools less efficient
Thursby and Thursby (2002)	AUTM and authors' own survey	Data envelopment analysis	Growth in university licensing and patenting can be attributed to an increase in the willingness of professors to patent and license, as well as outsourcing of R&D by firms; not to a shift toward more applied research

Table 19.1 (continued)

Author(s)	Data sets	Methodology	Key results
Chapple et al. (2005)	UK-NUBS/ UNICO survey – ONS	Data envelopment analysis and stochastic frontier analysis	UK TTOs exhibit decreasing returns to scale and low levels of absolute efficiency; organizational and environmental factors have considerable explanatory power
Carlsson and Fridh (2002)	AUTM	Linear regression	Research expenditure, invention disclosures, and age of TTO have a positive impact on university patenting and licensing

careers. Finally, there appear to be problems with staffing and compensation practices in the TTO. One such problem is a high rate of turnover among technology licensing officers, which is detrimental to the establishment of long-term relationships with firms and entrepreneurs. Other concerns are insufficient business and marketing experience in the TTO and the possible need for incentive compensation.

An interesting finding is that the variation in relative performance among TTOs cannot be completely explained by environmental and institutional factors, implying that organizational practices are likely to be an important determinant of relative performance. In a subsequent paper, Link and Siegel (2005) report that a particular organizational practice enhances technology transfer performance: the 'royalty distribution formula', which determines the fraction of revenue from a licensing transaction that is allocated to a faculty member who develops the new technology. Based on data from 113 US TTOs, the authors find that universities allocating a higher percentage of royalty payments to faculty members tend to be more efficient in technology transfer activities (closer to the 'frontier', in the parlance of SFE, stochastic frontier estimation). Organizational incentives for university technology transfer appear to be important. This finding is independently confirmed in Friedman and Silberman (2003) as well as in Lach and Schankerman (2004), using slightly different methods and data.

A theoretical paper by Jensen et al. (2003) models invention disclosures by faculty and university technology licensing as a game, in which the principal is the university administration, the faculty, and the TTO are agents who maximize expected utility. The TTO is treated as a dual agent, that is, an agent of both the faculty and the university. Faculty members must decide whether to disclose the invention to the TTO and at what stage; whether to disclose at an early embryonic stage or wait until it is a lab-scale prototype. The university administration influences the TTO and faculty members by establishing university-wide policies for the shares of licensing income and/or sponsored research. If an invention is disclosed, the TTO decides whether to search for a firm to license the technology and, in that case, then negotiates the terms of the licensing agreement with the licensee. Quality is incorporated in their model as a determinant of the probability of successful commercialization. According to the authors, the TTO engages in a 'balancing act', in the sense that it can influence the rate of invention disclosures; it must evaluate the inventions once they are disclosed; and it negotiates licensing agreements with firms as the agent of university administration.

The Jensen et al. (2003) theoretical analysis generates some interesting empirical predictions. For instance, in equilibrium, the probability that a university scientist discloses an invention and the stage at which he or she discloses it are related to the pecuniary reward from licensing, as well as faculty quality. The authors test the empirical implications of the dual agency model based on an extensive survey of the objectives, characteristics and outcomes of licensing activity at 62 US universities.[1] Their survey results provide empirical support for the hypothesis that the TTO is a dual agent. They also find that faculty quality is positively associated with the rate of invention disclosure at the earliest stage and negatively associated with the share of licensing income allocated to inventors.

Bercovitz et al. (2001) assess a key implementation issue in university management of technology transfer: the organizational structure of the TTO and its relationship to the overall university research administration. Based on the theoretical analysis of Alfred Chandler (1997) and Oliver Williamson (1964), who analyze the performance implications of four organizational forms: the functional or unitary form (U-form), the multidivisional (M-form), the holding company (H-form), and the matrix form (MX-form). The authors note that these structures have different implications for the ability of a university to coordinate activity, facilitate internal and external information flows, and align incentives in a manner that is consistent with its strategic goals with respect to technology transfer.

To test these assertions, they examine TTOs at Duke, Johns Hopkins and Penn State, and find evidence of alternative organizational forms at these three institutions. They attempt to link these differences in structure to variation in technology transfer performance along three dimensions: transaction output, the ability to coordinate licensing and sponsored research activities, and incentive alignment capability. While further research is needed to make conclusive statements regarding organizational structure and performance, the findings imply that organizational form does matter.

Other papers focus exclusively on the corporate perspective of formal university technology transfer. Hertzfeld et al. (2006) interviewed and then surveyed chief intellectual property attorneys at 54 R&D-intensive US firms concerning intellectual property protection mechanisms related to university patents. They found that firms express great difficulty in dealing with university TTOs on intellectual property issues, citing TTO staff inexperience; the TTO's lack of general business knowledge; and its tendency to overstate the commercial value of the patent. The authors report that in some cases firms decide to by-pass the TTO and deal directly with the university scientist or engineer.

Most empirical studies of TTO performance are based on US data. In recent years, several papers based on European Union data have been published. Using DEA and SFE methods, Chapple et al. (2005) find in a study of 50 UK universities that TTOs exhibit a low level of absolute efficiency in licensing activity and that there appear to be decreasing returns to scale. These findings indicate that growth in the size of TTOs is not necessarily accompanied by a corresponding growth in the business skills and capabilities of TTO managers. The findings imply a need to upgrade skills and capabilities and to reconfigure TTOs into smaller units, possibly with regionally based sector focus.

In sum, extant literature on university TTOs suggests that the key impediments to better university technology transfer performance tend to be organizational in nature (Siegel et al. 2003a; Siegel et al. 2003b). These include incentive problems, relating both to pecuniary and non-pecuniary rewards, such as credit toward tenure and promotion, differences in organizational cultures between universities and (small) firms, as well as the staffing and compensation practices of the TTO itself.

REVIEW OF STUDIES OF ACADEMIC ENTREPRENEURSHIP

While licensing is traditionally the most popular mechanism for commercialization of university-based technologies, universities are increasingly emphasizing the entrepreneurial dimension of technology transfer. The Association of University Technology Managers (AUTM, 2008) reports that the number of startup firms at US universities rose from 35 in 1980 to 555 in 2007. This rapid increase in startup activity attracts considerable attention in academic literature. Some researchers focus on the university as the unit of analysis, while others analyze entrepreneurial agents (either academic or non-academic entrepreneurs).

Studies using the university as the unit of analysis typically focus on the role of university policies in stimulating entrepreneurial activity. Roberts and Malone (1996) speculate that Stanford generated fewer startups than comparable institutions in the early 1990s because the institution refused to sign exclusive licenses to inventor–founders.

Degroof and Roberts (2004) examine the importance of university policies relating to startups in regions where environmental factors (e.g. technology transfer and infrastructure for entrepreneurship) are not particularly conducive to entrepreneurial activity. A taxonomy of four types of startup policies was derived: (1) an absence of startup policies; (2) minimal selectivity/support; (3) intermediate selectivity/support; and (4) comprehensive selectivity/support. Consistent with Roberts and Malone (1996), they find that comprehensive selectivity/support is the optimal policy for generating startups that exploit knowledge with high growth potential. However, such a policy is an ideal that may not be feasible, given resource constraints. The authors conclude that while spinout policies do matter in the sense that they affect the growth potential of ventures; it may be more desirable to formulate these policies at a higher level of aggregation than the university.

Table 19.2 summarizes some of the key theoretical and empirical papers on academic entrepreneurship. DiGregorio and Shane (2003) directly assess the determinants of startup formation using AUTM data from 101 universities and 530 startups. Based on estimates of count regressions of the number of university-based startups, they conclude that the two key determinants of startups are faculty quality and the ability of the university and inventor(s) to assume equity in a startup in lieu of licensing royalty fees. Interestingly, the availability of venture capital in the region where the university is located and the commercial orientation of the university (proxied by the percentage of the university's research budget that is derived from industry) are found to have an insignificant impact on the rate of startup formation. The authors also find that a royalty distribution formula that is more favorable to faculty members reduces startup formation, a finding confirmed by Markman et al. (2005a). DiGregorio and Shane (2003) attribute this result to higher opportunity costs associated with launching a new firm, relative to licensing the technology to an existing firm.

O'Shea et al. (2005) extend these findings in several ways. First, they employ a more sophisticated econometric technique employed by Blundell et al. (1995) on innovation counts, which accounts for unobserved heterogeneity across universities due to 'history

Table 19.2   Key studies of academic entrepreneurship

Author(s)	Unit of analysis	Data/ methodology	Key results
DiGregorio and Shane (2003)	University-based startups	AUTM survey/count regressions of the determinants of the no. of startups	Two key determinants of startup formation: faculty quality and the ability of the university and inventor(s) to take equity in a startup, in lieu of licensing royalty fees; a royalty distribution formula that is more favorable to faculty members reduces startup formation
O'Shea, Allen, and Arnaud (2005)	University-based startups	AUTM survey/count regressions of the determinants of the no. of startups	A university's previous success in technology transfer is a key determinant of its rate of startup formation
Franklin et al. (2001)	TTOs and university-based startups	Authors' quantitative survey of UK TTOs	Universities that wish to launch successful technology transfer startups should employ a combination of academic and surrogate entrepreneurship
Lockett et al. (2003)	TTOs and university-based startups	Quantitative and qualitative surveys of UK TTOs	Universities that generate the most startups have clear, well-defined spinoff strategies, strong expertise in entrepreneurship, and vast social networks
Lockett and Wright (2005)	TTOs and university-based startups	Survey of UK TTOs/count regressions of the determinants of the no. of startups	A university's rate of startup formation is positively associated with its expenditure on intellectual property protection, the business development capabilities of TTOs, and the extent to which its royalty distribution formula favors faculty members
Clarysse et al. (2005)	TTOs and university-based startups	Interviews and descriptive data on 50 universities across seven European countries	Five incubation models identified. Three match resources, activities and objectives: low selective, supportive and incubator. Two do not: competence deficient and resource deficient
Markman et al. (2005a)	TTOs and university startups	AUTM survey, authors' survey/ linear regression analysis	The most attractive combinations of technology stage and licensing strategy for new venture creation – early stage technology and licensing for equity – are least likely to be favored by the university (due to risk aversion and a focus on short-run revenue maximization)
Markman et al. (2005b)	TTOs and university-based startups	AUTM survey, authors' survey/ linear regression analysis	There are three key determinants of time-to market (speed): TTO resources, competency in identifying licensees, and participation of faculty–inventors in the licensing process

Author(s)	Unit of analysis	Data/ methodology	Key results
Bercovitz and Feldman (2008)	Medical School researchers at Johns Hopkins and Duke	Determinants of the probability of filing an invention disclosure	Three factors influence the decision to disclose inventions: norms at the institutions where the researchers were trained and the disclosure behaviors of their department chairs and peers
Audretsch (2000)	Entrepreneurs in the life sciences	101 founders of 52 biotech firms/ hazard function regression analysis	Academic entrepreneurs tend to be older, more scientifically experienced
Louis et al. (1989)	Faculty members in the life sciences	778 faculty members from 40 universities/ regression analysis	Key determinant of faculty-based entrepreneurship: local group norms; university policies and structures have little effect
Lowe and González (2007)	Faculty members	150 faculty members from 15 universities/ regression analysis	Faculty members are more productive researchers than observationally equivalent colleagues before they established their firms. The research productivity of these academics did not decline in the aftermath of their entrepreneurial activity
Zucker, Darby, and Brewer (1998)	Relationships involving 'star' scientists and US biotech firms	Scientific papers, data on biotech firms from the North Carolina Biotechnology Center (1992) and Bioscan (1993)/ count regressions	Location of star scientists predicts firm entry in biotechnology
Zucker, Darby and Armstrong (2000)	Relationships involving 'star' scientists and US biotech firms	Scientific papers reporting genetic-sequence discoveries/count regressions	Collaboration between star scientists and firm scientists enhances research performance of US biotech firms, as measured using three proxies: no. of patents granted, no. of products in development, and no. of products on the market
Zucker and Darby (2001)	Relationships involving 'star' scientists and Japanese biotech firms	Data on biotechnology firms and the Nikkei biotechnology directory	Collaboration between star scientists and firm scientists enhances research performance of Japanese biotech firms, as measured using three proxies: no. of patents granted, no. of products in development, and no. of products on the market
Vanaelst et al. (2006)	Start-ups and entrepreneurial team members	Interview data and comparative univariate analysis	Some researchers actively involved in the first phase of the spin-off exit; new members enter, especially those with commercial human capital; some faculty remain with university but work part-time in a technology development role for spin-off

and tradition'. This type of 'path dependence' would seem to be quite important in the university context. Indeed, the authors find that a university's previous success in technology transfer is a key explanatory factor of startup formation. Consistent with DiGregorio and Shane (2003), they also find that faculty quality, commercial capability, and the extent of federal science and engineering funding are also significant determinants of higher rates of university startup formation.

Franklin et al. (2001) analyze perceptions at UK universities regarding entrepreneurial startups that emerge from university technology transfer. The authors distinguish between academic and surrogate (external) entrepreneurs and 'old' and 'new' universities in the UK. Old universities have well-established research reputations, world-class scientists, and are typically receptive to entrepreneurial startups. New universities, on the other hand, tend to be weaker in academic research and less flexible with regard to entrepreneurial ventures. They find that the most significant barriers to the adoption of entrepreneurial-friendly policies are cultural and informational. The universities generating the most startups (i.e. old universities) are those that have the most favorable policies regarding surrogate (external) entrepreneurs. The authors conclude that the best approach for universities that wish to launch successful technology transfer startups is a combination of academic and surrogate entrepreneurship. This would enable universities to simultaneously exploit the technical benefits of inventor involvement and the commercial know-how of surrogate entrepreneurs.

In a follow-up study, Lockett et al. (2003) find that universities generating the most startups have clear, well-defined strategies regarding the formation and management of spinouts. These schools tend to use surrogate (external) entrepreneurs, rather than academic entrepreneurs, to manage this process. It also appears as though the more successful universities have greater expertise and vast social networks that help them generate more startups. However, the role of the academic inventor was not found to differ between the more and less successful universities. Finally, equity ownership is more widely distributed among the members of the spinout company in the case of the more successful universities.

Based on an extended version of the same database, Lockett and Wright (2005) assess the relationship between the resources and capabilities of UK TTOs and the rate of startup formation at their respective universities. In doing so, the authors apply the resource-based view (RBV) of the firm to the university. RBV asserts that an organization's superior performance (in the parlance of strategic management, its 'competitive advantage') is related to its internal resources and capabilities. They are able to distinguish empirically a university's resource inputs from its routines and capabilities. Based on estimation of count regressions (Poisson and negative binomial), the authors conclude that there is a positive correlation between startup formation and the university's expenditure on intellectual property protection as well as the business development capabilities of TTOs and the extent to which its royalty distribution formula favors faculty members. These findings imply that universities wishing to spawn numerous startups should devote greater attention to recruitment, training and development of technology transfer officers with broad-based commercial skills. These results are important for the following section.

Markman et al. (2005a) develop a model linking university patents to new-firm creation in university-based incubators, with university TTOs acting as intermediary. They focus on universities because such institutions are responsible for a substantial fraction of technology-oriented incubators in the USA. While there are some qualitative studies of university TTO licensing (e.g. Bercovitz et al., 2001; Siegel et al., 2003; Mowery et al., 2001), these are based on data from elite research universities only (e.g. Stanford, UC Berkeley and MIT) or from a small sample of more representative institutions. These results may not be generalizable to the larger population of institutions, which often do not enjoy the same favorable environmental conditions. To build a theoretically saturated model of TTOs' entrepreneurial development strategies, the authors collected qualitative and quantitative data from virtually the entire population of university TTOs.

A surprising conclusion of Markman et al. (2005a) is that the most 'attractive' combinations of technology stage and licensing strategy for new venture creation, i.e. early-stage technology, combined with licensing for equity, are least likely to be favored by the university and thus not likely to be used. That is because universities and TTOs typically focus on short-term cash maximization, and are extremely risk-averse with respect to financial and legal risks. Their findings are consistent with evidence presented in Siegel et al. (2003a), who find that TTOs appear to do a better job of serving the needs of large firms than small entrepreneurial companies. The results of these studies imply that universities should modify their technology transfer strategies if they are serious about promoting entrepreneurial development.

In other studies the authors use the same database to assess the role of incentive systems in stimulating academic entrepreneurship and the determinants of innovation speed, or time to market (Markman et al. 2004, 2005a). One interesting result of Markman et al. (2004) is that there is a positive association between compensation to TTO personnel with both equity licensing and startup formation. On the other hand, royalty payments to faculty members and their departments are either uncorrelated or even negatively correlated with entrepreneurial activity. This is consistent with DiGregorio and Shane (2003).

In Markman et al. (2005b), the authors find that speed matters, in the sense that the 'faster' the TTO can commercialize technologies protected by patents, the greater the returns to the university and the higher the rate of startup formation. They also report that there are three key determinants of speed: TTO resources, competency in identifying licensees, and participation of faculty–inventors in the licensing process.

Nerkar and Shane (2003) analyze the entrepreneurial dimension of university technology transfer, based on an empirical analysis of 128 firms founded between 1980 and 1996 to commercialize inventions owned by MIT. They begin by noting that there is an extensive literature in management that suggests that new technology firms are more likely to survive if they exploit radical technologies (e.g. Tushman and Anderson, 1986) and if they possess patents with a broad scope (e.g. Merges and Nelson, 1990). The authors propose that the relationships between radicalness and survival with scope and survival are moderated both by the market structure and level of concentration in the firm's industry. Specifically, they assert that radicalness and patent scope increase the probability of survival more in fragmented industries than in concentrated sectors. They estimate a hazard function model using the MIT database and find empirical support for these hypotheses. Thus the effectiveness of the technology strategies of new firms may be dependent on industry conditions.

Several studies focus on individual scientists and entrepreneurs in the context of university technology transfer. Audretsch (2000) examines the extent to which entrepreneurs at universities differ from other entrepreneurs. He analyzes a data set on university life scientists in order to estimate the determinants of the probability that they will establish a new biotechnology firm. Based on a hazard function analysis, including controls for the quality of the scientist's research, measures or regional activity in biotechnology, and a dummy for the career trajectory of the scientist, the author finds that university entrepreneurs tend to be older and more scientifically experienced.

There is also evidence on the importance of norms, standards and culture in this context. Based on a qualitative analysis of five European universities that had outstanding performance in technology transfer, Clarke (1998) concludes that the existence of an entrepreneurial culture at those institutions was a critical factor in their success. Roberts (1991) finds that social norms and MIT's tacit approval of entrepreneurs were critical determinants of successful academic entrepreneurship at MIT.

Louis et al. (1989) analyze the propensity of life-science faculty to engage in various aspects of technology transfer, including commercialization. Their statistical sample consists of life scientists at the 50 research universities receiving the most funding from the National Institutes of Health. The authors find that the most important determinant of involvement in technology commercialization was local group norms. They report that university policies and structures had little effect on this activity.

The unit of analysis in Bercovitz and Feldman (2008) is also the individual faculty member. They analyze the propensity of medical school researchers at Johns Hopkins and Duke to file invention disclosures, a potential precursor to technology commercialization. The authors find that three factors influence the decision to disclose inventions: norms at the institutions where the researchers were trained; disclosure behaviors of their department chairs; and the disclosure behavior of their peers.

The series of seminal papers by Lynne Zucker and Michael Darby with various collaborators explore the role of 'star' scientists in the life sciences on the creation and location of new biotechnology firms in the USA and Japan. In Zucker et al. (2000), the authors assess the impact of these university scientists on the research productivity of US firms. Scientists either resigned from the university to establish a new firm or kept their faculty position but worked very closely with industry scientists. In the life sciences, a star scientist is one who has discovered more than 40 genetic sequences, and affiliations with firms are defined through co-authoring between the star scientist and industry scientists. Research productivity is measured using three proxies: number of patents granted, number of products in development, and number of products on the market. Ties between star scientists and firm scientists are found to have a positive effect on these three dimensions of research productivity, as well as other aspects of firm performance and rates of entry in the US biotechnology industry (Zucker, Darby and Armstrong, 1998; Zucker, Darby and Brewer, 1998).

In Zucker and Darby (2001), the authors examine detailed data on the outcomes of collaborations between 'star' university scientists and biotechnology firms in Japan. Similar patterns emerge in the sense that they find that such interactions substantially enhance the research productivity of Japanese firms, as measured by the rate of firm patenting, product innovation and market introductions of new products. However, they also report an absence of geographically localized knowledge spillovers resulting from university technology transfer in Japan, in contrast to the USA, where they found that such effects were strong. The authors attribute this result to institutional difference between Japan and the USA in university technology transfer. Whereas in the USA, it is common for academic scientists to work with firm scientists at the firm's laboratories, in Japan, firm scientists typically work in the academic scientist's laboratory. Thus, according to the authors, it is not surprising that the local economic development impact of university technology transfer appears to be lower in Japan than in the USA.

Networks of academic scientists who become entrepreneurs may be important influences on the performance of university startups. Mustar (1997) classified startups depending on their cooperation arrangements with other public and/or private bodies and highlighted the relationship between the breadth of the social network, the growth trajectory, and the attrition rate. Nicolaou and Birley (2003) recognized that differences in the embeddedness of academics in a network of ties external or internal to the university may be associated with different growth trajectories.

SYNTHESIS AND RECOMMENDATIONS

The extant academic literature on university technology transfer and academic entrepreneurship provides some important lessons for university administrators who wish to stimulate this activity. Before addressing the important aspects of incentives and culture, the university administration must first make it clear that technology commercialization is a key strategic priority of the institution. This strategic choice should be reflected in resource allocation patterns; for instance, hiring individuals with strong technical and commercial backgrounds to staff the TTO.

The university must also decide on which mode of technology commercialization to stress: whether it is licensing, startups, sponsored research or other mechanisms of technology transfer focused on directly stimulating economic and regional development, such as incubators and science parks. Institutions choosing to stress the entrepreneurial dimension of technology transfer need to address skill deficiencies in TTOs, reward systems inconsistent with enhanced entrepreneurial activity, and education/training for faculty members, post-docs and graduate students relating to interactions with entrepreneurs. Business schools at these universities can play a major role in addressing these skill and educational deficiencies through the delivery of targeted programs to technology licensing officers and members of the campus community wishing to launch startup firms.

They also need to make sure that the TTO is working closely with the university's technology incubator and research park, especially if startup creation is a key strategic goal. Licensing and sponsored research generate a stream of revenue, while equity from startups can generate large payoffs in the long term. Universities wishing to stress economic and regional development (as many public universities might wish to do) should focus on startup creation, since these companies can potentially create jobs in the local region or state. Note also that while a startup strategy entails higher risk, since the failure rate of new firms is quite high, it also can potentially yield higher returns if the startup goes public. It is also important to note that a startup strategy entails additional resources if the university chooses to assist the academic entrepreneur in launching and developing their startup.

A review of the literature also reveals the high potential opportunity cost of commercialization and the need to modify promotion and tenure requirements to reflect the growing importance of commercialization. Specifically, universities placing a high priority on technology commercialization should modify their promotion and tenure guidelines to place a stronger positive weight on technology transfer activities in the promotion and tenure decision. This will require a great deal of tenacity on the part of academic administrators since there will be resistance from conventional academics to this change. I believe that such changes are warranted at institutions that wish to do so, although I do not underestimate the difficulty of changing norms, standards and values among entrenched tenured faculty. Finally, a switch from standard compensation to incentive compensation for technology licensing officers could also result in more licensing agreements.

It has also been difficult for universities to attract and retain TTO personnel with the appropriate skill sets to support an aggressive commercialization strategy. Traditionally, there is an emphasis in TTOs on legal skills, with an eye to protecting the university's intellectual property portfolio. However, an expansion of technology commercialization will require the creation and development of university-based startups, which means that TTO employees must also be adept at opportunity recognition, marketing, finance and other aspects of commercialization. They also need to be adept at interacting with venture capitalists and angel investors.

NOTE

1.   See Thursby et al. (2001) for an extensive description of this survey.

REFERENCES

Association of University Technology Managers (AUTM) (2008), *The AUTM Licensing Survey*, Fiscal Year 2007, Norwalk, CT: AUTM, Inc.

Audretsch, D.B. (2000), 'Is University Entrepreneurship Different?', mimeo, Indiana University.

Bercovitz, J.E.L. and M.P. Feldman (2008), 'Academic entrepreneurs: organizational change at the individual level', *Organization Science*, **19** (1), 69–89.

Bercovitz, J.E.L., M.P. Feldman, I. Feller and R. Burton (2001), 'Organizational structure as determinants of academic patent and licensing behavior: an exploratory study of Duke, Johns Hopkins, and Pennsylvania State Universities', *Journal of Technology Transfer*, **26** (1–2), 21–35.

Blundell, R., R. Griffith and J. Van Reenen (1995), 'Dynamic count data models of technological innovation', *Economic Journal*, **105** (429), 333–44.

Carlsson, B. and A. Fridh (2002), 'Technology transfer in United States universities: a survey and statistical analysis', *Journal of Evolutionary Economics*, **12** (1–2), 199–232.

Chandler, A.D. Jr (ed.) (1977), *The Visible Hand: The Managerial Revolution in American Business*, Cambridge, MA: Havard University Press.

Chapple, W., A. Lockett, D.S. Siegel and M. Wright (2005), 'Assessing the relative performance of university technology transfer offices in the U.K.: parametric and non-parametric evidence', *Research Policy*, **34** (3), 369–84.

Clarke, B.R. (ed.) (1998), *Creating Entrepreneurial Universities: Organizational Pathways of Transformation*, Oxford: Pergamon.

Clarysse, B., M. Wright, A. Lockett, E. van de Elde and A. Vohora (2005), 'Spinning out new ventures: a typology of incubation strategies from European research institutions', *Journal of Business Venturing*, **20** (2), 183–216.

Degroof J.J. and E.B. Roberts (2004), 'Overcoming weak entrepreneurial infrastructure for academic spin-off ventures', *Journal of Technology Transfer*, **29** (3–4), 327–52.

DiGregorio, D. and S.A. Shane (2003), 'Why do some universities generate more start-ups than others?', *Research Policy*, **32** (2), 209–27.

Foltz, J.D., B.L. Barham and K. Kim (2007), 'Synergies or trade-offs in university life science research', *American Journal of Agricultural Economics*, **89** (2), 353–67.

Franklin, S., M. Wright and A. Lockett (2001), 'Academic and surrogate entrepreneurs in university spin-out companies', *Journal of Technology Transfer*, **26** (1–2), 127–41.

Friedman, J. and J. Silberman (2003), 'University technology transfer: do incentives, management, and location matter?', *Journal of Technology Transfer*, **28** (1), 17–33.

Hertzfeld, H.R., A.N. Link and N.S. Vonortas (2006), 'Intellectual property protection mechanisms in research partnerships', *Research Policy*, **35** (6), 825–38.

Jensen, R., J.G. Thursby and M.C. Thursby (2003), 'The disclosure and licensing of university inventions: the best we can do with the s**t we get to work with', *International Journal of Industrial Organization*, **21** (9), 1271–300.

Lach, S. and M. Schankerman (2004), 'Royalty sharing and technology licensing in universities', *Journal of the European Economic Association*, **2** (2–3), 252–64.

Link, A.N. and D.S. Siegel (2005), 'Generating science-based growth: an econometric analysis of the impact of organizational incentives on university–industry technology transfer', *European Journal of Finance*, **11** (3), 169–81.

Lockett, A. and M. Wright (2005), 'Resources, capabilities, risk capital and the creation of university spin-out companies', *Research Policy*, **34** (7), 1043–57.

Lockett, A., M. Wright and S. Franklin (2003), 'Technology transfer and universities' spin-out strategies', *Small Business Economics*, **20** (2), 185–201.

Louis, K.S., D. Blumenthal, M.E. Gluck and M.A. Stoto (1989), 'Entrepreneurs in academe: an exploration of behaviors among life scientists', *Administrative Science Quarterly*, **34** (1), 110–31.

Lowe, R., and C. González-Brambila (2007), 'Faculty Entrepreneurs and Research Productivity', *The Journal of Technology Transfer*, **32** (3), 173–194.

Markman, G., P. Phan, D. Balkin and P. Gianiodis (2004), 'Entrepreneurship from the ivory tower: do incentive systems matter?,' *Journal of Technology Transfer*, **29** (3–4), 353–64.

Markman, G., P. Phan, D. Balkin and P. Gianiodis (2005a), 'Entrepreneurship and university-based technology transfer', *Journal of Business Venturing*, **20** (2), 241–63.

Markman, G., P. Phan, D. Balkin and P. Gianiodis (2005b), 'Innovation speed: transferring university technology to market', *Research Policy*, **34** (7), 1058–75.

Merges, R. and R.R. Nelson (1990), 'On the complex economics of patent scope', *Columbia Law Review*, **90** (4), 839–916.

Mowery, D.C., R.R. Nelson, B. Sampat and A.A. Ziedonis (2001), 'The growth of patenting and licensing by U.S. universities: an assessment of the effects of the Bayh–Dole Act of 1980', *Research Policy*, **30** (1), 99–119.

Mustar, P. (1997), 'Spin-off enterprises: how French academies create hi-tech companies: the condition for success or failure', *Science and Public Policy*, **24** (1), 37–43.

Nerkar, A. and S. Shane (2003), 'When do startups that exploit academic knowledge survive?', *International Journal of Industrial Organization*, **21** (9), 1391–410.

Nicolaou, N. and S. Birley (2003), 'Social networks in organizational emergence: the university spinout phenomenon', *Management Science*, **49** (12), 1702–25.

O'Shea, R., T. Allen and A. Arnaud (2005), 'Entrepreneurial orientation, technology transfer, and spin-off performance of U.S. universities', *Research Policy*, **34** (7), 994–1009.

Roberts, E.B. (ed.) (1991), *Entrepreneurs in High Technology, Lessons from MIT and Beyond*, New York: Oxford University Press.

Roberts, E. and D.E. Malone (1996), 'Policies and structures for spinning off new companies from research and development organizations', *R&D Management*, **26** (1), 17–48.

Rogers, E.M., Y. Yin and J. Hoffmann (2000), 'Assessing the effectiveness of technology transfer offices at U.S. research universities', *The Journal of the Association of University Technology Managers*, **12**, 47–80.

Siegel, D.S., D. Waldman and A.N. Link (2003a), 'Assessing the impact of organizational practices on the relative productivity of university technology transfer offices: an exploratory study', *Research Policy*, **32** (1), 27–48.

Siegel, D.S., D. Waldman, L. Atwater and A.N. Link (2003b), 'Toward a model of the effective transfer of scientific knowledge from academicians to practitioners: qualitative evidence from the commercialization of university technologies', *Journal of Engineering and Technology Management*, **21** (1–2), 115–42.

Thursby, J.G. and S. Kemp (2002), 'Growth and productive efficiency of university intellectual property licensing', *Research Policy*, **31** (1), 109–24.

Thursby, J.G., R. Jensen and M.C. Thursby (2001), 'Objectives, characteristics and outcomes of university licensing: a survey of major U.S. universities', *Journal of Technology Transfer*, **26** (1–2), 59–72.
Thursby, J.G. and M.C. Thursby (2002), 'Who is selling the ivory tower? Sources of growth in university licensing', *Management Science*, **48** (1), 90–104.
Tushman, M. and P. Anderson (1986), 'Technological discontinuities and organizational environments', *Administrative Science Quarterly*, **31** (3), 439–65.
Vanaelst, I., B. Clarysse, M. Wright, A. Lockett, N. Moray and R. S'Jegers (2006), 'Entrepreneurial team development in academic spinouts: an examination of team heterogeneity', *Entrepreneurship: Theory and Practice*, **30** (2), 249–91.
Williamson, O.E. (ed.) (1964), *The Economics of Discretionary Behavior: Managerial Objectives in a Theory of the Firm*, Englewood Cliffs, NJ: Prentice-Hall.
Wright, M., B. Clarysse, P. Mustar and A. Lockett (eds) (2007), *Academic Entrepreneurship in Europe*, Cheltenham, UK and Northampton, MA, USA: Edward Elgar.
Zucker, L.G. and M.R. Darby (2001), 'Capturing technological opportunity via Japan's star scientists: evidence from Japanese firms' biotech patents and products', *Journal of Technology Transfer*, **26** (1–2), 37–58.
Zucker, L.G. M.R. Darby and J. Armstrong (1998), 'Geographically localized knowledge: spillovers or markets?', *Economic Inquiry*, **36** (1), 65–86.
Zucker, L.G., M.R. Darby and J. Armstrong (2000), 'University science, venture capital, and the performance of U.S. biotechnology firms', mimeo, UCLA.
Zucker, L.G., M.R. Darby and M.B. Brewer (1998), 'Intellectual human capital and the birth of U.S. biotechnology enterprises', *American Economic Review*, **88** (1), 290–306.

20 The innovator's decision: entrepreneurship versus technology transfer
Daniel F. Spulber

INTRODUCTION

The connection between innovation and entrepreneurship is the subject of some debate. Are all innovators entrepreneurs? Are all entrepreneurs innovators? This debate is extremely important because of the critical role of innovation in fostering economic growth. Resolving the debate has major public policy implications because it can determine whether governments choose actions that encourage or discourage innovation. Fortunately, it is possible to disentangle these two distinct concepts. The discussion presented here attempts to resolve the debates by defining and specifying the relationship between innovation and entrepreneurship.

Innovation, which is the commercialization of invention, consists of two main actions: the innovator must obtain the invention and the innovator must provide the invention. The activities required to obtain the invention range from buying the invention from the inventor to developing the invention: license the invention from an inventor; purchase the invention from an inventor; hire an inventor to conduct research and to develop the invention; form a partnership with an inventor to conduct research and to develop the invention; and become an inventor and conduct R&D.

The activities required to provide the invention range from selling the invention to users to applying the invention in production and design and selling the results: license the invention to the user; sell the invention to a user; form a partnership with a user to apply the invention; and become a user of the invention by applying it in manufacturing and product design.

Entrepreneurship is the establishment of a firm; see Spulber (2009a). Clearly, therefore, not all innovators are entrepreneurs because obtaining and providing an invention can be carried out without establishing a firm. For example, an individual may act as an intermediary in the market for intellectual property without starting a firm. The individual may buy and resell an invention without the need for a firm. Buying and selling an invention is an innovation because it commercializes the invention. Say's (1852, 1982) classic work draws a careful distinction between the scientist, who develops the invention, and the entrepreneur, who organizes the application of discoveries. It bears emphasis that existing firms and nonprofit organizations also can engage in commercialization of inventions.

Perhaps more subtle and difficult is the question of whether all entrepreneurs are innovators. Again, the answer is no. Some firms simply add productive capacity to the market, performing tasks that are so unoriginal and routine that it would stretch matters to conceive of them as commercializing an invention. This is the familiar question of whether establishing a hot-dog stand represents entrepreneurship. The answer is yes because the hot-dog stand is a firm. The often-cited hot-dog stand usually does not

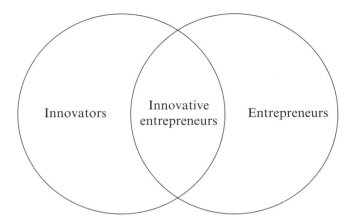

*Figure 20.1   Innovative entrepreneurs are at the intersection of innovators and
entrepreneurs*

involve innovation, although a new type of cooking system or new ingredients would do
the trick.

Therefore innovators and entrepreneurs are not the same, although the set of innovators and the set of entrepreneurs have an important intersection that defines the set
of innovative entrepreneurs, see Figure 20.1. Innovative entrepreneurs are those individuals who establish a firm to commercialize an invention. Innovators who are not
entrepreneurs engage in technology transfer; that is, they obtain and provide an invention without founding a firm. Entrepreneurs who are not innovators are referred to as
replicative entrepreneurs.

Having framed the connection between innovation and entrepreneurship, it becomes
possible to provide an economic analysis of when innovation involves entrepreneurship.
I introduce the concept of the innovator's decision to describe the innovator's choice
between innovation and technology transfer. An innovator becomes an entrepreneur when
establishing a firm is the most efficient way to commercialize an invention. An innovator
does not become an entrepreneur when intermediation without establishing a firm is the
most efficient way to commercialize an invention. The analysis shows that when there are
substantial imperfections in the market for ideas, the innovator chooses entrepreneurship.

If the innovator chooses entrepreneurship, the innovator must incur the costs and
risks of establishing a firm. The innovator's idea then will be embodied in the new firm.
The innovator enters the market for new firms and ultimately becomes an owner. If the
innovator chooses technology transfer, the innovator must incur the costs and risks of
selling or licensing the technology to others. The innovator's idea is an intermediary in
the market for disembodied ideas. The entrepreneur's idea involves new combinations of
technology and applications. The technology transfer can take the form of intellectual
property (IP), such as a patent, license or copyrighted work. The idea can be a blueprint,
scientific result, technical description, product design or a business plan.

The main implication of the innovator's decision is that entrepreneurship overcomes
imperfections in the market for ideas. First, it may be difficult to enforce the innovator's
IP rights so that revealing the idea to a potential buyer may subject the innovator to

expropriation. Second, due to bureaucratic decision-making, the existing firm may not be able to evaluate accurately the quality of the innovator's idea. Third, the quality of the idea is not observable to potential buyers, so that the market for ideas is subject to the problem of adverse selection. Fourth, the innovator and the acquirer of the technology may face costs of negotiating and writing a licensing contract that is contingent on the quality of the idea. Fifth, developing the idea may be costly, so that the developer must determine whether or not the expected benefits of development cover the costs of development. This complicates the adverse selection problem since the idea is observable to the entrepreneur but not to the potential acquirer. Sixth, technology transfer may require the innovator to invest in a costly signal that conveys information about the quality of the idea. The innovator pursues the commercialization strategy of entrepreneurship to overcome these obstacles in the market for ideas.

Entrepreneurs play a central role in the modern economy because they are the prime movers – the makers of firms. Entrepreneurs are fundamental to economic equilibrium because they set the economy in motion. Firms are responsible for practically all economic activity outside of government: innovating, pricing, contracting, employing resources, labor and capital goods, raising financial capital, organizing production, and marketing goods and services. In equilibrium, firms create markets as well as organizations, making both types of institutions endogenous. Economic equilibrium, including prices, allocation of goods and the structure of transactions, thus depends on the actions of entrepreneurs. The discussion draws upon the microeconomic analysis in Spulber (2009a) in which not only entrepreneurs, but also firms, markets and organizations are endogenous.

Entrepreneurs are major contributors to economic growth, development and prosperity; see Audretsch et al. (2006), Schramm (2006) and Baumol et al. (2007). Baumol (1968) emphasizes the function of the entrepreneur as locating new ideas, putting them into effect, and exercising leadership; see also Baumol (1993, 2002, 2005). Casson (1982, p. 97) finds that the entrepreneur builds the firm to handle the complexities of intermediation: 'Among these purpose-built organizations are market-making firms;' see also Casson (1987, 1997, 2003). The innovator's reward results from the firm's residual returns obtained by owning the firm or by divesting ownership. These issues are addressed in Spulber's (2009a) dynamic economic theory of the entrepreneur.

The innovator's decision has to do with the commercialization of an invention. It differs from Arrow's (1962, 1969) discussion of the incentive to invent. Arrow assumes that the inventor is a monopolist; that is, the inventor can choose a royalty to extract monopoly rents for his invention. The inventor is able to appropriate the private information that the invention represents. Arrow compares a competitive situation, in which the inventor sells the invention to all producers in a competitive product market, with a monopoly situation, in which the inventor is also a vertically integrated monopoly producer, so that the inventor himself employs the invention in the product market. Arrow shows that the inventor's profit is greater in the competitive situation than in the monopoly situation. Arrow's result is that a competitive product market provides a greater incentive to invent than a monopolistic product market. The incentive to invent depends on improvement in comparison to the initial technology.

The innovator's decision that is studied here is closely related to work on R&D and entrepreneurship. Gromb and Scharfstein (2002) compare innovation by entrepreneurs with that by managers of established firms. Gans et al. (2002) show that the returns to innovators from cooperating with existing firms is increasing in property rights protections and decreasing in the associated transaction costs. Gans and Stern (2000) look at an R&D race where the winner can license the technology and faces the possibility of imitation; see also Salant (1984), Katz and Shapiro (1987) and Reinganum (1981, 1982, 1989). Some related issues arise in studies of venture capital financing. Hellmann and Puri (2000) show that venture capital financing favors innovators over initiators and tends to speed the time to market for new high-tech ventures. Industrial organization models of entry and firm survival provide insights into the entrepreneurial startups. Geroski (1995) finds that entry often appears relatively easy but survival is not.

The chapter is organized as follows. The next section presents a Coasian analysis of the innovator's decision. Then I examine the effect of intellectual property rights on the innovator's choice between entrepreneurship and technology transfer. The fourth section considers how the architecture of existing firms affects the innovator's decision. The fifth section considers the effects of asymmetric information and adverse selection on the innovator's choice. After that I examine licensing royalties and the innovator's decision. The seventh section considers risk and the development of the idea, followed by an examination of the entrepreneur's signaling of the idea. The final section concludes.

THE INNOVATOR'S DECISION: A COASIAN ANALYSIS

The classic example of entrepreneurial innovation is Schumpeter's (1934) description of how the power loom was introduced to the weaving industry. The innovator need not be the inventor of the power loom, nor the producer of the power loom, nor the enterprise that uses the power loom. The innovators contribute only 'the will and the action' (Schumpeter, 1934, p. 137). The innovators are entrepreneurs because 'The introduction is achieved by founding new businesses, whether for production or for employment or for both' (ibid., p. 132). The risks of establishing a firm include not only business risks but the possibility of failure when entrepreneurs compete with existing firms as well as among themselves; Spulber (2009b) considers a model of competition among entrepreneurs. Schumpeter's (1942) 'creative destruction' refers to the exit of firms that occurs as a result of entrepreneurial competition.

Schumpeter (1934, p. 75) identifies entrepreneurship as 'the fundamental phenomenon of economic development. The carrying out of new combinations we call "enterprise"; the individuals whose function it is to carry them out we call "entrepreneurs"'. He further observes (ibid., p.66) that 'new combinations are, as a rule, embodied, as it were, in new firms which generally do not arise out of the old ones but start producing beside them'. The innovator becomes an entrepreneur when the new combinations are embodied in a firm. When innovators engage in market transactions to transfer the technology without establishing a firm, the new combinations are not embodied in a firm.

The innovator's decision refers to the innovator's choice between two alternative methods of commercializing an invention – entrepreneurship and technology transfer. Ronald Coase's insight about the nature of the firm provides valuable guidance. The innovator faces a tradeoff between the transaction costs of establishing a firm and the transaction costs of transferring technology. The choice between entrepreneurship and technology transfer depends in large part on a comparison of these transaction costs.

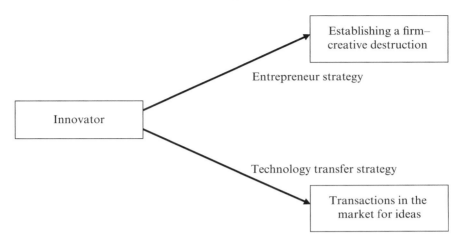

Figure 20.2   The innovator's decision: entrepreneurship versus technology transfer

(The choice between entrepreneurship and technology transfer also may be affected by the innovator's preferences, and endowment and the availability of credit needed to establish a new firm, but these issues are beyond the scope of the present chapter.) The innovator's strategic decision is represented in Figure 20.2.

The innovator's decision involves a crucial complication. There may already be firms in the relevant industry. For Schumpeter (1942, p. 83), 'every piece of business strategy . . . must be seen in its role in the perennial gale of creative destruction'. If the innovator engages in technology transfer, existing firms are potential partners and customers. However, if the innovator chooses entrepreneurship, existing firms are potential competitors. Then, entrepreneurship leads to what Schumpeter termed 'creative destruction' – the new firm is established beside the old firms and competes with them. The difference between coopera-tion and competition potentially changes the pattern of payoffs considerably.

When creative destruction is inefficient, the entry of new firms causes private costs to diverge from social costs. Ronald Coase's (1960) classic article, 'The problem of social cost', offers an important insight known as the 'Coase theorem'. The theorem can be summarized as follows. When property rights are well defined and when there are no transaction costs, the creators of a nuisance and the parties harmed by the nuisance will negotiate an efficient allocation. If the creators of a nuisance have property rights, the parties harmed by the nuisance will pay the creators of the nuisance to abate. If the parties harmed by the nuisance have property rights, the creator of the nuisance will need to pay them compensation and choose to abate. In either situation, the marginal private costs of the nuisance will equal the marginal private costs of abatement, thus yielding an efficient outcome regardless of the assignment of property rights.

A Coasian theorem can be obtained for entrepreneurial innovation. The socially costly activity is competitive entry by the entrepreneur when creative destruction is inefficient. The transaction costs in question are the costs of bargaining between the innovator and the owners and managers of the existing firm. In contrast to nuisance law, the property rights in question are not the destructive activity itself. The analogy with nuisance law and property rights is not perfect. In the case of creative destruction, the entry of new firms is the activity causing the social cost. Here, property rights to enter the market are well defined since the entrepreneur has a right to establish a new firm. The incumbent can pay the innovator not to enter in return for the transfer of the technology

The property rights that are in question have to do with intellectual property (IP). When IP rights are well defined, the innovator can sell the idea to the incumbent firm, which provides a basis for bargaining. When IP rights are not well defined or are not protected by law and business reputation, the innovator and the entrepreneur may not have a basis for bargaining over technology transfer.

I begin by establishing a Coasian theorem of entrepreneurship. I show that when there are no transaction costs and when IP rights are well defined, the entrepreneur and the existing firm are able to negotiate an efficient allocation rather than engaging in competition. When there are transaction costs in the market for ideas and IP rights are not well defined, a more general characterization of creative destruction is necessary. Then, transaction costs and intellectual property rights help to explain the puzzle of entrepreneurial innovation.

The process of creative destruction does not refer to the sunk costs of the existing firm. Those costs are not recoverable by definition. Sunk costs should have no bearing on economic decisions because such decisions are forward looking. They depend only on the prospective costs and benefits affected by the decisions. The process of creative destruction includes the ongoing value of the existing firm, its facilities, capital equipment, organizational capital, brand name and so forth.

Assume for the purposes of the present discussion that as a result of creative destruction, the entrepreneurial entrant displaces the existing firm. This assumption can be modified to allow for post-entry competition. For example, there may be monopolistic competition between entrepreneurs and existing firms offering differentiated products. In this setting, the entry of new firms reduces the profits of existing firms but all firms may survive. As another example, it may take time for entrepreneurs to displace existing firms, so that creative destruction takes place gradually. However, to highlight the main issues surrounding the innovator's decision, it is sufficient to assume that creative destruction is the replacement of the existing firm by the new firm.

Let θ denote the innovator's idea, which is defined as the insight needed to commercialize an invention. Thus the innovator's idea is not the same as the invention. Given the innovator's idea, suppose that the cost of obtaining the invention is $C(\theta)$, which can include related transaction costs. Suppose that the market value of providing the invention is $V(\theta)$, which can include related transaction costs. Denote the net benefits of innovation excluding transaction costs by

$$\Pi(\theta) = V(\theta) - C(\theta) \qquad (20.1)$$

Let the transaction costs of technology transfer be $T(\theta)$ and let the transaction costs of establishing a firm be $K(\theta)$.

Suppose technology transfer involves selling to an existing firm. The existing firm incurs adjustment costs from applying the invention. The existing firm's technology is represented by the value x, which is less than the value of the innovator's idea, $\theta > x$. The adjustment costs that the existing firm would incur by adopting the new technology are represented by the linear costs, $A(\theta - x)$, which is increasing in the difference in quality between the innovator's idea and the existing technology. For ease of presentation,

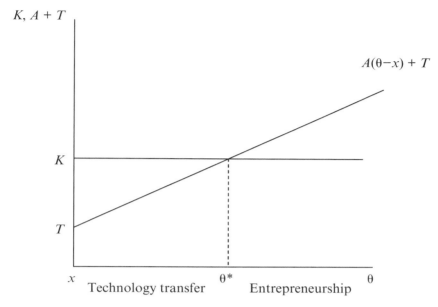

Figure 20.3   The critical value of the innovator's idea

suppose that both technology transfer and entrepreneurship are economically feasible, $\Pi(\theta) \geq T(\theta) + A(\theta - x)$ and $\Pi(\theta) \geq K(\theta)$. The existing firm's benefits need not be compared to the existing firm's profits from old technology because the alternative to adoption is entry of the new firm. If the innovator establishes a firm, creative destruction takes place and the existing firm does not survive.

The definition of efficiency in commercializing technology must account for transaction costs. Technology transfer is efficient if the transaction costs of establishing a firm are greater than the transaction costs and adjustment costs of technology transfer:

$$K(\theta) > T(\theta) + A(\theta - x)$$

Establishing a firm, which results in creative destruction, is efficient if the transaction costs of establishing a firm are less than or equal to the transaction costs and adjustment costs of technology transfer to the existing firm:

$$K(\theta) \leq T(\theta) + A(\theta - x)$$

Creative destruction is efficient if and only if this condition holds.

Consider a basic example to illustrate the main points. Suppose that the costs of establishing a firm do not depend on the properties of the innovator's idea, $K(\theta) = K$. Suppose also that the transactions costs of technology transfer do not depend on the properties of the innovator's idea, $T(\theta) = T$. This implies that creative destruction will be inefficient for incremental inventions and efficient for substantial inventions. This determines a critical value of the innovator's idea above which creative destruction is efficient, see Figure 20.3.

$$\theta^* = x + (K - T)/A \qquad\qquad (20.2)$$

When the value of the innovator's idea is less than the critical value, technology transfer is efficient. When the value of the innovator's idea is greater than or equal to the critical value, the innovator will become an entrepreneur and creative destruction will occur. The incremental innovation depends on the difference between the costs of establishing a firm and the costs of transferring the technology divided by the existing firm's adjustment cost parameter.

When creative destruction is efficient, the innovator will have an incentive to become an entrepreneur. When creative destruction is inefficient, the innovator and the owners of the existing firm have an incentive to avoid these inefficiencies. This suggests a Coasian theorem for creative destruction. If creative destruction is efficient, then there is no possibility of any payments from the existing firm to the entrepreneur that will deter entry. The innovator will choose to become an entrepreneur. If creative destruction is inefficient, the existing firm will bear the transaction costs of technology transfer and pay the innovator an additional royalty R in the range

$$\Pi(\theta) - A(\theta - x) - T(\theta) \geq R \geq \Pi(\theta) - K$$

The innovator can sell his idea to the existing firm at a price that captures the benefits of the innovation and avoids the costs of creative destruction. Then the innovator will choose not to become an entrepreneur.

This discussion establishes that entrepreneurship occurs if and only if creative destruction is efficient. The royalty will depend on the relative bargaining power of the innovator and the existing firm. For example, if there is more than one existing firm, the innovator can extract all the rents from his innovation, $\Pi(\theta) - A(\theta - x) - T(\theta)$. If there is more than one innovator, the existing firm need only pay the entrepreneur's net earnings from entry, $\Pi(\theta) - K$.

The efficiency of entrepreneurship with transaction costs is closely related to Coase's (1937, 1988, 1994) analysis of the nature of the firm. When there are high transaction costs in the market for ideas, the innovator commercializes his idea himself. The innovator becomes an entrepreneur when the transaction costs of establishing a firm are less than the transaction costs of transferring ideas in the market and adjusting the technology of the existing firm. The entrepreneur internalizes the commercialization of his decision. The entrepreneur vertically integrates two activities – discovery of the idea, and establishment of the firm based on that idea. The entrepreneur embodies the idea in a new firm when doing so entails lower transaction costs than transferring a disembodied idea and transforming the existing firm.

INTELLECTUAL PROPERTY RIGHTS

Arrow (1962) pointed out that an inventor may have problems realizing the value of his invention due to the risks of disclosing the information to a potential buyer who may appropriate the invention. For similar reasons, the innovator's ability to transfer the technology to the existing firm depends on legal protections for intellectual property

(IP). The preceding discussion assumed that the innovator had IP protection for his idea. When intellectual property rights are not well defined, creative destruction can occur even when it is inefficient. The market for ideas may not form. As a legal institution, IP rights are the outcome of policy decisions and the evolution of legal institutions. A general analysis would require a more complete characterization of corporate law, agency and partnership, contracts and property law, which is beyond the scope of the present discussion.

When IP rights are not well protected, the innovator must establish a firm as a means of protecting the returns to his idea. This outcome can occur when the property rights obtained by establishing a firm have better legal protections than intellectual property. If the innovator faces a risk that the existing firm will imitate or expropriate the technology without penalty, the incentives to license the idea will be reduced or eliminated. If the innovator can protect his idea by embodying the technology in a firm, then entrepreneurship yields benefits in comparison to licensing.

Suppose that the innovator must reveal the idea θ if he wishes to sell it to the existing firm. Let β be the probability that the existing firm can take the idea after observing it. The probability β represents the likelihood of imitation or the likelihood of expropriation. If the existing firm imitates or expropriates the innovator's idea, the innovator will not be able to establish a firm using that idea. The expected return from revealing the idea to the existing firm reflects the likelihood of retaining the intellectual property, $1 - \beta$.

The same definition of the efficiency of creative destruction still applies. The range of outcomes of bargaining also is the same. However, for any given royalty R, the innovator expects to receive $(1 - \beta)R$. The range of expected returns to the innovator from offering the innovation to the existing firm must be adjusted for the likelihood of expropriation;

$$(1 - \beta)[\Pi(\theta) - A(\theta - x) - T] \geq R \geq (1 - \beta)[\Pi(\theta) - K]$$

If the existing firm has all the bargaining power, the innovator would expect the royalty $R = \Pi(\theta) - K$ and would always choose to become an entrepreneur. Therefore, when the existing firm has all of the bargaining power, creative destruction will result even if it is inefficient.

Suppose that the innovator has all of the bargaining power, so that the royalty will be $R = \Pi(\theta) - A(\theta - x) - T$. Then, there is a critical value of the entrepreneur's idea that solves

$$\beta\Pi(\theta^{**}) + (1 - \beta)[A(\theta^{**} - x) + T] = K$$

Creative destruction will occur when the innovator's idea is greater than or equal to the critical value. Observe that

$$\beta\Pi(\theta) + (1 - \beta)[A(\theta - x) + T] > \Pi(\theta) - A(\theta - x) - T(\theta)$$

This holds since, by assumption, $\Pi(\theta) - A(\theta - x) - T(\theta) > 0$. This implies that the critical value θ^{**} is less than the critical value θ^* above which creative destruction is efficient. Therefore, when the innovator has all the bargaining power, there is a range of values of the innovator's idea between θ^{**} and θ^* such that creative destruction occurs even though it is inefficient.

Imperfect protections for IP lead to self-selection in the market for ideas. Innovators with low-quality ideas, $\theta \leq \theta^{**}$, transfer their technology to existing firms. Innovators with higher-quality ideas, $\theta > \theta^{**}$, protect their IP by establishing a firm. If innovators do not have sufficient IP rights, a market for technology transfer cannot develop and entrepreneurship increases as a means for protecting IP.

James Anton and Dennis Yao (1994) consider the possibility of expropriation and show that the inventor's wealth affects his decision to reveal his invention to a potential buyer. Anton and Yao (1995) look at entrepreneurs who are employees of firms, discover a significant invention, and then leave to start a new firm The employee has three options: keep silent and leave to start a new firm; reveal the invention to the employer in hopes of a reward; or negotiate a reward with the employer before revealing the invention. Dealing with the employer also can result in a new firm is the form of a spinoff. Anton and Yao (2004) find that large inventions are protected by secrecy when property rights are weak. Anton and Yao (2002) find that expropriable partial disclosure can act as a signaling device; see also Anton and Yao (2003).

THE ARCHITECTURE OF EXISTING FIRMS

The innovator may encounter all kinds of barriers in seeking to commercialize his idea. One particular problem in transferring the technology may be bureaucratic inertia and resistance from existing firms. Existing firms may be reluctant to adopt an idea that they did not invent themselves, the familiar 'not invented here' objection. Existing firms may be unable to properly evaluate the potential of a new idea, or entrenched interests in the firm may resist technology changes that would displace existing business activities, even if such changes were profitable. Managers of existing firms may make economically inefficient decisions due to imperfect incentives as a result of costly contracting, adverse selection and moral hazard problems. Due to information asymmetries, managers' incentives may not be perfectly aligned with the objectives of the firm's shareholders.

The inability of existing firms to evaluate new ideas accurately has been widely discussed. Errors in judgment experienced by individuals extend to organizations. Notably, Arrow (1962, p. 171) points out that the transmission of knowledge is imperfect due to costly communication and errors in judgment. The possibility of impediments to commercialization of economically desirable innovations is referred to by Acs et al. (2004) as a 'knowledge filter'.

The ability of existing firms to evaluate the innovator's idea affects the commercialization decision. The greater the ability of existing firms to evaluate the innovator's idea, the more likely the innovator can sell the idea to an existing firm. When existing firms cannot evaluate the innovator's idea accurately, the innovator will have an incentive to establish a firm to commercialize his idea. This section introduces a model of the industry that seeks to explain imperfections in commercialization.

Existing firms may reject some ideas that should be accepted, yielding Type-I errors. Existing firms may accept some ideas that should be rejected, yielding Type-II errors. The architecture of existing firms is a critical determinant of their ability to judge the innovator's idea. Sah and Stiglitz (1986) contrast two types of market architectures. A large centralized firm may be organized as a hierarchy, in which decision-makers at higher levels of the organization review decisions by those at lower levels. In contrast, in a decentralized market, individual firms make some types of decisions independently. Sah and Stiglitz refer to a market with a centralized firm as a hierarchy, and they refer to a market with multiple firms making independent decisions as a polyarchy.

This section considers the implications of hierarchies and polyarchies for entrepreneurship. The innovator attempts to sell his idea to existing firms. When hierarchies and polyarchies have different abilities to judge the quality of the idea, the result will be different effects on the commercialization decision. A market organized as a polyarchy chooses to approve a greater proportion of existing projects, as shown by Sah and Stiglitz (1986). In our framework, the result is that when existing firms are organized as a hierarchy, rather than as a polyarchy, more entrepreneurship results.

Representing ideas by θ, define a screening function, $p(\theta)$, as the probability a decision-maker approves of the idea. A perfect screening function would approve good projects by setting $p(\theta) = 1$ for $\theta > 0$ and would reject bad projects by setting $p(\theta) = 0$ for $\theta = 0$. Instead, assume that the screening function is imperfect, so that $0 < p(\theta) < 1$ for all θ. Suppose that the screening function can distinguish between projects by ranking them properly so that $p(\theta)$ is strictly increasing in θ.

Consider two market architectures. The market is organized as a hierarchy if it has one existing firm with m organizational levels. For the hierarchy to approve of the idea, a decision-maker at a lower level of the firm must first approve the idea, and then a decision-maker at a higher level of the firm must also approve the idea. The likelihood of a hierarchy with m levels approving the idea is $(p(\theta))^m$.

The market is organized as a polyarchy if there are m existing firms, any of which can approve of the idea. The likelihood of at least one firm approving the idea is equal to one minus the probability that all firms will reject the idea, $1 - (1 - p(\theta))^m$.

The hierarchy is less likely to approve the idea than the polyarchy. To see why, first let $m = 2$. When the screening function is imperfect, that is $0 < p < 1$,

$$p^2 + (1 - p)^2 < 1$$

This implies that

$$p^2 < 1 - (1 - p)^2$$

so that the two-level hierarchy is less likely to approve an idea than the two-member polyarchy. Since p is such that $0 < p < 1$, for $m > 2$

$$p^m + (1 - p)^m < p^2 + (1 - p)^2 < 1$$

This implies that

$$p^m < 1 - (1 - p)^m$$

Thus the m-level hierarchy is less likely to approve the project than the m-member polyarchy. The hierarchy is more likely to reject ideas that should be accepted, and thus commits more Type-I errors. The polyarchy is more likely to accept ideas that should be rejected, and thus commits more Type-II errors.

The innovator who submits an idea θ to the existing firm organized as an m-level hierarchy expects to obtain $(p(\theta))^m\theta$. The innovator who submits an idea θ to a poly-archy with m existing firms expects to obtain $[1 - (1 - p(\theta))^m]\theta$. The expected return is greater when the market is organized as a polyarchy than when it is organized as a hierarchy.

Suppose that there is a continuum of innovators with ideas uniformly distributed on the unit interval. The return to setting up a firm is $\theta - K$ for an entrepreneur with an idea θ. This implies that more innovators become entrepreneurs when the existing market is organized as a hierarchy than when it is organized as a polyarchy. The curve $(p(\theta))^m\theta$ lies everywhere below the curve $[1 - (1 - p(\theta))^m]\theta$. Both curves are monotonically increas-ing. Therefore the set of innovators θ such that the returns to establishing a firm $\theta - K$ is greater than the returns to selling the idea must be larger if the market is organized as a hierarchy than if it is organized as a polyarchy.

To illustrate this result with an example, suppose that the two curves each intersect the return to establishing the firm at just one point. Then, let θ^* be the critical idea for the market organized as a hierarchy

$$(p(\theta^*))^m\theta^* = \theta^* - K$$

The set of entrepreneurs when the existing firm is a hierarchy consists of entrepreneurs with high-quality ideas, $[\theta^*, 1]$. Let θ^{**} be the critical idea for the market organized as a polyarchy

$$[1 - (1 - p(\theta^{**}))^m]\theta^{**} = \theta^{**} - K$$

The set of entrepreneurs when the existing firm is a polyarchy again consists of entre-preneurs with high-quality ideas, $[\theta^{**}, 1]$. These critical values are represented in Figure 20.4. The set of entrepreneurs is greater when the existing firm is a hierarchy than when it is a polyarchy. This is because the marginal entrepreneur has a lower-quality idea when the existing firm is a hierarchy than when it is a polyarchy

$$\theta^* < \theta^{**}$$

The reason that there is more entrepreneurship when the existing firm is a hierarchy is that the existing firm rejects more ideas than does a polyarchy composed of many exist-ing firms.

The greater the number of decision makers m, the greater the performance gap between the hierarchy and the polyarchy. The hierarchy accepts fewer ideas as the number of levels, m, increases while the polyarchy accepts more ideas as the number of members, m, increases. In the limit, almost all innovators become entrepreneurs if faced with a hierarchical firm with large m. Almost all innovators sell their idea to an existing firm if faced with a polyarchy with many existing firms, m.

When the existing firm is a hierarchy, bureaucratic decision-making can prevent the acceptance of ideas. The hierarchical firm accepts fewer ideas relative to a market with many firms each of which independently evaluates the new idea. The architecture of the market for ideas is thus an important determinant of entrepreneurship.

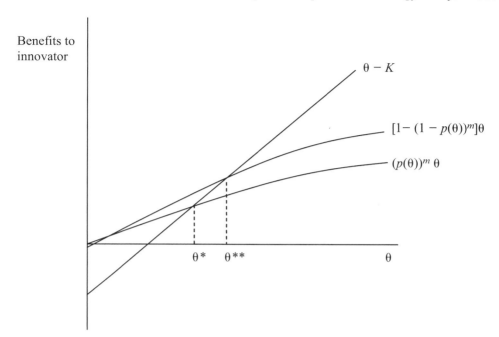

Figure 20.4 The critical values of the innovator's idea with a hierarchy and with a polyarchy

ADVERSE SELECTION

Adverse selection is an important determinant of entrepreneurship. It will be shown that the entrepreneur's problem is closely related to Akerlof's (1970) market for 'lemons'. Suppose there are only two types of ideas, low-quality ideas and high-quality ideas. The potential buyers of the idea are existing firms. Let $\theta \in \{\theta_L, \theta_H\}$ represent the two types of ideas, where

$$\theta_L < \theta_H$$

It is not possible for existing firms to observe whether the quality of the idea is either high or low. Let θ_L and θ_H be the value of the idea to an existing firm. An existing firm can only observe the quality of the idea by purchasing it. Each innovator can contract with at most one existing firm. Suppose for now that new entrants and existing firms do not compete with each other.

There is a population of innovators. A proportion of innovators, α, has a high-quality idea, θ_H. The rest of the innovators, with proportion $(1 - \alpha)$, have a low-quality idea, θ_L. Let the proportion of innovators with high-quality ideas be such that $0 < \alpha < 1$. Suppose that an innovator's idea can be sold to at most one existing firm. Since the quality of an idea is unobservable, existing firms have a willingness to pay equal to the expected value of an idea,

$$E\theta = (1 - \alpha)\theta_L + \alpha\theta_H$$

The innovator can credibly reveal the quality of an idea by establishing a firm. Let $K > 0$ be the cost of establishing a firm. Let θ_L and θ_H be the value of the firm that embodies the innovator's idea. Suppose that either type of firm is viable, $\theta_L > K$. Suppose for now that the innovator can afford the cost of establishing a firm. The model corresponds exactly Akerlof's (1970) 'market for lemons'.

The existing firm's cost of adopting the new technology is normalized to zero. This means that it is less costly to transfer the innovator's idea to an existing firm than to establish a new firm that embodies the idea. This implies that updating the existing firm is more efficient than establishing a new firm. If, conversely, the cost of transferring the innovator's idea to an existing firm were more costly than establishing a new firm, entrepreneurship would be more efficient. The purpose of assuming instead that establishing a new firm is less efficient is to consider how transaction costs in the market for ideas affect entrepreneurship.

The problem of adverse selection does not prevent the formation of a market for ideas if

$$(1 - \alpha)\theta_L + \alpha\theta_H \geq \theta_H - K$$

The expected value of a disembodied idea is greater than or equal to the value of setting up a firm. Then, both types of innovators can sell their ideas to existing firms. All innovation takes place through the market for ideas. No new firms are established.

Adverse selection can prevent the formation of a market for ideas if the expected value of a disembodied idea is less than the return to establishing a firm,

$$(1 - \alpha)\theta_L + \alpha\theta_H < \theta_H - K$$

Then, bad ideas drive good ones out of the market for ideas. Those innovators with high-quality ideas strictly prefer to establish a firm. Those with high-quality ideas self-select by becoming entrepreneurs. Because those innovators with high-quality ideas become entrepreneurs, only those with low-quality ideas enter the market for ideas. Since it is costly to establish a firm, existing firms will be able to purchase low-quality ideas. Existing firms are able accurately to infer the quality of the idea because only low-quality ideas are offered for sale in disembodied form. Entrepreneurship occurs if the proportion of good ideas is low. The critical value of the proportion of good ideas is

$$\alpha^* = 1 - K/(\theta_H - \theta_L)$$

Entrepreneurship occurs when $\alpha < \alpha^*$. The critical value of α is decreasing in the cost of establishing a firm, K, and increasing in the difference between high-quality and low-quality ideas. When the difference between the two types of ideas is significant, the critical value α^* approaches one and entrepreneurship is more likely to occur.

LICENSING CONTRACTS

The innovator can make the existing firm's royalty payment contingent on the quality of the idea. The innovator can license the technology with a contingent royalty contract based on the returns obtained by using the invention. With a contingent contract, the existing firm pays the innovator based on the firm's performance.

Suppose that it is feasible to offer the innovator a completely contingent royalty. The efficient royalty essentially gives the existing firm to the innovator minus a lump-sum transfer to the owners of the existing firm. The completely contingent royalty equals

$$R(\theta) = \theta - J$$

where $0 \leq J \leq K$. The lump-sum transfer to the owners of the existing firm reflects the relative bargaining power of the owners and the innovator. Given the completely contingent royalty, the innovator prefers to sell the technology rather than to establish the new firm. The outcome is efficient since it is less costly to transfer the technology rather than to establish a new firm.

It may not be feasible to write a complete contingent contract due to the transaction costs of bargaining and monitoring such contracts. Another possibility is a constant royalty per unit of returns for the existing firm. The existing firm pays the licensing royalty only after applying the innovator's idea. The existing firm offers a per-unit royalty r and pays $r\theta_H$ for a high-quality idea and pays $r\theta_L$ for a low-quality idea. The profit-maximizing firm has two options. The existing firm can pay a high royalty that can attract both types of innovators. The existing firm can pay a low royalty that attracts only innovators with low-quality inventions. The lowest royalty that will attract innovators with both types of ideas makes the high-quality innovator indifferent between selling the idea and starting a firm,

$$r_H \theta_H = \theta_H - K$$

This will attract innovators with both types of inventions since, for the low-quality idea,

$$r_H \theta_L > \theta_L - K$$

Alternatively, the lowest royalty that attracts only the innovator with a low-quality idea equals

$$r_L \theta_L = \theta_L - K$$

The existing firm earns an expected profit from offering the low royalty equal to

$$\pi_L = (1 - \alpha)(1 - r_L)\theta_L = (1 - \alpha) K$$

The existing firm earns an expected profit from offering the high royalty equal to

$$\pi_H = (1 - r_H)E\theta = KE\theta/\theta_H$$

The existing firm offers the low royalty if $\pi_H \geq \pi_L$, which is equivalent to $E\theta \geq (1 - \alpha) \theta_H$, or

$$\alpha \geq \frac{\theta_H - \theta_L}{2\theta_H - \theta_L} = \alpha^{**}.$$

In this case, the existing firm offers high royalties and entrepreneurship does not occur. Entrepreneurship occurs when $\alpha < \alpha^{**}$. Then, innovators with high-quality ideas establish firms and innovators with low-quality ideas license their ideas. Therefore, when the proportion of innovators that have high-quality ideas is less than the critical value α^{**}, entrepreneurship takes place. With licensing, the critical value of α does not depend on the cost of establishing a firm. The critical value depends on the relative quality of the two types of ideas.

RISK AND DEVELOPMENT OF THE IDEA

The innovator's commercialization decision is affected by the riskiness of the idea. The innovator must choose whether or not to develop the idea. If the innovator sells the idea, it will be developed by the existing firm. If the innovator becomes an entrepreneur, the innovator must bear the risk of developing the idea. If the development of the idea is successful, the entrepreneur can establish a firm and obtain the resulting rewards. If the development of the idea is not successful, the entrepreneur will not receive any rewards.

Suppose that there is one existing firm and one innovator. The innovator has an idea, θ, which is his private information. The existing firm's beliefs about the innovator's idea are represented by a uniform distribution on the unit interval. Suppose that the existing firm has market power and makes the innovator a first-and-final offer of a lump-sum royalty, R.

Suppose the innovator's idea must be developed before it can yield market returns. If the innovator sells the idea to the existing firm, then the existing firm develops the idea. If the innovator chooses to become an entrepreneur, he develops the idea himself. Developing an idea of type θ results in a profit π, which is uniformly distributed on the interval $[A - \theta, A + \theta]$, where A is a positive parameter. The expected value of the profit from the developed innovation is A and the variance of the profit from the developed innovation is var $\pi = \theta^2/3$. The probability density of π is $1/(2\theta)$. Assume that $A + K < 1$. Assume that $A > K$, which implies that $A + \theta > K$ for all ideas, θ.

If the innovator chooses to become an entrepreneur, he observes π costlessly. Then, the entrepreneur successfully establishes a firm if $\pi \geq K$, and earns $\pi - K$. If $\pi < K$, the development is not successful and the entrepreneur receives no rewards. The ability to observe π before paying the cost of establishing the firm allows the entrepreneur to obtain the benefits of a successful development of the idea. As a result, the entrepreneur benefits from greater variance of profits. The greater the value of θ, the higher is the quality of the idea for the entrepreneur. The expected benefit of the entrepreneur is positive if the upper bound on profits, $A + \theta$, is greater than the cost of establishing the firm. The value of the idea θ to the entrepreneur equals

$$U(\theta) = \int_K^{A+\theta} \frac{\pi - K}{2\theta} d\pi = \frac{(A + \theta - K)^2}{4\theta}$$

The marginal value of the idea is increasing in θ since

$$U'(\theta) = \frac{1}{4}\left[1 - \frac{(A - K)^2}{\theta^2}\right]$$

Note that $A + \theta > K$ implies that $\theta^2 > (A - K)^2$. The entrepreneur is made better off by having a more risky idea. The value of the idea is convex in the quality of the idea, θ,

$$U''(\theta) = \frac{(A - K)^2}{2\theta^3}$$

The entrepreneur benefits from risk by having the real option to decide whether or not to invest in establishing the firm. The entrepreneur invests in establishing the firm if the anticipated profit exceeds the cost of setting up the firm. This helps to explain the traditional emphasis on the entrepreneur benefiting from risk. The entrepreneur does not bear risk in the same manner as the investor, except to the extent that the entrepreneur supplies his own funds. Instead, the entrepreneur experiences the risks associated with the development of his idea. This makes the entrepreneur prefer more risk.

Stiglitz and Weiss (1981) employ a similar information structure to study the effects of adverse selection on bank credit. They find that debt makes the borrower favor risk. The observation that the entrepreneur prefers more risk is similar. Like a borrower, the entrepreneur benefits from the upside of the development process by having the option to establish the firm.

If the innovator forgoes the option of entrepreneurship, he can commercialize his idea by selling it to an existing firm at a lump-sum royalty, R. The innovator sells the idea to the existing firm only if the royalty is greater than or equal to the benefit from becoming an entrepreneur, $R \ge U(\theta)$. Recall that the entrepreneur's benefit function is increasing in the variance parameter, θ, so that there is a critical value θ^* defined by

$$U(\theta^*) = R$$

Innovators with low-variance parameter values, θ in $[0, \theta^*]$ sell their ideas to the existing firm. Innovators with high-variance parameter values, θ in $[\theta^*, 1]$, become entrepreneurs and establish firms.

The existing firm is risk neutral and is unaffected by the variance in the development process. The existing firm chooses the royalty based on the tradeoff between the amont paid to the innovator and the likelihood of obtaining the idea. The existing firm's profit equals $(A - R)\theta^*(R)$. The profit-maximizing royalty solves

$$(A - R)d\theta^*(R)/dR - \theta^*(R) = 0$$

Substituting for $d\theta^*(R)/dR = 1/U'(\theta^*)$ and solving for θ^* gives

$$\theta^* = A + K$$

Then, the royalty offered by the existing firm equals

$$R^* = \frac{A^2}{A + K}$$

The innovators with the most risky projects choose to become entrepreneurs. The number of entrepreneurs is

$$n^* = 1 - \theta^* = 1 - A - K$$

The number of entrepreneurs is decreasing in the expected value of the developed idea and in the cost of establishing the firm. The greater the cost of establishing the firm, the lower is the royalty offered by the existing firm. The royalty offered by the existing firm is increasing in the expected value of the developed idea. The effects of adverse selection are reflected in the number of innovators that choose to become entrepreneurs.

SIGNALING

The innovator may face transaction costs associated with explaining his idea to the existing firm. The idea may be unobservable and difficult to illustrate. It may be necessary for the innovator to invest in a costly signal that is observable to the existing firm. If the costs of signaling are relatively low, the innovator can convey the necessary information to the existing firm and transfer the technology. If the costs of signaling are relatively high, the innovator will choose to become an entrepreneur and establish a firm.

The basic issues can be illustrated by adapting Spence's (1974) signaling model. Suppose that there are two types of innovators in the population, those with low-quality ideas, θ_L, and those with high-quality ideas, θ_H. The innovator's idea is his private information and is unobservable to the existing firm. The innovator can provide a signal s to the existing firm. The signal can be a costly business plan, presentation or prototype. The cost of the signal is s/θ, which is increasing in the signal and decreasing in the quality of the idea.

The existing firm offers the innovator a royalty payment that equals the expected value of the idea given the signal,

$$R(s) = E[\theta \mid s]$$

Under some conditions, the market equilibrium with signaling is separating.[1] At a separating equilibrium, innovators with different ideas choose different signals, s_L and s_H. The existing firm offers different royalties based on the signals, R_L and R_H.

For an equilibrium to be separating, the outcomes must involve choices that are incentive compatible for the innovators. The innovator with the low-quality idea reveals his idea in equilibrium and receives a royalty equal to the value of his idea, $R_L = \theta_L$. The innovator with the low-quality idea will not invest in producing a signal, so that $s_L = 0$. The innovator with the low-quality idea must prefer the outcome to choosing the same signal as the innovator with the high-quality idea,

$$\theta_L \geq \theta_H - s_H/\theta_L$$

For the innovator with the high-quality idea to prefer investing in a signal, incentive compatibility requires that

$$\theta_H - s_H/\theta_H \geq \theta_L$$

Combining these two inequalities gives bounds on the value of the signal of a high-quality idea,

$$\theta_L(\theta_H - \theta_L) \leq s_H \leq \theta_H(\theta_H - \theta_L)$$

This range defines a continuum of separating equilibria.

Consider the equilibrium at which the innovator chooses the least costly signal. The innovator with the low-quality ideas chooses $s_L = 0$ and the innovator with the high-quality idea chooses the signal

$$s_H = \theta_L(\theta_H - \theta_L)$$

The cost of signaling determines the outcome of the commercialization decisions of innovators. The innovator with the low-quality idea faces no signaling costs. Therefore, rather than pay the costs of establishing a firm, the innovator with the low-quality idea prefers to sell this idea to the existing firm. The innovator with the high-quality idea chooses to signal the quality of the idea and sell to the existing firm if the costs of establishing a firm are greater than or equal to the costs of signaling

$$K \geq s_H/\theta_H = (\theta_L/\theta_H)(\theta_H - \theta_L)$$

Otherwise, if $K < s_H/\theta_H$, signaling is not worthwhile. The inventor with the high-quality idea becomes an entrepreneur when

$$K < (\theta_L/\theta_H)(\theta_H - \theta_L)$$

When the value of the high-quality idea is sufficiently great, the innovator chooses entrepreneurship. Thus, rewriting the preceding inequality gives a condition on θ_H,

$$\theta_H > \theta_L^2/(\theta_L - K)$$

which is sufficient for the high-quality innovator to choose to establish a firm.

CONCLUSION

The innovator faces a fundamental decision in choosing how to commercialize an idea. Commercializing an idea involves obtaining and providing an invention to the market. The innovator can choose to become an entrepreneur and establish a firm to carry out these tasks. Alternatively, the innovator may choose the option of technology transfer involving a variety of transactions, including spot transactions, contracts and partnerships. The choice between entrepreneurship and technology transfer involves substantial differences in rewards, risks, transaction costs, information and property rights. How the innovator resolves this decision has important consequences for market structure and technological change.

The innovator's decision is a choice between competition and cooperation. The entrepreneurship choice requires competing with existing firms and other entrepreneurs, and potentially displacing them with a better technology. The technology transfer choice requires cooperating with existing firms that will purchase or license the new technology. The discussion introduced a Coasian theorem of creative destruction. When efficient bargaining between innovators and existing firms is feasible, the innovator will choose entrepreneurship if and only if it is socially efficient to do so.

However, when efficient bargaining between innovators and existing firms is not feasible, entrepreneurship addresses imperfections in the market for ideas through creative destruction. When IP rights of innovators are not protected sufficiently, the innovator will establish a firm as a means of protecting the returns to his IP. When existing firms make inefficient technology adoption decisions, entrepreneurship provides an alternative means of innovation. Due to asymmetric information about innovators' ideas, adverse selection prevents the formation of a market for ideas when the expected value of a disembodied idea is less than the return to establishing a firm. When it is not feasible for innovators and existing firms to write efficient contracts, due to the transaction costs of bargaining and monitoring, entrepreneurship provides a way for innovators to realize the returns to their ideas. When uncertainty in the development process creates risk, entrepreneurship provides a way to address development decisions. When signaling the value of innovators' ideas is costly, entrepreneurship provides a more efficient way to use the innovators' information.

The innovator's decision helps to explain why the entrepreneur chooses to embody the technology in the new firm rather than to license the technology to other individuals or to other firms. This applies to new products, new processes, new business methods and new forms of organization. By establishing firms, innovators commercialize invention in the most efficient way. Innovators achieve their commercialization goals through entrepreneurship. Therefore entrepreneurship and creative destruction are necessary and valuable mechanisms for overcoming imperfections in markets for technology.

ACKNOWLEDGMENT

Daniel F. Spulber gratefully acknowledges the support of a research grant from the Ewing Marion Kauffman Foundation.

NOTE

1.   This depends on the restriction placed on out-of-equilibrium beliefs. See Banks and Sobel (1987) for the D2 criterion refinement, and applications by Banks (1992) and Besanko and Spulber (1992).

REFERENCES

Acs, Z.J., D.B. Audretsch, P. Braunerhjelm and B. Carlsson (2004), 'The missing link: the knowledge filter and entrepreneurship in endogenous growth', CEPR Working Paper No. 4358, Industrial Organizations, London.

Akerlof, G.A. (1970), 'The market for "lemons": quality uncertainty and the market mechanism', *The Quarterly Journal of Economics*, **84** (3), 488–500.

Anton, J.J. and D.A. Yao (1994), 'Expropriation and inventions: appropriable rents in the absence of property-rights', *The American Economic Review*, **84** (1), 190–209.

Anton, J.J. and D.A. Yao (1995), 'Starts-ups, spin-offs, and internal projects', *Journal of Law, Economics, & Organization*, **11** (2), 362–78.

Anton, J.J. and D.A. Yao (2004), 'Little patents and big secrets: managing intellectual property', *Rand Journal of Economics*, **35** (1), 1–22.

Anton, J.J. and D.A. Yao (2002), 'The sale of ideas: strategic disclosure, property rights, and contracting', *Review of Economic Studies*, **69** (240), 513–31.

Anton, J.J. and D.A. Yao (2003), 'Patents, invalidity, and the strategic transmission of enabling information', *Journal of Economics & Management Strategy*, **12** (2), 151–78.

Arrow, K.J. (1962), 'Economic welfare and the allocation of resources for invention', in R. Nelson (ed.), *The Rate and Direction of Inventive Activity: Economic and Social Factors*, Princeton, NJ: Princeton University Press, pp. 609–25.

Arrow, K.J. (1969), 'Classificatory notes on the production and transmission of technological knowledge', *The American Economic Review*, **59** (2), 29–35.

Audretsch, D.B., M.C. Keilbach and E.E. Lehmann (eds) (2006), *Entrepreneurship and Economic Growth*, Oxford: Oxford University Press.

Banks, J.S. (1992), 'Monopoly pricing and regulatory oversight', *Journal of Economics & Management Strategy*, **1**, 203–33.

Banks, J.S. and J. Sobel (1987), 'Equilibrium selection in signaling games', *Econometrica*, **55** (3), 647–61.

Baumol, W.J. (1968), 'Entrepreneurship in economic theory', *The American Economic Review, Papers and Proceedings*, **58** (2), 64–71.

Baumol, W.J. (ed.) (1993), *Entrepreneurship, Management, and the Structure of Payoffs*, Cambridge, MA and London: MIT Press.

Baumol, W.J. (ed.) (2002), *The Free-Market Innovation Machine: Analyzing the Growth Miracle of Capitalism*, Princeton, NJ: Princeton University Press.

Baumol, W.J. (2005), 'Entrepreneurship and invention: toward their microeconomic value theory', *Joint Center AEI–Brookings Joint Center for Regulatory Studies*.

Baumol, W.J., R.E. Litan and C.J. Schramm (eds) (2007), *Good Capitalism, Bad Capitalism, and the Economics of Growth and Prosperity*, New Haven, CT and London: Yale University Press.

Besanko, D. and D.F. Spulber (1992), 'Sequential equilibrium investment by regulated firms', *Rand Journal of Economics*, **23** (2), 153–70.

Casson, M. (ed.) (1982), *The Entrepreneur: An Economic Theory*, Totowa, NJ: Barnes & Noble.

Casson, M. (ed.) (1987), *The Firm and the Market: Studies on Multinational Enterprise and the Scope of the Firm*, Cambridge, MA: MIT Press.

Casson, M. (ed.) (1997), *Information and Organization: A New Perspective on the Theory of the Firm*, Oxford: Clarendon Press.

Casson, M. (ed.) (2003), *The Entrepreneur: An Economic Theory*, 2nd edn, Cheltenham, UK and Northampton MA: Edward Elgar.

Coase, R.H. (1937), 'The nature of the firm', *Economica*, **4**, 386–405.

Coase, R.H. (1960), 'The problem of social cost', *Journal of Law and Economics*, **3**, 1–44.

Coase, R.H. (1988), 'The nature of the firm: origin, meaning, influence', in O.E. Williamson and S.G. Winter (eds), *The Nature of the Firm: Origin, Evolution, Development*, New York: Oxford University Press, pp. 34–60.

Coase, R.H. (1994), 'The institutional structure of production', in Ronald H. Coase, *Essays on Economics and Economists*, Chicago, IL: University of Chicago Press, pp. 3–14.

Gans, J.S. and S. Stern (2000), 'Incumbency and R&D incentives: licensing the gale of creative destruction', *Journal of Economics & Management Strategy*, **9** (4), 485–511.

Gans, J.S., D.H. Hsu and S. Stern (2002), 'When does start-up innovation spur the gale of creative destruction?', *Rand Journal of Economics*, **33** (4), 571–86.

Geroski, P.A. (1995), 'What do we know about entry?', *International Journal of Industrial Organization*, **13** (4), 421–40.

Gromb, D. and D. Scharfstein (2002), 'Entrepreneurship in equilibrium', NBER Working Papers, London, London Business School.

Hellmann, T. and M. Puri (2000), 'The interaction between product market and financing strategy: the role of venture capital', *The Review of Financial Studies*, **13** (4), 959–84.

Katz, M.L. and C. Shapiro (1987), 'R&D rivalry with licensing or imitation', *The American Economic Review*, **77** (3), 402–20.

Reinganum, J.F. (1981), 'Dynamic games of innovation', *Journal of Economic Theory*, **25** (1), 1–41.

Reinganum, J.F. (1982), 'A dynamic game of R and D: patent protection and competitive behavior', *Econometrica*, **50** (3), 671–88.

Reinganum, J.F. (1989), 'The timing of innovation: research, development, and diffusion', in R. Schmalensee and R.D. Willig (eds), *Handbook of Industrial Organization*, Vol. 1, New York: Elsevier Science Publishers, pp. 849–908.

Sah, R.K. and J.E. Stiglitz (1986), 'The architecture of economic systems: hierarchies and polyarchies', *The American Economic Review*, **76** (4), 716–27.

Salant, S.W. (1984), 'Preemptive patenting and the persistence of monopoly: comment', *The American Economic Review*, **74** (1), 247–50.

Say, J.-B. (ed.) (1852), *Cours Complet d'Économie Politique: Pratique*, vols I and II, 3rd edn, Paris: Guillaumin et Cie.

Say, J.-B. (ed.) (1841) [1982], *Traité d'Économie Politique*, 6th edn, Geneva: Slatkine.

Schramm, C.J. (ed.) (2006), *The Entrepreneurial Imperative: How America's Economic Miracle Will Reshape the World (and Change your Life)*, New York: HarperCollins.

Schumpeter, J.A. (ed.) (1934), *The Theory of Economic Development: An Inquiry into Profits, Capital, Credit, Interest and the Business Cycle*, reprinted 2007, New Brunswick, NJ: Transaction Publishers.

Schumpeter, J.A. (ed.) (1942), *Capitalism, Socialism, and Democracy*, New York: Harper & Brothers.

Spence, A.M. (ed.) (1974), *Market Signaling: Informational Transfer in Hiring and Related Screening Processes*, Cambridge, MA: Harvard University Press.

Spulber, D.F. (ed.) (2009a), *The Theory of the Firm: Microeconomics with Endogenous Entrepreneurs, Firms, Markets, and Organizations*, Cambridge: Cambridge University Press.

Spulber, D.F. (2009b), 'Competition among entrepreneurs', *Industrial and Corporate Change*, advance access, 17 July 2009.

Stiglitz, J.E. and A. Weiss (1981), 'Credit rationing in markets with imperfect information', *The American Economic Review*, **71** (3), 393–410.

21 What do scientists think about commercialization activities?

Werner Bönte

INTRODUCTION

The commercialization of knowledge generated by universities and public research institutions is an important driver of economic growth in developed economies since the innovative activities of firms are often dependent on access to related academic research, with innovations in some industries significantly affected by academic research (Mansfield, 1995; Jaffe, 1989; Cohen and Levinthal, 1990). The inflow of knowledge from public research institutions is especially important for firms operating in fields with high speeds of technological change, like biotechnology, new materials and nanotechnology (Cockburn and Henderson, 2000; Pavitt, 1998; Zucker et al., 1998).

There are two major channels through which scientific knowledge is transferred to the private sector. First, firms may benefit from academic research because scientists present their results at conferences or publish them in scientific journals. Consequently, this publicly available knowledge can be used by firms and may positively affect the firms' innovation process. Second, academic researchers may be directly engaged in commercialization activities, like patenting, joint research with private firms, contract research, consulting and university-spinoffs. One might speculate that not just firms, but also scientists, might be interested in the transfer of scientific knowledge.

However, in spite of the importance of academic research for firm innovation, recent European innovation data show that 'the link between publicly financed science and innovative industry is rather weak' (Parvan, 2007, p. 1). One explanation for this weak link may be that many firms are unaware of the commercial potential of academic research or that they are reluctant to engage in collaboration with universities or public research institutions. Another explanation is that scientists are principally interested in basic research and refuse to engage in commercialization of their research results.

While empirical studies are starting to analyze firm incentives to engage in collaboration with universities (Veugelers and Cassiman, 2005), our knowledge about scientists' incentives to engage in commercialization activities is still limited. What do scientists think about commercialization of their research results? This study contributes to the understanding of scientists' attitudes toward commercialization of their scientific research results. Scientists face several trade-offs when deciding whether to engage in commercialization activities or not. Potential benefits from commercialization activities are reputational rewards or financial benefits. Potential drawbacks of such activities are reduction in time for own research or costs of commercialization. Moreover, commercialization of research may conflict with scientific identity of open science if scientists subscribe to the idea of open science.

In order to shed light on the relevance of these trade-offs, this study analyzes empirically factors that may influence scientists' commercialization activities. In particular, we investigate whether personal characteristics and scientific environment affect scientists' attitudes toward commercialization. The empirical analysis is based on a sample of scientists working at the research institutes of the Max Planck Society in Germany. These scientists assess various factors that may affect commercialization activities. They conduct basic research in various fields of life sciences, natural science, mathematics, technology and computer science, as well as the social sciences. Max Planck scientists work in the same institutional setting and are not obliged to attract external funding. Given the absence of internal institutional pressure to commercialize findings, Max Planck scientists represent a suitable sample for an empirical analysis of scientists' individual attitudes toward commercialization.

The rest of this chapter is structured as follows. The next section discusses trade-offs when deciding about engagement in commercialization activities. The third section describes the Max Planck Scientists' Survey. The fourth section presents the empirical analysis and estimation results, and the final section concludes.

SCIENTISTS' ATTITUDES TOWARD COMMERCIALIZATION ACTIVITIES

Scientists face trade-offs when deciding about engagement in commercialization activities. On the one hand, they may benefit from commercialization activities. For instance, such activities may lead to an increase in income, available resources or reputation. On the other hand, such engagement may have several drawbacks. They may be associated with high costs, they may reduce scientists' time for own research and they may conflict with scientists' support of open science. Moreover, these trade-offs may depend on the scientist's field of research as well as the availability and quality of support by technology transfers offices. In what follows, these trade-offs will be discussed in more detail.

The main justification for public funding of basic research is the public-good characteristic of knowledge resulting from scientific research activities (Arrow, 1962; Scherer, 1982). The idea of open science with free dissemination is especially important in academic science, since scientists doing basic research contribute to the stock of freely available knowledge (Dasgupta and David, 1987). According to the Mertonian norm of communism, scientists have an incentive to give up intellectual property rights in exchange for recognition and esteem (Merton, 1973). This incentive leads to communist activity in the sense that scientists share their work with the community for the common good. Moreover, researchers are interested in an early publication of their research results since priority in discovery is the key to scientific recognition (Merton, 1957; Stephan, 1996). When researchers communicate an advance in knowledge, they are rewarded by the scientific community for being first (David, 2003; Hong and Walsh, 2009). In contrast, commercialization of research results may imply that the dissemination of knowledge must be restricted in order to appropriate the financial benefits from research results. Consequently, there might be a conflict between the idea of open science and the commercialization of research results. For instance, scientists may refuse to engage in research cooperation with private firms if the latter try to appropriate the returns from new knowledge by protecting it through patenting or secrecy. Hence open science may represent a major obstacle to the commercialization of scientific research results.

However, it is argued that there has been a change in the culture of science since the mid-1980s. Science is coming under increasing pressure to make research results relevant to industry (Cohen et al., 1998; Hong and Walsh, 2009), and scientific success is increasingly evaluated by commercial success (Hackett, 1990). Hence commercialization of research results may lead to increasing scientific reputation among researchers. Owen-Smith and Powell (2003) argue that commercialization success and the attention of corporate partners make scientists visible in their research field. These scientists are often able to attract attention and funding, which, in turn, may lead to greater reputation. Such feedback loops seem plausible as researchers' quality and their commercial success are shown to be complements (Thursby et al., 2001). Consequently, reputational rewards from commercialization activities may be an important benefit accruing from such activities. However, reputation may not be an end in and of itself. Over the course of a scientific career, recognition of colleagues potentially translates into pecuniary rewards in terms of well-paid research positions, well-funded research projects or laboratories (Stephan, 1996; Hong and Walsh, 2009).

Direct monetary returns may be a further important driver for scientists to commercialize their research. For instance, starting a business based on research results may allow a scientist to earn extra money. Consulting is another way to receive extra money from science (Bains, 2005). Moreover, the results of studies analyzing the disclosure of research results by scientists indicate that adequate royalty payments to scientists effectively motivate them toward commercializing their research results (Jensen et al., 2003; Thursby et al., 2001).

A potential downside of commercialization activities is the reallocation of time from research to activities related to the commercialization of research results. Stern (2004) argues that scientists have a preference for doing research rather than working on possible industrial applications. Therefore it seems reasonable that scientists prefer to allocate as much time as possible to academic research. Several empirical studies analyze whether commercialization activities actually 'crowd out' basic research. Most existing studies analyzing the relationship of research output and commercialization efforts detected a complementary relationship. Empirical studies based on US data suggest that patenting and invention disclosure have a positive impact on publication output (Agrawal and Henderson, 2002; Azoulay et al., 2006). This result is confirmed by empirical studies based on European data (Breschi, 2007). Hence patents and licenses may be complementary to fundamental research as conflicts between research and commercialization time are not prevalent. However, whether this is also true for other commercialization activities, such as university spinoffs, consulting or cooperation with private firms is unclear. Hence it is important to know whether scientists believe that such substitutive relationships between own research and commercialization activities exist.

Of course, the assumed commercialization potential of a scientist's own research results is an important factor for engaging in commercialization activities. A scientist working in a field of research where commercialization activities are common and who is engaged in research that is suited for commercialization is more likely to be engaged in commercialization activities than one who is not. However, it is not only important whether research has really commercial potential or not, but also whether a scientist believes that the research has commercial potential. A scientist may think, for instance, that the research is too basic to be commercialized, although objectively it has commercialization potential. Technology transfer offices (TTOs) are another important factor. Time-intensive tasks associated with patenting are often carried out by TTOs. These offices also often support commercialization costs or help establish links between scientists and private firms. Hence TTOs are a gateway to university and public research institute results. Many empirical studies analyze the productivity of TTOs and its determinants (Rothaermel et al., 2008). However, it is also important to know scientists' opinion about TTOs. If scientists believe that TTOs are not needed to help with the commercialization process, they may not contact them. If this opinion is based on ignorance, the effectiveness of TTOs is significantly diminished.

In the empirical part of this chapter, scientists' assessment of benefits and drawbacks associated with commercialization activities is analyzed. In particular, measures of reputational rewards, costs of commercialization, reduction in time for own research, and financial benefits are used. Moreover, measures of open science identity, the assessment of the commercialization potential of research results, and importance of TTOs are analyzed.

The relationship between these measures and personal characteristics is also investigated. For instance, the position or career stage of a researcher is an important indicator for scientific expertise and human capital, which in turn may affect attitudes toward commercialization activities. Zucker et al. (2002) and Audretsch and Stephan (1996) found that star scientists are important research partners for firms.

Age represents another important factor that may affect attitudes toward commercialization. As mentioned above, it is argued that the culture of science is changing over time. One might therefore argue that attitudes of older researchers may differ from those of younger researchers. For instance, older researchers may follow the norm of open science while this norm is less relevant for younger scientists (Bercovitz and Feldman, 2008). Moreover, a scientist's gender may be relevant. Results of prior empirical studies suggest that female scientists are less likely to sell their science commercially (Stephan and El-Ganainy, 2007), and to disclose fewer inventions (Thursby and Thursby, 2005). Other variables included in the empirical analysis are citizenship to control for country effects and work experience in industry.

DATA SOURCE AND MEASUREMENT

Max Planck Scientists' Survey

This study is based on a survey within the Max Planck Society (MPS), which is an independent, publicly funded research organization in Germany. Currently, the MPS maintains more than 9000 scientists working at 80 institutes in various research fields. The Max Planck institutes are classified in three sections: the biology and medicine section; the chemistry, physics and technology section; and the humanities section. Research fields within the biology and medicine section include genetics, infection biology, cognition research and neuroscience, among others. Astrophysics, material sciences, climate research and energy and plasma physics are the core fields of the chemistry, physics and technology section. Humanities research within the MPS mainly focuses on cultural studies, jurisprudence and social sciences.

Although the MPS consists of many very different institutes, the institutional setting is identical throughout. All institutes select and carry out their research autonomously and independently within the aforementioned scope of the MPS. Each institute administers its own budget, which can be supplemented by third-party funds. Research results are made public and accessible to all, enabling an external committee of experts to regularly (usually biannually) evaluate the research going on in MPS institutes. Academic freedom of researchers is emphasized by the MPS and supported by the institutional design of MPS institutes. Scientists are free to process their research topics, as they feel the research should be done to achieve scientific excellence. Leading researchers from outside the MPS are appointed as directors of MPS institutes. MPS institutes are established only where the world's leading researchers are found and directors of MPS institutes are free to design their research topics and make decisions about resource allocation. This academic freedom may explain why MPS scientists have won a majority of Germany's Nobel prizes awarded since the Second World War.

Hence the identical structure of MPS institutes allows for surveying scientists working under a similar institutional setting, albeit working in different fields of research. Thus scientists' individual attitudes toward commercialization can be analyzed since attitudes are not affected by differences in the institutional setting.

In order to analyze scientist commercialization incentives, a bilingual survey capturing possible stimuli of and barriers to scientific commercialization was developed.[1] The questionnaire contains questions with regard to each individual scientist's commercialization activities, attitudes toward such activities, as well as questions on each scientist's research experience, industrial experience, education, demographics and risk-taking behavior. Survey questions were developed with the aim of quantitatively analyzing commercialization activities of scientists at the individual level. Questions were improved during a pilot study conducted in August and September 2007. The pilot study was performed with randomly contacted scientists based at non-MPS German research organizations.

Before interviewing scientists of the Max Planck Society, the executive directors and heads of administration of 78 MPS institutes were contacted and asked for permission to survey the scientists in their institute. Two institutes covering art history were not included in the study as these institutes are situated outside Germany, in Italy. Out of the 78 institutes asked, 67 allowed us to perform our survey, providing us with the scientists' contact phone numbers. The population for the survey consisted of 7808 scientists working for these 67 different MPS institutes. The phone survey was administered by TNS Emnid GmbH, a professional opinion research institute based in Germany. Trained interviewers, fluent in both English and German, from TNS Emnid GmbH contacted scientist from mid-October to mid-December 2007. The data set includes data from 2604 conducted interviews, indicating a response rate of 33.35 percent.

Measurement of Factors that Influence Scientists' Commercialization Activities

In order to analyze individual scientists' attitudes toward commercialization activities, the scientists' assessment of several statements concerning commercialization activities and science is used.

Scientists were asked to what degree they agree or disagree with these statements, using the following explanation:

> We would like to consider factors influencing commercialization activities of research. By commercializing we include patenting results, research collaboration with the private sector, consulting activities and starting businesses. In case you have experience with such activities, please give a general answer and do not evaluate a specific research project. In case you do not have any experience, please indicate your personal presumption. For the following statements please indicate to what degree you agree or disagree with the statements on a scale from 1 to 5; 1 meaning 'strongly disagree', 2 'disagree', 3 'either', 4 'agree', and 5 'strongly agree'.

The following statements were read to the scientists by the interviewer, and scientists were asked to what extent they agree.

- Open science: 'My research results should be freely available to any other researchers and businesses.'
- Reputational rewards: 'Commercialization activities increase the reputation of a scientist in my scientific community.'
- Reduction in time for own research: 'Commercialization activities are time consuming and reduce time for my research.'
- Low financial benefits: 'There is little, if any, money to be made from commercialization.'
- Commercialization costs: 'The costs of commercialization, e.g. patent applications, fees associated with starting a business, are very high.'
- Commercialization potential of research results – own research group: 'My research group focuses on basic research which is not suitable for commercialization.'
- Commercialization potential of research results – own research field: 'Commercialization activities are common in my scientific community.'
- Relevance of TTOs: 'Institutions, such as technology transfer offices, are needed to deal with the commercialization process, e.g. patent application process, finding licensees, finding venture capitalists.'

The 5-point scale responses to these statements are used as indicators. Note that scientists with and without experience in the commercialization of research results assessed the statements. Hence the statements reflect the scientists' general attitude toward benefits and drawbacks of commercialization activities, regardless of commercialization experience. Moreover, the survey contains information about personal characteristics such as age, work experience in industry, citizenship, gender, affiliation to one of the three MPS sections, time worked for Max Planck Society and research position. The last item distinguishes between PhD students, post-doctoral research fellows, group leaders and directors of research groups. The empirical analysis is based on a sample of scientists for which complete data for all variables exist. The size of the sample is therefore restricted to 1979.

EMPIRICAL RESULTS

The average scores for each factor influencing commercialization activities are reported separately for PhD students and senior researchers in Figure 21.1. One might expect that

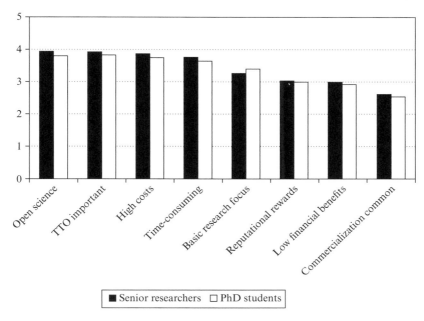

Note: Number of senior researchers is 964. Number of PhD students is 1015.

Figure 21.1   Scientists' attitudes toward commercialization – average scores

attitudes of more experienced researchers might differ from those of young scholars. The results, however, suggest that the responses of PhD students and senior researchers (post-doctoral research fellows, group leaders and directors) are remarkably similar. The scores are slightly higher for senior researchers, with the exception of the statement about the research focus of the group, but the ranking of the average scores is the same. The statement about open science exhibits the greatest agreement while the statement that commerciali-zation is common has the least agreement. This suggests that many scientists, irrespective of whether they are senior researchers or PhD students, support the idea of open science and think that commercialization is not common in their field. This may reflect the orientation of the Max Planck Society. However, if scientists assess the basic research focus of their own research group, only 50 percent agree that their group's research is too basic to be commercialized. Moreover, many scientists agree with the statement that technology transfer offices are relevant to deal with the commercialization process.

Figure 21.2 reports the average scores for senior researchers with and without com-mercialization experience. In the survey, scientists were asked whether they have expe-rience with starting new firms, patenting, disclosure of inventions, cooperations with private firms or consulting. Scientists reporting that they do not have experience with one of these activities form the group of scientists without experience. In our sample of 964 senior researchers, 55.6 percent, report that they have commercialization experience.

Here, remarkable differences between both groups exist. There are significant dif-ferences between both average responses as well as in the ranking. For the group of

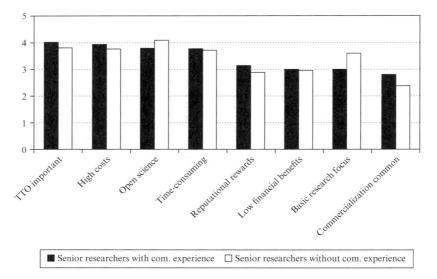

Note: Number of senior researchers with commercialization experience is 536. Number of senior researchers without commercialization experience is 428.

Figure 21.2   Senior researchers' attitudes toward commercialization – average scores

researchers without commercialization experience, the open science statement exhibits the highest average score, while the average score of this statement is significantly lower for the group of researchers with commercialization experience. In contrast, the TTO statement exhibits the highest score for the group of researchers with commercialization experience and TTOs are perceived as more important for the commercialization process by scientists with commercialization than by those without any such experience. As one might expect, senior researchers with commercialization experience rate the commercialization potential of their research (own group and own scientific community) higher than researchers without commercialization experience.

   The correlations among the factors influencing commercialization activities are also analyzed. The correlation matrix of pairwise correlations is presented in Table 21.1. Although many of the correlations are statistically significant, the values of most correlations are low, suggesting that factors are only weakly correlated. The strongest correlation exists between two measures capturing the research focus of a scientist's research group and the commonness of commercialization in a scientist's scientific field. However, the correlation is still relatively low (0.4205), which suggests that the two measures reflect different things. The indicator for reputational rewards is positively correlated with commonness of commercialization in a scientist's field but negatively correlated with the basic research focus of a group. The opposite is true for the indicator of open science. Moreover, there is a negative correlation between open science and reputation. This result may reflect the conflict between the norm of open science and commercialization activities. Moreover, the indicator reflecting the relevance of TTOs is positively correlated with cost and time demand of commercialization activities. This

Table 21.1   Correlation matrix

	C1	C2	C3	C4	C5	C6	C7	C8
Reputational rewards (C1)	1							
Low financial benefits (C2)	−0.0459 (0.0411)	1						
Time-consuming (C3)	−0.0938 (0.0000)	0.0958 (0.0000)	1					
High costs (C4)	0.0016 (0.9439)	0.0538 (0.0166)	0.2486 (0.0000)	1				
Open science (C5)	−0.1311 (0.0000)	0.0303 (0.1773)	0.0926 (0.0000)	−0.0142 (0.5270)	1			
TTO important (C6)	0.1146 (0.0000)	−0.0124 (0.5802)	0.0943 (0.0000)	0.1904 (0.0000)	−0.0024 (0.9153)	1		
Basic research focus (C7)	−0.2134 (0.0000)	0.1235 (0.0000)	0.1203 (0.0000)	−0.0400 (0.0753)	0.2154 (0.0000)	−0.0972 (0.0000)	1	
Commercial. common (C8)	0.2573 (0.0000)	−0.0706 (0.0017)	−0.1032 (0.0000)	0.0045 (0.8398)	−0.1472 (0.0000)	0.0634 (0.0048)	−0.4205 (0.0000)	1

Notes: The total sample comprises 1979 scientists. Numbers in parentheses are the exact significance levels.

implies that scientists who assume that these problems are relevant also find TTOs more important.

Next, the relationship between a scientist's assessment of the factors influencing commercialization activities and personal characteristics, such as commercialization experience, age, gender or career stage, is investigated. Moreover, the average score for each respective measure at the institute level is included (corrected for each scientist's individual score) in order to capture institute effects that may influence a scientist's attitudes. Individual attitudes may stem from institute culture or social influence of colleagues. Since the dependent variables are ordinal variables (5-point scales), an ordered probit model is used. Moreover, observations may not be independent across the scientists. Scientists belonging to the same Max Planck institute may share unobserved similarities that violate the assumption of independent observations. Hence robust standard errors are reported that correct for clustering effects at the institute level.

The results are reported in Tables 21.2 and 21.3. There is a statistically significant relationship between the average score of other scientists working at the same Max Planck institute and a scientist's individual assessments of reputational rewards, open science identity, commonness of commercialization in research field and basic research focus of research group. For the latter two variables this result suggests that scientists share to some extent the opinion about commercialization potential of their research results. One would expect this result if scientists belonging to the same institute are engaged in related fields of research. However, a striking result of the empirical analysis is that scientists' assessment of reputational rewards and open science are also influenced by institute effects, which may suggest that shared scientific norms can explain to some extent scientists' attitudes toward commercialization. In contrast, the assessment of costs and

Table 21.2   Determinants of factors influencing scientists' commercialization activities

	(1) Reputational rewards	(2) Low financial benefits	(3) Time-consuming	(4) High costs
Institute average	0.587***	−0.108	−0.330	−0.0150
	(0.0978)	(0.191)	(0.275)	(0.246)
Comm. experience (1 = yes)	0.223***	0.0211	−0.0240	0.0892
	(0.0533)	(0.0576)	(0.0595)	(0.0556)
Age (log of years)	0.0560	0.756***	0.220	0.0309
	(0.138)	(0.154)	(0.143)	(0.103)
Industry work experience (1 = yes)	0.133**	−0.0788	−0.0643	−0.0550
	(0.0538)	(0.0613)	(0.0599)	(0.0584)
German citizenship	−0.108*	0.0682	0.237***	0.359***
	(0.0634)	(0.0530)	(0.0500)	(0.0504)
Gender (1 = female)	0.114*	0.0148	−0.131**	−0.175***
	(0.0608)	(0.0651)	(0.0524)	(0.0494)
Post-doc.	0.0516	−0.129*	0.0535	0.149**
	(0.0616)	(0.0673)	(0.0625)	(0.0670)
Group leader	−0.0594	0.130	0.198**	0.212***
	(0.0975)	(0.0951)	(0.0991)	(0.0687)
Director	−0.220	−0.164	0.211	0.195
	(0.163)	(0.187)	(0.152)	(0.191)
Life sciences	0.200***	−0.156*	−0.0970	0.334***
	(0.0630)	(0.0835)	(0.106)	(0.104)
Chemistry, physics & technology	0.199***	−0.0931	−0.129	0.105
	(0.0569)	(0.0790)	(0.110)	(0.103)
Pseudo R^2	0.0221	0.0095	0.0129	0.0245
Wald test	$\chi 2(11)$	$\chi 2(11)$	$\chi 2(11)$	$\chi 2(11)$
	334.83***	47.55***	96.35***	164.30***

Notes: Results of ordered probit estimations. Robust standard errors that are adjusted for clusters (institutes) are reported in parentheses. *, ** and *** denote significance at the 10, 5 and 1 percent levels respectively. Number of observations: 1979.

time demand associated with commercialization activities as well as the assessment of the relevance of TTOs appear idiosyncratic, i.e. only determined by scientists' individual opinions.

There is a statistically significant relationship between commercialization experience and the assessment of reputational rewards, open science relevance of TTOs as well as commercialization potential of research. One might argue that commercialization experience influences scientists' attitudes. However, this result should be interpreted with caution because endogeneity problems are likely to exist: it may be that commercialization experience influences the scientists' assessment, but it is also likely that attitudes toward commercialization affect commercialization behavior. For instance, open science identity may be viewed as something fundamental, i.e. the identity of a scientist that does

Table 21.3   Determinants of factors influencing scientists' commercialization activities

	(1) Open science	(2) TTO important	(3) Commercialization common	(4) Basic research focus
Institute average	0.390**	0.172	0.802***	0.612***
	(0.170)	(0.252)	(0.0479)	(0.0670)
Comm. experience (1 = yes)	−0.277***	0.145**	0.397***	−0.417***
	(0.0469)	(0.0662)	(0.0656)	(0.0507)
Age (log of years)	0.491***	0.173	−0.286**	0.364***
	(0.120)	(0.147)	(0.140)	(0.113)
Industry work experience (1 = yes)	−0.155***	−0.0605	0.0850	−0.140**
	(0.0577)	(0.0722)	(0.0687)	(0.0661)
German citizenship	−0.0920	0.0620	−0.296***	0.130**
	(0.0593)	(0.0594)	(0.0598)	(0.0549)
Gender (1 = female)	−0.240***	−0.285***	−0.0791	−0.0239
	(0.0499)	(0.0390)	(0.0581)	(0.0509)
Post-doc.	0.0530	0.0415	0.0576	−0.132**
	(0.0679)	(0.0592)	(0.0596)	(0.0625)
Group leader	−0.0448	0.121	0.0171	−0.178**
	(0.0789)	(0.0983)	(0.100)	(0.0750)
Director	0.144	−0.0111	0.186	−0.335**
	(0.173)	(0.182)	(0.145)	(0.139)
Life sciences	−0.160**	0.273***	0.209***	−0.154***
	(0.0638)	(0.0857)	(0.0719)	(0.0582)
Chemistry, physics & technology	−0.107**	0.00889	0.106	−0.0829
	(0.0538)	(0.0731)	(0.0755)	(0.0566)
Pseudo R^2	0.0203	0.0202	0.0626	0.0400
Wald test	$\chi 2(11)$	$\chi 2(11)$	$\chi 2(11)$	$\chi 2(11)$
	141.38***	180.75***	581.92***	370.93***

Notes: Results of ordered probit estimations. Robust standard errors that are adjusted for clusters (institutes) are reported in parentheses. *, ** and *** denote significance at the 10, 5 and 1 percent levels respectively. Number of observations: 1979.

not change over time. In this case a scientist following Mertonian norms is less likely to be engaged in commercialization activities. This would explain the negative coefficient of the open science variable, but causality would run from open science identity to commercialization behavior. It is an interesting result that experience does not seem to affect the assessment of monetary benefits, time demand, and costs associated with commercialization activities.

Concerning a scientist's age, the results suggest that the older a scientist is – *ceteris paribus* – the more likely it is that the scientist agrees with the statement that little, if any, money is to be made from commercialization, that he or she agrees with the idea of open science and that he or she thinks that the commercialization potential of their own research is low. One explanation for the last result is that older scientists are actually engaged in research fields with limited commercialization potential. Another explanation is that only older scientists believe that this is the case, while younger scientist would rate the commercialization potential as higher. The finding that older scientists are more likely to follow the Mertonian norm of open science may point to change in the culture of science, implying that younger scientists are more prone to commercialization activities. Citizenship also influences scientists' attitudes toward commercialization activities. Scientists with German citizenship are more likely to think that commercialization activities are associated with high costs, that they are time-consuming, and that the research has low commercialization potential. Moreover, gender seems to be relevant. Females rate the drawbacks of commercialization activities as less relevant than males, they are less likely to agree with the idea of open science and they assess TTOs as less important than do males.

Research position is also relevant. Group leaders are more likely to agree with the statements that commercialization activities are time-consuming and associated with high costs. This result can be explained by the fact that group leaders are often managing directors responsible for organizing routine activities. Moreover, senior researchers – and especially directors – are less likely to agree with the statement that research of the group is too basic and not suitable for commercialization. This may suggest that senior researchers are better informed about the commercialization potential of research results. The results suggest that there are differences between the three sections of the Max Planck Society. In particular, scientists in the life sciences section are more likely to report that their research has commercialization potential. Moreover, scientists from life sciences and the chemistry, physics and technology sections are less likely to agree with the idea of open science when compared to scientists in the humanities section.

In order to check the robustness of the results, a similar analysis based on the sample of senior scientists is performed. The analysis is restricted to senior researchers because it is likely that the latter engage voluntarily in commercialization activities while PhD students are typically supervised by senior researchers. Moreover, dummy variables reflecting the research field of the scientists' PhD theses are included and a variable reflecting the relevance of time spent at the MPS, i.e. years a scientist worked for MPS divided by scientist's age, is added. These results are reported in Tables 21.4 and 21.5. By and large, the results are hardly affected.

The estimated coefficients of dummy variables reflecting the field of PhD are statistically significant in some cases. Results suggest that scientists with a PhD in chemistry are more likely to agree with the statements that commercialization activities increase reputation and that commercialization is common in their field of research. In contrast, they disagree with the statement that research in their group is too basic and not suitable for commercialization, that commercialization activities are time-consuming and that not much money can be made from commercialization. This result is plausible. Scientists with a PhD in biology are less likely to agree with the idea of open science. Moreover, the variable reflecting the time spent at the MPS also has a statistically significant impact. The longer the period of time scientists have worked for the MPS (relative to their age), the more likely it is that they will assess the financial benefits from commercialization activities as low, agree that such activities are time-consuming and costly, agree with the idea of open science and will report that their research (group and scientific community) has low commercialization potential. There are at least two

Table 21.4   *Determinants of factors influencing scientists' commercialization activities –*
sample of senior researchers (1)

	(1) Reputational rewards	(2) Low financial benefits	(3) Time-consuming	(4) High costs
Institute average	0.340**	−0.297	−0.268	0.0902
	(0.133)	(0.302)	(0.386)	(0.283)
Comm. experience (1 = yes)	0.266***	−0.0657	−0.00897	0.113
	(0.0888)	(0.0749)	(0.0802)	(0.0777)
Age (log of years)	−0.249	0.576**	0.243	−0.253
	(0.204)	(0.225)	(0.213)	(0.194)
Years at MPS/age	0.0216	0.770*	0.468*	0.509*
	(0.380)	(0.397)	(0.277)	(0.305)
Industry work experience (1 = yes)	0.0800	−0.102	−0.0617	−0.00849
	(0.0889)	(0.0887)	(0.0912)	(0.0921)
German citizenship	−0.0796	0.0729	0.247***	0.366***
	(0.0741)	(0.0729)	(0.0682)	(0.0757)
Gender (1 = female)	0.0502	0.0984	−0.132	−0.188**
	(0.0934)	(0.0822)	(0.0837)	(0.0830)
Group leader	−0.0739	−0.00532	0.0974	0.0483
	(0.0956)	(0.0883)	(0.0962)	(0.0741)
Director	−0.193	−0.0140	0.134	0.0953
	(0.167)	(0.189)	(0.160)	(0.193)
PhD biology	0.0727	−0.123	−0.0563	0.0158
	(0.112)	(0.108)	(0.126)	(0.125)
PhD chemistry	0.308***	−0.216**	−0.200*	−0.0171
	(0.111)	(0.0986)	(0.116)	(0.138)
PhD physics	0.0308	−0.0954	−0.0958	−0.147
	(0.122)	(0.121)	(0.0976)	(0.125)
PhD mathematics	−0.0688	−0.131	0.171	−0.508***
	(0.288)	(0.241)	(0.254)	(0.179)
PhD medical science	0.0580	0.00541	−0.464**	−0.0978
	(0.249)	(0.213)	(0.233)	(0.248)
PhD engineering	0.660***	0.0687	0.0143	0.263
	(0.252)	(0.268)	(0.225)	(0.252)
Life sciences	0.306*	−0.0922	−0.106	0.452***
	(0.170)	(0.135)	(0.201)	(0.167)
Chemistry, physics & technology	0.262	0.0771	−0.163	0.335*
	(0.166)	(0.143)	(0.200)	(0.173)
Pseudo R^2	0.0274	0.0194	0.0210	0.0308
Wald test	$\chi 2(17)$	$\chi 2(17)$	$\chi 2(17)$	$\chi 2(17)$
	153.72***	64.46***	86.78***	97.03***

Notes: Results of ordered probit estimations. Robust standard errors that are adjusted for clusters (institutes) are reported in parentheses. *, ** and *** denote significance at the 10, 5 and 1 percent levels respectively. Number of observations: 964.

Table 21.5   Determinants of factors influencing scientists' commercialization activities –
sample of senior researchers (2)

	(1) Open science	(2) TTO important	(3) Commerciali- zation common	(4) Basic research focus
Institute average	0.0842	0.0680	0.636***	0.338***
	(0.194)	(0.326)	(0.0710)	(0.0910)
Comm. experience (1 = yes)	−0.364***	0.223***	0.418***	−0.563***
	(0.0889)	(0.0852)	(0.0859)	(0.0842)
Age (log of years)	0.458*	−0.0364	0.0901	0.378*
	(0.237)	(0.249)	(0.208)	(0.211)
Years at MPS/age	0.799**	0.246	−1.191***	1.041***
	(0.386)	(0.396)	(0.314)	(0.335)
Industry work experience (1 = yes)	−0.154*	−0.147	0.0300	−0.176**
	(0.0893)	(0.0909)	(0.0910)	(0.0851)
German citizenship	−0.244***	0.0550	−0.182**	−0.0802
	(0.0728)	(0.0897)	(0.0808)	(0.0740)
Gender (1 = female)	−0.112	−0.206***	−0.0646	−0.0843
	(0.0841)	(0.0737)	(0.0927)	(0.0983)
Group leader	−0.0869	0.0529	−0.0470	−0.0712
	(0.0890)	(0.0741)	(0.104)	(0.0690)
Director	0.0478	−0.0452	0.108	−0.267*
	(0.191)	(0.192)	(0.147)	(0.147)
PhD biology	−0.236**	0.0896	−0.0444	−0.0879
	(0.108)	(0.159)	(0.0966)	(0.115)
PhD chemistry	−0.185	0.0760	0.359***	−0.293**
	(0.151)	(0.136)	(0.135)	(0.140)
PhD physics	0.127	−0.0383	0.0676	0.140
	(0.119)	(0.130)	(0.136)	(0.142)
PhD mathematics	0.308	−0.392*	−0.406	−0.0323
	(0.310)	(0.223)	(0.298)	(0.199)
PhD medical science	−0.00254	0.508**	−0.00935	0.0288
	(0.169)	(0.201)	(0.159)	(0.200)
PhD engineering	−0.183	0.234	0.0966	−0.417**
	(0.269)	(0.376)	(0.304)	(0.192)
Life sciences	−0.188	0.246	0.572***	−0.272**
	(0.155)	(0.197)	(0.138)	(0.122)
Chemistry, physics & technology	−0.273*	0.0484	0.220	−0.180
	(0.159)	(0.164)	(0.167)	(0.126)
Pseudo R^2	0.0303	0.0243	0.0751	0.0555
Wald test	$\chi2(17)$	$\chi2(17)$	$\chi2(17)$	$\chi2(17)$
	92.54***	156.18***	424.12***	237.62***

Notes: Results of ordered probit estimations. Robust standard errors that are adjusted for clusters
(institutes) are reported in parentheses. *, ** and *** denote significance at the 10, 5 and 1 percent levels
respectively. Number of observations: 964.

explanations for this result: first, attitudes of scientists change over time. Second, the focus of research conducted at the institutes of the Max Planck Society has shifted to research with a greater commercialization potential. In both cases the results point to a change in the scientific culture.

CONCLUSION

According to the results of this study, scientists face several trade-offs when deciding about engagement in commercialization activities. Scientists may benefit from commercialization activities if these lead to an increase in income and reputation. The downside of such activities is the reduction in time for research and the costs of commercialization, or there may be a conflict between commercialization and the idea of open science. Based on the Max Planck Scientists' survey, this study analyzes empirically scientists' attitudes toward commercialization activities.

The results suggest that many scientists believe in the idea of open science. However, scientists with commercialization experience are less likely to agree with this idea than those without commercialization experience. This result may point to a conflict between the idea of open science and engagement in commercialization activities. Moreover, older researchers are more likely to agree with the idea of open science than younger scientists. This may imply that life-cycle effects are relevant or there might be a change in scientific culture.

According to the scientists' assessments, technology transfer offices (TTOs) are important for dealing with the complicated commercialization process. Scientists with commercialization experience are more likely to agree with this than scientists without commercialization experience. Scientists in the life sciences section of the Max Planck Society, such as those with a PhD in medical science, find TTOs especially relevant.

Reputational rewards from commercialization activities are also relevant. In particular, scientists with a PhD in chemistry or engineering assume that commercialization activities increase a scientist's reputation. Moreover, the results show that there is an institute effect. A scientist tends to rate reputational rewards as more relevant if other scientists of the same Max Planck institute also rate reputational rewards as important.

In contrast, no such institute effects seem to exist with respect to the assessment of drawbacks of commercialization activities, such as reduction in time for own research, costs of commercialization or low financial benefits from commercialization activities. However, many scientists agree with the statement that costs of commercialization are high. Hence assessment of costs, time demand and financial benefits seem to be idiosyncratic. Moreover, there are no differences between assessments of scientists with and without commercialization experience.

The data set also contains information about scientists' assessment of commonness of commercialization activities in their scientific field and the suitability of the research results of their research group for commercialization. Although MPS focuses on basic research, many scientists report that commercialization is common and that the research of their group is suited for commercialization. Moreover, these assessments are not idiosyncratic since significant institute effects exist.

Interestingly, career stage does not seem to be very important. For instance, our results suggest that the attitudes toward commercialization activities of PhD students and senior researchers are quite similar. However, with respect to the assessment of the commercialization potential of own research, there is a difference between senior scientists and PhD students. The latter evaluate the potential as lower, which may be due to the lack of experience.

Other individual characteristics, such as age, gender and citizenship, also have significant effects on scientists' assessments. For instance, older scientists who worked for the Max Planck Society over a relatively long period are more likely to agree with the statement that financial benefits from commercialization activities are low, that such activities are costly and time-consuming, and that research has low commercialization potential. German scientists tend to rate costs and time demand associated with such activities as a greater problem than other scientists. Female scientists, however, assess cost of commercialization as less important.

Suggestions for future research include investigation of whether relationship between age and open science identity is due to life-cycle effects or to change in scientific culture. Moreover, the effects of gender and citizenship on attitudes toward commercialization activities need further explanation. Finally, an important question is whether the attitudes toward commercialization activities influence scientists' future engagement in such activities.

NOTE

1. The survey was conducted in either English and German, depending on the scientist.

REFERENCES

Agrawal, A. and R. Henderson (2002), 'Putting patents in context: exploring knowledge transfer from MIT', *Management Science*, **48** (1), 44–60.

Arrow, K. (1962), 'Economic welfare and the allocation of resources for invention', in R. Nelson (ed.), *The Rate and Direction of Inventive Activity: Economic and Social Factors*, Princeton, NJ: Princeton University Press, pp. 609–26.

Audretsch, D. and P. Stephan (1996), 'Company–scientist locational links: the case of biotechnology', *American Economic Review*, **86** (3), 641–52.

Azoulay, P., W. Ding and T. Stuart (2006), 'The impact of academic patenting on the rate, quality, and direction of (public) research output', NBER Working Paper.

Bains, W. (2005), 'How academics can make (extra) money out of their science', *Journal of Commercial Biotechnology*, **11** (4), 353.

Bercovitz, J. and M. Feldman (2008), 'Academic entrepreneurs: organizational change at the individual level', *Organization Science*, **19** (1), 69.

Breschi, S. (2007), 'The scientific productivity of academic inventors: new evidence from Italian data', *Economics of Innovation and New Technology*, **16** (2), 101–18.

Cockburn, I. and R. Henderson (2000), *Publicly Funded Science and the Productivity of the Pharmaceutical Industry*, vol. 1, Cambridge, MA: MIT Press.

Cohen, W., R. Florida, L. Randazzese and J. Walsh (1998), *Industry and the Academy: Uneasy Partners in the Cause of Technological Advance. Challenges to the Research University*, Washington, DC: Brookings Institution.

Cohen, W. and D. Levinthal (1990), 'Absorptive capacity: a new perspective on learning and innovation', *Administrative Science Quarterly*, **35**, 128–52.

Dasgupta, P. and P. David (1987), 'Information disclosure and the economics of science and technology', in G. Feiwell (ed.), *Arrow and the Ascent of Modern Economic Theory*, London: Macmillan, pp. 519–42.

David, P. (2003), 'The economic logic of open science and the balance between private property rights and the public domain in scientific data and information: A primer', Stanford Institute for Economic Policy, Research Discussion Paper.

Hackett, E. (1990), 'Science as a vocation in the 1990s: the changing organizational culture of academic science', *The Journal of Higher Education*, **61** (3), 241–79.

Hong, W. and J. Walsh (2009), 'For money or glory? Commercialization, competition, and secrecy in the entrepreneurial university', *Sociological Quarterly*, **50** (1), 145–71.

Jaffe, A. (1989), 'Real effects of academic research', *American Economic Review*, **79** (5), 957–70.

Jensen, R.A., J.G. Thursby and M.C. Thursby (2003), 'Disclosure and licensing of university inventions: the best we can do with the s**t we get to work with', *International Journal of Industrial Organization*, **21** (9), 1271–300.

Mansfield, E. (1995), 'Academic research underlying industrial innovation', *Review of Economics and Statistics*, **77**, 55–65.

Merton, R. (1957), 'Priorities in scientific discovery: a chapter in the sociology of science', *American Sociological Review*, **22** (6), 635–59.

Merton, R. (1973), *The Sociology of Science: Theoretical and Empirical Investigations*, Chicago, IL: University of Chicago Press.

Owen-Smith, J. and W. Powell (2003), 'The expanding role of university patenting in the life sciences: assessing the importance of experience and connectivity', *Research Policy*, **32** (9), 1695–711.

Parvan, S. (2007), 'Community innovation statistics', *Science and Technology*, **72**, 1–8.

Pavitt, K. (1998), 'The social shaping of the national science base', *Research Policy*, **27** (8), 793–805.

Rothaermel, F.T., S.D. Agung and L. Jiang (2008), 'University entrepreneurship: a taxonomy of the literature', *Industrial and Corporate Change*, **16** (4), 691–791.

Scherer, F. (1982), 'Inter-industry technology flows and productivity measurement', *Review of Economics and Statistics*, **64** (4), 627–34.

Stephan, P. (1996), 'The economics of science', *Journal of Economic Literature*, **34** (3), 1199–235.

Stephan, P. and A. El-Ganainy (2007), 'The entrepreneurial puzzle: explaining the gender gap', *The Journal of Technology Transfer*, **32** (5), 475–87.

Stern, S. (2004), 'Do scientists pay to be scientists?', *Management Science*, **50** (6), 835.

Thursby, J.G., R. Jensen and M. Thursby (2001), 'Objectives, characteristics and outcomes of university licensing: a survey of major US universities', *The Journal of Technology Transfer*, **26** (1), 59–72.

Thursby, J.G. and M.C. Thursby (2005), 'Gender patterns of research and licensing activity of science and engineering faculty', *The Journal of Technology Transfer*, **30** (4), 343–53.

Veugelers, R. and B. Cassiman (2005), 'R&D cooperation between firms and universities. Some empirical evidence from Belgian manufacturing', *International Journal of Industrial Organization*, **23** (5–6), 355–79.

Zucker, L., M. Darby and M. Brewer (1998), 'Intellectual human capital and the birth of US biotechnology enterprises', *American Economic Review*, **88** (1), 290–306.

Zucker, L., M. Darby and J. Armstrong (2002), 'Commercializing knowledge: university science, knowledge capture, and firm performance in biotechnology', *Management Science*, **48** (1), 139.

PART V

FIRMS AND INNOVATION

22 Small firms and innovation
Simon C. Parker

This chapter discusses the role of small firms in the process of innovation. The chapter advances theoretical arguments about the role of small firms in the innovative process, before reviewing evidence about their innovative contribution.

Although it is common nowadays to talk about 'entrepreneurship' rather than 'small firms', most new ventures start small, so for most practical purposes the set of new firms roughly approximates the set of small firms. The focus on small versus large firms (rather than new versus incumbent firms) is not just a historical legacy; it also reflects data availability, since data on innovation are more abundant when small firms rather than individual entrepreneurs are the unit of analysis. Few nascent entrepreneurs innovate very much, which is reflected for example by the fact that the Panel Study of Entrepreneurial Dynamics (PSED) devotes virtually no attention to the innovation issue (Gartner et al., 2004).

Innovation, deemed by Joseph Schumpeter to be a central aspect of entrepreneurship, has long attracted policy interest. Arguably, policy-makers are not chiefly interested in innovation as an end in itself, but more as a means to an end – or more precisely, several ends, such as innovation, wealth creation and growth. For example, it is known that industries with high rates of entry by small firms tend not only to be more innovative, but also enjoy high rates of productivity growth on average (Geroski and Pomroy, 1990; Cosh et al., 1999). And more innovative new entrants tend to enjoy superior post-entry performance (Vivarelli and Audretsch, 1998; Arrighetti and Vivarelli, 1999).

Joseph Schumpeter believed that large incumbents would ultimately dominate the innovation process by exploiting their economies of scale. Schumpeter predicted that the vast majority of R&D and innovations would eventually be conducted by large firms, while small firms would merely become the repositories of low-level imitation: 'relics of a bygone age'. Subsequently this view has been challenged on both theoretical and empirical grounds. Both theory and evidence are now considered in turn.

THEORETICAL ARGUMENTS

The first column of Table 22.1 lists several reasons why large firms might possess advantages at innovation over small firms. The second column lists some counter-arguments.

As Table 22.1 shows, there are four major areas of theoretical disagreement about the role small firms are likely to play in innovative activity. The first major difference relates to economies of scale, the basis of Schumpeter's predictions mentioned above. A modern articulation of this view is found in Klepper (1996), in which early innovators rapidly achieve scale, providing greater incentives to implement incremental process innovations than their smaller rivals. Klepper's key insight is that large firms can spread the costs of developing new innovations over a massive scale, so that innovations that yield

Table 22.1   Relative advantages of innovation by firm size

Large-firm innovation advantages	Small-firm innovation advantages
1. Scale economies • spread high fixed R&D costs over larger output • generate economies of scope • free limited managerial attention	1. Diseconomies of scale • less bureaucracy in small firms • shorter lines of communication • greater agility and lower agency costs
2. Innovation is less risky • size and market power • diversification of product lines	2. Greater incentives to innovate • easier to incentivise agents in small firms • to overcome entry barriers and competition
3. Larger firms can afford to spend more on R&D	3. Diminishing marginal returns to R&D; entrepreneurs can exploit knowledge spillovers
4. 'Efficiency effect' favours large incumbents	4. 'Replacement effect' favours small entrants

cost reductions of a given percentage rate yield greater absolute profit margins in larger firms. This enables large firms to reduce costs and expand scale even more. This self-reinforcing process forces out smaller rivals and chokes off entry, eventually culminating in highly concentrated oligopolistic market structures. Hence innovation interacts with scale to entrench large-firm competitive advantage. Scale economies in production might also provide 'economies of scope', thereby increasing profits from innovation (Acs and Audretsch, 2003). And senior managers of large firms can more easily delegate operational tasks to more junior managers, freeing up precious managerial attention needed to identify new ideas and innovations (Gifford, 1998).

On the other hand, large firms can be prone to diseconomies of scale, potentially making innovation more difficult. Large firms can suffer from bureaucratic inertia, which is antithetical to innovation (Link and Rees, 1990; Freeman and Engel, 2007). Indeed, it has been claimed that incumbents are not only relatively poor at pioneering radical innovations, but also struggle to develop incremental ones (Henderson and Clark, 1990). It could be that managers in existing firms fail to spot new opportunities because they follow internal routines that blind them to new trends in the market. If they act quickly, entrepreneurs located outside large firms might therefore be well placed to develop innovative ideas untrammelled by conventional corporate thinking (Pavitt et al., 1987; Freeman and Engel, 2007).

There also tend to be shorter lines of communication in small firms (Fielden et al., 2000). This information sharing promotes tighter links between work colleagues and fosters greater trust. There can also be greater ease of technology diffusion between networks of small firms, especially those involved in clusters that generate opportunities for cross-organizational learning (Morgan, 1997). And new, small ventures might be more agile and responsive to opportunities created by changing demand and demographic patterns (Bannock, 1981).

The second set of entries in Table 22.1 recognizes that incentives to innovate are also likely to differ by firm size. Large diversified firms can not only use exiting marketing channels to sell innovative products to numerous customers quickly and easily, but can also spread the risks of innovation, giving them greater incentives to develop radical innovations. On the other hand, large bureaucratic firms might find it costly to overcome agency problems and to provide the high-powered incentives required to motivate their workers to develop radical innovations (Holmstrom, 1989). Facing sufficiently high costs to incentivize effort in these cases, large firms may optimally pass over uncertain new technology development in favour of more routine ones, despite the more modest average returns of the latter (Bhide, 2000). Furthermore, incremental changes in corporations most easily satisfy objective external processes of scrutiny. And small firms may have to innovate in order to overcome entry barriers and to cope with retaliatory conduct by incumbents (Acs and Audretsch, 1989). This argument highlights important strategic and industry dimensions of small-firm innovation activity.

The third point in Table 22.1 draws on evidence that larger firms tend to perform more R&D (Cohen and Klepper, 1992). Larger firms usually have easier access to finance, through reinvested profits and bank loans, in order to finance expensive innovation. Yet there can be diminishing returns to R&D, which weigh on large firms more than on small firms. That attenuates the large firm R&D advantage (Acs and Audretsch, 1991). Small firms can also compensate for limited direct R&D spending by exploiting knowledge spillovers that leak out of larger organizations (see below).

Finally, Table 22.1 contrasts the so-called 'efficiency' effect with the 'replacement' effect. The efficiency effect recognizes that incumbents have greater incentives to innovate and retain monopoly profits than new entrants. The latter can at best obtain duopoly profits by exploiting an innovation opportunity in the same market (Gilbert and Newbery, 1982). The urge to preserve market share driven by monopoly profit incentives might explain why corporate giants in the IT world like Intel, Microsoft and Cisco continually innovate, sometimes radically. The replacement effect, on the other hand, recognizes that large incumbents might be unwilling to destroy their monopoly rents by engaging in paradigm-shifting innovations that render existing products obsolete (Arrow, 1962). That is, by definition, not a problem for new entrants. If the efficiency effect is strong enough, monopoly positions in product markets will tend to last, which might explain persistent innovation by incumbents in some industries, such as IT products (Klepper, 1996; Klepper and Simons, 2000). But in sectors open to drastic innovations, the replacement effect is more likely to dominate (Reinganum, 1983), entailing a strong tendency to entry.

EMPIRICAL EVIDENCE

The evidence relating to the role of large versus small firms, and radical versus incremental innovation, speaks to two issues. One concerns whether small firms are more or less innovative than large firms, and the other concerns whether large firms are responsible for a disproportionate number of incremental innovations while small firms are associated with more radical product introductions.

An important preliminary question is how to measure innovation. Researchers typically utilize one or more of the following measures: R&D expenditures, the number of patents, expert evaluations of the impact of innovations, and the rate of commercialization of inventions. The first two measures are skewed in favour of large firms and suffer from numerous methodological limitations (Acs and Audretsch, 2003). Among these, R&D is an input rather than an output measure; and many patents never lead to useful innovations in practice. The last two measures are perhaps the most informative, although it is important to use objective data rather than subjective self-assessments.

Aggregate cross-industry evidence paints a mixed picture about the contributions of small and large firms to aggregate levels of innovative activity. Large firms certainly perform the bulk of R&D spending and patenting activity (Cohen and Klepper, 1992; Almeida and Kogut, 1997; Sørensen and Stuart, 2000), though, consistent with the right-hand-side entry of point 3 of Table 22.1, small firms enjoy greater marginal growth benefits than large firms from additional R&D spending (van Praag and Versloot, 2007). However, as noted above, R&D is an input, not an output. In terms of innovative output, smaller and younger firms appear to enjoy pronounced advantages over their larger and older counterparts, at least in some industries (Scherer, 1980, pp. 407–38, 1984, 1991; Acs and Audretsch, 1988; Audretsch, 1991; Cohen and Klepper, 1996; Klepper, 1996). For example, according to Scherer (1991), in the 1980s 'small' US firms (defined as those with fewer than 500 employees) created 322 innovations per million employees compared with 225 per million in large firms. In a similar vein, Acs and Audretsch (1990, ch. 2) reviewed four databases measuring technological innovation on the basis of their peer-reviewed 'importance'. These authors estimated that small firms contribute around 2.4 times as many innovations per employee as large firms. The SBA (2003) estimates that small firms represent one-third of the most prolific patenting companies that have registered 15 or more US patents. Small firms' patents are twice as closely linked to scientific research as those of large firms, being more 'high-tech and leading-edge'. Moreover, their patents are on average more highly cited than those of large firms. In particular, new ventures hold more highly cited patents in the biotechnology industry than incumbent firms, in both the USA and France (Gittelman, 2006). Reflecting these findings, many famous radical innovations originated in small rather than large firms. Examples include the airplane, FM radio, the zipper, and the personal computer, among many others (Baumol, 2007). This evidence supports the contention that small firms specialize in radical innovations while large firms focus on incremental innovations.[1]

Further evidence of this kind comes from Prusa and Schmitz's (1991) analysis of the software industry, in which new firms provided the majority of 'category-opening' products in the 1980s, developing six times as many of these products in absolute terms as large firms. Prusa and Schmitz (1991) observed that existing firms had a comparative advantage in incremental improvements within existing product categories, consistent with the 'replacement effect' argument that incumbents avoid introducing competence-destroying technologies.[2] Further buttressing this point, Audretsch (2003) observed greater displacement of incumbents by entrants in innovative industries, suggesting that new firms have a 'more pronounced Schumpeterian creative destruction' innovation impact in these industries compared with incumbents.

On the other hand, large firms have produced many path-breaking innovations, too. A study of consumer durables and office products in the USA concluded that, in these sectors at least, incumbents and large organizations introduced the majority of radical product innovations over the last 60 years of the twentieth century (Chandy and Tellis, 2000). Furthermore, King and Tucci (2002) chronicle how experienced incumbents successfully rode each new technological wave that hit the hard disk-drive industry in the

USA. Incumbents may not have been the first ones into the market, but their survival rates exceeded those of new entrants. Indeed, later entry by incumbents does not necessarily point to failure or irrationality (Berchicci and Tucci, 2006; Bayus and Agarwal, 2007). Baum et al. (1995) report that the shift from analogue to digital technology in the facsimile transmission business enhanced the competitiveness of incumbents and reduced the new firm formation rate. These findings are all broadly consistent with Klepper's (1996) evolutionary perspective in which early innovators continue to grow by exploiting ever-increasing incentives to innovate, owing to ever-increasing economies of scale. The evidence from a range of US industries, including tyres, autos, penicillin and TVs, seems to confirm the innovative advantage of large, long-established incumbents.

There is greater disagreement among researchers about whether startups are more or less likely than established firms to commercialize inventions generated by universities. Mansfield (1991) claimed that small firms have an advantage over large firms in this regard, but Lowe and Ziedonis (2006, p. 180) detected few such differences between start-ups and established firms. Both sets of authors agree, however, that small start-ups bring commercial applications based on academic research to market more quickly than large firms. On the negative side, entrepreneurs continue to pursue unsuccessful commercializations for longer than established firms, perhaps because of over-optimism, and thereby can destroy value (Astebro, 2003; van Praag and Versloot, 2007).

Building on work by Jaffe (1989), Acs et al. (1994) argue that new small ventures exploit knowledge that spills over from universities and large companies. Based on estimates derived from a simple econometric model,[3] Acs et al. (1994) claim that knowledge spillovers are more decisive in promoting innovative activity of small firms than of large corporations. Other evidence is consistent with these findings. An analysis of Canadian biotech firms in the 1990s shows that entrants are attracted to incumbents' R&D resources within a 500-metre radius, but not outside this radius (Aharonson et al., 2007).

This suggests the existence either of agglomeration benefits (access to pools of labour or specialized inputs) or knowledge spillover externalities, which dissipate rapidly with distance. Aharonson et al. (2007) also observe that entry rates are significantly higher if technologically similar incumbents and firms with university alliances are situated close by. In their commanding survey of the evidence base on innovation, technological change and small firms, Acs and Audretsch (2003) conclude that economies bestowed through geographical proximity and spatial clusters might be more important for producing innovative output than 'traditional' scale economies, at least in some industries.[4]

In absolute terms, while it might be true that large firms have been the most important sources of innovations in the US economy, small firms have bucked the trend in several industries, including computers, process control instruments and biotechnology (Acs and Audretsch, 1990; Gittelman, 2006). That is, small-firm innovative advantage in the USA tends to be in different industries to those where large firms have an innovative advantage (Acs and Audretsch, 1988; Prevenzer, 1997). As a generalization, large firms have a comparative advantage in exploiting efficient internal 'routinized regimes' to develop innovations (including radical ones) in capital-intensive, concentrated and unionized industries that produce differentiated products (Acs and Audretsch, 1991). Precisely this outcome has been observed in manufacturing, for example (Tether et al., 1997; Craggs and Jones, 1998). In contrast, small firms have a comparative advantage in exploiting their 'entrepreneurial regimes' in industries where human capital and skilled labour are important productive factors (Pavitt et al., 1987; Acs and Audretsch, 1987a, 1987b, 1988, 1991; Marvel and Lumpkin, 2007). This nuanced picture does not provide unambiguous support for Schumpeter's prediction of ever-increasing concentration of innovation in large firms.

As always in discussions about the contributions made by entrepreneurs, it is important to retain a sense of perspective. At the level of the individual entrepreneur, most start-ups are in mundane non-innovative trades such as hairdressing and car-mechanic businesses (Storey, 1994). Real innovation appears to be confined to a small handful of businesses run by a few talented, visionary and determined entrepreneurs.

CONCLUSION

This chapter provides a brief overview of the role of small firms in innovation. While small firms do not perfectly capture contemporary notions of entrepreneurship, this construct arguably remains a useful lens through which the entrepreneurial innovation process can be viewed. The chapter systematically compared small firms with their larger counterparts, in an effort to put the distinctive aspects of small firm innovation into sharper relief.

Most of the prior studies discussed in this chapter are based on fairly aggregated data. It would be helpful if future data-gathering efforts paid greater attention to the innovative activities of nascent entrepreneurs. This might shed light on several interesting aspects of the entrepreneurial innovation process that were neglected here, including the roles of learning, team formation and alliance/joint venturing strategies, among others. It would also be interesting to explore whether the properties of innovating small firms are replicated in the very early stages of venture formation, and the process by which these properties evolve into the outcomes discussed in this chapter.

NOTES

1. Also consistent with these arguments is differences in innovation strategies by firm size: 'Entrepreneurs commercialise innovations to a larger extent, but score lower on the adoption of innovations than their [larger] counterparts' (van Praag and Versloot, 2007, p. 377).
2. For similar evidence from the US cement, minicomputer and airline industries, see Tushman and Anderson (1986).
3. Acs et al. (1994) estimated a 'knowledge production function' of the form

$$I_{ik} = \beta_{ok} + \beta_{1k} \ln RD_i + \beta_{2k} UR_i + \beta_{3k} \ln(UR.GC)_{ik} + u_{ik}$$

   where i indexes firms and k the type of firm (small – under 500 employees – or large), I is the number of innovations in 1982, UR_i is expenditure on university research that may be accessible to firm i, and RD is industry R&D that may be accessible to i. GC is a measure of geographical propinquity of university and industrial research: this captures spillover effects. Acs et al. (1994) estimated this function by tobit and found that β_1 was largest for large firms while β_2 was largest for small firms. Also, β_3 was positive but insignificant for large firms (= 0.033, with t-statistic 0.687), but positive and significant for small firms (= 0.111, with $t = 1.965$).
4. For other evidence that the presence of external knowledge sources (e.g. large R&D-intensive firms and universities) in regions increases the innovative output of firms located in those regions, see Jaffe (1989), Jaffe et al. (1993), Audretsch and Feldman (1996), SBA (2002) and Aharonson et al. (2007).

REFERENCES

Acs, Z.J. and D.B. Audretsch (1987a), 'Innovation in large and small firms', *Economics Letters*, **23**, 109–12.

Acs, Z.J. and D.B. Audretsch (1987b), 'Innovation, market structure, and firm size', *Review of Economics and Statistics*, **49**, 567–74.

Acs, Z.J. and D.B. Audretsch (1988), 'Innovation in large and small firms: an empirical analysis', *American Economic Review*, **78**, 678–90.

Acs, Z.J. and D.B. Audretsch (1989), 'Small firm entry in manufacturing', *Economica*, **56**, 255–65.

Acs, Z.J. and D.B. Audretsch (1990), *Innovation and Small Firms*, Cambridge MA: MIT Press.

Acs, Z.J. and D.B. Audretsch (1991), 'R&D, firm size and innovative activity', in Z.J. Acs and D.B. Audretsch (eds), *Innovation and Technological Change*, Ann Arbor, MI: University of Michigan Press, pp. 39–59.

Acs, Z.J. and D.B. Audretsch (2003), 'Innovation and technological change', in Z.J. Acs and D.B. Audretsch (eds), *Handbook of Entrepreneurship Research: An Interdisciplinary Survey and Introduction*, Boston, MA: Kluwer, pp. 55–79.

Acs, Z.J., D.B. Audretsch and M.P. Feldman (1994), 'R&D spillovers and recipient firm size', *Review of Economics and Statistics*, **100**, 336–67.

Aharonson, B.S., J.A.C. Baum and M.P. Feldman (2007), 'Desperately seeking spillovers? Increasing returns, industrial organisation and the location of new entrants in geographic and technological space', *Industrial & Corporate Change*, **16** (1), 89–130.

Almeida, P. and B. Kogut (1997), 'The exploration of technological diversity and the geographic localisation of innovation', *Small Business Economics*, **9** (1), 21–31.

Arrighetti, A. and M. Vivarelli (1999), 'The role of innovation in the post entry performance of new small firms: evidence from Italy', *Southern Economic Journal*, **65**, 927–39.

Arrow, K. (1962), 'Economic welfare and the allocation of resources for invention', in R. Nelson (ed.), *The Rate and Direction of Inventive Activity*, Princeton, NJ: Princeton University Press, pp. 602–29.

Astebro, T. (2003), 'The return to independent invention: evidence of risk-seeking, extreme optimism or skewness-loving?', *Economic Journal*, **113**, 226–39.

Audretsch, D.B. (1991), 'New-firm survival and the technological regime', *Review of Economics and Statistics*, **73**, 441–50.

Audretsch, D.B. (2003), 'Entrepreneurship policy and the strategic management of places', in D.M. Hart (ed.), *The Emergence of Entrepreneurship Policy*, Cambridge: Cambridge University Press, pp. 20–38.

Audretsch, D.B. and M.P. Feldman (1996), 'R&D spillovers and the geography of innovation and production', *American Economic Review*, **86**, 630–40.

Bannock, G. (1981), *The Economics of Small Firms: Return from the Wilderness*, Oxford: Basil Blackwell.

Baum, J., H. Korn and S. Kotha (1995), 'Dominant designs and population dynamics in telecommunications services', *Social Science Research*, **24**, 97–135.

Baumol, W.J. (2007), 'Small firms: why market-driven innovation can't get along without them', paper presented at IFN Conference, Stockholm, September.

Bayus, B.L. and R. Agarwal (2007), 'The role of pre-entry experience, entry timing, and product technology strategies in explaining firm survival', *Management Science*, **53** (12), 1887–902.

Berchicci, L. and C.L. Tucci (2006), 'Entrepreneurship, technology and Schumpeterian innovation: entrants and incumbents', in M. Casson, B. Yeung, A. Basu and N. Wadeson (eds), *The Oxford Handbook of Entrepreneurship*, Oxford: Oxford University Press, pp. 332–50.

Bhide, A.V. (2000), *The Origin and Evolution of New Businesses*, Oxford: Oxford University Press.

Chandy, R.K. and G.J. Tellis (2000), 'The incumbent's curse? Incumbency, size and radical product innovation', *Journal of Marketing*, **64** (3), 1–17.

Cohen, W.M. and S. Klepper (1992), 'The trade-off between firm size and diversity in the pursuit of technological progress', *Small Business Economics*, **4**, 1–14.

Cohen, W.M. and S. Klepper (1996), 'A reprise of size and R&D', *Economic Journal*, **106**, 925–51.

Cosh, A.D., A. Hughes and E. Wood (1999), 'Innovation in UK SMEs: causes and consequences for firm failure and acquisition', in Z.J. Acs and B. Carlsson (eds), *Entrepreneurship, Small and Medium Sized Enterprises and the Macro Economy*, Cambridge: Cambridge University Press, pp. 329–66.

Craggs, P. and P. Jones (1998), 'UK results from the Community Innovation Survey', *Economic Trends*, No. 539.

Fielden, S.L., M.J. Davidson and P.J. Makin (2000), 'Barriers encountered during micro and small business start-up in North West England', *Journal of Small Business and Enterprise Development*, **7**, 295–304.

Freeman, J. and J.S. Engel (2007), 'Models of innovation: startups and mature corporations', *California Management Review*, **50** (1), 94–119.

Gartner, W.B., K.G. Shaver, N.M. Carter and P.D. Reynolds (2004), *Handbook of Entrepreneurial Dynamics*, Thousand Oaks, CA: Sage Publications.

Geroski, P.A. and R. Pomroy (1990), 'Innovation and the evolution of market structure', *Journal of Industrial Economics*, **38**, 299–314.

Gifford, S. (1998), *The Allocation of Limited Entrepreneurial Attention*, Boston, MA: Kluwer.

Gilbert, R. and D. Newbery (1982), 'Pre-emptive patenting and the persistence of monopoly', *American Economic Review*, **72**, 514–26.

Gittelman, M. (2006), 'National institutions, public–private knowledge flows, and innovation performance: a comparative study of the biotechnology industry in the US and France', *Research Policy*, **35**, 1052–68.

Henderson, R. and K.B. Clark (1990), 'Architectural innovation: the reconfiguration of existing product technologies and the failure of established companies', *Administrative Science Quarterly*, **35**, 9–20.

Holmstrom, B. (1989), 'Agency costs and innovation', *Journal of Economic Behavior & Organization*, **12**, 305–27.

Jaffe, A.B. (1989), 'Real effects of academic research', *American Economic Review*, **79**, 957–70.

Jaffe, A.B., M. Trajtenberg and R. Henderson (1993), 'Geographic localisation of knowledge spillovers as evidenced by patent citations', *Quarterly Journal of Economics*, **63**, 577–98.

King, A. and C.L. Tucci (2002), 'Incumbent entry into new market niches: the role of experience and managerial choice in the creation of dynamic capabilities', *Manchester School*, **48** (2), 171–86.

Klepper, S. (1996), 'Entry, exit, growth and innovation over the product life cycle', *American Economic Review*, **86**, 562–83.

Klepper, S. and K.L. Simons (2000), 'Dominance by birthright: entry of prior radio producers and competitive ramifications in the US television receiver industry', *Strategic Management Journal*, **21**, 997–1016.

Link, A.N. and C. Rees (1990), 'Firm size, university research and the returns to R&D', *Small Business Economics*, **2**, 25–33.

Lowe, R.A. and A.A. Ziedonis (2006), 'Over-optimism and the performance of entrepreneurial firms', *Management Science*, **52** (2), 173–86.

Mansfield, E. (1991), 'Academic research and industrial innovation', *Research Policy*, **20**, 1–12.

Marvel, M.R. and G.T. Lumpkin (2007), 'Technology entrepreneurs' human capital and its effects on innovation radicalness', *Entrepreneurship Theory & Practice*, **31** (6), 807–28.

Morgan, K. (1997), 'The learning region: institutions, innovation and regional renewal', *Regional Studies*, **31**, 491–503.

Pavitt, K., M. Robson and J. Townsend (1987), 'Technological accumulation, diversification and organisation in UK companies, 1945–1983', *Manchester School*, **35**, 81–99.

Praag, C.M. van and P.H. Versloot (2007), 'What is the value of entrepreneurship? A review of recent research', *Small Business Economics*, **29** (4), 351–82.

Prevenzer, M. (1997), 'The dynamics of industrial clustering in biotechnology', *Small Business Economics*, **9**, 255–71.

Prusa, T.J. and J.A. Schmitz (1991), 'Are new firms an important source of innovation?', *Economics Letters*, **35**, 339–42.

Reinganum, J. (1983), 'Uncertain innovation and the persistence of monopoly', *American Economic Review*, **73**, 741–8.

SBA (2002), 'The influence of R&D expenditures on new firm formation and economic growth', Research Summary, 222, Washington, DC

SBA (2003), *The State of Small Business*, Washington, DC: Office of Advocacy, Small Business Administration.

Scherer, F.M. (1980), *Industrial Market Structure and Economic Performance*, Chicago, IL: Rand McNally College Publishing.

Scherer, F.M. (1984), *Innovation and Growth: Schumpeterian Perspectives*, Cambridge, MA: MIT Press.

Scherer, F.M. (1991), 'Changing perspectives on the firm size problem', in Z.J. Acs and D.B. Audretsch (eds), *Innovation and Technological Change*, Ann Arbor, MI: University of Michigan Press, pp. 24–38.

Sørensen, J.B. and T.E. Stuart (2000), 'Aging, obsolescence, and organizational innovation', *Administrative Science Quarterly*, **45** (1), 81–112.

Storey, D.J. (1994), *Understanding the Small Business Sector*, London: Routledge.

Tether, B.S., I.J. Smith and A.T. Thwaites (1997), 'Smaller enterprises an innovation in the UK: the SPRU Innovations Database revisited', *Research Policy*, **2**, 19–32.

Tushman, M. and P. Anderson (1986), 'Technological discontinuities and organisational environments', *Administrative Science Quarterly*, **31**, 439–65.

Vivarelli, M. and D.B. Audretsch (1998), 'The link between the entry decision and post-entry performance: evidence from Italy', *Industrial & Corporate Change*, **7**, 485–500.

23 Start-ups in innovative industries: causes and effects
Michael Fritsch

THE ROLE OF INNOVATIVE START-UPS

Policy-makers seem to be convinced that new businesses generate economic growth. For a long time, however, empirical analyses of the effect of new business formation on development have been rather rare (see Carree and Thurik, 2010, and Fritsch, 2008, for an overview). Recent research strongly suggests that not all new businesses have the same importance for growth. There is considerable indication that particularly well-prepared, innovative start-ups may stimulate economic development while the effect of non-innovative new businesses that replicate already existing products and processes is rather small or may even be negative.[1] This rather plausible result suggests that innovative start-ups are of great importance for economic development.

This contribution investigates the role and the effects of innovative start-ups for growth. In the next section, I introduce an important distinction between different types of effects that new businesses have on economic development and that the innovativeness of an entry plays an important role for these effects. The third section discusses different ways to identify innovative start-ups and provides empirical evidence showing that highly innovative new businesses are a rather rare event. I then investigate the typical backgrounds of founders and specific characteristics of innovative new businesses, subsequently reviewing their effects on employment and growth in the fifth section. The sixth section discusses what policy could do to stimulate a larger number of promising innovative start-ups. The final section summarizes the results and identifies some important questions for further research.

HOW CAN (INNOVATIVE) START-UPS AFFECT REGIONAL DEVELOPMENT?

The way in which the entry of new businesses shapes the development of a region[2] can be interpreted as a challenge–response interaction that leads to a process of creative destruction as described by Joseph A. Schumpeter (1942). Accordingly, an entry of a new business should be regarded as an increase in competition that may require a reaction by the incumbents. Several effects of this competitive process on regional growth can be distinguished:

1. The setting up of new businesses leads to additional demand for resources. It has a positive effect on employment because extra personnel are needed to operate the additional capacities ('direct employment effect').

2. The effects of competition between the new and the incumbent businesses on input as well as on output markets spur market selection. As far as this market selection process works, according to a 'survival of the fittest' scenario, the least productive firms must either reduce their level of economic activity or exit the market ('displacement effect'). Because such a scenario leads to an increase in average productivity, employment should decrease if output remains at a constant level. Hence, although starting a new business means creating additional capacities, the effect of new business formation on the number of jobs in the economy is not necessarily positive; it could be negative.
3. The increased productivity and other effects of competition between the new businesses and the incumbents (e.g. product innovation) may lead to improvements on the supply side of the economy that result in greater competitiveness and growth.

This review of the different impacts of new business formation on market processes makes very clear that the evolution of the new businesses, its direct contribution to employment and innovative change, represents only a portion of its total effect. Other effects that the start-ups have on development occur rather indirectly on the supply side of the economy. As far as the market process is working according to a survival of the fittest scenario, the direct employment effects, i.e. the growth of new businesses and the displacement of incumbents, should sum up to a decline in employment. Hence, under such conditions employment growth from new business formation can result only from improvements on the supply side.[3]

The following supply-side effects may be distinguished:

*   *Securing efficiency and stimulating productivity increase* by contesting established market positions. Not only the actual entry but also the very possibility of an entry should force the incumbents to perform more efficiently (Baumol et al., 1988).
*   *Acceleration of structural change*: frequently it can be observed that structural change is mainly accomplished by a turnover of the respective economic units, i.e. by entries of new firms joined by exits of old-established incumbents. In this case, the incumbents do not undergo necessary internal changes but rather are substituted by newcomers.[4] This type of process has been emphasized by J.A. Schumpeter's (1911/1934, 1942) concept of 'creative destruction' and by Alfred Marshall's (1920) analogy of a forest in which the old trees must fall in order to make way for the new ones.
*   *Amplified innovation*, particularly the creation of new markets. There are many examples of radical innovations introduced by new firms (Acs and Audretsch, 1990; Audretsch, 1995; Baumol, 2004).
*   *Greater variety* of products and problem solutions. If the product program of a newcomer differs from those of the incumbents, or if an entrant introduces significant process innovation, this leads to a greater availability of goods and problem-solving methods. Such an increased variety implies a higher probability of finding a supply with a better match for customer preferences. Increased variety due to new supplies may stimulate an intensified division of labor as well as follow-up innovation and can, therefore, generate significant impulses for economic development.[5]

Empirical analyses of the employment effects of new businesses have provided clear indication that indirect employment effects of new business formation are quantitatively much more important than their direct effects (Fritsch and Noseleit, 2009a, 2009b). A simple explanation for the larger indirect employment effects may be seen in the greater numbers of incumbents as compared to the entries. If the relatively many incumbents react to the challenge exerted by newcomers, this may produce more employment. It is plausible to assume that well-prepared, innovative new businesses represent a much greater challenge that requires a stronger reaction than non-innovative, replicative entries.[6] They may, therefore, have a stronger effect on development. This is the main reason for a growth-oriented policy to focus on innovative start-ups that can be regarded 'productive entrepreneurship' in the sense of Baumol (1990).

This view on the effects of new business formation on economic development has three important implications:

1. For the emergence of the supply-side effects, it is of critical importance that market selection works in accordance with a 'survival of the fittest' scenario. If the market mechanism forced the relatively efficient firms to exit and allowed the inefficient firms to survive, the result would be a decrease in the economy's competitiveness. Hence policy should avoid anything that leads to a distortion of market selection according to a 'survival of the fittest', e.g. subsidizing entries.
2. Improvements may occur on the side of the start-ups as well as on the side of the incumbents. The emergence of these improvements, therefore, does not necessarily require that the newcomers are successful and that they survive. As long as entries induce improvements by incumbents, positive supply-side effects are generated, even if most of the new businesses fail and exit the market shortly after entry. Therefore even the failed start-ups may make a significant contribution to the improvement of supply and competitiveness.
3. The intensity of the challenge in terms of competitive pressure that the newcomers exert on the incumbents depends critically on the quality of the start-ups, particularly the innovativeness of the supplied goods and services. Other aspects of the quality of a new business that determine the challenge for the incumbents is the qualification of the entrepreneur, the amount and quality of resources that are mobilized for the new business, the marketing strategy that is pursued, as well as the newcomer's productivity.

WHAT IS AN INNOVATIVE START-UP?

There is no common definition of which type of new business should be regarded as innovative. For our purposes here it is sufficient to state that a new business is a new economic entity that supplies new products, uses new ways of production or accesses new markets of suppliers or consumers (Schumpeter, 1911/1934). Using such a broad definition of innovation leaves room for distinguishing between different types of innovation (product, process, organizational, procurement and marketing innovation), as well as different degrees of innovativeness. In order to qualify as a start-up, an economic entity should be a new organization, not a takeover of an already existing company, but it could be a spin-off that emerges out of an existing firm. According to such a wide definition, innovative new businesses may be manifold.

Empirical identification of innovative start-ups is a delicate task. If data for individual firms are available, one could, for example, use the share of inputs or value added devoted to R&D as a definition. Accordingly, firms or industries are often classified as 'innovative' if they devote more than 3.5 percent of their inputs to R&D and they are regarded high-tech if this share is more than 8.5 percent (Grupp et al., 2000, p. 18; OECD, 2005, pp. 166–71). Since it is not entirely clear what inputs or activities should be counted as R&D and because not all innovations in the broad sense outlined above require any significant R&D, this method of defining an innovative firm or start-up is somewhat imprecise. Using the innovativeness of the product or the respective production process also does not lead to sufficient clarity, since there may well be quite different opinions about what is a new product or a new process.

A frequently applied method for distinguishing between innovative and non-innovative businesses is based on their industry affiliation. A well-known classification of this type has been proposed by the OECD (2005). This list is mainly based on the knowledge and R&D intensity of industries as well as on the innovativeness of their product programs. It distinguishes between 'high-technology', 'medium-high-technology', 'medium-low-technology' and 'low-technology' industries. While this classification is limited to manufacturing industries, certain service sector industries may also be classified as being 'knowledge-intensive'.[7] Such an industry classification according to innovativeness has a number of problems. First, what may be a non-innovative product or industry in one country may be quite innovative in another. It may, therefore, be appropriate to adjust this classification to the specific characteristics of countries. Second, industries and products may change their innovative quality over time so that respective adjustments are desirable. Third, industry affiliation is a rather fuzzy concept because there are innovative and not-so-innovative firms in all industries. Hence, even a well-developed up-to-date version of such an industry classification leads to only a diffuse picture of innovative and non-innovative entries. Given the limited availability of data on innovation, this is, however, often the only feasible way to identify such new businesses.

Another way of identifying innovative start-ups is venture capital (VC) investment into a firm. VC is equity financing for innovative young businesses. VC investors normally make a detailed assessment of the prospects of an innovation project before they risk their money. Hence start-ups receiving VC should be of relatively high quality, particularly with regard to innovation. A disadvantage of this method of identifying innovative start-ups is that it selects only new businesses with a rather high level of innovativeness. Although one may expect a relatively pronounced role of these entries for economic development, other less innovative new businesses that may also make a significant contribution to growth are completely disregarded. Moreover, it is not entirely clear to what extent VC firms are biased in their decision to invest into a certain venture in favor of firms that are located in spatial proximity (Sorenson and Stuart, 2001; Fritsch and Schilder, 2008). It may also be important to distinguish between VC from purely private financiers and VC from public or semi-public banks because public investors may follow specific strategies and apply different criteria for evaluating investments (Schäfer and Schilder, 2009).

It is common practice in the literature to regard spin-offs from universities and other research institutes as innovative. While this may largely hold for firms founded by faculty, it may not be entirely true for start-ups by students, which should be much more numerous given the relationship between the number of faculty and the number of students.

A HIGHLY INNOVATIVE START-UP IS A RARE EVENT!

Generally, the number of highly innovative new businesses tends to be rather small. According to the commonly used German definition of innovative industries (Grupp et al., 2000; see Table 23A.1 in the Appendix for details), there were, on average, 1014 start-ups per year in high-tech manufacturing industries in the 1997–2008 period, which comprises only 0.38 percent of all new businesses (Table 23.1).[8] Combined with the 1709 start-ups per year in 'technologically advanced' (non-high-tech) manufacturing industries, these two categories make up 1.02 percent of all new ventures. The shares of new businesses in technology-oriented services (6.56 percent), as well as in non-technology-oriented consulting (6.28 percent), turn out to be much larger, which is partly a result of the relatively imprecise definition of service industries.

Compared to start-ups in highly innovative industries, the number of these new and young businesses attracting VC is quite small. Obviously, the emergence of a new business that is sufficiently qualified to receive VC is a rather rare event. In Germany fewer than 400 start-ups appeared to be sufficiently promising to VC investors to receive first-round financing in 2007 (BVK, 2008, p. 9). Taking the total number of start-ups in Germany as recorded in the ZEW Founder Panels as about 244000 (Table 23.1), this is only three out of every 2000 new businesses. For the USA and the UK, the two nations with the most advanced VC industries, these shares are even lower. According to the 2009 *Yearbook* of the US National Venture Capital Association (NVCA, 2009, pp. 11, 31), the number of new businesses receiving first-round VC financing in 2008 amounted to 1179. Compared to the more than 2000000 new companies set up in the USA each year, this makes one out of every 2000 new businesses.[9] The British Venture Capital Association (BVCA, 2009, p. 12) reports 269 early-stage investments in the UK during

Table 23.1   Average number of start-ups and shares of start-ups in different types of industry, Germany 1997–2008

Sector	Average number of start-ups	Percentage share
All industries	243728	100
High-tech manufacturing	929	0.38
Technologically advanced manufacturing (non-high-tech)	1567	0.64
Non-technology-intensive manufacturing	10234	4.20
Technology-oriented services	15994	6.56
Non-technology-oriented consulting	15312	6.28

Source: Own calculations based on the ZEW-Founder Panels.

2008. Assuming that the UK had about 250000 start-ups that year, the share of VC-backed new businesses is about one in a thousand. A problem in calculating such ratios is that the information on the overall number of start-ups may not be comparable between countries. In particular, there are considerable differences between countries with respect to the inclusion of small-scale start-ups, such as firms with no employees or part-time entrepreneurship, which may make up a considerable share of the overall number of new businesses. Notwithstanding such differences, we can say that highly innovative new businesses comprise only a tiny fraction of all start-ups.

Because highly innovative start-ups tend to be clustered in space (Bade and Nerlinger, 2000), there are many regions where promising new business rarely emerge. Regions with no or only low levels of highly innovative start-ups tend to be rather remote, sparsely populated, and without higher education institutions (Audretsch et al., 2006; Bade and Nerlinger, 2000; Bosma, 2009).

WHO STARTS HIGHLY INNOVATIVE FIRMS?

Although it is easy to find simple examples of highly innovative entrepreneurs without significant formal education, most founders of innovative firms are well educated, often holding an academic degree.[10] Hence academics are a main source of founders of highly innovative new firms. Among the academic professions, engineers and natural scientists play a prominent role in this respect.[11] Since start-ups tend to be located close to the founder's residence, regions with large high-quality universities, particularly if they have departments of natural sciences and engineering, tend to experience relatively large numbers of innovative start-ups.

Two principal sources of innovative spin-outs of universities may be distinguished: students and faculty. Because the number of students tends to be much larger than the number of faculty, they should also generate a larger number of start-ups. However, information concerning the number of new business formations by members of these two groups is incomplete. This is especially true of information related to innovative start-ups founded by former students. While the 100 highest-ranked US research universities spawn a median of two faculty spin-offs per year, some universities, particularly MIT, report much larger numbers (Åstebro and Bazzazian, 2011). Some university-specific alumni surveys also show large differences in the percentage of students founding a business sometime after leaving their *alma mater*, albeit immediately or after a number of years. Figures range from 5 percent for Harvard Business School (1997–2004 students only; Lerner and Malmendier, 2007) to 24 percent for MIT (Roberts and Eesley, 2009), Stanford Business School (Lazear, 2005) and Tsinghua University in China, and up to 36 percent for Halmstadt University in Sweden (Eriksson, 1996). These figures clearly suggest enormous differences in the fertility of universities with regard to the emergence of new firms.

A recent German study found that only about 25 percent of the academic start-ups in innovative industries are set up during the time at university or directly after graduation (Mueller, 2010). A study of start-ups in innovative industries in the German State of Thuringia applying a different methodology indicates an even lower percentage (Cantner and Goethner, 2010). The overwhelming majority of these academic founders first chose to work as dependent employees before setting up their own business.

Gaining practical experience by working in a firm for some time after university education may, on the one hand, add important elements to a founder's qualification and increase their chances of success. On the other hand, however, the academic knowledge acquired at university may become somewhat outdated and obsolete. A recent study by Mueller (2009) for Germany related the time between leaving academia and starting a firm in an innovative industry to the new business's employment growth. Taking employment growth of the firm as a criterion for the founder's qualification, the author concludes that depreciation of academic knowledge occurs rather rapidly and is only slightly compensated by practical experience gained while working as a dependent employee. The study found that the highest employment growth is for new businesses established 3 to 5 years after leaving academia.

The observation that most founders in innovative industries with an academic background do not set up their business directly following graduation but after having worked for some time as a dependent employee draws the attention to spinoffs from incumbent private firms. Several empirical studies (for an overview see Klepper, 2009) show that smaller firms and relatively successful firms tend to spawn more spinoffs per employee than larger and older firms. Klepper (2007, 2009) shows that a typical motive for an innovative spinoff is disagreement with the former employer in the fields of business strategy and innovative development. Quite frequently, the founder of a spinoff saw no sufficiently satisfying possibility of realizing his or her ideas in their old firm, such that setting up their own business appeared the only feasible way to pursue their concept. Typically, spinoffs enter the same market as the incubating firm. In many cases the combined market share of the incumbent and the spinoff is greater than the market share of the incubator before the spinoff occurred, indicating that the additional competition by the spinoff is not a zero-sum game (Klepper, 2009) for the parties directly involved. Since many spinoffs locate in proximity to their incubators, they can be regarded a main driver in the formation of spatial clusters.

An important issue distinguishing many founders of highly innovative start-ups from those of not so innovative new ventures is the special need for support. If the idea of starting an own business is based just on a concept or an invention, then considerable effort and time may be necessary to transform this idea into a marketable product. In most cases this requires more resources than the potential founder has available on his/her own. Moreover, intensive advice by experienced experts may be required for a successful development of the product and business concept. In principle, VC firms fulfill this role. VC firms are, however, reluctant to engage in this 'seed phase' due to the high risk of failure during such early stages of projects. Hence there is a considerable danger that promising concepts are not pursued because of lagging resources; thus appropriate support could make a considerable difference in realizing these projects, ultimately making them ready for VC. The important question here is, however: what kind of support would be adequate and who should provide it? The available evidence strongly suggests that money alone is not the solution. The average founder of a high-tech business is an engineer or natural scientist with little substantial knowledge of how to manage a business. In many cases, such founders are focused mainly on technical possibilities and do not sufficiently account for consumer valuation of the product. Intensive coaching may be of great help to avoid mistakes and to increase the likelihood of economic success.

WHAT DO INNOVATIVE START-UPS CONTRIBUTE TO EMPLOYMENT AND GROWTH?

By bringing something new to the market, innovative start-ups can be a particular challenge for incumbent businesses and may cause considerable changes. One important observation is that new firms are less reluctant to introduce radical innovations than incumbents (Geroski, 1995; Baumol, 2004; Klepper, 2009). New and small firms have contributed a substantial share of twentieth-century technical breakthroughs, such as the airplane, personal computer, Internet services and many, many more (Baumol, 2004). Two principal explanations are offered for this observation. First, as new firms are being created, they are inherently more flexible and open for completely new products and processes, as opposed to long-, particularly large, established firms. Second, incumbent firms may be more interested in exploiting the profit possibilities of their existing product program than in searching for new opportunities, particularly if the new products may contest and 'cannibalize' their established ones (Geroski, 1995, p. 431; Klepper and Sleeper, 2005). Due to the reluctance that this sort of incumbent firms have towards new ideas, establishing one's own business may appear to be the only or the most promising possibility for inventors to commercialize their knowledge (Audretsch, 1995; Klepper, 2009). As a result, small and new businesses make an important contribution to technological development, even though the bulk of R&D expenditure is by large incumbent firms that mainly generate incremental innovations. This suggests an important role of start-ups as a driver of technological development, particularly in the early 'entrepreneurial' stage of a product life cycle (Audretsch, 1995; Winter, 1984).

It is well known that new businesses have a greater propensity to fail, termed the 'liability of newness', and this also holds for innovative start-ups. Empirical studies show that, on average, only 50 to 60 percent of new businesses last longer than five or six years. In setting the conceptual framework for the analysis of effects of new business formation on regional development, it was earlier argued that even those new businesses that are not economically successful and exit after some time may still make a significant contribution to economic development through stimulating improvements by the incumbents. This may be especially true for highly innovative start-ups, since they should be a considerably larger challenge for the incumbents firms than purely replicative entries. The likelihood of failure for innovative start-ups may differ from that for non-innovative entries for several reasons. On the one hand, it may be argued that innovative products, particularly if they are introduced in the early stage of a product life cycle, may benefit from new and growing demand. On the other hand, there is always some uncertainty with regard to the market success of new products, which may be particularly true for markets in the early stages of the life cycle, which can be a rather volatile environment. Moreover, innovative start-ups with high levels of R&D will have a greater risk of failure because the success of R&D activity is, by its very nature, uncertain. This applies particularly to those young firms that do not have a fully developed product at the time of start-up. If they are successful, they may, however, grow at high rates.

The empirical evidence with regard to the survival chances of innovative start-ups when compared to new businesses in other sectors is not entirely clear. While both Audretsch (1995) for the USA and Audretsch et al. (2000) for the Netherlands detect a relatively high risk of failure for start-ups in industries characterized by relatively high R&D levels,

Metzger and Rammer (2009), based on the ZEW Founder Panels, find a slightly higher survival rate for innovative industries in Germany. A multivariate analysis of German start-ups with data of the establishment file of the German Social Insurance Statistics by Fritsch et al. (2011) detects a greater probability of failure for start-ups in high-tech manufacturing but not for those in advanced manufacturing industries. Both German studies show that entries in German high-tech and technologically advanced manufacturing industries, as well as those in technology-oriented services, create on average more jobs per start-up than entries in non-innovative, low-tech and non-knowledge-intensive industries.

In order to assess the overall growth impact of new firms, Audretsch et al. (2006) included the start-up rate (number of start-ups over population) in a regional production function as an input, together with capital, labor and R&D investment. In their analysis for West Germany they find that start-ups in both the high-tech industry and in the information and communication industry had a statistically significant impact on the regional level of output, as well as on the level of labor productivity. The coefficients for start-ups in these industries for explaining regional GDP are smaller than for the start-ups in all industries. When labor productivity is used as dependent variable, the coefficient for high-tech entrepreneurship is higher. Causal interpretation of these results is, however, problematic since they are based on a pure cross-sectional analysis that is limited to the level of GDP and productivity as dependent variable, not to the development of these output indicators.

Analyzing the overall effect of new business formation on regional employment for Portuguese regions, Baptista and Preto (2010) find that the overall effect of knowledge-based firms on regional employment is substantially larger for businesses in knowledge-based industries than for start-ups in other industries. In particular, the displacement effects as well as the supply-side effects of new businesses in knowledge-based industries are much more pronounced than in non-knowledge-intensive industries. An assessment of the effects of start-ups in different industry groups on overall regional employment for West Germany concludes that there is a highly significant impact of new business formation in knowledge-intensive services, while the start-up rate in innovative manufacturing industries remains insignificant (Fritsch and Schroeter, 2011). The reason for this non-significant effect of manufacturing start-ups may be the fact that it is a rather small share of all new businesses. Moreover, as start-ups in innovative manufacturing industries tend to operate to a greater extent in interregional markets than do those in non-innovative industries, these may have larger indirect effects outside the regions than is accounted for when the employment change within the same region is the dependent variable.

Summarizing these findings, we can say that the direct employment effects of start-ups in innovative industries tend to be greater than those of new businesses in non-innovative industries. Assuming that innovative entries exert a greater challenge to incumbent businesses than replicative start-ups, the indirect effects should also be stronger. There are, however, only two studies (Baptista and Preto, 2011; Fritsch and Schroeter, 2011) confirming this conjecture empirically for entries in knowledge-intensive services. The principal effects of innovative start-ups on economic development are expected via their contribution to innovative change; however, such effects are difficult to measure and may be widely dispersed across regions. There is no doubt that these effects can be rather substantial and that a considerable effect is felt only in the long run.

WHAT CAN POLICY DO TO STIMULATE INNOVATIVE START-UPS?

Our review of the development of innovative start-ups shows that such firms, if they survive, tend to create, on average, more jobs than other types of entries. Probably more important than the employment within these new businesses are its indirect effects on employment in incumbent firms and its contribution to innovative change, which can hardly be comprehensively assessed in quantitative terms. This includes the role that innovative new businesses may play as incubators for spinoffs and the formation of innovative clusters that could be an important driver of long-run regional development.

Highly innovative start-ups have specific needs when compared with less innovative new businesses. In particular, many need intensive advice and comprehensive coaching in the process of business formation. And they may require other types of financing, particularly equity (VC) instead of bank loans, in order to develop their product and to bring it to the market. Since VC firms are hesitant to invest in innovative projects that are in their early stages of development and where considerable R&D is needed in order to make the product marketable, providing financial support to make innovative new ventures ready for VC investment could be particularly important.

Policy can follow three strategies in order to stimulate innovative start-ups. These strategies are complementary rather than conflicting. A first strategy would be to create favorable conditions for innovative start-ups. A second strategy could consist of a 'pick the winner' approach that tries to support those firms that are expected to be economically successful and to create large numbers of jobs. The third option is a 'make more winners' policy trying to increase the number of highly innovative and successful start-ups.

Creating Favorable Conditions for Innovative New Businesses

A main task of a policy that tries to create favorable conditions for innovative start-ups is to safeguard the availability of the resources that these new ventures require. This particularly concerns access to cutting-edge scientific knowledge, to financing and to qualified labor. The provision of knowledge and qualified labor particularly concerns education and research. This includes questions such as the access to education, the quality of research, the presence and the functioning of technology transfer offices as well as legal regulations that govern the different channels of knowledge transfer such as intellectual property-rights legislation. A basic precondition for a well-functioning VC market is an appropriate institutional environment (Lerner, 2009). This includes issues such as, again, the protection of intellectual property rights (e.g. patents), appropriate taxation schemes as well as the existence of markets for equity where VC firms can take public the companies they have invested in. However, since VC investors tend to be highly selective, many promising innovative new ideas will not receive capital from private sources even if these conditions are fulfilled and the VC market works properly. Therefore additional public support, e.g. by providing some type of public VC, may be a reasonable option.

Many universities and other public research organizations nowadays try to encourage and to support their innovative spinoffs in their early stages. Such activities may create considerable social benefits; however, the respective incubator organizations are able to appropriate only a small part of these returns (see Åstebro and Bazzazian, 2011, for an overview). Hence it may be reasonable to provide some compensation for these positive externalities in order to provide an incentive for increasing such support toward the social optimum as well as to induce respective activities in research institutions that largely abstain from facilitating start-ups. However, given that the larger share of innovative new businesses by founders with an academic background are set up a considerable time after the founder has left academia (see above), it would be desirable that these potential founders also have the possibility to enjoy comparable types of support. While previous research has directed much attention to how universities and other public research organizations support their immediate spinoffs, little is known about appropriate policies directed to those would-be high-tech entrepreneurs who have lost contact with their former academic incubator.

One rather popular policy tool is the establishment of science parks, where innovative young businesses can find appropriate space, advice and, potentially, benefit from spatial proximity to other firms working in related fields. In most cases, the resident young firms in such science parks benefit from some form of public assistance, particularly below-market rents for floor space. The empirical evidence about the effectiveness of science parks is, however, mixed (Lindelöf and Löfsten 2003; Siegel et al. 2003; Westhead, 1997). In a nutshell, the effects of science parks are highly dependent on the quality of the science park management, particularly the advice and coaching provided, as well as the efforts made to connect the firms with potential cooperative partners and financiers. Many science parks suffer from low numbers of high-tech start-ups in the region; hence low-tech businesses are often admitted in order to utilize the existent capacities.

Pick the Winners or Make More Winners?

If science parks are selective, accepting only highly innovative firms, and if tenants can benefit from some form of public support, this type of instrument can be regarded as part of a pick the winner policy that tries to support only those new businesses that are expected to be economically successful. The same holds for policy programs that provide R&D subsidies for innovative new ventures like the SBIR program in the USA. Such a pick the winner approach is, however, faced with a number of serious problems. One of these is the pretense of knowledge involved with the identification of those ventures selected to receive public support. Another problem is that such a policy discriminates against non-supported firms, which may result in distorted competition. Because of such problems, picking winners is a delicate task and much depends on the quality of the selection made.

Compared to policies that try to pick winners, a make more winners strategy that attempts to increase the number of successful innovative start-ups by creating a fertile seedbed for this type of venture may be more promising. One reason for this is that the specific problems of highly innovative businesses may prevent many of these projects from being realized. One can therefore suspect that the numbers of highly innovative entries can be increased if policy provides support in overcoming these hurdles. This may hold particularly for those potential founders that are not in close contact with an academic institution. However, little is known about such founders and appropriate ways to pave their way into entrepreneurship.

An important element of a make more winners strategy is to provide knowledge about entrepreneurship and management during education. Empirical studies suggest that exposure to entrepreneurship in university education does not lead to an increase of entrepreneurial intentions among students, but to better judgment of their own abilities and willingness to start their own business, which may lead to a greater self-selection into entrepreneurship (Graevenitz et al., 2010). Analyses of founder characteristics clearly show, however, that direct exposure to entrepreneurship, such as having self-employed family members or knowing someone who started a new business, significantly increases the probability of an individual of starting a firm (Parker, 2009). Hence entrepreneurship may be self-energizing in that existent self-employed persons encourage people around them to start their own businesses, thus spreading the entrepreneurial 'culture'.

To follow a make more winners strategy by trying to increase the number of high-quality start-ups means actively creating an entrepreneurial culture. For innovative start-ups this includes building a high-quality university system that provides cutting-edge scientific knowledge and technology, facilitating access of talented people to higher education, as well as effective technology transfer. Such a policy should be embedded in framework conditions that are favorable for innovative start-ups.

SUMMARY AND CONCLUSIONS

There is compelling evidence suggesting that innovative start-ups make an important contribution to economic development. Although completely accurate identification of innovative start-ups is impossible, one can say that available data clearly suggest that the emergence of highly innovative new businesses is a rather rare event. In highly developed countries, such as the USA, the UK, or Germany, only about one in a thousand new businesses, or even fewer than that, are innovative and promising enough to attract VC investors. But even when applying a wider definition, the number of innovative new businesses remains rather small. One reason for this is probably the fact that they are faced with specific problems such as high uncertainty about R&D results and about demand for the product, which makes it difficult for them to get the necessary financial resources. It does not appear far-fetched to assume that there would be potential for greater numbers of highly innovative start-ups if these problems could be mitigated. In order to be effective, such a strategy needs to be embedded in framework conditions that are conducive to innovative start-ups. Moreover, a make more winners strategy that exposes individuals to entrepreneurship and creates an entrepreneurial culture could be a promising way of setting the stage for more innovative new businesses.

Although our knowledge about innovative start-ups has increased considerably during recent years, the picture remains rather vague and unclear in many respects. There is no question that the subject deserves considerable further research. A main area for further investigation is the effects of innovative start-ups on technological change, competitiveness and growth. We should in particular learn more about the indirect effects that innovative new businesses have on the incumbents and on the development of the market. Another largely unexplored field is start-ups by former students, particularly those new businesses that are set up by people with an academic background several years after they left the academic sphere. The available empirical analyses of the role that academic institutions play as incubator for innovative start-ups focuses more or less entirely on new businesses by faculty or students who emerged immediately when leaving their *alma mater*. Since the majority of start-ups by academic founders are set up a considerable time after graduation, these studies heavily underestimate the role of academia as an incubator of new firms. Our lack of knowledge about these academic start-ups also implies deficits in evaluating the long-term effects of entrepreneurship education on new business formation, particularly on the gestation of innovative start-ups.

NOTES

1. Baptista and Preto (2011), Engel and Metzger (2006), Fritsch and Schroeter (2011), Metzger and Rammer (2009), Shane (2009).
2. Empirical studies on the effect of new business formation on employment should preferably be carried out at a regional level because an analysis at the level of industries leads to serious difficulties in the interpretation of the results. The reason is that if industries follow a life cycle, then the number of entries and the start-up rate will be relatively high in the early stages of the life cycle when the industry is growing, and relatively low in later stages, when the industry is stagnant or declining (Klepper, 1996). Obviously, the resulting positive correlation between the start-up rate and the development of industry employment in subsequent periods may be considerably shaped by the industry life cycle and cannot be unequivocally regarded as an effect of entry on development. Indeed, entirely different results are found if, for example, the relationship between the level of start-ups and subsequent employment change is analyzed at the level of regions and on the level of industries (see Fritsch, 1996). Therefore geographical units of observation are much better suited for such an analysis than industries.
3. If the process of market selection does not work as it should, and allows the survival of relatively unproductive competitors, this would weaken the competitiveness of the economy and, thus, cause the supply-side effects to become negative.
4. Such a process could, for example, be observed in the transformation of former socialist economies of Central and Eastern Europe, where new firms – the bottom-up component – had a considerably stronger impact on structural change, cf. Brezinski and Fritsch (1996) and the contributions in Pfirrmann and Walter (2002).
5. See Saviotti and Pyka (2004) for a more detailed discussion of the relationship between variety and economic development.
6. Falck (2007) found that new businesses surviving for at least five years ('long-distance runners') had a significantly positive impact on GDP growth while the effect of entries that stayed in the market for only one year ('mayflies') was statistically insignificant or significantly negative. Fritsch and Noseleit (2009b) arrived at a similar conclusion in an analysis at the regional level. If survival and success can be regarded as an indication for the quality of a start-up, then these results suggest that not all entries are of equal importance for economic development but that it is the quality of the newcomers that plays a decisive role.
7. Since many service firms do not have a standardized product program but provide support according to the individual needs of their customers, they are not innovative in the same sense as manufacturing firms. Hence service industries that may be relevant for innovation processes are entirely defined according to the knowledge intensity of their inputs. These knowledge-intensive service industries comprise, for example, 'computer services', 'R&D in natural sciences and engineering' or 'business consultancy'.
8. Data are taken from the Founder Panels of the Center for European Economic Research (ZEW–Mannheim). See Almus et al. (2000) for a description of this database.
9. Shane (2009) reports that since the year 1970 VC firms in the USA have invested on average in about 820 new firms per year.
10. A recent representative study of start-ups in innovative industries that occurred in the German State of Thuringia found that 72 percent of these ventures involved a founder with a completed academic degree. In 14.5 percent of cases the founder was still studying or ended his/her university education without completing their degree. Only 13.5 percent of the start-ups did not involve a founder with some kind of academic background (Cantner and Goethner, 2010).
11. The vast majority of the academic founders of German start-ups in innovative industries earned their academic degree in engineering, natural sciences (including medicine), mathematics or computer sciences (Metzger et al., 2010).

REFERENCES

Acs, Z. and D.B. Audretsch (1990), *Innovation and Small Firms*, Cambridge, MA: MIT Press.
Almus, M., D. Engel and S. Prantl (2000), 'The ZEW Firm Panels and the Mannheim Enterprise Panel (MUP) of the Centre for European Economic Research (ZEW)', *Journal of Applied Social Science Studies (Schmollers Jahrbuch – Zeitschrift für Wirtschafts- und Sozialwissenschaften)*, **120**, 301–8.
Åstebro, T. and N. Bazzazian (2011), 'Universities, entrepreneurship and local economic development', in M. Fritsch (ed.), *Handbook of Research on Entrepreneurship and Regional Development*, Cheltenham, UK: and Northampton, MA, USA: Edward Elgar.
Audretsch, D.B. (1995), *Innovation and Industry Evolution,* Cambridge, MA: MIT Press.
Audretsch, D.B., P. Houweling and A.R. Thurik (2000), 'Firm survival in the Netherlands', *Review of Industrial Organization*, **16**, 1–11.
Audretsch, D.B., M. Keilbach and E. Lehmann (2006), *Entrepreneurship and Economic Growth*, Oxford: Oxford University Press.
Bade, F.-J. and E.A. Nerlinger (2000), 'The spatial distribution of new technology-based firms: empirical results for West Germany', *Papers in Regional Science*, **79**, 155–76.
Baptista, R. and M.T. Preto (2011), 'Regional and business dynamics', *Small Business Economics*, **32** (forthcoming).
Baumol, W.J. (1990), 'Entrepreneurship: productive, unproductive and destructive', *Journal of Political Economy*, **98**, 893–921.
Baumol, W.J. (2004), 'Entrepreneurial enterprises, large established firms and other components of the free-market growth-machine', *Small Business Economics*, **23**, 9–21.
Baumol, W.J., J.C. Panzar and R.D. Willig (1988), *Contestable Markets and the Theory of Industry Structure*, rev. edn, San Diego, CA: Harcourt Brace Jovanovich.
Bosma, N. (2009), 'The geography of entrepreneurial activity and regional development', PhD dissertation, University of Utrecht, Netherlands.
Brezinski, H. and M. Fritsch (1996), *The Economic Impact of New Firms in Post-Socialist Countries: Bottom Up Transformation in Eastern Europe*, Cheltenham, UK and Northampton, MA, USA: Edward Elgar.
BVCA (The British Private Equity and Venture Capital Association) (2009), *Private Equity and Venture Capital Report on Investment Activity 2008*, London: BVCA.
BVK (German Private Equity and Venture Capital Association) (2008), *Early Stage-Venture Capital 2007*, http://www.bvkap.de/media/file/168.BVK_Teilstatistik_Early_Stage2007_310308.pdf, accessed 6 July 2009.
Cantner, U. and M. Goethner (2010), 'Academic spin-offs and innovative start-ups: two of the same kind?', Friedrich Schiller University, Jena (mimeo).
Carree, M.A. and R. Thurik (2010), 'The impact of entrepreneurship on economic growth', in Z.J. Acs and D.B. Audretsch (eds), *Handbook of Entrepreneurship Research*, 2nd edn, Boston, MA: Kluwer, pp. 557–94.
Engel, D. and G. Metzger (2006), 'Direct employment effects of new firms', in Michael Fritsch and Juergen Schmude (eds), *Entrepreneurship in the Region*, New York: Springer, pp. 75–93.
Eriksson, E.-L. (1996), 'Akademiskt Företagande – från student till företagare', Företagsekonomiska Institutionen, Lund, Lunds Universitet: Licentiatavhandling, 149.
Falck, O. (2007), 'Mayflies and long-distance runners: the effects of new business formation on industry growth', *Applied Economics Letters*, **14**, 1919–22.
Fritsch, M. (1996), 'Turbulence and growth in West Germany: a comparison of evidence by regions and industries', *Review of Industrial Organization*, **11**, 231–51.
Fritsch, M. (2008), 'How does new business formation affect regional development?', *Small Business Economics*, **30**, 1–14.
Fritsch, M. and F. Noseleit (2009a), 'Investigating the anatomy of the employment effects of new business formation', *Jena Economic Research Papers,* 001–2009, Friedrich Schiller University and Max Planck Institute of Economics, Jena.
Fritsch, M. and F. Noseleit (2009b), 'Start-ups, long- and short-term survivors and their effect on regional employment growth', *Jena Economic Research Papers,* 081–2009, Friedrich Schiller University and Max Planck Institute of Economics, Jena.
Fritsch, M. and D. Schilder (2008), 'Does venture capital investment really require spatial proximity? An empirical investigation', *Environment and Planning A*, **40**, 2114–31.
Fritsch, M., F. Noseleit and Y. Schindele (2011), 'Success or failure? Business-, industry- and region-specific determinants of survival – A multidimensional analysis for German manufacturing', mimeo, Friedrich Schiller University, Jena.
Fritsch, M. and A. Schroeter (2011), 'Does innovation make a difference? Employment effects of start-ups in innovative and non-innovative industries', *Jena Economic Research Papers*, 011-2011, Friedrich Schiller University and Max Planck Institute of Economics, Jena.

Geroski, P. (1995), 'What do we know about entry?', *International Journal of Industrial Organization*, **13**, 421–40.

Graevenitz, G. von, D. Harhoff and R. Weber (2010), 'The effects of entrepreneurship education', *Journal of Economic Behaviour & Organization*, **76**, 90–112.

Grupp, H., A. Jungmittag, U. Schmoch and H. Legler (2000), 'Hochtechnologie 2000: Neudefinition der Hochtechnologie für die Berichterstattung zur technologischen Leistungsfähigkeit Deutschlands', Karlsruhe and Hannover: FhG-ISI and NIW.

Klepper, St. (1996), 'Entry, exit, growth, and innovation over the product life cycle', *American Economic Review*, **86**, 562–83.

Klepper, St. (2007), 'Disagreements, spinoffs, and the evolution of Detroit as the capital of the U.S. automobile industry', *Management Science*, **53**, 616–31.

Klepper, St. (2009), 'Spinoffs: a review and synthesis', *European Management Review*, **6**, 159–71.

Klepper, St. and S. Sleeper (2005), 'Entry by spinoffs', *Management Science*, **51**, 1291–306.

Lazear, E.P. (2005), 'Entrepreneurship', *Journal of Labor Economics* **23**, 649–80.

Lerner, J. (2009), *Boulevard of Broken Dreams. Why Public Efforts to Boost Entrepreneurship and Venture Capital Have Failed – and What to Do about it*, Princeton, NJ: Princeton University Press.

Lerner, J. and U. Malmendier (2007), 'With a little help from my (random) friends: success and failure in post-business school entrepreneurship', Working Paper, Harvard University.

Lindelöf, P. and H. Löfsten (2003), 'Science park location and new technology-based firms in Sweden – Implications for strategy and performance', *Small Business Economics*, **20**, 245–58.

Marshall, A. (1920), *Principles of Economics*, 8th edn, London: Macmillan.

Metzger, G. and Ch. Rammer (2009), 'Unternehmensdynamik in forschungs- und wissensintensiven Wirtschaftszweigen in Deutschland' ('Firm dynamics in research- and knowledge intensive industries in Germany'), Mannheim: ZEW (Studien zum deutschen Innovationssystem Nr. 05-2009).

Metzger, G., D. Heger, D. Hoewer and G. Licht (2010), 'High-Tech-Gründungen in Deutschland' ('High-tech start-ups in Germany'), Mannheim: ZEW.

Mueller, K. (2009), 'Employment growth in newly established firms – is there evidence for academic entrepreneur's human capital depreciation?', Mannheim: Centre for European Economic Research (ZEW Discussion Paper No. 09-050).

Mueller, K. (2010), "Academic spin-off's transfer speed – analyzing the time from leaving university to venture", *Research Policy*, **39**, 189-199.

NVCA (National Venture Capital Association) (2009), *Yearbook 2009*, Arlington, VA, NVCA, http://www.nvca.org/index.php?option=com_docman&task=doc_download&gid=446&ItemId=93, accessed 6 July 2009.

Organisation for Economic Co-operation and Development (OECD) (2005), *OECD Handbook on Economic Globalisation Indicators*, Paris: OECD.

Parker, S. (2009), *The Economics of Entrepreneurship*, Cambridge: Cambridge University Press.

Pfirrmann, O. and G.H. Walter (2002), *Small Firms and Entrepreneurship in Central and Eastern Europe: A Socio-Economic Perspective*, Heidelberg: Physica.

Roberts, E.B. and C. Eesley (2009), *Entrepreneurial Impact: The Role of MIT*, Kansas City: Kauffman Foundation.

Saviotti, P.P. and A. Pyka (2004), 'Economic development, variety and employment', *Revue Économique*, **55**, 1023–49.

Schäfer, D. and D. Schilder (2009), 'Smart capital in German start-ups – an empirical analysis', *Venture Capital*, **11**, 163–83.

Schumpeter, J.A. (1911/1934), *Die Theorie wirtschaftlicher Entwicklung*, Berlin: Duncker & Humblot; English edition: *The Theory of Economic Development*, Cambridge, MA: Cambridge University Press, 1934.

Schumpeter, J.A. (1942), *Capitalism, Socialism and Democracy*, New York: Harper & Row.

Shane, S. (2009), 'Why encouraging more people to become entrepreneurs is bad public policy', *Small Business Economics*, **33**, 141–9.

Siegel, D.S., P. Westhead and M. Wright (2003), 'Assessing the impact of university science parks on research productivity: exploratory firm-level evidence from the United Kingdom', *International Journal of Industrial Organization*, **21** (9), 1357–69.

Sorensen, O. and T.E. Stuart (2001), 'Syndication networks and the spatial distribution of venture capital investments', *American Journal of Sociology*, **106**, 1546–88.

Westhead, P. (1997), 'R&D "inputs" and "outputs" of technology-based firms located on and off science parks', *R & D Management*, **27**, 45–62.

Winter, S.G. (1984), 'Schumpeterian competition in alternative technological regimes', *Journal of Economic Behavior and Organization*, **5**, 287–320.

APPENDIX

Table 23A.1   Classification of German industries according to their innovativeness

	NACE
High-tech manufacturing industries	
Processing of nuclear fuel	2330
Manufacture of pesticides and other agro-chemical products	2420
Manufacture of basic pharmaceutical products	2441
Manufacture of explosives	2461
Manufacture of engines and turbines, except aircraft, vehicle and cycle engines	2911
Manufacture of weapons and ammunition	2960
Manufacture of computers and other information-processing equipment	3002
Manufacture of other electrical equipment n.e.c.	3162
Manufacture of electronic valves and tubes and other electronic components	3210
Manufacture of television and radio transmitters and apparatus for line telephony and line telegraphy	3220
Manufacture of instruments and appliances for measuring, checking, testing, navigating and other purposes, except industrial process control equipment	3320
Manufacture of industrial process control equipment	3330
Manufacture of aircraft and spacecraft	3530
Technologically advanced manufacturing industries	
Reproduction of computer media	2233
Manufacture of industrial gases	2411
Manufacture of industrial gases	2412
Manufacture of other inorganic basic chemicals and other organic basic chemicals	2413/2414
Manufacture of synthetic rubber in primary forms	2417
Manufacture of paints, varnishes and similar coatings, printing ink and mastics	2430
Manufacture of pharmaceutical preparations	2442
Manufacture of glues and gelatines	2462
Manufacture of essential oils	2463
Manufacture of photographic chemical material	2464
Manufacture of other chemical products n.e.c.	2466
Manufacture of pumps and compressors	2912
Manufacture of taps and valves	2913
Manufacture of bearings, gears, gearing and driving elements	2914
Manufacture of agricultural tractors	2931
Manufacture of other agricultural and forestry machinery	2932
Manufacture of machine-tools	2940
Manufacture of machinery for mining, quarrying and construction	2952
Manufacture of machinery for food, beverage and tobacco processing	2953
Manufacture of machinery for textile, apparel and leather production	2954
Manufacture of machinery for paper and paperboard production	2955
Manufacture of other special purpose machinery n.e.c.	2956
Manufacture of office machinery	3001
Manufacture of electric motors, generators and transformers	3110

Table 23A.1   (continued)

	NACE
Manufacture of accumulators, primary cells and primary batteries	3140
Manufacture of lighting equipment and electric lamps	3150
Manufacture of television and radio receivers, sound or video recording or reproducing apparatus and associated goods	3230
Manufacture of medical and surgical equipment and orthopaedic appliances	3310
Manufacture of optical instruments and photographic equipment	3340
Manufacture of motor vehicles	3410
Manufacture of parts and accessories for motor vehicles and their engines	3430
Manufacture of railway and tramway locomotives and rolling stock	3520
Technology-intensive services	
Telecommunications	642
Computer and related activities	72
Research and experimental development on natural sciences and engineering	731
Architectural and engineering activities and related technical consultancy	742
Technical testing and analysis	743
Non-technical consulting	
Research and experimental development on social sciences and humanities	732
Legal activities	7411
Accounting, book-keeping and auditing activities; tax consultancy	7412
Market research and public opinion polling	7413
Business and management consultancy activities	7414
Advertising	744

24 Innovation and the evolution of industries: a tale of incentives, knowledge and needs
Uwe Cantner and Marco Guerzoni

INTRODUCTION

This chapter is about the co-evolution of technology and markets. Since our goal is to understand the way these forces impact the advancement of industry, these cannot effectively be independently analyzed.

Classical economists recognized that the link between technological evolution and market forces is the trigger of industrial revolution, as well as the consequential tumultuous process of economic growth: 'In turning from the smaller instruments in frequent use to the larger and more important machines, the economy arising from the increase of velocity becomes more striking' (Babbage, 1832, pp. 4–36). However, Adam Smith noted that the use of 'more important machines' is limited by the extent of the market. He described the combined effect of innovation, which creates new markets, and of new markets, which creates incentives for innovation. Karl Marx highlighted the role of machines as the main source of productivity increases as well. Marx also recognized that low wages lead to demand shortages.

Despite the awareness of the classical economists, the analysis of the co-evolution of technology and markets as the principal determinants of industrial dynamics is abandoned in traditional neoclassical theory.

A certain extension of this approach is found only in the search for incentives responsible for the direction and nature of technological progress. The so-called demand-pull approach looks at the demand side of the economy, considering product innovations as initiated by demand. On the other hand, changes in relative prices are considered responsible for certain factor-saving directions taken by technological progress.

Conversely, the role of technology is completely removed from the realm of the discipline: technological progress is treated as an exogenous variable and is therefore banned from the extra-economic sphere. For this reason, these approaches are not explicitly discussed here. These factors are characterized by the assumption of reactive behavior as used in neoclassical economics for all kinds of exogenous changes (preferences, relative factor price changes, income changes etc.). The economic processing of technological changes does not signify anything, but simply follows the market forces in which economic development is pushed by an exogenous technology shock. Within this theoretical frame, the emphasis on technological progress as the most important source of economic dynamics is of no use analytically because, as a black-box phenomenon, technological progress eludes economic interpretation.

Regardless of whether technological-push or demand-pull approaches are considered, typically both actors react only to economic changes. New technological know-how is a pure public good that each economic actor can appropriate at no cost and which is

– externally to the economic sphere – generated (invention) and adapted for economic purposes (innovation). Therefore innovative activities and the existence of spillover effects constitute no economic problem at all.

In this chapter, we review and discuss contributions that consider innovation both as a key factor of advancement and as an endogenous dimension of any economic system. The chapter consists of two focused discussions.

The next section discusses the evolution of technology and markets from the firm perspective. The emergence of new industrial economics takes into account the notion that firms or actors consciously and actively invest resources in order to achieve new technological know-how useful for economic purposes. Consequently, technological progress becomes an endogenous phenomenon, i.e. it is based on economically motivated decisions. Compared to traditional neoclassical economics, the new industrial economics performs much better in analyzing the importance of technological progress. However, in an effort to achieve static equilibrium solutions, it sacrifices some important aspects.

The third section highlights the role of the demand side in shaping competitive conditions and technological trajectories. We review two streams of literature concerning this issue. The first conceives of demand as a pure incentive effect, as in the neoclassical tradition. The second regards demand as a possible source of innovative ideas.

Within each section, we shall proceed symmetrically. Indeed, both technology-push and demand-pull contributions are neither monolithic nor homogeneous; a second divide intersects both streams of literature. There is a cross-section of literature both consistent with mainstream economics and focused on the monetary incentive of the firm to innovate. On the firm side, this is translated into the analysis of the impact of markets and institutions on the rewards of innovation. On the demand side, this framework results in the analysis of market size as the main pull mechanism.

A second approach deviates from mainstream economics, sacrificing the analytical tractability of the issues and highlighting the role of knowledge embedded in the innovation process. Therefore the focus is on the learning process within firms as a necessary condition for innovation. The demand side here is conceived as a flow of information from users and consumers to producers.

The organization of the chapter will reflect the historic structure of the literature. Specifically, this chapter shows how these approaches emerged, the critiques each confronted and, finally, their refinement. The conclusions also reveal future challenges in the field of the economics of innovation.

SUPPLY AND INNOVATION

Why do firms engage in innovative activities and invest in R&D? How are these activities related to the firm environment in general and specifically to the structure and dynamics of the market/industry?

Firms engage in innovative activities if they see an economic or technological opportunity. Analytical approaches construe these two aspects quite differently. The differences first accrue to the assumptions about the behavior of the economic actors and the ability of each to identify or to anticipate those opportunities. Second, there are sizable differences in the consideration of economic chances and of technological opportunities. On this basis, we can distinguish roughly two main camps: the first, based on neoclassical thinking, assumes perfectly rational agents whose only task is to design optimal R&D projects. On this approach, technological opportunities are always there and have only to be exploited, or as Dasgupta and Stiglitz (1980a, p. 272, fn. 1) put it: 'It is as though Mother Nature has a patent on all techniques of production . . . and that society has to pay x to purchase the right to use the technique of production . . .'. In this sense, the intensity and direction of innovative activities depend entirely on the economic incentives offered, mainly the potential of the profit. These profits in turn are dependent on the competitive situation facing a firm and are partially intertwined with the conditions for appropriating innovation rents and hence technological spillovers.

The other camp renders innovative agents boundedly rational in the sense that each neither has all information at hand nor is well equipped to solve each problem (Simon, 1955). In this sense, agents need to explore technological opportunities for innovative success, and require respective knowledge and competencies. The availability of each governs the intensity and direction of innovative activities. The ways actors acquire and build up these competencies and transform them into competitiveness are at the core of the analysis. Market conditions providing the financial resources for appropriate investments are crucial; technological spillovers are considered more a device for learning than a source of profit-diminishing imitation. Summing up, we can distinguish between incentives-based and knowledge-based theories. The following subsections will discuss both in detail.

Innovation and Economic Incentives

The origins: Schumpeter and first IO analyses
When addressing innovation activities of firms in industrial organization (IO), the neo-Schumpeterian hypotheses are an obvious point of departure. Schumpeter, in *Capitalism, Socialism and Democracy* (1943), postulates that large firms are the main driver of innovations and technological change (Schumpeter Mark II). In the alternative Schumpeter approach, formulated in *The Theory of Economic Development* (1912), entrepreneurs and therefore small firms are considered the engine of innovative change (Schumpeter Mark I). This Schumpeterian controversy led to the two neo-Schumpeter hypotheses. The first focuses on the firm and suggests that large firms are more innovative than small firms. The second argues on the basis of industry or market structure that innovation activities are more intense in more concentrated sectors. Finally, these hypotheses were taken up by industrial economics from the 1960s onward and were discussed first within the structure–conduct–performance approach of IO.

The seminal work by Arrow (1962) is considered the first approach to look at the relationship between the benefits accruing to innovative activities and the R&D costs involved in the context of different market structures. His analysis looks at the economic incentives of the actors to engage in R&D activities under alternative market structures. To make that analysis as simple as possible, he compares a monopoly and a situation of perfect competition in which innovative activities do not alter the respective market structure. Arrow shows that the differential profit in the case of perfect competition is always larger than that in the monopoly. The reason is to be seen in a lower profit in the case of the monopoly: the profit after innovation partly replaces the profit before innovation. In the case of perfect competition, this replacement does not apply, and the full amount of innovation rents is gained. Consequently, the economic incentives for innovative activities are higher in perfect competition than in monopoly, so one should expect more intense innovation in the former case. Hence Arrow falsifies the Schumpeter hypotheses within this IO framework.

Besides the criticism of Demsetz (1969), who identifies the non-comparability of the situations of monopoly and perfect competition within the Arrow approach, other criticism refers to the purely static character of the analysis as well as to the neglect (i) of the interdependence of market structure and innovative activities (Reinganum, 1989; Gilbert and Newberry, 1982); (ii) of oligopolistic competition (by focusing only on monopoly and perfect competition) (Dasgupta and Stiglitz, 1980a); and (iii) of technological interdependencies among innovators and (potential) imitators (Levin and Reiss, 1984).

The economics of R&D and new industrial economics
The latter three issues are taken up by the approach of new industrial economics by addressing the issues of the incentive to innovate, the bidirectional influence of the market structure, and the role of technological spillovers. The analyses are mainly of a game-theoretic type, where strategic choices of profit-maximizing firms refer not only to quantity or to price but also to R&D expenditures. The equilibrium-oriented modeling approach allows for welfare analysis by investigating the private and the social gains from innovative activities.

The models developed can be distinguished by the way (i) R&D expenditures affect innovation; and (ii) market competition and market structure are taken into account. Regarding the effect of R&D expenditures, three alternative lines of research have been taken: one states that the level of R&D is positively correlated to the economic reward (e.g. Dasgupta and Stiglitz, 1980a; Levin and Reiss, 1984); a second approach relates the level of R&D to the likelihood of success (e.g. Sah and Stiglitz, 1987); and a third line suggests a negative relationship between the level of R&D and the time to introduce a new product or new process (e.g. Dasgupta and Stiglitz, 1980b; Kamien and Schwartz, 1980). As modeling devices, non-tournament models assume either a non-monopolistic or endogenous market structure, whereas in tournament models (as well as in contest models) innovation competition allows only for one winner and thus always leads to a monopoly.

Contest models   A core issue in understanding innovation incentives is the relationship between the appropriability of innovation rents and the rate of technical progress. That is addressed in so-called contest models. Here firms announce R&D expenditures, allowing them to create an innovation, and then protect it with a patent, thereby allowing the earning of economic rents. These models show that the announced level of R&D is lower, the lower the degree of patent protection, and hence the incentive to engage in innovation is reduced (Witt, 1987). These models can be criticized on two grounds: first, as these are deterministic (e.g. Barzel, 1968; Scherer, 1967; Dasgupta and Stiglitz, 1980b; Gilbert and Newberry, 1982; Katz and Shapiro, 1985), they can be interpreted as auction models, where competing firms make offers and only the winner of the auction will then manage R&D activities (e.g. Dasgupta and Stiglitz, 1980b). It is quite obvious that this pattern is not a 'race'; the competitive aspect here refers to a potential competition

– which might be quite 'tough' (Reinganum, 1989, p. 855). Second, the appropriability conditions for innovation rents depend not only on the public-good character of know-how, but also on the market structure after innovation. Two separate lines of modeling take up these two aspects: non-tournament models and patent races.

Non-tournament models   Dasgupta and Stiglitz (1980a) criticized Arrow (1962) and suggested a model in which R&D competition and innovation were modeled as non-tournament. Many competing firms producing homogeneous outputs spend R&D to generate technologically equivalent and perfectly protected improvements of their respective production technologies, leading to lower unit costs. The incentive to spend on R&D activities does not depend on possible imitative activities of competitors, but on market structure and the features of technology. Therefore technological-innovation-related revenues are determined by the economic interdependence of the firms. Within a competitive surrounding allowing for market entry innovation, revenue will be zero in market equilibrium.

Given these assumptions, a number of relationships between market size and R&D decisions can be deduced. Generally valid results cannot be found in this model, only solutions dependent on certain parameters of demand and unit cost elasticity. In most cases, however, the rate of progress is greater in markets with a higher degree of monopoly. Schumpeter's argument of a positive relationship between market power and innovation rate seems here to be validated.

Technological spillovers are discussed in Levin and Reiss (1984), Spence (1984) as well as d'Aspremont and Jacquemin (1988), who enhance the Dasgupta and Stiglitz framework. Both Levin and Reiss (1984) and Spence (1984) show that spillover effects generally lead to a reduction of individual R&D expenditures and therefore have a negative incentive effect on R&D, with the exception of complementary R&D projects. Despite the incentive-reducing effect, spillovers reduce inefficiencies due to R&D duplication and enhance welfare. D'Aspremont and Jacquemin (1988) show this to take place when the intensity of spillover effects is high.

Tournament models or patent races   Non-tournament models attempt to explain how market forces influence R&D levels and rates of technological progress. However, these models do not discuss any strategic behaviors implemented by actors to defend their technologically or economic leading positions. In addition, patterns such as creative destruction (Reinganum, 1985) and success-breeds-success (Dasgupta, 1986) are not taken into account. On the contrary, tournament or patent race models do exactly that.

In these models, technological competition is interpreted as a race for a certain patent. The firm that introduces an innovation first enjoys patent protection and the resulting temporary monopoly. Investing in R&D activities is meant to increase the probability of success earlier than competitors. For the 'losers', the R&D expenditures spent are lost. The level of investments depends on two effects that impinge upon the expected rewards: the profit motive and the competitive threat. The former consists of the difference between the profit before and after successful innovation. The latter ensues by comparing the profit in the case of a successful innovation and the profit in the case in which the competitor wins. Both differences should be positive for an innovative engagement to be considered worth being pursued.

The interplay of these two effects generates asymmetric incentive structures for the incumbent monopolist and other firms willing to enter the market. Reinganum (1985) shows that, in the case of a drastic innovation, the incumbent and the potential entrant face the same competitive threat, whereas the incumbent's profit motive is much smaller (as the current monopoly profit is challenged). Hence the follower has a greater incentive to engage in R&D, which increases the probability of success, and the monopoly position consequently is more likely to change from the incumbent to the entrant, the case of creative destruction. In case of a non-drastic innovation, however, the incumbent invests more in R&D because it faces a greater competitive threat. Thus it will have a higher probability of success and of keeping the monopoly position. Taking into account technological spillovers between firms reinforces the tendency for creative destruction and weakens the continuation of monopoly position.

Extending the analysis to include the success-breeds-success pattern – as opposed to the leapfrogging pattern – requires a dynamic model with a sequence of several patent races. Reinganum (1985) also analyzes the case of a sequence of patent races. For drastic innovations, the respective patent races in the sequence are independent of each other, so that the sequential character of the model is not essential and static solutions apply. For non-drastic innovations, however, this independence does not hold, and winning a specific patent race is not just worthwhile for profit reasons but also for gaining strategic advantages for future races.

Drawing on stochastic models, only in a few cases are they analytically solvable, and simulation techniques as in Beath et al. (1989) need to be applied. In set-ups where spillover effects among firms are restrained, backward firms are not able to compete for the same stage within the innovation sequence as the leading firms. However, they 'approach' step by step the position of the leading firms. These are the catch-up type of models. Beath et al. (1989) combine the R&D decision with Bertrand and Cournot behavior on the market. Their simulation analyses show that Bertrand behavior tends to reinforce dominance and thus the catch-up type. Otherwise, Cournot behavior sustains leapfrogging.

Innovation and the Generation of New Knowledge

Empirics first: the neo-Schumpeter hypotheses revisited and other regularities

We now leave the realm of the incentives-based theory to move toward a more empirically grounded and knowledge-based approach to industrial dynamics. IO research addresses the neo-Schumpeter hypotheses mainly from a theoretical point of view. Associated empirical work on the validation of these hypotheses provides weak evidence for the hypothesis that large size or concentrated markets lead to greater innovative activities. Instead, other industry- or technology-specific factors show larger explanatory power. Including other variables, such as technological opportunity and conditions of appropriability, leads to a drastic reduction in the significance of the coefficients for concentration. Particularly in the context of the neo-Schumpeterian hypotheses, the variance of R&D intensity is barely explained by the concentration variable, whereas the industry variable explains 32 percent. In other studies, 4 percent of variance is explained by concentration, whereas more than 50 percent is explained by variables representing demand, opportunities and appropriability (Levin et al., 1985). Consequently, technological characteristics, demand-side characteristics (e.g. product diversification), as well as aspects of strategic interaction (e.g. intensity of price competition), show higher validity than the factors central to the hypotheses tested. In addition, a causality problem is involved in interpreting these empirical findings, as it is not clear whether innovative activities determine structural variables or the other way round. As a consequence, the application of a dynamic view on industrial innovative activities promises better results with respect to the changing and complex causality relationships.

Moreover, other empirical works highlight facts (often already labeled as stylized facts) related to the dynamics of entry and exit (Geroski, 1995; Audretsch, 1995; Doms et al., 1995; Malerba and Orsenigo 1997; Klepper and Simons, 2005; Cantner et al., 2009, 2010), to market turbulence, to the persistence of firm performance differences (Mueller and Cable, 2008; Auerswald, 2010; Caves and Barton, 1990; Cantner and Krüger, 2004), to the size distribution of firms, to patterns of firm growth (Simon, 1955; Ijiri and Simon, 1977; Bottazzi and Secchi, 2006; Cefis et al., 2007), and to a long-term perspective, just as in the industry life-cycle discussion.

These dimensions of the dynamics of industries infer that structural characteristics used traditionally, such as firm size and age, the intensity of competition (market concentration) and barriers to entry (scale economies etc.), are only partially able to explain the dynamics of firms and industries. As these rather incentive-based factors seem unable to fully account for industry dynamics, an alternate line of research emerged, focusing on the knowledge and capabilities of actors and firms as well as on the search and learning processes involved in building them. The approach directly addressing four characteristic of technology – opportunities, appropriability conditions, cumulativeness of technological change, and the specific nature of knowledge – is known by the acronym OACK.

OACK serves as a basis for investigating industrial dynamics and industrial evolution by looking at innovative activities and market structure as complex and mutually dependent phenomena. It further finds that the various ways agents compete and the level of competition itself depends on the degree of heterogeneity of innovative activities and successes. The heterogeneity across firms in innovation implies both the presence of idiosyncratic capabilities (absorptive, technological, etc.) and that firms not only do different things but, and most importantly, when they do the same thing, they know how to do it in different ways. This focus on the underlying capabilities for innovation activities alludes to behavioral foundations and the innovations' embeddedness in the prevailing technological environment. We now describe how the OACK approach has been useful to classify innovative activities.

Innovative patterns and their classification in the OACK approach

Understanding innovative activities requires opening up the black box (Rosenberg, 1976) in which actors both acquire and apply new concepts in order to create new combinations. A first step is to briefly address the rather general pattern of the innovation process in modern manufacturing, as suggested by Dosi (1988):

1. Endogeneity of innovative activities
2. Uncertainty
3. Partial dependence on contacts to science

4. Learning-by-doing, learning-by-using, learning-by-innovating, learning-by-inventing
5. Cumulativeness.

Features (1) and (2) point to the fact that economic actors (primarily firms) are engaged in innovation and are thereby confronted with strong and therefore non-calculable uncertainty (Knight, 1921; Arrow, 1991). This implies that designing optimal R&D methods is impossible and that the search for new ideas is a trial-and-error process. Hence an understanding of the economic agent different to the *homo oeconomicus* is required. Drawing on Simon (1955), we use the concept of bounded rationality, which questions the assumption of ubiquitous information (substantial rationality) available to agents, as well as the assumption of unbounded capabilities (procedural rationality) to use this information. The resulting notion of bounded rationality seems to be especially relevant, for actors are engaged in innovative (and imitative) activities. The act of creating something new, as an experimental activity, is essentially linked to imperfect information and imperfect abilities to use it.

The notion of bounded rationality entered the theory of the firm with Cyert and March (1963) as stable behavioral traits, and with Nelson and Winter (1982) when they added the concept of routines, a form of adaptive control with a more flexible behavior. Routines are behaviors that show stability over time as they are based on idiosyncratic knowledge and competencies. Routines change, however, if the rewards do not reach the desired level. A further strategic dimension of routines has been developed within the dynamic capability view of the firm (DCV), as introduced by Teece (1988) drawing on the resource-based view of the firm (e.g. Penrose, 1959; Wernerfelt, 1984). The inherent distinctive knowledge and competencies of individual firms are simply seen as a major resource (characterized as being valuable, rare, imperfectly tradable and non-substitutable) contributing to competitiveness. Since these resources are developed and implemented over time, these are termed dynamic capabilities in order to stress their role in long-term strategic planning. Other firms must incur non-negligible costs and build up respective absorptive capacities (Cohen and Levinthal, 1989) in order to try replicating the knowledge and competencies these capabilities represent.

Features (3) to (5) fit into the dimension of the OACK approach. These indicate how innovative actors act in this trial-and-error process. Actors gain information and expertise from the learning process and then build up dynamic capabilities. The latter, in turn, enables exploration of new opportunities and exploitation of existing ones (Rosenberg and Nelson, 1994, Zucker et al., 1998; Mowery et al., 2004). To the extent that learning relates to the accumulation of personal experience, actors are diverse in terms of their technological (as well as economic) knowledge. As an important consequence of this heterogeneity, the traditional conception of knowledge as a quasi-public good (Arrow, 1962) must be reconsidered. Knowledge seems to have a tacit component (Polanyi, 1967) and, therefore, may not be transferable at all (Cowan et al., 2000) or only at a certain price as a latent public good (Nelson, 1991). These features increase the appropriability of knowledge and reduce the importance of patent protection, otherwise prominent in traditional approaches. Because of the stickiness of knowledge, the social dimension of learning assumes a central role and the means by which knowledge is extracted from external sources such as science or competitors becomes crucial.

Based on the elements of the OACK approach and combining them with the general pattern of innovation in manufacturing, several broad classifications are suggested to deal with emerging patterns. Two of them, by Pavitt (1984) and by Malerba and Orsenigo (1995, 1997), are prominent.

The Pavitt classification distinguishes by sector-specific organization of innovation activities and the specific features of technological change. In the end, four different classes are identified: science-based industries; supplier-dominated industries; production-oriented industries with specialized suppliers; and scale-intensive sectors. This classification accounts for a first clear relationship between the way firms organize the activities to create/use new know-how and the structural dimensions of the sector in which they work.

The classification by Malerba and Orsenigo is oriented toward linking the pattern of innovation activities with the pattern of learning in firms. This exercise leads to two classes of sectors or so-called regimes. A first class contains sectors of an entrepreneurial regime with a larger number of predominantly small firms, low market concentration and market turbulence, easy market entry and exit, and low stability in the ranking of innovators (Schumpeter Mark I). These features are related to high technological opportunities, weak conditions of appropriability and a low degree of cumulativeness of technological knowledge. Consequently, market competition is intense and always fed by new ideas from within and from outside (entering firms) the market.

The sectors of the second class belong to a routinized regime. Large firms are more frequent, operating in more concentrated markets with low market share turbulence, high stability in innovator ranking, and a low market entry rate. The appropriability conditions for new knowledge are considerably high, and knowledge is intensively cumulative. As a result, we observe a considerably low intensity of competition among firms pursing innovation activities in a routinized way, continuously building up competitive advantage in a success-breeds-success manner.

This difference in the organization of innovative activities across industries may be related to a fundamental distinction between Schumpeter Mark I and Schumpeter Mark II models. Schumpeter Mark I is characterized by 'creative destruction', with technological ease of entry and a major role played by entrepreneurs and new firms in innovative activities. By contrast, Schumpeter Mark II is characterized by 'creative accumulation', with the prevalence of large established firms and the presence of relevant barriers to the entry for new innovators.

Technological regimes and Schumpeterian patterns of innovation change dynamically over time. According to an industry life-cycle view, the Schumpeter Mark I pattern of innovative activities may turn into a Schumpeter Mark II pattern (Klepper, 1996), but in the presence of a major technological discontinuity, a Schumpeter Mark II pattern may be replaced by a Schumpeter Mark I. If we introduce into the evolution of industry the role of both technology and knowledge, the dynamic features of system need also a revision.

Industrial Dynamics

Industry dynamics refers to an approach that looks at the change of industries over time (Malerba and Orsenigo, 1996) where innovative activities are a major driver of the dynamics.

Basic dynamic mechanisms and pattern

Combining the elements of the OACK approach with the behavioral foundations of innovative activities suggests that 'different agents (firms) know how to do different things in different ways (domains, levels of performance, etc.)' (Malerba and Orsenigo, 2000, p. 295). Consequently, the heterogeneity of firms in a sector or market can be related to differences in knowledge and competencies acquired over time. Those differences contribute to differential competitiveness and successes.

In this sense, the knowledge and competence specificities of firms are the major determinants of the industrial structure and its evolution over time. Two kinds of mechanisms driving that dynamics of industries have been identified: (1) mechanisms leading to the advance of knowledge and to the generation of innovations and (2) mainly market-based mechanisms for selecting between different new combinations. The interdependency of these two mechanisms will be discussed in the next section.

First, the cumulativeness of knowledge due to a firm-specific process of learning leads to a specific, path-dependent development of individual firm competencies. This specificity generates differences in firm performance, and path dependency makes it difficult for a follower to catch up to the leaders. Such a dynamic is labeled success-breeds-success, a term first used by Phillips (1971) to explain the development of the airplane industry. The success-breeds-success progression can be mitigated when agents can learn from others or imitate. This implies that backward firms can catch up to the knowledge or innovation leader (Verspagen, 1992; Cantwell, 1993). Complete equality or even overtaking may be constrained either by imperfect transferability of tacit knowledge (Polanyi, 1967) or by the lack of absorptive capacities (Cohen and Levinthal, 1989) by the lagging firm.

Second, firm heterogeneity caused by different innovative successes requires an understanding of market competition different from the allocative conception in neoclassical economics. Markets in this context are seen as a platform upon which competition among heterogeneous agents or better heterogeneous products takes place. With respect to innovation activities, different ideas and the different knowledge stocks and competencies behind them are in competition (Metcalfe, 1994; Nelson and Winter, 1982).

In this context, markets serve a twofold purpose. First, markets are a selective mechanism and work efficiently if, step by step, poorly performing ideas are eliminated and better ideas allowed to survive. The second aspect refers to Hayek's notion of competition as a discovery process, which allows firms to learn more about the viability of new ideas. This leads to a more complete picture, as the success of the market or failure of a firm provides information about the comparative evaluation of the product or new idea. This information can be used to adjust and to design further innovation activities. In this sense, the aforementioned search and learning mechanism is nicely combined with the mechanism of selective competition.

The concert of mechanisms

In the view of the empirical findings presented above and the literature on the behavioral foundations of innovative agents, there have been various attempts to formally analyze these phenomena. We briefly mention those that look at dynamics and at innovation. A first group of models attempts to reconcile the empirical regularities with the equilibrium approaches of industrial organization (e.g. Jovanovic, 1982; Ericson and Pakes, 1995; Sutton, 1998), thereby leaving out heterogeneity of actors or learning processes.

A second group of models deviates from equilibrium analysis and takes more of an evolutionary or neo-Schumpeterian perspective. The modeling exercises have analytical solutions only when the set-up is rather simple. However, more complicated relationships and the representation of heterogeneous agents with idiosyncratic paths of development often require simulation techniques to identify characteristic patterns of development. This group contains models in the evolutionary tradition of Nelson and Winter (Nelson and Winter 1982; Dosi et al., 1995), industry life-cycle models (Klepper, 1996, 2002; Klepper and Simons, 2000), history-friendly models (Malerba et al., 1999; Malerba and Orsenigo, 2002), and more macro-level models, by linking innovation and industry evolution to structural change and the changing sectoral composition of the economy (Metcalfe, 1998; Dopfer et al., 2004; Dosi, 2001; Saviotti, 1996).

Innovation–market feedbacks   In general, these models are based on the feedback effects between market competition and innovation activities (e.g. Mazzuccato and Semmler, 1999; Cantner et al., 2009; Klepper, 1996; 2002). Regarding medium-term dynamics, depending on the relationship between market success and innovative activities/successes, one can distinguish a reinforcing interaction leading to a success-breeds-success and monopolistic pattern meanwhile retarding relationships that allow turbulence in market shares and continuous leapfrogging in technological leadership. These results complement empirical regularities like persistent technological or economic performance differences in the former case, and market turbulences with high entry and exit rates in the latter case. Technological spillovers affect such patterns by smoothing turbulences and slowing down the tendency toward monopolization, whereas strong conditions of appropriability reinforce those dynamics.

Industry life-cycle features   Recent work on the industry life cycle (ILC) shows how, for narrowly defined markets or sectors (e.g. automobile, tire, laser, TV, penicillin), the mechanisms present in the previous sections interact and shape the pattern of industrial dynamics over a longer period of time. The life cycle starts with an entrepreneurial phase. The high intensity of competition over time may lead to the establishment of a technological standard or dominant design. This process is often accompanied by a sharp shakeout of firms that do not successfully help to establish that standard or fail to adapt to it. Moreover, this standard serves as a major barrier to further entry. The industry then develops into the phase of a routinized regime with less intense competition and stability of market shares.

This development is driven by a change in the major orientation of innovation activities. The process of standardization usually exhausts this phase of product competition, and innovation activities become more process oriented. The long-run pattern of the ILC suggests a succession of industrial structures. Among the main driving forces behind this development are the knowledge and competencies of firms in that sector. Klepper and Simons (2000, 2005), as well as Cantner et al. (2007, 2009, 2010) look at the importance of various knowledge components for ILC development. They distinguish between knowledge acquired by firms before they entered an industry, while being active in that industry, and knowledge related to innovative activities. The time of entry is also considered in relation to knowledge accumulation in the industry. Pre-entry experience, early entrance (and thus high post-entry experience), and degree of innovativeness turned out to be the most important factors for firm survival. Looking at the relative importance of those knowledge categories for survival, it turns out that the disadvantage of lower accumulated knowledge because of a late date of entry can be compensated by innovation knowledge.

The systemic view Another dimension of firm-heterogeneity-based differences in knowledge and competencies is the deliberate exchange of technological know-how (Allen, 1983). Especially in the case of complex technologies, which are based on a larger number of knowledge components and competencies, the exchange of know-how and the cooperation of firms in developing innovations are vital. This cooperative element of innovative activities is at the core of so-called sectoral systems of innovation (Malerba, 2004) in such sectors as automobiles and pharmaceuticals. Large and small firms cooperate and a specific division of labor is agreed upon. This obviously shapes the structure of an industry, often with large core firms and small 'satellite' firms.

DEMAND AND INDUSTRIAL DYNAMICS

In the previous section, we discussed the evolution of technology and markets from a firm perspective. The ability of firms to respond strategically to external stimuli, as well as their attempts to change the competitive environment, is the central force shaping the dynamics of industries and economies. In this section, we deal with the complementary role of users and consumers both in designing markets and in pulling innovations.

The role of demand in innovation processes is explicitly discussed by Adam Smith: the extent of a market limits the division of labor, which in Adam Smith's view is the main trigger for increasing returns leading to new product and process innovations. Indeed,

> this great increase of the quantity of work which, in consequence of the division of labour, the same number of people are capable of performing, is owing to three different circumstances; . . . and lastly, to the invention of a great number of machines which facilitate and abridge labour, and enable one man to do the work of many. (Smith, 1776, ch. 3)

However, the division of labor is limited by the extent of the market, because

> when the market is very small, no person can have any encouragement to dedicate himself entirely to one employment, for want of the power to exchange all that surplus part of the produce of his own labour, which is over and above his own consumption, for such parts of the produce of other men's labour as he has occasion for. (Ibid.)

The role of increasing returns in the economic process is analyzed by Young (1928), although mainly in heterodox approaches to economics of innovation (Dosi, 1988). By contrast, the explicit tie connecting market size and innovation made by Adam Smith is rarely discussed. A notable exception is the work by the sociologist of invention, Gilfillan (1935a), who not only revisits the ideas of Smith, but also suggests an additional role played by the demand side in the innovation process.

On the one hand, Gilfillan (1935a) suggested that the pace of technology should be faster in those sectors in which the number of potential adopters, and thus firms' incentives to innovate, are higher. On the other, based on a vast qualitative analysis on the shipping industry, he suggests that demand not only provides incentives, but also draws attention to new needs to be addressed by the supply side. In his words, 'there exists a technological lag, a chronic tendency of technology to lag behind demand,' (Gilfillan, 1935b, p. 1); thus only users and consumers can reveal to firms the route to go to satisfy their needs.

These two mechanisms linking demand and innovation, that is, demand as incentive and demand as source of information, can be identified in the literature along two distinct but similar paths: at first, they flourish both in academia and among policy-makers, but they eventually run into diminishing returns when facing incontestable empirical rejections and critics. In the first stage, the solid critiques confronted jeopardize the idea of demand as a determinant of innovation, but ultimately the critiques suggest and compel a sound refinement to the theory. As these two streams of literature are identified and subsequently traced, note that the incentive mechanism is consistent with a mainstream approach where technological choice is driven by market incentives. By contrast, the latter strongly departs from neoclassical economics by disregarding information flow as a relevant problem, but rather considering information as a quasi-public good reproducible at zero marginal cost.

Schmookler (1962, 1966) empirically tested the 'demand-pull' hypothesis, where technological change is pulled by the existence or emergence of new markets because human needs precede technological solutions. He reviews the innovation activity in the railway industry, captured by the numbers of patents, and compares it with the evolution over time of different economic indicators such as stock prices and gross capital formation. He shows that peaks in innovative activities lag behind those capturing the economic performance. Building upon the assumption that economic performance proxies demand as total expenditure, he concludes that 'the influence [upon innovation] of the latter [unfolding economic needs] has been substantial' (Schmookler, 1962, p. 20).

Contemporaneously, Arrow (1962) reveals the mechanism beneath this incentive effect. In the attempt to illustrate the impact of market structure on the propensity to innovate, which we mentioned in the previous section, he analytically states that incentives to innovate are equal to the increase in the mark-up per unit produced by an innovation multiplied by the units sold in the market. The simplicity and the analytical tractability of this proposition make the use of this concept widespread not only in the economic analysis of innovation and technological change (see, among others, Kennedy, 1964; Drandakis and Phelps, 1965; Samuelson, 1965; Hayami and Ruttan, 1970; Acemoglu and Linn, 2005), but also new growth theories (Aghion and Howitt, 1992; Grossman and Helpman, 1991, Romer, 1986, 1990).

Both the Arrow and Schmookler approaches, despite the clarity of the reasoning and their results, run into diminishing returns when confronted with undeniable empirical rejections. Scherer (1982) reruns Schmookler's analysis on a larger data set and rejects the demand-pull hypothesis when using the whole sample. However, when including only capital-goods industries in the analysis, Schmookler's results appear to be valid. Schmookler's hypothesis seems to work only in industries with large firms, facing a stable homogeneous demand, and mainly engaged in incremental product innovations or process innovation.

Overall, the demand-pull hypothesis has an explanatory power of innovation, but the range of its applicability is reduced. Specifically, the main result is that the concept cannot be applied without explicitly referencing the structure of the industry and the joint evolution of the technology side.

Schmookler's approach also fails to explain the dynamic nature of the phenomenon. In Adam Smith's view, the size of the market not only enables innovation, but endogenously generates a further stage where innovation itself expands demand: for instance, that might occur by allowing a lower price or by introducing new products. A further criticism in this direction is that of Kleinknecht and Verspagen (1990), which clearly addresses the problem of endogeneity in technological change; they correct the spurious relationship of innovation and the level of investment by controlling potential latent variables such as sector size. In addition, they test for reverse causality and find evidence of a co-evolution of demand and technology. This is the only paper in economics of innovation that is truly in the spirit of the Smithian increasing returns of demand and technology.

Similarly to Schmookler, Arrow's approach underwent heavy empirical falsification of the mechanism he described. The main result of new growth theory is the prediction of growth with scale effect: if Arrow's incentives mechanism acts as a multiplier, an increase in the market size creates larger incentives and, thus, permanently stimulates growth. Jones (1995) empirically rejects the hypothesis of growth with scale effect on a sample of OECD countries. In conclusion, once the inherent statistical flaws of the early Schmookler analysis are corrected, the magnitude of the demand-pull effect is reduced but the underlying theoretical paradigm still holds.

Young (1998) suggests a possible refinement of the concept, which can explain the lack of scale effect without dismissing the role of demand. He retrieves the 'principle of equivalent solutions' (Gilfillan, 1935b), which states that different innovations fulfilling the same need might coexist. If an economy is large enough and consumers exhibit heterogeneous preferences, firms can find it profitable to investigate alternative solutions to the same technological problem. On the one hand, this dynamic increases variety, thus resulting in higher welfare for users and consumers. On the other hand, it divides the available resources into different streams of R&D (one for each equivalent solution), which reduces the speed of technological improvement, consequently hindering growth. Young (1998) develops a growth model in which rents provided by an increase in the size of the market can be dissipated by developing more than one solution, with the purpose of satisfying a heterogeneous market.

Similarly, Acemoglu and Linn (2005) formalize the same idea and successfully test it empirically using the pharmaceutical market. Foellmi and Zweimüller (2002, 2005) focus on consumers' heterogeneity in terms of income: the more skewed the income distribution, the less homogeneous the final demand, and the weaker the incentives to invent. Ultimately, a large market increases the overall incentive for innovation, but consumer heterogeneity can simultaneously trigger an increase in the variety of alternative solutions, thus hindering growth. Any empirical studies focusing on the relationship between market size and innovation must take into account the mutual crowding-out effect of various equivalent solutions.

Demand as Source of Knowledge

As Gilfillan (1935b) suggests, demand can be interpreted not only as the size of the market providing incentives for invention, but also as a useful source of information to direct research toward the actual needs of potential buyers. The underlying hypothesis of the mechanism is that needs are anticipated in the market, not created by technology. Once again, together with incentives, knowledge is considered as the driving mechanism of the innovative process. Gilfillan's approach has been widely analyzed since the 1960s.

Myers and Marquis (1969) discuss the results of a survey investigating the economic and technological background of 567 innovations in five different industries. They conclude that for about 75 percent of the innovations tested, demand factors were prominent, thus setting an empirical milestone in innovation studies. Indeed, a number of empirical studies followed: Isenson (1969), Rothwell and Freeman (1974), Freeman (1968), Berger (1975), Boyden (1976), Lionetta (1977) and Gilpin (1975). These studies examine the role of demand in anticipating technology and find a tendency of technology to lag behind human needs: 'What is important is what consumers or producers need or want rather than the availability of technological options' (Gilpin, 1975, p. 65).

This paradigm was accepted until the end of the 1970s, when two disruptive articles by Mowery and Rosenberg (1979) and Dosi (1982) tackled its underlying assumptions. These authors explain that the theoretical flaw of those earlier studies was the inability to distinguish demand from the 'limitless set of human needs' (Dosi, 1982, p. 150). For this reason, demand-led studies could simply capture the idea that successfully realized innovations obviously meet some needs, but they could not explain the 'why of certain technological developments instead of others and of a certain timing instead of other' (ibid.). This critique is important because it hits those studies at their core assumption. Since then, innovation studies have mostly focused on the technology side (Freeman, 1994).

However, a few scholars still engage in this research agenda and manage to overcome this critique by refining the conceptualization of the demand side. These researchers try to leave a vague idea of demand by focusing on consumers with very well-defined needs. Teubal (1979), for instance, suggests that the influence of demand upon innovation depends on 'need determinateness, the extent to which preferences are specified (or need satisfaction is expressed) in terms of product classes, functions and features' (Teubal, 1979, cited in Clark, 1985, p. 244).

Von Hippel (1977) introduces the concept of lead users, those users familiar with problems and conditions that the rest of the market will face in the future. An innovator can gain useful insights into users' needs only from these lead users. The stream of literature linked with lead users is flourishing in the managerial literature (Foxall, 1987; von Hippel and Finkelstein, 1979; Parkinson, 1982; Shaw, 1985; Spital, 1978; Voss, 1985; Urban and von Hippel, 1988; Herstatt and von Hippel, 1992; Knodler, 1993; Morrison et al. 2000; Franke and Shah, 2001).

Malerba et al. (2003) develop a model in which a group of users exhibits selective preference for an innovation because they have diverse needs from the rest of the market. Those experimental users allow the creation of a niche market that acts as an incubator for the new technology. In diffusion studies, a similar idea is presented. A new product or process is introduced into the market only if a minimum threshold number of pioneers exists, that is, users with explicit and stringent needs to be fulfilled (Rogers, 1995).

Furthermore, both Windrum and Frenken (2003) and Windrum (2005) highlight the fact that users with diverse preferences can drive innovation cycles in mature industries. Specifically, both show that in some industries, such as the camera and computer industries, the presence of market niches can pull innovation with the purpose of satisfying particular market niches. Along the same line, Christensen (1997), Adner (2002), and Adner and Levinthal (2001) suggest that disruptive technology can emerge when markets realize that a product can be used in a different way by users with particular needs. They conceive a product as a bundle of characteristics and suggest that, if some characteristics are improved instead of others, a target consumer of a good can be created.

These studies share the perspective that not all users and consumers can provide firms with useful information, but rather only sophisticated consumers or consumers able to specify their needs with high accuracy (Guerzoni, 2007, 2010). In other words, what really matters in the information flow from market to firms is not the limitless set of human desires, but a small subsample of demand consisting of users with well-defined needs.

Thus we can say that the literature on demand and innovation can be divided into two streams. On the one hand, demand can be conceived as the market size and act as an incentive upon firms in order to pull innovation. On the other hand, demand can provide the firm with useful information to direct R&D. Critics of these studies forced both streams to be refined over time: demand might well play a role as incentive, but it should be controlled for its heterogeneity. The role of demand as source of information is also undeniable, but only those consumers well aware of their preferences are able to serve this purpose.

CONCLUSIONS

In the early age of economics, innovation was considered an endogenous factor of growth and development and was, therefore, widely analyzed. Over time, the role of innovation was elminated from the realm of economic studies.

This chapter tracked the efforts of scholars of economic innovation to keep the co-evolution of technology and markets as the key units of analysis to explain the development of industries.

This literature consists of two complementary building blocks. On the one side, the issue can be tackled by highlighting the role of firms and entrepreneurs in actively shaping the competitive environment and reacting to change by introducing product, process and organizational innovation. Conversely, the focus can be set on the demand side, which provides not only incentives, but also relevant information to direct R&D efforts along the right path. This dichotomy is known in the literature as the 'technology push vs. demand pull debate' (Freeman, 1994).

In our chapter, we kept this separation for illustrative purpose only: indeed, once we acknowledge that technology and markets co-evolve, any clear-cut distinction is impossible, as well as any superiority of one effect over the other. A second large divide exists in the literature. One stream of literature reduces the problem of innovation to simply a matter of rewards to innovation. Incentives clearly play a role in defining opportunities and constraints, but they are only one side of the same coin. The other side considers innovation as the end result of a complex process of learning that simultaneously takes place both in the firms and in the consumers. Innovation itself should be conceptualized as the process of matching available technological opportunities with well-defined needs.

Further challenges for the issue rely precisely on improving the understanding of this process by looking at the interaction of the two divides. First, both users' and firms' impact upon innovation should be simultaneously taken into account because of the relevant feedbacks among different actors in the system. Second, and for analogous reasons, the big divide between incentive-based and knowledge-based approaches must be bridged. Indeed, the degree of availability of knowledge heavily impinges upon the distribution of expected profit. Alternatively, it is partly endogenously determined by incentives to invest in codification, knowledge transfer and absorptive capabilities.

REFERENCES

Acemoglu, Daron and Joshua Linn (2005), 'Market size in innovation: theory and evidence from the pharmaceutical industry', *Quarterly Journal of Economics*, **119**, 1049–90.
Adner, Rod (2002), 'When are technologies disruptive? A demand-based view of the emergence of competition', *Strategic Management Journal*, **23**, 667–88.
Adner, Rod and Daniel Levinthal (2001), 'Demand heterogeneity and technology evolution: implications for product and process innovation', *Management Science*, **47**, 611–28.
Aghion, Philippe and Peter Howitt (1992), 'A model of growth through creative destruction', *Econometrica*, **60**, 323–51.
Allen, R.C. (1983), 'Collective invention', *Journal of Economic Behaviour and Organisation*, **4**, 1–24.
Arrow, Kenneth J. (1962), 'Economic welfare and the allocation of resources for invention', in Richard R. Nelson (ed.), *The Rate and Direction of Inventive Activity: Economic and Social Factors*, National Bureau of Economic Research, Conference Series, Princeton, NJ: Princeton University Press, pp. 609–25.
Arrow, K.J. (1991), 'The dynamics of technological change', in OECD (ed.), *Technology and Productivity: The Challenge for Economic Policy,* Paris, OECD, pp. 473–6.
Audretsch, D.B. (1995), 'Innovation, growth and survival', *International Journal of Industrial Organization*, **13** (4), 441–57.
Auerswald, P.E. (2010), 'Entry and Schumpeterian profits: how technological complexity affects industry evolution', *Journal of Evolutionary Economics*, **20** (4), 553–82.
Babbage, C. (1832), *On the Economy of Machinery and Manufactures*, Teddington: Echo Library.
Barzel, Y. (1968), 'Optimal timing of innovations', *Review of Economics and Statistics*, **50**, 348–55.
Beath J., Y. Katsoulacos and D. Ulph (1989), 'The game-theoretic analysis of innovation: a survey', *Bulletin of Economic Research*, **41** (3), 164–84.
Berger, Alan J. (1975), 'Factors influencing the locus of innovation activity leading to scientific instrument and plastics innovation', SM thesis, Cambridge, MA: Sloan School of Management, MIT.
Bottazzi G. and A. Secchi (2006), 'Gibrat's law and diversification', *Industrial and Corporate Change*, **15** (5), 847–75.
Boyden, Julian W. (1976), 'A study of the innovative process in the plastics additives industry', SM thesis, Cambridge, MA: Sloan School of Management, MIT.
Cantner, U. and J.J. Krüger (2004), 'Geroski's stylized facts and mobility in large German manufacturing firms', *International Journal of Industrial Organisation*, **24** (3), 267–83.
Cantner, U., K. Dressler and J. Krüger (2007), 'Die Evolution der deutschen Automobilindustrie (1886–1939) – Die Rolle technologischen Wissens und seiner Anwendung', in R. Walter (ed.), *Innovationsgeschichte*, Stuttgart: Franz Steiner Verlag, pp. 333–52.
Cantner, U., J. Krüger and K. von Rhein (2009), 'Knowledge and creative destruction over the industry life cycle – the case of the German automobile industry', *Economica*, **76** (301), 132–48.
Cantner, U., J. Krüger and K. von Rhein (2010), 'Knowledge compensation in the German automobile industry', *Applied Economics*, doi: 10.1080/00036840902762738.
Cantwell, J. (1993), 'Technological competence and evolving patterns of international production', in H. Cox, J. Clegg and G. Ietto-Giles (eds), *The Growth of Global Business*, London: Routledge, pp. 19–37.
Caves, R.E. and D.R. Barton (1990), *Efficiency in U.S. Manufacturing Industries*, Cambridge, MA: MIT Press.
Cefis, E. M. Ciccarelli and L. Orsenigo (2007), 'Testing Gibrat's legacy: a Bayesian approach to study the growth of firms', *Structural Change and Economic Dynamics*, **18**, 348–69.
Christensen, Clayton M. (1997), *The Innovator's Dilemma: When New Technologies Cause Great Firms to Fail*, Cambridge, MA: Harvard Business School Press.
Clark, Kim (1985), 'The interaction of design hierarchies and market concepts in technological evolution', *Research Policy*, **14**, 235–51.

Cohen, W.M. and D. Levinthal (1989), 'Innovation and learning: the two faces of R&D', *Economic Journal*, **99** (397), 569–96.
Cowan, R., P.A. David and D. Foray (2000), 'The explicit economics of knowledge: codification and tacitness', *Industrial and Corporate Change*, **9** (2), 211–53.
Cyert, R.M. and J.G. March (1963), *A Behavioural Theory of the Firm*, Englewood Cliffs, NJ: Prentice-Hall.
Dasgupta, P. (1986), 'The theory of technological competition', in J.E. Stiglitz and F. Mathewson (eds), *New Developments in the Analysis of Market Structure*, London and Cambridge, MA: Macmillan, pp. 519–47.
Dasgupta, P. and J.E. Stiglitz (1980a), 'Industrial structure and the nature of innovative activity', *Economic Journal*, **90**, 266–93.
Dasgupta, P. and J.E. Stiglitz (1980b), 'Uncertainty, industrial structure and the speed of R&D', *Bell Journal of Economics*, **11**, 1–28.
D'Aspremont, C. and A. Jacquemin (1988), 'Cooperative and noncooperative R&D in duopoly with spillovers', *American Economic Review*, **78**, 1133–7.
Demsetz, H. (1969), 'Information and efficiency: another viewpoint', *Journal of Law and Economics*, **12**, 1–22.
Doms, M., T. Dunne and M.J. Roberts (1995), 'The role of technology use in the survival and growth of manufacturing plants', *International Journal of Industrial Organization*, **13** (4), 523–42.
Dopfer, K., J. Foster and J. Potts (2004), 'Micro-meso-macro', Schumpeter Conference, Milan 2004.
Dosi, Giovanni (1982), 'Technological paradigms and technological trajectories: a suggested interpretation of the determinants and directions of technical change', *Research Policy*, **11**, 147–62.
Dosi, G. (1988), 'The nature of the innovative process', in G. Dosi, C. Freeman, R. Nelson, G. Silverberg and L. Soete (eds) (1988), *Technical Change and Economic Theory*, London: Pinter Publishers, pp. 221–38.
Dosi, G. (2001), *Innovation, Organization and Economic Dynamics: Selected Essays*, Cheltenham, UK and Northampton, MA, USA: Edward Elgar.
Dosi, G., O. Marsili, L. Orsenigo and R. Salvatore (1995), 'Learning, market selection and the evolution of industrial structures', *Small Business Economics*, **7** (6), 411–36.
Drandakis, Emmanuel M. and Edmond S. Phelps (1965), 'A model of induced invention, growth and distribution', *Economic Journal*, **76**, 823–40.
Ericson, R. and A. Pakes (1995), 'Markov perfect industry dynamics: a framework for empirical work', *Review of Economic Studies*, **62**, 53–82.
Foellmi, Reto and Josef Zweimüller (2002), 'Heterogeneous Mark-ups, Demand Composition, and the Inequality–Growth Relation', Royal Economic Society Annual Conference 76, London, UK: Royal Economic Society.
Foellmi, Reto and Josef Zweimüller (2005), 'Income distribution and demand-induced innovations', CEPR Discussion Paper 4985.
Foxall, Gordon R. (1987), 'Strategic implications of user-initiated innovation', in R. Rothwell and J. Bessant (eds.), *Innovation: Adaptation and Growth*, Amsterdam: Elsevier, pp. 25–36.
Franke, Nikolaus and Sonali Shah (2001), 'How communities support innovative activities: an exploration of assistance and sharing among end-users', MIT Sloan School of Management Working Paper no. 4164.
Freeman, Chris (1968), 'Chemical process plant: innovation and the world market', *National Institute Economic Review*, **45**, 29–57.
Freeman, Chris (1994), 'The economics of technical change', *Cambridge Journal of Economics*, **18**, 479–82.
Geroski, P.A. (1995), 'What do we know about entry?', *International Journal of Industrial Organization*, **13** (4), 421–40.
Gilbert, R.J. and D.M.G. Newberry (1982), 'Preemptive patenting and the persistence of monopoly', *American Economic Review*, **72**, 514–26.
Gilfillan, Seabury C. (1935a), *The Sociology of Invention*, Chicago, IL: Follett Publishing Company.
Gilfillan, Seabury C. (1935b), *Inventing the Ship*, Chicago, IL: Follett Publishing Company.
Gilpin, Robert (1975), *Technology, Economic Growth and International Competitiveness*, study prepared for the Subcommittee on Economic Growth of the Congressional Joint Economic Committee, Washington, DC: US Government Printing Office.
Grossman, Gene and Elhanan Helpman (1991), *Innovation and Growth in the Global Economy*, Cambridge, MA: MIT Press.
Guerzoni, M. (2007), 'Size and sophistication: the two faces of demand', CESPRI Working Papers no. 197, Università Bocconi, Milan, Italy.
Guerzoni, M. (2010), 'The impact of market size and users' sophistication on innovation: the patterns of demand and the technology life cycle', *Economic of Innovation and New Technology*, forthcoming.
Hayami, Yujiro and Vernon W. Ruttan (1970), 'Factor prices and technical change in agricultural development: the U.S. and Japan, 1880–1960', *Journal of Political Economy*, **77**, 1115–41.
Herstatt, Cornelius and Eric von Hippel (1992), 'From experience: developing new product concepts via the lead user method: a case study in low tech field', *Journal of Product Innovation Management*, **9**, 23–221.
Isenson, R.S. (1969), 'Project Hindsight: an empirical study of the sources of ideas utilized in operational

weapon systems', in William H. Gruber and Donald G. Marquis (eds), *Factors in the Transfer of Technology*, Cambridge, MA: MIT Press, pp. 155–76.

Ijiri, Y. and H. Simon (1977), *Skewed Distributions and the Size of Business Firms*, Amsterdam: North Holland.

Jones, Charles I. (1995), 'R&D-based models of economic growth', *Journal of Political Economy*, **103**, 759–84.

Jovanovic, B. (1982), 'Selection and the evolution of industry', *Econometrica*, **50** (3), 649–70.

Kamien, M. and N. Schwartz (1980), *Market Structure and Innovation*, Cambridge: Cambridge University Press.

Katz, M.L. and C. Shapiro (1985), On the Licensing of Innovations, Rand Journal of Economics 16, 1985, 504–20.

Kennedy, Charles (1964), 'Induced bias in innovation and the theory of distribution', *Economic Journal,* **74**, 541–7.

Kleinknecht, Alfred and Bart Verspagen (1990), 'Demand and innovation: Schmookler re-examined', *Research Policy*, **19**, 387–94.

Klepper, S. (1996), 'Entry, exit, growth and innovation over the product life cycle', *American Economic Review*, **86**, 562–83.

Klepper, S. (2002), 'Firm survival and the evolution of oligopoly', *RAND Journal of Economics*, **33** (1), 37–61.

Klepper, S. and K.L. Simons (2000), 'The making of an oligopoly: firm survival and technological change in the evolution of the U.S. tire industry', Journal of Political Economy, **108** (4), 728–60.

Klepper, S. and K.L. Simons (2005), 'Industry shakeouts and technological change', *International Journal of Industrial Organization*, **23** (1–2), 23–43.

Knight, F.H. (1921), *Risk, Uncertainty and Profit*, New York: Kelley.

Knodler, Janet T. (1993) 'Early examples of user-based industrial research', *Business and Economic History,* **22**, 285–94.

Levin, R.C., W.M. Cohen and D.C. Mowery (1985), 'R&D appropriability, opportunity, and market structure: new evidence on some Schumpeterian hypotheses', *The American Economic Review*, **75** (2), 20–24.

Levin, R.C. and P.C. Reiss (1984), 'Tests of a Schumpeterian model of R&D and market structure', in Z Griliches (ed.), *R&D, Patents, and Productivity*, Chicago, IL and London: University of Chicago Press, pp. 175–204.

Lionetta, William G. (1977), 'Sources of innovation within the pultrusion industry', unpublished S.M. thesis, Sloan School of Management, Cambridge, MA: MIT.

Malerba, F., (2004), 'Sectoral systems of innovation: basic concepts', in F. Malerba (ed.), *Sectoral Systems of Innovation: Concepts, Issues and Analysis of Six Major Sectors in Europe*, Cambridge: Cambridge University Press, pp. 9–35.

Malerba, F., R. Nelson, L. Orsenigo and S. Winter (1999), 'History friendly models of industrial evolution: the computer industry', *Industrial and Corporate Change*, **1**, 3–41.

Malerba, F. and L. Orsenigo (1995), 'Schumpeterian patterns of innovation', *Cambridge Journal of Economics*, **19**, 47–65.

Malerba, F. and L. Orsenigo (1996), 'The dynamics and evolution of industries', *Industrial and Corporate Change*, **5** (1), 51–87.

Malerba, F. and L. Orsenigo (1997), 'Technological regimes and sectoral patterns of innovative activities', *Industrial and Corporate Change*, **6**, 83–117.

Malerba, F. and L. Orsenigo (2000), 'Knowledge, innovation activities and industrial evolution', *Industrial and Corporate Change*, **9** (2), 289–313.

Malerba, F. and L. Orsenigo (2002), 'Innovation and market structure in the dynamics of the pharmaceutical industry and biotechnology: towards a history friendly model', *Industrial and Corporate Change*, **11** (4), 667–703.

Malerba, F., R. Nelson and L. Orsenigo (2003), 'Demand, innovation and the dynamics of market structure: the role of experimental users and diverse preferences; KITeS Working Paper, Milan.

Mazzucato, M. and W. Semmler (1999), 'Market share instability and stock price volatility during the industry life-cycle: the US automobile industry', *Journal of Evolutionary Economics*, **9** (1), 67–96.

Metcalfe, S. (1994), 'Competition, Fisher's principle and increasing returns to selection', *Journal of Evolutionary Economics*, **4**, 327–46.

Metcalfe, S. (1998), *Evolutionary Economics And Creative Destruction*, London: Routledge.

Morrison, Pamela D,. John H. Roberts and Eric von Hippel (2000), 'Determinants of user innovation and innovation sharing in a local market', *Management Science*, **46**, 1513–27.

Mowery, D., R. Nelson, B. Sampat and A. Ziedonis (2004), *Ivory Tower and Industrial Innovation: Technology Transfer Before and After Bayh–Dole*, Stanford, CA: Stanford University Press.

Mowery, David C. and Nathan Rosenberg (1979), 'The influence of market demand upon innovation: a critical review of some recent empirical studies', *Research Policies* **8**, 102–53.

Mueller D. and J.R. Cable (2008), 'Testing for persistence of profits' differences across firms', *International Journal of the Economics of Business*, **15** (2), 201–28.

Myers, Summer and Donald G. Marquis (1969), *Successful Industrial Innovation*, Washington, DC: National Science Foundation.
Nelson, R. and S. Winter (1982), *An Evolutionary Theory of Economic Change*, Cambridge, MA: Harvard University Press.
Nelson, R.R. (1991), 'Why do firms differ, and how does it matter?', *Strategic Management Journal*, **12**, Special Issue: Fundamental Research Issues in Strategy and Economics, 61–74.
Parkinson, S.T. (1982), 'The role of the user in successful new product development', *R & D Management*, **12**, 123–31.
Pavitt, K. (1984), 'Sectoral patterns of technical change: towards a taxonomy and a theory', *Research Policy*, **13**, 343–73.
Penrose, E. (1959), *The Theory of the Growth of the Firm*, London: Basil Blackwell.
Phillips, A. (1971), *Technology and Market Structure: A Study of the Aircraft Industry*, Lexington, MA: Heath, Lexington Books.
Polanyi, M. (1967), *The Tacit Dimension*, New York: Anchor Books.
Reinganum, J.F. (1985), 'Innovation and industry evolution', *Quarterly Journal of Economics*, **100**, 81–99.
Reinganum, J.F. (1989), 'The timing of innovation: research, development, and diffusion', in R. Schmalensee and R.D. Willig (eds), *Handbook of Industrial Organization*, Volume I, Elsevier Science Publishers, pp. 849–908.
Rogers, Everett (1995), *Diffusion of Innovations*, 4th edu, New York: The Free Press.
Romer, Paul M. (1986), 'Increasing returns and long-run growth', *Journal of Political Economy*, **94**, 1002–37.
Romer, Paul M. (1990), 'Endogenous technological change', *Journal of Political Economy*, **98**, 71–102.
Rosenberg, N. (1976), Perspectives on Technology, Cambridge: Cambridge University Press.
Rosenberg, N. and R. Nelson (1994), 'American universities and technical advance in industry', *Research Policy*, **23** (3), 323–48.
Rothwell, Roy and Chris Freeman (1974), 'SAPPHO updated – Project SAPPHO Phase II', *Research Policy* **3**, 258–91.
Sah, R.K. and J.E. Stiglitz (1987), 'The invariance of market innovation to the number of firms', *Rand Journal of Economics*, **18**, 98–108.
Samuelson, Paul (1965), 'A theory of induced innovations along Kennedy–Weisacker lines', *Review of Economics and Statistics*, **47**, 444–64.
Saviotti, P. (1996), *Technological Evolution, Variety and the Economy*, Cheltenham, UK and Northampton, MA, USA: Edward Elgar.
Scherer, F.M. (1967), 'Research and development resource allocation under rivalry', *Quarterly Journal of Economics*, **81**, 359–94.
Scherer, F.M. (1982), 'Demand pull and technological invention: Schmookler revisited', *Journal of Industrial Economics*, **30**, 225–37.
Schmookler, Jakob (1962), 'Economic sources of inventive activity', *Journal of Economic History*, **22** (1), 1–20.
Schmookler, Jakob (1966), *Invention and Economic Growth*, Cambridge, MA: Harvard University Press.
Schumpeter, J. (1942/1950), *Capitalism, Socialism and Democracy*, New York: Harper Brothers.
Schumpeter, J.A. (1935/1912), *Theorie der Wirtschaftlichen Entwicklung*, Berlin: Duncker & Humblot, 5.Auflage, 1935.
Schumpeter, Joseph A. (1943), *Capitalism, Socialism and Democracy*, London: George Allen & Unwin.
Shaw, Brian (1985), 'The role of the interaction between the user and the manufacturer in medical equipment innovation', *R&D Management*, **15**, 283–92.
Simon, H.A. (1955), 'A behavioural model of rational choice', *Econometrics*, **19**, 99–118.
Smith, A. (1776), *An Inquiry into the Nature and Causes of the Wealth of Nations*, London: W. Strahan and T. Cadell.
Spence, M. (1984), 'Cost reduction, competition, and industry performance', *Econometrica*, **52**, 101–21.
Spital, Clifford F. (1978), *The Role of the Manufacturer in the Innovation Process for Analytical Instruments*, PhD diss., Sloan School of Management, MIT, Cambridge, MA.
Sutton, J. (1998), *Technology and Market Structure: Theory and History*, Cambridge, MA: MIT Press.
Teece, D.J. (1988), 'Technological change and the nature of the firm', in G. Dosi, C. Freeman, R. Nelson, G. Silverberg and L. Soete (eds), *Technical Change and Economic Theory*, New York: Pinter, pp. 256–81.
Teubal, Morris (1979), 'On user needs and need determination: aspects of the theory of technological innovation', in Michael J. Baker (ed.) *Industrial Innovation: Technology, Policy, Diffusion*, London: Macmillan.
Urban, Glen and Eric von Hippel (1988), 'Lead user analysis for the development of new industrial products', *Management Science*, **34**, 569–82.
Verspagen, B. (1992), *Uneven Growth between Interdependent Economies*, Maastricht: UPM.
Von Hippel, Eric (1977), 'Transferring process equipment innovations from user-innovators to equipment manufacturing firms', *R&D Management* **8**, 13–22.

Von Hippel, Eric and Stan N. Finkelstein (1979), 'Analysis of innovation in automated clinical chemistry analyzers', *Science & Public Policy*, **6**, 24–37.
Voss, Christopher A. (1985), 'The role of users in the development of applications software', *Journal of Product Innovation Management*, **2**, 113–21.
Wernerfelt, B. (1984), 'A resource-based view of the firm', *Strategic Management Journal*, **5**, 171–80.
Windrum, Paul (2005), 'Heterogeneous preferences and new innovation cycles in mature industries: the amateur camera industry 1955–1974', *Industrial and Corporate Change*, **14**, 1043–74.
Windrum, Paul and Koen Frenken (2003), 'Successive cycles of innovation: the importance of user heterogeneity and design complementarities for radical product innovations in the camera and computer industries', paper presented at the SPRU conference 'What do we know about innovation?', University of Sussex, 13–15 November.
Witt, U. (1987), *Individualistische Grundlagen der evolutorischen Ökonomik*, Tübingen: J.C.B. Mohr (Paul Siebeck).
Young, A. (1928), 'Increasing returns and economic progress', *Economic Journal*, **38**, 529.
Young, A. (1998), 'Growth without scale effect', *Journal of Political Economy*, **106**, 41–3.
Zucker, L.G., M.R. Darby and M.B. Brewer (1998), 'Intellectual human capital and the birth of U.S. biotechnology enterprises', *American Economic Review*, **88** (1), 290–306.

25 How do young innovative companies innovate?

Gabriele Pellegrino, Mariacristina Piva and Marco Vivarelli

INTRODUCTION

Both the scientific community and policy-makers are showing increasing interest in the role that young innovative companies (YICs) play in the new technology implementation process, as these ultimately contribute to the renewal of the industrial structure and to aggregate economic growth.[1] For instance, one possible explanation of the transatlantic productivity gap could be found in the revealed capacity of the US economy to generate an increasing number of young innovative firms that manage to survive and introduce new products at the core of emerging sectors. On the contrary, young European firms reveal lower innovative capacity and most are doomed to early failure, the process resulting in churning rather than in innovative industrial dynamics (see Bartelsman et al., 2004; Santarelli and Vivarelli, 2007).

There are several different sources of innovation at the firm level; together with in-house and external R&D activities, technological acquisition (TA) in its embodied (machinery and equipment) and disembodied forms must be taken into account. This input–output framework can be seen as an extension of the 'knowledge production function' (KPF, initially put forward by Griliches, 1979), a tool for describing the transformation process running from innovative inputs to innovative outputs.

While most previous microeconometric research focuses on the R&D–Innovation–Productivity chain (see next section), few studies explicitly discuss the role of TA and the possible differences in the KPF across firms of different ages. By using microdata from the European Community Innovation Survey 3 (CIS 3) for the Italian manufacturing sector, the main novelty of this chapter lies in the authors' investigation of whether R&D and TA lead to significant differences in determining innovative output in firms of different ages. In particular, it will be tested whether the KPF of YICs exhibits some peculiarities in comparison with the KPF of mature incumbent firms.

The remainder of the chapter is organized as follows: a discussion of the theoretical framework on which this work is based is followed by a description of the data and indicators used in the empirical analysis and by discussion of the adopted econometric methodology. Subsequently, the empirical outcomes derived from the descriptive analysis and the econometric estimates are discussed. The fifth section concludes the chapter by briefly summarizing the main findings.

THE LITERATURE

Previous economic literature takes R&D and patents as a starting point for the analysis of innovative activities across economies, industries and firms. In particular, the relationship between innovative inputs and outputs explicitly appears as one of the components of those analyses whose main target is to measure the returns to innovation. In this stream of literature, the first contribution to discuss the innovative input–output relationship is by Griliches (1979, 1990), through a three-equation model in which one of the equations is what he called the knowledge production function (KPF), a function intended to represent the transformation process leading from innovative inputs (R&D) to innovative outputs (patents).[2] Similarly, the KFP is also included in models by Crèpon et al. (1998) as well as Lööf and Heshmati (2001).

So far the theoretical framework described provides the background for understanding the link between innovative inputs and outputs, and for the empirical assessment of this relationship. However, for the particular purpose of this chapter, most empirical studies suffer from two principal limitations. First, the relationship between innovation inputs and innovation outputs is not the primary focus but rather a secondary equation, ancillary to the authors' main purpose of investigating firms' performance in terms of productivity and/or profitability. Second, and more important, the KPF is traditionally simplified as a link between R&D investment and patenting activity. Historically driven by the relative ease of data availability compared to other innovation measures, there is room for a more comprehensive approach to the determinants of innovativeness. In particular, innovation surveys provide more precise and comprehensive measures of both innovative inputs and outputs.[3]

Consistently, different innovation outputs can be seen as the outcomes of several innovation inputs and not only as the consequence of formal R&D investments.[4] For instance, it is important to consider the role of technological acquisition (TA), both through 'embodied technical change'[5] acquired by means of investment in new machinery and equipment, as well as through the purchasing of external technology incorporated in licenses, consultancies and know-how (Freeman, 1982; Freeman et al., 1982; Freeman and Soete, 1987).

This chapter represents an attempt to open up this broader perspective. Once it is recognized that innovative inputs are not confined just to formal R&D and that innovative output can be measured by (more satisfactory) indicators,[6] the way for a deeper analysis of firms' peculiarities in the KPF is paved. In this framework, firms adapt an innovative strategy specific to their own particular economic environment by choosing the most effective combination of innovative inputs and outputs. In doing so, they distribute economic resources between formal in-house and external R&D, technological change embodied in machinery and equipment and the purchasing of external know-how and licenses.

In particular, we wonder whether YICs differ from mature incumbents in their input–output innovative relationships. Are YICs more R&D-based and conducive to a science-based reorientation of the current industrial structure?[7] Or, on the contrary, are YICs weaker than innovative incumbents and, consequently, less R&D-based and thus dependent on external knowledge provided by larger mature firms and research institutions?

The hypothesis that small and newly established firms are more science-based and technologically advanced is consistent with the entrepreneurial process of 'creative destruction' (Schumpeter, 1934; the so-called Schumpeter Mark I), while the process of 'creative accumulation' calls for large and established firms to take a leading role in the innovative process (Schumpeter, 1942; Schumpeter Mark II). Adopting evolutionary terminology, the former context can be seen as an 'entrepreneurial regime', where new firms and the industrial dynamics are the basic factors of change, while the latter can be considered a 'routinized regime', where larger and older incumbents are the engines of change and lead the innovative process (see Winter, 1984; Malerba and Orsenigo, 1996; Breschi et al., 2000).

Indeed, when focusing on all the industrial sectors and not just the emerging or the high-tech ones, several arguments sustain the view that larger mature firms might turn out to be more R&D based than their younger counterparts. First, mature larger incumbents are not affected by liquidity constraints since they have both easier access to external finance and more internal funds to support R&D activities that are both costly and uncertain. Second, larger incumbent firms possess a higher degree of market power and so enjoy a higher degree of 'appropriability' (Gilbert and Newbery, 1982). Empirically, Cohen and Klepper (1996) provide stylized facts supporting the view that the likelihood of a firm carrying out R&D increases with size, while Mairesse and Mohnen (2002) highlight scale economies and the differences in the organization of work that make larger established incumbents more inclined to carry out R&D activities. Third, learning economies (see Arrow, 1962; Malerba, 1992) are often crucial in innovative dynamics and older, experienced firms are obviously at an advantage from this perspective.

However, not all innovative firms are large established corporations. Indeed, economic literature supports the hypothesis that small and young firms face a different technological and economic environment from large mature firms with respect to innovative activities (see Acs and Audretsch, 1988, 1990; Acs et al., 1994). In particular, as discussed above, R&D does not represent the sole input through which firms can produce some innovative outcomes. While the financial and competitive reasons discussed can hamper an R&D-based innovative strategy for YICs, it seems much easier for them to rely on the market and choose 'to buy' instead of 'to make' technology (Acs and Audretsch, 1990). One of the hypotheses tested in this chapter is whether innovation outcomes in YICs rely more on external sources of knowledge than on formal in-house R&D. This hypothesis appears more plausible in a middle-technology economy, such as that of Italy, where middle-tech and traditional sectors represent the core of the industrial structure (for recent evidence on the crucial role of embodied technical change and other external sources of knowledge in spurring innovation in the medium and low-tech sectors, see Santamaría et al., 2009).

In the specific Italian 'national innovation system' (see Freeman, 1987; Lundvall, 1992 and Nelson, 1993, for an introduction to the concept, and Malerba, 1993, for an application to the Italian case), New Technology-Based Firms (NTBFs) may be an exception, while for YICs the main way to acquire knowledge might be through embodied technical change and technological acquisition (for previous evidence on the role of embodied technological change in fostering innovation in Italian manufacturing firms, see Santarelli and Sterlacchini, 1990; Conte and Vivarelli, 2005).

DATA SET, INDICATORS AND METHODOLOGY

The empirical analysis is carried out using microdata drawn from the third Italian CIS, conducted over a three-year period (1998–2000) by the Italian National Institute of Statistics (ISTAT). This survey is representative at both the sector and the firm size level of the entire population of Italian firms with more than ten employees. The CIS 3 data set adopts a weighting procedure that relates the sample of firms interviewed to the entire population[8] (ISTAT, 2004).

The data set comprises a set of general information (main industry of affiliation, group belonging, turnover, employment, exports) and a (much larger) set of innovation variables measuring the firms' innovativeness, economic and non-economic measures of the effects of innovation, subjective evaluations of factors hampering or fostering innovation, participation in cooperative innovation activities and access to public funding. The response rate is 53 percent, determining a full sample size of 15 512 firms, 9034 of which (58.24 percent) are in the manufacturing sector, our focus of attention. The manufacturing sample is then cleaned of outliers and firms involved in mergers or acquisitions during the previous three years, which would have biased our results.[9] We end up with 7965 innovating and non-innovating firms.

The subsample of innovators is then selected following the standard practice of identifying innovators as those firms declaring that in the previous three years they had introduced product or process innovations, or had started innovative projects (then dropped or yet to complete at 31 December 2000). The same definition was implemented by ISTAT as a filter to save non-innovators having to answer all the questions not relevant to them (with the risk of non-innovating firms not responding to the rest of the questionnaire). Thus firms identified as non-innovators skipped a large number of 'innovation questions', leaving us with very little information about their propensity to innovate or to invest in innovative inputs. This means that the CIS database provides information relevant to this study only for innovative firms; therefore only these firms are considered in the following analysis,[10] a total of 3045 firms. This sample is further reduced to 2713 firms by keeping only firms investing in at least one of the four innovative inputs we focus on. Finally, young firms with fewer than eight years of activity were identified as YICs (293 out of 2713).[11]

Innovative Outputs

Innovative outputs can be distinguished by their position in the innovation process. For instance, while patents are better defined as the outcome of the inventive process, product innovation properly represents the result of the market-oriented innovative process. However, even though product innovation is driven by demand considerations, it represents a pre-market result. In contrast, the share of sales deriving from innovative products (Mairesse and Mohnen, 2002) represents an *ex post* result in which the market has positively welcomed the new products introduced by the firm (Barlet et al., 2000).

Taking these considerations and the interpretative background discussed earlier into account, this chapter uses two available output indicators for the empirical analysis: namely, the introduction of product innovation (*PROD*), and the share of turnover (sales) derived from innovative products (*TURNIN*).[12] It is worth noting that this sales-weighted measure of innovation is the only continuous output indicator provided by the

CIS and it indicates the intensity of innovation (Lööf and Heshmati, 2002; Mairesse and Mohnen, 2002).

Innovative Inputs

Bearing in mind the theoretical discussion presented in the second section, four innovative inputs are used in this chapter: (1) in-house and external expenditures in formal R&D (*intra muros* R&D = IR); (2) R&D outsourced to other firms or research institutes (*extra muros* R&D = ER); (3) expenditures in embodied technological change (innovative investment in equipment and machinery = MAC); and (4) expenditures in technology acquisition (disembodied technology such as know-how, projects and consultancies, licenses and software = TA).

Control Variables

CIS 3 provides further information on firms beyond their innovative activity. Econometric estimates in this chapter adopt some of these indicators as further controls and explanatory variables. Attention is paid to the following control variables:

1. Firm's export propensity (*EXPint*): global competition can spur innovation and capabilities, while technologically inactive firms are doomed to exclusion from the international arena (e.g. Archibugi and Iammarino, 1999; Narula and Zanfei, 2003).
2. Firm membership in an industrial group (*IG*): Mairesse and Mohnen (2002) underline the expected innovative benefits due to easier access to (internal) finance and to the effect of intra-group knowledge links for firms that are members of industrial groups.
3. Firm access to policy support (*SUPPORT*): a government subsidy or a fiscal incentive should increase a firm's innovative performance, although the empirical evidence on this is quite controversial.[13]
4. Firm participation in a cooperation agreement (*COOP*): for research regarding the important role of cooperation agreements in affecting the innovative output of firms, see Cassiman and Veugelers (2002), Piga and Vivarelli (2003, 2004), Fritsch and Franke (2004).
5. Appropriability: the availability and use of different instruments for achieving a larger degree of appropriability of the innovation rent, such as patents (*PATENT*), trademarks, secrecy etc. (*PROT*) (see Levin et al., 1987) should positively affect the innovative performance.
6. While the recognized obstacles to innovation (such as financial constraints or organizational hindrances) (*HURDLE*) should obviously hinder innovative performance, the occurrence of other forms of innovation (such as organizational change, see Bresnahan et al., 2002; Hitt and Brynjolfsson, 2002; Piva et al., 2005) (*OTHERIN*) should complement the four innovative inputs described in the previous section.

Finally Pavitt's sectoral dummies (Pavitt, 1984) were added to the econometric specification in order to control for the different sectoral technological opportunity and appropriability conditions.

Table 25.1   The variables

Innovative input variables

IRint	Internal R&D expenditure in 2000, normalized by total turnover
ERint	External R&D expenditure in 2000, normalized by total turnover
MACint	Investments in innovative machinery and equipment in 2000, normalized by total turnover
TAint	Technological acquisitions in 2000, normalized by total turnover

Innovative output variables

TURNIN	Share of firm's total sales due to sale of new products
PROD	Product innovation: dummy = 1 if TURNIN > 0

Firm's general characteristics

EXPint	Export intensity ((turnover from export) / turnover)
IG	Dummy = 1 if belonging to an industrial group

Innovative-relevant information

SUPPORT	Dummy = 1 if the firm has received public support for innovation
COOP	Dummy = 1 if the firm takes part in cooperative innovative activities
PATENT	Dummy = 1 if the firm uses patents
PROT	Dummy = 1 if the firm adopts other instruments of protection than patents
HURDLE	Dummy = 1 if the firm has faced some kind of obstacle to innovation
OTHERIN	Dummy = 1 if the firm has realized managerial, strategic or organizational innovation

Pavitt sectoral dummies

SB	Dummy = 1 if science-based firm
SI	Dummy = 1 if scale intensive firm
SS	Dummy = 1 if specialized supplier firm
SD	Dummy = 1 if supplier-dominated firm

Table 25.1 briefly describes the variables used in the empirical analysis, while Table 25.2 reports the corresponding descriptive statistics.[14]

Econometric Issues

Equation (25.1) describes the general specification adopted for the aggregate empirical test of the innovative input–output relationship:

$$TURNIN_i = C + \beta_1 IRint_i + \beta_2 ERint_i + \beta_3 MACint_i + \beta_4 TAint_i + \Sigma \beta_J X_{ji}$$

$$+ \Sigma \gamma_k PAVITT_{ki} + \varepsilon \tag{25.1}$$

where C is the constant, i is the firm-index, *TURNIN* represents the innovative output in terms of the percentage of sales due to innovative products, *IR*, *ER*, *MAC* and *TA* indicate the innovative inputs we are interested in, **X** is the vector of the (max $j = 8$)

Table 25.2 Descriptive statistics

	All firms				Mature firms				Young firms (YICs)			
	2713 OBS		2098 OBS		2420 OBS		1870 OBS		293 OBS		228 OBS	
	MEAN	SD	MEAN	SD	MEAN	SD	MEAN	SD	MEAN	SD	MEAN	SD
Innovative input variables												
IRint	0.013	0.026	0.015	0.028	0.013	0.025	0.015	0.027	0.014	0.032	0.017	0.036
ERint	0.002	0.009	0.002	0.010	0.002	0.008	0.002	0.009	0.002	0.011	0.003	0.013
MACint	0.035	0.078	0.028	0.067	0.034	0.076	0.027	0.063	0.042	0.091	0.038	0.093
TAint	0.002	0.018	0.002	0.015	0.002	0.017	0.002	0.013	0.004	0.023	0.004	0.025
Innovative output variables												
TURNIN	30.260	29.364	39.131	27.710	29.781	29.982	38.541	27.375	34.218	32.129	43.973	29.949
PROD (dummy)	0.773	0.419	1	0	0.773	0.419	1	0	0.778	0.416	1	0
Firm's general characteristics												
EXPint	0.254	0.285	0.278	0.290	0.259	0.286	0.283	0.290	0.215	0.279	0.235	0.286
IG (dummy)	0.291	0.454	0.318	0.466	0.290	0.454	0.318	0.466	0.300	0.459	0.316	0.466
Innovative-relevant information												
SUPPORT (dummy)	0.533	0.499	0.539	0.499	0.533	0.499	0.536	0.499	0.536	0.499	0.566	0.497
COOP (dummy)	0.161	0.368	0.192	0.394	0.162	0.369	0.193	0.395	0.150	0.358	0.180	0.385
PATENT (dummy)	0.348	0.476	0.413	0.492	0.354	0.478	0.420	0.494	0.293	0.456	0.360	0.481
PROT (dummy)	0.679	0.467	0.756	0.430	0.683	0.465	0.758	0.428	0.642	0.480	0.737	0.441
HURDLE (dummy)	0.402	0.490	0.424	0.494	0.397	0.489	0.418	0.493	0.440	0.497	0.474	0.500
OTHERIN (dummy)	0.841	0.365	0.886	0.318	0.838	0.369	0.884	0.320	0.874	0.333	0.899	0.302
Pavitt sectoral dummies												
SB (dummy)	0.116	0.320	0.134	0.341	0.113	0.316	0.130	0.337	0.140	0.347	0.167	0.373
SI (dummy)	0.284	0.451	0.250	0.433	0.282	0.450	0.248	0.432	0.300	0.459	0.267	0.444
SS (dummy)	0.280	0.449	0.314	0.464	0.282	0.450	0.318	0.466	0.266	0.443	0.285	0.452
SD (dummy)	0.320	0.466	0.301	0.459	0.323	0.468	0.304	0.460	0.293	0.456	0.281	0.450

control variables and *PAVITT* are the sectoral dummies (science-based, scale-intensive and specialized suppliers, with the suppliers-dominated as the default category; $k = 3$). Consistently with the dependent variable, the four innovative inputs were normalized by sales; this makes the inputs homogeneous to the output and also controls for the scale effect due to the different sizes of the investigated firms.

As a consequence of the questionnaire's design, the adopted sales-weighted measure of a firm's innovativeness (*TURNIN*) assumes a positive value only for firms that have introduced product innovation (*PROD*). This raises an obvious problem of sample selection that has to be dealt with. In particular, equation (25.1) was tested jointly with a selection probit equation (25.2) of the type:

$$P(PROD_i = 1) = C + \beta_1 IRint_i + \beta_2 ERint_i + \beta_3 MACint_i + \beta_4 TAint_i$$

$$+ \Sigma\beta_J Z_{ji} + \Sigma\gamma_k PAVITT_{ki} + \varepsilon_i \qquad (25.2)$$

where $\mathbf{Z}$ is an extended vector of controls in equation (25.1), with $\mathbf{X} \in \mathbf{Z}$.[15]

Both the high values of the correlation coefficients (ρ) between the selection and the main equation and the statistical significances of the Mills ratios in the three models (all firms, mature firms, YICs) (see Table 25.3) confirm the validity of the choice of a Heckman-type (see Heckman, 1979) specification.

EMPIRICAL RESULTS

Table 25.3 reports the econometric results of the sample selection model applied to the entire sample and separately to the two subsamples comprising the mature incumbents and the YICs. As can be seen, in-house R&D is important in increasing the likelihood of product innovation for the entire sample, although this link is less significant for the YICs. More importantly, and in contrast with the mature firms, innovation intensity (*TURNIN*) is not related to internal R&D (*IR*) as far as the YICs are concerned. Far from being NTBFs, Italian YICs do not turn out to be R&D-based, but rather depend on external sources of knowledge.

The above result becomes obvious if we turn our attention to the other three innovative inputs. Neither external research (*ER*) nor technological acquisition (*TA*) seem to play a significant role in spurring product innovation in Italian manufacturing firms. However, in contrast with what happens for well-established incumbents, its impact is positive, although not significant, with regard to the YICs. Although statistically insignificant, this outcome suggests a possible role of *ER* and *TA* in facilitating innovation in the young firms.

Much more statistically robust is the outcome concerning the 'embodied technical change' variable, *MAC*. While rendering product innovation less likely,[16] *MAC* is positively and significantly (1 percent) linked to the innovation intensity in all the three models.

However, the coefficient is more than double the size for YICs. This means that Italian YICs are particularly dependent on the embodied technical change incorporated in machinery and equipment purchased from external sources. Together with what was found in relation to the non-significant impact of *IR*, this means that the investigated

Table 25.3 The sample selection estimates

	All firms		Mature firms		YICs	
	PROD	*TURNIN*	*PROD*	*TURNIN*	*PROD*	*TURNIN*
Constant	−0.19**	16.32***	−0.16*	19.91***	−0.25	11.97
	(−2.13)	(3.01)	(−1.79)	(3.60)	(−0.83)	(0.85)
IRint	15.17***	128.87***	15.23***	128.32***	14.42*	79.93
	(7.20)	(4.62)	(6.91)	(4.29)	(1.90)	(1.16)
ERint	7.75	25.89	8.47	−1.26	2.59	135.70
	(1.24)	(0.37)	(1.25)	(−0.02)	(0.14)	(0.79)
MACint	−1.11***	31.62***	−1.38***	26.78**	0.19	68.25***
	(−3.23)	(3.07)	(−3.61)	(2.32)	(0.20)	(3.03)
TAint	−0.32	−35.37	−0.25	−68.99	−0.90	37.25
	(−0.20)	(−0.87)	(−0.15)	(−1.47)	(−0.21)	(0.43)
EXPint	0.10	2.98	0.11	1.54	0.04	16.83**
	(0.89)	(1.29)	(0.93)	(0.65)	(0.11)	(2.14)
IG	0.01		0.02		−0.11	
	(0.19)		(0.24)		(−0.48)	
SUPPORT	−0.09		−0.13**		0.38*	
	(−1.43)		(−2.00)		(1.88)	
COOP	0.37***	3.30*	0.38***	2.99*	0.53	1.49
	(3.55)	(1.86)	(3.39)	(1.65)	(1.44)	(0.25)
PATENT	0.48***		0.47***		0.66**	
	(6.21)		(5.85)		(2.20)	
PROT	0.46***	5.34**	0.43***	4.68**	0.72***	5.68
	(6.95)	(2.41)	(6.12)	(2.11)	(3.50)	(0.75)
HURDLE	−0.01	−2.05	−0.022	−2.80**	0.08	2.44
	(−0.09)	(−1.60)	(−0.34)	(−2.11)	(0.39)	(0.57)
OTHERIN	0.42***	6.98***	0.45***	6.18**	0.15	5.28
	(5.47)	(2.97)	(5.54)	(2.52)	(0.58)	(0.76)
SB	0.18	8.25***	0.13	6.12***	0.56	19.75***
	(1.46)	(3.67)	(1.03)	(2.63)	(1.38)	(2.81)
SI	−0.08	−0.10	−0.08	0.09	−0.26	−0.61
	(−1.20)	(−0.06)	(−1.13)	(0.05)	(−1.15)	(−0.11)
SS	0.35***	7.45***	0.37***	6.68***	0.20	6.74
	(4.41)	(4.05)	(4.30)	(3.53)	(0.80)	(1.18)
ρ		0.62		0.48		0.85
Mills λ		18.04***		13.57**		27.20*
		(2.98)		(2.19)		(1.75)
No. of firms	2713	2098	2420	1870	293	228

Notes: z-statistics in parentheses. * significant at 10%; ** 5%; *** 1%.

YICs lack endogenous technological capabilities, while they are massively dependent on technologies coming from other firms through input–output relationships. On the whole, these results highlight a potential weakness of Italian YICs, which seem to lack an endogenous capacity to sustain their own innovative activities.

Briefly looking at the control variables, not surprisingly it is clear that exporting and science-based YICs are more likely to perform better in terms of innovative intensity. Instead, and in contrast with the mature firms, YICs do not seem to be established enough to be responsive to variables such as *HURDLE, OTHERIN* and *PROT.* This can be seen as a sign that these firms are still too young and inexperienced to set up a proper appropriability regime and to develop complementary innovative strategies.

CONCLUDING REMARKS

This chapter discusses the determinants of innovative output in YICs and mature firms by looking both at firms' internal and external R&D activities and at the acquisition of external technology in its embodied and disembodied components. These input–output relationships are tested through a sample selection procedure that takes into account the fact that our measure of innovative performance only refers to product innovation.

Looking at the aggregate results, it turns out that in-house R&D is closely linked to innovative performance, while external R&D does not seem to play a relevant role in Italian manufacturing. However, once the YICs are distinguished from the established firms, in the former, internal R&D expenditures no longer play a role in increasing inno- vation intensity, although it does increase the probability of engaging in product innova- tion. The crucial innovative input for YICs turns out to be the external acquisition of technology in its embodied component (*MAC*). This input is also positive and significant with regard to the mature firms, but it more than doubles in the case of the YICs.

These results suggest that in a intermediate-technology context such as Italian manu- facturing where middle-tech and traditional sectors represent the core of the industrial structure, on average YICs cannot be considered as new technology-based firms. Rather, they appear to be entrepreneurial entities that need to acquire external knowledge in order to foster their own innovation activity and are therefore crucially dependent on the external environment.

ACKNOWLEDGMENT

The authors would like to thank Andrea Conte, Giovanni Seri and the ADELE Laboratory at ISTAT in Rome for the provision of CIS 3 data.

NOTES

1. For instance, several EU member states have introduced new measures to support the creation and growth of YICs, especially by improving their access to funding (see BEPA, 2008; Schneider and Veugelers, 2008).
2. The other two equations in Griliches's simultaneous model represent the production function (augmented by the innovation term) and the determinants of R&D investment. See also Hall (1996, 2000), Mairesse and Mohnen (2002), Harhoff et al. (2003) and Hall et al. (2005).
3. Patents turn out to be a very rough proxy of innovation for several reasons: (1) not all innovations are patented (firms generally prefer other ways of protecting innovations, see Levin et al., 1987); (2) patents are very rare among small innovative firms and YICs; (3) patents differ greatly in inherent importance; (4)

firms in different sectors have very different propensities to patent (see Archibugi and Pianta, 1992; Patel and Pavitt, 1995).

4. This broader perspective is also endorsed in methodological advice as to the collection of data regarding innovation; in particular, this is well represented by the shift from the R&D-focused Frascati Manual ('Guidelines for the collection of R&D data', first published in 1963) to the *Oslo Manual* in the 1990s (OECD, 1997).
5. The embodied nature of technological progress and the effects related to its spread in the economy were originally discussed by Salter (1960); in particular, vintage capital models describe an endogenous process of innovation in which the replacement of old equipment is the main way through which firms update their own technologies (see also Jorgenson, 1966; Hulten, 1992; Greenwood et al. 1997).
6. See Nelson and Winter (1982) and Dosi (1988) for an extended and more articulated view of the innovative process across firms.
7. This seems to be the view implicitly accepted in the literature on the so-called 'New Technology-Based Firms' (NTBFs; see Storey and Tether, 1998; Colombo and Grilli, 2005), where only YICs in the high-tech sectors are analyzed; in contrast, in this chapter YICs across all sectors are studied. While in this study we compare YICs with mature innovative incumbents, a related stream of literature investigates the role of innovation in facilitating the entry and post-entry performance of newborn firms (see Audretsch and Vivarelli, 1996; Arrighetti and Vivarelli, 1999; Cefis and Marsili, 2006). Finally, in this chapter only innovative firms are studied, while another related field of study investigates the different propensity to innovate according to a firm's age (see Hansen, 1992; Huergo and Jaumandreu, 2004).
8. Firm selection was carried out through a 'one-step stratified sample design'. The sample in each stratum was selected with equal probability and without reimmission. The stratification of the sample was based on the following three variables: firm size, sector, regional location. Technically, in the generic stratum h, the random selection of $n_{\{h\}}$ sample observations among the $N_{\{h\}}$ belonging to the entire population was realized through the following procedure:

    *   a random number in the 0–1 interval was attributed to each N_h population unit;
    * N_h population units were sorted by increasing values of the random number;
    *   units in the first n_h positions in the order previously mentioned were selected.

    Estimates obtained from the selected sample are very close to the actual values in the national population. The weighting procedure follows Eurostat and *Oslo Manual* (OECD, 1997) recommendations: weights indicate the inverse of the probability that the observation is sampled. Therefore sampling weights ensure that each group of firms is properly represented and correct for sample selection. Moreover, sampling weights help in reducing heteroscedasticity commonly arising when the analysis focuses on survey data.
9. In fact, mergers and acquisitions may break the link between innovative inputs and outputs (a link that must be studied within the context of a single firm).
10. Given that our aim is to analyze the nature of the relationships within the innovative process (and not, for example, the effect of different inputs in determining the probability of innovating), this data limitation does not raise a problem of selection bias. Since we are interested in the internal mechanisms of the innovative process, we focus on a randomly selected sample of innovative firms (i.e. randomness must hold *within* the innovative subsample, not in comparison with the non-innovative one where such mechanisms are obviously absent). For a study based on a comparison *between* innovative and non-innovative Italian firms, see Parisi et al. (2006).
11. As far as the age of the firms in the 'young firms' subsample is concerned, the threshold of eight years was chosen to take into account the trade-off between a lower age and the representativeness of the subsample of YICs (here almost 10 percent of the entire sample). However, the estimates used here were replicated using a larger sample of young firms no more than ten years old. The results, available from the authors upon request, do not change substantially.
12. It is worth emphasizing the link adopted in the questionnaire design; this link goes from product innovation to the sales ratio indicator since only firms that have introduced product innovation can record a positive percentage of their sales as being derived from product innovation. This raises an issue of sample selection that will be discussed in the next methodological subsection.
13. In fact, while public funding should stimulate (in absolute terms) both the input and the output side of innovation, a crowding-out effect seems to operate, displacing (totally or partly) privately funded innovation activities. Using a data set of firms that benefited from the Small Business Innovation Research Program, Wallsten (2000) even comes to the conclusion that R&D grants completely crowd out firm-financed R&D spending, dollar for dollar. The view of Gonzáles et al. (2005) is much more optimistic: they found no evidence of crowding out. Using an unbalanced panel of more than 2000 Spanish manufacturing firms, the authors show that government intervention stimulates R&D activities. Midway between

14. In Appendix 25A.1 the sectoral compositions of the two subsamples of mature firms and YICs are reported: as can be seen, with regard to most sectors no significant differences emerge; however, to be on the safe side, all the regressions were controlled for Pavitt's sectoral dummies. In Appendix 25A.2, the correlation matrix for the entire sample is reported; as can be seen, all the correlation coefficients are less than 0.371, showing that data are not affected by serious collinearity problems. Corresponding tables for the subsamples of only the innovative firms are available upon request. Finally, Appendix 25A.3 reports the CIS questions on the basis of which the variables were constructed.

15. **X** and **Z** were differentiated, taking into account the statistical significance of the different controls in the two equations, the occurrence of convergence in all the three models and the need for a homogeneous comparison between them. However, results are robust to different specifications of the sample selection model (available upon request).

16. This result is consistent with previous studies (see Conte and Vivarelli, 2005) and is not surprising; indeed, it can be seen as a direct consequence of the sample selection procedure. In fact, MAC is strictly related to process innovation, which is the innovative category excluded in the selected sample. The 615 excluded firms are those only engaged in process innovation, while the 2098 firms included are those exhibiting either product innovation only or product and process innovation jointly.

REFERENCES

Acs, Z.J. and D.B. Audretsch (1988), 'Innovation in large and small firms: an empirical analysis', *The American Economic Review*, **78** (4), 678–90.
Acs, Zoltan J. and David B. Audretsch (1990), *Innovation and Small Firms*, Cambridge, MA: MIT Press.
Acs, Z.J., D.B. Audretsch and M.P. Feldman (1994), 'R&D spillovers and recipient firm size', *The Review of Economics and Statistics*, **76** (2), 336–40.
Archibugi, D. and S. Iammarino (1999), 'The policy implications of the globalisation of innovation', *Research Policy*, **28** (2–3), 317–36.
Archibugi, Daniele and Mario Pianta (1992), *The Technological Specialization of Advanced Countries: A Report to the EEC on International Science and Technology Activities*, Boston, MA: Kluwer Academic Publishers.
Arrighetti, A. and M. Vivarelli (1999), 'The role of innovation in the post-entry performance of new small firms: evidence from Italy', *Southern Economic Journal*, **65** (4), 927–39.
Arrow, K. (1962), 'The economic implications of learning by doing', *Review of Economic Studies*, **29** (3), 155–73.
Audretsch, D. and M. Vivarelli (1996), 'Determinants of new-firm startups in Italy', *Empirica*, **23** (2), 91–105.
Barlet, Corinne, Emmanuel Duguet, David Encaoua and Jacqueline Pradel (2000), 'The commercial success of innovations: an econometric analysis at the firm level in French manufacturing', in David Encaoua, Bronwyn H. Hall, François Laisney and Jacques Mairesse (eds), *The Economics and Econometrics of Innovation*, Boston, MA: Kluwer Academic Publishers, pp. 435–56.
Bartelsman, E., J. Haltiwanger and S. Scarpetta (2004), 'Microeconometric evidence of creative destruction in industrial and developing countries', IZA Discussion Paper No. 1374.
BEPA (2008), *Innovation and Growth in the EU: The Role of SME Policy*, Brussels: European Commission.
Breschi, S., F. Malerba and L. Orsenigo (2000), 'Technological regimes and Schumpeterian patterns of innovation', *The Economic Journal*, **110** (463), 388–410.
Bresnahan, T.F., E. Brynjolfsson and L.M. Hitt (2002), 'Information technology, workplace organization and the demand for skilled labor: firm-level evidence', *Quarterly Journal of Economics*, **117** (1), 339–76.
Busom, I. (2000), 'An empirical evaluation of the effects of R&D subsidies', *Economics of Innovation and New Technology*, **9** (2), 111–48.
Cassiman, B. and R. Veugelers (2002), 'R&D cooperation and spillovers: some empirical evidence from Belgium', *The American Economic Review*, **92** (4), 1169–84.
Cefis, E. and O. Marsili (2006), 'Survivor: the role of innovation in firm's survival', *Research Policy*, **35** (5), 626–41.
Cohen, W.M. and S. Klepper (1996), 'A reprise of size and R&D', *The Economic Journal*, **106** (437), 925–51.
Colombo, M.G. and L. Grilli (2005), 'Founders' human capital and the growth of new technology-based firms: a competence-based view', *Research Policy*, **34** (6), 795–816.
Conte, A. and M. Vivarelli (2005), 'One or many knowledge production functions? Mapping innovative activity using microdata', IZA Discussion Paper No. 1878.
Crépon, B., E. Duguet and J. Mairesse (1998), 'Research, innovation and productivity: an econometric analysis at the firm level', *Economics of Innovation and New Technology*, **7** (2), 115–58.

Dosi, G. (1988), 'Sources, procedures, and microeconomic effects of innovation', *Journal of Economic Literature*, **26** (3), 1120–71.

Freeman, Christopher (1982), *The Economics of Industrial Innovation*, 2nd edn, London: Pinter.

Freeman, Christopher (1987), *Technology Policy and Economic Performance. Lessons from Japan*, London: Pinter.

Freeman, Christopher, John Clark and Luc Soete (1982), *Unemployment and Technical Innovation: A Study of Long Waves in Economic Development*, London: Pinter.

Freeman, Christopher and Luc Soete (1987), *Technical Change and Full Employment*, London: Basil Blackwell.

Fritsch, M. and G. Franke (2004), 'Innovation, regional knowledge spillovers and R&D cooperation', *Research Policy*, **33** (2), 245–55.

Gilbert, R. and D. Newbery (1982), 'Preemptive patenting and the persistence of monopoly', *The American Economic Review*, **72** (3), 514–26.

Gonzáles, X., J. Jaumandreu and C. Pazó (2005), 'Barriers to innovation and subsidy effectiveness', *The RAND Journal of Economics*, **36** (4), 930–49.

Greenwood, J., Z. Hercowitz and P. Krusell (1997), 'Long-run implications of investment-specific technological change', *The American Economic Review*, **87** (3), 342–62.

Griliches, Z. (1979), 'Issues in assessing the contribution of research and development to productivity growth', *The Bell Journal of Economics*, **10** (1), 92–116.

Griliches, Z. (1990), 'Patent statistics as economic indicators: a survey', *Journal of Economic Literature*, **28** (4), 1661–707.

Hall, Bronwyn H. (1996), 'The private and social returns to research and development', in Bruce L.R. Smith and Claude E. Barfield (eds), *Technology, R&D, and the Economy*, Washington, DC: Brookings Institution and American Enterprise Institute, pp. 140–83.

Hall, Bronwyn H. (2000), 'Innovation and market value', in Ray Barrell, Geoff Mason and Mary O'Mahoney (eds), *Productivity, Innovation and Economic Performance*, Cambridge: Cambridge University Press, pp. 177–98.

Hall, B.H., A. Jaffe and M. Trajtenberg (2005), 'Market value and patent citations', *Rand Journal of Economics*, **36** (1), 16–38.

Hansen, J.A. (1992), 'Innovation, firm size, and firm age', *Small Business Economics*, **4** (1), 37–44.

Harhoff, D., F.M. Scherer and K. Vopel (2003), 'Citations, family size, opposition, and the value of patent rights', *Research Policy*, **32** (8), 1343–64.

Heckman J. (1979), 'Sample selection as a specification error', *Econometrica*, **47** (1), 153–61.

Hitt, Laurin M. and Erik Brynjolfsson (2002), 'Information technology, organizational transformation, and business performance', in Nathalie Greenan, Yannick L'Horty and Jacques Mairesse (eds), *Productivity, Inequality, and the Digital Economy. A Transatlantic Perspective*, Cambridge, MA: MIT Press, pp. 55–91.

Huergo, E. and J. Jaumandreu (2004), 'How does probability of process innovation change with firm age', *Small Business Economics*, **22** (3–4), 193–207.

Hulten, C.R. (1992), 'Growth accounting when technical change is embodied in capital', *The American Economic Review*, **82** (4), 964–80.

ISTAT (2004), '*Statistiche sull'Innovazione delle Imprese. Settore Industria. Anni 1998–2000*', Rome: ISTAT.

Jorgenson, D.W. (1966), 'The embodiment hypothesis', *Journal of Political Economy*, **74** (1), 1–17.

Levin, R., A. Klevorick, R. Nelson and S. Winter (1987), 'Appropriating the returns from industrial R-D', *Brookings Papers of Economic Activity*, **3**, 783–831.

Lööf, H. and A. Heshmati (2001), 'On the relationship between innovation and performance: a sensitivity analysis', ECIS – Stockholm School of Economics, Working Paper Series in Economics and Finance No. 446.

Lööf, H. and A. Heshmati (2002), 'Knowledge capital and performance heterogeneity: a firm-level innovation study', *International Journal of Production Economics*, **76** (1), 61–85.

Lundvall, Bengt-Åke (1992), *National Systems of Innovation*, London: Pinter.

Mairesse, J. and P. Mohnen (2002), 'Accounting for innovation and measuring innovativeness: an illustrative framework and an application', *The American Economic Review, Papers and Proceedings*, **92** (2), 226–30.

Malerba, F. (1992), 'Learning by firms and incremental technical change', *Economic Journal*, **102** (413), 845–59.

Malerba, Franco (1993), 'The National System of Innovation: Italy', in Richard R. Nelson (ed.), *National Systems of Innovation: a Comparative Study*, Oxford: Oxford University Press, pp. 230–60.

Malerba, F. and L. Orsenigo (1996), 'Schumpeterian patterns of innovation', *Cambridge Journal of Economics*, **19** (1), 47–65.

Narula, Rajneesh and Antonello Zanfei (2003), 'The international dimension of innovation', in Jan Fagerberg, David C. Mowery and Richard R. Nelson (eds), *The Oxford Handbook of Innovation*, Oxford: Oxford University Press, pp. 318–45.

Nelson, Richard R. (1993), *National Innovation Systems: A Comparative Analysis*, Oxford: Oxford University Press.

Nelson, Richard R. and Sidney G. Winter (1982), *An Evolutionary Theory of Economic Change*, Cambridge, MA: Harvard University Press.

OECD (1997), *Oslo Manual: The Measurement of Scientific and Technological Activities. Proposed Guideline for Collecting and Interpreting Technological Innovation Data*, Paris: OECD.

Parisi, M.L., F. Schiantarelli and A. Sembenelli (2006), 'Productivity, innovation and R&D: micro evidence for Italy', *European Economic Review*, **50** (8), 2037–61.

Patel, Pari and Keith Pavitt (1995), 'Patterns of technological activity: their measurement and interpretation', in Paul Stoneman (ed.), *Handbook of the Economics of Innovation and Technological Change*, Oxford: Blackwell Publishers, pp. 14–51.

Pavitt, K. (1984), 'Sectoral patterns of technical change: towards a taxonomy and a theory', *Research Policy*, **13** (6), 343–73.

Piga, C.A. and M. Vivarelli (2003), 'Sample selection in estimating the determinants of cooperative R&D', *Applied Economics Letters*, **10** (4), 243–6.

Piga, C.A. and M. Vivarelli (2004), 'Internal and external R&D: a sample selection approach', *Oxford Bulletin of Economics and Statistics*, **66** (4), 457–82.

Piva, M., E. Santarelli and M. Vivarelli (2005), 'The skill bias effect of technological and organisational change: evidence and policy implications', *Research Policy*, **34** (2), 141–57.

Salter, W.E.G. (1960), *Productivity and Technical Change*, Cambridge: Cambridge University Press.

Santamaría, L., M.J. Nieto and A. Barge-Gil (2009), 'Beyond formal R&D: taking advantage of other sources of innovation in low- and medium-technology industries', *Research Policy*, **38** (3), 507–17.

Santarelli, E. and A. Sterlacchini (1990), 'Innovation, formal vs. informal R&D, and firm size: some evidence from Italian manufacturing firms', *Small Business Economics*, **2** (2), 223–8.

Santarelli, E. and M. Vivarelli (2007), 'Entrepreneurship and the process of firms' entry, survival and growth', *Industrial and Corporate Change*, **16** (3), 455–88.

Schneider, C. and R. Veugelers (2008), 'On young innovative companies: why they matter and how (not) to policy support them', Department of Economics, Copenhagen Business School Working Paper 4-2008.

Schumpeter, Joseph A. (1934) *The Theory of Economic Development*, Cambridge, MA: Harvard University Press.

Schumpeter, Joseph A. (1942), *Capitalism, Socialism and Democracy*, New York: Harper & Brothers.

Storey, D.J. and B.S. Tether (1998), 'New technology-based firms in the European Union: an introduction', *Research Policy*, **26** (9), 933–46.

Wallsten, S.J. (2000), 'The effects of government–industry R&D programs on private R&D: the case of the Small Business Innovation Research Program', *The RAND Journal of Economics*, **31** (1), 82–100.

Winter, S.G. (1984), 'Schumpeterian competition in alternative technological regimes', *Journal of Economic Behavior and Organization*, **5** (3), 287–320.

APPENDIX 25A.1

Table 25A.1 *Sectoral composition and average employment of the firms belonging to the two subsamples: YICs and mature firms*

Industry	YICs			Mature firms		
	No. of firms	%	Av. emp.	No. of firms	%	Av. emp.
Manufacture of food products and beverage	14	4.8	136	152	6.3	210
Manufacture of textiles	13	4.4	107	110	4.5	205
Manufacture of wearing apparel; dressing and dyeing of fur	6	2.0	47	43	1.8	131
Manufacture of leather and related products	7	2.4	73	58	2.4	83
Manufacture of wood and of products of wood and cork, exc. furniture	9	3.1	26	80	3.3	55
Manufacture of paper and paper products	8	2.7	65	72	3.0	89
Printing and reproduction of recorded media	10	3.4	34	124	5.1	97
Manufacture of coke and refined petroleum products	5	1.7	139	18	0.7	52
Manufacture of chemicals and chemical products	27	9.2	191	200	8.3	189
Manufacture of rubber and plastics products	15	5.1	62	151	6.2	128
Manufacture of other non-metallic mineral products	17	5.8	37	152	6.3	173
Manufacture of basic metals	18	6.1	133	94	3.9	335
Manufacture of fabricated metal products	26	8.9	79	194	8.0	115
Manufacture of machinery and mechanical equipment	37	12.6	197	292	12.1	252
Manufacture of office machinery and computers	7	2.4	26	33	1.4	82
Manufacture of electrical equipment	13	4.4	96	154	6.4	174
Manufacture of radio, television and communication equipment	9	3.1	277	97	4.0	222
Manufacture of medical, precision and optical instruments	23	7.8	118	126	5.2	75
Manufacture of motor vehicles, trailers and semi-trailers	11	3.8	77	84	3.5	460
Manufacture of other transport equipment	8	2.7	73	49	2.0	646
Other manufacturing	8	2.7	53	124	5.1	91
Waste collection, treatment and disposal activities; materials recovery	2	0.7	15	13	0.5	17
Sample	293	100		2420	100	

APPENDIX 25A.2

Table 25A.2   Correlation matrix (entire sample: 2713 firms)

	PROD	IRint	ERint	MACint	TAint	EXPint	OTHERIN	IG	SUPPORT	COOP	PATENT	PROT	HURDLE
PROD	1.000												
IRint	0.186	1.000											
ERint	0.093	0.245	1.000										
MACint	−0.159	−0.069	−0.046	1.000									
TAint	−0.007	0.026	0.044	0.034	1.000								
EXPint	0.160	0.050	0.041	−0.167	−0.037	1.000							
OTHERIN	0.223	0.062	0.049	−0.093	0.027	0.163	1.000						
IG	0.110	0.024	0.057	−0.115	−0.008	0.243	0.109	1.000					
SUPPORT	0.021	0.178	0.061	0.060	0.003	0.055	0.031	0.000	1.000				
COOP	0.156	0.173	0.168	−0.074	0.014	0.159	0.105	0.249	0.118	1.000			
PATENT	0.253	0.096	0.102	−0.141	0.020	0.304	0.171	0.241	0.055	0.196	1.000		
PROT	0.306	0.150	0.099	−0.134	−0.003	0.240	0.311	0.185	0.059	0.186	0.370	1.000	
HURDLE	0.083	0.100	0.091	−0.018	0.036	0.048	0.139	0.000	0.002	0.093	0.116	0.152	1.000
SB	0.108	0.234	0.220	−0.054	0.001	0.048	0.059	0.050	0.019	0.127	0.135	0.140	0.051
SI	−0.139	−0.077	−0.090	0.107	0.017	−0.149	−0.073	−0.015	0.008	−0.031	−0.121	−0.126	−0.058
SS	0.138	0.065	0.037	−0.094	−0.024	0.154	0.010	0.041	0.031	0.077	0.114	0.059	0.042
SD	−0.073	−0.149	−0.100	0.024	0.006	−0.038	0.020	−0.059	−0.051	−0.130	−0.086	−0.031	−0.020

APPENDIX 25A.3

Table 25A.3   The questionnaire

Innovative input variables

Did your enterprise engage in the following innovation activities in 2000?

IR: Intramural research & experimental development (R&D)	All creative work undertaken within your enterprise on a systematic basis in order to increase the stock of knowledge, and the use of this stock of knowledge to devise new applications, such as new and improved products (goods/services) and processes (including software research)
ER: Acquisition of R&D (extramural R&D)	Same activities as above, but performed by other companies (including other enterprises within the group) or other public or private research organizations
MAC: Acquisition of machinery and equipment	Advanced machinery, computer hardware specifically purchased to implement new or significantly improved products (goods/services) and/or processes
TA: Acquisition of other external knowledge	Purchase of rights to use patents and non-patented inventions, licenses, know-how, trademarks, software and other types of knowledge from others for use in your enterprise's innovations

---

Innovative output variable: *TURNIN*

Estimate how your turnover in 2000 was distributed between:
- New or significantly improved products (goods or services) introduced during the period 1998–2000
- Unchanged or only marginally modified products (goods or services) during the period 1998–2000

Firm's general characteristics

IG	• Is your enterprise part of an enterprise group?

Innovative-relevant information

SUPPORT	• Did your enterprise receive any public financial support for innovation activities during the period 1998–2000? (from: local or regional authorities; central government; the European Union) • Has your enterprise received funding from the EU's 4th (1994–98) or 5th (1998–2002) Framework Programmes for RTD?
COOP	• Did your enterprise have any cooperation arrangements on innovation activities with other enterprises or institutions during 1998–2000?
PATENT	• Did your enterprise, or enterprise group, have any valid patents at the end of 2000 protecting inventions or innovations developed by your enterprise?
PROT	• During the period 1998–2000, did your enterprise, or enterprise group, make use of any of these other methods to protect inventions or innovations developed in your enterprise? (such as registration of design patterns; trademarks; copyright; secrecy; complexity of design; lead-time advantage on competitors)

Table 25A.3   (continued)

Innovative-relevant information	

OTHERIN	• Did your enterprise during the period 1998–2000 undertake any of the following activities?
	  – Strategy (implementation of new or significantly changed corporate strategies)
	  – Management (implementation of advanced management techniques within your enterprise)
	  – Organization (implementation of new or significantly changed organizational structures)
	  – Marketing (changing significantly your enterprise's marketing concepts/strategies)
	  – Aesthetic change (significant changes in the aesthetic appearance or design or other subjective changes in at least one of your products)

HURDLE	• Did your enterprise experience any hampering factors during the period 1998–2000? Economics factors (excessive perceived economic risks; innovation costs too high; lack of appropriate sources of finance); internal factors (organizational rigidities within the enterprise; lack of qualified personnel; lack of information on technology; lack of information on markets); other factors (insufficient flexibility of regulations or standards; lack of customer responsiveness to new goods or services)

26 Entrepreneurship, innovation and institutions
Erik Stam and Bart Nooteboom

INTRODUCTION

In a context of increasing international competition and ageing populations, many Western governments feel the urge to stimulate innovation in order to secure long-term wealth creation. This means that next to the traditional economic criteria of efficiency and equity, innovation is now a more central criterion for economic policy. Innovation is also seen as a tool to move nations through economic crises more quickly and position the nations to have a stronger economy as crises ease. Economic crises may also yield an opportunity to turn destruction into the creative destruction of innovation. Several policy instruments are considered in innovation policy, ranging from investments in public R&D, subsidizing private R&D and cooperation for innovation, to stimulating entrepreneurship. The latter area is receiving increasing attention in innovation policy. The popularity of a policy instrument is not necessarily an indication of consensus about its effectiveness, or clarity about its content. Entrepreneurship is a fuzzy concept that is used in a confusing way not only in policy, but in academia as well. The same is true for innovation. Nevertheless, there are multiple arguments that innovation is a key mechanism through which entrepreneurs drive economic growth (see, e.g., Audretsch et al., 2006; Baumol, 2002; Landes, 1998; Rosenberg and Birdzell, 1986).

In this chapter we provide a definition of entrepreneurship in the context of innovation, and discuss its role within a cycle of innovation. This cycle of innovation reflects the growth of knowledge in society: innovation is based on the knowledge base of a society and expands this innate knowledge base (cf. Nooteboom, 2000; Metcalfe, 2002). Increasing the set of future economic choices seems to be a reasonable policy in a context of radical uncertainty (Moreau, 2004, p. 866):

> One of the main roles of public policy is indeed to minimise the risks of technological or behavioural lock-in by maintaining some diversity among the characteristics of market participants and thus in the economic trajectories followed. The central policy problem becomes that of increasing the probability and the profitability of experimental behaviour. Thus the attention of the evolutionary policy-maker shifts away from efficiency towards creativity. Nelson and Winter (1982) underline that when the neoclassical hypothesis of a given opportunity set is relaxed, the role of the state becomes to discover and to extend this opportunity set rather than to choose among this set to maximise a hypothetical social welfare function.

Different types of innovation along the cycle of innovation are realized with different forms of entrepreneurship, which are constrained or enabled by different legal institutions. One of the key roles of governments is to design, change or destroy institutions in order to improve societal welfare. Governments typically have the authority to do this. We explicitly take the destruction of institutions into account, because (a) it is often much harder to abolish institutions than to create them, and (b) 'inefficient economic institutions are the rule, not the exception' (North, 1990a, p. 191). The question is what governments should do in the context of innovation policy. Here, social scientists can make a contribution by providing insight into what entrepreneurship and innovation are (theories about these phenomena), and how institutions affect them in reality (empirical evidence about their effects). This requires social scientists to be engaged scholars (cf. Van de Ven, 2007) and to provide new policy options as an honest broker between the academic world and the policy world (Pielke, 2007). With respect to institutions, the demand for social science knowledge is derived from the demand for institutional change (Ruttan, 2006; 2008). Advances in social science could then be useful in policy practice. The key question of this chapter is: how can policy best enable innovation-based entrepreneurship? The answer is derived from looking at both theoretical tenets and empirical evidence using an institutional design perspective, which aims at providing arguments for the design, change and/or destruction of institutions, given the goals of the governments. This perspective is closely linked to the new institutional economics (North, 1990b; Williamson, 2000) and mechanism design theory (Cramton, 2008; Myerson, 2008; Ruttan, 2008).

Traditionally economics deals principally with institutions in a minimal form, e.g. the necessity of institutions that secure property rights for markets to work. New approaches recognize that different institutions are appropriate in different circumstances, and deal with the positive and normative aspects of institutional diversity (cf. Djankov et al., 2003). According to the institutional economic approach to entrepreneurship, the rules of the game (institutions) that specify the relative payoffs to different entrepreneurial activities play a key role in determining whether entrepreneurship is allocated in productive or unproductive ways (Baumol, 1990; cf. Murphy et al., 1991).

From a policy perspective the issue at stake is how to design an innovation policy that targets but does not attempt to predetermine the outcomes of industrial development (as was the case with state investment planning in targeted industrial policies). This kind of innovation policy design falls between the targeted industrial policies that are (to some extent) determined by special interest groups on the one extreme, and general economic policies (like fiscal incentives for innovation investments and public investments in education and research) at the other. Targeted industrial policies are a reflection of a belief in the ability to optimally plan the allocation of resources in society. This is at odds with the fundamentally uncertain and unpredictable nature of innovation. The latter characteristics do not preclude any role for government, however. The role of government is to design institutions that enable the creativity that facilitates innovation, ultimately supporting economic progress (cf. McCloskey, 1997). From an institutional design perspective, social science knowledge can play an important role in the rational design of institutional reform and institutional innovation.

This chapter starts with a discussion of the nature of entrepreneurship and its relation to innovation. The next section provides a conceptual elaboration of innovation along a cycle in which exploration and exploration follow upon each other: this goes beyond the Schumpeterian notion of the innovation process that runs from exploration to exploitation only. We place the roles of entrepreneurship in innovation policy within this cycle of innovation. After these conceptual investigations of entrepreneurship and innovation, institutions move centre stage. In this final section we provide an overview of some (empirically tested) institutions that enable or restrain particular types of entrepreneurship. Examples of these institutions are intellectual property rights and the Small Business Innovation Research programme (for new technology-based firms), employment protection (for high-growth start-ups) and non-compete covenants (for spin-offs).

ENTREPRENEURSHIP AND INNOVATION

What is meant by entrepreneurship and how does it relate to innovation? Entrepreneurship and innovation are fuzzy concepts with multiple meanings. Innovation and entrepreneurship are often regarded as overlapping concepts. This can be traced back to the definition entrepreneurship put forward by Schumpeter (1934, p. 74), who defines entrepreneurs as individuals carrying out new combinations (i.e. innovations). Schumpeter distinguishes four roles in the process of innovation: the inventor, who invents a new idea; the entrepreneur, who commercializes this new idea; the capitalist, who provides the financial resources to the entrepreneur (and bears the risk of the innovation project); and the manager, who takes care of the routine day-to-day corporate management. These roles are usually filled by different individuals (see, e.g., Kenney, 1986). The literature on entrepreneurship recognizes a variety of entrepreneurial roles in economic change, all implicitly carrying with them an economically positive connotation. However, if entrepreneurs are defined to be persons who are ingenious and creative in finding ways that add to their own wealth, power and prestige (Baumol, 1990), then it is expected that not all activities will deliver a productive contribution to society (cf. Murphy et al., 1991). There are various other reasons why many entrepreneurs do not directly contribute to an increase in national income: some entrepreneurship is more adequately characterized as a non-profit-seeking activity (cf. Benz, 2006). Greater independence and self-fulfilment are more often mentioned as important motivations to become self-employed than increasing earning power (EOS Gallup, 2004). Empirical studies show that (on average) entry into self-employment has a negative effect on the monetary income of individuals (Hamilton, 2000; Parker, 2004). Being an entrepreneur may be rewarding because it entails substantial non-monetary benefits, like greater autonomy, broader skill utilization, and the possibility to pursue one's own ideas; i.e. more freedom (cf. Sen, 1999). These wide-ranging effects of entrepreneurship are reflected in the various aims of entrepreneurship policy, ranging from employment growth (lowering unemployment), flexibility of the economy, innovativeness of the economy, individual development, emancipation of females, and integration of ethnic minorities into host societies.

There are dozens of definitions of entrepreneurship (Hebert and Link, 1989; Thurik and Van Dijk, 1998). There is certainly no one answer to the question of what the phenomenon of entrepreneurship 'truly' is. Rather than looking for any essentialist, 'really true' definition of entrepreneurship, we prefer to study different forms and functions of entrepreneurship. Taking all entrepreneurship definitions together, they broadly reflect two relatively distinct (but partly overlapping) phenomena (cf. Davidsson, 2004). The first of those is the phenomenon that some people, rather than working for somebody else under an employment contract, strike out on their own and become self-employed.[1]

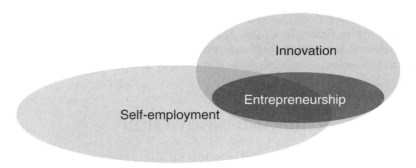

Figure 26.1   Entrepreneurship, innovation and self-employment

This involves some element of innovation at start-up, and some degree of innovativeness is needed to survive. However, innovation is not central to this phenomenon. The second phenomenon involves the development and renewal of any society, market, economy or organization based on micro-level actors who have the initiative and perseverance to make change happen. Here, 'entrepreneurship' means the creation of new economic activities and organizations ('Schumpeterian entrepreneurship') as well as the transformation of existing ones ('corporate entrepreneurship').

In the context of this chapter we focus on this second phenomenon, 'entrepreneurship'. Some self-employed are innovative but most are not, and it is innovation that we are interested in. In order to narrow down the discussion, we propose a working definition of entrepreneurship as 'the introduction of new economic activity by an individual that leads to change in the marketplace' (cf. Davidsson, 2004). Change in the marketplace generally entails new kinds of value for users, or new ways to provide or deliver existing values. This means that we exclude some other interpretations of entrepreneurship (as non-innovative self-employment) and parts of the innovation phenomenon (see Figure 26.1). For example, we exclude non-market activities such as not-for-profit endeavours, changes in contract (e.g. from employee to self-employed) and internal, administrative or organizational changes that do not appreciably affect markets, but include intra-preneurship that is driven by individual action and changes the marketplace. We also exclude mere contemplation of new ideas or introduction of fatally flawed ones that do not change the market (directly or indirectly, via learning mechanisms). We thus do not include novelty and creativity in all domains of human behaviour in our concept of entrepreneurship.

Consistent with our definition of entrepreneurship as the introduction of new economic activity by an individual that leads to change in the marketplace, we can formulate several necessary conditions for entrepreneurship (cf. Shane, 2003, pp. 6–8):

- existence of entrepreneurial opportunities (environmental changes: technological, political/regulatory, social/demographic);
- difference between people (in their willingness and ability to perceive and act upon an opportunity);
- risk bearing: does demand exist? Can the entrepreneur compete with others? Can the value chain be created? etc.;

- organizing (realizing the opportunity); either creating a firm, adapting a firm, or using the market mechanism (e.g. licensing);
- innovation: recombination of resources into a new form that is by implication not a perfect imitation of what has been done before, and thus involves a change in the marketplace.

These are necessary conditions for entrepreneurship. However, there are contingencies, such as whether the individuals discovering an opportunity are employees or independent individuals, and whether new firms (spin-offs or independent start-ups) or incumbent firms (acquisitions or corporate venturing) are used for the realization of the opportunity. We first review the first necessary condition: the existence of entrepreneurial opportunities.[2]

Entrepreneurial Opportunities

Because the range of options and the consequences of exploring new ideas are unknown, entrepreneurial decisions cannot be made through an optimization process in which mechanical calculations are made in response to a given set of alternatives (Baumol, 1993). People must be able to identify new means–ends relationships that are generated by a given change in order to discover entrepreneurial opportunities. Even if a person possesses the prior information necessary to discover an opportunity, he or she may fail to do so because of an inability to see new means–ends relationships. Unfortunately, visualizing these relationships is difficult. History is rife with examples in which inventors failed to see commercial opportunities (new means–ends relationships) that resulted from the invention of important technologies – from the telegraph to the laser.

Every entrepreneur who starts a new business has ideas. The real challenge is to discover an opportunity that is more than just a simple idea. These opportunities can be radical (Schumpeterian) or incremental (Kirznerian). Entrepreneurial opportunities may originate from changes in the environment. These can be technological, social, demographic, political or regulatory changes, but also general shocks to the economy (cf. Shane, 2003). First, technological change, often based on progress in the research base of society (e.g. biomedical knowledge, or nanotechnology), is a prime source of entrepreneurial opportunities for new technology-based firms. Together social and demographic changes can be quantitative changes, such as ageing population that offers new opportunities for entrepreneurs. It may also involve more qualitative changes: changing preferences or wants, for example reflected in the increase in the creative industries that satisfy new wants, or in the trend towards health and nutrition with its resulting demand for the supply of diet and organic food. In that sense people's necessities are few but their wants are endless. Finally, political and regulatory changes, such as deregulation, privatization and liberalization, open up opportunities for entrepreneurship. Examples of privatization as sources of entrepreneurial opportunities are the outsourcing of municipal services and the privatization of the health-care market, which have provided opportunities for high-growth start-ups.

Until now, we have largely left the definition and the discussion about the nature of innovation implicit. We deal explicitly with it in the next section.

CYCLE OF INNOVATION

Innovation is about the development of new knowledge introduced to the economy. This means that it starts with the cognition of the actors involved. This cognition is constructed from interactions of practices (see Nooteboom, 2000, 2008). Based on this insight, we arrive at an innovation process as a cycle or spiral of idea generation followed by development, commercialization, market penetration, diffusion, consolidation and differentiation, which lead to the beginning of invention. Thus this cycle of innovation goes beyond (neo-)Schumpeterian theory, which includes only the notion of invention as new combinations, and the subsequent commercialization and production (Schumpeter, 1934). Where new combinations come from in invention is left unexplained. We see innovation as a cumulative process with discontinuities: today's innovation stands on the shoulders of yesterday's innovation, to paraphrase Merton (1993). Innovation is highly cumulative – building on earlier inventions, development and applications – but also discontinuous in its creative destruction. This nature of innovation – and growth of knowledge more generally – explains why the economy is never in equilibrium (Metcalfe, 2002). The cycle of innovation explains how exploitation and exploration succeed each other and emerge from each other (see Figure 26.2).[3]

The proposal of a cycle of discovery (Nooteboom, 2000) was originally inspired by the work of Piaget on the development of intelligence in children.[4] Here it is applied at the level of firms, products and technologies within economies. How can such a shift of the level of analysis be justified? The claim here is that the cycle goes beyond empirical phenomena of child development. It represents a more general 'logic' of composition and break-up on the basis of experience, in an alternation of reducing variety of content, in the move towards consolidation (the upper half of Figure 26.2), an opening up of variety of context, in generalization (the lower half of Figure 26.2), which leads on to a renewed opening of content, in novel combinations. A basic idea of the cycle is that application of existing knowledge and competence in novel contexts (e.g. new applications of theory and technology, new markets for existing products, new jobs for people), called 'generalization', leads to 'differentiation' of existing practice for the sake of adaptation to the new selection environment. The new selection environment offers room to deviate from the previously consolidated institutions that resulted from a previous innovation. In adapting a product or practice to new conditions, one first taps into earlier experience

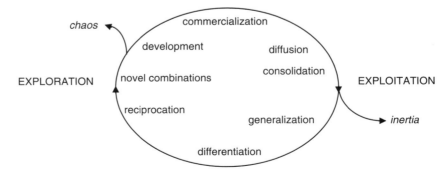

Figure 26.2   Cycle of innovation

about how things might be done differently, based on experience from earlier rounds of innovation. If differentiation does not suffice in order to survive, or to profit from newly emerging opportunities, a further step is to allow oneself to be inspired by foreign practices encountered in the new environment, which appear successful or promising where one's own practice seems to fail. This leads to experiments with combinations of known elements from existing practice and new elements from unfamiliar, local practices, called 'reciprocation'. This yields hybrid practices. The history of technology offers many examples of the importance of hybrids in the development of radical innovations (Mokyr, 1990). The significance of hybrids is that they allow one to explore the potential of novel elements without immediately surrendering the basic logic, structure, design principles or architecture of established practice. The problem with hybrids is that they yield inefficiencies and inconsistencies in the system ('spaghetti'), with overlaps, redundancies, misfits and 'work-arounds' to resolve them. That leads to more radical, architectural change, in Schumpeterian 'novel combinations'. The period of hybridization gives insight into the elements one would most like to preserve, given their performance in the hybrid, and the logic and architectural directions in which one might go in the future. Here, at this stage, small changes in design principles or basic logic can yield drastic changes in the functioning of the whole. At the same time, the inefficiencies and contradictions of hybrids also form a stumbling block: they may be seen as evidence of failure and lack of perspective for the innovation. Progress then depends on the perseverance of the entrepreneur or inventor. Also, the inefficiencies of reciprocation and hybridization are difficult to sustain under the pressures of competition. This frequently leads to failure – because problems do indeed prove to be insurmountable or ongoing efforts and uncertainty cannot be sustained – but occasionally it leads to a breakthrough. The cyclical process of innovation indicates how one can set out in exploration along a path of exploitation. Crucial for the process, in the stages of generalization and reciprocation, is the opening to novel contexts, with new challenges and opportunities, and openness in the form of curiosity and attention to unfamiliar practices and perspectives, and the willingness and opportunity to engage in experiments, and tolerance of the problems with hybrids. The cycle is illustrated in Figure 26.2.

So far, the discussion of the cycle concerns the bottom half of Figure 26.2, in the transition from exploitation to exploration, which is relatively new in the innovation literature. The top half of Figure 26.2 is more consistent with established innovation theory. Along the top half, in the emergence of a new idea or practice, in a novel combination, there is search for technical feasibility and commercial viability[5] of a new technology[6] or product and its optimal configuration, in the emergence of what in the innovation literature is called the 'dominant design' (Utterback, 1994; Geroski, 2003). This leads to what is called 'consolidation'. In that process, if a breakthrough of an innovation succeeds, it faces the need to replace old practices: in Schumpeterian terms, 'creative destruction'. Here, one runs into the problem that existing institutions, in the form of standards and regulations (technical, safety, commercial, fiscal, legal, administrative), market structures (distribution channels, installation, maintenance, repair), schooling and training, as well as established commercial positions, which form the existing selection environment, can block entry and change. In other words, in order to break through, innovation requires institutional change. As a result, due to institutional barriers, radical innovations can often break through only later, and initially can succeed only where they can be fitted into the prevailing order of existing institutions and market structures. They need to prove their worth and their potential more extensively before obstacles can be cleared. It is a well-known phenomenon that innovations initially do not find their application where their potential is highest but where the obstacles are lowest.

Hence openness of markets for new product entry, with a critical attitude towards established interests and institutions, is an issue for innovation policy. One policy implication is that enabling entrepreneurs goes beyond helping them to find their way through the thickets of rules and regulations. It also requires gathering insights as to how obstacles may be changed to accommodate the shifts of innovation.

In the movement towards consolidation, goals, means and causal relationships between them become clear. As uncertainty decreases and familiarity with the novelty increases among potential users, demand increases, new producers jump into the emerging market, and price competition intensifies. Pressure on price creates pressure towards efficiency, on the basis of process innovation (by large firms: see Falck, 2009). For pressures towards efficiency, standard economic analysis applies. Market mechanisms are needed to ensure optimal allocation of scarce resources (allocative efficiency) to known goals and means. In the drive towards efficiency, opportunities are taken to increase productive efficiency, by increase of scale, enabled by growing demand, which leads to concentration and the 'shake-out' of less efficient producers. Here, usually in competition policy, mechanisms are oriented towards removing barriers to entry (see Audretsch et al., 2001).

The fall of profits, in the transition from product innovation to process innovation during consolidation, yields an argument for trying to be a leader in the early stage of innovation, because thereby one captures the high profits of early partial monopoly before imitation sets in (cf. Schumpeter, 1942). As a follower, one enters at the stage of consolidation, where users profit from lower prices, but high profits have eroded. Furthermore, early leaders may construct entry barriers to followers. As the history of capitalism has shown, only an extremely small percentage of all start-ups make it to the position of industry leader (e.g. Microsoft, Apple, Cisco and Dell in ICT industries).

Ongoing progress throughout the cycle is by no means guaranteed. The cycle is not to be seen as a logically necessary sequence but as a heuristic that generally works. In trying novel combinations, one may get caught in ongoing uncertainty and chaos (see Figure 26.2), unable to settle the inconsistencies between new goals, means and connecting causalities. Prototypes, may continually fail to become viable, either technically or commercially. Rival designs, prototypes or technical standards may continue to compete for a long time, and for the duration potential users are hesitant to commit themselves. After consolidation, one may get caught in inertia (see Figure 26.2), particularly if there are no opportunities or incentives to escape to new contexts of application, or barriers to novel conditions being imposed from outside. In consolidation, institutions shift to accommodate the innovation, and once that has happened there are often strong pressures towards 'isomorphism' (DiMaggio and Powell, 1983), with strong pressures to conform, by 'coercion, mimesis (imitation) or normative pressures'. Vested economic interests protect existing institutions with installed bases of both tangible and intangible investments, existing competencies and efficiencies (accumulated in learning by doing), as well as market positions. Therefore innovation requires openness to novel contexts of application, e.g. global markets, or new users or suppliers, as arenas for exploration and sources of novel challenges. Stages of the cycle may be skipped, in a leap to novel combinations without much intervening differentiation or reciprocation. The process may not proceed beyond any given stage. For example, differentiation, as a step in exploitation, may not proceed to reciprocation and novel combinations.

Note that progress along the cycle is full of stress and potential conflict. In order to survive in novel contexts, innovators need to adapt their existing practices. In novel combinations, innovators encounter stress in trying to have their innovation accepted, and established practices encounter the stress of creative destruction.

The cycle of innovation provides the dynamic basis for the systemic view of innovation and innovation policy, in which innovation policy is concerned with stimulating and matching the knowledge-producing elements (exploration) and knowledge-exploiting elements (exploitation) of an economy. The cycle of innovation operates, more or less perfectly, depending on institutional conditions that inhibit or enhance the component processes of generalization (opening up to new contexts); differentiation (deviation from established practice to survive in the new context); reciprocation (opening up to contributions from unfamiliar ideas or practices); experimentation with hybrids and new principles, interpretive schemes or architectures; convergence to a dominant design; and institutional change to accommodate the novelty. Innovation policy is not about the determining the content of innovation, but about enabling innovation processes. Crucial in this policy is the opening to new contexts with new challenges and opportunities, opening to collaboration for the exploration of novel combinations, opening in the form of curiosity and attention to foreign practices, and the preparedness to engage in experiments with elements from those and with surprising hybrids.[7]

Entrepreneurship in the Innovation Cycle

It is customary to distinguish between equilibrium-breaking, Schumpeterian entrepreneurship that yields 'creative destruction', and 'Kirznerian' entrepreneurship (Kirzner, 1973), which finds new market niches for existing or adapted products, in a process of what economists call 'arbitrage', and thereby tends towards equilibrium. We can recognize this in the cycle of innovation: the movement towards consolidation can perhaps be seen as equilibration, and the movement away from it as disequilibration. Instead of two kinds of entrepreneurship, we can identify a larger range of types, all along the cycle of innovation. Thus there are entrepreneurs who make a new idea technically feasible, commercially feasible, productively efficient (e.g. Henry Ford in the automobile industry), eliminate entry barriers, carry it into new markets or applications, differentiate it, bring in new elements, in hybrids, or bring together elements from different practices in new architectures and thereby produce new concepts.

Note that in the step of generalization the actor who takes an existing product or practice into a new context is not necessarily an existing producer or practitioner. It may be an outside entrepreneur or user stepping in, or an employee spinning off from an existing firm, adopting the product or practice with his own specific experience and perspective. This, however, may already happen prior to consolidation, so that exploration may set in when exploitation has not yet settled down. Entrepreneurs adopting the innovation will inevitably, and not necessarily deliberately, colour their use of it according to their perspective, and seeing that the product is on its way to widespread diffusion and consolidation, with an erosion of profit, may already differentiate it deliberately. What we are saying here is that disequilibration may take place even during equilibration, which seems to make nonsense of the very notion of equilibration. Why would entrepreneurs move towards equilibrium if they know that it will erode profits?

INSTITUTIONS ENABLING/CONSTRAINING ENTREPRENEURSHIP

The economy would be in chaos without institutions,[8] one might even argue that economics – production, distribution and consumption – would not exist without institutions. Institutions are the rules that constrain behaviour – and in that way often reduce uncertainty, and transaction costs in particular, and enable (inter)actions. The most basic institutions that enable capitalist economies are property rights and the rule of law. In this paper we focus on how entrepreneurship, specified along the cycle of innovation, is enabled and constrained by institutions. A key question is which (formal) institutions governments should design to enable entrepreneurship, i.e. the introduction of new economic activity by an individual that leads to change in the marketplace. In practice, institutions are often not the product of intentional design,[9] and are often the outcome of a political process in which the interests of many stakeholders have to be satisfied. However, that does not mean that there is no scope for institutional design.[10]

The relationship between institutions and entrepreneurship seems paradoxical, as the former reduces uncertainty in order to enable behaviour (North, 1990b), while the latter involves judgement under uncertainty (Knight, 1921; Casson, 2003). This paradox is resolved by distinguishing different types of uncertainty (cf. Milliken, 1987; Van Waarden, 2001). For example, financial institutions are necessary to let financial markets work, so that entrepreneurs can acquire capital for investments with uncertain future returns. The latter uncertainties relate to whether the new product is technically viable, commercially viable, and whether the firm will not be outcompeted by rivals, while the former institutions for example reduce the uncertainties related to the value of money and creditworthiness of firms. Furthermore, institutions may also constrain the making of constraints and enable escape from constraints, creating uncertainty by keeping avenues towards innovation open, as in competition policy, or other elimination of entry barriers, which create the uncertainty of novel entry into markets.

The question of which institutions governments should design to enable entrepreneurship is not about more or less state or market, since markets require institutions that often only states can construct; it is about how the state can enable entrepreneurs to change the market. This also means that it might have to design institutions that constrain vested interests, or to abolish institutions that serve vested interests, in order to let entrepreneurs flourish.

In order to focus our discussion of how institutions affect entrepreneurship, we shall discuss particular types of entrepreneurship that according to the literature have relatively strong positive effects on economic growth: new technology-based firms, spin-offs,[11] and high-growth start-ups. Spin-offs and new technology-based firms are likely to be better indicators of exploitation of unused ideas than the general population of new firms, while they may also be involved in the exploration of ideas that have emerged out

Table 26.1   Types of entrepreneurship and legal institutions

Type of entrepreneurship	Position at the cycle of innovation	Legal institutions	Enabling/constraining effects
New technology-based firms	Novel combinations	Intellectual property rights	Markets for technology
New technology-based firms	Novel combinations – development – commercialization	Small Business Innovation Research (SBIR) programme	Sourcing of radical small firms innovations; commercialization of public research
Spin-off firms	Generalization, differentiation	Non-compete covenants (labour market)	Exploitation of ideas
High-growth start-ups	Commercialization – generalization	Employment protection (labour market)	Reallocation of labour

of the former exploitation of knowledge. High-growth start-ups are even stronger indicators of successful exploitation on a relatively large scale.

New Technology-based Firms and Patents

Entrepreneurs wanting to develop new technologies and introduce them to the market face Arrow's disclosure problem (Arrow, 1962): the value of a new technology to any one buyer may be decreasing in the number of other potential buyers who have been able to evaluate the new technology due to information leakages in the valuation process (value rivalry). There is thus a risk of expropriation of the 'rights' to use this new technology of the inventor if this invention has not been registered and protected by patent rights. The enforcement of patents or licensing agreements acts as an entry barrier that significantly reduces the potential for user reproducibility. Patent rights explicitly prevent would-be buyers from using the idea for commercial gain without the permission of the technology seller. The legal institution that solved this disclosure problem is the protection of intellectual property rights via patents (see Gans and Stern, 2010). New firms that specialize in the development of new technologies can thus claim the property rights of the inventions involved and gain from trading the use rights of this invention with licensing on a market for technology (cf. Arora et al., 2001). The availability of intellectual property protection by patents has been instrumental in the rise of the number of new firms in knowledge-intensive sectors like biotech and R&D services.[12]

New Technology-based Firms and SBIR

The Small Business Innovation Research (SBIR) programme is a public procurement programme aimed to subcontract socially relevant (i.e. fulfilling a public need) innovative research to small businesses. The programme's central goals are (1) meeting federal research needs with small business and (2) fostering commercialization of federally funded research (Cooper, 2003). The US Congress enacted the SBIR programme in the early 1980s as a response to the loss of US competitiveness in global markets, especially in the face of the 'Japanese threat' (see Audretsch, 2003). The birth of the SBIR programme was the result of lobbying activities by the National Science Foundation (NSF) and the Small Business Administration (SBA) (Obermayer, 2009). There was no clear design, but the programme was constructed and evolved through a trial-and-error process taking into account both the political and administrative viability of the programme. The US regulation underpinning the SBIR programme requires that 2.5 per cent of all federal government agency external R&D budgets be distributed to small innovative businesses. Each year the SBIR programme makes more than 4000 awards to US small businesses, amounting to over $2 billion in value (Connell, 2006). The SBIR consists of three phases: feasibility, development and commercialization. Phase I is oriented towards determining the scientific and technical merit (technological creativity) along with the feasibility (economic creativity) of a proposed research idea. A Phase I award (typically around $100000) provides an opportunity for a small business to establish the feasibility and technical merit of a proposed innovation. This is a step generally ignored by private venture capital. Phase II awards are more selectively aimed at developing new technologies and products, which involves about 50 per cent of the phase I award winners, and delivers up to $750000. Phase III awards are funded from mainstream (i.e. non-SBIR budgets), and add probably again as much as Phase I and II in total to overall R&D expenditure on SBIR projects (Connell, 2006). These Phase III projects also bring small businesses the opportunity to win valuable sole supplier contracts with federal agencies. Some of the most innovative US companies, like Genzyme, Amgen, and Genentech – all three university spin-offs – as well as Apple Computer, Compaq, Intel and Qualcomm received early-stage SBIR finance. Lerner (1999) shows that SBIR-funded firms enjoyed substantially greater employment and sales growth than other similar firms. It is not just the size of the subsidy that is important for the recipients: these awards also have an important certification function, increasing the trustworthiness of the recipients (Lerner, 1999; cf. Toole and Turvey, 2009). This implies that the programme's project review and selection process identifies the quality of projects and firms, so that information asymmetries are reduced that are normally an important cause of the failure of financial markets to provide investment capital to these projects and firms.

From an innovation policy point of view, the SBIR programme has the general purpose of stimulating technological innovation, and the more specific purpose to tap into the pool of innovative potential of small businesses to meet federal R&D needs on the one hand, and to increase private sector commercialization of inventions derived from federal R&D; i.e. to stimulate novel combinations, technology development and commercialization in the innovation cycle. The evolutionary design of the programme facilitates maximum experimentation, with minimal financial losses per experiment. The programme also reduces the inherent uncertainty involved in technological innovation concerning the functionality of the technology, the ability to produce new technology-based products, and the demand for the new product. In combination with providing 'venture capital' for product development, the SBIR programme reduces multiple barriers to technological innovation that are said to be especially harmful for new and small technology-based firms (cf. Hall, 2002).

The programme reduces the typical large-firm bias in public procurement. Public procurement in general, and innovation procurement in particular, favours large firms for logical reasons: due to accountability of these larger and often long-established parties, and the relatively low transaction costs for government procurement to a small set of large established firms. Procurement to a large set of small and new firms incurs more search costs, contract costs and control costs. This problem is even more severe when the 'product' subcontracted involves high uncertainties and many intangible assets, as is the case with subcontracting of innovative research. However, the downside of subcontracting to large established firms is that relatively incremental innovations will be sourced, due to the small variety of potential innovations, and the relative inert nature of larger, long-established firms. The problem then is how to source more radical forms of innovation, and solving the two (capital and product) market problems for new tech-based firms. The SBIR programme turned out to be an institutional change that solved these problems.

Spin-offs and Non-compete Agreements

Spin-off firms are a specific form of employee mobility, in which employees leave their former employer to pursue opportunities in their newly created and owner-managed legal entity. These entrepreneurs introduce ideas from their prior work experience to new contexts (generalization), and sometimes substantially differentiate these ideas in order to adapt to new selection environments (differentiation).

A number of studies show that one particular legal constraint on employee mobility – employee non-compete agreements[13] – lowers the ability of employees to move from one firm to another (Gilson, 1999; Fallick et al., 2006; Marx et al., 2009). These employee non-compete agreements are intended to help firms protect their investments in human capital, intellectual property[14] and relationships: firms can increase their productivity by training their workers, by developing new products and processes, as well as by building valuable relationships with customers and suppliers (see Franco and Mitchell, 2008). These non-compete agreements may also reflect the vested interests of incumbents that want to restrict the possibility of employees striking out on their own, and exploiting their knowledge outside the former employer. In this respect, employee non-compete agreements may be a constraint on the creation of spin-off firms, which has been confirmed by several studies (Stuart and Sorenson, 2003; Samila and Sorenson, 2009).

High-growth Start-ups and Employment Protection

Labour market regulations leading to large hiring and firing costs are negatively associated with new firm formation (Van Stel et al., 2007). This finding might reflect different mechanisms: relatively high opportunity costs for employees to become self-employed, constraints on the flexibility of highly uncertain innovative start-ups, or potential problems with attracting personnel for a growing new venture. There is some empirical evidence for all three mechanisms: Robson (2003) found that stricter employment protection legislation in OECD countries reduces self-employment;[15] Bosma et al. (2009b) found that the probability of individuals in European countries to start an innovative firm is negatively related to the strictness of employment protection, and Bosma et al. (2009a) found the same relation for the probability to start a new firm with high growth expectations. See Henrekson and Johansson (2009) for an extensive discussion of the effects of labour market institutions on the prevalence of high-growth firms.

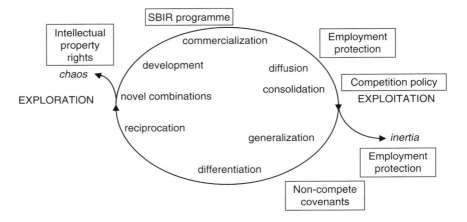

Figure 26.3   Institutions along the cycle of innovation

An overview of the reviewed institutions and their place along the innovation cycle is shown in Figure 26.3.

CONCLUSIONS

In this chapter we provide a definition of entrepreneurship in the context of innovation, and discuss its role in a cycle of innovation. This cycle of innovation reflects the growth of knowledge in society: innovation is founded on the knowledge base of a society and expands this knowledge base. Different types of innovation along the cycle of innovation are realized with different forms of entrepreneurship, which are constrained or enabled by different institutions. One of the key roles of governments is to design, change or destroy institutions in order to improve welfare in society. The key question of this chapter is: how can policy best enable innovation-based entrepreneurship? We take an institutional design perspective, which aims to provide arguments for the design, change and/or destruction of institutions, given the goals of government. This is illustrated by how four different formal institutions enable or constrain different types of entrepreneurship through the innovation cycle. These illustrations also show that it is not fruitful to see these institutions as either designed or as evolving spontaneously: the selection and consequential design and creation of institutions is both intended and unintended, which means that institutional learning becomes crucial.

The translation of scientific insights into the world of policy practice has several caveats. First, the success of institutional design in the context of innovation policy remains uncertain due to unforeseen interdependencies and unintended side-effects. Bringing the nuances and contingencies in the effects of institutional change centre stage might constrain the adoption of these insights into the world of policy practice. However, this should not be a licence for the exclusive use of slogans and sound-bites in the policy debate. The message should be simple enough to be communicated to a broad non-scientific audience, but should have enough causal depth and contextual sensitivity to avoid harmful translations of academic insight.

The second caveat concerns the dangers of evidence-based policy. Evidence-based in social sciences means building on academic publications in social science fields. In contrast to, for example, the research field of medicine, replication research is not greatly valued in social sciences (cf. Davidsson, 2004, ch. 9; Evanschitzky et al., 2007). There is a tendency to publish success studies, thus undersampling failures or zero-effect outcomes (cf. Denrell, 2003). This means that the social science knowledge base on the effects of institutions on entrepreneurship and innovation more broadly is not likely to be an unbiased pool of insights for the design of institutions. In order to become a reliable pool of insights, social sciences should become more like the medical sciences and emphasize replication studies (over time and different contexts), and engage as scholars with the actors involved in order to uncover the ways in which institutions affect their behaviour (cf. Van de Ven, 2007).

NOTES

1. In a similar way, entrepreneurship is often equated with self-employment and SMEs in other EU documents (EOS Gallup, 2004; European Commission, 2006).
2. We are agnostic on the extent to which these opportunities are to be discovered or created (cf. Sarasvathy et al., 2003).
3. Normally a linear approach is taken for explaining processes of innovation, ranging from the linear model of science to innovation (Bush, 1945), to innovation diffusion models (Rogers, 1962), to more recent innovation chain approaches (Roper et al., 2008).
4. For a survey of Piaget's work, both theoretical and empirical, including criticism, see Flavell (1967).
5. Entrepreneurs make conjectures about new combinations that are uncertain – that is, one cannot know (or even calculate the probability) *ex ante* whether these conjectures will be correct (Knight, 1921). Several types of uncertainty can be distinguished, e.g., technical, market and competition. The entrepreneur does not know in advance if the good or service she is producing will work, and, if so, if it can be produced at a cost lower than the price at which it will be sold (technical uncertainty). The entrepreneur also does not know if demand will exist for the product, and, if so, if customers will adopt in large enough volumes, quickly enough, and at a high enough price, to make the effort profitable (market uncertainty). Finally, the entrepreneur does not know if she will be able to appropriate the profits from the exploitation of the opportunity or if they will dissipate to competitors. This uncertainty will be resolved only with entry into the market (Rosenberg and Birdzell, 1986, pp. 257–8); hence the description of the market as a discovery process.
6. In contrast to Schumpeter's time, the invention need not to be turned into a product in order to enter the market, since there are now well-functioning markets for technology (see Arora et al., 2001). Companies that enter technologies markets do not have to invest in production-related activities but can focus their efforts on building stocks of intellectual property. The choice of entering the product or technology market is highly dependent on the appropriability regime and the extent to which complementary assets are held by existing companies (Teece, 1986).
7. The Renaissance in Europe was accompanied by a lively interest and use of many things that could be found elsewhere (Mokyr, 1990). This stands in contrast to China, for example, which from around 1400 lost its prior advantage by closing itself off to foreign influences. Perhaps this helps to explain why the first two industrial revolutions occurred in Europe.
8. Expanding on this: according to Hobbes (1651), society will be in chaos without institutions.
9. Hayek (1978), for example, held that institutional change emerges out of organic processes, which he termed 'spontaneous order'.
10. This very much resembles mechanism design theory, which evaluates how the rules that govern exchange and allocation affect the efficiency of alternative (market) institutions (Myerson, 2008; Roth, 2008).
11. The focus here is on corporate spin-offs. University spin-offs differ in two important ways. First, non-compete covenants are not a relevant issue for employees in (non-competing) public sector organizations. Second, the nature of innovation in university spin-offs mainly involves the upper half of the innovation cycle, i.e. the process from invention to commercialization. Institutional conditions that are important for

12. university spin-offs relate to the incentives for academic entrepreneurship (see Henrekson and Rosenberg, 2001), and the provision of seed capital and lead users (e.g. via the SBIR programme).
12. However, there is increasing evidence on the malfunctioning of the (US) patent system: see Jaffe and Lerner (2004); Bessen and Meurer (2008).
13. The fact that this is a non-*compete* agreement means that this institution is of less relevance in non-competitive settings of public research institutes and their potential spin-offs.
14. Marx et al. (2009) showed that patents (the regular legal protection of inventions) and non-compete agreements are complements, not substitutes. Both are legal institutions to control knowledge, either embodied knowledge (non-compete agreements) or codified knowledge (patents).
15. This is not that obvious, as the reverse might also be logical: strict employment protection legislation may promote self-employment by encouraging employers to contract out work to self-employed workers.

REFERENCES

Arora, A., A. Fosfuri and A. Gambardella (2001), 'Markets for technology and their implications for corporate strategy', *Industrial and Corporate Change*, **10**, 419–51.
Arrow, K. (1962), 'Economic welfare and the allocation of resources for invention', in *The Rate and Direction of Inventive Activity: Economic and Social Factors*, Princeton, NJ: Princeton University Press, pp. 609–25.
Audretsch, D.B. (2003), 'Standing on the shoulders of midgets: the U.S. Small Business Innovation Research Program (SBIR)', *Small Business Economics*, **20**, 129–35.
Audretsch, D.B., W.J. Baumol and A.E. Burke (2001), 'Competition policy in dynamic markets', *International Journal of Industrial Organization*, **19**, 613–34.
Audretsch, D.B., M.C. Keilbach and E.E. Lehmann (2006), *Entrepreneurship and Economic Growth*, Oxford: Oxford University Press.
Baumol, W.J. (1990), 'Entrepreneurship: productive, unproductive, and destructive', *Journal of Political Economy*, **98** (5), 893–921.
Baumol, W. (1993), 'Formal entrepreneurship theory in economics: existence and bounds', *Journal of Business Venturing*, **8**, 197–210.
Baumol, W.J. (2002), *The Free-Market Innovation Machine: Analyzing the Growth Miracle of Capitalism*, Princeton, NJ: Princeton University Press.
Benz, M. (2006), 'Entrepreneurship as a non-profit-seeking activity', Institute for Empirical Research in Economics Working Paper no. 243, University of Zurich.
Bessen, J. and M.J. Meurer (2008), *Patent Failure: How Judges, Bureaucrats, and Lawyers Put Innovators at Risk*, Princeton, NJ: Princeton University Press.
Bosma, N., V. Schutjens and E. Stam (2009a), 'Two faces of entrepreneurship. Drivers of innovative and replicative entrepreneurship', paper presented at the DIME workshop 'Regional Entrepreneurship as a source of Perpetuation and Change', 15–17 October Jena.
Bosma, N., V. Schutjens and E. Stam (2009b), 'Entrepreneurship in European regions: implications for public policy', in J. Leitao and R. Baptista (eds), *Public Policies for Fostering Entrepreneurship: A European Perspective*. New York: Springer, pp. 59–89.
Bush, V. (1945), *Science: The Endless Frontier*, Washington, DC: United States Government Printing (http://www.nsf.gov/about/history/vbush1945.htm).
Casson, M. (2003), *The Entrepreneur: An Economic Theory*, Cheltenham, UK and Northampton, MA, USA: Edward Elgar.
Connell, D. (2006), *'Secrets' of the World's Largest Seed Capital Fund: How the United States Government Uses its Small Business Innovation Research (SBIR) Programme and Procurement Budgets to Support Small Technology Firms*, Cambridge: Centre for Business Research, University of Cambridge.
Cooper, R.S. (2003), 'Purpose and performance of the Small Business Innovation Research (SBIR) program', *Small Business Economics*, **20**, 137–51.
Cramton, P. (2008), 'Innovation and market design', in J. Lerner and S. Stern (eds), *Innovation Policy and the Economy*, Chicago, IL: National Bureau of Economic Research, pp. 113–37.
Davidsson, P. (2004), *Researching Entrepreneurship*, New York: Springer.
Denrell, J. (2003), 'Vicarious learning, undersampling of failure, and the myths of management', *Organization Science*, **14** (3), 227–43.
DiMaggio, P.J. and W.W. Powell (1983), 'The iron cage revisited: institutional isomorphism and collective rationality in organizational fields', *American Sociological Review*, **48**, 147–60.
Djankov, S., E. Glaeser, R. La Porta, F. Lopez-de-Silanes and A. Shleifer (2003), 'The new comparative economics', *Journal of Comparative Economics*, **31**, 595–619.

EOS Gallup (2004), 'Flash 160 "Entrepreneurship"', survey for Directorate General Enterprise – European Commission, Brussels: EOS Gallup.

European Commission (2006), Report on the implementation of the Entrepreneurship Action Plan, Brussels: European Commission – DG Enterprise and Industry.

Evanschitzky, H., C. Baumgarth, R. Hubbard and J.S. Armstrong (2007), 'Replication research's disturbing trend', *Journal of Business Research*, **60**, 411–15.

Falck, O. (2009), 'Routinization of innovation in German manufacturing: the David–Goliath symbiosis revisited', *Industrial and Corporate Change*, **18** (3), 497–506.

Fallick, B., C.A. Fleischman and J.B. Rebitzer (2006), 'Job-hopping in Silicon Valley: some evidence concerning the microfoundations of a high-technology cluster', *Review of Economics and Statistics*, **88**, 472–81.

Flavell, J.H. (1967), *The Developmental Psychology of Jean Piaget*, Princeton, NJ: Van Nostrand.

Franco, A.M. and M.F. Mitchell (2008), 'Covenants not to compete, labor mobility, and industry dynamics', *Journal of Economics and Management Strategy*, **17**, 581–606.

Gans, J.S. and S. Stern (2010), 'Is there a market for ideas?', *Industrial and Corporate Change*, **19** (2), 805–37.

Geroski, P. (2003), *The Evolution of New Markets*, Oxford: Oxford University Press.

Gilson, R.J. (1999), 'The legal infrastructure of high technology industrial districts: Silicon Valley, Route 128, and covenants not to compete', *New York University Law Review*, **74**, 575–629.

Hall, B. (2002), 'The financing of research and development', *Oxford Review of Economic Policy*, **18**, 35–51.

Hamilton, B.H. (2000), 'Does entrepreneurship pay? An empirical analysis of the returns to self-employment', *Journal of Political Economy*, **108**, 604–31.

Hayek, F. (1978), *New Studies in Philosophy, Politics, Economics, and the History of Ideas*, London: Routledge & Kegan Paul.

Hebert, R.F. and A.N. Link (1989), 'In search of the meaning of entrepreneurship', *Small Business Economics*, **1** (1), 39–49.

Henrekson, M. and D. Johansson (2009), 'Competencies and institutions fostering high-growth firms', *Foundations and Trends in Entrepreneurship*, **5** (1), 1–80.

Henrekson, M. and N. Rosenberg (2001), 'Designing efficient institutions for science-based entrepreneurship: lessons from the US and Sweden', *Journal of Technology Transfer*, **26** (3), 207–31.

Hobbes, T. (1651), *Leviathan* (reprint 1968), Harmondsworth: Penguin.

Jaffe, A.B. and J. Lerner (2004), *Innovation and Its Discontents: How Our Broken Patent System is Endangering Innovation and Progress, and What to Do About It*, Princeton, NJ: Princeton University Press.

Kenney, M. (1986), 'Schumpeterian innovation and entrepreneurs in capitalism: a case study of the US biotechnology industry', *Research Policy*, **15**, 21–31.

Kirzner, I.M. (1973), *Competition and Entrepreneurship*, Chicago, IL: University of Chicago Press.

Knight, F.H. (1921), *Risk, Uncertainty and Profit*, Boston, MA: Hart, Schaffner & Marx.

Landes, D.S. (1998), *The Wealth and Poverty of Nations: Why Some Are So Rich and Some So Poor*, New York: W.W. Norton.

Lerner, J. (1999), 'The government as venture capitalist: the long-run effects of the SBIR program', *Journal of Business*, **72** (3), 285–97.

Marx, M., D. Strumsky and L. Fleming (2009), 'Mobility, skills, and the Michigan noncompete experiment', *Management Science*, **55** (6), 875–89.

McCloskey, D. (1997), *The Vices of Economists; The Virtues of the Bourgeoisie*, Amsterdam: Amsterdam University Press.

Merton, R.K. (1993), *On the Shoulders of Giants*, Chicago, IL: University of Chicago Press.

Metcalfe, J.S. (2002), 'Knowledge of growth and the growth of knowledge', *Journal of Evolutionary Economics*, **12** (1), 3–15.

Milliken, F. (1987), 'Three types of perceived uncertainty about the environment: state, effect, and response uncertainty', *Academy of Management Review*, **12** (1), 133–43.

Mokyr, J. (1990), *The Lever of Riches: Technological Creativity and Economic Progress*, Oxford: Oxford University Press.

Moreau, F. (2004), 'The role of the state in evolutionary economics', *Cambridge Journal of Economics*, **28**, 847–74.

Myerson, R.B. (2008), 'Perspectives on mechanism design in economic theory', *American Economic Review*, **98** (3), 586–603.

Murphy, K.M., A. Schleifer and R.W. Vishny (1991), 'The allocation of talent: implications for growth', *Quarterly Journal of Economics*, **106** (2), 503–30.

Nelson, R.R. and S. Winter (1982), *An Evolutionary Theory of Economic Change*, Cambridge, MA: Belknap Press.

Nooteboom, B. (2000), *Learning and Innovation in Organizations and Economies*, Oxford: Oxford University Press.

Nooteboom, B. (2008), 'Learning, discovery, and collaboration', in B. Nooteboom and E. Stam (eds), *Micro-foundations for Innovation Policy*, Amsterdam: Amsterdam University Press, pp. 75–102.

North, D.C. (1990a), 'Institutions and a transaction-cost theory of exchange', in J.E. Alt and K.A. Shepsle (eds), *Perspectives on Positive Political Economy*, New York: Cambridge University Press, pp. 182–94.

North, D.C. (1990b), *Institutions, Institutional Change and Economic Performance*, Cambridge: Cambridge University Press.

Obermayer, A.S. (2009), 'The role of Senator Ted Kennedy in the birth of the Small Business Innovation Research Programme', mimeo.

Parker, S.C. (2004), *The Economics of Self-employment and Entrepreneurship*, Cambridge: Cambridge University Press.

Pielke, R. (2007), *The Honest Broker: Making Sense of Science in Policy and Politics*, Cambridge: Cambridge University Press.

Robson, M.T. (2003), 'Does stricter employment protection legislation promote self-employment?', *Small Business Economics*, 21 (3), 309–19.

Rogers, E.M. (1962), *Diffusion of Innovations*, New York: Free Press.

Roper, S., J. Du and J.H. Love (2008), 'Modelling the innovation value chain', *Research Policy*, 37, 961–77.

Rosenberg, N. and L. Birdzell (1986), *How the West Grew Rich*, New York: Basic Books.

Roth, A.E. (2008), 'What have we learned from market design?', *Economic Journal*, 118, 285–310.

Ruttan, V.W. (2006), 'Social science knowledge and induced institutional innovation: an institutional design perspective', *Journal of Institutional Economics*, 2 (3), 249–72.

Ruttan, V.W. (2008), 'Induced technical change, induced institutional change and mechanism design', Staff Paper P08-1, Department of Applied Economics, University of Minnesota.

Samila, S. and O. Sorenson (2009), 'Non-compete covenants: incentives to innovate or impediments to growth', SSRN Working Paper 1411172.

Sarasvathy, S.D., N. Dew, S.R. Velamuri and S. Venkatamaran (2003), 'Three views of entrepreneurial opportunity', in Z.J. Acs and D.B. Audretsch (eds), *Handbook of Entrepreneurship Research*, Boston, MA: Kluwer, pp. 141–60.

Schumpeter, J.A. (1934), *The Theory of Economic Development*, Cambridge, MA: Harvard University Press.

Schumpeter, J.A. (1942), *Capitalism, Socialism, and Democracy*, New York: Harper & Brothers.

Sen, A. (1999), *Development as Freedom*, Oxford: Oxford University Press.

Shane, S. (2003), *A General Theory of Entrepreneurship: The Individual–Opportunity Nexus*, Cheltenham, UK and Northampton, MA, USA: Edward Elgar.

Stuart, T.E. and O. Sorenson (2003), 'Liquidity events and the geographic distribution of organizational foundings', *Administrative Science Quarterly*, 48, 175–201.

Teece, D. (1986), 'Profiting from technological innovations: implications for integration, collaboration, licensing and public policy', *Research Policy*, 15, 285–305

Thurik, A.R. and B. Van Dijk (1998), 'Entrepreneurship: visies en benaderingen', in D.P. Scherjon and A.R. Thurik (eds), *Handboek ondernemers en adviseurs in het MKB*, Dordrecht: Kluwer Bedrijfsinformatie, pp. 127–47.

Toole, A.A. and C. Turvey (2009), 'How does initial public financing influence private incentives for follow-on investment in early-stage technologies?', *Journal of Technology Transfer*, 34, 43–58.

Utterback, J. (1994), *Mastering the Dynamics of Innovation*, Boston, MA: Harvard Business School Press.

Van de Ven, A. (2007), *Engaged Scholarship*, New York: Oxford University Press.

Van Stel A., D. Storey and A.R. Thurik (2007), 'The effect of business regulations on nascent and young business entrepreneurship', *Small Business Economics*, 28 (2), 171–86.

Van Waarden, F. (2001), 'Institutions and innovation: the legal environment of innovating firms', *Organization Studies*, 22 (5), 765–95.

Williamson, O.E. (2000), 'The new institutional economics: taking stock, looking ahead', *Journal of Economic Literature*, 38 (3), 595–613.

27 The propensity to patent an innovation: comparing entrepreneurial with routinized innovators
Alfred Kleinknecht and Gerben van der Panne

INTRODUCTION

Patents are a frequently used innovation indicator as patent records are publicly available and easily accessible. Moreover, patent data are classified by technical fields, and patent time series allow for the convenient study of historical trends. As frequently argued, there are two major drawbacks associated with this indicator. First, not all patents relate to innovations, i.e. the market introduction of a product or service. Little is known about 'sleeping' patents that are never translated into commercial use. Second, many innovators do not seek patent protection. Often alternative mechanisms of protection are considered more efficient. Among the latter, secrecy and time-lead on competitors (Levin et al., 1987), and the protection of tacit knowledge by keeping qualified people in the firm (Brouwer and Kleinknecht, 1999) tend to rank higher than patents. In this chapter we explicitly address what F.M. Scherer once called the 'propensity to patent'. This propensity might vary substantially across industries, types of innovation or other dimensions.

When investigating interfirm differences in the propensity to patent, comparisons between R&D data and patents are less helpful since any deviation between the two may also be ascribed to a more or less efficient use of R&D inputs. Moreover, standard R&D data are a deficient indicator of innovation in small firms (Kleinknecht et al., 2002). This chapter therefore uses a direct measure of the 'output' of the innovative process: a firm's announcement of the market introduction of a new product. In the second section we describe our database of new-product announcements and provide descriptive information. The third section discusses earlier research and our hypotheses. The fourth documents a multivariate analysis of factors that affect the probability that a firm will seek patent protection for its newly announced product. Conclusions are provided in the fifth, and final, section.

THE NEW-PRODUCT ANNOUNCEMENT DATA

The data were collected by systematically screening new-product announcements in the Netherlands, using 43 trade journals published during September 2000–August 2002. The 43 journals cover new-product announcements from all sectors of manufacturing and services in the Netherlands. Similar data collection methods have been used before. An early example is the US Small Business Administration database, collected by The Futures Group (1984) in 1982, that lead to a series of research papers surveyed by Acs and Audretsch (1993). In Europe, similar databases have been compiled in the Netherlands (see several chapters in Kleinknecht and Bain, 1993), the UK (Coombs et al., 1996), Italy (Santarelli and Piergiovanni, 1996), Spain (Flor and Oltra, 2004) and Finland (Saarinen, 2005).

Learning from earlier rounds of data collection, our data collection procedure deliberately deviated from the earlier approaches in three respects:

1. We confined the collection of data to what we consider 'innovations'. We omitted advertisements and cases of mere product differentiation, using the following selection criterion: from the edited parts of the journals, we took only announcements that report at least one characteristic feature (concerning functionality, efficiency or other significant product characteristics) that distinguishes the new product from preceding versions or substitutes. In total, 1585 cases were found.
2. The innovating firms were sent a questionnaire addressing background information about the firm, its innovation activities, networks and properties of the announced product. The response rate was 66.6 percent (1056 firms).
3. Firms were explicitly asked whether the firm developed the product, perhaps in collaboration with others. Out of the 1056 firms, 658 (62.3 percent) reported that their innovation was imported, that is, the new-product-announcing firm was simply serving as a distribution channel for innovations developed abroad. These cases were omitted from the database. The high share of imported innovations reflects the economic openness of a small country like the Netherlands. Those 37.7 percent of cases (398) that were developed by the firms themselves are the starting point of our analysis.

Obviously, the data collection method does not follow standard statistical procedures, and we make no claim that the database is statistically representative. The data deviate strongly from other innovation data (such as the CIS) with respect to the age distribution of innovators. Half of the innovating firms in our database were founded after 1985, one-quarter after 1994 and 10 percent after 1998. About one-third of the firms founded after 1996 were founded with the explicit goal of developing and launching the new product announced in the journal. This age structure indicates an important advantage of our data collection method: it is suitable for tracing very small and young innovators. (For details about the database see Van der Panne, 2004.) Very little is known about these entrepreneurial firms as they tend to be neglected in official R&D and innovation surveys, which often have cut-off points at 10 or 20 employees.

In spite of being, on average, quite young and small, the new-product announcing firms appear to be remarkably technology-driven. Almost 80 percent report engaging in R&D activities on a permanent basis; the remainder consider R&D to be an occasional activity. R&D as a percentage of sales is high, with a median of 8 percent. A total of 47.7 percent report having acquired some patents during the last three years. The share of announced products that are protected by patent applications is 34.5 percent.[1] Further descriptive data are summarized in Tables 27.1 and 27.2. Within the group of new-product-announcing firms, the group of innovators younger than ten years stands out on several indicators: these are more likely to have collaboration arrangements with customers, apply more frequently for patent protection for new products, and have higher R&D intensities, to name three.

Table 27.1   Descriptive statistics

	All firms, $n = 398$	Firms <10 years old, $n = 133$	Manufacturing firms, $n = 184$	Service firms, $n = 214$
Shares of innovators collaborating with customers (%)	35	42.3	33.5	36.4
Firm age (years, median)	16	3	25	12
Firm size (numbers of employees, median)	22	6	40	13
R&D activities on a permanent basis (%)	79.0	79.7	85.9	73.1
Shares of experienced innovators, i.e. firms having acquired patents in the past three years (%)	47.7	51.1	51.7	44.3
Shares of firms that applied for a patent related to the new product announced (%)	34.5	47.2	33.7	35.1
Share of firms that were founded with the explicit mission of realizing the new-product announcement (%)	37.1	37.1	50.0	31.3
R&D intensities (median) (%)	8.0	20.0	5.0	9.5
Shares of firms with products new to the market (other than new to the firm) (%)	74.3	81.3	74.3	74.4
Shares of firms with new (other than incrementally improved) products (%)	52.7	59.3	48.0	56.7

Table 27.2   Patenting by 398 firms that announced new products in the Netherlands

Number of firms that have:	Totals	NL	EU	Outside EU
Patented only in NL	38	38		
Patented only in EU	55		55	
Patented only outside EU	33			33
Patented in NL and EU	20	20	20	
Patented in NL and outside EU	1	1		1
Patented in EU and outside EU	8		8	8
Patented in NL, EU and outside EU	32	32	32	32
Totals	187	91	115	74

Table 27.2 shows numbers of patent applications either at a national, a European or an outside European scale, or some combination of these possibilities. The number of observations does not allow separate analyses of patenting by country or by world region. We confine ourselves to analyzing factors that affect the probability that an innovator will apply for any type of patent protection.

DETERMINANTS OF THE PROPENSITY TO PATENT

Earlier Research

Three studies examine the relationship between measures of innovative output and patents. Comparing data on US new-product announcements with US patent data, Acs and Audretsch (1989) conclude from cross-industry regressions that 'patents vary with company R&D, total R&D, and skilled labor in the same manner as does innovative activity'. In general, the results support the validity of patent counts as a measure of innovative activity.' (1989, p. 180). This result is challenged by Arundel and Kabla (1998), who find differences across industries in the shares of innovation cases that are patented. It should be noted, however, that the data used by Acs and Audretsch (1989) cover many small and medium-sized firms in the USA, while Arundel and Kabla (1998) sample the largest firms from all EU countries. In a third study, using a representative manufacturing sample from the Netherlands, Brouwer and Kleinknecht (1999) analyze somewhat different data. While Arundel and Kabla (1998) used numbers of innovation cases that are patented, Brouwer and Kleinknecht (1999) used two different types of information: (1) qualitative data on the appreciation by innovative firms of patents as a protection against imitators; and (2) the relationship between a firm's score on the indicator of innovative output from the Community Innovation Survey (CIS), measuring shares in sales of innovative products, and actual patent applications, also reported in the CIS.

The qualitative data by Brouwer and Kleinknecht (1999) essentially confirm the results of Arundel and Kabla (1998): there is considerable variation in the appreciation of patent protection by innovators across industries, and the variation across industries observed in the Arundel and Kabla (1998) and the Brouwer and Kleinknecht (1999) studies are quite similar. The second data set used by Brouwer and Kleinknecht allows for a more detailed multivariate analysis. Confronting shares of innovative products in total sales with numbers of patent applications filed at the European Patent Office, and controlling for other factors, systematic deviations between the two indicators become visible. Firms having the same score on innovative output have a significantly different score on patent applications along the following dimensions:

- compared to larger firms, smaller innovators have a significantly lower probability of applying for at least one patent;
- given that smaller innovators apply for patents, however, they file applications in higher numbers than do larger innovators;
- firms that collaborate on R&D file significantly more patent applications;
- firms in high-technological opportunity sectors tend to file significantly more patent applications than firms in low-technological opportunity sectors.

This implies that if one were to rely exclusively on patents as an innovation indicator, the share of small firms that innovate would be underestimated while the innovation intensity of small innovators would be overestimated. Second, the innovation activities of firms that do not collaborate on R&D would be undercounted, and that would also be true for firms in low-technological opportunity sectors (for details see Brouwer and Kleinknecht, 1999).

It should be noted that Brouwer and Kleinknecht (1999) derive results from the Community Innovation Survey (CIS), which is based on representative sampling of firms with ten or more employees in the manufacturing and service industries of the Netherlands. The database used in the present chapter consists of many small and young entrepreneurial firms and it comes close to the type of innovation data from the USA used by Acs and Audretsch (1989). While the CIS may cover many firms that fit into the Schumpeter II 'routinized' innovation model in which path-dependent historical accumulation of knowledge is important, many firms in the new-product announcement database may better fit into the Schumpeter I 'entrepreneurial' innovation model that is rather based on spontaneously available knowledge. The patenting behavior of such small, entrepreneurial firms is only sparsely researched. The question is whether patterns found in the CIS data do or do not hold for entrepreneurial firms.

Hypotheses

For the sake of comparability between 'routinized innovators' and 'entrepreneurial innovators', the analysis follows the Brouwer and Kleinknecht (1999) study using CIS data. In doing so, it is unfortunately not possible to use detailed sector dummies, as numbers of innovators by industry are often quite small. Firm size and firm age are controlled for. Firm size and age can be taken as indicators of general experience and organizational learning that should result in a more professional attitude toward intellectual property protection. The nature of R&D activity is also controlled for: does R&D occur only occasionally or is it a permanent activity? Control for such factors appears relevant as the Brouwer and Kleinknecht study indicated that although small firms have lower probabilities of applying for any patent, if small firms do apply, they apply for higher numbers of patents. This points to a 'threshold' problem, possibly related to incurring the information costs for the first patent. In principle, smaller firms are likely to have less market power than have larger firms, and thus should be keener to seek legal protection for the knowledge. Brouwer and Kleinknecht (1999) show that this is indeed the case: once a firm passes the threshold of the first patent, it applies for patents in greater numbers than do larger firms. But many do not pass the threshold. The open question is whether this also holds for technology-driven entrepreneurial firms.

While Brouwer and Kleinknecht (1999) use a simple dummy variable for firms that collaborated on R&D, this study uses richer information: the number of R&D collaboration partners. There are two reasons to expect that R&D collaborators will have a higher propensity to seek patent protection. First, the firms may not fully trust the partners; before giving the collaboration partners insight into precious knowledge, firms might wish to legally protect it. Second, patenting also means that knowledge becomes codified. Codified knowledge can more easily be used as an asset in contract negotiations. These two motives are confirmed by Blind et al. (2006). The authors add a third, strategic, motive: 'A powerful patent portfolio may also attract interesting cooperation partners' (Blind et al., 2006, p. 666). This argument, however, suggests that causality is opposite to what is assumed in this model. However, such opposite causality is hardly relevant in this case, as this study measures patenting and R&D collaboration not at the firm level, but rather at the project level. Given the time delay between a patent application and the publication of the application by the Patent Office, it is not very likely that the decision to apply for patent protection for a certain product will attract collaboration partners for that same product. Finally, one should note that a 'powerful patent portfolio' is unlikely to be relevant for the small entrepreneurial firms dominating the database, but rather for bigger firms. Therefore an R&D collaboration measure is included as an independent variable for which a positive sign is expected.

In a study on patenting behavior, it is also important to distinguish by type of innovation. Our database allows classifying by degree of innovativeness along two lines: (1) radically new versus incrementally improved products; and (2) products new to the firm (but already known in the market) versus products new to the market. 'Radically new' and 'new to the market' innovations are expected to have higher probabilities of being patented.

Besides estimating the model for the total sample, the model is estimated separately for firms younger than ten years and for firms ten years or older. Younger firms are assumed to generally follow an 'entrepreneurial' ('Schumpeter I') innovation model, while older firms rather follow a 'routinized' ('Schumpeter II') innovation regime. The outcomes for the older firms are expected to resemble the results found by Brouwer and Kleinknecht (1999), while the 'entrepreneurial' firms might deviate.

RESULTS

The logit estimates of factors influencing the probability that an innovator will achieve patent protection are summarized in Table 27.3. Looking at the estimates for the total sample (Model I) and at the separate estimate on firms with the age of ten years and more (Model III), three results that are consistent with the expectations are found. First, as in Brouwer and Kleinknecht (1999), R&D collaborators are significantly more likely to patent than firms that innovate on a stand-alone basis.[2] Second, firms launching products that are not only new to the firm but also new to the market have higher propensities to patent. Third, a higher propensity to patent also holds for firms that launch new (other than incrementally improved) products.

It should be noted that the database severely limits our possibilities for analyzing inter-industry differences in the propensity to patent. This is for two reasons. First, detailed industry dummies cannot be introduced due to low numbers of innovators in several industries. Second, standard industry classifications often are not meaningful for highly innovative firms. One should realize that Schumpeterian 'new combinations', by definition, deviate from standard economic activities that can be conveniently grouped into well-defined industry classes. Innovators engage in an uncertain search process with sometimes surprising outcomes. An example in the database is a firm that started as a chemical firm and developed into a producer of chemical measurement devices. In other words, the uncertain search process can lead to an untidy industry classification. This may explain why, in various tentative estimates not shown here, few comprehensive differences in patenting propensities across industries were found. Surprisingly, even a simple 'manufacturing' versus 'services' dummy proved insignificant. It is reassuring, however, that all the tentative experiments with industry dummies had only a negligible influence on the coefficients of other variables.

In conclusion, it is not possible to reproduce the results on inter-industry differences

Table 27.3   *Factors affecting the probability of a new product-announcing firm achieving patent protection (summary of logit estimates; coefficients (z-values in brackets)*

Exogenous variables	Model I Total sample:	Model II Firms <10 years old	Model III Firms of 10 and more years old
Number of partners for R&D	0.17	0.19	0.18
collaboration	(2.93)**	(1.79)*	(2.43)**
R&D activities on a permanent basis	−0.19	0.02	−0.32
	(−0.54)	(0.05)	(−0.63)
Control dummies for product characteristics:			
Product is new to the market, other	1.12	0.69	1.41
than new to the firm	(2.95)**	(1.18)	(2.63)**
Product is radically new, other than	0.83	0.42	0.95
incrementally improved	(2.80)**	(0.88)	(2.42)**
Constant term	−2.30	−1.47	−2.82
	(−4.72)**	(−1.85)*	(4.24)**
Number of observations	251	90	161
Pseudo R^2	0.10	0.05	0.13

Notes: ** Significant at 5% level; * significant at 10% level.

in the propensity to patent reported by Arundel and Kabla (1998) and Brouwer and Kleinknecht (1999). The difference between the latter two studies and this one seems to come mainly from the fact that Arundel and Kabla used data from Europe's largest firms and Brouwer and Kleinknecht used CIS data that, while covering also smaller size classes, still ignored firms below ten workers. One should note that firms with fewer than ten workers represent 116 out of 398 firms (29 percent) in the database. In the latter two studies, industry classifications seem to be more meaningful than among our small and young innovators.

Unexpectedly the dummy variable on 'permanent' versus 'occasional' R&D activities is insignificant. Seemingly, the high innovation intensities of entrepreneurial firms dominate other effects such as a more 'professionalized' attitude toward innovation. It should be added that in earlier estimates, not shown here, dummies for firms that are spin-offs from larger firms are included. However, in all versions, this variable was far from significant.

The most striking result is found when separating the younger firms from older ones; see Models II and III. In fact, all the variables that were significant among the older firms (and a bit less so in our total sample) are insignificant for younger firms. For firms less than ten years old, no single systematic factor that makes a difference for the propensity to patent is found. Not surprisingly, in the estimate for the young innovators, R^2 is low. The above conclusions also hold when the demarcation line for a young firm changes from less than ten years to less than five years.

It is interesting to see that innovators younger than ten years have a considerably higher propensity to seek patent protection for newly announced products (see Table 27.1 above). Among firms less than ten years old, 47 percent applied for such a patent, while in the group of ten and more years old, the corresponding percentage is only 27 percent. Experiments with the size variable, not shown here, reveal that there is no linear relationship between firm size and the propensity to patent, neither in the total sample, nor in the group of younger or older firms. A dummy for less than ten years old (versus ten years and more), however, is significant for all estimates. This suggests that there is a meaningful difference between the young, 'entrepreneurial' innovators and the older, 'routinized' innovators.

CONCLUSIONS

Research by Arundel and Kabla (1998) shows that a firm's propensity to patent an innovation differs considerably across industries. Using quite different data, Brouwer and Kleinknecht (1999) confirmed those results and added that the patenting propensity differs by firm size and between innovators that do or do not collaborate on R&D. In this chapter, the results of these two studies is only partly reproduced, in part due to the use of data strongly influenced by small and young firms with high innovation intensities. In particular, the data are less suitable for analyzing inter-industry differences in the patent propensity, as young innovators are difficult to classify correctly by sectors. Many of their innovative activities (with often uncertain outcomes) might cut across standard industry definitions; in the long run, they might even force statistical agencies to revise their industry classifications.

For firms of ten years and older, one result by Brouwer and Kleinknecht (1999) is reproduced: firms collaborating on R&D have significantly higher probabilities of seeking patent protection for innovations. Moreover, it is plausible that we find higher patenting probabilities among firms that have new (other than incrementally improved) products and among firms that offer products that are 'new to the market', other than only 'new to the firm'. It is interesting, however, that all those results do *not* hold for firms less than ten years old. In fact, seeking for factors that influence a young firm's propensity to patent, no significant variables are found. It looks as if the decision whether or not to seek patent protection for an innovation is a random-walk process among those young and highly innovative firms. One can only say that almost half of these firms (47 percent as opposed to 27 percent of the older firms) apply for patent protection of their newly announced products, but it seems hard to find variables that predict to which half a young firm is likely to belong.

The difference between younger and older firms (taking ten years as a division line) is a reasonable proxy for the distinction between a Schumpeter I ('entrepreneurial') and a Schumpeter II ('routinized') innovation model. Almost all innovators in the databases used by Arundel and Kabla (1998) and by Brouwer and Kleinknecht (1999) (and most of the older firms in our database) are likely to fit into a Schumpeter II model. For this 'routinized' innovation model, processes of path-dependent historical knowledge accumulation, experience and organizational learning are of obvious importance, and this offers possibilities for predicting their patenting behavior. On the other hand, the patenting behavior of young firms that seem to fit into the Schumpeter I ('entrepreneurial') garage business model is hard to predict. All that can be said is that these are highly technology-driven firms. The patenting activity is substantially higher than among the older firms. Seemingly, however, there is too much turbulence in this group to allow an estimate of a meaningful model of patenting behavior.

NOTES

1. This percentage is based on 354 (out of 398) firms that answered the question on patenting in our survey. The percentage of patenting innovators underlying our estimate (34.7 percent) differs slightly, as only 251 firms had no item non-response to the various variables used in the estimate.
2. Note that information about numbers of partners is used for R&D collaboration, while Brouwer and Kleinknecht (1999) use a simple dummy for firms that collaborate on R&D.

REFERENCES

Acs, Z.J. and D.B. Audretsch (1989), 'Patents as a measure of innovative activity', *Kyklos*, **42**, 171–80.
Acs, Z.J. and D.B. Audretsch (1993), 'Analysing innovation output indicators: the US experience', in A. Kleinknecht and D. Bain (eds), *New Concepts in Innovation Output Measurement*, London: Macmillan, pp. 10–41.
Arundel, A. and I. Kabla (1998), 'What percentage of innovative activity is patented?', *Research Policy*, **27**, 127–41.
Blind, K., J. Edler, R. Frietsch and U. Schmoch (2006), 'Motives to patent: empirical evidence from Germany', *Research Policy*, **35**, 655–72.
Brouwer, E. and A. Kleinknecht (1999), 'Innovative output and a firm's propensity to patent. An exploration of CIS micro data', *Research Policy*, **28**, 615–24.
Coombs, R. P. Narandren and A. Richards (1996), 'A literature-based innovation output indicator', *Research Policy*, **25**, 403–13.
Flor, M.L. and M.J. Oltra (2004), 'Identification of innovating firms through technological innovation indicators: an application to the Spanish ceramic tile industry', *Research Policy*, **33** (2), 323–36.
Futures Group, The (1984), *Characterization of Innovations Introduced on the US Market in 1982*, report by K.L. Edwards and T.J. Gordon, Glastonbury, CT, May (mimeo).
Kleinknecht, A. and D. Bain (eds) (1993), *New Concepts in Innovation Output Measurement*, London: Macmillan.
Kleinknecht, A., K. van Montfort and E. Brouwer (2002), 'The non-trivial choice between innovation indicators', *Economics of Innovation and New Technology*, **11**, 109–21.
Levin, R.C., A. Klevorick, R.R. Nelson and S. Winter (1987), 'Appropriating the returns from industrial research and development', *Brookings Papers on Economic Activity*, **3**, 783–820.
Saarinen, J. (2005), *Innovations and Industrial Performance in Finland, 1945–1998*, PhD thesis, Department of Economic History, University of Lund.
Santarelli, E. and R. Piergiovanni (1996), 'Analyzing literature-based innovation output indicators: the Italian experience', *Research Policy*, **25**, 689–711.
Van der Panne, G. (2004), *Entrepreneurship and Regional Knowledge Spillovers*, PhD thesis, TU Delft, Faculty of Technology, Policy and Management.

28 Business–public research collaborations, entrepreneurship and market orientation: impact on innovativeness in regional clusters

Andreas Eisingerich and Tobias Kretschmer

The potential of a regional cluster to create jobs and wealth, and to sustain the region's economic well-being is seen as particularly important by business leaders and policy-makers. Economists and geographers have long argued that firms accumulate significant benefits from co-location, and a significant body of scholarship studies the social and economic processes driving agglomeration. Researchers examining determinants and outcomes of successful clusters of co-located organizations consider (1) the embeddedness of economic action (Piore and Sabel, 1984; Storper, 1997); (2) the sharing and creation of knowledge (Maskell and Lorenzen, 2004; Powell et al., 1996; Tallman et al., 2004); and (3) agglomeration effects (Henderson, 1974; Marshall, 1920; Mills, 1967).

While there is extensive literature on the perceived success of exemplary clusters (see, e.g., Bresnahan et al., 2001; Rosenberg, 2002; Saxenian, 1994), a clear understanding of the unique factors sustaining the innovativeness of clusters across geographic regions and industrial sectors is still lacking. Owen-Smith and Powell (2004) highlight the important role of universities in spreading new knowledge across proximate actors. While most agree on the importance of new knowledge, little about the potential of research institutions to act as key determinants of a cluster's success is known. In this study, this gap in the current literature is addressed through the exploration of the various elements of business–public research collaborations that can sustain cluster innovativeness and performance over time.

Entrepreneurship, whether conceptualized as the creation of new organizations (Dobrev and Barnett, 2005), development and commercialization of new products and processes (Schumpeter, 1934), or the exploitation of new markets (Lumpkin and Dess, 1996) is considered key to social and economic development. For example, creating new jobs facilitates social mobility of actors (Carroll and Hannan, 2000), which in turn may foster flexibility, responsiveness to change and innovativeness. Despite the body of research on the clustering of entrepreneurial action (Saxenian, 1994; Schoonhoven and Romanelli, 2000; Stuart and Sorenson, 2003), there is little consideration of either the relationship between entrepreneurship and business–public research collaborations or its combined impact on cluster innovativeness. In this study, we address this gap in the literature by directly assessing the relationships between business–public research collaborations and entrepreneurship on the one hand with levels of entrepreneurship and innovativeness within clusters on the other.

Theories embracing the idea that firms located in clusters may be more innovative than other firms traditionally focus on the transmission of tacit knowledge (Audretsch, 1998; Jaffe et al., 1993), enhanced access to information (Audretsch and Feldman, 1999), and the role of sophisticated consumers (Porter, 1998). Proponents of these theories argue that actors within a cluster may innovate more because there is greater likelihood of tacit knowledge exchange, thus providing a larger pool of ideas. In addition to this, demanding, knowledgeable consumers can provide further stimuli to innovate and commercialize new ideas. However, these models fail to consider whether actors have the capacity and willingness to generate and disseminate market intelligence in the first place. Because a company's innovativeness can be strongly related to its ability to understand and trade upon exogenous factors influencing consumers' current and future needs, our purpose in this study is to examine the following connections. First, we examine the extent market orientation within clusters, as defined by Kohli and Jaworski (1990), is positively related to a cluster's overall innovativeness. Second, we assess the extent to which the generation and dissemination of market intelligence becomes more important to actors' capacity to develop new innovations as environmental uncertainty increases.

This study provides a conceptual framework in which to propose how and why business–public research collaborations can foster innovation within regional clusters. Specifically, we propose that the links between business and public research institutions have a significant impact on innovation by catalyzing entrepreneurial action in a cluster. Further, we posit that the positive relationship between collaboration and innovation in clusters increases as the environment becomes more uncertain. We also identify a cluster's collective market orientation as a determinant of innovation in clusters. Our findings support the proposition that companies and research institutions can work together to drive economic activity and innovation within clusters. Theoretical and practical contributions of the study are discussed.

CONTRIBUTION OF THIS STUDY

Researchers run the risk of being seduced by the glamour of the 'cluster brand' (Martin and Sunley, 2003) at the cost of rigorous analysis and examination of whether regional clusters can sustain economic action and entrepreneurial activities. Fascinated by the performance of Silicon Valley, numerous clusters around the globe tried to replicate its formula for success (Rosenberg, 2002). This fascination of using the 'cluster brand' has created an entire industry of consultants and policy advisers keen to copy the success of Silicon Valley for regional and national governments. However, lessons learned from a small number of well-known success stories in specific sectors, such as information technology, may not be applicable to other clusters and sectors around the world.

By employing a design for our study that differentiates itself in terms of the number and breadth of clusters studied, using a common methodological framework, we seek to extend current research on clusters and innovation. Specifically, we examine ten clusters across four industries in North America and Europe identifying key determinants of cluster innovativeness. We argue that actors' ability both to generate and disseminate market intelligence and to exploit collaborative linkages between business and public research organizations can act as an important source of innovativeness within clusters. Given the substantial costs involved in both public and private research, it is even more important to identify and trade upon potential synergies created by the market-oriented cooperation between public research institutions and industry.

This study proceeds as follows. In the next section, we present our research methodology. Then we combine our findings with existing work to develop a series of testable propositions. Specifically, we outline the roles of market orientation, entrepreneurship and the collaboration between business and research institutions in driving and sustaining innovation within a cluster. Finally the theoretical and practical contributions as well as the implications of the study are discussed, along with the limitations and potential avenues for future research.

METHODOLOGY

Analysis and Procedures

We conducted in-depth field research across ten industrial clusters to incorporate a wide range of perspectives and experiences to accommodate the diverse nature of sectors and regional clusters (Eisenhardt, 1989, 1991; Miles and Huberman, 1984). The use of replication logic in multiple-case studies helps ensure external validity as well as construct and internal validity (Eisenhardt, 1989, 1991; Yin, 1994). Using multiple sources of evidence gives us an overview of the shared views of cluster participants and observers.

In-depth interviews with over 100 general managers/chief executive officers help us understand the phenomena as expressed by cluster members and observers in their own words (Taylor and Bogdan, 1998). While Box 28.1 summarizes interview questions, it can only partly convey the content of our rich discussions, as interviewees frequently provided additional and complementary comments. We combined our primary data with archival data and industry publications to avoid 'elite bias' (Seidler, 1974) and to interpret and validate new lines of thinking regarding the effects of cluster networks. Methodologically, the goal of this study was to accurately describe network phenomena within clusters through an iterative process of theory development (Eisenhardt, 1989, 1991) using multiple sources of evidence (Miles and Huberman, 1984).The specific details of data collection are recorded in the Appendix.

Research Setting: Industrial Clusters in North America and Europe

Based on the review of extant literature and in-depth analyses of regional clusters, industrial clusters with varying levels of environmental uncertainty were selected: biotechnology, chemicals, information technology and the automotive sector. Following Kohli and Jaworski (1990), three components of environmental uncertainty are considered: (1) market turbulence or the rate of change in the composition of customers and their preferences; (2) competitive intensity; and (3) technological turbulence or the rate of technological change. Lant et al.'s (1992) approach to examine companies operating under different degrees of environmental uncertainty is also employed and, thus, analyzed the environmental complexity, predictability and frequency of change faced by firms operating in individual clusters.

During the pre-study interviews it became apparent that it was more difficult for biotechnology firms to gauge future sales levels for existing products and markets than for chemical firms. Similarly, firms in the information technology and biotechnology sectors

BOX 28.1   INTERVIEW ITEMS

Collaboration between business and public research institutions

- To what extent do you collaborate with public research institutions (such as universities, think-tanks, research hospitals etc.)?
- What are the positive and negative consequences of collaborations with public research institutions?
- When are collaborations with public research institutions not very important to business innovativeness?
- To what extent do collaborations between public research institutions and industry impact overall levels of innovation within a cluster?
- How do formal linkages with research organizations preclude you from dealing with your exchange partners informally over time?
- To what extent does regional proximity/cluster membership make any difference to the effectiveness of industry–public research collaborations?

The role of entrepreneurship

- How do collaborations with public research organizations make any difference to the way you think of new business opportunities?
- What are the major costs/benefits associated with these collaborations?
- What does the term 'entrepreneurship' mean to you?
- How do your linkages with public research organizations affect the way you try to do new business?
- To what extent does the collaboration between industry and public research organizations impact levels of entrepreneurial action in a cluster?

The role of market orientation

- What does the term 'market orientation' mean to you?
- Has your market orientation changed since you started to operate in this cluster?
- Which role does the generation and dissemination of market intelligence play for your business?
- What are the positive and negative consequences of being market oriented to your business?
- When is being market oriented not very important to overall levels of innovation in a cluster?

Entrepreneurship and innovation in clusters

- What characteristics of a cluster foster or discourage entrepreneurship and innovation?

- Do you think this cluster is more/less innovative than other comparative clusters?
- Which factors are key to sustaining a cluster's innovativeness over time?
- To what extent does entrepreneurship impact levels of innovativeness in a cluster?

had to cope with more frequent environmental changes, such as technological change, product obsolescence and the development of new markets, than chemical firms. On the other hand, global competition, pressure to consolidate and volatile prices of raw materials led to intensified competition in an uncertain market environment, forcing companies in the automotive sector to redefine the competitive advantages addressing changing market conditions.

Regarding R&D efforts, information technology and biotechnology firms explore new applications of the current capabilities building on a diverse set of approaches. While chemical companies focused most of itsresources on maximizing efficiency of extant processes, the majority of firms in the automotive sector experimented with emerging technologies in addition to process innovations reducing the costs of production. Interview respondents underscored the importance of timely results in the information technology and biotech sectors.

Geographic clusters for the study were identified on the following bases: first, clusters with similar structures were identified to the greatest possible degree. More specifically, all clusters in the sample were strongly linked to the economic, research and cultural capitals of their respective economic region. In addition, clusters had a large number of economic activities centered on public research facilities. Second, clusters in the sample had relatively less-developed venture capital communities. At the same time public organizations played an important role in the funding and dissemination of research activities in all the clusters. Third, European clusters were similar in age and stages of development. These basic similarities helped with the analysis and interpretation of collected data. Specifically, comparing similar clusters enabled controlling for 'extraneous variation' (Eisenhardt, 1989, p. 536) and, thus presented more convincing results.

The 'embedded' rather than holistic multiple-case study approach (Yin, 1994) is taken in order to discuss the impact of network characteristics on cluster performance. Accordingly, each cluster analysis consisted of a 'whole' study in and of itself. Therefore individual field results were not pooled across clusters. Rather, archival data analyses and in-depth interviews led to insights for each cluster. Each case's conclusions were then considered to be findings needing replication by other individual cluster cases.

DETERMINANTS OF CLUSTER INNOVATIVENESS

In this section the expectations of the impact of business–public research collaborations, entrepreneurship and levels of market orientation on the innovativeness of clusters are formalized. Figure 28.1 illustrates the proposed relationships between these variables. Specifically, both market orientation and business–public research collaborations are

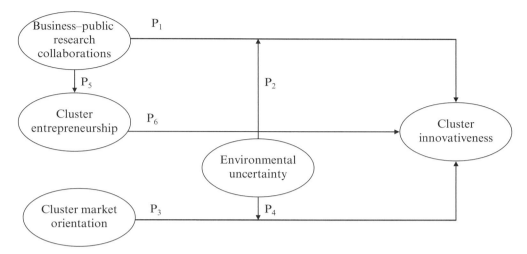

Figure 28.1   Business–public research collaborations, entrepreneurship, market orientation and cluster innovativeness

expected to have positive relationships with a cluster's innovativeness. Further, when environmental uncertainty is high, both levels of market orientation and business–public research collaborations should have stronger effects on clusters' innovativeness. The role of entrepreneurship to mediate the relationship between collaboration and cluster innovativeness is further examined. The detailed rationale behind these propositions is provided below.

Business–Public Research Collaborations

By facilitating the openness necessary to develop new knowledge and innovation, public research institutions, such as universities, think tanks and research hospitals, can contribute substantially to the agility of, and innovation in, regional clusters. In this study, public research institutions are observed acting as catalysts of innovation and business activity within regional clusters for a number of reasons. First, researchers at university and other public institutions are frequently embedded in global innovation networks. Researchers often form small, highly focused groups of shared interests. In addition to their international links, these research groups can consistently attract the most promising talents in the field. By offering access to a global network of expertise, public research institutions can help cluster members to side-step dysfunctional forces of collective inertia and reduced competitive vigilance. In the face of increasing R&D costs, internationalization of research activities and shorter invention and development cycles, the ability to trade upon an international network of experts is likely to take on added significance. As the director of a public research hospital put it:

> Now, I can draw on my own research but I can also draw on the expertise of all my colleagues who may have something bundle-able. In the end, it allows me to offer a more valuable and stronger package.

During our research, interviewees often argued that the locus of research development and competition in the research environment of the early 2000s is not individual people but is instead research networks composed of people working in different institutions around the world. One common misconception is that research performed in public institutions, such as universities and research hospitals, is static, archaic and protected from competition. Contrary to popular belief, academic research can be fiercely competitive. For example, when the deputy director of a biotechnology think tank was questioned about the significance of competition, he replied:

> In life sciences, competition is the most important topic of all. Information spreads extremely fast in this area of work. Right now, there are hundreds of scientists competing with each other globally day by day. Everyone wants to come first.

Because of fierce competition, researchers at university and research hospitals work hard to stay on top of current developments and seek to collaborate with the best partners in the field. Conversely, businesses may be forced to focus on short-term results and consequently are unable to devote sufficient time and resources to basic research. By dedicating significant resources to fundamental research and exploiting networks of cutting-edge research capabilities, public research institutions enable private companies to take advantage of an entire pool of potential business opportunities. As the head of a major research center explained it:

> I see innovation as the strongest engine of economic development. Most radical innovations were discovered by accident, and it may take some time to see the real potential of them. In this place, we work to make sure the pipeline of ideas does not dry up. We lay the eggs and business may find ways of turning them into gold.

More specifically, business–public research collaborations can create synergies facilitating access to a diverse set of actors, thus enhancing opportunity scanning, fostering outreach and the agility to innovate, all necessary to avoid suffocation and potential lock-in. Past research underscores the importance of links to a diverse set of exchange partners as key indicators of actors' adaptability (Burt, 1992; McFadyen and Cennalla, 2004). Because public research institutions may exhibit different cultures, policies and strategies from private businesses, regional clusters connecting companies with public research actors are more likely to provide an environment that results in sustainable and successful evolutionary business strategies. As the general manager of a biotechnology company put it:

> It frequently happens that we face hurdles in certain areas, and it really helps to take a step back, go to the experts in that field and ask for some assistance. Very often their [academics'] approach is different from ours, and they may approach the issue from an angle we never thought of.

In addition to increasing the likelihood of complementarities, exchanges between business and public research institutions can enhance actors' capability of adaptive behavior and problem solving. In this study it was observed that clusters characterized by a critical amount of internal diversity created catalytic reactions and ultimately exploited existing ideas more fully. Diversity creates further diversity through ongoing innovation (Grabher and Stark, 1997), and links between actors are unique to specific regional clusters. These links are difficult, if not impossible, to transfer, and therefore can represent a crucial source of a cluster's sustainable competitive advantage. For instance, when asked about the major factors driving the success of one particular regional cluster in our sample, the director of research at a public hospital said:

> Being able to work as part of a team is one of the major success factors of scientists in this region. And my personal opinion is that researchers and scientists mainly stay and work here for many, many years, because of the trust and collaboration they can get. I think this is very unique about this place. You can go and pack your books into a suitcase, but you cannot take the research environment with you.

Diversity, however, is of limited use without communication and interaction. Actors must establish ties with each other in order to facilitate exchange of capabilities and resources, thus fully unlocking the potentials of diversity. Clusters with diverse, but isolated, members may have the same chance of suffering from inertia as inward-focused clusters. Cooperative ties between companies and public research institutions foster internal diversity as more business opportunities are exploited, resulting in an increasing number of new products and services. Universities facilitate the early establishment of links between people who will work at different institutions at later stages of their careers. Regional proximity, on the other hand, reduces the perceived costs of getting hold of each other and further enhances cooperation, as individuals are more likely to casually interact with each other. As exchange facilitates the exploration and exploitation of opportunities actors within a cluster may benefit from a virtuous cycle of enhanced innovativeness. Accordingly, on the basis of these arguments we offer the following propositions:

P_1 *Business–public research collaboration will be positively related to cluster innovativeness.*

P_2 *The positive effects of business–public research collaboration on cluster innovativeness will increase as environments become more uncertain.*

Market Orientation and Innovation within Clusters

In the past, new product development was mainly determined by individual companies' capabilities to collect and understand information about their customers and competitors. However, as competition has gradually shifted from among individual integrated firms to among clustered networks of organizations, a firm's market orientation, as defined by Kohli and Jaworski (1990), not only affects the company's responsiveness to competition and customer needs but can impact the entire network of companies of which it is a part. This is because individual companies can learn from, and take advantage of, each other's market orientation. As Achrol and Kotler (1999) suggest, companies that integrate and expand information flows may benefit from more effective coordination of actions and consequently higher product innovation performance (Han et al., 1998).

Specifically, the high social and formal connectivity within clusters facilitates the rapid recognition of change, as actors observe each other's offerings in the marketplace. Because actors continuously observe and adjust to change, they develop intuition regarding future changes in competitive pressures, technology and customer wants. Both the speed and the depth of the challenges to established ideas and assumptions may have to increase to successfully exploit changes in technology, competition and customer wants. Because actors are more directly affected by, but may also more easily observe, each other's portfolio of initiatives in the same cluster, market-oriented clusters are likely to be characterized by high levels of innovation. As the chief executive officer in an information technology company put it:

> I don't think [business name] would be as flexible and innovative somewhere else, and I will tell you why. Most importantly, an entire ecosystem has evolved and developed around us and a couple of other companies in this cluster. We might not be tightly linked with every single business, but we watch carefully what they are doing to identify opportunities. It's this collective alertness that steers our business toward where markets are heading.

As actors can more easily observe, assess and integrate each other's changing product and service offerings within a cluster, organizations are forced to create more differentiated value propositions and new sources of demand. Accordingly, high levels of market orientation may not only increase competition within a cluster but also enhance the competitiveness of its actors. Vertical and horizontal network relations within a cluster enable firms to observe the success or failure of various forms of customization, as they may share direct or indirect links with customers and partnering firms.

Moreover, as market orientation levels within a cluster increase, localized business can supply a greater number and variety of products and services. This takes on added significance as the value chains of more and more businesses consist of networks of firms, including suppliers of specialized inputs, manufacturers of complementary products and providers of complementary services that can increase innovation by facilitating greater specialization of both inputs and outputs (Anderson et al., 1994; Wathne and Heide, 2004). According to Piore and Sabel (1984), for instance, 'flexible specialization' may lead to improved efficiency, reduced input prices and greater speed to market from the collective market orientation within a cluster. As the chief executive officer at a supplier of automotive parts put it:

> [Business name] would not be able to operate as effectively elsewhere, where firms do not know our customers. Our partners must also understand the businesses of our customers. How can we offer the right product and make a profit when our partners have no idea about what we are trying to achieve?

Therefore, in addition to accessing larger pools of ideas and innovations (Audretsch and Feldman, 1999) and taking advantage of a greater variety of specialized suppliers, actors may also greatly benefit from high levels of market orientation within a cluster. First, high levels of collective market orientation can lead to 'flexible specialization' where firms share time and effort involved in observing and understanding market trends. To develop and design competitive products and services, firms need detailed information about changing technologies, competition and customer needs. Because it is costly and time-consuming to collect relevant information, actors' ability to build on each other's market intelligence can act as a source of competitive advantage. Essentially, high levels of market orientation within a cluster may allow individual firms to gain access to a greater depth and breadth of information than isolated firms.

Actors outside a cluster, on the other hand, cannot benefit from a cluster's collective market orientation for a number of reasons. A body of extant research illustrates that firms apply very different coordination mechanisms according to different contexts (Carson et al., 2003; Langfred, 2004; McEvily et al., 2003). More specifically, information spreads faster within industrial clusters through an abundance of weak and strong ties facilitated by geographic proximity (Dyer and Singh, 1998; Kogut, 2000; Maskell and Lorenzen, 2004; Powell et al., 1996; Tallman et al., 2004). Furthermore, regional proximity may foster trust between actors and take on added significance for inter-organizational cooperation, exchange of information and learning.

Trust can facilitate effective interaction between organizations (Arrow, 1974; Barney and Hansen, 1994; Dyer and Chu, 2003; Zaheer et al. 1998). When discussing the benefits of trust during our study, many interviewees talked about issues relating to transaction costs (Williamson, 1975, 1985). For instance, the director of an information technology company argued:

> I would say [business name] has two different kinds of partners. First, companies we can trust to work with us and, second, companies working according to contracts. The latter cannot be relied on to do anything that is not written in the contract. It's a completely different story with most of our local partners. We share a culture of getting things done. I give them a call and settle things on the spot. They know [business name] does the same when they are in similar situations.

Coleman (1984) corroborates the importance of 'social trust' among regionally proximate actors to facilitate activities within a whole environment of potential business partners through lowering contract costs. Clustering can play an even more significant role in knowledge exchange. Because of its complex, tacit and 'sticky' nature, knowledge is especially difficult to transfer and absorb (Kogut and Zander, 1992; Nelson and Winter, 1982; Szulanski, 1996). Close regional proximity, however, facilitates frequent interpersonal contact and informal relations between firms, enabling more effective knowledge exchange. First, shared values combined with reputational effects may create a socioeconomic environment with reduced uncertainty and enhanced cooperation among cluster members. Moreover, because of increased interpersonal contact, co-location can also enable firms to improve their absorptive capacity (Cohen and Levinthal, 1990; Zahra and George, 2002) and increase the potential for 'collective learning' (Lawson and Lorenz, 1999). As confirmed by numerous respondents, information related to market orientation is extraordinarily difficult to exchange, let alone absorb, when partners do not share a common mindset about customers and markets. For instance, the director of a company in the new media industry said:

> It is almost as if we were talking about two different things. We say A and they understand B. Our people believe markets will go this way, and they think it will go the other way. But I can understand where they are coming from because I have visited their place and I could see that companies operate differently there. I mean, we share so many common things here. I never have to start explaining local customer behavior to a partner that works here.

Rapid technological progress and changes in competition or customer needs make it even more difficult for firms to predict environmental circumstances. For example, communicating in a foreign language is already a formidable task. Similarly, high environmental uncertainty is likely to aggravate existing coordination problems between firms. First, the higher environmental uncertainty, the more asymmetric is information distributed (Akerlof, 1970) and, thus, the higher the threat of opportunistic behavior by a firm. Accordingly, trust is more important in uncertain economic environments. Information asymmetry and speed of environmental progress, however, may not only act as a barrier to trusting relationships but also make exchanging information more difficult. Regional proximity, on the other hand, may help actors cope by facilitating continuous observation, benchmarking and monitoring what other firms are doing in the same cluster.

In summary, clustered firms are more likely to share common formal and social information channels unavailable to firms outside a cluster. Shared history, trust and common understanding of phenomena can also enhance cluster members' ability to interpret, and learn from, each other's strategies. Because firms outside a cluster may not be able to make full use of market-related information available to clustered firms, clusters may benefit from high rates of successful innovation that cannot be imitated easily by non-cluster firms. Based on these arguments, we propose:

P_3 *Collective market orientation within a cluster will be positively related to cluster innovativeness.*

P_4 *The positive effects of collective market orientation within a cluster on cluster innovativeness will increase as environments become more uncertain.*

Business–Public Research Collaborations: Impact on Entrepreneurship

While collective resources, such as local access to a large pool of well-trained and specialized labor, can be an important asset to regional clusters (Marshall, 1920; Porter, 1998), the comments of a chief scientific officer at a biotechnology company indicate that something else may be needed in addition to highly skilled labor:

> The university has one of the most dominant publication records, it has the best citation record and, yet, we get the least number of true biotech companies created here. The technology transfer from universities to the private sector is just terrible. In order to make business work, companies and universities have to work more closely together.

This emphasizes the need to understand what determines levels of entrepreneurship in regional clusters. Although entrepreneurship is frequently thought of as the act of an individual (Stevenson et al., 1999), it is often shaped by social, economic and institutional forces surrounding the entrepreneur (Stuart and Sorenson, 2003). According to McMullen and Shepherd (2006), uncertainty can be responsible for preventing prospective entrepreneurial action from taking place, so that fewer actors may engage in entrepreneurial activities when they perceive the environment as unpredictable (Hayek, 1945; Kirzner, 1979; Milliken, 1987). It is further suggested that less entrepreneurial action takes place when actors lack sufficient knowledge to act upon a number of options (Duncan, 1972; Milliken, 1987; Shane and Venkataraman, 2000). Because the inability of an actor to create and trade upon market opportunities is frequently offset by others (Schumpeter, 1934), a cluster's ability to foster entrepreneurial action takes on added significance.

Business–public research collaborations help actors reduce perceived uncertainty in several ways. First, knowledge developed at research institutions may provide actors with tools to reduce uncertainty and combine extant resources profitably. For instance, labor mobility and knowledge flows from public to private research institutes and companies have been argued to be one of the most significant determinants of innovation in clusters (Jaffe et al. 1993; Owen-Smith and Powell, 2004; Saxenian, 1994). However, when researchers leave public institutions to work in a cluster's private sector, the divide between business and research institutions is likely to remain or grow even larger. The chief executive officer at a biotechnology company described the outcome of hiring a public researcher as follows:

> He is an enormous talent and we are glad to have him with us, but at the same time I must admit that we lost our connection with [university name] because of that. Unfortunately he was pretty much the only person willing to work with business there.

Entrepreneurial skills and market information can be transmitted between private firms and public research institutions in a variety of ways, but one of the most effective is close collaboration. As scientists at private and public institutions continue to learn from each other, more academic researchers are more likely to see the benefits from commercialization of innovation. During our study, we observed that numerous academic researchers are still uneasy about, if not hostile to, the idea of commercializing their innovations and links between business and academia in general. Conversely, many researchers would like to see their discoveries make significant contributions to society. As researchers at public institutions gain experience in working with business, they are likely to become more confident in exploiting the practical sides of collaboration to maximize their impact on society. Therefore a 'knowledge spiral' (Nonaka and Takeuchi, 1995) can begin when people in companies and public institutions start talking to each other about their respective approaches, goals and values. By doing so, actors can gain a deeper understanding of one another's perspectives and cooperate more effectively (Mohrman et al., 2001).

As the skills required to commercialize discoveries are substantially different from those needed to write publishable studies, only a small number of academic researchers feel comfortable managing the commercialization of work on their own. As the chief financial officer at a biotechnology company noted:

> In reality, the naive scientist one can watch in Hollywood movies, working by himself somewhere in a dark laboratory does not exist anymore. Scientists are self-confident and they have confidence in their work. But without any business experience, they still find it extremely difficult to commercialize innovations.

Scientists at public institutions, however, may acquire some of this expertise through collaboration with business partners. As a result, entrepreneurial activity should increase as more inventions are commercialized and more scientists are willing to license technologies out of their own university or public research lab and start their own businesses. Because academics founding their own company can continue to draw on the knowledge of colleagues and often maintain their ties with university and other public research institutions, they act as successful bridges between business and academic research. This is confirmed by numerous biotechnology companies founded by people who worked in public institutions, developed links with business partners and consequently started their own company in the clusters, as with MIT spin-offs populating Massachusetts Route 128 (Shane and Stuart, 2002).

Taiwan provides another case of how an intellectual property infrastructure (Di Gregorio and Shane, 2003) and intensified links between business and public research institutions can facilitate academic entrepreneurial activities (Chang et al., 2003). Through this, the number of university campus tenant business ventures in Taiwan increased from 18 in 1997 to 937 in 2003 (Chang et al., 2005). During our study, we found that partnerships with public research institutions often benefit companies, thereby enhancing entrepreneurial activities in a region. Managerial decision-makers can gain high value-added understanding of fundamental principles underlying current technologies and are thus in a better position to estimate future growth areas, avoid speculative solutions and make better decisions overall. Small and medium-sized enterprises without sufficient funds to invest in own R&D projects can especially benefit from collaborations with research organizations.

Through their prior experiences, academic researchers continue to work on practices that are likely to drive future innovation. The director of an information technology company reported the following experience:

> I saw that [business name] was not moving fast enough. We kept reinventing the wheel over again. In terms of technology development, the collaboration with [name of university] did not make much difference, but the impact on our long-term strategy was critical. I think they really helped us get a clearer picture of what we have to do to stay competitive in the long term.

Earlier economic environments may have been more stable and predictable than today (Greenwood and Hinings, 1996). In many industries today, the capability of identifying practices that will influence the future can be one of the most critical sources of competitive advantage. Therefore, we propose:

P₅   Enhanced business–public research collaborations within a cluster will be positively related to a cluster's overall level of entrepreneurship.

Entrepreneurship and Innovativeness within Clusters

New organizations do not just create additional jobs, but also act as catalysts of change. By creating jobs, new organizations create opportunities for people to make full use of their skills. For example, employees' ability to choose organizations based on their human capital is likely to affect social mobility (Carroll and Hannan, 2000), which can have an important and positive effect on innovation levels.

The ability of cluster members to (1) generate and pursue creative ideas, (2) mobilize and coordinate resources to develop those ideas into promising innovations, and (3) commercialize inventions successfully is likely to depend greatly on the depth and breadth of entrepreneurship within a cluster. For instance, by actively seeking solutions to present and future customer needs, entrepreneurship can trigger innovative processes. Because each entrepreneurial organization will seek novel ways of meeting customer needs to benefit from differentiation and economic rents, clusters characterized by high levels of entrepreneurship can host members possessing more heterogeneous knowledge and strategies. Access to heterogeneous information can be especially important for actors' ability to generate and trade upon new ideas (Coleman, 1988; McEvily and Zaheer, 1999; McFadyen and Cennalla, 2004; Rodan and Galunic, 2001), reduce lock-in effects and ossification (Pouder and St John, 1996; McFadyen and Cennalla, 2004) and take advantage of new opportunities (Burt, 1992).

In other words, entrepreneurship combines resources and brings together complementary assets to stimulate innovation that may lead to reduced production costs, enhanced output volumes and profitability. The creative combination of resources may defray production costs and minimize risks associated with the development and production of new goods (Hagedoorn, 1993; Nohria and Garcia-Pont, 1991). Because clusters with high levels of entrepreneurship are likely to host a large set of diverse actors, members can take advantage of highly specialized service activities for a single stage of production. Greater specialization, in turn, may enable companies to devote more funds to the innovation of new products and services (Feldman, 2000; Storper, 1997).

In short, by founding new business ventures, entrepreneurship can play a crucial role in developing new economic opportunities, stimulating heterogeneity, facilitating change, enhancing actors' absorptive capacities and fostering the development of new intellectual capital. Accordingly, we propose:

P_6 *A cluster's overall level of entrepreneurship will be positively related to its overall cluster innovativeness.*

GENERAL DISCUSSION

This study examines the role of both business and public research institutions in driving innovation in clusters. It suggests that the development and exploitation of new ideas and knowledge can benefit from stronger business–public research collaborations with universities, think-tanks and research hospitals. Economic action and entrepreneurial activities within clusters can also be fostered by exchanging resources between actors in business and research arenas. As entrepreneurial action is an important driver of innovation, the synergies and opportunities created through collaborative work are particularly relevant. Further, we study cluster members' ability to generate and disseminate market intelligence to examine a cluster's ability to reinvent itself and achieve high innovation rates over long periods of time. The propositions we generate from our interviews are suggestive of some real effects of cluster policy and structure on entrepreneurial and innovative activity, although they will of course have to be tested in a larger-scale empirical study.

The examination of both business ventures and research institutions in clusters fills a significant gap in the literature. While the extant body of literature contains numerous studies on well-known success stories, academic research has not yet explored the impact of collaboration between firms and research institutions on cluster innovativeness across different clusters, which is surprising given the amount of money invested in research by firms and public institutions. Increased willingness by universities to engage in technology transfer and commercialization of innovation highlights the importance of evaluating the benefits of cooperation between industry players and research institutions. Our analysis demonstrates the links between innovation, entrepreneurship and collaborations between companies and research institutions within clusters, and underscores the roles of both private and public actors in driving entrepreneurial action and innovation.

This study offers another contribution by employing in-depth case analyses of ten different clusters across four industries of varying environmental uncertainty in North America and Europe. Although respondents confirmed that the positive impact of collaboration on innovativeness increases as environmental circumstances become more uncertain, we find that companies in less volatile sectors (e.g. chemicals) can also benefit from working with scientists at university and other research institutions. Indeed, entrepreneurial activity within clusters is enhanced by initiatives designed to exploit synergies of collaboration between research institutions and companies. Our interviews also suggest that the positive relationship between levels of entrepreneurial action and business–public research collaborations is not significantly affected by the culture of different countries. More specifically, the proposed relationships were confirmed in both North America and Central Europe. By looking at numerous collaborations between actors in business and research institutions in different sectors and countries, we found that entrepreneurial activities increased as more actors engaged in such collaborative efforts.

Interestingly, most of our interviewees did not utilize all the potential benefits from collaborative action, as there are still barriers between the business and academic arenas. Specifically, conflicting performance criteria and attitudes by actors in industry and academia represent hurdles to successful industry–academia linkages. For instance, academic researchers are evaluated on the basis of the quality and number of their publications, while firms focus on developing commercially valuable processes and products that can be protected by patents. Although academic researchers may be interested in collaborating with industry partners, many decide not to because of fear that such cooperation can delay or put limitations on publication. As their career hinges on their publication output, they are often reluctant to devote time and energy to the commercialization of innovations. Conversely, companies frequently make quick decisions and, thus, may be reluctant to work with academics facing less time pressure to deliver patentable results.

It was interesting to see that many interview respondents viewed their situation as not ideal. Indeed, many interviewees thought of incentive systems that would consider commercialization of knowledge in addition to the quality and number of publications. Further, the importance of fundamental research must be communicated to companies, so that knowledge and innovations can be transformed into commercially usable forms. In examining small- and medium-sized businesses, we observed that these companies benefit most from technology transfers and research conducted at universities and public hospitals. As small- and medium-sized businesses may not be able to afford costly R&D efforts, but generate a large number of jobs and can be highly flexible and innovative in their business approach, links with research institutions would help in turning ideas and inventions into jobs and wealth within a cluster.

Our study suggests that economic action, entrepreneurial activity and levels of innovation within clusters can be increased when barriers to collaboration between industry and research institutions are overcome. Academic institutions increasingly set up technology transfer offices acting as bridges between industrial partners and academic researchers.

The most successful technology transfer officers have an academic background as well as a history in business, which enables them to communicate credibly and effectively the benefits of collaborative projects between actors in industry and academia. Although some academic researchers still oppose the commercialization of ideas, we noted that younger faculty members are increasingly receptive to linkages with industry partners. Further, we found that science students were keen on attending courses introducing concepts of technology transfer and commercialization of innovation, a development supported by the findings of our study.

Although this study involved the collection of data in ten regional clusters across four industries, the generalizability of the propositions is limited by the relatively small number of cases. Larger-scale quantitative efforts may provide additional insights and inspire greater confidence in the findings of this study. Furthermore, this study covers only two Western industrialized economies. It would be interesting to see results from a similar study in developing countries.

Another important limitation of our analysis is the omission of other factors influencing the proposed relationships. For example, the availability of seed funds, grants and loan funds makes a significant difference to actors' ability to transform knowledge into commercially usable products and processes. In both North American and European clusters, public institutions provided seed funding to assist the early development phases of commercialization. During this study, however, we observed that many actors could not fully exploit all commercial potential because of limited funds available. This suggests that especially small- and medium-sized businesses require access to funds to unlock the benefits of university–industry collaboration. Furthermore, the impact of business–public research collaborations on levels of entrepreneurial action and innovation within clusters may be affected by issues related to legal ownership of intellectual property. For example, American universities have strong incentives to set up technology transfer offices, specializing in the commercialization of knowledge because intellectual rights are awarded to them rather than to faculty members. We found, however, that numerous academic researchers set up their own business ventures when patents were granted to them. North American researchers, for example, are free to choose between making use of the services offered by public technology transfer offices or commercialize innovations themselves. Thus further work may extend our analysis by shedding additional light on the linkages between levels of entrepreneurial action, innovation and collaboration between industry and research institutions within clusters.

CONCLUSION

This study underscores the important role of business–public research collaborations in driving levels of entrepreneurial activities and innovation within clusters. By doing so, it suggests that links between companies and research institutions, such as universities and research hospitals, should be strengthened in order to facilitate entrepreneurial action that can consequently catalyze economic growth in a cluster, and advance new technologies to create and exploit new market opportunities. The findings of this study also identify entrepreneurship as a key link between effective collaboration and levels of innovation within clusters. More specifically, we suggest that to increase a cluster's overall ability to innovate, collaborations between business and research institutions may first have to foster entrepreneurial action within the cluster. In addition, we show that a cluster's innovativeness is also determined by its collective market orientation. These findings take on added significance considering the large amounts of money invested in private and public research activities as well as funds provided by public organizations to encourage business–public research collaborations and address the recent call for applying management theory to major public issues (Rynes and Shapiro, 2006) by providing a more effective guide for managers and policy-makers to master the challenge of sustainable cluster performance.

REFERENCES

Achrol, R.S. and P. Kotler (1999), 'Marketing in the network economy', *Journal of Marketing*, **63**, 146–63.

Akerlof, G. (1970), 'The market for lemons: qualitative uncertainty and the market mechanism', *Quarterly Journal of Economics*, **84**, 488–500.

Anderson, J.C., H. Håkansson and J. Johanson (1994), 'Dyadic business relationships within a business network context', *Journal of Marketing*, **58** (October), 1–15.

Arrow, K.J. (1974), *The Limits of Organization*, New York: Norton & Co.

Audretsch, D.B. (1998), 'Agglomeration and the location of innovative activity', *Oxford Review of Economic Policy*, **14** (2), 18–29.

Audretsch, D.B. and M.P. Feldman (1999), 'Innovation in cities: science-based diversity, specialization, and localized competition', *European Economic Review*, **43**, 409–29.

Barney, J.B. and M.H. Hansen (1994), 'Trustworthiness as a source of competitive advantage', *Strategic Management Journal*, **5** (2), 175–90.

Bresnahan, T., A. Gambardella and A. Saxenian (2001), '"Old economy" inputs for "new economy" outcomes: cluster formation in the new Silicon Valleys', *Industrial and Corporate Change*, **10** (4), 835–60.

Burt, R.S. (1992), *Structural Holes: The Social Structure of Competition*, Cambridge, MA: Harvard University Press.

Carroll, G.R. and M.T. Hannan (2000), *The Demography of Corporations and Industries*, Princeton, NJ: Princeton University Press.

Carson, S.J., A. Madhok, R. Varman and G. John (2003), 'Information processing moderators of the effectiveness of trust-based governance in inter-firm RandD collaboration', *Organization Science*, **14** (1), 45–56.

Chang, Y.C., Y.Y. Chu, S.C. Hung and B.W. Lin (2003), 'Science and technology drivers in a knowledge based economy', APEC-STPRC Final Report, Taiwan.

Chang, Y.C., M.H. Chen, M. Hua and P.Y. Yang (2005), 'Industrializing academic knowledge in Taiwan', *Research Technology Management*, July–August, 45–50.

Cohen, W.M. and D.A. Levinthal (1990), 'Absorptive capacity: a new perspective on learning and innovation', *Administrative Science Quarterly*, **35**, 128–52.

Coleman, J.S. (1984), 'Introducing social structure into economic analysis', *American Economic Review*, **74** (2), 84–8.

Coleman, J.S. (1988), 'Social capital in the creation of human capital', *American Journal of Sociology*, **94**, 95–120.

DiGregorio, D. and S. Shane (2003), 'Why do some universities generate more start-ups than others?', *Research Policy*, **32** (2), 209–27.

Dobrev, S.D. and W.P. Barnett (2005), 'Organizational roles and transition to entrepreneurship', *Academy of Management Journal*, **48** (3), 433–49.

Duncan, R.B. (1972), 'Characteristics of organizational environments and perceived environmental uncertainties', *Administrative Science Quarterly*, **17**, 313–27.

Dyer, J.H. and W. Chu (2003), 'The role of trustworthiness in reducing transaction costs and improving performance: empirical evidence from the United States, Japan, and Korea', *Organization Science*, **14** (1), 57–68.

Dyer, J.H. and H. Singh (1998), 'The relational view: cooperative strategy and sources of interorganizational competitive advantage', *Academy of Management Review*, **23**, 660–79.

Eisenhardt, K.M. (1989), 'Building theories from case study research', *Academy of Management Review*, **14**, 532–50.

Eisenhardt, K.M. (1991), 'Better stories and better constructs: the case for rigor and comparative logic', *Academy of Management Review*, **16**, 620–27.

Feldman, M.P. (2000), 'Location and innovation: the new economic geography of innovation, spillovers, and agglomeration', in G.L. Clark, M.P. Feldman and M.S. Gertler (eds), *The Oxford Handbook of Economic Geography*, Oxford: Oxford University Press, pp. 373–94.

Glaser, B.G. and A. Strauss (1967), *The Discovery of Grounded Theory: Strategies for Qualitative Research*, New York: Aldine Publishing Company.

Grabher, G. and D. Stark (1997), 'Organising diversity: evolutionary theory, network analysis and postsocialism', *Regional Studies*, **31** (5), 533–44.

Greenwood, R. and C.R. Hinings (1996), 'Understanding radical organizational change: bringing together the old and the new institutionalism', *Academy of Management Review*, **21**, 1022–54.

Hagedoorn, J. (1993), 'Understanding the rationale of strategic technology partnering: interorganizational modes of cooperation and sectoral differences', *Strategic Management Journal*, **14**, 371–85.

Han, J.K., N. Kim and R.K. Srivastava (1998), 'Market orientation and organizational performance: is innovation a missing link?', *Journal of Marketing*, **62**, 30–45.

Hayek, F.A. (1945), 'The use of knowledge in society', *American Economic Review*, **35**, 519–30.

Henderson, J.V. (1974), 'The sizes and types of cities', *American Economic Review*, **64**, 640–56.

Jaffe, A.B., M. Trajtenberg and R. Henderson (1993), 'Regional localization of knowledge spillovers as evidenced by patent citations', *Quarterly Journal of Economics*, **63**, 577–98.

Kirzner, I.M. (1979), *Perception, Opportunity, and Profit: Studies in the Theory of Entrepreneurship*, Chicago, IL: University of Chicago Press.

Kogut, B. (2000), 'The network as knowledge: generative rules and the emergence of structure', *Strategic Management Journal*, **21**, 405–25.

Kogut, B. and U. Zander (1992), 'Knowledge of the firm, combinative capabilities, and the replication of technology', *Organization Science*, **3**, 383–97.

Kohli, A.K. and A.B. Jaworski (1990), 'Market orientation: the construct, research propositions, and managerial implications', *Journal of Marketing*, **54** (2), 1–18.

Kumar, N., L.W. Stern and J.C. Anderson (1993), 'Conducting interorganizational research using key informants', *Academy of Management Journal*, **36**, 1633–51.

Langfred, C.W. (2004), 'Too much of a good thing? Negative effects of high trust and individual autonomy in self-managing teams', *Academy of Management Journal*, **47** (3), 385–99.

Lant, T.K., F.J. Milliken and B. Batra (1992), 'The role of managerial learning and interpretation in strategic persistence and reorientation: an empirical exploration', *Strategic Management Journal*, **13** (8), 585–608.

Lawson, C. and E. Lorenz (1999), 'Collective learning, tacit knowledge and regional innovative capacity', *Regional Studies*, **33**, 305–17.

Lumpkin, G.T. and G.G. Dess (1996), 'Clarifying the entrepreneurial orientation construct and linking it to performance', *Academy of Management Review*, **21**, 135–72.

Marshall, A. (1920), *Principles of Economics*, (8th edn), London: Macmillan.

Martin, R. and P. Sunley (2003), 'Deconstructing clusters: chaotic concept or policy panacea?', *Journal of Economic Geography*, **3** (1), 5–35.

Maskell, P. and M. Lorenzen (2004), 'The cluster as market organization', *Urban Studies*, **41** (5/6), 991–1009.

McEvily, B. and A. Zaheer (1999), 'Bridging ties: a source of firm heterogeneity in competitive capabilities', *Strategic Management Journal*, **20**, 1133–58.

McEvily, B., V. Perrone and A. Zaheer (2003), 'Trust as an organizing principle', *Organization Science*, **14** (1), 91–103.

McFadyen, A.M. and A.A. Cennalla (2004), 'Social capital and knowledge creation: diminishing returns of the number and strength of exchange relationships', *Academy of Management Journal*, **47**, 735–46.

McMullen, J.S. and D.A. Shepherd (2006), 'Entrepreneurial action and the role of uncertainty in the theory of the entrepreneur', *Academy of Management Review*, **31** (1), 132–52.

Miles, M.B. and M.A. Huberman (1984), *Qualitative Data Analysis*, Thousand Oaks, CA: Sage Publications.

Milliken, F.J. (1987), 'Three types of perceived uncertainty about the environment: state, effect, and response uncertainty', *Academy of Management Review*, **12**, 133–43.

Mills, E.S. (1967), 'An aggregative model of resource allocation in a metropolitan area', *American Economic Review*, **57**, 197–210.

Mohrman, S.A., C.B. Gibson and A.M. Mohrman (2001), 'Doing research that is useful to practice: a model and empirical exploration', *Academy of Management Journal*, **44** (2), 357–75.

Nelson, R.R. and S.G. Winter (1982), *An Evolutionary Theory of Economic Change*, Cambridge, MA: Harvard University Press.

Nohria, N. and C. Garcia-Pont (1991), 'Global strategic linkages and industry structure', *Strategic Management Journal*, **12**, 105–24.

Nonaka, I. and H. Takeuchi (1995), *The Knowledge Creating Company*, New York: Oxford University Press.

Owen-Smith, J. and W. Powell (2004), 'Knowledge networks as channels and conduits: the effects of spillovers in the Boston biotechnology community', *Organization Science*, **15**, 5–21.
Piore, M.J. and C.F. Sabel (1984), *The Second Industrial Divide*, New York: Basic Books.
Porter, M.E. (1998), 'Clusters and competition: new agendas for companies, governments, and institutions', in M.E. Porter (ed.), *On Competition*, Cambridge, MA: Harvard Business Books, pp. 197–287.
Pouder, R. and C. St John (1996), ' Hot spots and blind spots: geographical clusters of firms and innovations', *Academy of Management Review*, **21**, 1192–225.
Powell, W.W., K.W. Koput and L. Smith-Doerr (1996), 'Interorganizational collaboration and the locus of innovation: networks of learning in biotechnology', *Administrative Science Quarterly*, **41**, 116–45.
Rodan, S. and C. Galunic (2001), 'More than network structure: how knowledge heterogeneity influences managerial performance and innovativeness', *Strategic Management Journal*, **25**, 541–62.
Rosenberg, D. (2002), *Cloning Silicon Valley: The Next Generation of High-tech Hotspots*, London: Pearson Education.
Rynes, S.L. and D.L. Shapiro (2006), 'Public policy and the public interest: what if we mattered more?', *Academy of Management Journal*, **48** (6), 925–7.
Saxenian, A. (1994), *Regional Advantage: Culture and Competition in Silicon Valley and Route 128*, Cambridge, MA: Harvard University Press.
Schoonhoven, C.B. and E. Romanelli (2000), *The Entrepreneurship Dynamic: The Origins of Entrepreneurship and its Role in Industry Evolution*, Stanford, CA: Stanford University Press.
Schumpeter, J.A. (1934), *The Theory of Economic Development*, Cambridge, MA: Harvard University Press.
Seidler, J. (1974), 'On using informants: a technique for collecting quantitative data and controlling for measurement error in organizational analysis', *American Sociological Review*, **39**, 816–31.
Shane, S. and T. Stuart (2002), 'Organizational endowments and the performance of university start-ups', *Management Science*, **48** (1), 154–71.
Shane, S. and S. Venkataraman (2000), 'The promise of entrepreneurship as a field of research', *Academy of Management Review*, **25**, 217–26.
Stevenson, H., H.I. Grousbeck, M.J. Roberts and A.V. Bhide (1999), *New Business Ventures and the Entrepreneur*, New York: McGraw-Hill.
Storper, M. (1997), *The Regional World: Territorial Development in a Global Economy*, New York: Guilford Press.
Stuart, T.E. and O. Sorenson (2003), 'Liquidity events and the regional distribution of entrepreneurial activity', *Administrative Science Quarterly*, **48**, 175–201.
Szulanski, G. (1996), 'Exploring internal stickiness: impediments to the transfer of best practice within the firm', *Strategic Management Journal*, **17**, 27–44.
Tallman, S., M. Jenkins, N. Henry and S. Pinch (2004), 'Knowledge, clusters, and competitive advantage', *Academy of Management Review*, **29**, 258–71.
Taylor, S.J. and R. Bogdan (1998), *Introduction to Qualitative Research Methods*, New York: John Wiley & Sons.
Wathne, K.H. and J.B. Heide (2004), 'Relationship governance in a supply chain network', *Journal of Marketing*, **74** (January), 73–86.
Williamson, O.E. (1975), *Markets and Hierarchies*, New York: Free Press.
Williamson, O.E. (1985), *The Economic Institutions of Capitalism*, New York: Free Press.
Yin, R.K. (1994), *Case Study Research: Design and Methods*, Thousand Oaks, CA: Sage.
Zaheer, A., B. McEvily and V. Perrone (1998), 'Does trust matter? Exploring the effects of interorganizational and interpersonal trust on performance', *Organization Science*, **9** (2), 141–59.
Zahra, S.A. and G. George (2002), 'Absorptive capacity: a review, reconceptualization, and extension', *Academy of Management Review*, **27**, 185–203.

APPENDIX: METHODOLOGY

This appendix provides a detailed discussion of the data collection methodology. During the pre-study stage, extant theories were drawn upon to conduct pilot face-to-face interviews, involving open-ended, moderately directive interview questions. To accommodate the diverse nature of sectors and regions in which clusters are found, qualitative data were collected from companies in four industries: (1) biotechnology; (2) information technology; (3) chemicals; and (4) automotive. As the purpose of the pre-study analysis was to elicit propositions, grounded theory-building techniques were employed (Glaser and Strauss, 1967; Miles and Huberman, 1984). As interview data were collected and analyzed, new findings were constantly integrated clarifying particular issues and revising the framework.

Following Porter's (1998) approach, initially regional concentrations of firms in the same industrial sector were found in order to identify the constituent parts of clusters at a location. The second step was to look horizontally for industries passing through common channels or producing complementary products. Based on the literature review and the preliminary findings from five pilot interviews, a stratified sampling plan to ensure that the sample included firms and organizations within multiple clusters across industries in North America and Europe was used. The final sample was drawn after an in-depth analysis of company websites.

Throughout the study, a key informant methodology requiring one respondent from each organization was employed. The use of single informants is common in organizational level research and is especially appropriate when only a limited number of employees in a firm can reasonably be expected to have complete and detailed knowledge about the phenomena under investigation (Kumar et al., 1993). In other words, key informants are not expected to be statistically representative of members of the organization but, due to their specialized knowledge, they are able to generalize patterns of behavior after summarizing observed and/or expected organizational relationships (Seidler, 1974). A relatively large sample of interviewees was sought for three reasons. First, a large sample size increases the number of responses from which meaningful inferences can be derived. Second, given that the sample covers four industries across ten clusters, a large data set increases the potential for studying differences between clusters in both the number and strength of collaborations between companies and research institutions. In addition, the sample should reflect a diverse set of organizations. Accordingly, different-sized firms are selected, ranging from five employees to several tens of thousands, and organizations with different (1) strategies and scope (e.g. universities, trade associations, venture capital companies); (2) age; (3) country of origin; and (4) various roles (servicing, technology etc.).

Once the nature and structure of each identified cluster was understood, a letter introducing ourselves and explaining our research project was sent to potential key informants in order to avoid cold calling. Subsequently each informant was called to discuss and answer questions regarding our study. Ultimately, over 50 in-depth interviews across four European clusters were arranged. Of the individuals interviewed, the majority held general managerial positions in private and public institutions. Additionally, university professors across a range of subjects and leaders of public or university-affiliated R&D organizations were interviewed. As we wanted to explore how individuals frame and understand specific concepts and relationships, a semi-structured interview protocol was followed, permitting us to begin our investigation with propositions-directed questions, while engaging in an iterative process of refinement and picking up on interviewees' additional or complementary comments that formed an integral part of the study's findings. Interviews were conducted carefully, explaining and clarifying the questions as well as adding questions to follow up on interesting ideas and to direct the questions toward neglected areas. All but two interviews were recorded; in those cases where the tape recorder malfunctioned, detailed notes were recorded immediately following the interview. In most cases, tours of the organization were taken, allowing dialogue with regular employees. These conversations enabled access to a wide range of experiences and perspectives in the course of the data collection.

The second stage of our study involved transcribing the interviews conducted in the first round. In this stage, we also conducted a formal coding analysis of the data using NVivo software. The information obtained from the interviews was then tested against archival data and industry reports of the time. Our framework and interview questions were refined with each visitation to the data and the initial research propositions. Next, the findings from the first round of interviews were discussed with industry experts and business scholars. This ensured that the framework and the representation of phenomena were accurate and meaningful. From the analysis of our first-round data, it was found that public research institutions and universities play a particularly important role in biotechnology industries. Accordingly, the second-round sample includes more individuals working in public research organizations. Following the same approach as for our first-round sample, we contacted key informants in four North American clusters and arranged over 70 in-depth interviews.

In the third stage of our study, 79 face-to-face, semi-structured interviews in four different North American clusters were conducted. As in the first-round sample, we interviewed key informants engaged in (1) biotechnology, (2) chemicals, (3) information technology, and (4) automotive business areas. Semi-structured interviews were open-ended and carried out over a four-month period. In most cases, an invitation to tour and meet other people in the organization was extended. In 17 cases invitations for follow-up meetings were extended. The sample attempts to reflect a diverse set of organizations in order to obtain a rich set of ideas and insights. All but one interview were recorded.

In the fourth stage, all recorded interviews from the second round were transcribed and analyzed, using NVivo analysis software. A cross-country analysis, comparing findings from the North American and European clusters, was then conducted. To ensure construct validity, telephone interviews with four experts in their respective industry were held. Telephone interviews lasted around one hour and helped us to verify interview data with industry reports at the time. During the fifth stage of our study, two European clusters from our original sample were revisited and two additional European clusters were analyzed for a total of 11 interviews.

PART VI

THE MAKING OF THE ENTREPRENEUR

29 The genetics of entrepreneurship
Nicos Nicolaou and Scott Shane

INTRODUCTION

Perhaps the most common question that practitioners ask about entrepreneurship is 'Are entrepreneurs born or made?' Unfortunately, despite more than 40 years of research, scholars have only recently tried to provide an answer to this question. Using the techniques of behavioral genetics, researchers have begun to explore whether there is an innate component in entrepreneurial activity.

Despite the newness of the effort, this investigation has had significant influence on the field of entrepreneurship, as exemplified by this chapter. Initial studies show that some portion of the identification of entrepreneurial opportunities, the tendency to be an entrepreneur and entrepreneurial performance are genetic. Therefore, while handbooks on entrepreneurship have not traditionally considered the genetics of entrepreneurship, recent discoveries necessitate this discussion.

This chapter reviews the recent findings on the genetics of entrepreneurship. It examines the evidence for the effect of genes on opportunity discovery, the tendency to start a business and entrepreneurial performance. It identifies the different ways genes are thought to affect entrepreneurial activity. It reviews the methodologies used by researchers to identify genetic effects; and it outlines the direction of future research in this area. Finally, the chapter draws implications from these results for both research and practice.

THE EVIDENCE FOR THE HERITABILITY OF ENTREPRENEURIAL ACTIVITY

Heritability measures how much genetic factors influence a phenomenon of interest; it identifies the percentage of difference in observed behavior that is the result of genetic factors (psych.colorado.edu, 2009). If something has zero heritability, then genetic factors do not influence individual-level variation in the phenomenon. But if something has a non-trivial heritability, then genetics should be incorporated into explanations of it.

Many aspects of business, including financial risk taking (Zyphur et al., 2009), job turnover (McCall et al., 1997), job satisfaction (Arvey et al., 1989), job attitudes (Arvey et al., 1994), work values (Keller et al., 1992) and leadership (Arvey et al., 2007), are heritable. That is, genetics affects many aspects of business. In particular, occupational choice shows substantial heritability.

Heritability of Occupational Choice

As early as 1932, researchers found statistical evidence of the heritability of work-related interests (Carter, 1932). Genetic factors influence whether people want to become doctors or salespeople, or any number of other occupations.

Researchers have documented substantial heritability of work interests in both twin and adopted children using all major vocational instruments available (Moloney et al., 1991; Arvey and Bouchard, 1994; Grotevant et al., 1977). Combined studies of twins reared separately and adopted children show that approximately 33 percent of the variance between people in vocational interests is genetic (Betsworth et al., 1994).

Heritability of the Decision to become an Entrepreneur

Because entrepreneurship is a job, prior research on the heritability of occupational choice suggests that the decision to become an entrepreneur is also heritable. In a study of identical and fraternal twins in the UK, Nicolaou et al. (2008a) found heritabilities of 48 percent for the tendency to be self-employed, 39 percent for the number of years self-employed, 37 percent for the tendency to be an owner–operator of a business, 37 percent for the number of businesses owned and operated, 41 percent for having started a business, 42 percent for the number of businesses started, 41 percent for the tendency to have engaged in the start-up process, and 42 percent for the number of start-up efforts. Moreover, the researchers found that these heritability estimates remained the same after controlling for a variety of potentially confounding factors.

Two additional studies replicated these heritability estimates. Zhang et al. (2009) examined a sample of Swedish twins and found heritability estimates of 60 percent for entrepreneurship among women. In a sample of US twins, Nicolaou and Shane (2009b) estimate the heritability of self-employment to be 48 percent.

Moreover, Nicolaou and Shane (2009b) show that the heritability of the decision to be an entrepreneur is related to the general heritability of occupational choice. Specifically, they investigated the heritability of three additional occupational choices in the same data set in which they examined the heritability of self-employment: the decision to be a manager, a salesperson and a teacher. The results showed that being a manager, salesperson or teacher have heritability estimates of 30 percent, 46 percent and 43 percent, respectively. That is, in the same sample, the heritability estimates for being a manager, salesperson, teacher and entrepreneur are of similar magnitudes.

Heritability of Opportunity Recognition

Previous research shows that many entrepreneurs found companies to pursue specific business opportunities that they identify (Baron, 2007; Baron and Ensley, 2006; Casson and Wadeson, 2007; Gaglio and Katz, 2001; Shane and Venkataraman, 2000; Venkataraman, 1997). This link between recognizing opportunities and founding companies raises the question of whether opportunity recognition itself is heritable. This pattern is plausible because opportunity recognition is largely a cognitive function and research shows strong heritability for many aspects of brain function (McGue and Bouchard, 1989).

Measuring opportunity recognition through a scale created from the literature on the topic (e.g. Baron and Ozgen, 2007; Singh et al., 1999), Nicolaou et al. (2009) found the heritability of opportunity recognition to be 45 percent in a sample of UK twins.

Heritability of Entrepreneurial Performance

Not only do researchers find evidence of the heritability of the decision to be an entrepreneur and the identification of entrepreneurial opportunities, but they also find evidence of the heritability of entrepreneurial performance. In an examination of self-employed identical and fraternal twins from the USA, Nicolaou and Shane (2009c) estimate the heritability of self-employment income to be 74 percent. That is, the amount of money made by self-employed people is highly heritable.

In short, opportunity recognition, the decision to be an entrepreneur and entrepreneurial performance are all highly heritable, with estimates of heritability being of similar magnitude to that of other types of occupational choice.

POTENTIAL MECHANISMS FOR THE EFFECT OF GENES ON ENTREPRENEURSHIP

While the estimates of the heritability of opportunity recognition, the decision to found a business and performance in running a company are intriguing, these are merely facts showing that genetic factors influence entrepreneurship. These estimates do not explain *how* genes affect entrepreneurship. For that, we need a theory. At this point, researchers have not yet formulated a complete theory of how genes affect opportunity recognition, the decision to become an entrepreneur or entrepreneurial performance. However, they have begun to identify the mechanisms through which genes exert influence.

Researchers do not believe that one single gene governs entrepreneurship. Unlike Huntington's disease, a disorder for which a single gene *determines* whether or not a person is afflicted, there is no single gene that *determines* whether people recognize opportunities, start businesses, or make money in their entrepreneurial endeavors. Rather, researchers believe that a set of genes collectively influence the *probability* that these outcomes will occur.

Moreover, researchers do not believe that genes influence entrepreneurial activity directly. Genes only provide instructions that tell the human body how to create different proteins from amino acids (small organic molecules that are the components from which proteins are made). Therefore genes cannot directly affect behavior (Arvey and Bouchard, 1994). Instead, the genes that provide instructions for proteins implicated in brain structure, neurotransmitters and glandular systems exert an influence on entrepreneurial activity because the glandular and nervous systems affect behavior (Arvey and Bouchard, 1994).

Researchers believe that genes influence entrepreneurial activity in four *complementary* ways: through direct physiological effects; by co-varying with individual attributes; through correlations with environments; and through interactions with environments.

Direct Physiological Effects

Genes are thought to influence entrepreneurial activity through direct physiological effects, such as through their effects on neurotransmitter activity (Pinker, 2009; Rutter, 2006). Nerve cells communicate using chemicals called neurotransmitters. Different people have different versions of genes that influence the amount of different neurotransmitters in their brains. The amounts of neurotransmitters, in turn, influence how people feel, think, and behave (Arvey and Bouchard, 1994).

Consider the example of serotonin. This neurotransmitter calms anxiety by affecting how nerves communicate with each other. As a result, serotonin levels affect how people feel physically in response to taking chances. People with higher serotonin levels feel less anxious than people with lower serotonin levels in response to the same objective level of risk. Although no research has yet tested the hypothesis, genetic variations in serotonin levels might increase the odds of taking risky decisions, such as quitting a job to found a company.

Similarly, the genes that influence hormone production, such as testosterone, might also influence entrepreneurial activity. Base levels of testosterone are over 80 percent heritable (Meikle et al., 1988). As a result, some people's genes lead their bodies to produce more testosterone.

This genetically induced variation in testosterone levels might affect the odds that people start businesses. People whose bodies produce higher levels of testosterone feel a greater physical boost from activities that involve aggression, dominance and risk taking. Starting a business might be the kind of activity that is more common among high-testosterone individuals. White et al. (2006) examined this hypothesis using a sample of male MBA students. They found that higher-testosterone men were more likely to have been involved with new venture creation.

Genetic Co-variation with Individual Attributes

Genes are thought to influence entrepreneurial activity through co-variation with individual-level attributes that affect entrepreneurial activity. Among the attributes thought to influence entrepreneurial activity through genetic co-variation are intelligence, personality, temperament and cognition. All of these attributes are influenced by neurobiological and hormonal systems, are heritable (Ilies et al., 2006), and have been associated with entrepreneurship.

While no studies have yet examined genetic co-variation of intelligence, temperament or cognitive factors with entrepreneurship, several studies show evidence of genetic co-variation of personality traits with dimensions of entrepreneurial activity. Nicolaou et al. (2008b) show that sensation seeking, a personality characteristic that leads to greater pursuit of new experiences (Zuckerman, 1994; Stephenson et al., 2003; Zuckerman et al., 1978; Lusher et al. 2000), partially 'mediates' the heritability of entrepreneurship.

Shane et al. (2009) find that extraversion and openness to experience mediated the genetic influence on entrepreneurship in two different samples of UK and US twins. Specifically, they showed that genetic factors were responsible for 62 and 60 percent of the phenotypic correlation between extraversion and being an entrepreneur in the UK and US samples, respectively, and between 85 and 74 percent of the phenotypic correlation between openness to experience and being an entrepreneur in the UK and US samples, respectively.

Researchers also find evidence of genetic co-variation of personality with opportunity recognition. Shane et al. (2010) found that genetic factors account for 62 percent of the phenotypic correlation between openness to experience and opportunity recognition, suggesting that the same genes influence both the personality characteristic and the identification of opportunities.

Finally, researchers find evidence of genetic co-variation with entrepreneurial performance. Examining a sample of self-employed identical and fraternal twins from the USA, Nicolaou and Shane (2009c) showed that 61 percent of the phenotypic correlation between extraversion and self-employment income and 38 percent of the phenotypic correlation between openness to experience and self-employment income, and 100 percent of the phenotypic correlation between agreeableness and self-employment income, is genetic.

Gene–Environment Correlations

Genes are thought to influence entrepreneurial activity through gene–environment correlations. This phrase refers to the tendency for people's genetic make-up to affect the odds that they experience certain environments (Plomin and Bergeman, 1991; Plomin et al., 2008). Because the environments that people face are influenced by their genetic propensities, some people's genetic make-up may increase their odds of being in environments where the chances of starting a business are higher.

Evocative, active and passive are three different forms of gene–environment correlation (Plomin et al., 1977; Rutter and Silberg, 2002). Evocative gene–environment correlations are present when individuals evoke reactions from others based on their genetic predispositions. For instance, professors might be more inclined to encourage MBA students with innate entrepreneurial interests to take their courses. As a result, the innate entrepreneurial interests might increase the odds that people start businesses by putting them in courses in which they develop business plans to start companies.

The active type occurs when people actively pursue situations that fit their genetic predispositions. For example, a person with innate entrepreneurial interests might be more likely to attend events at which investors in start-ups are found.

Passive gene–environment correlations are present when one's family environment is associated with their genetic propensities (Plomin et al., 2008). For instance, a person with innate entrepreneurial interests might learn more about entrepreneurship as a child because his or her parents are more likely to have a family business and talk about running a business at the dinner table.

Gene–Environment Interactions

Genes are thought to influence entrepreneurial activity through interactions between genes and environmental factors. These interactions occur when possession of a particular version of a gene makes a person more sensitive to external factors that increase the odds of displaying a behavior (Rowe, 2003).

No research has yet examined gene–environment interactions in entrepreneurship.

But it is possible to hypothesize these effects. For example, some people might have a version of a gene that increases their odds of taking risks. However, even with this genetic variant, a person will not start a business unless they receive the appropriate stimulus from the environment. If the person gains access to information that facilitates the identification of a new business idea, having the genetic predisposition to take risks might increase the odds of starting a business. However, in the absence of the environmental trigger or the genetic predisposition, business formation is less likely to occur.

METHODOLOGY OF RESEARCH ON THE GENETICS OF ENTREPRENEURSHIP

Researchers use both quantitative and molecular genetics techniques to study the effect of genes on entrepreneurship.

Quantitative Genetics

Behavioral geneticists explore hereditary differences in behavior through studies of twins and adopted children. Examination of twins permits the identification of the share of behavior that comes from genetic and environmental factors because identical twins have identical DNA, while, on average, half of fraternal twins' segregating genes are the same. If identical and fraternal twins do not face different environments – an assumption that has been tested extensively and been shown to be robust (Hettema et al., 1995; Kendler and Prescott, 2006; Scarr and Carter-Saltzman, 1979) – the difference in the proportion of shared genes is the source of differences in behavior between pairs of fraternal and identical twins.

By examining the association between pairs of identical and fraternal twins on aspects of entrepreneurship, researchers can identify the portion of variance attributable to genetic factors. If a behavior is 100 percent genetically determined, a perfect correlation would exist between two identical twins, but the correlation between two fraternal twins would be only 0.50. If a behavior has no genetic effect, the correlations between behaviors of identical and fraternal twins would be the same. If the correlation between identical twins is greater than that between their fraternal counterparts, genes must influence the phenomenon being measured. And because entrepreneurial activity cannot change a person's genetic make-up, genetics must be the cause of the activity and not the other way around.

Behavioral geneticists also look at how similar the behavior of adopted children is to that of their adoptive and biological parents. Adopted children have both 'genetic' parents (birth parents who gave their children for adoption) and 'environmental' parents (the adoptive parents who are not biologically related to their children) (Plomin et al., 2008). Because adopted children share their biological parents' genes but and not their adoptive guardians' DNA, genetic factors must account for correlations between the entrepreneurial activities of children and their biological parents. Genetic influence can also be estimated by comparing the correlation for entrepreneurial activity between 'genetic-plus-environmental' parents and their children, with the correlation between adopted parents and their adopted children. If the correlation between 'genetic-plus-environmental' parents and their children is higher than the correlation between adopted parents and their adopted children, this would suggest that genetic factors impact entrepreneurial activity.

Molecular Genetics

Molecular geneticists examine how genes influence entrepreneurial activity by identifying specific genes that are related to the activity through association and genome-wide association studies.

In association studies, researchers collect data on whether or not people have a particular version of a gene that they think is related to some dimension of entrepreneurship, as well as whether or not the people show evidence of that entrepreneurial dimension. Then the researchers look to see if the variant of the gene and the dimension of entrepreneurship are correlated.

In genome-wide association studies, scientists search the complete genome for small variations that are more common among people with certain characteristics instead of looking for the correlation between a version of a particular gene and an aspect of entrepreneurial activity (Hirschhorn and Daly, 2005). Adjusting for the large number of correlations that they are exploring, the researchers identify the genes that are significantly associated with the aspect of entrepreneurial activity that they are investigating.

FUTURE RESEARCH ON THE GENETICS OF ENTREPRENEURSHIP

So, where does the field go from here? The answer is 'many places' because much remains unexplored in the genetics of entrepreneurship. No one has yet identified specific genetic polymorphisms that are associated with any aspect of entrepreneurship. Identifying polymorphisms associated with important dimensions of entrepreneurship, such as opportunity recognition, the tendency to start a business, the attraction of resources and entrepreneurial performance, is an important step in developing a full-fledged understanding of the genetics of entrepreneurship.

To do this, scientists are now conducting molecular genetics studies. This effort involves genome-wide association studies to identify specific genes associated with different dimensions of entrepreneurship, most notably the identification of opportunities and the decision to found a business. It also involves candidate gene studies in which theory is used to specify genes that are thought to influence some dimension of entrepreneurship.

The effort to identify the genes associated with different dimensions of entrepreneurship will likely require an investigation of many genes. Not only is it possible that different genes affect different dimensions of entrepreneurial activity, but it is also likely that each gene has only a tiny effect on entrepreneurial activity. Research shows that explaining a noticeable amount of variance on most behavioral outcomes requires aggregating the effects of many genes because the effect of the average gene is small. Because no studies have yet examined the effects of individual genes on entrepreneurship, researchers do not yet know how many genes are needed to account for a sizable portion of most entrepreneurial activities.

Even though the effect of each gene may be small, we may be able to identify much the variance between people in their entrepreneurial activities by looking at the combined effect of many genes. For instance, one study found that a group of 59 genes explained 38 percent of the variance in novelty seeking and 32 percent of the difference in persistence (Comings et al., 2001), two dimensions of human behavior thought to influence entrepreneurship. Efforts to investigate dimensions of entrepreneurship might reveal that as many genes need to be aggregated to account for a similar portion of the variance in entrepreneurial activity.

Researchers will also need to specify how the genes combine to influence entrepreneurship. Genes sometimes have additive effects on behavior, while at other times they have multiplicative effects. For instance, the DRD4 and COMT genes interact to influence novelty seeking (Strobel et al., 2003). The interaction of these genes might have similar effects on entrepreneurship, given the association of novelty seeking with entrepreneurial activity. On the other hand, these two genes might have additive effects on entrepreneurial activity or no effect at all. And these are only the interactions between two genes. Three or more genes may also combine, additively or multiplicatively, to influence entrepreneurial activity.

Researchers also need to test for interactions between specific genes and environmental stimuli on different dimensions of entrepreneurship. For example, scientists might explore whether the provision of capital to people who have a genetic predisposition to engage in entrepreneurial activity trigger those people to start companies.

It is important to examine gene–environment interactions because most genes are pleiotropic, which means that a single gene influences multiple behaviors. Because many genes affect more than one outcome, having a variant of a gene that makes a person more likely to start a business doesn't mean that the person will do so. The genetic endowment might also predispose the person to engage in other activities. Take, for example, the effect of versions of several dopamine receptor genes, which have been found increase the odds that people will seek novelty. Some people might seek this novelty by forming new businesses, while others might do so by engaging in extreme sports. The pleiotropic nature of the genes means that the environmental triggers that the predisposed people respond to – perhaps information about business opportunities and new sports – might account for the way the genetic predisposition manifests itself.

Researchers also need to examine gene–environment correlations. A handful of genes can have a substantial effect on entrepreneurial activity because our genes influence our tendency to choose situations that reinforce our genetic predispositions. Thus a small genetic difference might lead to a tiny innate advantage at something that increases the odds of being in entrepreneurial settings – perhaps the ability to tolerate the stress of making decisions under uncertainty. Because people choose settings in which they are most comfortable, this initial small difference leads to a set of subsequent choices that can result in very large downstream effects (Dawkins, 1982).

THE BOUNDARIES OF GENETIC RESEARCH ON ENTREPRENEURSHIP

Because genetics research is often misunderstood, we would like to outline the boundaries of how genetics affects entrepreneurship. First, genes do not *determine* anything about entrepreneurship, whether that is the identification of opportunities, the decision to start a firm, or entrepreneurial performance. Genes only *influence* the odds that people engage in entrepreneurship. Therefore genetics research on entrepreneurship should not be confounded with biological determinism (Turkheimer, 1998).

Second, no genes provide instructions specifically for entrepreneurial activity. Being a business founder or recognizing opportunities are complex phenotypes, making the chances that a version of a single gene has a strong direct effect on any aspect of entrepreneurial activity. Because human beings had largely the same genes in prehistoric times that they have now, the genes that affect the odds of going into business for oneself probably encode for something else that was present in prehistoric times, such as intelligence or temperament.

Third, genetic research on entrepreneurship is explicitly '*interactionist*'. Genetic investigations do not imply that environmental conditions don't matter for entrepreneurship. Quite the opposite: most researchers believe that the environment matters more than genes in explaining entrepreneurship. Nevertheless, the effects of genes are non-trivial and an understanding of entrepreneurship depends on explanations of how genetics and the environment *complement* each other.

Fourth, genetic research on entrepreneurship does *not* claim that genetics accounts for racial or ethnic differences. Pseudo-scientific efforts to use genetics to explain racial or ethnic differences in other fields of inquiry have adversely affected the reputation of genetics research. Research shows that the differences in the attributes that genes affect are individual level differences (Plomin, 1999).

IMPLICATIONS OF RESEARCH ON THE GENETICS OF ENTREPRENEURSHIP

Genetics research on entrepreneurship has implications for both research and practice. In the subsections below, we outline the implications for theorizing about entrepreneurship, for undertaking empirical research to test those theories, and for making practical use of the results.

Implications for Theorizing about Entrepreneurship

Research on the genetics of entrepreneurship will facilitate the development of better theories about entrepreneurship. Consider, for example, the explanation for the oft-found correlation between parents and children in entrepreneurial activity (Shapero and Sokol, 1982; De Wit and Van Winden, 1989; Butler and Herring, 1991; Taylor, 1996; Burke et al., 2000; Uusitalo, 2001; Aldrich and Kim, 2007; Sorenson, 2007; Fairlie, 1999). The prevailing explanation for this empirical pattern – one provided in hundreds of articles – is that parents teach their children about entrepreneurship during childhood (Krueger, 1993). An alternative explanation – one that is unfortunately not found in any of the articles – is that genetic factors passed from parents to children predispose the children of entrepreneurs to become entrepreneurs. Evidence of the heritability of entrepreneurship combined with evidence that the 'shared environment' has no effect on the odds of being an entrepreneur indicates that the commonly offered explanation – learning in childhood – is probably incomplete. An alternative explanation for higher frequency of entrepreneurship among the children of entrepreneurs is the genetic transmission of entrepreneurial predispositions.

Research on the genetics of entrepreneurship also helps to develop accurate theories of 'why' and 'how' people identify opportunities. Take, for example, theories of opportunity recognition that are based solely on access to information. The genetic correlation between recognition of opportunities and the personality characteristic of openness to experience indicates that part of the variance across people in the identification of entrepreneurial opportunities is explained by the same genetic factors that affect openness to experience (Nicolaou et al., 2009). Because opportunity recognition is heritable and partially the result of genetically influenced individual differences, purely environmental explanations for opportunity identification are, at best, incomplete, and, at worst, incorrect.

Exploration of the genetics of entrepreneurship helps researchers to develop more comprehensive explanations of entrepreneurship. For example, research to date does not account for all of the variation across people in opportunity recognition or the decision to start a business (Aldrich and Kim, 2007). While accepting that environmental factors matter too, a genetic approach to entrepreneurship suggests that incorporating biological explanations will help us to develop a comprehensive understanding of the phenomenon (White et al., 2006; Nicolaou et al., 2008b). The size of the genetic component in the dimensions of entrepreneurship examined to date is simply too large to simply ignore.

Genetics research contributes to the development of a process theory of entrepreneurship. Research shows that common genes influence the recognition of opportunities and the decision to become an entrepreneur. These empirical patterns suggest that part of the mechanism for how people become entrepreneurs lies in how genetic differences lead to variation in the tendency to become open to experience, which influences the probability of identifying new business opportunities. The odds of recognizing opportunities, in turn, affect the probability that a person will become an entrepreneur.

Taking a genetic approach helps link research on entrepreneurship to broader theories of human behavior. Prior research shows substantial heritability of vocational interests (McGue and Bouchard, 1989, Gottfredson, 1999; Moloney et al., 1991; Betsworth et al., 1994). The fact that similar heritability estimates are found for the occupations of teacher, manager, salesperson and entrepreneur suggests that genetics influences the choice of entrepreneurship as a vocation in the same ways that it influences the choice of other occupations.

Implications for Conducting Entrepreneurship Research

Genetics can be used to improve entrepreneurship research methodology. First, it facilitates the identification of a control group for entrepreneurs. When examining how environmental factors affect entrepreneurship, scholars need a control group with which to compare entrepreneurs. Some scholars select managers (Brockhaus, 1980; Busenitz and Barney, 1997); others use the overall population (Gartner and Carter, 2003). The differences in choice of control groups undermine the validity of the research because one cannot tell whether any observed differences result from the difference between the alternative control groups or between the chosen control group and the experimental group.

Knowledge of pleiotropic genetic influences would improve the choice of control group. To explore how environmental factors influence entrepreneurship (e.g. does easy credit increase the odds that people will start businesses?), the correct comparison group is the set of people whose decisions are influenced by the same genetic factors. For example, if the same genes influence the tendency to be both a manager and an entrepreneur, then managers are the right control group for exploring the effect of the ease of access to credit on the decision to be an entrepreneur.

Genetics research also helps researchers to more accurately measure the effect of environmental influences on entrepreneurship using non-experimental data (Kohler et al., 2005). Because genes can influence both environmental factors and dimensions of entrepreneurship, scholars need to use co-twin control designs, which hold constant the effect of unobserved genetic endowments on the environmental factors, allowing entrepreneurship scholars to better measure the effect of environmental factors on entrepreneurship.

Implications for Practice

Genetics research on entrepreneurship has implications for practice. First, it can provide information on how managers investors and entrepreneurship educators might best enhance entrepreneurial activity. These efforts will be more effective if they are focused on influencing variables whose co-variation with entrepreneurship is mostly environmental, rather than variables whose co-variation with entrepreneurship is mostly genetic.

The research to date shows that the co-variation between personality and whether or not a person becomes an entrepreneur is largely due to genetic factors. This empirical pattern suggest that attempts to train and provide incentives for people to become entrepreneurs should not focus on efforts to adjust their personalities, but, instead, should focus on factors less subject to genetic co-variation with decision to become an entrepreneur (perhaps access to capital). Knowing what variables are not the best to manipulate in efforts to encourage entrepreneurship through changes to environmental factors helps managers, educators and policy-makers to better encourage entrepreneurial behavior.

Nevertheless, if one were to try to change personality characteristics as a way of increasing the tendency of people to become entrepreneurs, such interventions would vary in their effectiveness depending on the personality characteristic one focused on. Research shows that environmental factors account for more of the co-variance between the personality characteristic of extraversion and the decision to become an entrepreneur, than between the personality characteristic of openness to experience and the decision to become an entrepreneur. This empirical pattern indicates that extraversion is a better candidate than openness to experience for efforts to change people's personalities as a way to increase their odds of starting businesses.

Similarly, common genetic effect on the recognition of opportunity and the decision to be an entrepreneur makes it difficult to increase entrepreneurship by improving opportunity recognition. Too much of the variance in the decision to become an entrepreneur comes from the same genetic sources that affect opportunity recognition for that factor to be an effective one for manipulation.

Research on gene–environment interactions has the potential to offer a variety of implications for the practice of entrepreneurship. If specific environmental triggers interact with genetic predispositions to affect entrepreneurship, then policy-makers, educators, and corporate managers need to think in terms of identifying the right triggers.

For instance, those individuals with a particular form of the DRD4 gene might be predisposed to engage in entrepreneurial activities only if faced with the right environmental stimulus. If those people were confronted with an environment conducive to productive entrepreneurship, they might start legitimate businesses, but if they were confronted with an unproductive environment, such as poverty, they might start criminal enterprises (Hamer and Copeland, 1999).

Although people can choose any occupation regardless of their genetic predispositions, research suggests that some people are innately predisposed to be better at entrepreneurial activity than others. This information might prove useful to people thinking of becoming entrepreneurs, financiers thinking of investing in their businesses, and career counselors seeking to advise people on whether they are a good fit for running their own businesses.

Ironically, the results of genetics research on entrepreneurship might help people figure out how to overcome their genetic predispositions. The patterns identified in this research are merely predispositions – and *not* deterministic relationships – and people can always overcome their genetic predispositions. But overcoming predispositions means acting against one's natural tendencies. While this can be done, it usually demands more conscious effort than working in accord with those tendencies.

CONCLUSION

Recent research indicates that some individuals are innately predisposed to recognize entrepreneurial opportunities, engage in entrepreneurial activity, and perform well at running their own business. Moreover, this research has shown that personality characteristics mediate genetic effects on the recognition of opportunities, the decision to be an entrepreneur, and performance at entrepreneurial activity. This evidence of biological underpinnings of entrepreneurship complements environmental explanations of why people become entrepreneurs, and what accounts for entrepreneurial performance. As a result, it improves our understanding of entrepreneurship and the normative implications we can draw from our research on it. However, much additional work is required in order to better understand how genes influence entrepreneurial behavior both alone and in interaction with environmental stimuli.

ACKNOWLEDGMENTS

Nicos Nicolaou is most grateful to Philip Zepter and Home Art and Sales Services AG for funding support.

REFERENCES

Aldrich, H. and P. Kim (2007), 'A life course perspective on occupational inheritance: self-employed parents and their children', in M. Ruef and M. Lounsbury (eds), *The Sociology of Entrepreneurship, Research in the Sociology of Organizations*, **25**, 33–82.

Arvey, R.D. and T.J. Bouchard (1994), 'Genetics, twins, and organizational behavior', *Research in Organizational Behavior*, **16**, 47–82.

Arvey, R.D., T. Segal and L. Abraham (1989), 'Job satisfaction: environmental and genetic components', *Journal of Applied Psychology*, **74** (2), 187–92.

Arvey, R.D., B.P. McCall, T.J. Bouchard, P. Taubman and M.A. Cavanaugh (1994), 'Genetic influences on job satisfaction and work values', *Personality and Individual Differences*, **17**, 21–33.

Arvey, R.D., Z. Zhang, B.J. Avolio and R.F. Kreuger (2007), 'Developmental and genetic determinants of leadership role occupancy among women', *Journal of Applied Psychology*, **92**, 693–706.

Baron, R.A. (2007), 'Behavioral and cognitive factors in entrepreneurship', *Strategic Entrepreneurship Journal*, **1**, 167–82.

Baron, R.A. and M.D. Ensley (2006), 'Opportunity recognition as the detection of meaningful patterns: evidence from comparisons of novice and experienced entrepreneurs', *Management Science*, **52**, 1331–44.

Baron, R.A. and E. Ozgen (2007), 'Social sources of information in opportunity recognition: effects of mentors, industry networks, and professional forums', *Journal of Business Venturing*, **22**, 174–92.

Betsworth, D., T. Bouchard, C. Cooper, H. Grotevant, J. Hansen, S. Scarr and R. Weinberg (1994), 'Genetic and environmental influences on vocational interests assessed using adoptive and biological families and twins reared apart and together', *Journal of Vocational Behavior*, **44**, 263–78.

Brockhaus, R.H. (1980), 'Risk taking propensity of entrepreneurs', *Academy of Management Journal*, **23**, 509–20.

Burke, A.E., F.R. FitzRoy and M.A. Nolan (2000), 'When less is more: distinguishing between entrepreneurial choice and performance', *Oxford Bulletin of Economics and Statistics*, **62**, 567–87.

Busenitz, L. and J. Barney (1997), 'Differences between entrepreneurs and managers in large organizations: biases and heuristics in strategic decision making', *Journal of Business Venturing*, **16**, 165–80.

Butler, J.S. and C. Herring (1991), 'Ethnicity and entrepreneurship in America: toward an explanation of racial and ethnic group variations in self employment', *Sociological Perspectives*, **34**, 79–94.

Carter, H. (1932), 'Twin similarities in occupational interests', *The Journal of Educational Psychology*, **23** (9), 641–55.

Casson, M. and N. Wadeson (2007), 'The discovery of opportunities: extending the economic theory of the entrepreneur', *Small Business Economics*, **28**, 285–300.

Comings, D.E., R. Gade-Andavolu, N. Gonzalez, S. Wu et al. (2001), 'The additive effect of neurotransmitter genes in pathological gambling', *Clinical Genetics*, **60**, 107–16.

Dawkins, R. (1982), *The Extended Phenotype*, Oxford: Oxford University Press.

de Wit, G. and F.A.A.M. Van Winden (1989), 'An empirical analysis of self employment in the Netherlands', *Small Business Economics*, **1**, 263–72.

Fairlie, R. (1999), 'The absence of African-American owned businesses: an analysis of the dynamics of self-employment', *Journal of Labor Economics*, **17** (1), 80–108.

Gaglio, C.M. and J.A. Katz (2001), 'The psychological basis of opportunity identification: entrepreneurial alertness', *Small Business Economics*, **16** (2), 95–111.

Gartner, W. and N. Carter (2003), 'Entrepreneurial behavior and firm organizing processes', in Z. Acs and D. Audretsch (eds), *Handbook of Entrepreneurship Research*, Boston, MA: Kluwer, pp. 195–222.

Gottfredson, L.S. (1999), 'The nature and nurture of vocational interests', in M.L. Savickas and A.R. Spokane (eds), *Vocational Interests: Their Meaning, Measurement, and Use in Counseling*, Palo Alto, CA: Davies-Black.

Grotevant, H., S. Scarr and R. Weinberg (1977), 'Patterns of interest similarity in adoptive and biological families', *Journal of Personality and Social Psychology*, **35** (9), 667–76.

Hamer, D. and P. Copeland (1999), *Living with Our Genes*, New York: Anchor Books.

Hettema, J.M., M.C. Neale and K.S. Kendler (1995), 'Physical similarity and the equal environment assumption in twin studies of psychiatric disorders', *Behavior Genetics*, **25**, 327–35.

Hirschhorn, J. and M. Daly (2005), 'Genome-wide association studies for common diseases and complex traits', *Nature Reviews*, **6** (2), 95–108.

Ilies, R., R. Arvey and T. Bouchard (2006), 'Darwinism, behavioral genetics, and organizational behavior: a review and agenda for future research', *Journal of Organizational Behavior*, **27**, 121–41.

Keller, L., T. Bouchard, R. Arvey, N. Segal and R. Dawes (1992), 'Work values: genetic and environmental influences', *Journal of Applied Psychology*, **77** (1), 79–88.

Kendler, K.S. and C.A. Prescott (2006), *Genes, Environment and Psychopathology*, New York: Guilford Press.

Kohler, H.-P., J.R. Behrman and A. Skytthe (2005), 'Partner+Children=Happiness? The effect of fertility and partnerships on subjective well-being', *Population and Development Review*, **31** (3), 407–45.

Krueger, N. (1993), *Growing Up Entrepreneurial*, Atlanta, GA: Academy of Management Proceedings.

Lusher, J., L. Ebersole and D. Ball (2000), 'Dopamine D4 receptor gene and severity of dependence', *Addiction Biology*, **5**, 469–72.

McCall, B., M. Cavanaugh and R. Arvey (1997), 'Genetic influences on job and occupational switching', *Journal of Vocational Behavior*, **50** (1), 60–77.
McGue, M. and T. Bouchard (1989), 'Genetic and environmental determinants of information processing and special mental abilities: a twin analysis', in R. Sternberg (ed.), *Advances in the Psychology of Human Intelligence*, Hillsdale, NJ: Lawrence Erlbaum, vol. **5**, pp. 7–45.
Meikle, A.W., J.D. Stringham, D.T. Bishop and D.W. West (1988), 'Quantitating genetic and nongenetic factors influencing androgen production and clearance rates in men', *Journal of Clinical Endocrinology and Metabolism*, **67**, 104–9.
Moloney, D., T. Bouchard and N. Segal (1991), 'A genetic and environmental analysis of the vocational interests of monozygotic and dizygotic twins reared apart', *Journal of Vocational Behavior*, **39**, 76–109.
Nicolaou, N. and S. Shane (2009a), 'Can genetic factors influence the likelihood of engaging in entrepreneurial activity?', *Journal of Business Venturing*, **24** (1), 1–22.
Nicolaou, N. and S. Shane (2009b), 'Entrepreneurship and occupational choice: genetic and environmental influences', Working Paper.
Nicolaou, N. and S. Shane (2009c), 'The genetics of entrepreneurial performance', Working Paper.
Nicolaou, N., S. Shane, L. Cherkas, J. Hunkin and T. Spector (2008a), 'Is the tendency to engage in entrepreneurship genetic?', *Management Science*, **54** (1), 167–79.
Nicolaou, N., S. Shane, L. Cherkas and T. Spector (2008b), 'The influence of sensation seeking in the heritability of entrepreneurship', *Strategic Entrepreneurship Journal*, **2**, 7–21.
Nicolaou, N., S. Shane, L. Cherkas and T. Spector (2009), 'Opportunity recognition and the tendency to be an entrepreneur: a bivariate genetics perspective', *Organizational Behavior and Human Decision Processes*, **110** (2), 108–17.
Pinker, S. (2009), 'My genome, my self', *New York Times Magazine*, 11 January, pp. 24–31; 46; 50.
Plomin, R. (1999), 'Genetics and general cognitive ability', *Nature*, **402**, C25–C29.
Plomin, R. and C.S. Bergeman (1991), 'The nature of nurture: Genetic influence on "environmental" measures', *Behavioral and Brain Sciences*, **14**, 373–427.
Plomin, R., J.C. DeFries and J.C. Loehlin (1977), 'Genotype–environment interaction and correlation in the analysis of human behavior', *Psychological Bulletin*, **84**, 309–22.
Plomin, R., J.C. DeFries, G.E. McClearn and P. McGuffin (2008), *Behavioral Genetics*, 5th edn, New York: Worth Publishers.
psych.colorado.edu/~carey/hgss/hgssapplets/heritability/heritability.intro.html (2009).
Rowe, D. (2003), 'Assessing genotype×environment interactions and correlations in a postgenomic world', in R. Plomin, J.C. DeFries, I.W. Craig and P. McGuffin (eds), *Behavioral Genetics in the Postgenomic Era*, Washington, DC: American Psychological Association.
Rutter, M. (2006), *Genes and Behavior*, Oxford: Blackwell.
Rutter, M. and J. Silberg (2002), 'Gene–environment interplay in relation to emotional and behavioral disturbance', *Annual Review Psychology*, **53**, 463–90.
Scarr, S. and L. Carter-Saltzman (1979). 'Twin method: defense of a critical assumption', *Behavior Genetics*, **9**, 527–42.
Shane, S., N. Nicolaou, L. Cherkas and T. Spector (2009), 'Genetics, the big five, and the tendency to be an entrepreneur', Working Paper.
Shane, S., N. Nicolaou, L. Cherkas and T. Spector (2010), 'Openness to experience and opportunity recognition: evidence of a common genetic etiology', *Human Resource Management*, **49** (2), 291–303.
Shane, S. and S. Venkataraman (2000), 'The promise of entrepreneurship as a field of research', *Academy of Management Review*, **25**, 217–26.
Shapero, A. and L. Sokol (1982), 'The social dimensions of entrepreneurship', in C.A. Kent, D.L. Sexton and K.H. Vesper (eds), *Encyclopedia of Entrepreneurship*, Englewood Cliffs, NJ: Prentice Hall, pp. 72–90.
Singh, R.P., G.E. Hills, R.C. Hybels and G.T. Lumpkin (1999), 'Opportunity recognition through social network characteristics of entrepreneurs', in *Frontiers of Entrepreneurship Research*, Wellesley, MA: Babson College, pp. 228–41.
Sorenson, J. (2007), 'Closure versus exposure: mechanisms in the intergenerational transition of self-employment', in M. Ruef and M. Lounsbury (eds), *Research in the Sociology of Organizations*, Amsterdam: JAI Press, pp. 83–124.
Stephenson M, R. Hoyle, P. Palmgreen and M. Slater (2003), 'Brief measures of sensation seeking for screening and large-scale surveys', *Drug and Alcohol Dependence*, **72**, 279–86.
Strobel, A., K. Lesch and B. Brocke (2003), 'Dopamine D4 receptor gene polymorphism and novelty seeking: evidence for a modulatory role of additional polymorphisms', paper presented at the 11th Biennial Meeting of the International Society for the Study of Individual Differences, Graz, Austria.
Taylor, M. (1996), 'Earnings, independence or unemployment: why become self-employed?', *Oxford Bulletin of Economics and Statistics*, **58** (2), 253–66.
Turkheimer, E. (1998), 'Heritability and biological explanation', *Psychological Review* **105**, 782–91.

Uusitalo, R. (2001), 'Homo Entreprenaurus?', *Applied Economics*, **33**, pp. 1631–8.
Venkataraman, S. (1997), 'The distinctive domain of entrepreneurship research', in J.A. Katz (ed.), *Advances in Entrepreneurship, Firm Emergence and Growth*, vol.3, Greenwich, CT: JAI Press, pp. 119–38.
White, R., S. Thornhill and E. Hampson (2006), 'Entrepreneurs and evolutionary biology: the relationship between testosterone and new venture creation', *Organizational Behavior and Human Decision Processes*, **100**, 21–34.
Zhang, Z., M. Zyphur, J. Narayanan, R. Arvey, S. Chaturvedi et al. (2009), 'The genetic basis of entrepreneurship: effects of gender and personality', *Organizational Behavior and Human Decision Processes*, **110** (2), 93–107.
Zuckerman, M. (1994), *Behavioral Expressions and Biosocial Bases of Sensation Seeking*, Cambridge: Cambridge University Press.
Zuckerman, M., S. Eysenck and H.J. Eysenck (1978), 'Sensation seeking in England and America: cross-cultural, age, and sex comparisons', *Journal of Consulting and Clinical Psychology*, **46**, 139–49.
Zyphur, M., J. Narayanan, R. Arvey and G. Alexander (2009), 'The genetics of economic risk preferences', *Journal of Behavioral Decision Making*, **22** (4), 367–77.

30 Entrepreneurship education
Oliver Falck, Robert Gold and Stephan Heblich

INTRODUCTION

In the USA, it seems that you cannot move without bumping into one; in Europe, they are fervently longed for; all over the world, universities are suspected of being their breeding ground. Entrepreneurs – those mystical beings who are believed to have such a positive influence on innovation and economic growth – are enjoying a global demand. As to what drives the entrepreneur, Schumpeter quite romantically describes it as 'the will to conquer', 'the dream and the will to found a private kingdom', and 'the joy of creating, of getting things done' (1912, p. 93). All well and good, but it does not explain where these Schumpeterian 'entrepreneurial endowments' (cf. Lazear, 2005) come from. In this chapter, we shed some light on this crucial question.

Are entrepreneurs born or made? Is it nature or nurture that is responsible for entrepreneurial endowments? We argue that such endowments are the result of a combination of innate genetics as well as education, i.e. socialization and schooling. In this chapter, we focus on the role of socialization and (pre-university) schooling, i.e. adolescents' education in a broader sense and, thus, focus on the early (in the life cycle) formation of entrepreneurial endowments. Early entrepreneurial endowments, unfortunately, are not directly observable, so we look at something that is – the 'entrepreneurial intentions' of university students, i.e. their desire to become an entrepreneur in future. In this context, Falck et al. (2009) show that entrepreneurial intentions expressed in adolescence strongly predict future actual entrepreneurship.

To identify a causal effect of endogenous entrepreneurial endowments from socialization and schooling on entrepreneurial intentions, we exploit the 1990 (re-)unification of the Federal Republic of Germany (FRG) and the German Democratic Republic (GDR) as quasi-natural experiment. We compare German university students in reunified Germany who were educated in the East (former GDR) with those who were educated in the West (former FRG). These two sets of students had radically dissimilar forms of socialization and schooling before 1990. Conditional on various background factors, we consider education under the East German system of a planned economy as socialist treatment. We assume that being treated with a socialist ideology in younger years 'cured' any entrepreneurial inclination. Accordingly, *ceteris paribus*, university students raised and educated in the GDR should be less interested in becoming entrepreneurs than fellow students brought up in the market-based economy of the FRG.

We find, in a first step, significantly lower entrepreneurial intentions among the treatment group of East German university students after reunification. This result is robust with the inclusion of university fixed effects and various control variables. In a second step, we focus on a subsample of those students who finished secondary education while Germany was still divided. When comparing the entrepreneurial intentions of East German students who finished secondary education under the socialist regime with those of West German students, the treatment effect is even stronger. We cautiously interpret this as a positive effect of a change in the schooling system on individual entrepreneurial endowments. These findings suggest that policy-makers can influence entrepreneurial endowments via the school system. In a third step, we assess the problem of selection into universities by restricting our sample to students from either East or West Germany who are attending a West German university that is not located in the region where they received their secondary education. This procedure should avoid a bias that could arise from comparing mobile students from East Germany to students in West Germany who did not move because mobility is possibly related to the presence or absence of entrepreneurial characteristics, for example attitudes toward risk. As the treatment effect of an education under a socialist regime remains significant, we are confident that we do indeed measure a causal effect.

The remainder of the chapter is organized as follows. The next section reviews some major contributions that analyze the formation of entrepreneurial endowments prior to university education. The third section introduces our empirical strategy, and the fourth describes our data set. In the fifth section, we present our analyses of the impact of schooling and socialization on university student entrepreneurial intentions. The final section concludes by discussing the implications of our work and offers some suggestions for further research.

THE FORMATION OF ENTREPRENEURIAL ENDOWMENTS

Economic research on what drives the formation of cognitive and non-cognitive skills usually adopts a life-cycle perspective; that is, every individual has certain innate biological characteristics that influence his or her endowments. Nicolaou et al. (2008) and Nicolaou and Shane (2009) analyze this in the context of entrepreneurship, and their results suggest that genetic factors are an important explanation of individual differences in the ability to identify entrepreneurial opportunities and for an overall tendency to become an entrepreneur. With these characteristics as the foundation, socialization and schooling further contribute to the development of entrepreneurial endowments.

As for socialization influences, parental role models are first and foremost. The fact that young children spend most of their time with their parents helps to explain the strong impact of parental background on the predilection for a certain occupation; or, as Marshall (1920) put it, 'as years pass on, the child of the working man learns a great deal from what he sees and hears going on around him'. Following research by Aldrich et al. (1998), Dunn and Holtz-Eakin (2000), and Hout and Rosen (2000), entrepreneurial parents leave an especially pronounced mark on their children due to 'their ability to provide contact between their children (while the children are relatively young) and the business workplace . . . As the child receives continued exposure to the family business, he picks up, almost without realizing it, a working knowledge of how to run a business enterprise' (Lentz and Laband, 1990, p. 564). Fairlie and Robb (2007) take this one step further and directly attribute the 'entrepreneurial' effect to adolescent work experience in the family business.

Children's peers also play an important role in the process of socialization (Bandura, 1977), and could very well have an impact on the formation of entrepreneurial endowments (Falck et al., 2009). Let us assume that some of a child's peers think of themselves and others as future entrepreneurs, although perhaps not with that exact terminology. These peers believe it would be 'cool' to be their own boss, run their own business, and not take orders from anyone else. These children are quite likely adventurous, fun to hang out with, and 'leaders of the pack' (cf. Akerlof and Kranton, 2002). And leadership, argues Baumol (1968), is one of the major ingredients of entrepreneurial success.[1] A child's entrepreneurial peers may playfully reinforce entrepreneurial endowments, setting the stage for Schumpeter's 'will to conquer' and 'will to found a private kingdom'.

There is not much literature directly on the influence of education on entrepreneurial endowments, aside from the now common notion that human capital has a positive impact on entrepreneurship (Evans and Leighton, 1989). However, following Lazear's (2005) idea of entrepreneurs being 'jacks-of-all-trades' who possess a balanced portfolio of cognitive and non-cognitive skills, extra-curricular activities might be more conducive to entrepreneurial endowments than math or science.

Along this line, Falck and Woessmann (2010) argue that competition between schools results in school administrators being innovative with regard to courses, teaching methods and, especially, extra-curricular activities, and that these latter can complement student qualifications beyond baseline educational goals. Such extra-curricular activities are likely to encourage or enhance entrepreneurial endowments such as social skills, innovativeness or the willingness to put ideas into action, all of which have the potential to shape student's intentions to become an entrepreneur. Consistent with their hypothesis, the authors find cross-country evidence for a positive effect of competition from private schools on system-wide student entrepreneurial intentions at the national level. In a similar study at the national level, Sobel and King (2008) observe that voucher programs in the USA create greater rates of youth entrepreneurship relative to traditional public schools without such programs.

These initial findings suggest that both socialization and schooling contribute to the development of those cognitive and non-cognitive skills and abilities generally falling under the rubric of entrepreneurial endowments. In the following section, we develop our empirical strategy to assess this issue and introduce our large sample of German university students. Based on this sample, we analyze the effect of socialization and schooling on individual entrepreneurial endowments. Specifically, we focus on how socialist education influences students' desire to become an entrepreneur.

EMPIRICAL STRATEGY

Our empirical strategy for identifying the impact of schooling and socialization on individual entrepreneurial endowments is threefold. First, we analyze the joint pre-university impact of socialization *and* schooling by comparing university students who were raised in West Germany with university students who were at least partly raised in East Germany before reunification in 1990. Here, our identification is based on the fact that these two groups experienced different educational treatments. East German university students were (at least partly) treated with socialization and schooling in a planned economy; West German students were treated with socialization and schooling in a free market economy.[2]

In a second step, we restrict our sample to university students who completed their secondary education before reunification in 1990. In this sample, university students were completely socialized and schooled either in a planned economy or in a free market economy. To address the problem of selection into universities, we restrict, in a third step, our sample to mobile students at West German universities, that is, those who left their 'familiar' environment in either West or East Germany to attend a university located in West Germany.[3] By focusing on mobile East and West German students, we deal with a potential bias that could arise from the fact that mobility might be related to the presence or absence of other entrepreneurial characteristics, for example, risk aversion.

This leaves us with the following estimation equation for the different samples of university students:

$$I_{imut} = \alpha + \alpha_m + \alpha_u + \alpha_t + \beta_1 D_{imut} + \mathbf{X}_{imut}\beta_2 + \varepsilon_{imut}$$

where the dependent variable I_{imut} is a binary variable that equals unity if student i studying major m at university u in survey wave t reports that he or she certainly wants to become an entrepreneur and zero otherwise. University student entrepreneurial intention is our 'as-close-as-possible' measure for entrepreneurial endowments. The explanatory variable D_{imut} is a dummy variable that equals unity if the university student was socialized and schooled in a German state formerly belonging to the GDR and zero if he or she went to school in West Germany. The matrix $\mathbf{X}_{imut}$ includes a set of individual characteristics and family background variables (cf. Parker, 2004 for an extensive overview). A detailed list of all control variables is provided in Table 30A.1 of the Appendix. Finally, we include a whole set of major fixed effects α_m, university fixed effects α_u, and survey wave fixed effects α_t; ε_{imut} is an error term. As our outcome variable is binary, we use both probit and linear probability models. We cluster our standard errors at the university level (cf. Moulton, 1986).

DATA

The data for our empirical analyses are derived from a survey regularly conducted among university students in Germany. The survey is part of a research project on the situation of students at German universities (*Studiensituation und studentische Orientierung*). The project is based at the University of Konstanz and is supported by Germany's Federal Ministry of Education and Research. The entire data set comprises ten waves of recurring surveys of university students. The university panel started in the winter term 1982/83 and was repeated every second or third year, with the most recent wave carried out during the 2006/07 winter term. Overall, the survey has 87 946 observations from 29 German universities, technical universities and universities of applied sciences, and covers questions about study progress, work and learning habits, leisure-time activities, attitudes and job preferences. Included questions provide information about student family background and schooling. Information about demographic variables, such as age or gender, is also available. Altogether, the survey thus draws a rich picture of the conditions and perspectives of students at German universities.

We focus on the three waves (Waves 5–7) conducted after reunification in 1990, which were collected in winter terms 1992/93, 1994/95 and 1997/98, giving us 23 542 observations. We restrict our analysis to this period to ensure that students educated in East German schools experienced at least several years of organized socialist treatment. Since we want to exploit the rich portfolio of possible control variables, we address a number of missing values in our multivariate regressions by imputing missing values of the control variables; replacing missing values with the variable mean in the case of metric variables; and creating an additional category for missing values in the case of categorical variables. Values are not imputed for either our dependent variable or for our explanatory variable of interest: the East–West indicator or for the university site, which we use to calculate cluster-robust standard errors. As this procedure does not directly effect the estimations of the coefficients of the respective variables, it enables us to make use of the full sample. Descriptive statistics of our sample and the main variables of interest are provided in Table 30.1.

RESULTS

Following the threefold strategy introduced earlier, we initially estimate the effect of socialization and schooling in East and West Germany, respectively, where we consider being partly raised in East Germany before reunification as non-entrepreneurial treatment. The upper part of Table 30.2 provides our basic estimations where we stepwise include controls. All estimations include university fixed effects, survey wave fixed effects, and major fixed effects. We report both probit (Table 30.2a) and linear probability (Table 30.2b) specifications.

In both panels of Table 30.2, Column (1) considers only those individual characteristics related to demographic variables of the respondents. The results suggest that East German students are significantly less likely to report entrepreneurial intentions than their West German counterparts. In a next step, in Column (2), we add controls for the students' previous and current education. Among other things, we control for grades in the high-school certificate, grades in intermediate examinations, and assess whether the respondents started their university studies immediately after finishing secondary school. In Column (3), we control for the student socialization. Specifically, we control for parental schooling and parental current occupation. In Column (4), we estimate a model containing control variables for the students' previous job experiences and future job prospects. For instance, we add a variable on prior occupation, current occupation and topic of study, as well as perceived problems in the future job market. Finally, in Column (5), we estimate a fully specified model containing all the control variables mentioned above. Across all specifications, the treatment effect remains robust, i.e. there is a significantly negative effect of socialist socialization and schooling on university student entrepreneurial intention.

In the bottom part of Table 30.2, we run the same regressions conducted in the upper part of the table, but focusing on the subgroup of students who completed secondary school while Germany was still divided and thus received either pure socialist or pure libertarian schooling and socialization. We expect these results to differ from the whole sample of students that also includes East German students who received a mixed education, or, in other words, who received at least some entrepreneurial treatment. Indeed,

Table 30.1   Descriptive statistics

	All students	Raised in FRG	Raised in GDR
Observations	23 543	17 953	5 514
Share of students with entrepreneurial intentions	22.82	23.52	20.53
Age (mean)	24.99	25.59	23.04
Share of female students	41.22	38.95	48.58
Average number of children	0.102	0.102	0.100
Marital status			
Married	7.3	7.56	6.44
Single, with permanent partner	49.71	49.99	49.01
Single, without permanent partner	42.23	41.63	43.94
Widowed/divorced	0.77	0.82	0.60
Share with at least one self-employed parent	24.47	25.81	20.22
Term (mean)	6.442	6.880	4.989
Majors			
Linguistic and cultural studies	2950	2367	570
Psychology	420	324	95
Pedagogics	1653	1226	422
Sport	254	165	89
Law	1735	1176	556
Social sciences	545	435	107
Economic sciences	3582	2691	879
Mathematics & natural science	3497	2878	616
Medicine	1823	1381	440
Agronomy, forestry, nutrition science	480	341	135
Engineering	5700	4259	1427
Arts	655	546	109
Other	163	112	49
Waves			
Wave 5: 1992/93	8709	6610	2053
Wave 6: 1994/95	8035	6262	1759
Wave 7: 1997/98	6799	5081	1702
Universities			
U Berlin (TU)	1556	1230	324
U Bochum	1548	1524	20
U Essen	1196	1188	5
U Frankfurt	1506	1472	29
U Freiburg	1779	1744	31
U Hamburg	2216	2160	53
U Karlsruhe	1842	1815	24
U München (LMU)	2059	2036	22
UAS Coburg	421	364	57
UAS Essen	299	290	6
UAS Frankfurt	477	469	8
UAS Hamburg	874	852	18
UAS Kiel	494	476	17

Table 30.1   (continued)

	All students	Raised in FRG	Raised in GDR
UAS Koblenz	416	407	9
UAS München	1 201	1 179	15
U Dresden	1 115	106	1 005
U Leipzig	1 295	153	1 140
U Magdeburg	687	35	647
U Potsdam	435	99	334
U Rostock	526	94	432
UAS Erfurt	209	37	172
UAS Magdeburg	198	23	173
UAS Stralsund	149	18	128

the impact of socialist education is stronger for those students who went to school exclusively in the GDR. Consequently the socialist treatment effect is smaller for those who at least had some years of schooling in reunified Germany.

In Table 30.3, we repeat the estimations from Table 30.2 for the subsample of students in West German university locations. Hence we exclude students at East German universities since the specific economic environment in the formerly socialist part of Germany might affect their entrepreneurial intentions. Moreover, we concentrate on those mobile students who finished school in East or West Germany and chose to attend a West German university located away from home. This procedure should mitigate the bias arising from comparing mobile students from East Germany to students in West Germany who did not move because mobility is possibly related to the presence or absence of certain entrepreneurial characteristics, for example, risk aversion. We use the full set of control variables for all specifications and report probit results (left panel) and linear probability model results (right panel) in Table 30.3. We consider different measures for mobility. Column (1) considers all mobile students at West German university locations who report that the university is not in their hometown. In a second step, we consider those students who report that they are at least 50 kilometers away from their hometown and, as shown in Column (2), the effect becomes stronger. In a third step, we retain only West German students who went to a different federal state to attend university (Column (3)). Here we find an effect similar to that reported in Column (1).

Overall, the results do not significantly change with a focus on those students who completed a pure GDR socialist education before the 1990 reunification. The results are presented in the lower part of Table 30.3. For this group, the coefficients are again somewhat higher. Continuing to find significant effects of schooling and socialization in the subsample of mobile East and West German university students at the same West German universities suggests that selection into universities is not predominant in our analysis.

Given that our results remain extremely robust to all specifications and control variables, we are confident that we can interpret the effect of being schooled and socialized in a non-entrepreneurial environment as having a causal effect on the entrepreneurial intentions of university students. Being raised in a non-entrepreneurial environment reduces the likelihood of having entrepreneurial intentions between around 4 and 7 percentage

Table 30.2a   Probit estimations for the whole sample

	(1)	(2)	(3)	(4)	(5)
All students					
Raised in GDR	−0.052***	−0.050***	−0.054***	−0.044***	−0.042***
	(0.012)	(0.013)	(0.013)	(0.012)	(0.013)
Controls: education	no	yes	no	no	yes
Controls: socialization	no	no	yes	no	yes
Controls: job experience & perspectives	no	no	no	yes	yes
Controls: individual characteristics	yes	yes	yes	yes	yes
No. of obs.	22 195	22 195	22 195	22 195	22 195
Pseudo-R^2	0.056	0.076	0.071	0.070	0.105
All students who finished school before 1990					
Raised in GDR	−0.082***	−0.073***	−0.090***	−0.077***	−0.073***
	(0.019)	(0.017)	(0.019)	(0.018)	(0.016)
Controls: education	no	yes	no	no	yes
Controls: socialization	no	no	yes	no	yes
Controls: job experience & perspectives	no	no	no	yes	yes
Controls: individual characteristics	yes	yes	yes	yes	yes
No. of obs.	10 733	10 733	10 733	10 733	10 733
Pseudo-R^2	0.059	0.073	0.073	0.075	0.104

Notes: The table reports probit models with marginal effects at the sample mean. The dependent variable, entrepreneurial intention, is unity if a student reports that he or she definitely wants to become a self-employed entrepreneur or freelancer, zero otherwise. All specifications include university fixed effects, survey wave fixed effects, and major fixed effects. The control variables are described in more detail in Table 30A.1. Cluster (university) robust standard errors are reported in parentheses. *Denotes 10% level of significance, **denotes 5% level of significance, ***denotes 1% level of significance.

points. Given that the mean share of students with entrepreneurial intentions is about 23 percent, this effect is economically important. Accordingly, we conclude that entrepreneurial education may indeed strengthen entrepreneurial endowments. When further distinguishing between the overall effect from socialization and the effect of schooling, we find that even a short period of schooling in a non-socialist regime increases the entrepreneurial intentions of university students, which again supports the idea that education in a market economy can have an impact on entrepreneurial intentions. Hence we conclude that education, either by parents, peers or schools, can result in an enhancement of entrepreneurial endowments.

Table 30.2b   OLS estimations for the whole sample

	(1)	(2)	(3)	(4)	(5)
All students					
Raised in GDR	−0.052***	−0.052***	0.054***	−0.045***	−0.045***
	(0.012)	(0.013)	(0.013)	(0.012)	(0.013)
Controls: education	no	yes	no	no	yes
Controls: socialization	no	no	yes	no	yes
Controls: job experience & perspectives	no	no	no	yes	yes
Controls: individual characteristics	yes	yes	yes	yes	yes
No. of obs.	22 195	22 195	22 195	22 195	22 195
Pseudo-R^2	0.059	0.075	0.076	0.074	0.106
All students who finished school before 1990					
Raised in GDR	−0.077***	−0.068***	−0.085***	−0.074***	−0.071***
	(0.017)	(0.015)	(0.018)	(0.017)	(0.016)
Controls: education	no	yes	no	no	yes
Controls: socialization	no	no	yes	no	yes
Controls: job experience & perspectives	no	no	no	yes	yes
Controls: individual characteristics	yes	yes	yes	yes	yes
No. of obs.	10 733	10 733	10 733	10 733	10 733
R^2	0.062	0.074	0.077	0.079	0.105

Notes: The table reports OLS estimation results where the dependent variable, entrepreneurial intention, is unity if a student reports that he or she definitely wants to become a self-employed entrepreneur or freelancer, zero otherwise. All specifications include university fixed effects, survey wave fixed effects, and major fixed effects. The control variables are described in more detail in Table 30A.1. Cluster (university) robust standard errors are reported in parentheses. *Denotes 10% level of significance, **denotes 5% level of significance, ***denotes 1% level of significance.

CONCLUSIONS

Our findings for a sample of German university students suggest that both socialization and schooling contribute to the development of entrepreneurial endowments that eventually impact on students' intentions to become an entrepreneur. In an attempt to learn more about the relative importance of socialization and schooling, we use the quasi-natural experiment resulting from the years around German reunification to consider the effect of pre-university education on students' entrepreneurial intentions. Using surveys of university students who experienced at least part of their secondary education under the socialist GDR regime and students from West Germany who were schooled under

Table 30.3   *Probit and OLS estimations for the subsample of West German university locations*

	Probit			OLS		
	(1)	(2)	(3)	(1)	(2)	(3)
Students in the West						
Raised in GDR	−0.062***	−0.072***	−0.063***	−0.063***	−0.073***	−0.063***
	(0.012)	(0.013)	(0.015)	(0.013)	(0.013)	(0.014)
Controls: education	yes	yes	yes	yes	yes	yes
Controls: socialization	yes	yes	yes	yes	yes	yes
Controls: job experience & perspectives	yes	yes	yes	yes	yes	yes
Controls: individual characteristics	yes	yes	yes	yes	yes	yes
No. of obs.	13033	7618	5340	13033	7618	5349
(Pseudo-) R^2	0.099	0.102	0.110	0.100	0.104	0.111
Students in the West who finished school before 1990						
Raised in GDR	−0.074***	−0.075***	−0.067***	−0.071***	−0.073***	−0.064***
	(0.018)	(0.020)	(0.020)	(0.018)	(0.019)	(0.019)
Controls: education	yes	yes	yes	yes	yes	yes
Controls: socialization	yes	yes	yes	yes	yes	yes
Controls: job experience & perspectives	yes	yes	yes	yes	yes	yes
Controls: individual characteristics	yes	yes	yes	yes	yes	yes
No. of obs.	6834	4114	3004	6834	4119	3009
(Pseudo-) R^2	0.097	0.105	0.117	0.099	0.106	0.119

Notes: Marginal effects are reported at the sample mean. The dependent variable, entrepreneurial intention, is unity if a student reports that he or she definitely wants to become a self-employed entrepreneur or freelancer, zero otherwise. All specifications include university fixed effects, survey wave fixed effects, and major fixed effects. The control variables are described in more detail in Table 30A.1. Cluster (university) robust standard errors are reported in parentheses. *Denotes 10% level of significance, **denotes 5% level of significance, ***denotes 1% level of significance.

an education system that embraced the values of a market economy, we find significant differences in entrepreneurial intentions. Furthermore, East German students completing their secondary education before reunification in 1990 have lower entrepreneurial intentions than those completing their secondary education after reunification. These results are robust for different specifications within groups of students at West German universities where we stepwise exclude less alike students and, thus, rule out selection into university and related biases.

Our findings suggest that entrepreneurial intentions are, to some extent, determined endogenously in the process of socialization and schooling. Our results further suggest that policy-makers can influence entrepreneurial endowments via the schooling system. However, at this point, we can only confirm that changes in the education system might have an effect on entrepreneurial endowments, but we cannot draw any conclusions about the most effective design for increasing these endowments. Determining this requires further empirical research.

The results from our study of the subsample of university students who finished their secondary education either in the GDR or in unified Germany, respectively, shows that teaching the values of a free market economy can affect the formation of entrepreneurial intentions, i.e. the interest in becoming an entrepreneur. This initial finding makes us confident that a specialized entrepreneurship education could increase entrepreneurial endowments, i.e. develop the preconditions for the development of this desire. However, work on how entrepreneurial courses at school influence individual entrepreneurial intentions does not go beyond case studies and thus there is great scope for future research.

NOTES

1. The entrepreneur's job is 'to locate new ideas and to put them into effect. He must lead, perhaps even inspire; he cannot allow things to get into a rut and for him today's practice is never good enough for tomorrow . . . He is the individual who exercises what in the business literature is called "leadership"' (Baumol, 1968, p. 65).
2. Note that we exclude students who completed secondary school in a country other than Germany from the whole analysis.
3. Note that West Germany is far from being equally familiar to West German students as there are considerable cultural differences between German regions, the result of Germany being heavily fragmented until 1870 (cf. Falck et al., 2010).

REFERENCES

Akerlof, G.A. and R.E. Kranton (2002), 'Identity and schooling: some lessons for the economics of education', *Journal of Economic Literature*, **40**, 1167–201.
Aldrich, H., L.A. Renzulli and N. Langton (1998), 'Passing on privilege: resources provided by self-employed parents to their self-employed children', *Research in Social Stratification and Mobility*, **16**, 291–317.
Bandura, A. (1977), *Social Learning Theory*, Englewood Cliffs, NJ: Prentice Hall.
Baumol, W. (1968), 'Entrepreneurship in economic theory', *American Economic Review*, **58**, 64–71.
Dunn, T. and D. Holtz-Eakin (2000). 'Financial capital, human capital, and the transition to self-employment: evidence from intergenerational links', *Journal of Labor Economics*, **18**, 282–305.
Evans, D.S. and L.S. Leighton (1989), 'Some empirical aspects of entrepreneurship', *American Economic Review*, **79**, 519–35.
Fairlie, R.W. and A. Robb (2007), 'Families, human capital, and small business: evidence from the characteristics of business owners survey', *Industrial & Labor Relations Review*, **60**, 225–45.
Falck, O. and L. Woessmann (2010), 'School competition and students' entrepreneurial intentions: international evidence using historical catholic roots of private schooling', PEPG Working Paper 10-01, Kennedy School of Government, Harvard University.
Falck, O., S. Heblich, A. Lameli and J. Suedekum (2010), 'Dialects, cultural identity, and economic exchange', IZA Discussion Paper No. 4743.
Falck, O., S. Heblich and. E. Luedemann (2009), 'Identity and entrepreneurship: do peers at school shape entrepreneurial intentions?', PEPG 09-05 Working Paper, Program of Education Policy and Governance, Kennedy School of Government, Harvard University.

Hout, M. and H. Rosen (2000), 'Self-employment, family background, and race', *Journal of Human Resources*, **35**, 670–92.

Lazear, E.P. (2005), 'Entrepreneurship', *Journal of Labor Economics*, **23**, 649–80.

Lentz, B.F. and S. Laband (1990), 'Entrepreneurial success and occupational inheritance among proprietors', *Canadian Journal of Economics*, **23**, 101–17.

Marshall, A. (1920), *Principles of Economics*, 8th edn, London: Macmillan.

Moulton, B.R. (1986), 'Random group effects and the precision of regression estimates', *Journal of Econometrics*, **32**, 385–97.

Nicolaou, N. and S. Shane (2009), 'Born entrepreneurs? The genetic foundations of entrepreneurship', *Journal of Business Venturing*, **23**, 1–22.

Nicolaou, N., S. Shane, J. Hunkin, L. Cherkas and T. Spector (2008), 'Is the tendency to engage in entrepreneurship genetic?', *Management Science*, **54**, 167–79.

Parker, S.C. (2004), *The Economics of Self-Employment and Entrepreneurship*, Cambridge: Cambridge University Press.

Schumpeter, J.A. (1912), *The Theory of Economic Development*, New York: Oxford University Press.

Sobel, R.S. and K.A. King (2008), 'Does school choice increase the rate of youth entrepreneurship?', *Economics of Education Review*, **27**, 429–38.

APPENDIX

Table 30A.1   Detailed variable description

Category	Variable	Description
Dependent variable	• Entrepreneurial intention	Question: *In which area do you want to be permanently employed in the future?* Option *self-employed (entrepreneur or freelancer)* Answers on a 4-point-scale Variable is unity if respondent chooses '*yes, certainly*' and zero otherwise
Explanatory variable	• Raised in the GDR	Variable is unity if respondent graduated from school in East Germany (former GDR), zero otherwise
Control: education	• Final degree aspired	Six categories indicating which degree the respondent finally wants to reach (Diploma, Magister Artium, state examination, etc.)
	• High school certificate	Demeaned variable indicating the grade reached in high school certificate
	• Immediate start	Variable is unity if respondent started studies immediately after school, zero otherwise
	• Intermediate examination	For categories indicating that intermediate examinations exist, whether the respondent has taken this examination and whether it was passed
Control: socialization	• School education father • School education mother	Categorical variable indicating the level of school education for the respondent's father and mother separately. Discriminates secondary school (8th grade), middle school (10th grade), high school (12th/13th grade), and no graduation (less than 8th grade)
	• Occupation father • Occupation mother	Categorical variable indicating the actual occupation of the respondent's mother, respectively, father. Discriminates public officials, white-collar workers in the public sector, white-collar workers in the private sector, blue-collar workers in the public sector, blue-collar workers in the private sector, self-employed, and others
Control: individual characteristics	• Field of study	Thirteen categories indicating the respondent's major: linguistic and cultural studies; psychology; pedagogics; sport; law; social sciences; economic sciences; mathematics & natural science; medicine; agronomy, forestry, nutrition science; engineering; arts; other
	• Wave	Wave 5: winter term 1992/93; Wave 6: winter term 1994/95, Wave 7: winter term 1997/98
	• Kind of studies	Four categories indicating whether respondent is obtaining first degree, second degree, doctoral degree, or doing other postgraduate courses
	• Term	Number of terms the respondent has already been studying his/her major

Table 30A.1   (continued)

Category	Variable	Description
	● Marital status	Four categories: married, not married but living with permanent partner, single without permanent partner, widowed/divorced
	● Children	Number of children
	● Age	
	● Sex	
	● University	Dummies for 23 German universities (universities, technical universities, and universities of applied sciences)
Control: job experience and perspectives	● Job experience	Binary variable indicating whether respondent has been employed before starting studies
	● Student job	Binary variable indicating whether respondent has ever had a student job
	● Decided	Binary variable indicating whether respondent has yet decided on a future occupation
	● Job perspectives	Categorical variable indicating the student's self-assessed job perspectives on a 4-point-scale, ranging from '*no problems finding an appropriate job*' to '*big problems finding a job at all*'

Index